California Political Almanac

D1738370

California Political Almanac
2007–2008

Edited by

A.G. Block
Gerald C. Lubenow
Institute of Governmental Studies

CQ PRESS

A Division of Congressional Quarterly Inc.
Washington, D.C.

CQ Press
1255 22nd Street, NW, Suite 400
Washington, DC 20037
202-729-1900; toll-free, 1-866-4CQ-PRESS (1-866-427-7737)
www.cqpress.com

Cover photo credits: Gov. Arnold Schwarzenegger in his Sacramento, Calif., office, March
2004 (AP Photo/Rich Pedroncelli) and on the steps of the Capitol in Sacramento, November
2003. (AP Photo/Eric Risberg).

∞ The paper used in this publication exceeds the requirements of the American National
Standard for Information Sciences—Permanence of Paper for Printed Library Materials, ANSI
Z39.48-1992.

Printed and bound in the United States of America

11   10   09   08   07   1   2   3   4   5

ISBN: 978-0-87289-504-1
ISSN: 1097-9166

Contents

Tables and Figures

Maps

The Editorial Team

The 2007–2008 edition of the *California Political Almanac* is the product of count-less hours of work by a team of veteran journalists, academics, and policy experts. They were aided in their labors by a cadre of dedicated graduate students from three entities at the University of California, Berkeley—the Graduate School of Journalism, the Institute of Governmental Studies, and the Goldman School of Public Policy—and by student interns from the University of California Center Sacramento.

The almanac editors owe special thanks to Jack Citrin, associate director of the Institute of Governmental Studies, and Gary Dymski, director of the University of California Center Sacramento. Without their generous financial, administrative, and intellectual support, this project would not have been possible.

A.G. Block, coeditor and principal writer, is director of the Public Affairs Journalism Program at the University of California Center Sacramento. He previously served as editor of *California Journal* magazine and coeditor of the 1997–1998 and 1999–2000 editions of the *California Political Almanac*.

Gerald Lubenow, coeditor, retired as director of publications and program director of the Center for Politics and Public Service at the Institute of Governmental Studies at the University of California, Berkeley. He formerly served as bureau chief for *News-week* in San Francisco and London.

John Decker is a consultant to the California legislature who has served as a budget expert for both Republican and Democratic staff. He is legislative fellow in residence at the Institute of Governmental Studies at the University of California, Berkeley. He wrote the essay on California's budget.

Robert Gunnison is director of school affairs at the University of California, Berkeley, Graduate School of Journalism and a past Sacramento bureau chief for United Press International and the *San Francisco Chronicle*. He coordinated and edited congressional and legislative profiles written by students from the Graduate School of Journalism.

Ethan Rarick is director of publications at the Institute of Governmental Studies. He served as executive editor and coordinated the team's editorial efforts with CQ Press.

Susan Rasky teaches at the University of California, Berkeley, Graduate School of Journalism. She previously covered Congress for the *New York Times*. She wrote the introduction to the almanac section on California's congressional delegation and edited congressional and legislative profiles written by students from the Graduate School of Journalism.

Peter Schrag is a noted author and public affairs columnist for the *Sacramento Bee* and a visiting scholar at the Institute of Governmental Studies at the University of California, Berkeley. Among his works are *California: America's High Stakes Experiment* and *Paradise Lost: California's Experience, America's Future*. He wrote the introduction to this volume.

Maria Wolf is publications editor for the Institute of Governmental Studies at the University of California, Berkeley.

Nik Bonovich is a political writer and analyst based in Los Angeles. His work has appeared in the *California Target Book, The Hotline,* and *Political Pulse*. He wrote various legislative and congressional profiles.

Chris Burnett is a professor of journalism and political science at California State University, Long Beach, and a past congressional correspondent for the *Columbus Dispatch*. He wrote various legislative and congressional profiles.

Bruce E. Cain is Robson Professor of Political Science at the University of California, Berkeley, and director of the Institute of Governmental Studies and the UC Washington Center. His books include *The Reapportionment Puzzle* and *The Personal Vote*. He co-authored the essay on term limits included in the *Almanac*'s introduction to the California legislature.

Jim Evans is communications director for California state senator Darrell Steinberg of Sacramento and a former managing editor of *California Journal*. He wrote an essay on the two-thirds vote requirement as part of the *Almanac*'s introduction to the California legislature.

John Howard is managing editor of *Capitol Weekly* in Sacramento. He was an editor and reporter for the Associated Press and *California Journal*, as well as Sacramento bureau chief for the *Orange County Register*. He wrote various congressional and legislative profiles, as well as profiles of Attorney General Jerry Brown and Lieutenant Governor John Garamendi.

Thad Kousser is on the faculty at the University of California, San Diego, and is the author of *Term Limits and the Dismantling of State Legislative Professionalism*. He co-authored the essay on term limits included in the *Almanac*'s introduction to the California legislature.

David Lesher is California director of the New America Foundation, a former editor of *California Journal,* and a former political reporter and editor with the *Los Angeles Times*. He wrote an overview for the *Almanac*'s introduction to the California legislature.

Cecilia O'Donnell is a senior at the University of California Santa Barbara. She researched California's bureaucracy, updated the section on California counties, and wrote several legislative profiles.

Dan Walters is a political columnist for the *Sacramento Bee* and editor of the first edition of *California Political Almanac*. Part of the historical essay in chapter 1 is derived from his original commentary.

University of California Center Sacramento
Eddie Boquilla
Will C. Douglas
Bjorn Francis
Jose San Mateo
Tezeta Stewartz
Saul Sugarman
Elizabeth Wilson

Graduate School of Journalism
Michael Fitzhugh
Heather Gehlert
Jeff Kearns
Lisa Lambert
Monica Mehta
Michael Rosen-Molina
Rebecca Ruiz
Leonie Sherman
Matt Wheeland
Chris Young

Institute of Governmental Studies
Shitel Rani Chanana
Michael Tamariz

Goldman School of Public Policy
Anat Shenker

Introduction: The New California

In the five years from 2002 to 2006, California had eight statewide elections, which must be some sort of record: In 2002, voters re-elected Gov. Gary Davis, a Democrat. In October 2003, barely eleven months later, they recalled him and replaced him with Republican Arnold Schwarzenegger. In 2004 they elected a legislature in which—notwithstanding the reputed unpopularity of its predecessors in opinion polls —not one seat changed party control (and Democrats maintained sizeable majorities in each house).

In 2005, at the special election Schwarzenegger had called, they repudiated the governor they'd elected just two years before. With the polls registering dismal approval ratings for the man who had nearly 70 percent positive ratings a year before and was now attacking the Democrats' "girlie men" and "special interests," they soundly defeated a Schwarzenegger-backed set of initiatives that would have capped spending, sharply cut the political power of public employee unions, and shifted control of the redistricting process from the legislature to an independent commission.

A year later, a year during which he radically changed his agenda and his tone, they re-elected him by a margin of nearly 18 points. When he began his second term in January 2007 with a call for "post-partisanship," he proposed an extraordinary agenda that included everything from health care for all Californians to the creation of low-carbon fuel standards to cut global warming, to the continuation of what he hoped would be an $80 billion infrastructure building program, now including prisons and dams as well as roads and schools, that he and the legislature had launched the year before—all with a promise that there'd be no new taxes.

In the meantime—counting all 10 statewide elections since March 2000—Californians had voted on 54 initiatives, putting the state in contention to break the mark of 62 set in the single decade of the 1990s. Among others, voters passed measures to toughen penalties for juvenile crime, outlaw gay marriage, and impose severe residence restrictions and monitoring on pedophiles. They voted for major new spending for child care (to come out of the general fund), a surtax on high incomes for mental health programs, plus billions in bonds for deficit reduction, stem cell research, and the first installment of the governor's long agenda of infrastructure projects.

None of these measures involved direct new taxation for the average resident. But they did mean still more debt and further deferral of the difficult choice between high-quality services and higher taxes. In addition, state and local agencies were running up tens of billions in unfunded health care liabilities for retired employees. Was this conservatism, liberalism, or what? What was going on here?

There's no end of explanations for California's quirky political behavior: Californians' relentless search for the perfection promised by the historic California dream; the complexity, dynamics, and diversity of a state of 36 million people; the gerrymandering of legislative districts, which, combined with the state's political geography, produces seats most of which are safely Democratic or Republican; the political shortsightedness associated with term limits; the essential dysfunctionality of the state's fiscal structure; the use of the initiative process to trump the liberal tilt of the legislature; the huge gap between the voting population—what Mark Baldassare of the Public Policy Institute of California calls the "exclusive electorate"—and the rest of the population. That electorate, which comprises barely over half of the state's adult residents, remains roughly 70 percent non-Hispanic white. It is older, more affluent, and more conservative than the population as a whole, in which whites are now just another minority and Latinos will eventually be an absolute majority.

But beneath all this political volatility and uncertainty a more profound and lasting change is under way: the emergence of a new California that's significantly—maybe radically—different from the California of a half century ago. Part of that change is the hollowing out of the state's middle class and the growing gap between the state's most affluent residents and its poorest. Another (somewhat related) part is the growing population of immigrants and their children: In 1960 nearly 80 percent of Californians were white Anglos; by 2006, when 26 percent of California's population was foreign born—the highest percentage since the decades after the Gold Rush—the number of non-Hispanic whites had declined to 46 percent and was certain to continue declining, not only as a percentage of the population, but in absolute numbers. At the same time, as large numbers of Latinos and Asians—both already artificial statistical conglomerates—married people of other ethnicities, even those categories became increasingly amorphous. Children born in California today, said essayist Richard Rodriguez, don't look like their grandparents. With the exception of some rural northern California counties and a few exclusive communities elsewhere, there are few all-white places left.

The ethnic data reflect a world of other changes—in the economy and in language, food, music, family relationships, and international connections. No one knows how many of the thousands of immigrant families in California now include a mixture of legal residents, illegal residents, and citizens. Hundreds of thousands of Californians, moreover, have strong family and residential ties to the places from which they came —in Mexico, El Salvador, the Philippines, India, China, Pakistan, Armenia; a fourth of California's school children come from homes where English is not the primary language. The largest source of foreign revenue in Mexico—roughly $20 billion in 2005—is remittances from immigrant workers in the U.S.; additional millions are raised by hundreds of hometown associations in this country for church renovations, school improvements, road work, and recreational facilities in Michoacan, Zacatecas, and other Mexican states, funds that are matched two to one or three to one by Mexican state and federal agencies.

Similarly, there are widespread connections between Silicon Valley and other high-tech sectors and trans-Pacific enterprises and schools, and in the constant movement of technicians and engineers between them. It's estimated that more than half of the Silicon Valley companies started since 1995 were founded by at least one immigrant. There are hundreds of cross-border and trans-Pacific trade, cultural, labor, educational, health, environmental, and other organizations. Thousands of workers and students cross the border daily to work or study in this country. A growing number of Mexican entrepreneurs live in Chula Vista and commute to Tijuana, and thousands of Californians go to Mexico for pharmaceuticals and dental care.

All of those things—the families, the trade, the cultures—raise a crucial question about much of California and the Southwest: Is the border still just a line or is it becoming a region that, like the globalized economy, is rapidly outgrowing and overgrowing the political institutions and ideas by which the world in general and the U.S. in particular still try to conduct their public business? NAFTA, the North American Free Trade Agreement, allows the free movement of goods and capital across the Canadian and Mexican borders, but it does not address labor, even though the former deeply affect the latter. Meanwhile, by making it more expensive and dangerous for illegal workers to follow the historic path—north in the spring, south in the winter—the nation's attempts to tighten border enforcement have had the paradoxical effect of sharply driving up the number of illegal residents in this country, first by discouraging the seasonal cross-border rotation of workers and then by encouraging workers who no longer go back to send for their families. Even though the dispersion of immigrants to other parts of the country has reduced California's dominance as the prime destination of Mexicans, the state still has far and away the largest share of newcomers.

To say that this new California has had enormous impact on state and national politics is probably an understatement, not only in the debate on immigration but on the choices voters make on taxation and public services and, of course, on the delivery of public services themselves. To what extent are Californians less willing to tax themselves for good schools if those schools are widely perceived to be serving other people's children, especially if many of those children aren't supposed to be here in the first place? To what extent do the children of recent immigrants, most of whom tend to earn low wages and thus pay proportionately less in taxes than the average worker, burden schools and other public services?

Conversely, since those children represent a sizeable part of California's future workforce, the preservation of a strong economy and the good jobs it provides depend in large measure on their education. California, in 2006 the world's sixth largest economy, once took for granted that the diversity of its economy and its strength in high technology, entertainment, financial services, and agriculture virtually guaranteed its future in global markets. But with the sharp rise in competition overseas, not only in technology and manufacturing but in high-tech services and specialty crop agriculture where the state had long led the world, nothing is assured. The education and welfare of those children, as Steven Levy of the Center for the Continuing Study of the California Economy points out, thus has to be regarded as a long-term investment, not just a present-day expense.

Given the many challenges the state faces in its overcrowded roads, its low-performing schools, its low college graduation rates, and in the broader issues raised by its multilingual, multicultural population, what's surprising is not the magnitude of California's problems or the uncertainty many people feel about how to address them, but the success the state has had in accommodating itself to the new California. While English is not the first language in the homes of most new immigrants, legal or illegal —as of course it wasn't a century ago either—the great majority of the second generation regards English as its prime, if not its only, language. In the third generation, almost no one speaks the old language.

There are now some 600,000 Latino-owned businesses in California; of Latinos who came here before 1980, 55 percent own their own homes, almost the state average. What those numbers reflect is a more pervasive mutual acculturation—the fact that fewer and fewer Californians notice the browning of the state, the increasing difficulty of telling who's what, either from appearance or accent. That's particularly true for the state's younger generation, the kids who don't look like their grandparents, who've grown up with the state's new complexion and rarely seem to notice. It's difficult to imagine that California would now pass another Proposition 187, the 1994 initiative that sought to prohibit illegal aliens from the state's public schools and that, paradoxically, energized a great wave of Latino naturalization and voter registration that, because GOP Gov. Pete Wilson was a chief sponsor of the measure, was overwhelmingly Democratic.

None of that means that California is now immune to the waves of nativism and racism that marked its past. Voters tell pollsters and interviewers again and again that they want the state to work. Despite his recent changes of agenda, making California government work has been a Schwarzenegger refrain since he first ran for office in 2003. But with only rare exceptions, Californians have voted again and again for the procedural status quo, rejecting Schwarzenegger's attempt to gain more control over what he called auto-pilot spending, turning down redistricting reform proposals, soundly opposing attempts to reduce the state requirement mandating a two-thirds majority in each house of the legislature to approve a budget or any tax increase, refusing to change the law to exempt nonviolent felonies as crimes qualifying as a third-strike and thus a mandatory 25-years-to-life prison sentence, and refusing to modify the state's strict term limits for legislators.

Was that all mistrust of the elected legislature, as the conventional wisdom had it, or was it also inchoate fear among those older, whiter, richer voters of the political power—present and future—of the state's new residents? Which is to say that perhaps the biggest gap, and the greatest difficulty in governing a state that many have often called ungovernable, is the distance between the new realities on the ground, where California, despite outbursts of ethnic tensions and the vitriol on some of the radio talk shows, seems to be working pretty well, and the creaky political institutions and attitudes that are supposed to govern and manage them. The call for a centrist "post-partisanship" era of collaboration, a theme that echoed his first inaugural just three years before, and his ambitious environmental and health care agenda reflected Schwarzenegger's unique circumstances. Here was a Republican governor of a major state who had been overwhelmingly re-elected in a Democratic year and who, had he not been constitutionally barred from the office, would now be on the short list of presidential possibilities. But that constitutional disability freed him from the constraints of presidential politics.

The governor nonetheless made it clear in a series of extravagant Hollywood-style presentations that he had great ambitions, both for his state and for himself. The prior year had produced that major infrastructure bond package, a much-heralded commitment to lower greenhouse gas emissions and a bill raising the state's minimum wage, all of which he cited as evidence that with bipartisan support California could make progress on crucial issues. (Only cynics noted that the bipartisanship was largely between the governor and legislative Democrats with few Republicans in the mix.) In proposing his 2007 agenda—the emissions reduction program, the health care proposal to cover all of California's 6.5 million uninsured, the major prison construction program to address the Herculean problems of a corrections system on the verge of collapse, and yet another $30 billion in construction projects in addition to the infrastructure bonds approved in 2006—Schwarzenegger, sounding ever more like Gov. Pat Brown, the symbol of the state's great era of ambitious development in the 1960s, would again make California a showcase for the nation.

None of that is guaranteed, especially in a state that has had a hard time making choices about taxes and spending and is riven by such deep economic, political, and social gaps. It isn't just gerrymandered districts but real political differences that help produce the partisanship. More prosaically, California has also had a chronic structural deficit—the gap between the projected rise in spending and the projected rise in revenues—and already has $120 billion in outstanding bond debt, either sold or authorized to be sold. If the strong economy that California enjoyed in 2005–2006 turns down, as it eventually will, it will be hard to sustain even current programs, let alone embark on any ambitious new initiatives.

Nonetheless, given California's size and demographics, the fact that many other states are now undergoing the challenges brought by immigration and the changing economy, and the near-certainty that within thirty or forty years much of the nation, with its growing Asian and Hispanic population, will probably look like California did in the 1990s, it is inevitable that California will remain, for better or worse, the model for the nation and, in many instances, for the world. No society in all history has ever attempted to forge a postindustrial high-tech economy and a harmonious democracy from such a wide spectrum of backgrounds, languages, and cultures. What is surprising is not that California faces huge challenges in that awesome self-imposed task, but that it is doing so well.

—Peter Schrag

1

The Political Scene: Enter Stage Left

Midway through the first decade of the 21st century, California politics is marked by an irony: the most recognizable politician in one of the most solidly Democratic states in the nation is a Republican.

Governor Arnold Schwarzenegger simply is larger than life. A pumped-up former body builder and global celebrity movie star who married into the Kennedy clan, Schwarzenegger at first towered over California's political landscape like the Colossus of Rhodes. Republicans hailed his rise to power during an unprecedented 2003 gubernatorial recall election as the opening gambit for the resurrection of a party long considered moribund on the left coast. Democrats, who have dominated Golden State politics for nearly a decade, cast a wary eye at this new high-energy foe—and at his envy-inflaming poll numbers.

But during his first two years in office, Schwarzenegger, like that ancient colossus, began to resemble swagger cast in bronze, immobile and incapable of affecting—let alone, controlling—the frenetic commerce swirling at his feet. Republicans still clung to the hope that he would save them; emboldened and combative Democrats increasingly poked him in the eye. Bipartisan rancor in the legislature, and between Democratic lawmakers and the governor, produced little in the way of productive solutions to the state's intractable problems. And all the while, his poll numbers fell and fell and fell.

Early in 2006—his re-election year—there were doubts that Schwarzenegger could win a second term. But by the end of the year, he had smashed his Democratic opponent and cruised back into office, illustrating again that California politics is an amusement park ride where wild ups and downs are the norm and the electorate hopes the car won't derail.

The past decade offers a glimpse.

It wasn't so long ago—1994, to be exact—that the California Republican Party was in the ascendancy without a global celebrity in its rocket pack. That year, it swept to victory at the business end of a wedge issue, illegal immigration, exploiting voter dissatisfaction with government generally and with Democrats specifically. The GOP re-elected a governor and attorney general, captured the offices of secretary of state, treasurer, and insurance commissioner, very nearly ended the career of a popular Democratic U.S. senator, and elected a majority in the state Assembly for the first time in more than two decades. The California results mirrored a national trend that saw Republicans capture both houses of Congress and make inroads in traditionally Democratic statehouses across the country.

Republicans thought their 1994 win would usher in a new era for their party and light the path to political dominance. Instead, they traded short-term wins for long-term losses by exploiting for political gain the ethnic diversity that has long been one of California's great strengths. The resulting backlash stove in the Republican house.

In 1996 Democrats took back the Assembly. Two years later, they demolished GOP candidates for governor and U.S. Senate, while little known and underfunded Democrats nearly ousted the incumbent Republican secretary of state and insurance commissioner. By 2002, Republicans were barely competitive in any statewide race, and the bench of potential candidates looked shopworn. The party had so little confidence in its ability to compete that it signed on to a 2001 reapportionment and redistricting scheme that guaranteed it minority status for the rest of the decade.

A Look Back

California is a political petri dish, and its political evolution reflects rapid socioeconomic change. As a social laboratory, California tests the ability of our traditional system of government to cope with change beyond the imagination of the system's creators. How California copes becomes an example for the nation, as states once ethnically homogenous confront the kind of diversity that has long been a staple of the California landscape.

To understand the political currents flowing through California in the 21st century, one must first understand its social and economic currents. According to the wave theory of social development—each wave consisting of economic change, followed by social change, followed by political change—California is in the third, or political phase, of its third wave.

The first wave lasted roughly a century, from the early days of settlement in the 1840s to the onset of World War II. After the Gold Rush, California in the late 19th century played a relatively unimportant role in the larger scheme of American history. It had a resource-based economy—mining, agriculture, and timber—and a decidedly rural ambience. Los Angeles, with its orange groves, vegetable fields, and low buildings, resembled an overgrown midwestern farm city, notwithstanding the presence of the Pacific Ocean and the few movie studios that had sprung up in the wake of World War I.

San Francisco had a more cosmopolitan reputation, along with cable cars and Chinatown, but it was the exception. Largely white and Republican, California was pretty much ignored by the rest of America, whose population was centered in the East and remained Eurocentric. With the exception of the Transcontinental Railroad, Californians tended to have a regional focus.

All of that changed on December 7, 1941, when the Japanese bombed Pearl Harbor and plunged the United States into a world war that had been raging in the Pacific for nearly a decade. Suddenly, America was forced to consider Asia as a factor in its future, and California was the lens through which the nation viewed the Pacific. Overnight, the state transformed itself into an industrial giant serving the war effort, sprouting dozens of aircraft assembly lines, shipyards, steel mills, and all the economic infrastructure of modern war. It became a staging arena for the Pacific campaign, a training ground and shipping point for soldiers, sailors, and airmen.

The war and the instant industrial changes it wrought jerked California into the 20th century—an economic transformation that bore with it rapid social impacts: Hundreds of thousands, then millions of Americans were drawn or sent to California to participate in the war effort. Although the state had always seen a steady flow of immigrants, it was nothing compared to what happened during World War II and continued almost unabated after the war. "Gone to California" became a terse explanation for the sudden absence of families in hundreds of midwestern, southern, and eastern communities. It was one of history's great migrations, one that had begun during the Great Depression, when refugees from the Dust Bowl, chronicled in John Steinbeck's *The Grapes of Wrath*, came to California in a desperate search for work and formed the nucleus of life and politics in the state's agricultural regions.

As the expanding industrialization of California created jobs, it drew immigrants who formed a new industrial middle class. They had vast ambitions for themselves and their families. They wanted schools, highways, parks, and homes. And during the postwar years, they provided the core backing for politicians who promised to fulfill their desires.

Johnson, Warren, and Nixon

California's prewar Republicanism was different from the conservative midwestern strain represented by the likes of Ohio's Robert Taft. Rooted in the abolitionism of the Civil War era and the prairie populism of William Jennings Bryan and Robert LaFollette, California Republicans were reformist and progressive. The state's great Republican reformer, Hiram Johnson, set the tone for the 20th century when he led efforts to break the stranglehold that Southern Pacific Railroad and other entrenched economic interests had on the legislature. Small farmers had battled for decades with the railroad over freight rates, clashes that were political and, in one instance, violent. With Johnson—governor and later U.S. senator—marshaling public opinion, California enacted a series of pioneering political reforms that included the initiative, referendum, and recall—processes originally designed to increase popular control of politicians that would echo down the decades as tools of a different class of special interests. In 2005 and 2006, the initiative would become the favorite club of Arnold Schwarzenegger after he had gained power via the recall.

Johnson set a tone of high-minded Republicanism that survived for decades. Democrats of the era were weak, able to elect only a single, one-term governor—Culbert Olsen in 1938—despite the dramatic rise of the Democratic Party nationally after Franklin Roosevelt became president in 1933. \

Olsen's GOP successor, Earl Warren, was of the Johnsonian mold, and he became the only governor ever elected three times, going on to fame as chief justice of the U.S. Supreme Court from 1953 to 1969. Warren was governor during and immediately after World War II, while the state was undergoing major economic and social change. He responded to California's growth with far-reaching investments in public infrastructure—schools, highways, parks, and other facilities—that served the state's fast-growing population and laid the foundation for even greater public works in the future.

During this period, California began developing a national reputation for political unpredictability and became a key battleground in the ideological wars sweeping America. Postwar California politics revolved mainly around Cold War issues, typified by the 1950 U.S. Senate contest between a young Republican congressman named Richard Nixon and liberal political activist Helen Gahagan Douglas. Nixon won a brutal, bigoted campaign in which he implied that Douglas was sympathetic to communism. The polarizing political battle launched Nixon and marked a turn away from centrist politics by both parties.

Democrats began veering to the left through such organizations as the California Democratic Council, established by Alan Cranston and other liberals to strengthen party identification in a state where cross-filing allowed candidates to obtain the nomination of both parties. The CDC battled more conservative elements then in control of the Democratic Party. Republicans took a turn to the right with conservatives such as U.S. Senator William Knowland, an Oakland newspaper publisher, assuming a larger role in the party as moderates of the Warren-Goodwin Knight faction fell from grace during a national political era notable for the rise of Republican U.S. Senator Joseph McCarthy of Wisconsin.

But social change in mid- to late-1950s California favored the Democrats. Immigrants, who had come to the Golden State to take jobs in the ever-expanding industrial economy, their ranks swollen by returning veterans, put down roots and became politically active, often as members of industrial unions. They expanded the Democratic Party base, especially after the Republicans' right turn alienated voters who had supported Warren's moderates.

Republicans were affected again in 1953 when Warren was removed from the scene by President Dwight Eisenhower, who appointed the California governor as chief justice of the U.S. Supreme Court. When Warren went east, the governorship fell to his lieutenant governor, Republican Goodwin Knight.

The New Breed

Jesse Unruh was the archetype of the postwar breed of lawmakers. He came to California from Texas during the war and stayed to attend the University of Southern California where he became active in campus politics as leader of a band of liberal veterans. Within years after graduating, Unruh was heavily involved in politics on a grander scale and won a seat in the state Assembly. It was the perfect territory for the consummate political animal, and his arrival coincided with the general rise of Democratic fortunes in the 1950s.

The 1958 election was the pivotal event in the postwar rise of the Democratic Party, a direct result of the social and economic changes brought about by World War II. Knowland, who had led the right-wing Republican contingent in the Senate during the early and mid-1950s, was openly hostile to Eisenhower's modern Republicanism, which included Warren's appointment to the Supreme Court. Knowland saw Eisenhower, Warren, Thomas E. Dewey, and other GOP leaders from the East as leading the party and the nation astray, refusing to confront expansionist communism around the globe and temporizing on such domestic issues as labor union rights and welfare spending.

Knowland, with presidential ambitions of his own, wanted to return the party to the right and seek the nomination when Eisenhower's second term ended in 1960. He thought the California governor's office would be a more powerful platform for a presidential campaign than his job as Republican leader of the Senate. His major impediment was Knight, the moderate Republican governor who didn't want to give up the job. Knight, who inherited the top spot when Warren left for the Court, won a term in his own right in 1954 and intended to seek re-election in 1958.

Knowland bullied Knight into a job swap. With the rightists firmly in control of the party machinery, Knight reluctantly agreed to run for Knowland's Senate seat in what became a historic miscalculation. Knowland, preoccupied with his quest for the White House, didn't bother to consider whether his forced switch with Knight would sit well with California voters. With arrogance bordering on stupidity, he assumed voters would do whatever he wanted them to do. He was wrong. Democrat Edmund G. "Pat" Brown, Sr., the liberal attorney general, was elected governor, while U.S. Representative Clair Engle captured Knowland's Senate seat. Knight might have been re-elected governor and Knowland given another term in the Senate had they not attempted the swap, but voters instead retired them both.

Democrats Take Over

1958 was a banner year for Democrats. They took firm control of the legislature, and over the next eight years, the most ambitious policy agenda in California history became reality. With Unruh as Assembly speaker, the early Brown years saw a torrent of liberal, activist legislation ranging from an ambitious water development scheme to pioneering civil rights and consumer protection measures. In terms of the sheer volume of construction on state projects, it is an era often cited by California's current governor, Arnold Schwarzenegger, as a model for the kind of investment that ought to be made in the state's infrastructure.

While Unruh sharpened the ideological focus of the Assembly, taking it to the left, the state Senate remained a bastion of rural conservatism. For a century, the Senate's 40 seats had been distributed on the basis of geography rather than population. No senator represented more than two counties, and giant Los Angeles County, with a third of the state's population, had just one senator. That system gave the Senate a decidedly rural flavor and a solid majority to conservative Democrats and Republicans. Even so, Brown guided much of his progressive agenda through the upper house, using his unmatched skills of personal persuasion on Democratic senators.

In 1966, as Brown was winding up his second term, the U.S. Supreme Court, still under Warren's leadership, handed down its far-reaching "one man-one vote" decision, which required state legislative seats to be apportioned by population. As Senate districts were redrawn in response to the ruling, there was a huge shift of power from rural to urban counties, strengthening not only Democrats generally but liberals within the party. That change didn't take effect until another man had assumed the governorship, however, the result of another clash between two big-name politicians.

The Rise of Ronald Reagan

Brown wanted to run for a third term in 1966, but Unruh thought—or so he later claimed—that Brown had promised to step aside in his favor. Whatever the truth, long simmering disputes between Unruh and Brown ruptured over Brown's decision to seek a third term, and both would suffer for it. Brown ran for his third term, but his break with Unruh, a rising level of social unrest, some public fumbles on Brown's part, and the appearance of an ex–movie actor named Ronald Reagan spelled disaster for those ambitions.

Reagan, a moderately successful B-movie leading man and television actor, was enticed to run against Brown by a consortium of wealthy southern California businessmen just as television emerged as a new and powerful factor in political campaigning. Televised debates had doomed Richard Nixon's bid for the presidency in 1960, leading to his hopelessly desperate run against Brown for the governorship in 1962. Two years later, Reagan made a powerful television speech for Barry Goldwater, the Republican presidential candidate. Reagan was, the businessmen decided, just the man to take on nontelegenic Pat Brown in 1966.

The GOP kingmakers were right. Even though the Democratic phase of the postwar political era was not yet concluded, and even though a large majority of California voters were Democrats, Reagan buried Brown's bid for a third term by emphasizing the incumbent's shortcomings and stressing his own conservative, get-tough attitude toward civic and campus unrest; namely, free speech and anti–Vietnam War protests at UC Berkeley and the 1965 riot in Watts. Reagan's strong win even swept several other Republicans into statewide office.

Two years earlier, Reagan's old Hollywood chum, song-and-dance man George Murphy, had defeated Pierre Salinger for a California Senate seat. Brown appointed Salinger, who had been John Kennedy's press secretary, to the Senate after Engle died during his first term. With Murphy in the U.S. Senate (he was defeated for a second term by John Tunney in 1970), Reagan in the governor's office, and Republicans holding other statewide offices, the GOP appeared once again to be on the rise. But it proved a short spurt. It would take another socio-economic cycle for Republicans to begin a sustained rise in influence among voters.

The GOP controlled the Assembly for two years in 1968–1969, but for most of Reagan's eight years as governor, he had to deal with a Democratic-controlled legislature. Unruh was gone after his losing run against Reagan in 1970, but another southern California liberal, Bob Moretti, took his place. There were occasional compromises between the conservative governor and liberal legislators, most notably on welfare reform, but it was a period remarkable for its dearth of serious policy direction from Sacramento. The Pat Brown–Jesse Unruh legacy was not undone, Reagan's rhetoric

Turnout of Registered Voters General Elections, 1912-2006			
Presidential Elections		**Nonpresidential Elections**	
Year	**Turnout percent**	**Year**	**Turnout percent**
1912	72	1914	79
1916	80	1918	59
1920	72	1922	65
1924	73	1926	63
1928	80	1930	64
1932	81	1934	75
1936	83	1938	75
1940	81	1942	59
1944	86	1946	63
1948	81	1950	73
1952	87	1954	70
1956	87	1958	80
1960	88	1962	79
1964	88	1966	79
1968	86	1970	76
1972	82	1974	64
1976	82	1978	70
1980	77	1982	70
1984	75	1986	59
1988	73	1990	59
1992	75	1994	61
1996	66	1998	58
2000	71	2002	51
2004	76	2003 (recall)	61
		2005 (special)	50
		2006	56

California Gubernatorial Voting Patterns

Democrats		Republicans	
Year	Votes (millions)	Year	Votes (millions)
1966	2.8	1966	3.7
1970	2.9	1970	3.4
1974	3.1	1974	2.9
1978	3.8	1978	2.5
1982	3.7	1982	3.8
1986	2.8	1986	4.5
1990	3.5	1990	3.8
1994	3.2	1994	4.4
1998	4.6	1998	3.1
2002	3.5	2002	3.1
2006	3.4	2006	4.9

The Candidates

1966	Reagan (R) Brown (D)	1990	Wilson (R) Feinstein (D)
1970	Reagan (R) Unruh (D)	1994	Wilson (R) Brown (D)
1974	Brown (D) Flournoy (R)	1998	Davis (D) Lungren (R)
1978	Brown (D) Younger (R)	2002	Davis (D) Simon (R)
1982	Deukmejian (R) Bradley (D)	2006	Schwarzenegger (R) Angelides (D)
1986	Deukmejian (R) Bradley (D)		

notwithstanding. But neither could liberals advance their agenda. It was a time of stalemate.

De-industrialization

Even as Reagan and Moretti battled in Sacramento, another economic and social-political cycle, largely unnoticed at the time, was beginning to manifest itself.

The period of intense industrialization in California began to wind down in the 1960s. Asia, principally Japan, had risen from the devastation of war to become a new industrial power. Californians began buying funny looking cars stamped "Made in Japan," and domestic automakers began shutting down plants in California. The steel for those cars was made not in Fontana but in Japan or Korea. Even tire production began to shift overseas. One factory at a time, California began to de-industrialize.

California was not the only state to experience damaging foreign competition in basic industrial production in the 1960s and 1970s, but what happened in California was unusual. The state underwent a massive economic transformation, from a dependence on basic industry to an economy rooted in trade (much of it with the nations of Asia), services, and certain kinds of highly specialized manufacturing, especially high-tech centered in the Silicon Valley south of San Francisco. Computers and associated devices and services—including a huge aerospace industry tied to Pentagon contracts—became the new backbone of the California economy, one that exploded with growth until a corrosive recession struck the state in 1990. But before the boom and the bust, there was a lull.

The rapid population growth that California had experienced during the postwar years slowed markedly in the 1970s as industrial job opportunities stagnated. California was still growing, even growing a bit faster than the nation as a whole, but the pace was much less dramatic. And California began to experience another phenomenon: an outflow of residents to other states.

In retrospect, that lull in growth may have been politically misleading. It persuaded the state's leaders, first Reagan and then his successor, Democrat Edmund G. "Jerry" Brown, that the infrastructure of services and facilities that had been built after World War II was adequate, that it was time to retrench, tighten budgets, and cut back on public works, whether they be state buildings in Sacramento or freeways in Los Angeles. It was a collective and indirect policy decision that would have serious adverse consequences in later years and lead Schwarzenegger and legislative leaders to attempt a reversal of course in 2006.

A Different Kind of Politician

Jerry Brown, son of the man Reagan defeated for governor in 1966, burst into state politics in 1970 as the elected secretary of state, a mostly ministerial office with few powers or opportunities for publicity. But Brown, a young former seminarian who was the personal antithesis of his back-slapping father, seized the moment.

The Watergate scandal had erupted in 1972, destroying Nixon's presidency and focusing public attention on political corruption. Brown grabbed the issue by proposing a political reform initiative and shamelessly pandering to the media, especially television. In 1974 he bested a field of relatively dull Democratic rivals, including Moretti, to win the party's nomination for governor, and then took on Houston Flournoy, the competent but colorless Republican state controller, who was a throwback to the era of Republican moderation.

Even so, it was whisker-close. Ultimately, Brown was elected not so much on his political acumen, but because of his name and the post-Watergate political climate, which had raised Democratic voter strength to near-record levels. At the height of Democratic power in 1976, 59 percent of California voters identified themselves as Democrats while just over 30 percent said they were Republicans. Democrats ran up huge majorities in the legislature; at one point after the 1976 elections, Republicans fell to just 23 seats in the 80-member Assembly. Even Orange County, the seemingly impregnable GOP bastion, had a Democratic registration plurality.

There was a spurt of legislative activity, much of it involving issues such as farm worker and bread-and-butter labor bills that had stalled in the Reagan years. Brown preached a homegrown political philosophy that defied easy categorization: liberal on civil rights, labor rights, and environmental protection but conservative on taxes and spending. Brown defined the philosophy in a series of slogan-loaded speeches in which he talked of teachers being content with psychic income rather than salary increases and of California facing an era of limits. It contrasted directly with the expansionist policies of his father and other postwar governors.

The Property Tax Revolt

At first, Brown was a hit. The words and a rather odd personal lifestyle drew attention from national political reporters starved for glamour in the post-Kennedy world of Jerry Ford and Jimmy Carter. A steady stream of pundits trekked to Sacramento and produced a flurry of effusively praiseful articles. Brown was a star, a Democratic Reagan, and Brown believed it. Scarcely more than a year after becoming governor, he was running for president. As Brown turned his political attention eastward—or skyward, according to some critics—he neglected California politics. And it was changing in ways that would profoundly influence the course of events into the next century.

As the state economy roared out of a mid-1970s recession, property values soared, and so, too, did property tax bills. It was an issue too prosaic for Jerry Brown, who had his sights set firmly on the White House. But it was just the ticket for two aging political gadflies, Howard Jarvis and Paul Gann.

Raising the specter of Californians being driven from their homes by skyrocketing property taxes, Jarvis and Gann placed on the ballot a radical measure to slash property taxes and hold them down forever. Republican candidates, seeking an issue to restore their political power, seized on Proposition 13, as the measure was numbered on the June 1978 ballot. Belatedly, Brown and legislative leaders devised a milder alternative for the same ballot.

Proposition 13 was enacted overwhelmingly, and Brown, then running for reelection against Attorney General Evelle Younger, did a 180-degree turn. Sensing that the tax revolt could be his political downfall, Brown proclaimed himself "a born-again tax cutter" and pushed a state tax cut as a companion to Proposition 13. Younger failed to exploit the opening in the fall campaign, and Brown breezed to an easy re-election victory in November. Almost immediately, the governor began plotting another run for the White House in 1980, this time as an advocate of balanced budgets, spending limits, and tax cuts. Brown was nothing if not ambitious and opportunistic, qualities that were to be his political undoing.

Brown's re-election aside, the 1978 elections marked the beginning of a long slide for the Democratic Party after two decades of dominance. Democrats suffered major losses in legislative races that year, and a flock of conservative Republicans, dubbing themselves "Prop. 13" babies, came to Sacramento—out of caves, liberals sniffed—to conduct ideological war.

In ensuing years, Republicans gained and lost legislative seats, with a net increase even in the face of a Democratic reapportionment plan in 1982 that was designed specifically to keep Democrats in power. Throughout the 1980s Democrats suffered a massive hemorrhage of voters. Their lead in party identification eroded year by year until it reached parity at about 45 percent each in the late 1980s. There was a corresponding shrinkage in the voter registration gap as well. In the mid-1970s, voter registration favored Democrats by, at most, a 57 percent to 34 percent margin. By the late 1980s, the Democrats had dipped to below 50 percent for the first time in a half-century while Republican registration climbed to nearly 40 percent. Democrats even lost a fraction of a point in 1988, when they committed $4 million to a huge voter registration drive in support of Michael Dukakis's presidential campaign. The slide continued in 1990, contributing to Democrat Dianne Feinstein's narrow loss to Republican Pete Wilson in their duel for the governorship.

Unofficial voter registration numbers were even worse for the Democrats. It was estimated that at least one million, and perhaps as many as two million, of California's 14-plus million registered voters didn't exist. The official euphemism for those phantom names is "deadwood," and it exists because California's voter registration laws make it difficult to drop people from the rolls when they die or move. Some mobile Californians may be counted two or three times as registered voters in different jurisdictions. And because Democrats are more likely to change addresses than Republicans, an adjustment for the deadwood tends to reduce Democratic ranks more dramatically.

It was generally acknowledged that stripping the voter rolls of duplicate or missing names would reduce official Democratic registration to 47 percent or 48 percent and raise Republican registration above 40 percent. That's why Democratic legislators resisted efforts to purge the rolls. Whatever the real number, the Democratic side declined and the Republican side gained. And some Democratic officials, most notably Secretary of State March Fong Eu, warned that the party was in danger of slipping into minority status.

The New Melting Pot

The roots of the trend may be found in the socio-economic currents in California during the late 1970s and 1980s. As the state's postindustrial economy shifted into high gear in the late 1970s, it created millions of jobs and, like the postwar period of industrialization, began attracting new waves of immigrants to fill them. But these immigrants didn't come from Indiana, Tennessee, and Texas. They came from Mexico, Taiwan, Korea, and the Philippines.

By the late 1980s, California's population was growing by some 2,000 people a day, and half of them were immigrants, mostly from other Pacific Rim nations with whom California was establishing ever-stronger economic ties. California was developing, in short, into the new American melting pot.

As newcomers poured into central cities, especially Los Angeles, San Francisco, and San Jose, there was an outpouring of Anglo families into the suburbs. And as those suburbs filled and home prices soared, there was an even more dramatic movement into the new suburbs springing up in former farm towns such as Modesto and

Stockton in northern California and Riverside and Redlands in southern California. These new white, middle-class suburbanites shifted political allegiance to the GOP and its promise of limited government and taxes. Areas once dependably Democratic, such as Riverside and San Bernardino counties, evolved into Republican registration majorities as they merged into suburbia. Prosperity encouraged the conversion, as did the popularity of Reagan in the White House.

A 1988 California Poll found Anglo voters favored Republicans by a 50 percent to 41 percent margin. That was critical because non-Anglos, while identifying with the Democratic Party by substantial margins, were not voting in numbers anywhere close to their proportions of the population. Exit polls in elections during the 1980s revealed that more than 80 percent of California voters were Anglos, even though they had dipped to under 60 percent of the population. It is a disconnect that continues today, although the gap is decreasing.

At the other extreme, Asians doubled their numbers in California between the late 1970s and the late 1980s, surpassing African Americans to become almost 10 percent of the population. Yet Asians accounted for just 2 percent to 4 percent of voters. The fast-growing Latino population was approaching one-fourth of the total by the late 1980s, but was only 6 percent or 7 percent of the voters until the 1992 election, when their numbers spiked upward a bit. Among non-Anglo minorities, only African Americans voted in proportion to their numbers—roughly 8 percent of the population and the electorate. But they are the slowest growing minority.

Thus, the 1980s saw a widening gap between the ethnic characteristics of California and those of voters, who not only were white but better educated, more affluent, and—perhaps most important—markedly older than the non-voters. By 1986, half of California's voters were over 50 years old, a reflection of the rapid aging of the Anglo population. That aging process continued as the state entered the 1990s and the baby boomers edged into middle age.

The Characteristic Gap

While California's population was moving in one direction—toward a multiracial, relatively young profile—the electorate was moving in another. And this characteristic gap was driving California politics to the right, toward a dominant mood of self-protection and reaction. Republicans scored well among older voters with appeals on crime, taxes, and, in 1994, illegal immigration. Democrats, hammered on these and other hot-button issues, scrambled to find some response and were mostly unsuccessful, despite a sharp but fleeting change in 1992.

The characteristic gap made itself evident on a variety of issues and contests, but was most noticeable when it came to taxation and spending. The Proposition 13 property tax revolt in 1978 and the subsequent passage of Proposition 4, a public spending limit promoted by Proposition 13 co-author Paul Gann in 1979, were the first signs that the climate had changed. Another indicator was the 1982 election of Republican George Deukmejian as governor on a no-new-taxes, tough-on-spending platform (along with a tough-on-crime stance). Deukmejian, a decent but uncharismatic former legislator and attorney general, represented a striking change of style from the unpredictable Jerry Brown.

Demands for more spending were coming from and for a growing, relatively young, non-Anglo population, while an older bloc of Anglo voters held political power. By the late 1980s, a majority of California's school children were non-Anglo, while less than a quarter of California voters had children in school—one example of how the characteristic gap affected political decision making. A 1987 poll conducted for the California Teachers Association revealed that older voters would kill any effort to raise state taxes for education. A CTA consultant noted that even arguments about grandchildren and overall societal need didn't work with those voters. If education was losing its basic political constituency—voters with children in public schools—major spending programs such as health and welfare services for the poor enjoyed even less support.

Deukmejian resisted new taxes, vetoed Democratic spending bills, trimmed the budget, and saw his popularity soar. He was re-elected by a landslide in 1986, defeating for the second time Los Angeles Mayor Tom Bradley. Even Deukmejian, who gloried in his "Iron Duke image," relented in 1989 as the Gann spending limit enacted by voters 10 years earlier squeezed the state budget. Under pressure from business interests to spend more to relieve traffic congestion, Deukmejian and legislative leaders finally reached agreement on a 1990 ballot measure to loosen the Gann limit and increase the gasoline tax. It passed, but other tax measures on the 1990 ballot were summarily rejected, indicating that only something as universal as transportation could overcome the continuing voter resistance to higher taxes.

The Essential Question

As California entered the 1990s, the essential public policy question was whether an aging Anglo population would continue to dominate the political agenda, even in the face of pressure from business executives for more spending on infrastructure to maintain a healthy business climate.

Democrats, watching an erosion of support among white, middle-class Californians, pinned their hopes at the start of the decade on a strategy of registering and organizing millions of non-Anglo voters. Former Governor Jerry Brown, who went into political exile after losing a U.S. Senate bid in 1982, returned to the stage in 1989 by winning the state Democratic Party chairmanship on a promise to bring more minorities and economically displaced whites into the party. Unfaithful, Republican-voting Democrats would, in effect, be banished from the party as it took a couple of steps to the left.

Simple as that sounds, it proved a complex task, beset by barriers of citizenship, language, and a tendency among refugees from authoritarian regimes to be apolitical. That tendency is most evident among Asians, whose cultural traditions discourage direct connections to government and politics. The number of Asian legislators rose from zero in 1990 to seven by 2007, and all but one were Democrats.

But Democrats have their own problems in creating a party image attractive to minorities who may be social and political conservatives. Some Democratic policy positions, such as pro-choice on abortion, are a hard sell to Latino voters, for instance. Prior to 1996, Republicans regularly garnered 40-plus percent of the Hispanic vote, and GOP candidates often fared even better among Asian voters.

There also are internal barriers, such as the traditionally powerful role that African Americans have played within the Democratic Party. Rhetoric about a Rainbow Coalition notwithstanding, minority groups do not automatically cooperate on matters political and there is, in fact, considerable friction.

While Jerry Brown raised millions of dollars during the first two years of his party chairmanship, he spent millions on staff and infrastructure, and when Democrats narrowly lost the governorship in 1990, many supporters of Democratic candidate Dianne Feinstein blamed Brown. The moderate Feinstein consciously attempted to woo middle-class white voters back from the Republicans, and her failure touched off another round in the Democrats' perennial debate over ideological positioning and tactics.

The issue was resolved when Brown was replaced as state party chairman by Phil Angelides, a one-time legislative staffer who had become a prominent and wealthy land developer in Sacramento and subsequently was elected state treasurer in 1998. Brown quit to run for the U.S. Senate but then, for reasons that remain unclear, switched course and made a run for the presidency that became one of the oddest footnotes to the 1992 campaign. He did not surface again as a candidate until a successful run for mayor of Oakland in 1998. Termed out of that office in 2006, he continued one of the state's most unusual political odysseys that year by being elected attorney general.

Angelides, who played a prominent role in Dukakis's 1988 presidential campaign, favored bringing back middle-class voters, which coincided nicely with the ascendancy of Bill Clinton as the party's presidential candidate in 1992. With Angelides' organizational and fundraising ability on conspicuous display, Democrats got their act together in California in 1992, signing up hundreds of thousands of new voters, especially in middle-class suburbs where reapportionment threatened the party's grip on the legislature and the congressional delegation. For the first time in more than a decade, Democratic voter strength increased, both in registration and party identification polls, albeit not dramatically.

Reapportionment Battles

The Democrats' new-found organizational strength was accompanied by a virtual disintegration of the Republican Party structure in the state because of deep divisions between moderates, led by Wilson, and a strong religious-right coalition. The GOP split, ironically, occurred just as the party won a hard-fought battle over reapportionment.

After the 1980 census, Democrats maintained their hold on the legislature and expanded their control of the state's congressional delegation with a highly partisan reapportionment plan that preserved their power in the face of real-world trends. The plan was approved by Brown and a state Supreme Court dominated by liberal Brown appointees.

The relative lull in California population growth during the 1970s meant that the state was awarded only two new congressional seats after the 1980 census, its delegation increasing from 43 to 45. Prior to the 1980s reapportionment, the 43-member delegation had been divided 22–21 in favor of Democrats. It was a fair division of the seats in terms of both overall party identification and congressional vote in the state, both of which were evenly divided between parties. But after the late U.S. Representative Phil Burton completed a gerrymandered plan he called "my contribution to modern art," the delegation was 28–17 in favor of Democrats. And it was so well done that Republicans were able to gain only two seats in subsequent elections, leaving the delegation at 26–19.

California's population growth was much higher in the 1980s. The state gained six million people between 1980 and 1990, roughly a quarter of total U.S. population growth. The state was awarded seven new congressional seats, giving it not only the largest congressional delegation in the nation but the largest of any state in history.

Republicans wanted redress. They believed they should have roughly half of the California seats, which would mean receiving all of the new ones. And it would have been difficult for the Democrats to pull a repeat of 1982, not only in congressional reapportionment, but in redrawing legislative districts.

For the reapportionment plan enacted after the 1990 census, conditions for Democrats were not as favorable and the stakes were much higher. After Deukmejian's decision not to run for a third term in 1990—which meant he wouldn't be available to veto any gerrymander drawn by majority Democrats in the legislature—GOP leaders, stretching as high as the White House, engineered a strategic coup. They persuaded Pete Wilson, the one-time San Diego mayor who had defeated Jerry Brown for a U.S. Senate seat in 1982 and won a second term handily in 1988, to run for governor in 1990.

Selection of a Democratic candidate didn't go as easily. Attorney General John Van de Kamp, a liberal with strong environmental and consumer credentials, was the early favorite. His only declared rival, Feinstein, refused to drop out, even when her campaign manager quit with a blast at her commitment to the race. Feinstein fashioned a decidedly more centrist image, arguing that a liberal such as Van de Kamp was headed for certain defeat at Wilson's hands. Among other things, she supported the death penalty, a litmus test for many Democrats.

Feinstein won the nomination and engaged in an expensive shootout with Wilson, her one-time political ally when she was mayor of San Francisco and he was a U.S. senator. Wilson won a narrow victory and became California's 36th governor, putting himself in position to protect Republican interests on reapportionment—as well as to confront the many problems of a fast-growing and diverse state, including a worsening budget crisis.

A final factor in reapportionment was that minority groups, especially those representing Hispanics, believed they, too, were damaged by the 1982 reapportionment. So they pressured Democrats for new representation in both congressional and legislative seats. Initially, Democrats—led by Assembly Speaker Willie Brown, Jr.—tried to negotiate their way out of their dilemma, offering Republicans guaranteed gains in both the legislature and Congress in return for equally strong guarantees that Democrats would retain control. There was a substantial sentiment among Republican politicians toward such a settlement, primarily because the alternative, throwing the issue to the courts, was less certain.

Brown tried to capitalize on the Republican divisions, openly courting conservative Assembly members who were at ideological odds with Wilson, promising them locked-in congressional seats if they would abandon the governor. Ultimately, Brown and a few right-wing plotters could not put together a veto-proof deal, and Democrats

Absentee Voting in Gubernatorial Elections Since 1974			
Year	**Percentage**	**Year**	**Percentage**
1974	4	1994	22
1978	5	1998	24
1982	6	2002	27
1986	8	2003	30
1990	18	2006	42

simply passed their reapportionment plan and allowed Wilson to veto it, thus moving the reapportionment debate to the state Supreme Court.

The court hired the same consultants it had used two decades earlier to draw reapportionment maps after a similar stalemate between the Democratic legislature and Reagan. Within weeks, the court's consultants had created 172 legislative and congressional districts that closely followed demographic trends—shifting more power from the cities to the suburbs, which enhanced Republican prospects, and creating more minority seats, especially Latino seats, within urban areas largely dictated by the federal Voting Rights Act.

Defeat from the Jaws of Victory

Wilson and Republican leaders were jubilant. They saw an unprecedented opportunity to seize control of the Capitol for the first time in decades—a prospect enhanced by the 1990 passage of Proposition 140, the term limits initiative, which eventually would force entrenched Democratic incumbents to surrender their seats. What looked good for Republicans on paper, however, needed first to overcome the party's own divisiveness.

The postwar history of the California Republican Party has been one of recurrent conflict between moderates and conservatives. In 1982, with the election of Deukmejian to the governorship (he defeated right-wing lieutenant governor Mike Curb in the primary) and Pete Wilson to the U.S. Senate, the centrists regained the influence they had lost during the Ronald Reagan and post-Proposition 13 years.

With patronage from the governor's office and the Senate, Republican moderates enjoyed a rebirth of influence within the party while right-wingers complained of being ignored. Their lone bastion was the Assembly Republican Caucus, which continued to be dominated by the "Proposition 13 babies."

Conservatives stopped short of open revolt. They didn't balk at having Wilson as their candidate for governor in 1990 because they wanted a winner who would protect the party on reapportionment. But issues such as abortion continued to divide the party bitterly as it sought a new direction in the post–Cold War, post-Reagan era.

Wilson had scarcely been inaugurated when sniping began. Conservatives were irritated by Wilson's selection of moderate state Senator John Seymour—a former conservative who had flip-flopped on abortion—as his successor in the U.S. Senate and were put off by Wilson's advocacy of new taxes during his first year in office to balance the state budget. The moderate-conservative split flared sharply late in the 1991 session of the legislature, when moderates, encouraged if not abetted by Wilson, seized control of the Assembly GOP caucus. And it raged throughout 1992.

The right recaptured the party apparatus and fielded numerous candidates for legislative and congressional seats while Wilson and the moderates belatedly challenged them in the June primaries. Conservatives won most of the head-to-head battles but several found themselves unelectable in swing districts where more moderate Republican candidates could have won.

After more than a dozen years of electoral gains, Republicans were hurt in 1992 by a rapidly deteriorating state economy; the unpopularity of Republican President George Bush, who virtually abandoned a state the GOP had won in the previous five presidential elections; the resurgent political activism of women over the issue of abortion; and, finally, the fact that California Democrats had gotten their act together under Angelides.

What had appeared to be a golden opportunity for Republicans to make legislative gains turned into a virtual wash while Democrats swept the presidential vote and two U.S. Senate seats. It was a Republican debacle that left open the question whether Wilson could win re-election in 1994.

Democrats emerged from the 1992 elections with high hopes for ousting Wilson with state Treasurer Kathleen Brown, daughter of one former governor and sister of another, as the presumptive Democratic candidate. Brown made up her mind to run in late 1992, as Wilson's popularity plummeted to record lows. One respected poll had her leading Wilson by a 23-point margin; the Eastern media flocked to California to anoint her as the new political star; and Brown easily bested a couple of Democratic foes in the primary.

But Brown's aura as a political dynamo was mostly myth, and her campaign foundered from the outset. She changed managers, slogans, and themes so many times that even the most dedicated watchers lost count. She raised immense amounts of money but could not buy ads on the last weekend of the campaign. And Wilson, starting early in 1994, began demonstrating the intensely focused, if graceless, campaign style that had previously vanquished two other Democratic stars, Jerry Brown and Feinstein.

A Focus on Immigration

Wilson focused on illegal immigration and crime as his issues, while Kathleen Brown tried, and failed, to develop alternative themes attractive to voters. The more she campaigned, in the primary and later against Wilson, the worse she did in the polls. Wilson pulled even in June, and then trounced her by 14 points in November. The massive nature of his win, coupled with his penchant for bashing President Clinton, propelled the governor into contention for the 1996 Republican presidential nomination. But Wilson's foray onto the national stage turned out to be his most embarrassing political venture. Saddled with a voice damaged by surgery and reminders of a '94 campaign promise to serve the entirety of his second term as governor, Wilson launched his presidential bid in August 1995 with a speech in front of the Statue of Liberty. But, plagued by months of internal turmoil within his campaign staff and stuck at the bottom of national polls, he pulled out before the end of the year.

More significant for his party, the tenor of Wilson's anti-immigration-fueled campaign, and his willingness to embrace an initiative—Proposition 187—to deny social and education benefits to illegal aliens, motivated many Latino immigrants to seek citizenship and register as Democrats. It was a movement that would reverberate negatively on the governor's party for the rest of the decade.

Meanwhile, the legislature increasingly withdrew into itself, preoccupied with such inside baseball as campaign strategy, fund raising, and partisan and factional power struggles. It seemed unable, or unwilling, to cope with the huge policy issues raised by the dynamics of the real world beyond the Capitol: population growth, ethnic diversity, transportation congestion, educational stagnation, environmental pollution. The legislature, recast by Unruh as a full-time professional body in the 1960s and once rated the best in the nation, faced policy gridlock and rising popular disgust with its antics, fueled by spiraling corruption scandals.

California's political demography is at least partially responsible for its legislative lethargy. Legislators are torn between the demands and aspirations of California's new immigrant-dominated population and the limits set by white, middle-class voters. And the very professionalism that was Unruh's proudest achievement contributed to the malaise. Full-time legislators, many of them graduates of the legislature's staff, are preoccupied with their political careers; legislative duties that conflict with those careers are shunted aside.

Legislative Reform and the Onset of Term Limits

Throughout the 1980s, critics proposed reforms to restore the legislature's luster, such as imposing limits on campaign spending and fund raising (which had increased geometrically) and providing public funds to campaigns. Voters endorsed a comprehensive reform initiative in 1988, but they also approved a more limited version placed on the ballot by some legislators and special-interest groups. The first provided public funds for campaigns while the second specifically barred such spending; the second gained more votes. The result was that most of the first initiative was negated, but nearly all of the second was later invalidated by the courts.

As a years-long federal investigation of Capitol corruption spawned indictments in 1989, the legislature began drafting reforms designed to raise its standing with an increasingly cynical public. These reforms, including tighter conflict-of-interest rules and a ban on speaking fees, were approved by voters in 1990. Voters also gave their blessing to an initiative—Proposition 140—that imposed tough term limits on lawmakers, eliminated their pensions, and sharply reduced the legislature's spending on operations.

Term limits and reapportionment produced bumper crops of new legislators in 1992 and 1994. Under the term limits law, Assembly members are limited to three two-year terms and senators to a pair of four-year terms. As the 1995 legislative session began, scarcely 20 of the Assembly's 80 members had more than two years' experience, and in 1996, the remaining older members gave up their seats. By 2005, every member serving in 1990 had been termed out of both houses of the legislature, stripping that body of its last vestige of institutional memory. And when the 2007–2008 legislature convened in December 2006, the Assembly welcomed 36 rookies—nearly half the entire house.

There is endless speculation as to the effects of term limits beyond creating turn-over. It is clear that the new legislators arriving in the Capitol are a more diverse group, with many newcomers emerging from local government rather than legislative staff. That has changed the dynamics of lobbying by making grass-roots organizations more important and one-on-one relationships less important. Power also shifted from the constantly changing Assembly to the more experienced Senate.

The 1994 elections produced a partisan shift. Republicans won a bare majority of the 80-member Assembly by picking up eight new seats, although the defection of one Republican left a historic 40–40 tie over the all-powerful Assembly speakership as the session began.

The deadlock lasted for seven weeks. Ostensibly, leaders of the two partisan factions, longtime Speaker Willie Brown and GOP leader Jim Brulte, were engaged in negotiations aimed at a bipartisan agreement on sharing power. But while negotiations came close to success, they faltered on the all-important issue of time. Democrats wanted an agreement for two years while Republicans insisted that if they regained a 41-seat majority, they wanted control.

The impasse was resolved when Democrats seized power through parliamentary maneuvers. Brown, presiding by dint of seniority, issued a series of procedural rulings that allowed Democrats to vote to oust Republican Assemblyman Richard Mountjoy, alleging that he had ceded his claim on the seat because he had been elected to the Senate in a special election. Brown and the Democrats then adopted new rules that provided at least the appearance of power-sharing with the Republicans, who vowed to recall Republican-turned-independent Paul Horcher, elect a successor to Mountjoy, and claim control of the house. This they did, but it took a year.

187 Comes Home to Roost

The chronic impotence of the legislature manifested itself in an explosion of initiative campaigns that took issues directly to voters, bypassing the Capitol altogether. Initiatives became so popular that lawmakers and even candidates for governor began sponsoring them as vehicles to make policy or gain favorable publicity. In 1990, gubernatorial candidate Wilson trumpeted an initiative to deal with crime, and seeking re-election in 1994, he backed the highly controversial Proposition 187.

The fallout from Proposition 187 did not significantly affect the elections of 1996, when another Republican-dominated initiative—Proposition 209—dealt a blow to state-sponsored affirmative-action programs and further solidified the growing perception of the Republican Party as not only Anglo, but anti-ethnic. The 187 fallout hit full force in the elections of 1998, when Latinos and other ethnic groups voted overwhelmingly for Democratic candidates and helped fashion the GOP debacle that forced the party to search for ways to reach beyond its shrinking white voter base and attract non-Anglos to its standard.

At the same time, there were warning signs that all was not well with Democrats, despite their triumphs of 1998, and the brightest red light went on in one of the state's strongest Democratic bastions—Oakland. In November, Jerry Brown, who had renounced his Democratic Party membership, won the nonpartisan office of mayor by campaigning against the Democratic-dominated political establishment. Four months later, in March 1999, a Green Party candidate named Audie Bock upset former Oakland Mayor Elihu Harris, a longtime Democratic Party figure who was trying to win a special election to the state Assembly, where he had served prior to becoming mayor. Harris lost even though he outspent Bock ten-to-one and had the full backing of Assembly Democrats. Although Harris was deeply flawed as a candidate, his loss coming on the heels of Brown's gave Democrats pause.

Scandals

Between 1999 and 2005, three meaty scandals forced the resignation of two state-wide constitutional officers—Republican Insurance Commissioner Charles Quackenbush (2000) and Democratic Secretary of State Kevin Shelley (2004)—and severely weakened the stature of a third, Governor Gray Davis, forcing a historic recall in 2003.

Quackenbush was undone by events that followed the 1994 Northridge earthquake. Insurance companies allegedly mishandled hundreds of millions of dollars worth of claims filed after the quake. After a series of investigations, Quackenbush's department recommended heavy fines for three major companies —State Farm, Allstate, and 20th Century Insurance—with the money earmarked for special funds designed to compensate homeowners. But Quackenbush and his top aides arranged to fine them much smaller amounts and funnel the money into nonprofit foundations established to promote his political career. For instance, Department of Insurance staff recommended that State Farm pay $2.38 billion in fines and $114.7 million into a policyholder fund. Quackenbush signed an agreement whereby State Farm paid $2 million to one of his foundations and a mere $5,000 to the department to cover administrative costs. Similar deals were cut with four other insurers.

After the *Los Angeles Times* detailed these arrangements late in 1999, Democratic lawmakers—using the oversight function of the Joint Legislative Audit Committee— launched an aggressive investigation of Quackenbush and his department, focusing on the foundations and Quackenbush's role in negotiating deals that benefited his career at the expense of policyholders. Hearings stretched through the spring and early summer of 2000, and Quackenbush was forced to resign. He subsequently left California and now is a deputy sheriff in Florida.

The next year, Davis was caught in an embarrassing scandal over his fund-raising activity, and though it did not force his resignation, the mess contributed to the view that Davis's administration was for sale. At the center of the scandal was a $95 million contract that the administration had signed with software giant Oracle. A state auditor's report found that the contract was overpriced and the software unnecessary. More significant was the $25,000 campaign contribution that Oracle bestowed on Davis's re-election campaign shortly after the contract was approved. Three Davis aides were fired over the incident, but the image persisted that the governor strong-armed contributions out of corporations who wanted to do business with the state.

In 2004, a different kind of scandal brought down Shelley, whose problems were threefold. First, $75,000 in campaign contributions were given to his election campaign by three people who received grant money that then-Assemblyman Shelley had steered to a nonprofit San Francisco center founded by a longtime Shelley ally and fund raiser. The contributions looked like campaign money laundering or, worse, a payback. Shelley received an additional $80,000 in contributions from other donors involved in real-estate transactions with the same ally, prompting an investigation by the state Department of Real Estate.

Second, the FBI was investigating Shelley's office for the way it distributed hundreds of thousands of dollars in federal grants designed to enhance nonpartisan efforts to increase voter participation. It was alleged that Shelley gave the money to Democratic cronies, who used it in a partisan effort to help Democrats.

Finally, there was Shelley himself. Throughout his legislative career and as secretary of state, Shelley was plagued by an anger-management problem that often saw the 6'5" official intimidate and berate employees and staff. Stories about Shelley were legendary, including one incident where a Capitol surveillance camera caught him lashing out at an employee whom he had just fired.

As the scandals and investigations widened, Shelley withdrew into a bunker, surrounded by staff and the massive state bureaucracy. Republicans in the legislature pressed for a full-scale investigation, like the one engineered by Democrats to topple Quackenbush. Legislative hearings began early in 2005, with Democrats seemingly content to concentrate on testimony from Shelley's underlings. Republicans clamored for Shelley himself to be subpoenaed—and grilled. Shelley ended it all when, on February 4, he announced that he would resign, effective March 1, 2005. Governor Schwarzenegger then appointed Republican moderate Bruce McPherson of Santa Cruz to replace Shelley. McPherson had been termed out of the legislature in 2004 after serving in the Assembly and Senate.

The Coming and Going of Gray

California's abruptly shifting politics are symbolized by the short, unhappy second term of Governor Gray Davis, a Democrat first elected in 1998 after serving what many considered the most complete gubernatorial apprenticeship in state history. Between 1975 and 1998, Davis had learned the business from the ground up, serving as chief of staff to Governor Jerry Brown, two terms in the Assembly, and two terms each as state controller and lieutenant governor.

Despite having "Experience Money Can't Buy" as his campaign slogan promised, Davis was ill-prepared when it came to leadership. A prodigious fundraiser, he set records for accumulating campaign money and had nearly $50 million in the bank for his re-election in 2002. But his frantic money-raising reinforced the image that Davis was for sale and presided over a pay-to-play administration.

His first term was a study in contrasts. The first two-plus years saw California steeped in prosperity, fueled in large measure by a boom in northern California's technology sector. The "dot-com" revolution, named for internet-based start up companies, poured billions of dollars in income-tax revenues into state coffers as entrepreneurs and their employees earned millions of dollars in stock options, bonuses, and inflated salaries. Davis and the legislature used the bloom-bloated revenues to bulk up the state budget, while securing tax cuts and tax breaks. Given the way budgets are created and maintained, the state was ill-prepared for the "dot-com bust" of 2000–2001, when billions in tax revenue disappeared along with the Internet-based companies that had created the boom. By 2003, the state had a budget gap in excess of $18 billion.

Davis's first term also was plagued in 2001 with an energy crisis that threatened to send rolling blackouts the length and breadth of California. The crisis was sparked, in part, by a deregulation of the energy industry that took place during the second Wilson administration. But the full impact of deregulation smashed headlong into the Davis administration when, after years of neglect in building new power plants and securing new and enhanced sources of electricity, the state was at the mercy of newly deregulated market forces—causing electricity prices to skyrocket some 900 percent in times of perceived shortage. As the state's energy providers—including the massive Pacific Gas & Electric and Southern California Edison—hemorrhaged money and careened toward bankruptcy, Davis was slow to respond. Nor did the governor inspire confidence in his leadership by loudly proclaiming that the "energy crisis" was not his fault; thus trying to deflect political blame with an electorate that wanted solutions, not excuses.

Republicans, bankrolled by national GOP interests, ran a series of TV ads blasting Davis, and his poll numbers plummeted from 57 percent in January 2001 to 36 percent in May. His administration ultimately negotiated long-term electricity deals at exorbitant rates with providers such as the now-defunct Enron Corporation, who it later was revealed had artificially driven up the price of electricity by "gaming" the California market.

As Davis's 2002 re-election approached, he was in danger of becoming the first sitting governor defeated for re-election in California since Culbert Olsen in 1942. His most serious threat was Richard Riordan, a moderate Republican completing his second term as mayor of Los Angeles. Riordan entered the GOP primary where he faced what was thought to be only token opposition from Secretary of State Bill Jones and conservative businessman William Simon—the son of Richard Nixon's secretary of the treasury and a neophyte politician. Less than two months before the election, Riordan led Simon by 37 points in the polls.

Davis and his political advisors launched a pre-emptive strike. In the weeks leading up to the March election, the Davis campaign aired $10 million in statewide TV ads that savaged Riordan and helped shape the GOP primary. Their goal was to derail Riordan, and it worked. In a stunning reversal of fortunes, Simon won the primary by 14 points.

During the fall campaign, the Simon campaign proved as inept as its candidate was energetic. Simon's most memorable gaffe took place during a televised debate with Davis, where the Republican nominee accused the Democratic governor of having accepted a campaign contribution on state property—a legal no-no that, if true, would have reinforced Davis's image as a mercenary whose governorship was for sale to the highest bidder. The Simon campaign later said it had a photo that verified the allegation. Unfortunately for Simon, the photo proved the opposite—the check was delivered to Davis in a private home.

Recall and Arnold

Davis squeaked past Simon to win his second term. But storm clouds already were gathering in the form of an embryonic recall effort launched by conservative groups not long after Davis was sworn in for a second term in January 2003. At first, the recall failed to gain much traction, primarily due to lack of ready cash for signature gathering and despite free publicity lavished on the effort by conservative radio talk-show hosts.

But in May, Darrell Issa, a conservative congressman from San Diego, pumped life into the recall by forming his own recall committee and seeding it with a $100,000 check. Eventually, Issa would funnel $2 million into the endeavor and—not surprisingly—declare himself a candidate for governor should the recall reach the ballot. Thanks to Issa's money, the recall gained momentum, with three separate campaigns eventually submitting 1.7 million signatures—far more than the 897,158 required to put it on the ballot. Then-Secretary of State Kevin Shelley announced in late July that it had qualified, and Lieutenant Governor Cruz Bustamante set the election for October 7.

In effect, the recall asked voters two questions: Should Gray Davis be recalled, and who should replace him as governor? The first question was a "yes" or "no." The second required voters to pick from among those who had filed to run as Davis's replacement. Eventually, 135 candidates would leap into the fray, but the next governor would come from a small slate of contenders with name ID, money, and professional campaign teams: Green Party activist Peter Camejo, former baseball commissioner Peter Ueberroth, pundit Arianna Huffington, Davis's 2002 opponent Bill Simon, and state Senator Tom McClintock.

But that dynamic changed dramatically with a pair of announcements, both on August 6.

The candidate who created the most public turmoil made his eleventh hour announcement not on a courthouse step or in front of the state Capitol but on "The Tonight Show with Jay Leno." Actor and businessman Arnold Schwarzenegger, one of the most recognized celebrities in the world, turned politics upside down when he said he would run—despite weeks of speculation that he would sit out the race. Schwarzenegger's candidacy immediately changed the tenor and scope of the recall, elevating it to international status and raising the odds that Davis would be swept from office. Schwarzenegger sucked the air out of most other GOP campaigns, eventually causing Simon and Ueberroth to drop out, although their names remained on the ballot.

For Davis, however, another significant candidate announced on the same day—Lieutenant Governor Cruz Bustamante, who defied efforts by party leaders to keep high-ranking Democrats on the sidelines. Bustamante's decision angered those who felt Davis might be saved if the party presented a united front. Bustamante's poor showing—he finished second, some 17 points behind Schwarzenegger—further alienated Democrats and demolished his statewide elective career. Termed out as lieutenant governor in 2006, he ran for state insurance commissioner and was soundly defeated by Republican Steve Poizner.

It is highly unlikely that Davis could have been saved from an angry and frustrated electorate seeking a scapegoat for a litany of woes, including the budget deficit, chronic energy shortages, and poor performing schools. Davis—despite his political pedigree—was a man without friends or real allies. He was not well liked by Democratic colleagues (never mind Republicans) and was despised by those who felt strong-armed by his mania for fund raising. In times of crisis, he proved to be a panicky, inept leader—a paper tiger whose first-term popularity reflected nothing more than the ephemeral sheen of prosperity.

On October 7, 2003, Davis was recalled in a historic election that saw Schwarzenegger installed in his place. Schwarzenegger had campaigned against "politics as usual" and promised to "blow up boxes" in Sacramento in order to cleanse the Capitol of special interests that he said were responsible for the state's financial woes. Within an hour after being sworn in as governor, Schwarzenegger signed an order that reduced the vehicle license fee—the fulfillment of a campaign promise that added more than $4 billion to the state's already alarming budget deficit.

Despite campaign promises to the contrary, Schwarzenegger steeped his first year in orthodoxy, attacking the massive budget deficit much the way Davis had sought to deal with it—with a combination of cuts and borrowing. He campaigned vigorously for a $15 billion bond on the March 2004 primary ballot, with the proceeds earmarked for deficit reduction. He cut deals with the education establishment to suspend constitutionally mandated school-funding guarantees to help the immediate fiscal crisis, promising in return to pay back what schools lost to the deal. He launched an effort to "reform" government through a performance-review commission, which issued a much-ballyhooed report after statewide hearings on government efficiency and operation. Once the ballyhoo subsided, the report sank into the traditional abyss reserved for comprehensive overall efforts.

Overall, however, Schwarzenegger's first year produced more confusion than results. Part of the problem stemmed from the way he constructed his inner circle of administrators and advisors. Many—Chief of Staff Pat Clarey and communications guru Rob Stutzman, for instance—were political conservatives. Others, such as Cabinet Secretary Terry Tamminen and senior advisor Bonnie Reiss—were liberals close to the governor's Democratic in-laws, the Kennedy clan. The conflicts inherent in this structure were most evident in the way the governor treated the legislature. At times, Schwarzenegger insisted that lawmakers were his partners in solving the state's problems. At other times, he referred to them as "girlie men" and threatened to take his case directly to the people in the form of initiatives if the legislature did not pass his agenda. The "good cop, bad cop" routine didn't work. The governor tried to play both roles, and ended up looking more like a Kindergarten Cop still learning the ways of Sacramento.

Midway through 2005, it was even unclear whether Schwarzenegger would seek re-election in 2006. He was said to be frustrated with the Capitol's incessant partisan bickering, and there were public and not-so-subtle signals from his wife, First Lady Maria Shriver, that she and their children had tired of the time he spent away from their Brentwood home.

Rumors aside, just the specter of a Schwarzenegger candidacy in 2006 helped shape the potential field of Democratic challengers. In April 2005, for instance, Attorney General Bill Lockyer, once considered a shoo-in to run for governor, opted to run for state treasurer instead. Lockyer's withdrawal left two major Democratic candidates in the race—Treasurer Phil Angelides and Controller Steve Westly. Their battle was expensive, with the wealthy controller largely self-funding and Angelides relying on close allies in the development world and traditional Democratic groups suspicious of Westly's past cooperation with Schwarzenegger.

Angelides prevailed, but events outside his control already had pre-ordained the election as Schwarzenegger—politically wounded by the erratic course he had plotted in 2005—staged a remarkable political resurgence that allowed him to brush aside his

Democratic foe even as he mostly ignored both his opponent and the campaign for governor.

A Not-So-Special Election

Throughout 2005, Schwarzenegger clashed with legislators over a variety of issues, notably public employee pensions, state spending, and the drawing of legislative districts. Along the way, the governor took on traditional Democratic allies, but it was an unfortunate set of foes for any politician because it included teachers, nurses, and rank-and-file law enforcement personnel such as police and firefighters.

As early as his 2005 state-of-the-state address, Schwarzenegger challenged lawmakers to enact his forthcoming agenda by a date certain or face the wrath of voters because he would take that agenda to the ballot and call a special election to accomplish what the legislature refused to do. That confrontational tone continued throughout 2005, with the governor refusing to compromise on his agenda and Democrats—prompted by labor groups—adamantly refusing to accede to his demands.

The result was an expensive statewide special election in November 2005 where voters were asked to decide the fate of eight initiatives, most backed by the governor and the business community—notably the California Chamber of Commerce and California Business Roundtable. Labor fought back, led by the nurses, teachers, and firefighters.

The result was a resounding defeat for Schwarzenegger and a change of approach for 2006. Chastened by his shellacking in the special election and facing re-election, Schwarzenegger began to rebuild his image, choosing cooperation over confrontation and working with Democratic lawmakers to fashion a productive legislative session in 2006.

The governor began his resurrection with an unprecedented apology to voters for putting them through both the expense and the angst associated with the special election. He admitted it was a mistake, promised to be more cooperative, then proceeded to join with the legislature to produce an increase in the minimum wage, key bills to address global warming, and more money for education.

More significant, Schwarzenegger proposed a bold plan to rebuild California's infrastructure, financed with a series of bonds. Although he initially called for more than $100 billion in bonds, the governor and lawmakers agreed to a more modest package, with the money to be spent for transportation, schools, housing, and flood protection. The bonds appeared as four measures on the November 2006 ballot—not coincidentally, the same ballot that contained Schwarzenegger's re-election.

The governor and legislative leaders—Democrats all—campaigned in tandem for the bonds, an odd alliance that hampered the efforts of Schwarzenegger's Democratic opponent, state Treasurer Phil Angelides. But Schwarzenegger didn't need help. By the end of the gubernatorial campaign, he had reconstructed his political image and swamped Angelides.

Taking strong cues from the electorate's attitude on confrontation and cooperation, Schwarzenegger entered his second and final term pledging to continue his collaboration with lawmakers. He described himself as a "centrist" and used the occasion of his inaugural and 2007 state-of-the-state address to propose, among other ideas, sweeping changes in health care coverage for Californians. Democrats applauded the governor's move even as they began to poke holes in his specific ideas. The noticeable difference, perhaps signaling a political maturity on the part of Schwarzenegger, was the governor's demeanor—he launched the effort without the "my way or the highway" rhetoric that had precluded any cooperation in 2005.

The governor's change of approach was founded in political realities gripping California and those who seek to govern it.

A More Independent Future

The political map of California has changed over the past decade. In 1995, 38 of the state's 58 counties had Democratic pluralities. That number had shrunk to 21 by 2005. A red-blue map of California shows that Democrats dominate the coast, while Republicans control inland areas. Democrats maintain overall hegemony because of their dominance in urban Los Angeles and the San Francisco Bay Area.

The most Democratic counties in California are Alameda, Imperial, San Francisco, Santa Cruz, Marin, and Los Angeles—all with more than 50 percent Democratic registration. By contrast, only one county—Placer—has better than 50 percent Republican registration. Of the top 10 Republican counties, only Orange (in eighth place) can be considered a population center.

But the real story does not involve Republicans or Democrats but those who have chosen to identify outside the two major parties—mostly decline to state. In 2007, Republicans and Democrats face an erosion of support clearly marked in voter-registration figures. In February 1995, 49 percent of voters signed up as Democrats, 37 percent as Republicans. Only 10 percent considered themselves decline to state. On the eve of the 2006 election, the Democrats' share had dropped to 42.5 percent, Republicans' to 34.3 percent. Decline to state registration had soared to more than 18.7 percent. In seven counties, decline to state broaches 20 percent of the electorate: San Francisco, Santa Clara, Alpine, Mono, Alameda, San Mateo, and San Diego. Much of the growth in more independent registration mirrors communities with growing ethnic populations, especially among Asians.

Capturing those voters has proven a particular knot for both parties, in part because each continues to elect legislators who pander to the extremes, while the electorate as a whole continues its relentless march toward moderation. Until the parties figure out a way to compete more effectively for registrants as well as votes, erosion will be the norm for Republicans and Democrats.

2

The Constitutional Officers

California has 12 constitutional officers, so named because their jobs are created and duties outlined in the state constitution. Each is elected to a four-year term in even-numbered nonpresidential years, and all are subject to term limits (two terms and out). Eight are elected statewide: governor, lieutenant governor, attorney general, secretary of state, treasurer, controller, insurance commissioner, and superintendent of public instruction. The remaining four, members of the State Board of Equalization, are elected from districts.

By far the most powerful constitutional officer is the governor who, by virtue of California's size and economic magnitude, can be one of the nation's most significant political players. Over the past half century, nearly every California governor entertained notions of running for president, and one—Ronald Reagan—occupied the White House from 1981 to 1988. In 1953 another California governor, Earl Warren, was appointed chief justice of the United States Supreme Court, where he used political and judicial skills to lead his colleagues through a momentous chapter in American history.

But the governor also can serve as a lightning rod for voter discontent. And in an era when it is becoming easier and more prevalent to express dissatisfaction through statewide ballot measures, the governor can be vulnerable to recall—as was demonstrated so emphatically in 2003 when Democrat Gray Davis was bounced from office less than a year into his second term and replaced with Republican Arnold Schwarzenegger.

As with legislators, term limits have prompted a game of musical chairs among constitutional officers. In 2006, three moved from one post to another after term limits forced them from their jobs: John Garamendi from insurance commissioner to lieutenant governor; Bill Lockyer from attorney general to treasurer; and John Chiang from Board of Equalization to controller. Four others tried to move but lost the election: Phil Angelides from treasurer to governor; Steve Westly from controller to governor; Cruz Bustamante from lieutenant governor to insurance commissioner; and Claude Parrish from Board of Equalization to treasurer.

GOVERNOR
Arnold Schwarzenegger (R)

Arnold Schwarzenegger

It is said that the conservative core of the state Republican Party never would have nominated Schwarzenegger to run for governor, that he needed an extraordinary circumstance to open a path to Sacramento. That path opened in 2003 with the recall of Gov. Gray Davis. Campaigning to replace Davis, Schwarzenegger was pro-choice, pro-environment, and indifferent on issues such as gay rights and gun control, an approach more reminiscent of a centrist Democrat than a mainstream California Republican.

Not that he wasn't willing to experiment once he took office. His first term as governor was marked by inconsistent political behavior and rookie mistakes, but after three years of wandering around the political spectrum, trying on various philosophies as though he were shopping for a suit, Schwarzenegger appears to be most comfortable in the centrist flannels that first defined him.

More significant, he has gained his sea legs and established himself as a governor in action as well as in name, willing to use his considerable celebrity and formidable power to lead a state that many observers believe is ungovernable on the natural. His interests are both grand and parochial—improving California while building a legacy for his governorship.

Schwarzenegger began his second term as governor in 2007 much the way he ended his first term just prior to his 2006 re-election, by proposing bold visions for his adopted state. In a series of speeches centered on his inaugural, Schwarzenegger called for greater access to health care, improved transportation systems, and greater efforts to clean up the environment and address problems associated with global warming. He called for a robust construction program for highways, schools, prisons, dams and water storage facilities, and universities.

And he implored lawmakers and other government officials to work in a spirit of cooperation, not confrontation—in direct contrast to the way he first began his unusual tenure as governor of the nation's most unusual state.

Even before he came to Sacramento, the Austrian-born, celebrity body builder/action-hero/businessman harbored ambitions for leadership and had confidence in his ability to bend others to his will. As biographer Laurence Leamer pointed out in his 2005 book, *Fantastic: The Life of Arnold Schwarzenegger,* Schwarzenegger holds powerful and mesmerizing leaders in great esteem and aspires to a destiny writ large.

Gubernatorial Elections 1902-2006

1902		
George C. Pardee (R)	49%	
Franklin K. Lane (D)	47%	

1946		
Earl Warren (R*)	92%	
Henry Schmidt (Pr)	7%	

1906		
James Gillett (R)	40%	
Theodore Bell (D)	38%	

1950		
Earl Warren (R*)	65%	
James Roosevelt (D)	35%	

1910		
Hiram Johnson (R)	46%	
Theodore Bell (D)	40%	

1954		
Goodwin Knight (R)	57%	
Richard Graves (D)	43%	

1914		
Hiram Johnson (Pg*)	50%	
John Fredericks (R)	29%	
J. B. Curtin (D)	13%	

1958		
Edmund "Pat" Brown (D*)	60%	
William Knowland (R)	40%	

1918		
William Stephens (R*)	56%	
Theodore Bell (I)	37%	

1962		
Edmund "Pat" Brown (D)	52%	
Richard Nixon (R)	47%	

1922		
Friend Wm. Richardson (R)	60%	
Thomas Woolwine (D)	36%	

1966		
Ronald Reagan (R)	57%	
Pat Brown (D*)	42%	

1926		
C. C. Young (R)	71%	
Justus Wardell (D)	25%	

1970		
Ronald Reagan (R*)	52%	
Jesse Unruh (D)	45%	

1930		
James Rolph, Jr. (R)	72%	
Milton Young (D)	24%	

1974		
Jerry Brown (D)	50%	
Houston Flournoy (R)	47%	

1934		
Frank Merriam (R)	49%	
Upton Sinclair (D)	38%	
Raymond Haight (C)	13%	

1978		
Jerry Brown (D*)	56%	
Evelle Younger (R)	37%	

1938		
Culbert Olson (D)	53%	
Frank Merriam (R*)	44%	

1982		
George Deukmejian (R)	49%	
Tom Bradley (D)	48%	

1942		
Earl Warren (R)	57%	
Culbert Olson (D*)	42%	

1986		
George Deukmejian (R*)	61%	
Tom Bradley (D)	38%	

Elections 1902-2006 cont.

1990			2002		
Pete Wilson (R)	49%		Gray Davis (D*)		47%
Dianne Feinstein (D)	46%		William Simon (R)		42%
1994			**2003** Recall of Gray Davis		
Pete Wilson (R*)	55%		Yes		55%
Kathleen Brown (D)	41%		No		45%
			Arnold Schwarzenegger (R)		49%
			Cruz Bustamanate (D)		32%
			Tom McClintock (R)		13%
1998			**2006**		
Gray Davis (D)	58%		Arnold Schwarzenegger (R)		56%
Dan Lungren (R)	38%		Phil Angelides (D)		39%

Parties: C= Commonwealth, D=Democrat, I =Independent, Pg=Progressive, Pr=Prohibition, R=Republican. Asterisk indicates incumbent. Both Stephens and Knight ran as incumbent governors because they were elevated from lieutenant governor when the previous governor vacated the office. Stephens took over when Hiram Johnson was elected to the U.S. Senate. Knight became governor when Earl Warren was named chief justice of the U.S. Supreme Court.

But his road to the governorship, while not an accident, relied on an extraordinary circumstance—the recall of a sitting governor. In large measure, it depended on the bad luck and ill-timed ineptitude of his predecessor—Gray Davis.

Davis, who became governor in 1998, was a bundle of contradictions. In many ways, he was the best-prepared chief executive in California history, having served apprenticeships as Governor Jerry Brown's chief of staff, a state legislator, state controller, and lieutenant governor. But despite his profound job experience, Davis lacked two essentials—political courage and, most significant, leadership. Not charisma, but command. Davis's two immediate predecessors, Republicans George Deukmejian and Pete Wilson, certainly lacked charisma, but each knew how and when to take decisive action.

Davis came to power in 1998 as a political centrist at a time of prosperity, the state's robust economy driven by explosive, if ephemeral, growth in the high-tech sector. Among other factors, the so-called "dot-com boom" poured billions of dollars in additional and unforeseen income tax revenues into state coffers—a tremendous boost to a state addicted to the income tax as its primary source of funding. Davis didn't so much lead as steer, and for the first two years of his administration, he enjoyed superb poll ratings, his popularity buoyed by the state's fiscal well-being.

Unfortunately for Davis, the prosperity was not permanent. By 2002, following a protracted energy crisis and the "dot com bust," California's economy had tanked and the state faced a growing budget deficit estimated at $24 billion.

In the midst of these calamities, Davis ran for re-election in 2002, winning a second term by the slimmest of margins over an exceptionally weak Republican opponent, conservative businessman Bill Simon. Voter turnout was at an all-time low, as were Davis's approval ratings—a signal that the electorate was grumpy, disaffected, and disenchanted with its choices for governor. A month after Davis was sworn in, an embryonic recall campaign took shape prompted by Republicans sensing a chance to reverse the election. The attempt to gather signatures for a recall sputtered through the late winter and spring until, on May 15, Darrell Issa, a wealthy Republican congressman from San Diego, seeded the effort with nearly half a million dollars. By July 23, the recall had qualified.

A gubernatorial recall asks two questions: (1) should the governor be bounced from office; and (2) who should replace the governor if he or she is recalled? Anyone interested in the job may file to run in the replacement phase, and there is no runoff; the candidate with the most votes is elected governor if the recall succeeds.

Under these circumstances, Davis's survival boiled down to a pair of factors, Democratic solidarity and the lack of a credible successor. The first required that no significant Democratic candidate go after Davis's job, giving voters a clear choice on recall: vote "no" or see a Republican take over. The second did not necessarily mean a potential successor with experience in elective office. On the contrary, voters seemed fed up with politics as usual. "Credible successor" meant a candidate who could capture the voters' imagination and allow them to dream of a plausible alternative.

Enter the Terminator

Most experienced politicians think carefully about how, where, and when they launch a bid for office, hoping the event will set a tone for the forthcoming campaign. When he announced for president in 1995, for instance, Wilson sought heft and credibility by using the Statue of Liberty as a prop.

Arnold Schwarzenegger revealed his decision to run for governor on "The Tonight Show with Jay Leno." It was a fitting venue. Schwarzenegger, after all, was every inch show biz—an actor whose talent was a light year short of an Oscar nomination but who had created an international celebrity out of whole cloth and Hollywood hype. His August 6 announcement immediately transformed the recall, riveting world attention on what Davis and Democrats hoped would be an obscure exercise in electoral gymnastics and super-sizing what U.S. Senator Dianne Feinstein characterized as "a carnival."

On the same day, Lieutenant Governor Cruz Bustamante—never a friend or even an ally to Davis—shattered Democratic solidarity by declaring his candidacy. With just two months left before the October 7 election, Davis's governorship was in deep, deep trouble. Politically, the governor shed his centrist outer shell and struggled to shore up long-neglected Democratic roots. He backed a flurry of labor-related bills, as well as another that would haunt his effort to survive—legislation granting California driver's licenses to illegal immigrants.

Eventually, 247 candidates offered themselves as successors to Davis, and 135 actually filed the necessary papers and paid the required fees to secure a place on the ballot. Among the more offbeat: actor Gary Coleman, stripper Angelyne, comedian Leo Gallagher, former Green Party Assemblywoman Audie Bock, *Hustler* publisher Larry

California Governors

Governor	Party	Inauguration
Peter H. Burnett	Independent	December 1849
John McDougal	Independent	January 1851
John Bigler	Democrat	Jan. 1852, Jan. 1854
J. Neeley Johnson	American	January 1856
John B. Weller	Democrat	January 1858
Milton S. Latham	Lecompton Democrat	January 1860
John G. Downey	Lecompton Democrat	January 1860
Leland Stanford	Republican	January 1862
Fredrick F. Low	Union	December 1863
Henry H. Haight	Democrat	December 1867
Newton Booth	Republican	December 1871
Romualdo Pacheco	Republican	February 1875
William Irwin	Democrat	December 1875
George C. Perkins	Republican	January 1880
George Stoneman	Democrat	January 1883
Washington Bartlett	Republican	January 1887
Robert W. Waterman	Republican	September 1887
Henry H. Markham	Republican	January 1891
James H. Budd	Democrat	January 1895
Henry T. Gage	Republican	January 1899
George C. Pardee	Republican	January 1903
James N. Gillett	Republican	January 1907
Hiram W. Johnson	Republican	January 1911
Hiram W. Johnson	Progressive	January 1915
William Stephens	Republican	January 1919
Friend Wm. Richardson	Republican	January 1923
C. C. Young	Republican	January 1927
James Rolph, Jr.	Republican	January 1931
Frank F. Merriam	Republican	June 1934, Jan. 1935
Culbert L. Olson	Democrat	January 1939

California Governors cont.		
Earl Warren	Republican*	Jan. 1943, Jan. 1947, Jan. 1951
Goodwin J. Knight	Republican	Oct. 1953, Jan. 1955
Edmund G. "Pat" Brown	Democrat	Jan. 1959, Jan. 1963
Ronald Reagan	Republican	Jan. 1967, Jan. 1971
Edmund G. "Jerry" Brown	Democrat	Jan. 1975, Jan. 1979
George Deukmejian	Republican	Jan. 1983, Jan. 1987
Pete Wilson	Republican	Jan. 1991, Jan. 1995
Gray Davis	Democrat	Jan. 1999, Jan. 2003
Arnold Schwarzenegger	Republican	Nov. 2003, Jan. 2007
*Earl Warren won both the Republican and Democratic primaries in 1946.		

Flynt, a Democrat named "Dan Feinstein," and Republicans named "Robert Dole" and "Michael Jackson." Davis's 2002 gubernatorial opponent, Bill Simon, joined the fray, as did former baseball commissioner Peter Ueberroth, but both dropped out under pressure from Republican kingmakers eager to unite behind a single—electable—nominee: Schwarzenegger.

The five most notable candidates—Schwarzenegger, Bustamante, GOP state Senator Tom McClintock, Green Party candidate Peter Camejo, and pundit Arianna Huffington—staged one televised debate, a September 24 soiree punctuated with bad jokes, condescending remarks, catty retorts, and ill-informed commentary. Of the five, only two comported themselves as adults: McClintock and Camejo. Moreover, the iconoclastic McClintock refused to bow out, causing some worry among Republicans that he would siphon enough votes away from Schwarzenegger to tip the election to Bustamante.

It was a needless bit of fretting. Schwarzenegger's team—borrowed from Pete Wilson—ran the campaign as if it was promoting "Terminator Ultimate," complete with elaborate stunts, photo ops, and interviews with media softies such as Larry King and Oprah. The candidate crisscrossed the state in a special bus followed by an entourage of international journalists and greeted by crowds keen to catch a glimpse of a celebrity who, by the way, was running for governor. He was high energy all the time, hammering at Davis on issues such as the driver's license bill and an increased "car tax" or VLF. He promised to "blow up boxes" once he came to Sacramento, to end the gridlock that seemed to paralyze the California government, to institute a bipartisan approach and wrench government out of the hands of "special interests"—whom he conveniently neglected to define. In the hands of a skilled pitchman like Schwarzenegger, the litany of messages tapped deep resentment among voters.

Not that Schwarzenegger himself was spared the rough-and-tumble. As Election Day approached, the *Los Angeles Times* welcomed him to big-time politics by reciting, in detail, his personal boorishness, including allegations that he groped and fondled women on the sets of various movies. Although miffed, the candidate did not deny the allegations but diffused them as best he could by apologizing for past behavior.

The *Times'* stories slowed but did not derail the Schwarzenegger campaign. When the votes were tallied on October 7, more than 55 percent of the electorate opted to recall Davis and nearly 49 percent chose Schwarzenegger to replace him, with Bustamante a distant second. It wasn't a majority, but it was more than enough. Schwarzenegger was governor.

Up from Nothing

As Schwarzenegger likes to remind the public, he arrived in the United States in 1968 at age 21, with $20 in his pocket. Even then, he was no common immigrant but a European bodybuilding champion who that year placed second in the Mr. Universe competition—a title he won the following year. Two years later, living in southern California, he began appearing as a bit player in movies. Not good movies, but movies nonetheless. He also launched his first business—a mail-order enterprise that sold training supplies for bodybuilders.

By the mid 1970s, he was the most successful bodybuilder in history and a self-promoting celebrity whose life was featured in a successful documentary film, "Pumping Iron." He landed more significant movie roles, with a breakthrough casting in 1980 as "Conan the Barbarian." Two years later, he made the first "Terminator" movie and became a box-office smash. He took the oath as an American citizen in 1983 and, four years later, married television news correspondent Maria Shriver, daughter of Sargent Shriver and a niece to John, Robert, and Edward Kennedy. He embellished his image with big cigars, racy motorcycles, involvement with Special Olympics, a knack for self-hype, and a portfolio of popular movies with the artistic flair of cage combat.

In less than two decades, Schwarzenegger had transformed himself from penniless immigrant to the embodiment of an American success story. He even dabbled in statewide politics in 2002 with passage of Proposition 49, the Schwarzenegger-sponsored ballot initiative that set aside money for after-school programs. That kind of accomplishment doesn't just happen. It is the result of some luck, true, but it is more the product of ambition, drive, and focus—traits that would serve him both well and ill in politics.

The Governator

If Schwarzenegger thrived on overcoming obstacles, he tackled the perfect job— governor of a state with financial problems of near mythic proportions. The centerpiece was a two-year budget gap between state revenues and spending that some estimated to be near $38 billion by the time he took office. Lurking along the periphery of the budget was a litany of festering problems such as high workers' compensation rates that lent credence to the notion that California was a rotten place to do business. Taken together, it was a tough nut for the most experienced government wonk, let alone a neophyte politician.

Yet it was a fiscal problem that Schwarzenegger exacerbated on his first day in office when, only moments after taking the oath on the Capitol steps, he plopped himself behind a desk and fulfilled his most prominent campaign promise—a rollback of

Salaries	
Governor	$206,500
Lieutenant Governor	$154,875
Attorney General	$175,525
Secretary of State	$154,875
Controller	$165,200
Treasurer	$165,200
Superintendent of Public Instruction	$175,525
Insurance Commissioner	$165,200
Members, Board of Equalization	$154,875
Speaker of the Assembly	$130,062
Senate President Pro Tem	$130,062
Assembly/Senate Minority Leader	$130,062
Assembly/Senate Majority Leader	$121,580
Legislator	$113,098
Chief Justice, Supreme Court	$217,902
Associate Justice	$209,521
Appellate Court Judge	$196,428
Superior Court Judge	$171,648
Legislators also receive tax-free per diem of $162 for attending legislative sessions.	

the car tax. With a flourish of his pen, Schwarzenegger added another $4 billion to the state debt.

But after reviewing his first eight months in office, *California Journal* reported that Schwarzenegger seemed "the natural politician." Journalist and Reagan biographer Lou Cannon, no stranger to celebrity governors, described his accomplishments: "persuaded voters to pass a $15 billion bond issue to refinance the state's debt, co-opted the Democratic-controlled legislature, reformed a troubled workers' compensation system, cut side deals with educators, unions, and Native American tribes, and even dazzled Californians who disagree with him."

Schwarzenegger's administration reflected his mixed outlook. It was an eclectic group, including environmentalist Terry Tamminen as head of the state Environmental Protection Agency, strawberry farmer A. G. Kawamura as secretary of Food and Agriculture, moderate Sunne Wright McPeak to head the Business, Transportation, and Housing Agency, and Shriver pal Bonnie Reiss, a Malibu liberal, as "senior advisor."

He recruited a flock of former Wilson aides from the business community and conservative ranks, including chief of staff Pat Clarey. Communications director Rob

Stutzman once worked for former Attorney General Dan Lungren and conservative state Senator Rob Hurtt. Former Los Angeles Mayor Richard Riordan, a moderate Republican, became his education secretary. Finance chief Donna Arduin was imported from Florida where she worked for conservative Governor Jeb Bush. Her chief deputy, Mike Genest, came from the Senate Republican Caucus fiscal staff.

Schwarzenegger was flamboyant and larger than life, breathing energy and panache into an office that had been occupied for 20 years by a trio of coma-inducing personalities. His poll numbers were staggering, his 65 percent approval rating higher than for any governor of the past half a century, including Ronald Reagan. He developed a close working friendship with the most powerful Democrat in Sacramento—the acerbic, chronically grumpy leader of the state Senate, John Burton, an old-line lefty from San Francisco who also happened to be well connected in Hollywood. He tended relationships inside the Capitol, mastering small gestures as well as big maneuvers. When Assembly Speaker Herb Wesson held an informal farewell buffet for Capitol reporters, for instance, Schwarzenegger dropped by for a few impromptu words of praise for the termed-out Democrat. It was a gesture no one could imagine from Gray Davis.

As he cultivated majority Democrats, Schwarzenegger at times ignored the legislature's Republican minority, which went along because, as one GOP insider told *California Journal*, "we have no place else to go." But the governor did not neglect his party's delegation altogether, appearing at GOP fundraisers, including one that netted some $300,000 for the re-election kitty of his old recall foe, Tom McClintock. By one estimate, Schwarzenegger used his star appeal to raise more than $18 million for Republican candidates during his first half-year in office. And he went to the wall for the most significant Republican issue in that debt-ridden year: opposition to anything that smacked of a tax increase. Reagan and Wilson before him each had confronted similar budget shortfalls with a combination of spending cuts and tax increases, but Schwarzenegger would have none of it. Instead, he relied on the same short-term fixes that Davis applied to the fiscal problem: cuts, creative math, and borrowing, including a campaign to pass a measure—Proposition 57—designed to ease the state's fiscal morass by selling bonds to pay off debt.

In September 2004, Schwarzenegger capped an amazing 11-month run with a rousing speech to the Republican National Convention in New York.

Amid all this cooperation and love, however, emerged hints of another Schwarzenegger—a more combative and pugnacious governor, more akin to the cutthroat bodybuilder who once belittled opponents to gain a competitive edge. When negotiations over the 2004 budget stalled, Schwarzenegger ridiculed legislators as "girlie men" during a televised interview. It was an unscripted, off-the-cuff moment, but he refused to back away from the comment, which instantly cemented itself into the lore of American politics and signaled a more troubled second year in office.

A Reversal of Fortunes

Nothing in politics lasts forever, especially not helium-filled poll numbers.

For the most part, Schwarzenegger traveled the route of bipartisan cooperation during his first year, a few incendiary off-road side trips notwithstanding. But a different governor took the wheel as the second year dawned, a more truculent and confrontational version who seemed to consider bipartisan teamwork like some odious diversion best Hummerized as road kill. His reasoning varied, but there was a feeling among some of the administration's more conservative allies that the previous year's cooperation had gained the governor little in the way of true reform. He had patched over critical problems but had not secured structural changes they felt were necessary to correct the state's fiscal wanderings. He also must have felt stung by media analyses that credited legislative Democrats with "rolling" the governor on the budget, on a spending cap, even on workers' compensation reform.

If Schwarzenegger became more combative, he wasn't alone in shattering the atmosphere of cooperation. Democrats, too, felt less like gubernatorial lap dogs, emboldened by what they perceived as the governor's mixed track record during the 2004 elections. Once again, he had demonstrated his ability to sell the public on a notion—he was able to help pass or defeat a number of ballot measures, winning approval of stem cell research and defeating a fix to the state's three-strikes law in criminal sentencing. The latter feat was especially noteworthy because the initiative had strong approval ratings until Schwarzenegger weighed in against it.

But the governor had less success promoting candidates and made not a dent in Democratic majorities in either the Senate or Assembly. To the contrary, it was all he could do to save embattled Republican incumbents. Not that the governor had much to work with when it came to legislative candidates; he was saddled with those promoted by Republican lawmakers. In several cases, the governor stumped for GOP contenders whose only qualification for office seemed to be a discernable pulse. Still, Democrats came away discounting the governor's coattails, and if he couldn't hurt them personally, Democrats felt less inclined to sell their philosophical souls in support of the administration's agenda. The fear factor was gone.

Nevertheless, in his 2005 state-of-the-state address, Schwarzenegger challenged the Democratic-controlled legislature to enact his agenda of fiscal and political reform by a certain date, or he would take that agenda to the voters as initiatives in a special election. Politically, he moved closer to the right, his agenda increasingly shaped by the California Chamber of Commerce and its influential president, Allan Zaremberg.

Democrats refused to move on that agenda with the alacrity deemed essential by the administration. Schwarzenegger tried to promote his views with the public, but his efforts were ham-handed, and he picked fights with a peculiar assortment of enemies. He engaged in verbal scuffles with teachers over tenure, merit pay, and competency, with public employees over pension reform, with nurses over staffing ratios in hospitals. A pension proposal, introduced as legislation, was drafted so poorly that it would have denied survivor benefits to the families of police officers and firefighters killed on the job. Nurses haunted his every public appearance. His political foes joined forces under the banner "Alliance for a Better California," and their continued pressure forced the governor to abandon efforts to impose merit pay on teachers and revamp public-pension programs.

At one point, Schwarzenegger engaged in a public shouting match with the education community over a deal made the previous year and involving school funding. Educators, including the powerful California Teachers Association, had agreed to help close the state budget gap by suspending the sacred Proposition 98 school-funding formula for 2004–2005. The governor, in return, promised to restore funding as soon as revenues improved. That improvement occurred in 2005–2006, but Schwarzenegger's budget proposal did not reflect his promise. The two sides snorted at each other all through the spring, with the debate trivialized at times into semantic arguments over the meaning of "promise." They argued over who would shovel the porch while the state's fiscal house was being buried by an avalanche.

The governor's more belligerent approach was a decided change of pace but hardly surprising. Schwarzenegger has admitted on numerous occasions that psychological intimidation was part of his competitive repertoire, so why not apply mental brinkmanship to Capitol politics? When negotiations bogged down with Democrats over a variety of issues, Schwarzenegger carried through with his promise to call a special election for November 2005. Eight initiatives qualified for that ballot, including three of special importance to Schwarzenegger: remove redistricting from the legislature, increase the time it takes to gain teacher tenure from two to five years, and dramatically enhance the governor's budgetary power in times of fiscal crisis.

To pay for the ballot campaign, Schwarzenegger continued what had been a frenetic fundraising campaign, raising tens of millions of dollars from business and Republican sources all over the country. In June, after he announced the special election, the governor embarked on a trip throughout California to sell his agenda, allowing his critics to accuse him of neglecting his duties as governor for the business of promoting his initiatives. Again, his focus was not surprising. He has said in interviews that he takes on one task at a time. In this case, the task was the election. Moreover, Schwarzenegger loves to campaign and only tolerates the daily routines of governing.

But the fundraising effort exposed duplicity in Schwarzenegger, who had said during the 2003 recall that because of his independent wealth he did not need to raise campaign cash and could not be bought by special interests. He cast Davis as a 24/7 fundraiser beholden to his financiers. But after taking the reins of government himself, Schwarzenegger spent a good part of his first term raising enough money from special interests to obliterate Davis's legendary reputation.

The public responded to the gridlock and the election, but not the way Schwarzenegger and his allies might have hoped. His poll numbers plummeted. A mid-June California Poll pegged his approval rating at 37 percent—down from 65 percent the previous September—and an *Oakland Tribune* headline proclaimed, "Governor looking a lot like Gray." More significant, a second June poll showed significant erosion in the number of Californians inclined to re-elect Schwarzenegger—from 56 percent in February 2005 to 39 percent by June. A snapshot without the context of a heated election campaign, the poll indicated that Schwarzenegger might lose his re-election to one of two Democratic challengers—Treasurer Phil Angelides and Controller Steve Westly.

Californians disagreed with the governor on the issues and, more significant, on the need for a special election, which could cost counties and the state an estimated $80 million. Soon after the poll appeared, the administration and legislators began signaling that a compromise on the 2005–2006 budget was in the air, and that the legislature might even put additional measures on the ballot that represented a covenant with the administration on reapportionment and fiscal reform—thereby trumping measures already qualified for the special election. The budget deal was announced on July 6, only seven days after the constitutional deadline—and "early" by recent standards. The governor signed the 2005–2006 budget on July 11.

The administration denied that overtures to the legislature were predicated on falling poll numbers, and, in a sense, his decision to call a special election helped spur Democrats to end the budget fight so they could concentrate on defeating the governor's initiatives. The urgency behind Democratic overtures on the budget was underscored when they capitulated on a key demand of the governor and his Republican allies in the legislature—abandonment of a plan to raise taxes on the wealthiest Californians to provide additional funding for K-12 education. Once Democrats caved in and the governor's weak poll numbers surfaced, a new more conciliatory tone emerged from the administration, marking yet another change of direction.

Schwarzenegger had hoped to use the budget agreement to build momentum and help resurrect his sagging popularity. But a mini scandal erupted only days after the budget signing when it was revealed that he had profited a little too handsomely from a business deal with the publisher of muscle and body building magazines, earning millions of dollars in outside income. The magazines relied heavily on the makers of dietary supplements for advertising—and Schwarzenegger's compensation was pegged to ad revenues. Significantly, a year earlier Schwarzenegger had vetoed a bill to help regulate those supplements, and the authors of the bill, Democratic state Senator Jackie Speier among others, charged the governor with a blatant conflict-of-interest. At first the governor's minions tried to pooh-pooh the situation, but after three days of flamingly bad publicity, Schwarzenegger announced he would sever all ties with the magazine publisher, although he refused to give back the more than $1 million he had earned in 2004.

Meanwhile, voters pummeled the governor's initiatives, defeating every one of them, some by substantial margins, in a special November 2005 statewide election. Labor groups—led by nurses, teachers, firefighters, and public employee unions— poured millions into the "anti-Arnold" effort, leaving the governor's image as a political dynamo in tatters.

His confidence shaken but not broken, a chagrined Schwarzenegger accepted his loss. More to the point, he turned his unbridled optimism loose on what was a political debacle, apologizing to the electorate for putting them through such a divisive election and vowing to cooperate once again with the legislature. It was no mere coincidence that he expressed this *mea culpa* on the eve of his 2006 re-election campaign, where polls showed he was vulnerable.

He cleaned house, sidelining some of the intractable conservative voices in his administration and turning more and more for advice and guidance to his politically astute wife, Maria Shriver. In the six months following the November 2005 election, The Associated Press reported, nearly half the governor's administrative staff departed, among them Stutzman and Clarey.

The result was a move back to the center where he joined with legislative Democrats on several fronts. They cooperated to pass a $43 billion package of bonds meant to repair the state's neglected infrastructure—money meant for roads, mass transit, affordable housing, schools and universities, and flood protection. Voters approved the bonds in November 2006. The governor broke with President George Bush and the federal administration over the issue of global warming, proclaiming the threat real and signing a bill that strengthened air quality regulations in California. Finally, Schwarzenegger agreed to an increase in the minimum wage—long a Democratic priority that had been thwarted by both governors Wilson and Davis.

The cooperative posture worked wonders on Schwarzenegger's approval rating, which steadily rose all through 2006 until he became unassailable at the polls in November. His Democratic opponent, Treasurer Phil Angelides, never gained much traction with the electorate, and Schwarzenegger spent most of the campaign season stumping for the infrastructure bonds and ignoring both Angelides and the race for governor. At one point, more than a month before Election Day, his re-election was declared a lock by no less an expert than Willie Lewis Brown, Jr., the former Democratic speaker of the Assembly and former mayor of San Francisco.

Brown's pronouncement proved accurate, as Schwarzenegger was re-elected with 56 percent of the vote. More notable, he held Angelides to under 40 percent, including in Angelides' home county of Sacramento.

Governor as Cartoon

If not seen as ordinary, most politicians come into office at least perceived as someone the average Californian might relate to on a gut level; slightly more ambitious, perhaps, slightly more thick-skinned, but not too far removed from the typical neighbor. An elected official, especially a governor or president, can evolve into a caricature of him- or herself, but that conversion takes time and exposure.

Not so Arnold Schwarzenegger. This governor came to office as a nation unto himself, a world celebrity who, despite humble beginnings, had long ago shed his public accessibility. Not merely a cartoon, he entered the world of politics as an entire comic strip, and his challenge—and that of his handlers—was to comport himself in ways that moved his image away from the one-dimensional and wrapped it in an aura of statesmanship and credibility.

At the outset, he and his team reinforced the cartoon image with stunts and ill-time rhetoric. The governor veered away from the notion that he would eventually be seen as Ronald Reagan rather than George Murphy or—worse— Jesse Ventura, the wrestler/actor-turned-politician who during one term as governor of Minnesota never outran the image of a buffoon.

Schwarzenegger initially displayed an inconsistency that made him difficult to predict or assess and hampered his ability to advance his agenda. His administration frequently played good cop/bad cop with Democrats in the legislature and with Democratic allies. The governor assumed both roles, and it became increasingly difficult to discover the real Arnold amid the bipolar mess that became his Capitol persona.

To his credit, Schwarzenegger corrected the problem and proved that he is no buffoon, though he still is given to bouts of outsized rhetoric that dents his credibility. When he unveiled his 2007–2008 budget, he declared he would eliminate a projected $5.5 billion deficit without raising taxes—a notion immediately characterized as unrealistic by the nonpartisan legislative analyst.

In the context of California, Schwarzenegger is a Republican in name only, a self-styled "centrist" whose political values are closest to the 20 percent of California voters who register decline to state. As such, his most challenging relationship is not with legislative Democrats but with their Republican counterparts, most of whom hew farther to the right than the governor.

Evidence of this challenge surfaced in the wake of the 2006 election when Republicans in the Assembly and Senate attempted coups against their caucus leadership. They succeeded in the Assembly where George Plescia was dumped in part because his caucus thought he had been too cooperative with the governor and Democrats during negotiations over the 2006 budget. He was replaced by Mike Villines, a Fresno lawmaker who vowed to be more assertive when pushing issues important to Republicans. Given that six Republican votes are needed to pass a budget, Villines's ascendancy signaled troubles ahead.

In the Senate, Republican leader Dick Ackerman survived the revolt, but the same point was made. Senate Republicans delivered a more concrete message shortly after the governor's inaugural when they denied their votes to one of his nominees for the state Board of Education—labor official Joe Nunez. The confirmation required a two-thirds approval, or 27 votes. Democrats provided 25, but Republicans either voted "no" or abstained, causing Nunez's nomination to fail.

Unlike other California governors, Schwarzenegger's political future does not include the presidency; he is precluded by law from holding the job because he was not born in the United States, and it would take an amendment to the U.S. Constitution for him to qualify. Instead, speculation about his future has centered on the U.S. Senate. Incumbent Democrat Barbara Boxer must stand for re-election in 2010, the same year Schwarzenegger is termed out of the governorship, and that fact presents him with an intriguing choice.

But at least one noted political observer—USC professor Sherry Bebitch Jeffe—believes Schwarzenegger has little interest in the Senate, where he would not be able to exercise executive power and would instead be junior among 100 members of an exclusive club where outsized egos are the norm. Jeffe speculates that the governor, should he choose to further his political career, might want a job closer to home, a job that will satisfy his executive itch and leave him alone in the spotlight—mayor of Los Angeles.

BIOGRAPHY: Born: Thal, Austria, July 30, 1947. Home: Los Angeles. Education: BA, University of Wisconsin-Superior. Military: Austrian Army, 1965. Family: wife Maria Shriver, four children. Religion: Catholic.

OFFICES: State Capitol Building, Sacramento, CA 95814; Phone: (916) 445-2841; Fax: (916) 445-4633; email: governor@governor.ca.gov; Web: www.governor. ca.gov; 2550 Mariposa Mall, Suite 3013, Fresno, CA 93721, Phone: (559) 445-5295, Fax: (559) 445-5328; 300 South Spring Street, Suite 16701, Los Angeles, CA 90013, Phone: (213) 897-0322, Fax: (213) 897-0319; 1350 Front Street, Suite 6054, San Diego, CA 92101, Phone: (619) 525-4641, Fax: (619) 525-4640; 455 Golden Gate Avenue, Suite 14000, San Francisco, CA 94102, Phone: (415) 703-2218, Fax: (415) 703-2803; 3737 Main Street, Suite 201, Riverside, CA 92501, Phone: (909) 680-6860, Fax: (909) 680-6863; 134 Hall of the States, 444 North Capitol Street NW, Washington, D.C. 20001, Phone: (202) 624-5270, Fax: (202) 624-5280.

Lieutenant Governors Since 1950

Goodwin J. Knight	Republican	elected 1950
Harold J. Powers	Republican	appointed 1953
Harold J. Powers	Republican	elected 1954
Glenn M. Anderson	Democrat	elected 1958, 1962
Robert Finch	Republican	elected 1966
Ed Reinecke	Republican	appointed 1969
Ed Reinecke	Republican	elected 1970
Mervyn Dymally	Democrat	elected 1974
Mike Curb	Republican	elected 1978
Leo T. McCarthy	Democrat	elected 1982, 1986, 1990
Gray Davis	Democrat	elected 1994
Cruz Bustamante	Democrat	elected 1998, 2002
John Garamendi	Democrat	elected 2006

ELECTED: 2003; TERM LIMIT: 2010
ELECTION HISTORY: None.
2003 RECALL ELECTION: Schwarzenegger (R) 49%
Bustamante (D) 32%
McClintock (R) 13%

LIEUTENANT GOVERNOR
John Garamendi (D)

John Garamendi

Few of California's statewide political figures are as hard to define and classify as John Garamendi, a ruggedly handsome rancher with a Harvard MBA who spent 16 years in the legislature before becoming California's first elected insurance commissioner in 1990. A moderate Democrat, Garamendi cut a dashing figure when he was first elected to the Assembly in 1974, drawing frequent comparisons to John F. Kennedy, his political idol. Like Kennedy, Garamendi was handsome, wealthy, ambitious, and idealistic, a devotee of physical contact sports—he was a wrestler and football star at the University of California, Berkeley—with a passion for political infighting. In the Kennedy mold, Garamendi showed elan and exhibited a sort of noblesse oblige in both his politics and his personal lifestyle. His annual barbecues at his sprawling Mokelumne Hill ranch are still remembered in the Capitol, and Garamendi's polished image was not so much a politician as that of a rural land baron and aristocrat, an odd combination in California's rough-and-tumble political wars. Like the Kennedys, Garamendi favored large families—he and his wife Patti have six children—and he seemed to have all the tools to one day become California's governor. He even served in the Peace Corps in Africa, another Kennedyesque role.

But his political plans often misfired when he tried to gain statewide office, and while he has lingered on the statewide stage, he has never secured the starring role. Veteran political observers contend Garamendi, while obviously talented and skilled as one of the legislature's top budget writers, suffers from a combination of personal arrogance and bad timing. In 1982 he was defeated in the Democratic gubernatorial primary by Los Angeles Mayor Tom Bradley, and 12 years later, he lost his second run for governor when Kathleen Brown beat him in the 1994 Democratic primary, which Garamendi entered after serving one term as insurance commissioner.

Garamendi was not the only family member to suffer defeats during this period; his wife Patti lost races for both the Assembly and Senate before taking a third beating in a race against Republican Richard Pombo in the 11th Congressional District. Her campaigns were poorly planned and executed, and they signaled the demise of Patti's elective political career, but not that of her husband.

After a four-year stint in the Clinton administration's Interior Department, where he played a significant role in the negotiations over the Headwaters Forest, Garamendi returned to statewide office by winning a second term as insurance commissioner in 2002, exploiting the scandal-plagued tenure of Republican Insurance Commissioner Charles Quackenbush who had been forced from office in the summer of 2000.

He's made one major political misstep since 2002. In 2003 he announced plans to run as a candidate to replace Democratic Governor Gray Davis in the recall election but withdrew the next day after heeding Democrats' demands to stay out of the race in order to protect Davis's chances—unsuccessfully, as it turned out—against Republican frontrunner Arnold Schwarzenegger.

Garamendi's biggest political liability doesn't stem from his campaigning, however; it arises from his role as an insurance regulator.

Throughout his statewide political career, Garamendi has been stalked by the specter of Executive Life, a troubled insurer with some 300,000 policyholders that Garamendi's Insurance Department seized in 1991. To raise money, Garamendi approved the sale of Executive Life and its hefty junk-bond portfolio to a group of French investors, who later resold the assets for many times what they paid. Garamendi later said he was outfoxed in the deal, and the investors, it developed, had the secret backing of the French government, an arrangement that violated U.S. law. A flurry of lawsuits—including attempts by Garamendi to overturn the deal—consumed years of court hearings, but the bottom line is that Garamendi's attempts to recover funds fell woefully short, totaling some $75 million, or 2 percent, of the nearly $4 billion that Garamendi said were due tens of thousands of beleaguered annuitants.

Garamendi, hoping to get Executive Life behind him as he started a 2006 run for lieutenant governor, approved the final settlement, but the case remained a political issue. Two of his primary rivals for the Democratic nomination came out of the state

Senate, where one—Jackie Speier—spent her final term as chair of the Senate Government Oversight Committee. Speier loudly, and frequently, demanded a full-blown legislative investigation into Garamendi's role in the Executive Life seizure, and she tried to make the most of Garamendi's track record during the campaign. Her committee launched an investigation, and Garamendi was forced to testify.

Garamendi, on the other hand, benefited from political geography because Speier had to share her electoral base with another female senator—Liz Figueroa of Fremont. Although all three candidates hailed from northern California, Garamendi was much better known in the south thanks to his frequent forays into statewide politics and his role as commissioner. In Los Angeles County, for instance, Garamendi captured 50,000 more votes than Speier and Figueroa combined. He outpolled the pair's combined vote in Orange, Ventura, Riverside and San Bernardino counties as well, then ran neck-and-neck with Speier in San Diego County. Garamendi's showing in the south more than offset Speier's strength in her native San Francisco Bay Area, where her candidacy was blunted by Figueroa.

Still, the election was close, with Garamendi besting Speier 43 percent to 40 percent. Figueroa was a distant third with 17 percent. His overall margin of victory over Speier was slightly more than 65,000—75 percent of it piled up in Los Angeles County.

Garamendi's tough political year did not end with the primary. His general election foe was conservative Republican Tom McClintock, an iconoclastic state senator from Thousand Oaks, running his fourth statewide race since 1994, when he ran a surprisingly credible race for state controller before losing to Democrat Kathleen Connell. Eight years later, he ran for the same post, coming within a hair's breadth of defeating Democrat Steve Westly.

But McClintock's most enduring image was constructed during the 2003 recall election against Governor Gray Davis. Pressured by Republicans to withdraw in favor of Schwarzenegger, McClintock brandished his conservatism as a sword, challenging his party to adhere to its conservative principles. In televised debates, McClintock appeared as the man of reason, outlining his values and priorities in a calm and rational voice. He often was characterized as "the adult in the room" that included Schwarzenegger and his chief Democratic rival, Lieutenant Governor Cruz Bustamante. McClintock finished a respectable third, using that momentum to fuel his run against Garamendi in 2006.

Garamendi enjoyed an early lead in the polls, but that edge began to erode as the campaign heated up after Labor Day. Executive Life was again the centerpiece as McClintock's campaign rolled out TV and radio ads featuring Executive Life policyholders who accused Garamendi of selling the insurance company to a "junk bond king" and losing policy holders billions of dollars. In late October, an independent auditor issued a report on Executive Life, and both sides tried to spin the results. Garamendi said it vindicated him; McClintock argued that the report didn't address potentially damaging allegations.

McClintock tried to run as a "team" with Schwarzenegger but the governor, while publicly supporting McClintock, paid little attention to his campaign. That allowed Garamendi to paint McClintock as too extreme for California, and, by Election Day, the race was too close to call.

It was a Democratic year, however, as Garamendi prevailed by 4 percent, buoyed by a 300,000-vote margin in Los Angeles County and another 300,000-vote bulge in the two counties that bracket San Francisco Bay—San Francisco and Alameda.

As lieutenant governor, Garamendi has no mandate, nor does he have an agency to administer, such as the Department of Insurance. Officially, he is president of the state Senate and can cast the deciding vote in case of a tie—a situation that never happens. He is a regent of the University of California and acts as governor when Schwarzenegger is incapacitated or out of state. Garamendi has said he will cause no mischief on those occasions.

BIOGRAPHY: Born: Camp Blanding, Florida, January 24, 1945. Home: Walnut Grove. Education: BS, UC Berkeley; MBA, Harvard. Military: None. Family: wife Patti, six children, nine grandchildren. Religion: Presbyterian.

OFFICES: State Capitol Building, Room 1114, Sacramento, CA 95814; Phone: (916) 445-8994; Fax: (916) 323-4998; email: john.garamendi@ltg.ca.gov, Web: www. ltg.ca.gov; 300 South Spring Street, Suite 12702, Los Angeles, CA 90013, Phone: (213) 897-7086, Fax: (213) 897-7156; 701 B Street, Suite 376, San Diego, CA 92101, Phone: (619) 525-4305, Fax: (619) 525-4071; 2550 Mariposa Mall, Room 5006, Fresno, CA 93721, Phone: (559) 445-5501, Fax: (559) 445-5415.

ELECTED: 1998; TERM LIMIT: 2006.

ELECTION HISTORY: Assembly, 1974–1976; state Senate, 1976–1989; insurance commissioner 1990–1994, 2002–2006

2006 ELECTION: Garamendi (D) 49%
McClintock (R) 45%

ATTORNEY GENERAL
Edmund G. "Jerry" Brown, Jr. (D)

Edmund G. Brown

California has no political dynasties, but Jerry Brown carries the name of a family that comes close.

His father, Edmund G. "Pat" Brown, served as a San Francisco prosecutor, state attorney general, and two-term governor, the first California governor born in the 20th century. Jerry, in a less conventional climb up the political ladder and far different temperamentally from his father, cut his political teeth in the 1960s as an elected trustee in the Los Angeles Community College District, then successfully ran, at 32, for secretary of state. Four years later he was elected governor, and won re-election in 1978. Like his father and sister Kathleen, who served as state treasurer and ran unsuccessfully for governor in 1994, Jerry is a Democrat.

Now, Jerry is back in state government as state attorney general, having overwhelmed Republican contender Charles Poochigian. Thus, Jerry holds the same job that his father had in the 1950s, making the Brown father-son team unique in Califor-

Attorneys General Since 1950

Edmund G. "Pat" Brown	Democrat	elected 1950, 1954
Stanley Mosk	Democrat	elected 1958, 1962
Thomas C. Lynch	Democrat	appointed 1964
Thomas C. Lynch	Democrat	elected 1966
Evelle J. Younger	Republican	elected 1970, 1974
George Deukmejian	Republican	elected 1978
John Van de Kamp	Democrat	elected 1982, 1986
Dan Lungren	Republican	elected 1990, 1994
Bill Lockyer	Democrat	elected 1998, 2002
Edmund G. "Jerry" Brown	Democrat	elected 2006

nia's two most powerful offices, although another father-son duo, Frank C. Jordan and Frank M. Jordan, served successively as secretary of state for nearly 60 years from 1911 on.

Jerry Brown is many things—shrewd, ambitious, peripatetic, cerebral, restless, disorganized, spiritual, arrogant, and, in his late 60s, newly married. But if he is defined by any single characteristic, it is political ambition. While he was governor, he ran for president twice. After his governorship, he lost a bid for the U.S. Senate, ran again for president, headed the state Democratic Party, served as a political talk-show host, and served two terms as mayor of Oakland. Brown, himself, said that he seemed to be constantly running for some office, and he noted that his father was involved in political campaigns nearly continuously since his early 20s. Politics, it seems, is part of Jerry's DNA.

He started by getting involved in Vietnam war protests in Los Angeles in the 1960s and organizing migrant farm workers with the late Cesar Chavez. In 1969, Brown was one of dozens of candidates for trustees of the then-newly formed Los Angeles Community College District. He was elected, observers said later, in part because his name was more familiar than others on the ballot and because it appeared near the top of a long line of contenders. Since then, his life has been one long political campaign.

"I look back on my father's career, he ran for his first office as a Republican when he was like 22, and then in 1939, the year after I was born, he ran for district attorney," Brown once said. "He ran every two to four years until 1966 when Ronald Reagan beat him. Then I ran for junior college board about three years later and I started running every year or two or four. I didn't realize until the end of that road that we have quite a propensity to run for office. I don't know whether it is inborn or taught, but I would be less than candid if I said I don't enjoy running for office. Now, what that means, I'll leave you to speculate."

Friends say Brown is the complete political animal who just "does what he does," and former girlfriend and rock singer Linda Ronstadt once said that she often thought of a Latin phrase, *Age quod agis*, when she performed. It means "Do what you are doing," and presumably she picked that up from the classically educated Brown, who once studied for the priesthood at the Sacred Heart Novitiate and speaks Latin.

But while Jerry Brown gets generally good marks for his political acumen, willingness to embrace new ideas, and ability to wield power, he gets less favorable reviews for governing. During his two terms as governor, his administration was seen as uneven at best, in part because Brown appeared preoccupied by his campaigns for the presidency. He was widely criticized for his handling of the Medfly infestation, which sent his approval ratings plunging in the polls. During his 1989–1991 stint as chairman of the state Democratic Party—a post he won by defeating Steve Westly, who later became state controller and was defeated by Phil Angelides in the 2006 Democratic gubernatorial primary—Brown left abruptly to run for the U.S. Senate, then changed his mind and ran for president.

His reputation for the unorthodox was heightened by his visits to Mother Theresa in India and his trips to Japan as part of his well-publicized interest in Zen Buddhism. During the 1990s, Brown hosted a talk radio show called "We the People," then dropped his Democratic Party affiliation and became a "Decline to State" as he prepared for a campaign for Oakland mayor. Liberal Democrats, already suspicious of Brown for dropping his party label, became even more critical as Brown moved to the right during his 1998–2006 stint as Oakland mayor.

The return of Brown to government means there are two stellar political performers in the capital firmament, though Brown plays a supporting role to film star-turned-governor Arnold Schwarzenegger. Politically, the two share one crucial characteristic—they move easily from one side of the political spectrum to the other in their quest for public support. In their playbook, partisan ideology and consistency count for less than pragmatism. In an era of an electorate marked by an increasing number of voters who decline to state a party affiliation, it is an effective formula. Schwarzenegger appears to have been dragged to his pragmatism by the defeat of his Republican-driven ballot propositions in a 2005 special election and the victory of a huge, bipartisan infrastructure bond package a year later.

Brown's willingness to change his political colors is more deeply held, best expressed in his oft-quoted "canoe theory" of politics, in which you "paddle a little to the left, then paddle a little to the right" to keep the canoe going down the middle. Quotes like that drew derision from a political press that is far more comfortable assessing partisanship than defining ideas. Brown, a graduate of UC Berkeley and Yale Law School comfortable with such then-unusual notions as state-backed space travel, wind power, and specialized commuter highway lanes, was an easy journalistic target. Chicago newspaper columnist Mike Royko dubbed Brown "Governor Moonbeam," and, though Royko years later apologized for the sobriquet, the name stuck.

Brown's penchant for surprises, a hallmark of his years in and out of political power, remains intact. The confirmed bachelor finally got married, in 2006, to his long-time partner Anne Gust, the former chief counsel for Gap who, Brown has announced, will be a top, unpaid adviser in his attorney general's office. Brown plans to live and work in Oakland with occasional commutes to the Justice Department headquarters in Sacramento.

Brown's relationship with the press, always turbulent, is likely to remain so. "I've been the most popular and the most unpopular governor in California, and that was a real learning experience," Brown once told a luncheon of the American Society of Newspaper Editors, "I don't hold you people responsible. I think you are determined by this pull in the marketplace with that little zone of discretion, the idiosyncratic excellence. No, the press is derivative. Something goes wrong, I would hold myself accountable. Often I got the upside, and I had to take the downside. What looked good one year, then gets tiring, and they use it against me."

BIOGRAPHY: Born: San Francisco, April 7, 1938. Home: Oakland. Education: BA, UC Berkeley; JD, Yale. Military: None. Family: wife, Anne Gust. Religion: Catholic.

OFFICES: 1300 I Street, Sacramento, CA 95814; Phone: (916) 324-5437; Fax: (916) 323-2137; Web address: http://www.ag.ca.gov. 300 South Spring Street, Los Angeles, CA 90013, Phone: (213) 897-2000; 110 West A Street, Suite 1100, San Diego, CA 92101, Phone: (619) 645-2001; 455 Golden Gate Avenue, Suite 11000, San Francisco, CA 94102, Phone: (415) 703-5500; 1515 Clay Street, Suite 2000, Oakland, CA 94612, Phone: (510) 622-2100; 2550 Mariposa Mall, Suite 5090, Fresno, CA 93721, Phone: (559) 445-6590.

ELECTED: 2006 TERM LIMIT: 2014

ELECTION HISTORY: Los Angeles Community College Board of Trustees, 1969–1974; Secretary of State, 1970–1974; Governor, 1974–1982; Mayor, Oakland, 1998–2006.

2006 ELECTION: Brown (D) 56%
Poochigian (R) 38%

CONTROLLER
John Chiang (D)

John Chiang

For the past four years, the office of state controller had been in the hands of California's resident political tyro—Democrat Steve Westly. Uber-ambition is to Westly what wizardry is to Harry Potter—it defines his essence, adds uniqueness to his character, and is more essential than integrity, intelligence, notions of public service, or glibness under fire.

In 2006 Westly merged ambition and opportunism, a combination that often forms a political fuel not unlike hydrogen—combustible, unstable, and highly unpredictable. The formula looks plausible on paper, but then, there is the *Hindenburg* to consider.

It is the reason Westly is no longer controller. He left the office after one term to pursue the grander vision of becoming governor. In that quest, the super-rich Democrat very nearly spent himself into the finals but fell short in his primary battle with state Treasurer Phil Angelides.

Controllers Since 1950		
Thomas Kuchel	Republican	elected 1950
Robert Kirkwood	Republican	appointed 1952
Robert Kirkwood	Republican	elected 1954
Allan Cranston	Democrat	elected 1958, 1962
Houston Flournoy	Republican	elected 1966, 1970
Kenneth Cory	Democrat	elected 1974, 1978
Gray Davis	Democrat	elected 1986, 1990
Kathleen Connell	Democrat	elected 1994, 1998
Steve Westly	Democrat	elected 2002
John Chiang	Democrat	elected 2006

Westly's run for governor created a vacancy for controller, and into the breech stepped Democrat John Chiang, chairman of the state Board of Equalization. Chiang first came to that elective office as an appointee in 1996, succeeding Democrat Brad Sherman who had been elected to Congress. Chiang had served as Sherman's chief aide, and he held the seat as a designee for two years before winning in his own right in 1998. He was re-elected in 2002 and termed out in 2006.

Chiang's original appointment generated controversy because then-Governor Pete Wilson, a Republican, had the power to appoint a successor, who had to be confirmed by the state Senate. Although Wilson grumped about Sherman naming a replacement, the governor never intervened, perhaps sensing that his nominee would not be confirmed by the Democratic-controlled legislature.

Chiang's quest for controller began with a minor upset over state Senator Joe Dunn in the June 2006 Democratic primary. An elective base in Los Angeles coupled with his Asian ethnicity helped Chiang overcome Dunn, a high-powered, well-heeled former Orange County trial lawyer. Although highly regarded in Sacramento, Dunn was unknown outside his Senate district and was unable to raise his profile during a busy primary campaign season.

In the 2006 general election, Chiang faced a conservative Republican, former Assemblyman Tony Strickland. Neither Chiang nor Strickland was well known to most voters, and the two candidates dwelt in obscurity for most of the fall, with Strickland's hopes riding in large measure on the alleged coattails of Arnold Schwarzenegger. Chiang pushed his financial expertise, citing Strickland's lack of economic experience, while Strickland campaigned on his fiscal conservatism.

The race remained relatively close until the last weeks when the playing field was skewed by infusions of cash and resources on behalf of Strickland. Working through independent expenditures, a group of Indian gambling tribes contributed nearly $1 million for television advertisements on behalf of the Republican. Their effort was augmented by a similar expenditure by Intuit, the software company that publishes "TurboTax." Intuit's motives were relatively clear. In addition to serving as controller,

Treasurers Since 1950

Charles G. Johnson	Progressive	elected 1950, 1954
Ronald Button	Republican	appointed 1956
Bert A. Betts	Democrat	elected 1958, 1962
Ivy Baker Priest	Republican	elected 1966, 1970
Jesse M. Unruh	Democrat	elected 1974, 1978, 1982, 1986*
Thomas Hayes	Republican	appointed 1989
Kathleen Brown	Democrat	elected 1990
Matthew K. Fong	Republican	elected 1994
Phil Angelides	Democrat	elected 1998, 2002
Bill Lockyer	Democrat	elected 2006

*Elizabeth Whitney served as acting treasurer following Unruh's death, August 1987-January 1989.

the winner of the race would become an *ex facto* member of the state Board of Equalization—a four-member tax panel evenly split between Republicans and Democrats. Thus, the controller would be the deciding vote on a panel that determined the fate of tax appeals by, among others, gaming tribes and software companies.

More significant for Intuit, Chiang championed a small pilot program called "ReadyReturn," which allowed the state to do income tax returns for some 11,000 taxpayers. Last year, under pressure from Intuit and others, the legislature allowed the program to die. During the campaign, Chiang proposed reviving it and expanding ReadyReturn to serve more than a million taxpayers. That possibility posed a threat to Intuit.

Labor groups responded to support for Strickland by diverting resources from the governor's race—where the result was never in doubt—to help bolster Chiang. Although money pumped into Strickland made the race interesting, 2006 was a Democratic year in an already Democratic state, and Chiang won by a comfortable margin.

As controller, Chiang sits on numerous boards including the State Lands Commission, the Franchise Tax Board, and the Board of Equalization. A former attorney with the state controller's office, Chiang worked as a tax specialist for the Internal Revenue Service. He spent his first term on the BOE championing reforms such as providing the disabled with help when filing sales and use taxes, and he has been active in organizing forums and seminars to help nonprofits, small businesses, and religious groups with various tax issues and procedures.

BIOGRAPHY: Born: New York City, July 31, 1962. Home: Chatsworth. Education: BA, University of South Florida; JD, Georgetown. Military: None. Family: wife Terry Chi. Religion: Catholic.

OFFICES: 300 Capitol Mall, 18th Floor, Sacramento, CA 95814; Phone: (916) 445-3208; Fax: (916) 322-4404; Web address: http://www.sco.ca.gov; 600 Corporate Pointe, Suite 1000, Culver City, CA 90230, Phone: (310) 342-5656, Fax: (310) 342-5670.
ELECTED: 2006 TERM LIMIT: 2014
ELECTION HISTORY: None.
2002 ELECTION: Chiang (D) 51%
                   Strickland (R) 40%

TREASURER
Bill Lockyer (D)

Bill Lockyer

Term limits have been dogging Democrat Bill Lockyer around the political landscape for more than a decade, forcing the career politician to be ever more creative in his quest to hang onto office. His elective career began more than 30 years ago when, in 1973, he won a seat in the state Assembly. He was elected to the state Senate in 1982, serving until term limits knocked him out in 1998. From 1993 to 1998, Lockyer served as Senate president pro tem, making him the most powerful Democrat in the Capitol.

In 1998, Locker extended his political career by becoming attorney general, and it was thought that his next step would be a reach for the top rung, governor. He announced a campaign for the post and began raising money. At the April 2005 Democratic state convention he passed out "Lockyer for Governor" buttons.

Two weeks later, he was out of the race, telling the *San Francisco Chronicle* that he had had it with the kind of nonstop partisan bickering now entwined with any governor's job description. Instead, Lockyer said, he would run for state treasurer—a lateral move politically, but a position that wields significant fiscal power.

Political motivation often is shaded with nuance, however. And although Lockyer may have cast a gimlet eye at life as governor, the 64-year-old politician likely glanced at realities posed by the financial portfolios of three potential opponents—Democrats Phil Angelides and Steve Westly and Republican incumbent Arnold Schwarzenegger. All are immensely wealthy.

Lockyer is no slouch when it comes to raising campaign money, but he is not personally rich. He has spent his entire adult life in public service, having served as a legislative aide before winning office. He earned a law degree through night school while serving in the legislature. He would have needed all the financial and manpower help he could muster to fend off Angelides and Westly in the Democratic primary. They both spent liberally in the gubernatorial primary won by Angelides.

Perhaps Lockyer also noted how his behavior over the past few years bruised feelings within the party. The most significant hiccup occurred in the aftermath of the 2003 recall against Governor Gray Davis when Lockyer admitted publicly that he had voted for Republican Arnold Schwarzenegger instead of the most prominent Democratic candidate—Lieutenant Governor Cruz Bustamante. He also dismissed allegations that Schwarzenegger had sexually harassed women as "frat boy behavior." In the minds of women and party faithful, those remarks cast Lockyer into company with Judas and Brutus.

When he became attorney general in 1998, Lockyer changed an office that had been held for the previous eight years by Dan Lungren, a conservative Republican now in Congress. He beefed up the civil rights division, which had languished under Lungren, and began an aggressive environmental program, taking on property owners over issues of coastal protection.

Personally, Lockyer has one of the more mercurial personalities in politics; he has been known to go from smiles and charm to red-faced invective quicker than a Johan Santana fastball. He is painfully aware that his personality is the stuff of Capitol legend, having once told the *Oakland Tribune* that he was "lovable" rather than "dysfunctional" or "strange." Eccentric or not, his legislative career was marked by a rare combination of deal-making skills and liberal philosophical purity. As attorney general, relieved of the necessity of deal-making, he concentrated on philosophy, placing an environmentalist and consumer-oriented stamp on the Justice Department.

Lockyer used the Justice Department to counter the whims of the state's celebrity Republican governor, including a lawsuit to keep a Schwarzenegger-backed redistricting initiative off the November 2005 special election ballot. He kept Schwarzenegger's pension-reform initiative off the same ballot because its sponsors considered Lockyer's title and summary so politically biased they withdrew the measure.

His decision to switch from the governor's race to the contest for state treasurer cleared the field. No Democrat stepped forward to challenge him in the primary— more correctly, to challenge his campaign wallet—and he drew a weak Republican opponent in the finals. Republican Claude Parrish was a two-term member of the state Board of Equalization whose campaign floated for about a nanosecond after leaving the dock and promptly sinking from view.

BIOGRAPHY: Born: Oakland, May 8, 1941. Home: Hayward. Education: BA, UC Berkeley; teaching credential, CSU Hayward; JD, McGeorge School of Law. Military: None. Family: wife Nadia, two children. Religion: Episcopalian.

OFFICES: 915 Capitol Mall, Suite 110, Sacramento, CA 95814; Phone: (916) 653-2995; Fax: (916) 653-3125; Web site: http://www.treasurer.ca.gov; 304 South Broadway, Suite 550, Los Angeles, CA 90013, Phone: (213) 620-4467, Fax: (213) 620-6309.

ELECTED: 2006 TERM LIMIT: 2014

ELECTION HISTORY: Assembly, 1973–1982; state Senate, 1982–1998; Attorney General, 1998–2006.

2006 ELECTION: Lockyer (D) 54%
                     Parrish (R) 37%

Secretaries of State Since 1950		
Frank M. Jordan	Republican	elected 1950, 1954, 1958, 1962, 1966
Pat Sullivan	Republican	appointed 1970
Edmund G. "Jerry" Brown	Democrat	elected 1970
March Fong Eu	Democrat	elected 1974, 1978, 1982, 1986, 1990
Bill Jones	Republican	elected 1994, 1998
Kevin Shelley	Democrat	elected 2002
Bruce McPherson	Republican	appointed 2005
Debra Bowen	Democrat	elected 2006

SECRETARY OF STATE
Debra Bowen (D)

Debra Bowen

Before term limits roiled California's political universe, secretary of state was one of the most stable positions in state government. With the exception of a three-year window between 1940 and 1943, the Jordans—father Frank C. and son Frank M.—held the job from 1911 to 1970. After Jerry Brown served one brief term (1971–1975), Democrat March Fong Eu settled in for another two decades. Republican Bill Jones followed with two terms—the most allowed under term limits. In all that time, spanning nearly a century, little in the way of controversy, corruption, or political angst radiated from what was largely a procedural and ministerial post.

Then, in 2002, came Kevin Shelley.

The scion of a San Francisco political dynasty founded by his father, former Mayor Jack Shelley, Democrat Kevin Shelley emerged from the legislature, where he had been majority leader of the Assembly. Intensely partisan and politically ambitious, Shelley initially drew praise for the nonpartisan way he handled the 2003 recall election against fellow Democrat Gray Davis. But Shelley soon became embroiled in a series of mushrooming scandals that centered on his fundraising and on the overly partisan way he spent federal money designed to promote voter participation. Halfway into his first term, Shelley resigned, allowing Governor Arnold Schwarzenegger to appoint a successor.

Schwarzenegger reached into the thin bag of Republican options and tapped a moderate, recently termed-out state senator from Santa Cruz, Bruce McPherson, whose reputation for bipartisan cooperation and courtliness made him the one GOP nominee who could slam dunk the Senate's confirmation process. As secretary of state, McPherson had to clean up the detritus of Shelley's brief but turbulent tenure, most important the distribution of federal voting-improvement funds. He also had to administer a controversial November 2005 special election packed with ballot propositions that included highly partisan political reform measures on redistricting, budgeting, and union-financing sought by Schwarzenegger. The initiatives failed spectacularly, prompting the governor to take a more conciliatory tone in dealing with legislative Democrats.

McPherson sought the job on his own in 2006 and drew a tough, principled state senator as an opponent. Debra Bowen had been a fixture around Sacramento since 1992 when she first won a seat in the Assembly from a district that leaned Republican. She walked a fine line between party loyalty and pragmatism, casting the deciding vote on the 1993 budget and then in 1994 publicly grousing about Democratic maneuvers that essentially cancelled Republican control of the Assembly. In most cases, she proved a reliable Democratic vote. She was, however, one of two Democratic senators removed—forcibly, some say—from the Senate Appropriations Committee during 2005 because she balked at voting the caucus line on the committee's suspense file.

Capitol insiders regard Bowen as one of the hardest-working members, as well as one of the legislature's most intelligent and forthright senators. More significant, they tapped her as "most likely to chair an ethics committee" in a 2006 survey by *Capitol Weekly*. Her legislative agenda has been hefty through the years, and she left some notable footprints when termed out in 2006. In addition to opening up legislative data to the public, Bowen has sponsored significant bills to protect consumer privacy, give consumers the tools to fight Internet "spam," require emission standards for small power plants, protect children in the state foster-care system, and shield seniors from elder abuse.

Bowen did not wait to jump into the race for secretary of state until Shelley had resigned in April 2005. Instead, she made it known that she would take on Shelley in the 2006 primary. Unlike fellow Democrats, who either remained silent on Shelley's troubles or tried to rally around the embattled incumbent, Bowen made no secret that her challenge was predicated on the fact that she had lost confidence in him. Her candidacy was seen as the first crack in Democratic solidarity on Shelley, and some believe that it helped grease his eventual demise.

Before taking on McPherson, Bowen had to get through the Democratic primary where she faced a Senate colleague—Deborah Ortiz of Sacramento. It was considered a competitive race, but Bowen raised far more money and put together a formidable campaign operation that helped her pile up 61 percent of the primary vote. She beat Ortiz in every population center save Sacramento, including a 117,000-vote margin in Los Angeles County.

Los Angeles also contributed heavily to Bowen's victory in the general election. In a contest decided by slightly more than 250,000 votes statewide, Bowen defeated McPherson in Los Angeles County by 448,000 votes.

As Bowen geared up to run for secretary of state, she rolled out a succession of bills that affect her new position. In 2005, she authored legislation that requires all election results to be audited using a paper record. In 2006, she sponsored bills that require a public audit of absentee and early-voted ballots and allow absentee voters to easily find out if their ballot arrived at the county elections office. Yet another bill eliminated restrictions on who can examine voting machines. She sponsored a bill to regulate signature gathering operations for initiatives, but Schwarzenegger vetoed it.

As she took the oath of office in January 2007, Bowen already had spread angst among some of her chief clients—county registrars of voters. A skeptic on the reliability of electronic voting machines in use throughout the state, Bowen promised to review those machines to ensure that they were both dependable and secure. That promise sent a shiver through counties that have invested millions of dollars in election equipment that Bowen's office might force them to replace. Bowen promised an "orderly and meticulous" review, telling the *Los Angeles Times* that "the integrity of elections is too important."

BIOGRAPHY: Born: Rockford, IL, October 27, 1955. Home: Marina del Rey. Education: BA, Michigan State University; JD, University of Virginia. Military: None. Family: husband, Mark Nechodom, one child. Religion: Decline to state. Occupation: Attorney.

OFFICES: 1500 11th Street, Sacramento, CA 95814; Phone: (916) 653-7244; Fax: (916) 653-4620; Web site: http://www.ss.ca.gov; 300 South Spring Street, 12th Floor, Los Angeles, CA 90013, Phone: (213) 897-6225, Fax: (213) 897-6855; 1350 Front Street, Suite 2060, San Diego, CA 92101, Phone: (619) 525-4406, Fax: (619) 525-4407; 455 Golden Gate Avenue, Suite 7300, San Francisco, CA 94102, Phone: (415) 557-0171, Fax: (415) 557-0169; 2497 West Shaw, Suite 101, Fresno, CA 93711, Phone: (559) 445-6018, Fax: (559) 445-6888.

ELECTED: 2006 TERM LIMIT: 2014.
ELECTION HISTORY: Assembly, 1992–1998; state Senate 1998–2006
2006 ELECTION: Bowen (D) 48%
McPherson (R*) 45%

SUPERINTENDENT OF PUBLIC INSTRUCTION
Jack O'Connell (Nonpartisan)

When it comes to issues that lather up most Californians, education ranks near the top, poll after poll. Yet California's system for governing public education is so convoluted it lacks even a scrap of accountability. Consider those with a hand in educating the seven million students who attend the state's 9,000-plus schools:

- A state Board of Education whose 11 members are appointed by the governor
- A secretary of education who is an appointed member of the governor's cabinet
- 58 elected county boards of education
- 58 county superintendents of schools
- 985 school districts of varying size, each with an elected board
- 985 district superintendents
- The legislature's Senate and Assembly Education Committees

Superintendents of Public Instruction Since 1950

Roy Simpson	elected 1950, 1954, 1958
Max Rafferty	appointed 1962, elected 1966
Wilson Riles	elected 1970, 1974, 1978
Bill Honig	elected 1982, 1986, 1990
Delaine Eastin	elected 1994, 1998
Jack O'Connell	elected 2002, 2006

Jack O'Connell

• The state Department of Education

And then there is the superintendent of public instruction. To the public, the nonpartisan superintendent—the only statewide constitutional officer whose lone focus is education—sits atop this gaggle of boards, officials, and committees, delivering edicts on policy, allocating resources, and generally orchestrating all things educational. Given the weighty subject, that mandate would make the superintendent a powerful political player—if only it were true.

In the practical world of California politics, the superintendent exercises virtually no power and wields little authority. Education policy is set by the state Board of Education. The governor and the legislature allocate money for schools. Textbooks are certified by the state board and selected by districts. And so on.

The superintendent's job is to oversee the Department of Education, which implements board policy and doles out resources according to formulas crafted by others. The superintendent's influence is entirely dependent on his or her ability to snuggle up to the governor or use a bully pulpit to generate public support for an issue. The position is not quite as ineffectual as that of, say, lieutenant governor, or the "bucket of warm spit" that former U.S. Vice President John Nance Garner once used to describe his job—but it is close.

A statewide, nonpartisan superintendent of schools was created by a 1912 ballot measure—one that shaped the inherent conflict in education governance by also establishing the state Board of Education. The bifurcated structure was an afterthought to the real battle that year over free textbooks in public schools. The legislature created the Department of Education in 1921.

Despite the fuzzy nature of the job, there is never a shortage of candidates to run for it, especially in an era when termed-out legislators scramble for a landing spot while thumb twiddling for something more significant. There have been six superintendents since 1950, but only one—the conservative Max Rafferty—parlayed the job into as much as a nomination for something more exalted. Rafferty won the Republican nomination for U.S. Senate in 1968 but lost the general election to Democrat Alan Cranston.

The current superintendent is Jack O'Connell, a Central Coast Democrat who spent 20 years in the legislature before being termed out of both houses in 2002—the same year he secured his present post.

The gregarious, self-deprecating O'Connell is a former high school teacher who was a popular legislator during two decades in Sacramento. He won his first election to the legislature in 1982 with generous help from Assembly Democrats, especially then-Speaker Willie Brown, Jr. Although he never would have come by his seat without Brown, O'Connell quickly shed the need for caucus largesse by establishing a presence in the Santa Barbara area and raising constituent service to an art form. Each weekend he tended voters' needs and concerns while sitting behind a card table randomly plunked down somewhere in his district. As a result, he was never seriously challenged in either his Assembly or Senate district, despite less-than-overwhelming Democratic registration. In 1988, the Democratic incumbent was also the GOP nominee as a write-in.

As a legislator, the former teacher established an expertise on education issues, chairing education committees in both houses and sponsoring bills that reduced class size in elementary schools and raised pay scales for beginning teachers. He served a term as speaker pro tem of the Assembly, which gave him wide exposure because he presided over the televised floor sessions. As a senator, he sponsored and campaigned for Proposition 39, the successful November 2000 ballot initiative that reduced the majority required to pass local school bond measures from two-thirds to 55 percent. His leap to superintendent in 2002 was considered a natural.

O'Connell was opposed for superintendent by Orange County school board member Katherine Smith, who offered only limited resistance. O'Connell—backed by a lifelong ally, the California Teachers Association, and by most education-related organizations—outspent Smith 45 to one and racked up more votes than any other candidate on the November 2002 ballot. The only heat-generating issue focused on each candidate's qualifications. Smith grumped that O'Connell's ballot designation included the word teacher even though he hadn't been within an area code of a classroom for 20 years. O'Connell, a former high school teacher, groused that Smith—who once taught in private schools—referred to herself as an educator even though she had been involved in real estate for the past three decades.

As superintendent, O'Connell immediately restored a strong working relationship with the governor's office—a problem during the eight-year tenure of his predecessor, Democrat Delaine Eastin. A former legislator herself, Eastin and Republican Pete Wilson regularly brawled over education policy during her first term, with Wilson treating Eastin's office like an irritating but ultimately irrelevant foghorn. Her status did not improve much during her second term even though Democrat Gray Davis succeeded Wilson. In a spectacular miscalculation, Eastin endorsed Davis's 1998 primary opponent, Democrat Al Checchi, a political blunder that soured her relationship with Davis from the get-go.

O'Connell, on the other hand, had been a consistent ally to the new governor and not only endorsed him early on but stuck by him when Davis's gubernatorial campaign struggled for traction in the primary. Unfortunately, Davis was recalled less than a year into O'Connell's first term as superintendent and replaced with Republican Arnold Schwarzenegger, who targeted teachers as a special interest with too much influence over education policy. That stance put him at odds with O'Connell, whose political base has long included both the California Teachers Association and the California Federation of Teachers.

With no real authority, O'Connell used his office as a sounding board to oppose many of the new governor's education proposals, including school funding reforms and a merit pay system to reward and punish teachers. He was especially critical of Schwarzenegger's refusal to honor school funding deals made with the education community to help alleviate the state's 2003–2004 budget crisis. On less combative fronts, O'Connell campaigned for healthier foods to be served in schools and for a system of universal preschool.

Republicans have criticized O'Connell for the way he has used what little authority remains to him, focusing on his slow implementation of a statewide high school exit exam and waivers to the state's algebra requirement granted to high school students. They also claim he has advocated raising taxes to give more money to schools.

O'Connell's re-election in 2006 was no-contest. Although he drew several opponents, none was formidable. O'Connell amassed 50 percent of the vote in the June primary, which in a nonpartisan race allowed him to avoid a November runoff. That gave O'Connell the welcome chance to devote more of his time to family matters, which became acute during 2005 and 2006 when his wife, Doree, was diagnosed with cancer.

Like many termed-out constitutional officers, O'Connell's political future is up in the air. He must leave this post in 2010 and has made some noise about running for governor in what promises to be a crowded Democratic primary. Well liked and well respected, the moderate O'Connell might prove underrated in a field that could include the likes of Los Angeles Mayor Antonio Villaraigosa, San Francisco Mayor Gavin Newsom, Attorney General Jerry Brown, former Controller Steve Westly, 2006 nominee Phil Angelides, and Congresswoman Jane Harman.

BIOGRAPHY: Born: Glen Cove, NY, October 8, 1951. Home: San Luis Obispo. Education: BA, CSU Fullerton; secondary teaching credential, CSU Long Beach. Military: None. Family: wife Doree Caputo, one child. Religion: Catholic.
OFFICE: 1430 N Street, Suite 5602, Sacramento, CA 95814; Phone: (916) 319-0800; Fax: (916) 319-0100; email: joconnell@cde.ca.gov; Web: www.cde.ca.gov.
ELECTED: 2002; TERM LIMIT: 2010
ELECTION HISTORY: Assembly 1982–1994; state Senate, 1994–2002.
2002 ELECTION (nonpartisan): O'Connell 62%
　　　　　　　　　　　　　　Smith 38%
2006 ELECTION (nonpartisan): O'Connell 52%
　　　　　　　　　　　　　　Knopp 17%
　　　　　　　　　　　　　　Lenning 14%
　　　　　　　　　　　　　　Bunting 8%
　　　　　　　　　　　　　　McKicken 8%

Insurance Commissioners Since 1990		
John Garamendi	Democrat	elected 1990
Charles Quackenbush	Republican	elected 1994, 1998
Henry Low	Democrat	appointed 2001
John Garamendi	Democrat	elected 2002
Steve Poizner	Republican	elected 2006

INSURANCE COMMISSIONER
Steve Poizner (R)

Steve Poizner

Poizner achieved two significant accomplishments in 2006: He finally secured an elective position after spending overwhelming amounts of personal cash in pursuit of an office; and he became the only Republican not named Schwarzenegger to be elected statewide since 1998.

A moderate, Poizner first burst on the political scene in 2004 when he tried to capture an Assembly seat from the Silicon Valley area of northern California. The district—the 21st—was heavily Democratic, which posed some challenges that Poizner tried to overcome with cash. His opponent was Democrat Ira Ruskin.

At the time, Poizner was a political neophyte whose one asset was a wallet the size of a Swiss bank. Poizner eventually spent nearly $7 million of his own money on the campaign, smashing all previous records for self-indulgence. Ruskin and his Democratic allies spent about a third as much.

The playing field was tilted heavily for Ruskin, given the district's 14-point Democratic registration edge, and Poizner sought to even the odds by piling bags of cash on his side of the table. He spent $500,000 on the primary, in which he was unopposed. He spent, he confessed, to build up his name, and throughout the summer his campaign was the single biggest advertiser on Bay Area television—running more ads than Dodge trucks and Viagra. After the primary frivolity, Poizner got serious about spending his money, writing checks to his campaign for $250,000 to $350,000 every 30 seconds and continuing to blanket the region with information about himself. It was estimated that his name ID was in the 80 percent range, meaning that four out of every five residents knew of him. What they may not have heard *about* him, however, formed the centerpiece of Ruskin's campaign—that he was the Republican candidate and that he had contributed to George Bush's re-election. Poizner's candidacy proved one point: That unless the opponent is a serial killer or CEO of an energy company, no amount of money—even $100 per vote—can win a district where Democrats enjoy a 14-point registration edge.

Poizner took that lesson to heart, eschewing another run for the legislature in 2006 and focusing instead on a statewide post, where the Democratic edge is far less significant. He chose to run for insurance commissioner, a job where self-funding is not only a virtue but a powerful campaign theme.

The commissioner is considered the most powerful regulator in California. The office oversees a $100-plus billion industry, sets insurance rates, has the authority to seize companies in trouble, audits insurers, and can bar companies from doing business in California. The commissioner holds sway over more than 300,000 agents and brokers and runs a department with a $200 million budget—financed mostly through fees on insurers. In that context, insurance money can be toxic because those who rely on it are instantly suspect. Poizner's ability to fund his own campaign set him on the high road and made it a clear path to the general election. No Republican could raise enough to take him on, and he had the Republican primary to himself.

Poizner drew one final piece of good fortune—the Democrat who chose to run for insurance commissioner was Lt. Governor Cruz Bustamante, arguably the weakest Democratic candidate for any statewide office. Not only did Bustamante raise money from the insurance industry, but despite his years in public office, the former Assembly speaker had wounded himself politically by running as a replacement candidate in the 2003 recall election against Gov. Gray Davis. Democrats were implored to stay out of that race to lend credence to the argument that the recall was a Republican plot. Bustamante's candidacy crippled that effort, and many Democrats never forgave him.

As he did with his Assembly race, Poizner spent early, often, and liberally—in excess of $9 million from his own fortune, which is estimated at close to $1 billion. That allowed him to cut through the white noise created by other campaigns—notably for governor—and raise his profile throughout the state. As expected, he ran on the theme of integrity, calling attention to his opponent's support from those he would regulate. Among those who endorsed him was Harvey Rosenfield, the consumer advocate and godfather of Proposition 103—the 1988 initiative that made the commissioner's job elected rather than appointed.

Poizner captured just over 50 percent of the vote, running well in normally Democratic strongholds such as Los Angeles, Contra Costa, San Mateo, and Santa Clara counties while piling up big margins in GOP enclaves. He won Orange County by 250,000 votes—the kind of margin other Republican candidates only dream about these days.

A self-styled moderate and coalition builder, Poizner is the prototype Silicon Valley entrepreneur turned politician. A native Texan, Poizner migrated to California in 1978, earning an MBA from Stanford. He made his fortune during the dot-com boom when his company, Snap Trak, developed the GPS-based technology which, among other things, allowed the pinpointing of 911 calls made from cellular phones. Snap Trak was subsequently sold to Qualcomm in March 2000 for close to $1 billion.

Poizner's political odyssey took a side tour in 2005 when Governor Schwarzenegger nominated him for a spot on the California Public Utilities Commission. Poizner eventually withdrew because he could not extract himself from financial entanglements associated with his billion-dollar portfolio. He later served as chair of a failed 2005 initiative to reform the redistricting process.

Poizner inherited a few land mines when he took office in January 2007. Just before leaving to become lieutenant governor, the previous commissioner—Democrat John Garamendi—issued what *Capitol Weekly* called "a barrage of new regulations" affecting the insurance industry. It was said that Garamendi's motives were less than pristine, that he wanted to force Poizner to either accept the new regulations or rescind them. The latter action could leave Poizner open to charges that he is anticonsumer, a label that could prove a liability for Poizner who is said to have ambitions for the governorship in 2010, when Arnold Schwarzenegger is termed out. As displayed in his past campaigns, Poizner certainly has the resources to mount that effort, and one of his rivals could be Garamendi.

BIOGRAPHY: Born: Houston, Texas, January 4, 1957. Home: Los Gatos. Education: BS, University of Texas; MBA, Stanford. Military: None. Family: wife Carol, one daughter. Religion: Jewish.
OFFICES: 300 Capitol Mall, Suite 1700, Sacramento, CA 95814; Phone: (916) 492-3500; Fax: (916) 445-5280; Web site: http://www.insurance.ca.gov; 300 South Spring Street, 13th Floor, Los Angeles, CA 90013, Phone: (213) 346-6464, Fax: (213) 897-9051; 45 Fremont, 23rd Floor, San Francisco, CA 94105, Phone: (415) 538-4010, Fax: (415) 904-5889.
ELECTED: 2006; TERM LIMIT: 2014
ELECTION HISTORY: None.
2006 ELECTION: Poizner (R) 51%
Bustamante (D) 39%

BOARD OF EQUALIZATION

From a felled redwood tree to recycled car tires, there is virtually no aspect of state commerce that is not touched by the state Board of Equalization. Created in 1879 by a constitutional amendment, the board's principal mandate is to ensure that all taxation is equal and uniform throughout the state.

Today the board has a finger on the economic pulse of virtually every aspect of commerce and government in California, collecting about $31 billion in taxes and fees each year. It administers four tax programs: property taxes, sales and use taxes, special taxes, and the tax appellate program. Its reach is broad. The board determines assessments and classifies properties. It adopts rules and regulations for county tax assessors and hears tax appeals from individuals and business owners. It administers a plethora of fees and taxes on such commodities as alcoholic beverages, cigarettes, insurance, fuel, timber, hazardous waste, and telephone service, and even administers a children's lead poisoning prevention fee. It also administers the sales and use taxes of numerous cities, counties, and transit districts.

But the board has been called an anachronism—outmoded, outdated, and outpaced by events it governs. Proposals have been advanced to consolidate it with the Franchise Tax Board and create a single tax agency. But the only such proposal to reach a governor's desk was vetoed by Governor Pete Wilson in 1994 and likely would find tough sledding in today's term-limit-obsessed legislature. Lawmakers see the board as

Board of Equalization Districts
Percent of Democrats and Republicans

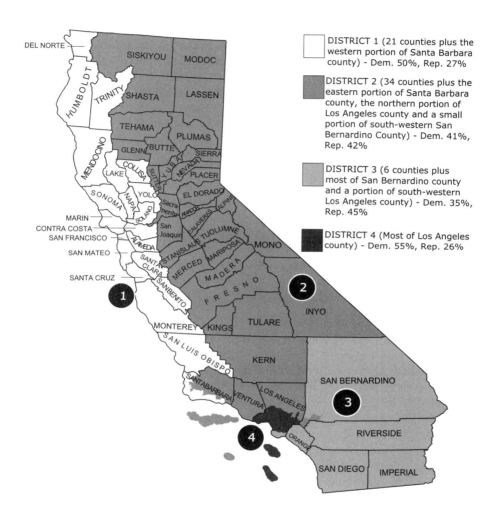

DISTRICT 1 (21 counties plus the western portion of Santa Barbara county) - Dem. 50%, Rep. 27%

DISTRICT 2 (34 counties plus the eastern portion of Santa Barbara county, the northern portion of Los Angeles county and a small portion of south-western San Bernardino County) - Dem. 41%, Rep. 42%

DISTRICT 3 (6 counties plus most of San Bernardino county and a portion of south-western Los Angeles county) - Dem. 35%, Rep. 45%

DISTRICT 4 (Most of Los Angeles county) - Dem. 55%, Rep. 26%

another rung on the electoral ladder and are loathe to erase a landing strip on the path to their next office.

The board consists of four elected members who are limited to two, four-year terms, and one *ex-officio* member—the state controller. Each member represents about one quarter of the state, or roughly nine million people.

Prior to the 1980s, the board was a political backwater, albeit a well-paid one, where members could expect to win re-election and serve comfortably until retirement. But no political office is a backwater these days. Even before term limits came to full flower, the board was used as a springboard rather than a retirement village. In

1994, member Matt Fong catapulted to higher office by becoming state treasurer and four years later, another member, Brad Sherman, was elected to Congress.

Term limits have made the board a comfortable place to bide time. In recent years, a pair of Democratic legislators occupied seats while waiting to return to Sacramento. In 1994 Johan Klehs of San Leandro won the first of two terms on the board before returning for a final term in the Assembly in 2002 and laying the groundwork for a run for state Senate. In 2002 termed-out Assemblywoman Carole Migden of San Francisco was elected to the board but served only half a term before capturing a state Senate seat. Also in 1994, Republican Dean Andal left the Assembly one term early, subsequently winning two terms on the board. Andal, who has yet to run for a third and final Assembly term, was replaced in 2002 by another Republican lawmaker—Bill Leonard, who had been termed out of both the Assembly and Senate.

The current board has two Democrats and two Republicans, with Democratic Controller Steve Westly tipping the balance of power.

Betty Yee (D)
1st District

Counties: Alameda, Colusa, Contra Costa, Del Norte, Humboldt, Lake, Marin, Mendocino, Monterey, Napa, San Benito, San Francisco, San Luis Obispo, San Mateo, Santa Barbara, Santa Clara, Santa Cruz, Solano, Sonoma, Trinity, Yolo
Voter Registration: 49% D – 26% R – 20% DS

Betty Yee

The 1st District extends along the California coast from the Oregon border to the northern portion of Santa Barbara County. In the 2001 redistricting, it ceded six spacious but sparsely populated northern California counties to the neighboring 2nd District, trading them for more densely populated territory in San Luis Obispo and Santa Barbara counties. The district's Democratic character remained the same, however.

San Francisco Democrat Carole Migden was elected to represent the 1st District in 2002, the year she was termed out of the Assembly, but it was commonly assumed that Migden would burn up less than a nanosecond as a member of the board. And in fact, Migden used a good portion of her first—and only—two years on the board cobbling together a foundation for her return to the legislature. Not that the hard-charging Migden ignored her duties; while on the board, she served a term as chair and pushed hard for closing corporate loopholes. But by 2005, she was gone, having won a seat in the state Senate in November 2004.

Migden's place was taken by her chief deputy, Betty Yee, who was appointed acting member, and then ran for the job on her own in 2006. Yee followed Migden to the board after long years of service as a fiscal and budgetary expert on the staff of the legislature and at the Department of Finance. She was chief deputy director for budget at Finance in the Davis administration and held staff positions with a variety of legislative Assembly and Senate committees, including Budget and Appropriations.

BIOGRAPHY: Born: San Francisco, October 19, 1957. Home: San Francisco. Education: BA, UC Berkeley; MA, Golden Gate University. Military: None. Family: Decline to state. Religion: Decline to state.
OFFICES: 450 N Street, MIC 71, Sacramento, CA 95814; Phone: (916) 445-4081; Fax: (916) 324-2087; email: Board.MemberD1@boe.ca.gov; 455 Golden Gate Avenue, Suite 10500, San Francisco, CA 94102, Phone: (415) 557-3000, Fax: (415) 455-0287.
APPOINTED: 2004; TERM LIMIT: 2010.
ELECTION HISTORY: None.
2006 ELECTION: Yee (D*) 65%
Neighbors (R) 29%

Bill Leonard (R)
District 2

Counties: Alpine, Amador, Butte, Calaveras, El Dorado, Fresno, Glenn, Inyo, Kern, Kings, Lassen, Los Angeles, Madera, Mariposa, Merced, Modoc, Mono, Nevada, Placer, Plumas, Sacramento, San Bernardino, San Joaquin, Santa Barbara, Shasta, Sierra, Siskiyou, Stanislaus, Sutter, Tehama, Tulare, Tuolumne, Ventura, Yuba
Voter Registration: 39% D – 43% R – 14% DS

Bill Leonard

The 2nd District is enormous as it runs along the Nevada-California border from Modoc to Inyo counties and through the Central Valley from the Oregon border to Kern County. It also juts west to slide along the Pacific Ocean at Santa Barbara and Ventura counties.

Republican in nature, the district has been represented since 1994 by legislative refugees—Dean Andal from 1994 to 2002 and, currently, Bill Leonard. Leonard's distinguished legislative career began in 1978 when he was first elected to the Assembly as a "Prop. 13 baby"—a nickname bestowed on GOP lawmakers who came to the legislature in the wake of Proposition 13. A staunch—some would say rigid—social and fiscal conservative, Leonard was one of the few Republican officials to oppose Proposition 140, the 1990 initiative that imposed term limits on the legislature. After it passed, he became adept at prolonging his elective career, participating in the first term-limits-prompted seat swap when, in 1996, he traded districts with then-Assemblyman Jim Brulte. Brulte, who had been termed out of the Assembly, ran for Leonard's Senate seat while Leonard, who had been termed out of the Senate, captured Brulte's Assembly district. It marked a second go-around for Leonard, who left the Assembly in 1988 to run for the Senate. Since his previous Assembly stint was completed prior to passage of Proposition 140, Leonard was entitled to three additional terms in the lower house. Legislative term limits finally caught up with him for good in 2002—the year he won a seat on the BOE. He was re-elected handily in 2006.

While a legislator, Leonard was often a member of leadership, serving as Senate Caucus chairman for a time and as Assembly minority leader from 1996 to 1998. His Assembly leadership ended abruptly after the disastrous election of 1998 when his caucus lost five seats. Although he was not entirely responsible for the debacle, Leonard resigned from leadership.

BIOGRAPHY: Born: San Bernardino, October 29, 1947. Home: Rancho Cucamonga. Education: BA, UC Irvine. Military: None. Family: wife Sherry, three children, one grandchild. Religion: Presbyterian.

OFFICES: 400 Capitol Mall, Suite 2340, Sacramento, CA 95814; Phone: (916) 445-2181; Fax: (916) 327-4003; email: Bill.Leonard@boe.ca.gov; 4295 Jurupa Avenue, Suite 204, Ontario, CA 91761, Phone: (909) 937-6106, Fax: (909) 937-7044.

ELECTED: 2002; TERM LIMIT: 2010.

ELECTION HISTORY: Assembly, 1978–1988, 1996–2002; state Senate, 1988–1996.

2002 ELECTION: Leonard (R) 59%
       Santos (D) 42%

2006 ELECTION: Leonard (R*) 56%
       Raboy (D) 38%

Michelle Steel (R)
District 3

Counties: Imperial, Los Angeles, Orange, Riverside, San Bernardino, San Diego.
Voter Registration: 34% D – 45% R – 17% DS

Michelle Steel

District 3 occupies the southern portion of California—minus Los Angeles and Ventura counties. As such, it takes in the Inland Empire and the coastal counties of Orange and San Diego that feed the Empire with its temper-fueling traffic gridlock.

Republican Claude Parrish was termed out in 2006 after proving that persistence pays off. He ran for—and failed to win—in three consecutive elections, starting in 1986. He finally succeeded in 1998 when his predecessor—an ageless Republican warlock named Ernie Dronenburg, Jr.—was pried out of office by term limits after 20 years on the BOE. Parrish ran for state treasurer in 2006 and was drubbed by Democrat Bill Lockyer.

Parrish's departure left a vacancy, and five Republicans sought to replace him in the 2006 primary. Only two had the name and resources to make a credible run—Assemblyman and former state Senator Ray Haynes and Michelle Steel, Parrish's chief deputy and the wife of former Republican Party chairman Shawn Steel.

At the outset, it was thought that Haynes had all the advantages. A veteran legislator, he represented Riverside County and was well known throughout the southland as a strong voice for conservative values.

But Haynes came late to the race, announcing his intentions in the summer of 2005, less than a year before the primary. At that point, Steel had been campaigning for the job for two years and had a monumental head start on Haynes in endorsements and fund raising. Among those who backed her were U.S. Reps. Ed Royce and Dana Rohrabacher, Van Tran, Mike Antonovich, Los Angeles Sheriff Lee Baca, and a host of Republican legislators. She was able to get to the right of Haynes politically with an endorsement from conservative icon Grover Norquist and prevented the influential California Republican Assembly from endorsing any candidate—a move considered a blow to Haynes.

The only controversy in the campaign centered on Steel's official ballot designation as "Equalization Member's Deputy." In a down-ticket contest where voters likely know nothing about either candidate, even on Election Day, a ballot designation may provide the sole rationale for someone's decision, and Steel's ability to associate herself with the job in question was a benefit.

Steel, who is Korean, received much financial support from the Korean community, which helped her build a $600,000 campaign treasury by the end of 2005. Her money allowed Steel to finish the campaign with a strong mail and phone-bank effort that Haynes could not begin to match. Still, the race was close, with Steel capturing 38 percent of the vote to Haynes 34 percent. Three other candidates split the balance. Steel easily defeated the Democrat in November.

BIOGRAPHY: Born: Seoul, Korea, June 21, 1955. Home: Palos Verdes. Education: BA, Pepperdine. Military: None. Family: husband Shawn, two children. Religion: Christian.

OFFICES: 450 N Street, Suite 77, Sacramento, CA 95814; Phone: (916) 445-5713; Fax: (916) 323-0546; email: Board.Member.Steel@boe.ca.gov; 550 Deep Valley Drive, Suite 355, Rolling Hills Estates, CA 90274; Phone: (310) 377-8016, (866) 910-9558; Fax: (310) 377-5731.

ELECTED: 2006. TERM LIMIT: 2014.

ELECTION HISTORY: None.

2006 ELECTION: Steel (R) 57%
Christian-Heising (D) 39%

Judy Chu (D)
4th District

Judy Chu

The 4th District is easy to peg on a map since it is most of urban Los Angeles County, including the city of Los Angeles. It also has served as a decent Democratic stepping-stone to higher office. Brad Sherman parlayed the BOE into a seat in Congress back in 1994, and his appointed successor, John Chiang, recently was elected state controller.

Chiang's departure opened a coveted seat on the BOE, and two Assembly Democrats squared off in the June primary. Judy Chu represented the San Gabriel Valley, while Jerome Horton came from Inglewood in a clash that featured Asian and African-American candidates. The race was expected to be competitive, but Chu won comfortably, amassing 50 percent of the vote to Horton's 32 percent, while two other Democrats split the rest. Given district registration, Chu was not seriously challenged in November 2006.

Chu first came to the legislature in 2001 by winning a special election after incumbent Gloria Romero won yet another special election to the state Senate. It was something of an ironic victory for Chu because her first foray into legislative politics resulted in a 1998 Democratic primary loss to Romero, a tussle that symbolized district competition for power between Asians and Latinos.

Chu rose through Assembly ranks to chair the important Appropriations Committee during her final term, and that position gave her a fund-raising base that helped her in her primary campaign. Her key legislation focused on hate crimes, but she carried tax legislation, including a bill that allows the state to more aggressively pursue delinquent taxpayers. Her tax-related package of bills was not without political purpose, given her subsequent run for the Board of Equalization. To get ready for that campaign, Chu announced in May 2005 that she would refuse to take the 12 percent pay raise granted to the legislature by an independent commission.

BIOGRAPHY: Born: Los Angeles, July 7, 1953. Home: Monterey Park. Education: BA, UCLA; PhD, California School of Professional Psychology. Military: None. Family: husband Michael Eng. Religion: Decline to state. Occupation: Professor.

OFFICES: 450 N Street, Suite MC71, Sacramento, CA 95814; Phone: (916) 445-4154; Fax: (916) 323-2869; email: judy.chu@boe.ca.gov; 660 South Figueroa Street, Suite 2050, Los Angeles, CA 90017, Phone: (213) 239-8506, Fax: (213) 239-8753.

APPOINTED: 2006. TERM LIMIT: 2014.

ELECTION HISTORY: Garvey School Board, 1985–1988; Monterey Park City Council, 1988–2001; Assembly, 2000–2006

2006 ELECTION: Chu (D) 65%
Forsch (R) 27%

3

The Omnipresent Bureaucracy

State bureaucracy is everywhere. It is Caltrans workers pruning oleander along state highways, janitors polishing floors in state buildings, DMV clerks renewing driver's licenses, investigators inspecting nursing homes, and education experts choosing new textbooks for high school students.

Working within a multitude of state agencies, boards, and commissions, the state's 325,000-plus employees oversee every aspect of state government. In one way or another, the state bureaucracy and its work force touch virtually every facet of life in California.

Some politicians—Governor Arnold Schwarzenegger among them—believe the bureaucracy is bloated, a "monster" in need of starvation, according to one memorable line from the governor. But state workers are hardly a drain on state resources, though they may, in the eyes of some critics, make a convenient scapegoat for California's fiscal troubles. Wrapped in red tape they may be, but bureaucrats are the technicians that keep the machinery of state government humming.

The salaries of this vast army of employees range from the low-end minimum wages of hourly workers to the cushy paychecks of politically connected commissioners, some of whose appointments earn them more than $100,000 a year. Governors, Assembly speakers, and Senate pro tems parcel out the choicest appointments as patronage plums, political rewards for party loyalists, and parking places for termed-out legislative allies. These patronage jobs have come under increasing scrutiny and heavier fire because the work involved is minimal, sometimes only requiring an appearance once or twice a month.

The State Work Force			
Year	Governor	Employees Per 1,000 Population	Employees
1978-79	Brown	9.6	218,530
1979-80	Brown	9.5	220,193
1980-81	Brown	9.5	225,567
1981-82	Brown	9.4	228,813
1982-83	Transition	9.2	228,489
1983-84	Deukmejian	8.9	226,695
1984-85	Deukmejian	8.9	229,845
1985-86	Deukmejian	8.7	229,641
1986-87	Deukmejian	8.6	232,927
1987-88	Deukmejian	8.6	237,761
1988-89	Deukemjian	8.7	248,173
1989-90	Deukmejian	8.7	254,589
1990-91	Transition	8.7	260,622
1991-92	Wilson	8.6	261,713
1992-93	Wilson	8.4	260,939
1993-94	Wilson	8.5	265,035
1994-95	Wilson	8.5	269,004
1995-96	Wilson	8.5	271,076
1996-97	Wilson	8.5	271,966
1997-98	Wilson	8.4	271,254
1998-99	Davis	8.6	282,860
1999-2000	Davis	8.9	296,076
2000-01	Davis	9.1	311,239
2001-02	Davis	9.3	323,603
2002-03	Davis	9.1	321,394
2003-04	Davis	8.8	316,860
2004-05	Schwarzenegger	8.6	313,684
2005-06	Schwarzenegger	8.6	317,593
2006-07	Schwarzenegger	9.1	340,120

Source: Governor's Proposed Budget, 2007-2008.

But while governors, their political appointees, and their legislative allies come and go, the bureaucracy remains. It is the one constant in state government.

BUSINESS, TRANSPORTATION, AND HOUSING AGENCY

Oversees 16 departments dealing with housing, business, and transportation including the California Highway Patrol, state Department of Transportation (CalTrans), Department of Motor Vehicles, Department of Alcohol and Beverage Control, and the Department of Real Estate. Acting Agency Secretary: Barry Sedlick. Office: 980 9th Street, Suite 2450, Sacramento, CA 95814; Phone: (916) 323-5400; Fax: (916) 323-5440; Web: www.bth.ca.gov. Employees: 43,676. 2007–2008 Budget: $18.1 billion.

Department of Alcohol Beverage Control

Licenses and regulates the manufacture, sale, purchase, possession, and transportation of alcoholic beverages. Director: Jerry Jolly. Office: 3927 Lennane Drive, Suite 100, Sacramento, CA 95834; Phone: (916) 419-2500; Fax: (916) 419-2599; Web: www.abc.ca.gov. Employees: 459. 2007–2008 Budget: $51.5 million.

Department of Corporations

California's investment and financing authority with exclusive power to bring both civil and administrative actions under the laws subject to the jurisdiction of the California Corporations Commissioner. Licenses and regulates a variety of businesses, including securities brokers and dealers, investment advisers and financial planners, and certain fiduciaries and lenders. Regulates the offer and sales of securities, franchises, and off-exchange commodities. Commissioner: Preston Dufauchard. Office: 1515 K Street, Suite 200, Sacramento, CA 95814; Phone: (916) 445-7205; Fax: (916) 445-7975. Web: www.corp.ca.gov. Employees: 277. 2007–2008 Budget: $33.9 million.

Department of Financial Institutions

Created in 1996 to consolidate the functions of the former Department of Banks and the Department of Savings and Loans. Oversees the operation of California's state-chartered financial institutions to protect the public from financial loss due to the failure of state-chartered institutions. Promotes sound financial services practices, licenses new financial institutions, promotes financial literacy, and examines financial institutions. Commissioner: Michael Kelley. Office: 111 Pine Street, Suite 1100, San Francisco, CA 94111; Phone: (415) 263-8555; Fax: (415) 989-5310. Web: www.dfi.ca.gov. Employees: 224. 2007–2008 Budget: $28.5 million.

Department of Housing and Community Development

Guides and supports public and private sector efforts to provide decent homes for every Californian, administers low-income housing programs and standards for manufactured homes. Director: Lynn Jacobs. Office: 1800 Third Street, Sacramento, CA 95814; Phone: (916) 445-4775; Fax: (916) 324-5107; Web: www.hcd.ca.gov. Employees: 597. 2007–2008 Budget: $968.6 million.

Department of Managed Health Care

Established in July 2000 as part of a sweeping package of reforms designed to ensure high-quality prevention and health care for Californians enrolled in managed-health-care plans. A first-in-the-nation innovative approach to ensuring aggressive prevention and high quality managed health care. Director: Lucinda Ehnes. Office: 980 9ᵗʰ Street, Suite 500, Sacramento, CA 95814; Phone: (916) 324-8176; Fax: (916) 322-9430. Web: www.hmohelp.ca.gov. Employees: 297. 2007–2008 Budget: $43.5 million.

Department of Motor Vehicles

Registers vehicles and vessels, issues and regulates driver's licenses, and oversees the manufacture, delivery, and disposal of vehicles. Director: George Valverde. Office: 2415 1st Avenue, Sacramento, CA 95818; Phone: (916) 657-6518; Fax: (916) 457-7582. Web: www.dmv.ca.gov. Employees: 8,280. 2007–2008 Budget: $996.2 million.

Department of Real Estate

Licenses real estate agents and developers, protects the public in offerings of subdivided property and investigates complaints. Real Estate Commissioner: Jeff Davi. Office: 2201 Broadway, Sacramento, CA 95818; Phone: (916) 227-0782; Fax: (916) 227-0777. Web: www.dre.ca.gov. Employees: 337. 2007–2008 Budget: $46.6 million.

Department of Transportation (Caltrans)

Builds, maintains, and rehabilitates roads and bridges; manages airport and heliport safety and access; regulates airport noise; helps local governments provide public transportation. Director: Will Kempton. Office: 1120 N Street, Suite 1100, Sacramento, CA 95814; Phone: (916) 654-5266; Fax: (916) 654-6608; Web: www.caltrans.ca.gov. Employees: 21,758. 2007–2008 Budget: $12.8 billion.

California Highway Patrol

Patrols state highways to ensure the safe, convenient, and efficient transportation of people and goods, monitors school bus and farm labor transportation safety, oversees the transport of hazardous waste, and provides security for state elected officials and the Capitol. Commissioner: Mike Brown. Office: 2555 1st Avenue, Sacramento, CA 95818; Phone: (916) 657-7152; Fax: (916) 657-7324; Web: www.chp.ca.gov. Employees: 11,012. 2007–2008 Budget: $1.83 billion.

Office of Patient Advocate

Established in July 2000, the Office of the Patient Advocate (OPA) is an independent office in state government charged with informing and educating consumers about their rights and responsibilities as HMO enrollees. Acting Director: Ed Mendoza. Office: 980 9th Street, Suite 500, Sacramento, CA 95814; Phone (916) 324-6407; Web: www.opa.ca.gov. 2007–2008 Budget: $2.4 million

Office of Real Estate Appraisers

Licenses and regulates residential and commercial real-estate appraisers. Acting Director: Anthony Majewski. Office: 1102 Q Street, Suite 4100, Sacramento, CA 95814; Phone: (916) 440-7878; Fax: (916) 440-7406; Web: www.orea.ca.gov. Employees: 26. 2007–2008 Budget: $4.2 million.

Office of Traffic Safety

Seeks to reduce fatalities, injuries, and economic loss due to motor-vehicle crashes. Director: Christopher Murphy. Office: 7000 Franklin Boulevard, Suite 440, Sacramento, CA 95823; Phone: (916) 262-0990; Fax: (916) 262-2960; Web: www.ots.ca.gov. Employees: 34. 2007–2008 Budget: $96.3 million.

HEALTH AND HUMAN SERVICES AGENCY

Administers state and federal programs for health care, social services, public assistance, job training, and rehabilitation. Duties are divided among the agency's 18 departments and commissions and the Managed Risk Medical Insurance Board. Agency Secretary: Kim Belshé. Office: 1600 9th Street, Suite 460, Sacramento, CA 95814; Phone: (916) 654-3454; Fax: (916) 654-3343; Web: www.chhs.ca.gov. Employees: 33,381. 2007–2008 Budget: $38.1 billion (state funds); $78.8 billion (total funds).

Department of Aging

Promotes the well-being of older adults and adults with disabilities. Director: Lynda Terry. Office: 1600 K Street, Sacramento, CA 95814; Phone: (916) 322-5290; Fax: (916) 324-1903; Web: www.aging.ca.gov. Employees: 134. 2007–2008 Budget: $65 million (state funds); $222 million (total funds).

Department of Alcohol and Drug Programs

Ensures that communities and individuals are free of alcohol and drug problems. Director: Kathryn Jett. Office: 1700 K Street, Sacramento, CA 95814; Phone (916) 445-1943; Fax: (916) 323-5873; Web: www.adp.ca.gov. Employees: 344. 2007–2008 Budget: $291 million (state funds); $662.7 million (total funds).

Department of Child Support Services

Promotes the well-being of children and the self-sufficiency of families by delivering child support establishment and collection services that help parents meet the financial, medical, and emotional needs of their children. Director: Gretta Wallace. Office: P.O. Box 419064, Rancho Cordova, CA 95741; Phone: (916) 464-5300; Fax: (916) 464-5065; Web: www.childsup@ca.gov. Employees: 519. 2007–2008 Budget: $319.8 million (state funds); $1.1 billion (total funds).

Department of Community Services and Development

Administers state and federal funds that provide programs for low-income individuals. The funds are distributed through a network of local agencies. Director: Lloyd Throne. Office: 700 North 10th Street, Suite 258, Sacramento, CA 95814; Phone (916) 341-4200; Fax: (916) 327-3153; Web: www.csd.ca.gov. Employees: 109. 2007–2008 Budget: $169.8 million (total funds).

Department of Developmental Services

Provides services and support for children and adults with developmental disabilities through state-operated developmental centers and contracts with various nonprofit agencies called regional centers. Director: Terri Delgadillo. Office: 1600 9th Street, Suite 240, Sacramento, CA 95814; Phone: (916) 654-1897; Fax: (916) 327-3153; Web: www.dds.ca.gov. Employees: 7,747. 2007–2008 Budget: $2.75 billion (state funds); $4.32 billion (total funds).

Department of Health Care Services

Formerly known as the Department of Health Services, the department's public health functions were split off into a new Department of Public Health. DHCS is in charge of preventive medical services, public water supplies, environmental health, epidemiological studies, rural and community health, radiologic health, and maternal and child health. Its Food and Drug Program seeks to protect consumers. Director: Sandy Shewry. Office: 1501 Capitol Avenue, Suite 6001, Sacramento, CA 95814; Phone: (916) 440-7500; Fax: (916) 440-7404; Web: www.dhs.ca.gov. Employees: 2,957. 2007–2008 Budget: $15 billion (state funds); $38.1 billion (total funds).

Department of Public Health

Formerly part of the Department of Health Services, the new Department of Public Health was created in 2006 to administer a range of public and environmental health programs. Director: Sandy Shewry. Office: 1501 Capitol Avenue, Suite 6001, Sacramento, CA 95814; Phone: (916) 440-7500; Fax: (916) 440-7404; Web: www.dhs.ca.gov. Employees: 3,284. 2007–2008 Budget: $1.1 billion (state funds); $3 billion (total funds).

Department of Mental Health

Provides care and treatment to the state's mentally ill in state hospitals and works with mentally ill inmates incarcerated with the Department of Corrections and California Youth Authority. Director: Stephen Mayberg. Office: 1600 9th Street, Suite 151, Sacramento, CA 95814; Phone (916) 654-2309; Fax: (916) 654-3198; Web: www.dmh.cahwnet.gov. Employees: 11,298. 2007–2008 Budget: $3.4 billion (state funds); $4.78 billion (total funds).

Department of Rehabilitation

Helps people with disabilities, particularly those with severe disabilities, obtain and retain employment and live independently in their communities. Director: Catherine Campisi. Office: 2000 Evergreen Street, Sacramento, CA 95815; Phone: (916) 263-8987; Fax: (916) 263-7474; Web: www.rehab.cahwnet.gov. Employees: 1,863. 2007–2008 Budget: $57.9 million (state funds); $389.7 million (total funds).

Department of Social Services

Operates state social service and income-assistance programs, which are managed and funded through a partnership of state, federal, and local governments. Benefits include welfare programs, social services, community care licensing, and disability evaluation. Provides social services to the blind, needy, elderly, and disabled, and seeks to protect children and adults from abuse, neglect, and exploitation. Director: Cliff Allenby. Office: 744 P Street, Suite 1740, Sacramento, CA 95814; Phone: (916) 445-6951; Fax: (916) 653-3173; Web: www.dss.cahwnet.gov. Employees: 4,236. 2007–2008 Budget: $8.9 billion (state funds); $18.8 billion (total funds).

Office of Statewide Health Planning and Development
Promotes health care accessibility by providing information about health care outcomes, ensuring the safety of buildings used to provide health care, insuring loans to encourage the development of health care facilities, and helps develop and sustain the capacity of communities to address local health care issues. Director: Dr. David Carlisle. Office: 1600 9th Street, Suite 433, Sacramento, CA 95814; Phone: (916) 654-1606; Fax: (916) 653-1448; Web: www.oshpd.ca.gov. Employees: 412. 2007–2008 Budget: $67.5 million (state funds); $77.5 million (total funds).

Emergency Medical Services Authority
Ensures quality patient care by administering a statewide system of emergency medical care, injury prevention, and disaster medical response. Director: Dr. Cesar Aristeigueita. Office: 1930 9th Street, Sacramento, CA 95814; Phone: (916) 322-4336; Fax: (916) 324-2875; Web: www.emsa.ca.gov. Employees: 54. 2007–2008 Budget: $14.4 million (state funds); $25 million (total funds).

Managed Risk Medical Insurance Board
Seeks to improve health by increasing access to affordable, comprehensive, quality health care coverage. Included in its mandate is the Healthy Families Program. Chair: Cliff Allenby. Executive Director: Lesley Cummings. Office: 1000 G Street, Suite 450, Sacramento, CA 95814; Phone: (916) 324-4695; Fax: (916) 324-4878; Web: www.mrmib.ca.gov. Employees: 85. 2007–2008 Budget: $498 million (state funds); $1.28 billion (total funds).

SECRETARY FOR EDUCATION
Advises the governor on education policy and legislation and administers the Academic Volunteer and Mentoring Program and the California Commission on Improving Life Through Service (federally funded under the AmeriCorps program). The secretary's role has grown through the years, fueled in part by squabbles between the governor and the elected superintendent of public instruction. That this office exists at cabinet level speaks to the hydra-like system of education governance—a system that includes the secretary and the superintendent, numerous levels of boards of education, all with separate mandates, as well as local superintendents of schools for districts and counties.

The current acting secretary, Scott Himelstein, replaced Alan Bersin, the former superintendent of San Diego schools. Office: 1121 L Street, Suite 600, Sacramento, CA 95814; Phone: (916) 323-0611; Fax: (916) 323-3753; Web: www.ose.ca.gov. Employees: 17. 2007–2008 Budget: $2.1 million.

Board of Education
Establishes policies and adopts regulations for schools from kindergarten through the 12th grade. Primary duties include selecting textbooks for grades K-8, developing curriculum frameworks, approving district waivers from regulations, and overseeing state testing programs, teacher credentialing, and school district reorganization. In the past, the board was seen as subservient to the elected superintendent of public instruction. But squabbles between board members, who are appointed by the governor for fixed terms, and past superintendents over budget and educational reforms led to a lawsuit between the board and then-Superintendent Bill Honig during the 1980s. The board prevailed, successfully wresting power away from the superintendent's office. The board has been the center of controversy regarding its appointees as well. Governor Arnold Schwarzenegger's attempt to re-appoint several members has run afoul of the state Senate, including Republican lawmakers withholding votes for teacher union official Joe Nunez in 2007. Members: Kenneth Noonan, president; Ruth Bloom, vice president; James Aschwanden; Alan Bersin; Yvonne Chan; Donald Fisher; Ruth Green; David Lopez; Jonathan Williams; Andrew Estep (student member). Executive Director: Roger Magyar. Office: 1430 N Street, Room 5111, Sacramento, CA 95814; Phone: (916) 319-8027; Fax: (916) 319-0175; Web: www.cde.ca.gov. Employees: 9. 2007–2008 Budget: $1.6 million.

Department of Education
Administers the K-12 education system by coordinating and directing the state's local elementary and high school districts. Administers education policies set by the Board of Education. Superintendent: Jack O'Connell. Office: 1430 N Street, Sacramento, CA 95814; Phone: (916) 319-0800; Fax: (916) 319-0100; Web: www.cde.ca.gov/eo. Employees: 2,520. 2007–2008 Budget: $59 billion.

University of California Board of Regents
Governs the 10 campuses of the University of California, five teaching hospitals, centers in Washington, D.C., and Sacramento, and manages three major laboratories operated under contracts with the U.S. Department of Energy. The 18 regents are appointed by the governor to 12-year terms and are considered among the most prestigious civic appointees in the state. Ex-officio Board members are Governor Arnold Schwarzenegger, Lieutenant Governor John Garamendi, Speaker of the Assembly Fabian Nunez, Superintendent of Public Instruction Jack O'Connell, UC President Robert Dynes, Alumni Association President Jefferson Coombs, and Vice President Stephen Schreiner. The regents (and the end of their terms): Chair: Richard Blum (2014); Vice Chair: Russell Gould (2017); William de la Pena (2018), Judith Hopkinson (2009), Eddie Island (2107), Odessa Johnson (2012), Joanne Corday Kozberg (2010), Sherry Lansing (2010), Monica Lozano (2013), George Marcus (2012), John Moores (2009), Gerald Parsky (2008), Norman Pattiz (2015), Peter Preuss (2008), Frederick Ruiz (2016), Leslie Tang Schilling (2013), Bruce Varner (2018), Paul Wachter (2016). Office: 1111 Franklin Street, Oakland, CA 94607; Phone: (510) 987-9074; Fax: (510) 987-9086; Web: www.ucop.edu. UC Employees: 74,852. 2007–2008 Budget: $19.8 billion.

University of California President and Chancellors

Robert Dynes, UC President; Robert Birgeneau (Berkeley), Larry Vanderhoef (Davis), Michael Drake (Irvine), Norman Abrams (Los Angeles), Roderic Park (Merced), France Cordova (Riverside), Marye Anne Fox (San Diego), J. Michael Bishop (San Francisco), Henry Yang (Santa Barbara), George Blumenthal (Santa Cruz)

Trustees of the California State Universities

Trustees set policy, make budget decisions, govern collective bargaining, and handle personnel matters, including appointment of the system and campus presidents. They are appointed by the governor for eight-year terms. The members oversee 24 campuses, with more than 400,000 students and 40,000 faculty and staff. Ex-officio members are Governor Arnold Schwarzenegger, Lieutenant Governor John Garamendi, Assembly Speaker Fabian Nunez, Superintendent of Public Instruction Jack O'Connell, and Chancellor Charles Reed. Trustees (and the end of their term): Chair: Roberta Achtenberg (2007); Vice Chair: Jeffrey Bleich (2010); Herbert Carter (2011), Carol Chandler (2012), Moctesuma Esparza (2008), Debra Farar (2014), Kenneth Fong (2013), Murray Galinson (2007), George Gowgani (2010), Melinda Guzman Moore (2012), R. William Hauck (2009), Raymond Holdsworth Jr. (2011), Ricardo Icaza (2008), Andrew LaFlamme (student-2007), Robert Linscheid (Alumni), Lou Monville (2014), Jennifer Reimer (student), Craig Smith (Faculty), Glen Toney (2013), Kyriakos Tsakopoulos (2009). Chancellor: Charles Reed. Office: 401 Golden Shore, Suite 641, Long Beach, CA 90802; Phone: (562) 951-4700; Fax: (562) 951-4986; Web: www.calstate.edu. Enrollment: 409,000 students. CSU Employees: 44,916. 2007–2008 Budget: $7.4 billion.

California State University Chancellor and Presidents

Charles Reed, CSU Chancellor; F. King Alexander (Long Beach), Ruben Arminana (Sonoma), Warren Baker (California Polytechnic, San Luis Obispo), Robert Corrigan (San Francisco), William Eisenhardt (California Maritime Academy), Alexander Gonzalez (Sacramento), Milton Gordon (Fullerton), Diane Harrison (Monterey Bay), Karen Haynes (San Marcos), Albert Karnig (San Bernardino), Don Kassing (San Jose), Jolene Koester (Northridge), James Lyons, Sr. (Dominguez Hills), Horace Mitchell (Bakersfield), J. Michael Ortiz (California Polytechnic, Pomona), Mohammad Qayoumi (East Bay), Rollin Richmond (Humboldt), James Rosser (Los Angeles), Richard Rush (Channel Islands), Hamid Shirvani (Stanislaus), Stephen Weber (San Diego), John Welty (Fresno), Paul Zingg (Chico).

Board of Governors, California Community Colleges

Sets policy and provides guidance for 72 districts and 109 campuses serving some 2.5 million students. A locally elected board manages each district, while the chancellor and board of governors provide systemwide leadership, a presence before the legislature, and policy guidance. Board members: Kay Albiani (president), Lance Izumi (vice president), George Caplan, Debbie Malumed, Barbara Davis-Lyman, Barbara Gothard, Rose Castillo-Guilbault, Benita Haily, Randall Hernandez, Bridget Howe, Kristin Jackson Franklin, John Koeberer, Pauline Larwood, Margaret Quinones, Gary Reed, Carolyn Russell, Tanna Thomas. Chancellor: Marshall Drummond. Office: 1102

Q Street, Sacramento, CA 95814; Phone (916) 445-8752; Fax: (916) 322-4783; Web: www.cccco.edu. System enrollment: 2.5 million students. Employees: 150. 2007–2008 Budget (all campuses): $7.9 billion.

Commission on Teacher Credentialing

In 1970 the California Legislature created a permanent, independent commission to enhance teacher training and upgrade teacher preparedness. In 1988 lawmakers strengthened the commission's autonomy as the state's primary policymaking body for the education profession and expanded its legal and regulatory authority. Its primary purpose is to improve teaching and learning in state schools. It sets standards and awards professional credentials. Commission members: Chair: David Pearson. Interim Executive Director: Dale Janssen. Office: 1900 Capitol Avenue, Sacramento, CA 95814; Phone (916) 445-0184; Fax: (916) 327-3166; Web: www.ctc.ca.gov. Employees: 160. 2007–2008 Budget: $58.9 million.

LABOR AND WORKFORCE DEVELOPMENT AGENCY

Created in 2002, this agency oversees seven major departments, boards, and panels that serve California businesses and workers. The first cabinet-level agency to coordinate workforce programs, it is designed to improve access to employment and training programs and to ensure that California businesses and workers have a level playing field in which to compete. Among its branches are the Agricultural Labor Relations Board, Employment Development Department, California Unemployment Insurance Appeals Board, and Department of Industrial Relations. Agency Secretary: Victoria Bradshaw. Office: 801 K Street, Suite 2101, Sacramento, CA 95814; Phone: (916) 327-9064; Fax: (916) 327-9158; Web: www.labor.ca.gov. Employees: 11,552. 2007–2008 Budget: $11.2 billion.

Agricultural Labor Relations Board

Created in 1975 by the Agricultural Labor Relations Act, the board is designed to provide stable relations between growers and farm workers. Chair: Irene Raymundo. Executive Secretary: J. Antonio Barbosa. Office: 915 Capitol Mall, Third Floor, Sacramento, CA 95814; Phone: (916) 653-3699; Fax: (916) 653-8750; Web: www.alrb. ca.gov. Employees: 39. 2007–2008 Budget: $5.1 million.

Unemployment Insurance Appeals Board

Hears appeals for unemployment and disability benefits. Members are appointed by the governor, state Senate Rules Committee, and Assembly speaker and are paid in excess of $100,000 per year. Chair: Ann Richardson. Executive Director: Juan Arcellana. Office: P.O. Box 944275, Sacramento, CA 94424; Phone: (916) 263-6722; Web: www.cuiab.ca.gov. Employees: 631. 2007–2008 Budget: $74.5 million.

Department of Industrial Relations

Handles a range of work-related endeavors, including workers' compensation, industrial safety (CalOSHA), labor standards, and labor statistics. Acting Director: John Rea. Office: 455 Golden Gate Avenue, San Francisco, CA 94012; Phone: (415)

703-5070; Fax: (415) 703-5058; Web: www.dir.ca.gov. Employees: 2,739. 2007–2008 Budget: $308 million (state funds); $384.5 million (total funds).

Employment Development Department

Assists employers and workers in finding jobs through hundreds of service locations throughout the state. Manages the unemployment insurance program, collects payroll taxes that support worker benefit programs, provides economic and labor market data, and administers the Job Training Partnership Act. Director: Patrick Henning. Office: 800 Capitol Mall, Suite 5000, Sacramento, CA 95814; Phone: (916) 654-8210; Fax: (916) 657-5294; Web: www.edd.ca.gov. Employees: 8,739. 2007–2008 Budget: $111.8 million (state funds); $10.8 billion (total funds).

DEPARTMENT OF CORRECTIONS AND REHABILITATION

Previously known as the California Adult & Youth Corrections Agency, the renamed department brought the Department of Corrections and the California Youth Authority under one roof, with one administrative team. Employs more than 65,000 employees with an annual budget in excess of $20 billion. It operates 33 prisons and 38 conservation camps, housing more than 167,000 inmates. The Youth Authority houses more than 3,600 juvenile offenders. The agency manages the state parole system, supervising 151,000 parolees. A troubled agency, its health program has been taken over by a federal court, which threatens to take over the entire agency. Agency Secretary: James Tilton. Office: 1100 11th Street, Suite 400, Sacramento, CA 95814; Phone: (916) 323-6001; Fax: (916) 442-2637; Web: www.cdcr.ca.gov. Employees: 65,973. 2007–2008 Budget: $20 billion.

Board of Parole Hearings

California's parole board combines the old Board of Prison Terms and Youth Authority Board. It sets terms and conditions for parole and conducts parole hearings for all prisoners sentenced to life terms with possibility of parole. Chair: James Davis. Office: 1515 K Street, Suite 600, Sacramento, CA 95814; Phone: (916) 445-4072; Fax: (916) 445-5242; Employees: 371. 2007–2008 Budget: $108.5 million.

RESOURCES AGENCY

Oversees 23 agencies, departments, boards, and commissions that manage the state's air, water, land, and wildlife. Agency Secretary: Mike Chrisman. Office: 1416 9th Street, Suite 1311, Sacramento, CA 95814; Phone: (916) 653-5656; Fax: (916) 653-8102; Web: www.resources.ca.gov. Employees: 16,486. 2007–2008 Budget: $13.2 billion.

Department of Boating and Waterways

Responsible for public boating facilities, water safety, beach erosion, small-craft harbor development, and yacht and ship brokerage licensing. Chair: H.P. Purdon; Director: Raynor T. Tsuneyoshi. Office: 2000 Evergreen Street, Suite 100, Sacramento, CA 95815; Phone: (916) 263-1331; Fax: (916) 263-0648; Web: www.dbw.ca.gov. Employees: 80. 2007–2008 Budget: $76.7 million.

Department of Conservation

Develops and manages the state's land, energy, mineral and farmland resources, and disseminates information on geology, seismology, mineral, geothermal, and petroleum resources, agricultural and open-space land, and container recycling and litter reduction. Director: Bridgett Luther. Office: 801 K Street, Sacramento, CA 95814; Phone (916) 322-1080; Fax: (916) 445-0732; Web: www.consrv.ca.gov. Employees: 675. 2007–2008 Budget: $1.3 billion.

Department of Fish and Game

Maintains all species of wildlife, provides recreational use of wild species, including hunting and fishing, facilitates the scientific and educational use of wildlife, and protects the economic benefits of natural species. Director: Ryan Broddrick. Office: 1416 9th Street, Sacramento, CA 95814; Phone: (916) 445-0411; Fax: (916) 653-1856; Web: www.dfg.ca.gov. Employees: 2,323. 2007–2008 Budget: $447 million.

Department of Forestry and Fire Protection

Provides fire protection on more than 31 million acres of California's privately owned woodlands and emergency services in 35 of the state's 58 counties. Director: Ruben Grijalva. Office: P.O. Box 944246, Sacramento, CA 94244; Phone: (916) 653-5121; Fax: (916) 653-4171; Web: www.fire.ca.gov. Employees: 5,724. 2007–2008 Budget: $1.3 billion.

Department of Parks and Recreation

Acquires, designs, develops, operates, maintains, and protects the state park system. Director: Ruth Coleman. Office: 1416 9th Street, Sacramento, CA 95814; Phone: (916) 653-8380; Fax: (916) 657-3903; Web: www.parks.ca.gov. Employees: 3,221. 2007–2008 Budget: $494 million.

Department of Water Resources

Plans, guides, develops, and conserves the state's water supply, forecasts future water supply needs, evaluates existing water resources, and explores their potential to meet state needs. Administers flood control programs, dam safety, and water management in the Central Valley. Works with federal government in the CALFED Bay-Delta Program. Director: Lester Snow. Office: 1416 9th Street, Suite 1115-1, Sacramento, CA 95814; Phone: (916) 653-5791; Fax: (916) 653-5028; Web: www.water.ca.gov. Employees: 2,929. 2007–2008 Budget: $8 billion.

California Conservation Corps

Manages a work force of some 2,000 youth at 21 sites across the state who perform conservation work, including flood control, fire restoration, tree planting, stream clearance, park maintenance, landscaping, and wildlife habitat restoration. Director: Will Semmes. Office: 1714 24th Street, Sacramento, CA 95816; Phone: (916) 341-3100; Fax: (916) 323-4989; Web: www.ccc.ca.gov. Employees: 308. 2007–2008 Budget: $102.7 million.

Energy Resources Conservation and Development Commission
Ensures reliable sources of energy to meet state needs. An independent commission, its budget is funneled through the Resources Agency. Chair: Jackalyne Pfannenstiel. Executive Director: Robert Therkelsen. Office: 1516 9th Street, Sacramento, CA 95814; Phone: (916) 654-4287; Fax: (916) 653-3478; Web: www.energy.ca.gov. Employees: 535. 2007–2008 Budget: $417.3 million.

State Lands Commission
Manages and protects all state lands received via statute from the federal government, including the beds of navigable waterways, off-shore submerged lands, state school, and granted lands. Chair: John Garamendi. Executive Officer: Paul Thayer. Office: 100 Howe Avenue, Suite 100 South, Sacramento, CA 95825; Phone: (916) 574-1900; Fax: (916) 574-1810; Web: www.slc.ca.gov. Employees: 212. 2007–2008 Budget: $28.6 million.

California Coastal Commission
Protects and enhances public access to coastal areas, including development, habitat protection, marine water quality, and scenic resources. The governor, Senate Rules Committee, and the speaker of the Assembly appoint 12 voting members. In years past, the commission has been the focal point for controversy over its handling of coastal issues and charges of bribery and corruption on the part of some commissioners. Chair: Patrick Kruer. Executive Director: Peter Douglas. Office: 45 Fremont Street, Suite 2000, San Francisco, CA 94105; Phone (415) 904-5200; Fax: (415) 904-5400; Web: www.coastal.ca.gov. Employees: 145. 2007–2008 Budget: $17 million.

ENVIRONMENTAL PROTECTION AGENCY
Coordinates the state's environmental regulatory programs and ensures fair and consistent enforcement of environmental law. Agency Secretary: Linda Adams. Office: 1001 I Street, Sacramento, CA 95814; Phone: (916) 445-3846; Fax: (916) 324-0908; Web: www.calepa.ca.gov. Employees: 4,781. 2007–2008 Budget: $1.47 billion (state funds); $1.72 billion (total funds).

Air Resources Board
Promotes clean air and protects public health by regulating pollutants released into the air by automobiles and industry. Chair: Robert Sawyer. Executive Officer: Catherine Witherspoon. Office: 1001 I Street, Sacramento, CA 95814; Phone (916) 322-2990; Fax: (916) 445-5025; Web: www.arb.ca.gov. Employees: 1,148. 2007–2008 Budget: $394.6 million (total funds).

Integrated Waste Management Board
Manages the state's solid waste disposal system. Chair: Margo Brown. Executive Director: Mark Leary. Office: 1001 I Street, Sacramento, CA 95814; Phone (916) 341-6000; Fax: (916) 341-6054; Web: www.ciwmb.ca.gov. Employees: 467. 2007–2008 Budget: $199.1 million (total funds).

Department of Toxic Substances Control

Protects the state from hazardous waste and regulates the use and disposal of hazardous materials. Director: Maureen Gorsen. Office: 1001 I Street, Sacramento, CA 95814; Phone: (916) 322-0476; Fax: (916) 327-0978; Web: www.dtsc.ca.gov. Employees: 1,016. 2007–2008 Budget: $84.2 million (total funds).

Department of Pesticide Regulation

Regulates the manufacture, use, distribution, and disposal of pesticides. Director: Mary-Ann Warmerdam. Office: 1001 I Street, Sacramento, CA 95814; Phone: (916) 445-4300; Fax: (916) 324-1452; Web: www.cdpr.ca.gov. Employees: 368. 2007–2008 Budget: $68.9 million (total funds).

State Water Resources Control Board

Works with nine regional water control boards to preserve and enhance the quality, allocation, and use of the state's water resources. Chair: Tam Dudoc. Executive Director: Celeste Cantu. Office: 1101 I Street, Sacramento, CA 95814; Phone: (916) 341-5250; Fax: (916) 341-5621; Web: www.waterboards.ca.gov. Employees: 1,596. 2007–2008 Budget: $834.5 million (total funds).

Office of Environmental Health Hazard Assessment

Protects public health through scientific evaluation of environmental risks posed by hazardous substances. Director: Joan Denton. Office: 1001 I Street, Sacramento, CA 95814; Phone: (916) 324-7572; Web: www.oehha.ca.gov. Employees: 119. 2007–2008 Budget: $17.5 million (total funds).

STATE AND CONSUMER SERVICES AGENCY

An omnibus agency that oversees consumer protection, school construction, government procurement, civil rights law enforcement, real estate development, the state personnel board, teachers' retirement, collection of state income taxes, services for crime victims, preparation of state building codes, and operation of the state museums in Los Angeles. Agency Secretary: Rosario Marin. Office: 915 Capitol Mall, Suite 200, Sacramento, CA 95814; Phone: (916) 653-4090; Fax: (916) 653-3815; Web: www.scsa.ca.gov. Employees: 16,039. 2007–2008 Budget: $24.9 billion.

Department of Consumer Affairs

Licenses and oversees 2.3 million Californians working in more than 200 professions, including doctors, accountants, contractors, and auto-repair technicians, to name a few. Supervises more than 40 boards, commissions, and task forces—many of them targeted for elimination by the governor's Performance Review Commission. Director: Charlene Zettel. Office: 400 R Street, Suite 3000, Sacramento, CA 95814; Phone: (916) 445-1254; Fax: (916) 445-8796; Web: www.dca.ca.gov. Employees: 2,757. 2007–2008 Budget: $447 million.

Department of General Services

A diverse department with six divisions and 23 offices, it manages and maintains state property, allocates office space, monitors contracts, and helps small and minority businesses obtain state contracts. Director: Ron Joseph. Office: 707 Third Street, West Sacramento, CA 96606; Phone: (916) 376-5000; Fax: (916) 376-5005; Web: www. dgs.ca.gov. Employees: 3,703. 2007–2008 Budget: $1.24 billion.

Department of Fair Employment and Housing
Enforces state civil rights laws that prohibit discrimination in housing, employment, and public services. Director: Suzanne Ambrose. Office: 455 Golden Gate Avenue, Suite 14500, San Francisco, CA 94102; Phone: (916) 557-2325; Fax: (916) 557-0855; Web: www.scsa.ca.gov. Employees: 228. 2007–2008 Budget: $24.4 million.

Department of Technology Services
The result of the consolidation of the Stephen P. Teale Data Center and the Health and Human Services Data Center, the department provides tech services to state government. Acting Director: Anna Brannen. Office: P.O. Box 1810, Rancho Cordova, CA 95741; Phone (916) 464-4018; Fax (916) 464-4287; Web: www.dts.ca.gov. Employees: 768. 2007–2008 Budget: $260 million.

Franchise Tax Board
Administers the personal income tax, bank, and corporation tax laws, and homeowner and renter assistance programs. Audits campaign expenditure and lobbyist reports under the Political Reform Act of 1974. Chair: John Chiang. Executive Officer: Selvi Stanislaus. Office: P.O. Box 115, Rancho Cordova, CA 95741; Phone: (916) 845-4543; Fax: (916) 845-3191; Web: www.ftb.ca.gov. Employees: 5,175. 2007–2008 Budget: $623.4 million.

State Personnel Board
Manages the state civil service system, hears appeals from disciplined employees, and runs the Career Development Program. President: Sean Harrigan. Executive Officer: Floyd Shimomura. Office: 801 Capitol Mall, Sacramento, CA 95814; Phone: (916) 653-1028; Fax: (916) 653-8147; Web: www.spb.ca.gov. Employees: 161. 2007–2008 Budget: $23.9 million.

Public Employees' Retirement System (CalPERS)
The nation's largest pension plan, PERS administers pension, disability, health, and death benefits to past and present public employees. Chief Executive Officer: Fred Buenrostro. Offices: 400 P Street, Sacramento, CA 95814; Phone: (916) 326-3829; Fax: (916) 326-3410; Web: www.calpers.ca.gov. Employees: 1,954. 2007–2008 Budget: $13.6 billion.

State Teachers' Retirement System (STRS)
The largest teacher retirement system in the country includes retirees, survivors, and disabled members. Chief Executive Officer: Jack Ehnes. Offices: 7667 Folsom Boulevard, Third Floor, Sacramento, CA 95826; Phone: (916) 229-3700; Fax: (916) 229-3704; Web: www.calstrs.com. Employees: 777. 2007–2008 Budget: $8.5 billion.

Victims Compensation and Government Claims Board
Oversees adjudication and disbursement of claims associated with crimes and claims against the state associated with accidents involving the government or government agencies. Chair: Rosario Marin. Offices: 630 K Street, Sacramento, CA 95814; Phone: (916) 323-3432; Web: www.boc.ca.gov. Employees: 297. 2007–2008 Budget: $139.5 million.

MISCELLANEOUS BOARDS, DEPARTMENTS, AND COMMISSIONS

Commission on Peace Officer Standards and Training
Sets standards and assists local and state entities with the training of law enforcement officers. Executive Director: Daria Rowert. Offices: 1601 Alhambra Boulevard, Sacramento, CA 95816; Phone: (916) 227-3909; Fax: (916) 227-3895; Web: www. post.ca.gov. Employees: 118. 2007–2008 Budget: $62.7 million.

State Compensation Insurance Fund
Provides employers with a permanent market for workers' compensation insurance. Employees: 6,768. 2007–2008 Budget: $4.2 billion.

Department of Personnel Administration
Represents the governor and the state in all employer-employee relations and serves as the governor's chief personnel policy advisor. Director: Marty Morgenstern. Offices: 1515 S Street, North Building No. 400, Sacramento, CA 95814; Phone: (916) 322-5193; Fax: (916) 322-8376; Web: www.dpa.ca.gov. Employees: 233. 2007–2008 Budget: $93.7 million.

Department of Food and Agriculture
Oversees the state's vast agricultural industry, including plants and animals. Secretary: A.G. Kawamura. Offices: 1220 N Street, Sacramento, CA 95814; Phone: (916) 654-0462; Web: www.cdfa.ca.gov. Employees: 1,816. 2007–2008 Budget: $294.5 million.

Fair Political Practices Commission
Created by Proposition 9, the Political Reform Act of 1974. Regulates public disclosure of campaign contributions and spending by all nonfederal candidates for public office, political-action and independent-expenditure committees, and ballot measure committees; spending disclosures by lobbyists; and conflict-of-interest rules and personal financial disclosures by public officials. Chair: Liane Randolph. Executive Director: Mark Krausse. Office: 428 J Street, Sacramento, CA 95814; Phone: (916) 322-5660; Fax: (916) 327-2026; Web: www.fppc.ca.gov. Employees: 78. 2007–2008 Budget: $10.6 million.

Lottery Commission

Oversees and runs the state lottery. Director: Anthony Molica. Office: 600 North 10th Street, Sacramento, CA 95814; Phone: (916) 323-7095; Fax: (916) 323-7087. The Lottery Commission is financed with proceeds from the lottery and does not draw on funds from the state general fund.

Public Utilities Commission

Provides the public with lowest reasonable rates for utilities and transportation services. President: Michael Peevey. Executive Director: William Ahern. Office: 505 Van Ness Avenue, San Francisco, CA 94102; Phone: (415) 703-2782; Fax: (415) 703-1758; Web: www.cpuc.ca.gov. Employees: 950. 2007–2008 Budget: $1.3 billion.

Horse Racing Board

Regulates pari-mutuel wagering for the protection of the betting public. Chair: Richard Shapiro. Executive Director: Ingrid Fermin. Office: 1010 Hurley Way, Suite 300, Sacramento, CA 95825; Phone: (916) 263-6000; Fax: (916) 263-6042; Web: www.chrb.ca.gov. Employees: 57. 2007–2008 Budget: $10.8 million.

Electricity Oversight Board

Ensures reliable electricity transmission and reasonable wholesale electricity market prices. Acting Executive Director: Erik Saltmarsh. Office: 770 L Street, Suite 1250, Sacramento, CA 95814; Phone: (916) 322-8601; Fax: (916) 322-8591; Web: www.eob.ca.gov. Employees: 22. 2007–2008 Budget: $4.1 million.

Milton Marks Little Hoover Commission

An oversight agency created in 1962 that investigates state operations and promotes efficiency, economy, and improved service. Executive Director: Stuart Drown. Offices: 925 L Street, Suite 805, Sacramento, CA 95814; Phone: (916) 445-2125; Fax: (916) 322-7709; Web: www.lhc.ca.gov. Employees: 9. 2007–2008 Budget: $1 million.

Bureau of State Audits

Audits state government operations and issues reports to promote the effective use of public funds. State Auditor: Elaine Howle. Offices: 555 Capitol Mall, Suite 300, Sacramento, CA 95814; Phone: (916) 445-0255; Fax: (916) 322-7801; Web: www.bsa.ca.gov. Employees: 147. 2007–2008 Budget: $15.9 million.

Department of Finance

Creates the governor's annual state budget. Director: Mike Genest. Office: 1145 Capitol Building, Sacramento, CA 95814; Phone: (916) 445-3878; Fax: (916) 324-7311; Web: www.dof.ca.gov. Employees: 542. 2007–2008 Budget: $84.4 million.

Military Department

Oversees the California National Guard and all of its components. Adjutant General: William Wade II, MG. Office: 9800 Goethe Road, Sacramento, CA 95826;

Phone: (916) 854-3000; Fax: (916) 854-3671. Employees: 780. 2007–2008 Budget: $131.8 million.

Department of Veterans' Affairs

Oversees California's veterans' homes and the affairs of all Californians who have served in the military, including the Cal-Vet home loan program. Secretary: Thomas Johnson. Office: 1227 O Street, Sacramento, CA 95814; Phone: (916) 653-2158; Fax: (916) 653-1960; Web: www.cdva.ca.gov. Employees: 1,606. 2007–2008 Budget: $394.6 million.

Governor's Office of Emergency Services

Provides emergency and disaster relief, planning, and coordination between state, federal, and local agencies. Director: Henry Renteria. Office: 3650 Schriever Avenue, Mather, CA 95655; Phone: (916) 845-8510l; Fax: (916) 845-8511; Web: www.oes. ca.gov. Employees: 563. 2007–2008 Budget: $1.3 billion.

4

Improved Finances: Coping with Uncertainty and Embracing Opportunities

After he was sworn into the state Senate, Sacramento's Darrell Steinberg made his way to a brief reception in the state Capitol. Unlike the weather outside, Steinberg was cheery and warm, happy to be back in the legislature. At the reception, he told supporters he looked forward to tackling tough issues using what he learned in six years in the Assembly. (He was termed-out in 2004.) He had, after all, successfully navigated the Byzantine byways of the budget when he chaired both the Assembly Appropriations and Budget committees.

But California's fiscal environment has changed since Steinberg served in the Assembly. The budget is much more sound. The rollover debt, which accumulated between 2000 and 2003, has been financed. Tax receipts are growing faster than expenditures. The legislative analyst believes that finances will steadily improve throughout this legislative session—and at least until 2012.

Voters, too, may have sensed better conditions as they approved major bond proposals in the November 2006 election. Their approval provides the governor and legislature with authority to borrow to acquire parkland, build schools, and improve freeways. Rather than attend to a growing deficit, Senator Steinberg and his fellow legislators can focus on how state finances might be better deployed to further California's social and economic interests.

To provide a perspective on the state's fiscal environment, this chapter briefly describes the budget ending on June 30, 2007, reviews the 2007–2008 budget, and closes by looking into the state's financial future to describe how budget decisions in the 2007–2008 session might affect the state's long-term finances and budget decisions.

Where the Money Goes

The state expects to spend a little over $102 billion from the General Fund in the year ending June 30, 2007. Though it will also spend another $30 billion from special funds in the same year, the legislature and governor tend to concentrate their budget efforts on spending from the General Fund. Special funds have prescribed uses, while General Fund money supports most state activities. As the legislature tries to balance its budget demands with available resources, General Fund revenues provide the most discretion for reallocating to respond to changing priorities.

From the General Fund, the legislature and governor allocated nearly 50 cents of every dollar to education, including K-12, community colleges, and the university systems. Another 28 cents went to health and social service programs. A dime went to the criminal justice system, primarily the state's prisons and correctional facilities. Seven cents pays for roads, capital projects, and pays off state debt. The last seven cents pays for all other state programs.

Table 1 displays General Fund allocations, by major program. In brief, these major programs include the following:

• **Education.** The education budget is primarily devoted to supporting programs in K-12 and community college districts, at a state General Fund cost of about $41 billion in 2006–2007. They also receive locally generated property tax revenues of about $13 billion. There are roughly 9,500 schools in the K-12 system and 109 colleges. The state constitution provides a minimum funding level, annually adjusted for changes in both the schools' average daily attendance and the economy.

• The University of California and state university systems received $2.7 billion and $2.9 billion, respectively. The Student Aid Commission, which provides financial aid through the Cal Grant program, received $800 million. In total, the three entities received nearly $6.5 billion in 2006–2007.

• **Health and Social Services.** In this area, the Medi-Cal program received the greatest amount of General Fund appropriations. The state coordinates its Medi-Cal expenditures with the federal program (especially Medicaid) to provide health services to low-income people. The state allocated over $16 billion to Medi-Cal in 2006–2007, an amount matched by the federal government. Local governments, mostly counties, also provide funding for these programs.

Two other health programs received large allocations in 2006–2007. Developmental services received $2.5 billion, and mental health got $1.6 billion. Mental health programs also receive special fund money from a voter-approved initiative that imposes a surcharge on the state's wealthiest individuals.

The state's largest social services program, known as SSI/SSP, assists aged, blind, and disabled people. The program is a joint federal/state program, and the state spent about $3.5 billion in 2006–2007.

The state extends assistance to families with children through the CalWORKs program, and it expects to spend nearly $2 billion from the General Fund. The program also receives federal grants through the federal Temporary Assistance for Needy Families program.

Table 1 Where the Money Goes Estimated General Fund Expenditures, By Major Program Areas, 2006–2007 Dollars in Millions		
	Amount	**Percent**
Education		
K-14	41,439.7	
University System and Financial Aid	6,489.5	
Subtotal, Education	47,929.2	47%
Health and Social Services		
Medi-Cal	13,823.9	
Other Health	5,602.5	
Social Services	9,545.4	
Subtotal, Health and Social Services	28,971.8	28%
Criminal Justice	10,676.8	10%
Debt and Capital Outlay	7,344.5	7%
Other	<u>7,195.4</u>	7%
Total	102,117.7	

The In-Home Supportive Services Program assists aged, blind, and disabled persons living at home. The state expects to spend over $1.4 billion on this program, though it covers only 32 percent of program costs. The federal government picks up 50 percent and counties cover 18 percent.

• ***Criminal Justice.*** Criminal Justice expenditures are primarily associated with running the state's prison system, at an expected cost of $8.2 billion. The system includes 33 prisons and eight youth facilities. The Judiciary, including the court system, is likely to cost another $2 billion.

• ***Debt and Capital Outlay.*** The state will allocate about $3.4 billion to service its General Obligation bonds, accounting for most of the debt costs. It will transfer about $2.6 billion from the General Fund to transportation projects and use about $700 million to make lease-payments, primarily to finance prisons and university facilities. These amounts do not reflect any allocation to service the debt on the rollover bond.

Of the remaining $7 billion, $1.5 billion financed resources, water, and environmental programs. Health benefits for retirees and state grants to local government cost about $1 billion each. The state's two main tax agencies received $700 million.

Table 2 Where the Money Comes From Estimated General Fund Revenues, By Major Tax, 2006–2007 Dollars in Millions		
	Amount	Percent
Personal Income Tax	52,000	55%
Sales Tax	27,610	29%
Corporation Tax	10,190	11%
All Other	5,028	5%
Total, General Fund Taxes	94,828	

Another $500 million is to be transferred to the state's reserve on June 30, 2007. The balance, about $2 billion, goes to other state administration.

Who Pays?

In 2006–2007, the state expects to deposit revenues and other resources totaling $95 billion into the General Fund. The single largest revenue source for these deposits is the personal income tax, which accounts for more than half of all General Fund revenue. The other two major revenue sources, the sales tax and the corporation tax, account for 29 percent and 11 percent respectively. There are many minor General Fund revenue sources, including the insurance tax; together they account for five percent of General Fund revenues. Table 2 displays the expected revenue by major tax source.

•   *Personal Income Tax.* The personal income tax is expected to generate around $52 billion in 2006–2007. Income tax rates are progressive, rising as incomes rise, from a low of 1.0 percent to a high of 9.3 percent. Voters approved a surcharge on high-income taxpayers earmarked for mental health programs.

Under a progressive tax system, taxpayers with higher incomes pay a larger share of their income in taxes than do taxpayers at lower income levels, and the current structure concentrates on a small portion of all taxpayers. Of the roughly 13.6 million full-year residents who filed personal income tax returns in 2001, 8 million returns (60 percent) generated less than 5 percent of the total taxes paid. Taxpayers with the top 10 percent of income paid 78 percent of the tax, while the top 5 percent paid 68 percent of the tax. Taxpayers with the top 1 percent of income paid nearly 50 percent of all the income tax in 2001.

•   *Sales Tax.* The legislative analyst expects the sales tax to generate around $28 billion for the General Fund in 2006–2007. The tax is on the final sale price of personal property, primarily retail transactions. The law exempts most food items, utilities, and prescription medicines. Automobile sales, including parts, generate one-fifth of all General Fund sales tax revenue. Together, department stores, restaurants, and bars generate about the same amount.

•   *Corporation Tax.* The analyst expects the Corporation Tax to generate about $10 billion. The law levies an 8.84 percent rate on corporate profits.

Shrinking Deficits Ahead: Proceed with Caution

In the 2006–2007 fiscal year, the state will spend $102.1 billion, but only take in $94.8 billion. The $7.3 billion difference between income and spending, known as the "operating deficit," is one indicator of fiscal health.

The state cannot sustain operating deficits for long periods, as the state constitution prohibits the state from ending the year with a planned deficit. In 2006–2007, the state ends the year in the black because it started the year with a $10.9 billion carry-over surplus. Using the carryover, it can finance the operating deficit and end the year with a positive balance of $3.6 billion.

For 2007–2008, the operating deficit is likely to narrow to about $5.5 billion. If the legislature and governor use the $3.6 billion carryover surplus to help fill the operating deficit—and if they pay off encumbrances (end-of-year expenditures totaling about $500 million)—they would face a lingering budget shortfall of about $2.4 billion.

Veterans of earlier fiscal fights can more easily manage this shortfall. It is one-third the size of the problem associated with the 2005 budget—the last spending plan considered during Steinberg's Assembly tenure. Table 3 displays the state's fiscal condition for the two years.

The governor and legislature can address the 2007–2008 shortfall by a combination of cutting programs and increasing General Fund resources.

When Governor Schwarzenegger presented his 2007 budget proposal on January 10, 2007, he assumed the state's fiscal condition was much healthier than described above. He assumed the state would prevail in its appeals of two superior court decisions for a savings of about $1.1 billion. He also estimated that revenues would be higher and baseline expenditures would be lower (for an improved baseline of about $1.2 billion). Taken together, these factors would nearly wipe out the $2.4 billion June 30, 2008, deficit. In his budget, he proposes shifting special funds into the General Fund and reducing programs so that the state ends the year with a $2.1 billion carryover surplus. According to the legislative analyst, the governor's January budget makes enough permanent changes to halve the state's ongoing deficits.

As an alternative to permanent cuts, the legislature and governor may be tempted to use some of the more clever budget-balancing schemes they applied to earlier budgets. For example, in 2003 they changed state accounting standards to shift costs into a later year and thereby improve the 2003–2004 ending balance. In the past, they have also overestimated revenues and underestimated expenses. Though these kinds of practices sometimes are dismissed as "tricks" because they seem to solve financial problems with slight-of-hand magic, they can be appropriate when the state expects to have excess revenue in future budget years. But, the state does not expect surpluses anytime soon. If the state were to engage in these kinds of cost- and revenue-shifts in 2007–2008, it would merely add to fiscal problems in subsequent years.

In whatever way they balance the 2007–2008 budget, the legislature and governor will consider how their solutions affect future year finances.

Assessing Future Finances

In looking at the state's longer-term finances, the Legislative Analyst's Office expects state finances to continue to improve. The analyst detailed for a five-year period

Table 3 General Fund Condition Carryover Surplus, Revenues, and Expenditures, 2006–2007 and 2007–2008 Dollars in Millions		
	2006-07	**2007-08**
Carryover Balance	10,868	3,578
Revenues and Transfers	94,828	100,120
Resources Available	105,696	103,698
Expenditures	102,118	105,588
Encumbrances		521
Ending Balance	3,578	-2,411

ending in 2012 the expected expenditure growth (by program) and revenue performance (by major tax). Overall, the analyst projects that General Fund spending will rise from $102.1 billion in 2006–2007 to $129.0 billion in 2011–2012, for an average annual growth of 4.8 percent. Revenues will grow slightly faster, at an average annual rate of 6.1 percent. As a result, the operating deficit will have steadily fallen to under $1.3 billion by the end of the projection period.

In the years covered by the projections, the analyst expects debt expenditures to grow fastest, from $4.2 billion to $6.9 billion, an average annual growth rate of nearly 11 percent. These higher debt costs are associated with the issuance of the bonds approved in November 2006. Other fast-growing programs include In Home Supportive Services, Developmental Services, SSI/SSP and Medi-Cal. Slower-than-average growth will occur in K-14 education, higher education, and general government. Table 4 displays the growth by major program.

The analyst expects the personal income tax to grow a little faster than the other taxes, but all the revenues will grow approximately with the economy over the projection period.

Projections Carry Uncertainties

The estimates contained in Table 4 are the analyst's best projections of likely costs. As with all projections, they are as accurate as the assumptions used in making the calculations. For expenditures, if economic or demographic factors vary significantly from the analyst's assumptions, the projections will be off. While all programs are subject to these potential variations, a handful of programs can make a disproportionate impact on the state's operating balance because of their size. They are:

Table 4 Projected Expenditures, 2006–2007 and 2011–2012 Dollars in Millions			
	2006-07	**2011-12**	**Average Annual Growth over Period**
Education			
K-14	41,157	50,646	4.1%
UC	2,918	3,464	3.5%
CSU	2,724	3,311	4.0%
Health and Social Services			
Medi-Cal	13,824	17,840	5.2%
CalWORKS	1,964	1,988	0.3%
SSI/SSP	3,543	4,848	6.5%
IHHS	1,446	2,285	9.6%
Developmental Services	2,491	3,797	8.8%
Other	5,705	7,247	4.9%
Corrections	8,471	11,082	5.5%
Proposition 42	2,616	1,888	-6.3%
Debt Service on Infrastructure Bonds	4,162	6,936	10.8%
Other	11,097	13,690	4.3%
	102,118	129,022	4.8%

• ***K-14 Schools.*** The analyst expects K-14 schools to receive $55.1 billion in 2006–2007 and $71.1 billion in 2011–2012. Of this amount, the General Fund will provide $41.2 billion in 2006–2007 and $50.2 billion in 2011–2012, with the difference made up by local property tax revenue. The analyst assumes moderate property tax revenue growth. If property tax revenues grow more quickly, the state General Fund will have to contribute less than projected.

The analyst also assumes that K-12 average daily attendance will fall for the years 2006–2007 through 2009–2010, and reduce General Fund costs. Should attendance be more robust, General Fund costs could increase.

•   *Medi-Cal.* The analyst expects Medi-Cal to receive $13.8 billion in 2006–2007, and increase each year of the projection to reach $17.8 billion in 2011–2012. The growth is driven by rising caseload and medical costs. The analyst assumes that, though medical-care costs will rise faster than the general inflation rate, state costs would be moderated by improving efficiencies (such as savings associated with shifting more patients to managed care). To the extent the state can keep cost increases closer to the general inflation rate, state costs will be lower than projected by the analyst.

•   *Corrections.* The analyst expects the corrections budget to increase from $8.5 billion in 2006–2007 to $11.1 billion in 2011–2012. The state has struggled to address continuing problems in its prisons. In recent years, it has lost a spate of court cases requiring improved inmate care and increased employee compensation. There are more cases pending. To the extent the courts decide against the state, corrections costs could increase from the projected amount.

•   *Higher Education.* Governor Schwarzenegger committed to funding UC and CSU at amounts much higher than projected by the analyst. In 2007–2008, costs would rise by $130 million if the legislature funded the governor's commitment. By the end of the projection period, the higher education costs would be $900 million.

•   *Revenues.* Of all the projections, revenues carry the greatest consequences for forecasting error. This is especially true of the state's income and corporation taxes. These taxes account for about two-thirds of the General Fund. If the revenue estimate is off by just 3 percent, revenues will be up by nearly $2 billion.

The state receives about 55 percent of all General Fund revenue from the income tax in 2006–2007, and revenue performance relies heavily on payments from the state's wealthiest taxpayers. If the tax situation changes for the state's wealthiest taxpayers, as it did during the capital gains bubble (1996–2000) and bust (2001–2002), the state's General Fund revenues will change.

Embracing the Opportunity

There are many financial uncertainties associated with the analyst's projections, and the uncertainties grow in the latter half of the projection period.

Despite the uncertainties, if revenues remain on target for 2007–2008, the governor and the legislature will likely have a respite from yawning deficits. Under these improved fiscal conditions, they can address some long-simmering problems. Because it has the time and resources, the legislature may wish to address the following issues in 2007–2008:

•   *Allocating the New Bond Funds.* The voters approved $46 billion of bond authority for schools, roads, housing, and resources. The bond authority provides a welcome opportunity to plan for and meet the future needs of Californians. Some of the money in the bonds, notably for housing, is already committed and earmarked. Most of the bond money, however, must be appropriated by the legislature. In making this appropriation, the legislature and governor can direct the bond funds to the best projects. To do so requires a considered review of the alternative uses of the bond funds. If the legislature and governor devote significant effort to identifying capital needs consistent with the bond authorizations, they can direct state funds to their highest and best use.

• *Anticipating Workforce Needs.* Within 10 years, much of the state's workforce will have retired or left state service. According to the Little Hoover Commission and the Schwarzenegger Administration, the state is not attracting, training, or retaining a sufficient number of qualified staff and managers. Though the California Program Review identified the problem and prescribed solutions, neither the legislature nor executive branch has embraced those solutions. In 2007–2008, they could address the problem with renewed vigor. If the state changes its recruitment, training, and compensation soon, it can ensure an adequate workforce after the baby boomers have left state service.

• *Financing Resource Protection.* The state has a large number of resource-stewardship entities, including the Department of Parks and Recreation, Coastal Conservancy, and Department of Fish and Game. There responsibilities for protecting the state's natural and cultural resources are very broad. Unfortunately, these entities have little hope of securing sufficient state funding to meet their responsibilities. The departments, together with private interests, have studied ways to supplement state support for these departments and stewardship programs. By committing to a broad discussion of state resource stewardship, the legislature and governor could lead the state into a new understanding and commitment to protect the state's natural and cultural heritage.

Shaping Public Finance

Compared to recent budgets, the 2007–2008 budget debate began with a much smaller deficit, so balancing it was a smaller challenge. With this respite from fiscal stress, the legislature and governor could address a number of long-neglected fiscal issues in crafting the budget. By taking considered action on some of these issues in 2007–2008, they can help improve state finances and service delivery.

The disposition of the 2007–2008 budget will have a greater resonance for Senator Steinberg, at the dawn of his Senate career, than it will on members who are already in the middle of their Senate tenure. He may have the opportunity to vote on seven more budgets, so he will be addressing the consequences of this year's budget decisions in each year through the end of his second term in 2014. He, together with the large bloc of other members first elected in 2006, have a particular interest in ensuring that this legislative session produces thoughtful, well-informed fiscal decisions.

—John Decker

5

The Judiciary

Their individual opinions and dissents can be quite unpredictable, but the three women and four men on the California Supreme Court seldom locate their majority too far from the political center. In that sense, and because by ethnicity as well as gender they are the most diverse court in the state's history, the current justices are probably a better reflection of California voters than any of their predecessors in the past two and a half decades. Since 1996, they have been led by Ronald George, who was elevated to chief justice by Governor Pete Wilson five years after Wilson first named him to the high court.

Veteran legal reporter Bob Egelko calls George the most politically adroit chief justice in decades, noting that he has cultivated three different governors, the legislature, and the media while "tiptoeing with his colleagues through the minefields of abortion, civil rights, prisoner releases, and the (2003 gubernatorial) recall." In 2004, the court added same-sex marriage to that minefield, delivering a unanimous but narrow verdict striking down San Francisco's attempt to legalize same-sex marriage and letting the broader constitutional questions about the rights of same-sex couples percolate through the lower courts.

By no means a liberal, George nonetheless has moved the court toward a more centrist stance and is often the swing vote in close cases. Although his court remains a friendly place for prosecutors and manufacturers, he has been viewed favorably by many of the state's criminal defense attorneys, who supported his retention at the ballot. In that arena, George also proved himself adept at political maneuvering, helping engineer two changes in election law that may have improved his own chances at the polls. The first eliminated any reference on the ballot to the length of court terms, which has been found to suppress support for justices seeking full, 12-year terms. (Those appointed to fill the remaining term of a justice who has left the court must seek retention for that term at the first gubernatorial election following their appointment.) The other change added each justice's career history to the statewide ballot pamphlet—minus the politically perilous mention of the name of the appointing governor.

Through most of the 1990s, the court enjoyed a period of relative anonymity. Justices faced no opposition at election time, were routinely confirmed on the ballot, and were rarely mentioned by statewide officeholders in campaigns. That abruptly changed in 1998 when, for the first time in 12 years, a pair of Supreme Court justices up for re-election came under attack. Anti-abortion foes, angered by the court's decision overturning parental consent laws on abortions for minors, took aim at George and Associate Justice Ming Chin, who had joined the court's 4–3 majority on the abortion ruling. Associate Justices Stanley Mosk and Janice Rogers Brown, who dissented on that ruling, ran without organized opposition.

Although unaccustomed to political campaigning, George and Chin did not sit idly by. They peppered the state with paid slate mailers, lined up endorsements from law enforcement, law firms and business groups, and won editorial endorsements from newspapers throughout the state. Their message was consistent: We are solid, mainstream jurists under assault by single-issue extremists.

The opposition, meanwhile, was severely underfunded, raising only $40,000, compared to $700,000 each for George and Chin. Operating as Citizens for Judicial Integrity, the campaign had the support of conservative Christian groups; its spokesman was a vice president of the California ProLife Council, who viewed the court's abortion ruling as a further erosion of parents' rights. Hampered by its lack of funding, the anti-court campaign had no paid TV advertising and only one radio ad that ran sporadically around the state. There was a brief flicker of interest when a group of conservative legislators called for the state Republican Party to oppose Chin and George. But party leaders, mindful of abortion's political pitfalls and unwilling to gamble on creating vacancies that might be filled by a Democratic governor, chose to avoid the battle. The election results were stunning. George was confirmed with a 75 percent majority, 18 points ahead of his vote percentage just four years earlier. Chin captured 69 percent, 13 points higher than his previous ballot confirmation as an appellate justice. With Mosk and Brown winning 70 and 76 percent, respectively, the court received its strongest public support since 1974.

The challenges to George and Chin were a faint echo of the attack against the state's highest judges in 1986, when a California electorate, enraged by the state Supreme Court's failure to affirm death sentences, ousted three sitting justices, including Chief Justice Rose Bird. In the emotional campaign to remove Bird and Associate Justices Cruz Reynoso and Joseph Grodin, all appointed by former Democratic Governor Jerry Brown, crime victims' groups argued that the justices were allowing their personal views against capital punishment to influence their interpretations of the law. Bird, the subject of controversy since her 1977 appointment as the first woman on the court, ran televised campaign ads, something previously unheard of in a Supreme Court election. She attacked then-Governor George Deukmejian for using the politics of death to advance his career.

"We need the death penalty. We don't need Rose Bird," Deukmejian told audiences as he campaigned for re-election in 1986. Voters agreed, handing him the opportunity to replace the three liberal jurists with conservatives. Deukmejian selected three appellate justices: John Arguelles, David Eagleson, and Marcus Kaufman, all three of whom stayed scarcely long enough to fatten their pensions. He elevated Malcolm Lucas, his former Long Beach law partner, to chief justice.

Under Lucas, the court was friendlier to business and less likely to overturn voter initiatives (it upheld ballot measures on term limits, insurance rates, restricting criminal defendants' procedural rights, and limiting local tax authorities). In other matters, the court issued a 1993 opinion with widespread implications for California's political process, refusing to revive a voter-approved initiative intended to reform the financing of legislative campaigns. Lucas wrote the lead opinion that buried Proposition 68, arguing that a rival measure, Proposition 73, remained the law despite the fact that the courts had struck down the contribution limits it sought to establish. The court's dissenters argued that the action killed "the only real chance at reforming the link between money and politics that the voters of California have had in a generation." The court weighed in on another political issue in 1992, agreeing to draw new boundary lines for legislative and congressional districts after Wilson vetoed the Democratic legislature's versions. A six-member majority led by Lucas established new district boundaries that were applauded by Republicans as their chance to level the political playing field and undercut the Democrats' decade-long dominance.

Whether the Lucas legacy gave voters all they asked for in 1986 is for historians to decide, but the court did make some significant changes. The most obvious occurred in death penalty cases, the focal point of the public's frustration with the Bird court, which had reversed 64 of the 68 death sentences it reviewed—with Bird voting to reverse in every case. The Lucas court tipped those numbers upside down, upholding 85 percent of its death penalty cases. But behind those numbers lurk other less successful aspects of the court's death penalty administration. By the time Lucas stepped down in 1996, only five defendants in cases his court heard had been executed. Although the death penalty was reinstated in 1978, legal challenges prevented anyone from being executed until convicted double murderer Robert Alton Harris died in San Quentin's gas chamber on April 21, 1992. Sentenced to death for the 1978 murders of two San Diego teenagers, Harris was the first person executed by the state in 25 years. The last had been police killer Aaron Mitchell in 1967. In 1996, two death row inmates—William George Bonin, the murderer of 14 teenage boys, and multiple killer Keith Daniel Williams—were put to death by lethal injection, the first such executions in California. In early 2005, California had 640 inmates on death row, but only 11 had been executed since the death penalty was restored. During the same period, according to a *Los Angeles Times* review of the state's death row cases in 2005, 28 inmates died naturally, 12 committed suicide, and two were killed in incidents on the San Quentin exercise yard. As Chief Justice George observed, "The leading cause of death on death row is old age."

A lack of lawyers willing to handle death penalty cases has created a nagging backlog that has left defendants waiting years to have their cases heard. George said that 115 death row inmates still have not been appointed lawyers for the first direct appeal to the state Supreme Court, a right mandated by state law. Another 149 lack lawyers for state *habeas corpus* and executive clemency petitions, according to the *Times*.

In 2001, the court lost its longest serving member, 88-year-old Stanley Mosk, an appointee of former Governor Edmund G. "Pat" Brown, and at the time the court's only Democrat. The legendary Mosk served 37 years on the state Supreme Court, writing landmark decisions on civil rights, free speech, and criminal justice. Smart, eloquent, and principled, Mosk was said by admirers to rank with Justices Matthew Tobriner and Roger Traynor as a giant of the country's judicial system whose trail-blazing opinions at the state level often presaged by years those that the United States Supreme Court would adopt. Among the 1,688 rulings he authored was the *Bakke* case in 1976 that struck down racially based university admissions. Although viewed as a liberal, Mosk was often a force for consensus on the court, particularly in his later years. In his sole appointment to the state's high court Governor Gray Davis named Carlos Moreno, a Democrat, to replace Mosk.

In 2005, Justice Janice Rogers Brown left the court after winning a difficult U.S. Senate confirmation to the United States Court of Appeals for the District of Columbia. President George W. Bush first nominated her to the influential federal appeals bench in July 2003, but Senate Democrats filibustered to block her and other conservative Bush judicial nominees. When Bush re-nominated Brown two years later, both Senators Dianne Feinstein and Barbara Boxer vigorously opposed the appointment. She was eventually confirmed under a complex deal brokered by 14 moderate senators of both parties. A staunch, though not entirely predictable conservative, Brown has been a lightening rod for controversy since Governor Pete Wilson named her to the state's high court in 1996 over the objections of a state bar committee that rated her unqualified because she lacked experience and was thought to infuse her politics into her judicial decisions. In the years since, court watchers have come to regard her as a bold, decisive thinker despite some firey solo opinions taking shots at the decisions of judicial colleagues on her own court, and on occasion at fellow conservatives on the United States Supreme Court. She was replaced on the court by another conservative woman—Carol Corrigan—but a justice known for her legal intelligence rather than her confrontational style. Corrigan was Governor Arnold Schwarzenegger's first, and to date only, high court appointment.

Chief Justice George's nonconfrontational style is generally admired by legal scholars, although some critics of his approach believe he has gone too far in trying to please the lawmakers who control his budget. George is the first chief justice to secure a substantial increase in state funding for trial courts, a task he pursued while touring courts in all 58 counties shortly after he was named chief justice. Through the late 1990s, he worked to improve the court's frayed relations with legislators, who did not take kindly to the 1991 ruling upholding term limits in which the Lucas court decried what it called an "entrenched, dynastic legislative bureaucracy" in the Capitol. Thanks to term limits, all the legislators who might have chafed at that language were gone as of 2004. George has improved relationships with the press corps, becoming more accessible than either of his predecessors. In response to a discussion with a group of reporters, George changed the court's schedule for filing opinions, and he often returns reporters' phone calls, a practice unheard of under his immediate predecessors.

STATE SUPREME COURT

Office of the Clerk, 350 McAllister St., San Francisco, CA 94102, Phone: (415) 865-7000, Fax: (415) 865-7183, Web: www.courtinfo.ca.gov/courts/supreme.

Chief Justice
Ronald M. George

Associate Justices:
Marvin R. Baxter
Ming W. Chin
Carol A. Corrigan
Joyce L. Kennard
Carlos R. Moreno
Kathryn M. Werdegar

Chief Justice

RONALD M. GEORGE

George, the 27th chief justice of the court, is considered an independent conservative who takes a pragmatic, thoughtful approach to cases. With associate justices known for their individual opinions, the George court is not divided along liberal-conservative lines but is constantly realigning into different majorities. Increasingly, the chief justice is seen as its ideological center. George was former Governor Pete Wilson's first appointee to the court, filling a seat that became vacant in 1991 when Justice Allen Broussard, the court's only African American at the time, retired. Five years later, Wilson elevated George to the top post, where his first major ruling overturned California's parental consent law for minors who seek abortions. George has steered the court clear of the kind

Ronald M. George

of controversies and political animosities that plagued his predecessors, and in 1998, despite an organized campaign by abortion foes to unseat him, voters reconfirmed him with a 75 percent majority.

Educated at Princeton University and Stanford University Law School, George was viewed in Los Angeles legal circles as a brilliant and ambitious judge who had long desired a seat on the state's highest court. He earned statewide attention in 1981 when, as a Superior Court Judge, he rejected a motion by then-Los Angeles County District Attorney John Van de Kamp to drop murder charges against Hillside Strangler suspect Angelo Buono. With George presiding over the trial, Buono was convicted of the gruesome sex-related murders of nine Los Angeles-area women.

BIOGRAPHY: Born: Los Angeles, March 11, 1940. Education: J.D., Stanford; A.B., Princeton. Family: married; three children.

CAREER: Appointed by Wilson, 1991; associate justice, 2nd District Court of Appeal, 1987–1991; Superior Court judge, Los Angeles County, 1977–1987; Municipal Court judge, Los Angeles, 1972–1977; deputy state attorney general, 1965–1972.

MARVIN BAXTER

As Appointments Secretary to Governor George Deukmejian for six years, Baxter appointed more than 700 judges. As Deukmejian's second term came to a close, Baxter became a nominee himself, accepting an appointment to the 5th District Court of Appeal in Fresno in 1988. In 1990, Deukmejian named him to the high court to replace Justice David Eagleson, who retired. Baxter faced the voters in 2002 and was confirmed for a new term of office that began on January 7, 2003. Baxter, who grew up in a farming community outside Fresno, has a bachelor's degree from Fresno State College and a law degree from Hastings College of Law. Regarded as the court's most pro-prosecution and consistent conservative, Baxter wrote the 2002 ruling upholding the Gray Davis administration's use of the Sexually Violent Predators Act to keep serial rapist Paul Ghilotti confined in a mental hospital after he had served his prison sentence.

Marvin Baxter

BIOGRAPHY: Born: Fowler, January 9, 1940. Education: J.D., Hastings College of Law; B.A., CSU-Fresno. Family: married, two children.
CAREER: Appointed by Deukmejian, 1990; associate justice, 5th District Court of Appeal, 1988–1990; governor's appointments secretary, 1983–1988; private law practice, 1969–1983; deputy district attorney, Fresno County, 1967–1969.

MING W. CHIN

A scholarly, hard-working conservative, Chin proved himself a prolific opinion writer during his first term on the bench. Appointed by Governor Pete Wilson to replace Justice Armand Arabian in January 1996, Chin voted with the court's majority in 1997 to strike down a law requiring parental consent for a minor's abortion. As a result, anti-abortion groups targeted him, along with Chief Justice George, when he sought retention in 2002.

As an appellate justice, Chin wrote a significant opinion holding that the scientific community was too split on the reliability of DNA evidence to make it admissible in a criminal trial. He also wrote the majority opinion that

Ming W. Chin

held that evidence of battered women's syndrome is relevant to the reasonableness of a defendant's belief in the need for self-defense.

BIOGRAPHY: Born: Klamath Falls, OR, August 31, 1942. Education: J.D., B.A., University of San Francisco. Family: married, two children.

CAREER: Appointed by Wilson, 1996; presiding justice, 1st District Court of Appeal, Division Three, 1994–1996; associate justice, 1st District Court of Appeal, 1990–1994; Alameda County Superior Court judge, 1988–1990; private law practice, 1973–1988; deputy district attorney, Alameda County, 1970–1972.

CAROL A. CORRIGAN

Corrigan grew up in the Central Valley, the daughter of a journalist. Before taking up the law, she flirted with a career in psychology after graduating from Holy Names College in Oakland, briefly attended a post-graduate program at Washington University in St. Louis, Missouri, and received her law degree from Hastings School of Law in San Francisco in 1975. Her legal career has followed the path of colleague Ming Chin, both having served at the Alameda County District Attorney's Office before becoming Alameda County Superior Court judges and appointees to the 1st District Court of Appeal, Division Three. She was named to the high court by Governor Arnold Schwarzenegger in December 2005 to replace Janet Rogers Brown, who had been named to the federal bench by President George W. Bush. She is considered a conservative on criminal matters although much more collegial than her predecessor. A former Democrat, she switched party allegiance not long after former Governor Pete Wilson named her to the appellate court in 1994—a move considered by some as a precursor to her nomination to the Supreme Court. Wilson did not elevate her to the Supreme Court, however.

Carol Corrigan

BIOGRAPHY: Born: Stockton, August 16, 1948. Education: J.D., Hastings College of the Law; B.A., Holy Names College. Family: single.

CAREER: Appointed by Schwarzenegger, December 2005; associate justice, 1st District Court of Appeal, Division Three, 1994–2005; Alameda County Superior Court judge, 1991–1994; judge, Oakland, Emeryville, Piedmont Judicial District, 1987–1991; senior deputy district attorney, Alameda County, 1985–1987; deputy district attorney, Alameda County, 1975–1985.

JOYCE LUTHER KENNARD

Kennard, an immigrant of Dutch-Indonesian ancestry and the first Asian-born justice in court history, came to the United States alone when she was 20. Her meteoric rise through the state court system began when Governor George Deukmejian appointed her to the Los Angeles Municipal Court in 1986. On the high court, she has a reputation for fierce independence and frequent dissents. Court watchers categorize her as moderate but unpredictable. In 2002, she wrote a major free-speech decision for a divided court permitting a San Francisco man to sue Nike over a public relations campaign in which the shoe and clothing manufacturer allegedly lied about working conditions in the factories of its Asian contractors. The opinion said the court was not preventing a business from defending its labor practices. "It means only that when a business enterprise, to promote and defend its sales and profits, makes

Joyce Luther Kennard

factual representations about its own product or its own operations, it must speak truthfully," Kennard wrote. She was the lone dissenter in another 2002 case, where the court upheld Proposition 21, a voter-approved initiative creating tougher penalties for juvenile crime. Kennard said the law should be struck down because it gives prosecutors arbitrary power to charge a juvenile in adult criminal court without review by a judge.

BIOGRAPHY: Born: Bandung, West Java, May 6, 1941. Education: J.D., M.P.A., B.A., USC; A.A., Pasadena City College. Family: married.

CAREER: Appointed by Deukmejian, 1989; Superior Court judge, Los Angeles, 1987–1989; Municipal Court judge, Los Angeles County, 1986–1987; senior attorney for former Associate Justice Edwin F. Beach, 2nd District Court of Appeal, 1979–1986; deputy attorney general, California Department of Justice, Los Angeles, 1975–1979.

CARLOS R. MORENO

Moreno, the lone Democrat on the state's high court, was appointed by Governor Gray Davis to replace the legendary Stanley Mosk, who died in the summer of 2001. Accepting the job meant giving up a life-time seat on the federal bench, where President Bill Clinton had placed him only three years earlier. But Moreno said he could have a much bigger impact in Sacramento, and court watchers seem to concur, describing him as a pivotal vote who can determine the outcome of cases when the justices are split. Moreno, although a centrist like the governor who appointed him, is seen as a strong and independent voice on the court. While he is seen as more conservative than Mosk on death penalty cases, he has been willing to argue

Carlos R. Moreno

for reversal of death sentences on occasion, and he has said that he pays close attention to how adequately defendants are represented in capital cases. In the 2002 Ghilotti case, Moreno dissented from the majority decision to block the serial rapist's release, which put him at odds with Governor Davis. Moreno won retention in 2002 to serve the last eight years of Mosk's term.

BIOGRAPHY: Born: Los Angeles, November 4, 1948. Education: J.D., Stanford; B.A., Yale. Family: married, two children.
CAREER: judge, United States District Court for the Central District of California, 1998–2001; Appointed by Davis, 2001, Superior Court judge, Los Angeles County, 1993–1998, Municipal Court judge, Compton Judicial District, 1986–1993; private law practice, 1979–1986; deputy city attorney, Los Angeles City Attorney's Office, 1975–1979.

KATHRYN MICKLE WERDEGAR

Werdegar was appointed to the California Supreme Court in 1994 by Governor Pete Wilson, her longtime friend and law school classmate at UC Berkeley's Boalt Hall. The first woman editor of the *University of California Law Review*, she transferred to George Washington University School of Law for her final year and graduated first in her class. Her career began in the U.S. Department of Justice's civil rights division under Robert Kennedy, where she wrote appellate briefs, drafted civil-rights-related legislation, and worked to release Martin Luther King, Jr., from prison. Because she was appointed to fill out the term of retiring Justice Edward Panelli, Werdegar was forced to run for retention shortly after joining the court

Kathryn Mickle Werdegar

and before she had issued any opinions. In the years since, she has emerged as one of the court's most frequent dissenters and is sometimes described by legal experts as the philosophical heir to the late Stanley Mosk, for years the only liberal on the panel. In 2001, she wrote a decision allowing Medicare beneficiaries to sue HMOs in state court. That same year, she was the lone dissenter when the court ruled that gunmakers can't be held liable for the criminal use of their weapons. Werdegar said gunmakers owe the public "a duty of care" in the way their weapons are designed, distributed, and marketed. In 2002, she was elected to a second term after a campaign co-chaired by Wilson and Democratic Senator Dianne Feinstein.

BIOGRAPHY: Born: San Francisco, April 5, 1936. Education: J.D., George Washington; B.A., University of California, Berkeley. Family: married, two children.
CAREER: Appointed by Wilson, 1994; associate justice, 1st District Court of Appeal, 1991–1994; senior staff attorney to California Supreme Court Justice Edward Panelli, 1985–1991; senior staff attorney, 1st District Court of Appeal, 1981–1985; associate dean for Academic and Student Affairs and associate professor, University of San Francisco School of Law, 1978–1981; attorney, California Continuing Education of the Bar, 1971–1978; consultant and author, California College of

Trial Justices, 1968–1971; special consultant, state Department of Mental Hygiene, 1967–1968; associate, UC Berkeley Center for Study of Law and Society, 1965–1967; consultant, California State Study Commission on Mental Retardation, 1963–1964; legal assistant, U.S. Department of Justice civil rights division, 1962–1963.

California Appellate Court Justices

Court of Appeal, 1st Appellate District, Division One, 350 McAllister St., San Francisco 94102; Phone: (415) 865-7300, Clerk's Office: (415) 865-7201 Fax: (415) 865-7309 .

Presiding Justice James J. Marchiano (2002, appointed to court 1998); Associate Justices Sandra L. Margulies (2002), William D. Stein (1988), and Douglas E. Swager (1995).

Court of Appeal, 1st Appellate District, Division Two, 350 McAllister St., San Francisco 94102; Phone: (415) 865-7300, Fax: (415) 865-7309.

Presiding Justice J. Anthony Kline (1982), Associate Justices Paul R. Haerle, (1994), James R. Lambden (1996), and James A. Richman, (2006).

Court of Appeal, 1st Appellate District, Division Three, 350 McAllister St., San Francisco 94102; Phone: (415) 865-7300, Fax: (415) 865-7309.

Presiding Justice William R. McGuiness (1998, appointed to court 1997); Associate Justices Peter J. Siggins (2005), Joanne C. Parrilli (1995), and Stuart R. Pollak (2002).

Court of Appeal, 1st Appellate District, Division Four, 350 McAllister St., San Francisco 94102; Phone: (415) 865-7300, Fax: (415) 865-7309.

Presiding Justice Ignazio J. Ruvolo (1996); Associate Justices Timothy A. Reardon (1990), Maria P. Rivera (2002), and Patricia K. Sepulveda (1998).

Court of Appeal, 1st Appellate District, Division Five, 350 McAllister St., San Francisco 94102; Phone: (415) 865-7300, Fax: (415) 865-7309.

Presiding Justice Barbara J. R. Jones (1998, appointed to 1996); Associate Justices Linda M. Gemello (2002), Mark B. Simons (2001), and vacant.

Court of Appeal, 2nd Appellate District, Division One, 300 South Spring St., Los Angeles 90031; Phone: (213) 830-7000

Presiding Justice Vaino Spencer (appointed to court and presiding since 1980); Associate Justices Robert M. Mallano (2000), Frances Rothschild (2005) and Miriam A. Vogel (1990).

Court of Appeal, 2nd Appellate District, Division Two, 300 South Spring St., Los Angeles 90013; Phone: (213) 830-7000.

Presiding Justice Roger W. Boren (1993, appointed to court 1987); Associate Justices Michael G. Nott (1990), Kathryn Doi Todd (2000), and Judith M. Ashmann-Gerst (2001) and Victoria M. Chavez (2006).

Court of Appeal, 2nd Appellate District, Division Three, 300 South Spring St., Los Angeles 90013; Phone: (213) 830-7000.

Presiding Justice Joan Dempsey Klein (1978); Associate Justices Richard D. Aldrich (1994), H. Walter Croskey (1987), and Patti S. Kitching (1993).

Court of Appeal, 2nd Appellate District, Division Four, 300 South Spring St., Los Angeles 90013; Phone: (213) 830-7000.

Presiding Justice Norman L. Epstein (2004, appointed to court 1990); Associate Justices Nora M. Manella (2006), Steven C. Suzukawa (2006), and Thomas Willhite (2005).

Court of Appeal, 2nd Appellate District, Division Five, 300 South Spring St., Los Angeles 90013; Phone: (213) 830-7000.

Presiding Justice Paul Turner (1991, appointed to court 1989); Associate Justices Orville A. Armstrong (1993), Sandy Kriegler (2005), and Richard M. Mosk (2001).

Court of Appeal, 2nd Appellate District, Division Six, 200 East Santa Clara St., Ventura, 93001; Phone: (805) 641-4700.

Presiding Justice Arthur Gilbert (1999, appointed to court 1982); Associate Justices Paul H. Coffee (1995), Steven Z. Perren (1999), and Kenneth R. Yegan (1990).

Court of Appeal, 2nd Appellate District, Division Seven, 300 South Spring St., Los Angeles 90013; Phone: (213) 830-7000.

Presiding Justice Dennis M. Perluss (2003, appointed to court 2001); Associate Justices Earl Johnson, Jr. (1982), Fred Woods (1988), and Laurie D. Zelon (2003).

Court of Appeal, 2nd Appellate District, Division Eight, 300 South Spring St., Los Angeles 90013; Phone: (213) 830-7000.

Presiding Justice Candace D. Cooper (1999); Associate Justices Laurence D. Rubin (2000), Paul Boland (2001), and Madeleine I. Flier (2003).

Court of Appeal, 3rd Appellate District, 914 Capitol Mall, Sacramento, 95814; Phone: (916) 654-0209.

Presiding Justice Arthur G. Scotland (1998, appointed to court 1989); Associate Justices Coleman A. Blease (1979), Richard Sims (1982), Rod Davis(1989), George Nicholson (1990), Vance W. Raye (1991), Fred K. Morrison (1994), Harry E. Hull, Jr. (1998), Ronald B. Robie (2002), M. Kathleen Butz (2003), and Tani Cantil-Sakauye (2005).

Court of Appeal, 4th Appellate District, Division One, 750 B Street, Suite 300, San Diego, 92101; Phone: (619) 645-2760.

Presiding Justice Judith McConnell (2003, appointed 2001); Associate Justices, Patricia D. Benke (1987), Richard D. Huffman (1988), Gilbert Nares (1988), Judith L. Haller (1994), Alex C. McDonald (1995), James A. McIntyre (1996), Terry B. O'Rourke (1998), Cynthia Aaron (2003), and Joan Irion (2003).

Court of Appeal, 4th Appellate District, Division Two, 3389 Twelfth Street, Riverside, 92501; Phone: (951) 248-0200.

Presiding Justice Manuel A. Ramirez (presiding since appointed 1990); Associate Justices Barton C. Gaut (1997), Thomas E. Hollenhorst (1998), Jeffrey King (2003), Art W. McKinster(1990), Douglas P. Miller (2006), Betty Ann Richli (1994).

Court of Appeal, 4th Appellate District, Division Three, 925 N. Spurgeon Street, Santa Ana, California 92701; Phone: (714) 558-6777

Presiding Justice David G. Sills (1990); Associate Justices Richard M. Aronson (2001), William W. Bedsworth (1997), Richard D. Fybel (2002), Raymond J. Ikola

(2002), Eileen C. Moore (2002), Kathleen E. O'Leary (2000), and William F. Rylaars-dam (1995).

Court of Appeal, 5th Appellate District, 2525 Capitol Street, Fresno, 93721; Phone: (559) 445-5491.

Presiding Justice James A. Ardaiz (1994, appointed 1987); Associate Justices Dennis A. Cornell (2000), Betty L. Dawson (2003), Gene M. Gomes (2002), Thomas A. Harris (1990), Bert Levy (1997), Steven M. Vartabedian (1989), and Rebecca A. Wiseman (1995).

Court of Appeal, 6th Appellate District, 333 West Santa Clara Street, Suite 1060, San Jose, 95113; Phone: (408) 277-1004.

Presiding Justice Conrad L. Rushing (2003, appointed 2002); Associate Justices Patricia Bamattre-Manoukian (1989), Wendy Clark Duffy (2005), Franklin D. Elia (1988), Richard J. McAdams (2003), Nathan D. Mihara (1993), and Eugene M. Premo (1988).

6

The Legislature

Historian and essayist Carey McWilliams once described California as "the great exception" because, for the first hundred years of its existence, the state at the western edge of the continent seemed a place apart, different in mood and temperament from anywhere else in the United States. But in his 2005 book about Edmund G. "Pat" Brown, biographer Ethan Rarick took the view that by the time Brown became governor in 1958, California had become the nation's trend-setting mainstream. Events, styles, and political moods that began in California soon spread east to engulf all of America.

But in this still-new 21st century, California, in a political sense, is once again "the great exception"—the only state in the nation led by a governor who gained office through a recall election. And although many states struggle with fiscal stability, California has become the mother ship of chronic budget deficits and dysfunctional legislatures.

Red ink and recalls were nothing new to California when Governor Gray Davis was targeted in the summer of 2003. Three of four previous governors—including iconic Ronald Reagan—had been in the crosshairs, although none of the efforts ever reached the ballot. Still, the 1968 effort to bounce Reagan gathered 550,000 signatures. And nearly half a dozen budgets have been in the red since 1991, when a third of the state's revenues were vaporized by recession.

In years past, the state and its legislature were able to weather fiscal and political crises. But in 2003 it foundered, and that crisis led, in no small measure, to the success of the recall effort against Davis and the rise to power of Republican Arnold Schwarzenegger. But as much as the recall was aimed at the governor, few doubt that had voters the means and legal procedure to do so, they would have recalled the legislature *en masse* at the same time, for the state's elective and deliberative body endured poll ratings even lower than that of the governor. Davis, it could be said, was the rooftop rod that attracted lightning meant as much for lawmakers as for himself.

California's crisis in government is a calamity rooted entirely in Sacramento. There has not been a flood or an earthquake or other natural disaster to speed the state toward the brink of financial ruin and political paralysis. There is no significant corruption scandal. And while the economy sputtered in the wake of the dot-com crash of 2000–2001, it has since recovered and is not to blame. This catastrophe took place while everyone was playing by the rules. Many of those rules, however, were set by an angry and disconnected electorate trying to restrain the power and scope of state government while ignorant or suspicious of the human frailties behind political collaboration.

And if ineffective government is rooted in Sacramento, the tap root descends directly through the legislature, which has been rendered ineffective by the merger of four factors: term limits, a closed primary system, a 2001 redistricting scheme that virtually eliminated competition in legislative districts, and the two-thirds vote required for the legislature to pass a budget.

The term limits set by voters in 1990 drastically changed the process of lawmaking by removing the entrenched class of career politicians and restricting their replacements to six years in the Assembly and eight years in the state Senate. In 2005, when the full effect of term limits finally engulfed the legislature, that body was more diverse in gender and ethnicity, but the critical human relationships that develop over time—through confrontation and compromise—had evaporated. There were no personal histories between individual conservatives and liberals such as Republican Ross Johnson and Democrat John Burton, forged during battles past and matured through time into mutual respect and, in a few cases, even friendship. Today, crossing the aisle is a perilous act, seen as traitorous and worthy of punishment or ostracism. Those who try, such as Republican Assemblyman Keith Richman and Democratic Assemblyman Joe Canciamilla, are marginalized by their parties and within their political caucuses.

Political peace missions have been nearly impossible since 2001 when lawmakers from both parties conspired to draw new boundaries for their political districts. The most recent redistricting and reapportionment concentrated Republican and Democratic voters into safe districts that ensure re-election for the incumbent party. Those new districts produced a generation of lawmakers who do not fear challenges from the other party but from ideologues within their own organization. Moderates who may appeal across party lines rarely survive primaries.

Few observers are surprised that California government, even one led by a charismatic moderate Republican, has spiraled into endless crisis. The building blocks have been piling up for years, clearly evident in the multi-year gridlock over financial restructuring, long-term construction plans, and health care. It is the logical result of a government that has grown more partisan, less experienced, more manipulated, and less visionary than at any time in its history.

In its August 2003 issue, *California Journal* magazine found wide agreement about the four significant contributors to the state's difficulties: term limits, the hardened politics created by the merger of safe legislative seats, a closed primary election system, and the two-thirds super majority required to pass a budget. At the time, those four ingredients combined with the recall election and Gray Davis's unprecedented unpopularity to create a monumental crisis of government.

For a time after the recall, the political stew that bedeviled Davis continued to plague Schwarzenegger—especially ideological rifts that hampered meaningful compromise among legislators. Early in his administration, Schwarzenegger was able to confront immediate budget problems by striking compromises with Democratic allies, especially in the education community, and by appealing directly to voters. The emphatic nature of the recall provided a rare window of opportunity for a very popular governor to strike deals with legislators fretting over their own fragile political fates.

But in his second year as governor, as the fear factor lessened among Democrats, Schwarzenegger, too, ran afoul of California's more intractable political problems. And, predictably, Schwarzenegger's once stratospheric approval ratings in polls began to plummet back to earth, and his inability to affect a working relationship with the legislature reinforced notions about paralysis in government.

The question for many in the wake of Davis's recall was whether he had been bounced from office for failing to govern a state that had become ungovernable. Some experts believe that the recall election itself was an expression of the tremendous anxieties afoot in America, stemming from the trauma of September 11 to criminal scandals that rocked Wall Street and saw the collapse of corporate giants such as World Com and Enron to the frightening experiences of war in Iraq and all the financial and personal insecurities produced by this series of unfortunate events.

But it is significant to note as well that while citizens and voters in all other states have experienced this same set of national and international crises, no other state has expressed its anxieties in quite the same way as California. No other governor has been recalled. Few state governments languish in the doldrums of fiscal crisis—even as their economies improve and more revenues flow into state coffers, as was the case in California in 2005. The super-heated voter reaction of 2003 was unique to California.

Here, then, is a more detailed look at key elements plaguing the legislature.

—*David Lesher*

Term Limits

Anyone who thought that solving fiscal crises would be easier after term limits took effect has been sorely disappointed. Term-limited legislators are no more likely to pass difficult budgets on time than their predecessors. Their "fresh" perspectives and "real world experiences" apparently succumb to partisan pressures and personal ambitions a nanosecond after stepping through the doors of the Capitol. California's budget process is predicated on compromise and bipartisanship, but political forces pull in opposite directions.

It is impossible to attribute to term limits all of the state's troubles overcoming massive structural deficit. But term limits have left lawmakers ill prepared to deal with a budget crunch compared to the veterans who faced a similar crisis in the early 1990s. Studies indicate that the legislature's collective experience level, knowledge of the budget, and willingness to engage in oversight has shrunk to an alarming level. Since the process is more flawed than in the past, it is likely the product—a budget—will be as well.

One dramatic difference between pre– and post–term limit legislators is the level of experience and expertise they bring to the process. In the Assembly particularly, committee chairs and staff often are new to their positions and to Sacramento. The Senate benefits from the regular flow of Assembly members and their staff to the upper house, but even that now is less than in years past because the most experienced legislators—those who had been elected prior to the advent of term limits in 1990—finally left the legislature for good at the end of 2004. Still, the Senate's modestly greater experience tends to balance off the Assembly, though it also leads to conflict in the way the two houses see problems such as budget deficits.

Lack of experience might be offset if members had incentives to learn as much as possible about the budget as fast as possible. Some do. But interviews with experienced budget staff suggest that many members do not invest much time and effort in building the budget. Budget subcommittees theoretically offer a chance for legislators to immerse themselves in the nitty-gritty of policy evaluation, information that might lead to serious negotiation and informed compromise. But new legislators, either daunted by the learning curve involved or motivated to make a mark quickly, do not take subcommittee work seriously.

Inexperience alone, however, does not explain the remarkable political polarization that has gripped the legislature and made tough problems even more difficult to solve. Term limits prevent members from anticipating a future in his or her house. This means they all have much less incentive to cooperate across party lines because there will be no time for a "go along to get along" attitude to pay off. Without a future voice in the policies that emerge from the house, individual members feel no ownership of policy decisions. Members cannot cooperate to increase taxes in times of fiscal crisis (as Governor Pete Wilson and top Republican legislators did in the early 1990s) and then fight another day to cut back these very taxes (as Wilson and his allies did in the mid 1990s) because another day does not come for this same set of legislators. Term limits erode the opportunities and incentives to govern responsibly.

Yet the very hope of term limits was that they would lead to above-the-fray statesmanship precisely because they erased everyone's political future. Proposition 140 would quickly send everyone back to their farms, homes, schools, and hardware stores, thus freeing them to stand up to tyrannical party leaders and greedy special interest groups in order to do what is best for California. But the initiative failed to produce a new breed of citizen legislator. Research has shown that newly elected Assembly members are not much different from their predecessors, other than being a bit younger and more likely to have served in local government.

Many new legislators do bring new ideas and energy, but most report that it takes a few sessions to learn how to channel ideas into policy. By then, their term is up. Bitten by the political bug, more than three-quarters of them run for another office. Instead of being freed from electoral pressures, they are ever more reliant on the favor of party leaders and campaign contributors—often those greedy special interests—as they seek to impress a new set of voters. Ironically, by severing the link between legislators and the constituents who knew them well as individuals, term limits have heightened the partisan solidarity that makes solving state problems so intractable.

—Bruce E. Cain and Thad Kousser

Partisan Redistricting and the Closed Primary

In recent years, the philosophical gap between legislative Republicans and Democrats has widened and hardened, with the two sides having increased difficulty resolving differences over a myriad of issues, from taxes to tort reform. Partisan brawls tend to bring the legislature to a standstill whenever a two-thirds majority is needed to approve legislation that must be passed; notably, a state budget.

One significant factor contributing to Capitol gridlock is the bipartisan redistricting adopted in 2001 and based on the 2000 Census. The vast majority of legislative and congressional districts created by that plan are so safe that most lawmakers win their office in partisan primaries rather than in the general election. The result is a legislature that is ideologically polarized because hardcore conservatives and hardcore liberals dominate the primary process.

In 1996 California voters adopted an open primary system that allowed voters to cast votes in any primary, regardless of party registration. Democrats could cross over to vote in Republican primaries, and visa versa, giving hope to moderates in districts where one party enjoyed a large registration edge because they could seek support from minority party voters who knew their nominee could never win a general election and thus were open to backing the most moderate majority party candidate.

The open primary was operational in 2000, but the courts struck it down in 2001, reinstating the previous system of closed primaries. That drove candidates back to the extremes because they no longer had to fear the wrath of crossover voters. Attempts to revive some form of open primary have failed, with the most recent effort Proposition 62 in 2004.

California's 2001 redistricting plan contributes to Capitol gridlock because much of what happens in legislatures throughout the country these days is driven by ideology, according to Alan Rosenthal, a professor at the Eagleton Institute of Politics at Rutgers University and a national expert on state legislatures. People in safe districts, Rosenthal said, can indulge their ideological positions.

An inevitable consequence of partisan redistricting is the disappearance of the political middle—moderate lawmakers who often provide compromise votes on contentious issues. In years past, budgets were passed when majority Democrats peeled off a few moderate Republicans willing to help reach the required two-thirds vote. But the new redistricting has made it more difficult to coax votes out of Republicans. As one former legislator put it, "Democrats get rewarded for providing service; Republicans are rewarded for cutting taxes"—a dynamic with no common ground.

The new, safe districts also change the political calculation for what it means to be at risk in an election. In competitive seats, incumbents facing challenges from the other party are wary of being considered too extreme. In safe districts, being "extreme" can be an asset, and serious challenges are likely to come from even more ideologically dogmatic members of one's own party—a risk that keeps incumbents and candidates tacking to the right or left.

Redistricting stripped Democrats of another tool once used to pressure Republicans on the budget and other critical issues, pointing out the consequences of cutting services in their districts. Democrats tried that tactic during the 2003 budget impasse, sending Democratic members into solid GOP districts to warn local officials about cuts supported by their Republican representatives. These Democrats quickly discovered that Republicans would suffer far greater consequences for helping to raise taxes than for spending cuts. The lesson: for that kind of pressure tactic to work, the district has to be competitive between the two parties.

The way new districts were drawn also enhanced the clout of legislative leaders when enforcing party discipline on legislators. The most effective display of that clout occurred in 2003 when the Republican leader of the state Senate, Jim Brulte of Rancho Cucamonga, threatened to campaign—in the primary—against any GOP incumbent supporting a tax increase, a threat delivered in person to Senate and Assembly Republicans and widely reported in the media. Afterward, no Republican even hinted at support for a tax hike, despite a massive budget deficit that defied compromise. Although no Democrat so bluntly intimidated members of his or her caucus, the message resonated. No Democrat wanted to face the wrath of, say, Sheila Kuehl, anymore than a Republican wanted to cross Brulte.

—A. G. Block

The Two-Thirds Vote

For the California Legislature to enact a budget, 27 of 40 state senators and 54 of 80 Assembly members must vote for it. Although Democrats currently hold a substantial majority in both houses, they still need eight Republicans to cross the line (six in the Assembly and two in the Senate). California is one of three states—including Arkansas and Rhode Island—with such a requirement.

Historically, the constitutional two-thirds requirement—passed by California voters in 1933—has been a significant obstacle, but one that could be overcome by an experienced legislature in which lawmakers on both sides could reach across the aisle. After term limits and the most recent drawing of new district lines, that kind of compromise is extremely difficult to fashion. Critics argue that term limits and redistricting converted the two-thirds vote from an inconvenience to a poison pill.

No less a budget expert than former Assembly Speaker Willie Brown, Jr., outlined the problem. "When I was in Sacramento, there were always 20% [of legislators] who wouldn't vote for a budget, no matter what, but everybody else recognized the need for a budget, and I could deal with them. Now, the person who crosses the line to vote on the budget is viewed as a traitor, not as a patriot."

Many Republicans, who happen to be the current minority party, argue that the two-thirds vote requirement keeps them involved in governing the state. The vote requirement, they believe, provides an important check on the majority, and without it, the state's fiscal woes would be worse. Others are not so sure. Some Republicans believe that the two-thirds requirement actually increases unnecessary spending by increasing the amount of pork in the budget. Democrats, they argue, dangle pet programs in front of Republicans to entice a few votes on the budget, making the budget process a bidding process.

Often, agreement on the budget results in short-term expediency at the expense of long-term fiscal soundness. During the late 1990s, when the California economy was booming and revenues were fat, Republicans agreed to spending increases for schools and other programs in exchange for tax cuts. But because of the way the state budget is built, those increases became permanent spending—even when revenues plummeted in subsequent years.

The two-thirds vote requirement allows both parties to dodge responsibility for budget quagmires. Democrats can avoid responsibility by claiming that they can't pass a budget with a simple majority, while Republicans avoid it by insisting they are in the minority. And voters do not seem motivated to change the system. In March 2004, they rejected Proposition 56, which would have reduced the threshold for passing a budget to 55%.

—Jim Evans

Resolutions

As author and journalist Lou Cannon once wrote, "California history offers no blueprint for resolving the state's chronic fiscal predicament, but it makes a strong case that political leaders are most apt to succeed when they take risks and set aside ideology in times of crisis."

Cannon cited the ability of past governors—notably Ronald Reagan and Pete Wilson—to work across party lines with Democrat-dominated legislatures to resolve fiscal crises in 1967 and 1991, respectively. In both cases, governors fashioned compromises with powerful legislative Democrats. In Reagan's case, it was Assembly Speaker Jesse Unruh; for Wilson, it was Willie Brown.

The display of professionalism by all sides in 1967 and 1991, Cannon noted, helped ease serious fiscal difficulties. Both governors accepted tax increases that they philosophically opposed; both Democratic leaders accepted what they believed were excessive spending cuts. Those incidents occurred in a different time, however. And although saddled with the two-thirds vote, leadership was not encumbered by the current partisan redistricting or by a legislature weakened by the full effects of term limits.

That scenario did not play out in 2005, when Schwarzenegger and Democrats took their squabbles to a special statewide ballot where voters promptly registered their disgust. Chastened by that experience, Schwarzenegger was much more accommodating in 2006, when he and the legislature's Democratic majority agreed on an increase in the minimum wage, a package of bonds to fund improvements to the state's aging infrastructure, and measures to address global warming. The governor and lawmakers promised to continue that cooperation—fashioned in the middle ground—in 2007 to address the state's growing crises in health care and prison reform, among other issues.

RATINGS

Ratings for each legislator are from a spectrum of seven ideological and trade groups. The score represents the percentage votes the officeholder cast in favor of bills of interest to that organization. Where "n/a" is listed, the legislator was not rated by that organization, usually because illness or extended absences kept the member away when votes were cast. Rating methodologies vary by organization. For a complete list and analysis of how each organization compiled its ratings, contact the group or visit the Web site listed below.

AFL-CIO: The California Labor Federation, affiliated with the American Federation of Labor–Congress of Industrial Organizations, represents the bulk of the state's labor groups and based its ratings on 26 Senate votes and 25 Assembly votes. Contact information: 1127 11th Street, Room 425, Sacramento, CA 95814, Phone: (916) 444-3676, Fax: (916) 444-7693, Web: www.calaborfed.org.

CAI: The Children's Advocacy Institute is part of the Center for Public Interest Law at the University of San Diego School of Law. It tracks legislation concerning children and based its ratings on 21 bills in seven categories: poverty, health/safety, child protection, juvenile justice, education, and miscellaneous. Contact information: 5998 Alcalá Park, San Diego, CA 92110, Phone: (619) 260-4806, Fax: (619) 260-4753, Web: www.caichildlaw.org.

CoC: The California Chamber of Commerce is the state's most influential business organization, with several of its executives having served in key positions with the Schwarzenegger administration. It tracked 17 bills in the Senate and 15 in the Assembly, dealing with such issues as public contracts, ports, hospital staffing, workers' compensation reform, and minimum wage. Contact information: P.O. Box 1736, Sacramento, CA 95812, Phone: (916) 444-6670, Fax: (916) 444-6685, Web: www.calchamber.com.

CLCV: The California League of Conservation Voters, the largest and oldest state political action committee, is the political arm for more than 100 environmental organizations. It tracked 10 Senate and 13 Assembly bills dealing with, among other issues, "green" schools, water quality, coastal contamination, port pollution, and junk mail. Contact information: 1212 Broadway, Oakland, CA 94612, Phone: (510) 271-0900, Fax: (510) 271-0901, Web: www.ecovote.org.

EQCA: Equality California is a civil rights and advocacy organization for the gay and lesbian community. It tracked 10 bills on issues such as same-sex marriage, nondiscrimination in employment, hate crimes, sexual harassment, and clean-needle exchange programs. Contact information: 1127 11th Street, Suite 208, Sacramento, CA 95814, Phone: (916) 554-7681, Fax: (916) 442-4616, Web: www.eqca.org.

CCS: The Congress of California Seniors is a statewide advocacy group that promotes the interests of seniors and their families. They based their ratings on six Senate and five Assembly bills on issues such as drug pricing, nursing home reform, energy rates and supplies, safety for the disabled, and homeowner protections. Contact information: 1228 N Street, Suite 30, Sacramento, CA 95814, Phone: (916) 442-4474, Fax: (916) 442-1877, Web: www.seniors.org.

CMTA: The California Manufacturers and Technology Association works to promote a friendly business climate on behalf of some 30,000 manufacturing and technology-related firms. It based its ratings on eight Senate and four Assembly bills, plus the Senate confirmation of Andrea Hoch as administrator of the Division of Workers' Compensation. Among its key issues are minimum wage, abusive and frivolous lawsuits and manufacturer liability. Contact information: 980 9th Street, Suite 2200, Sacramento, CA 95814, Phone: (916) 441-5420, Web: www.cmta.net.

FARM: The Family Farm Scorecard issued by the California Farm Bureau Federation. The score is based on 10 bills, seven from the Senate and three from the Assembly. Contact information: 2300 River Plaza Drive, Sacramento, CA 95833. Phone: (916) 561-5500, Web: www.cfbf.com.

NARAL: Pro-Choice California supports reproductive and human rights–related legislation, especially on the issue of abortion rights. Contact information: 111 Pine Street, Suite 1500, San Francisco, CA 94111. Phone: (415) 890-1020. Web: www. prochoicecalifornia.org.

Senate Districts

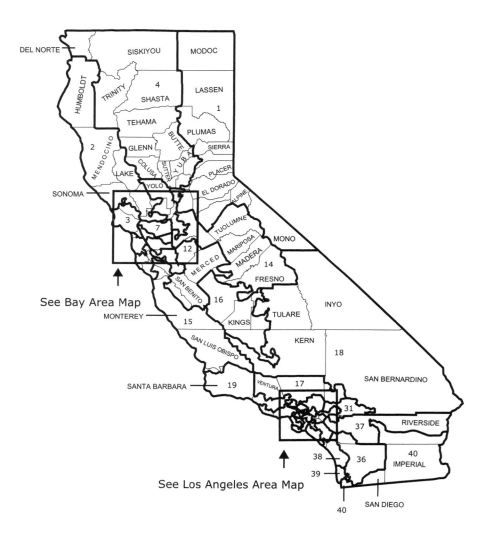

See Bay Area Map

See Los Angeles Area Map

Bay Area Senate Districts

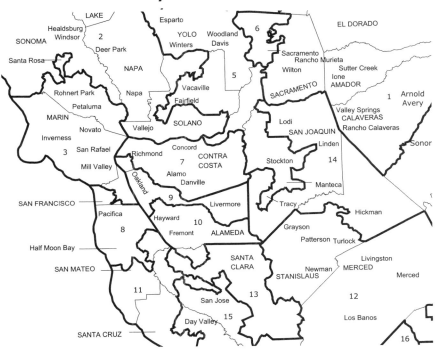

Los Angeles Senate Districts

Senate Members and District Numbers

1	Dave Cox R-Fair Oaks	21	Jack Scott D-Altadena
2	Pat Wiggins D-Santa Rosa	22	Gil Cedillo D-Los Angeles
3	Carole Midgen D-San Francisco	23	Sheila Kuehl D-Santa Monica
4	Sam Aanestad R-Grass Valley	24	Gloria Romero D-Los Angeles
5	Michael Machado D-Linden	25	Ed Vincent D-Inglewood
6	Darrell Steinberg D-Sacramento	26	Mark Ridley-Thomas D-Leimert Park
7	Tom Torlakson D-Antioch	27	Alan Lowenthal D-Long Beach
8	Leland Yee D-San Francisco	28	Jenny Oropeza D-Long Beach
9	Don Perata D-Oakland	29	Bob Margett R-Arcadia
10	Ellen Corbett D-San Leandro	30	Ron Calderon D-Montebello
11	Joe Simitian D-Palo Alto	31	Bob Dutton R-Rancho Cucamonga
12	Jeff Denham R-Salinas	32	Gloria Negrete McLeod D-Chino
13	Elaine Alquist D-Santa Clara	33	Richard Ackerman R-Irvine
14	Dave Cogdill R-Modesto	34	Lou Correa D-Santa Ana
15	Abel Maldonado R-Santa Maria	35	Tom Harman R-Huntington Beach
16	Dean Florez D-Shafter	36	Dennis Hollingsworth R-Murrieta
17	George Runner R-Lancaster	37	Jim Battin R-La Quinta
18	Roy Ashburn R-Bakersfield	38	Mark Wyland R-Del Mar
19	Tom McClintock R-Thousand Oaks	39	Christine Kehoe D-San Diego
20	Alex Padilla D-Los Angeles	40	Denise Moreno Ducheny D-San Diego

SENATE

SAM AANESTAD (R)
4th Senate District

Counties: Butte, Colusa, Del Norte, Glenn, Nevada, Placer, Shasta, Siskiyou, Sutter, Tehama, Trinity, Yuba
Cities: Rocklin, Lincoln, Nevada City, Redding, Yreka, Red Bluff, Chico, Paradise, Loomis
Ethnicity: 82% White, 12% Latino, 2% Black, 4% Asian
Voter Registration: 33% D – 46% R – 17% DS
President 04: 62% Bush, 37% Kerry

Sam Aanestad

The political story of the 4th District is one for the books. Not the history books, but the little volumes that teach Republican candidates how to campaign and GOP legislators how to identify land mines that might blow off a leg once they reach Sacramento.

This is safe Republican territory, made even more secure by the 2001 redistricting, and a place where elections are won and lost in the GOP primary. In 2002 that primary featured two members of the state Assembly who symbolized divisions within the party itself and who campaigned on a single theme: what it means to be a Republican in the intensely partisan universe of legislative politics. Sam Aanestad, an oral surgeon from Grass Valley, was the conservative; Dick Dickerson, a former Shasta County supervisor, the moderate. The key issue: Republican loyalty. The previous year, Dickerson was one of only four GOP lawmakers who joined with Democrats to vote for the state budget, and he tried to characterize that vote as good for the district. Aanestad, backed by a legion of conservative allies, cast it in a different light—treachery worthy of Benedict Arnold.

Much of Dickerson's political support came from labor, a traditional GOP adversary that reinforced Aanestad's message: Republicans could not count on his opponent. Labor poured more than $250,000 into independent expenditure campaigns in the district, but the effort backfired on Dickerson. One labor-inspired slate mailer included the hapless Dickerson in a list of endorsements that included the likes of Gray Davis, the Democratic candidate for governor. In fact, every other endorsement on the slate was a Democrat. With friends like these, Dickerson didn't need enemies.

In the context of 2002, election atmospherics gave a great boost to Aanestad, who defeated Dickerson by more than 12 percent. It was an election where conservative voters—motivated by fears that moderate Richard Riordan might capture the GOP nomination for governor—turned out in droves to vote for conservative businessman Bill Simon. In November, Aanestad brushed aside his Democratic opponent without flexing much of the considerable muscle he showed in defeating Dickerson. He easily won re-election in 2006 and is termed out in 2010.

Although he needs no prodding, the significance of the campaign has not been lost on Aanestad, who has hewn to the conservative line as a legislator. Solidly anti-tax, he has carried bills on charter school funding, high-speed pursuits by law enforcement officers, and the licensing of dentists. The state Charter Schools Foundation named him "legislator of the year" for 2006. As vice chairman of the Appropriations Committee, he is one of the Senate's leading anti-tax voices, but not the kind of lawmaker who either espouses or fosters the kind of bipartisan approach advocated by Gov. Arnold Schwarzenegger.

The district Aanestad represents underwent a major overhaul during the 2001 redistricting, as evidenced by the fact that a five-point Democratic voter registration edge became a 13-point deficit after mapmakers finished with it. While the old district was landlocked, the new version slides west along the Oregon border to pick up Del Norte County, including the state's most notorious prison at Pelican Bay outside

Crescent City. But the political change occurred in the south. Where once the district dipped into Yolo and Solano counties, it now avoids those Democratic enclaves, instead expanding east to add all of Butte and Yuba counties, plus the western chunk of Placer County that includes conservative foothill suburbs northeast of Sacramento.

Geographically, the district straddles Interstate 5 from the Oregon border to the outskirts of Sacramento. The demographics are not mixed; it is the whitest district in the Senate. Most of it is rugged and remote, with pockets of population scattered along the interstate and buffeting the state capital. As Anaestad's election demonstrates, it is politically very conservative.

BIOGRAPHY: Born: Bismarck, ND, July 16, 1946. Home: Grass Valley. Education: BA, UCLA; MPA, Golden Gate University; DDS, UCLA. Military: None. Family: wife Susan, three children. Religion: Christian. Occupation: Oral Surgeon

OFFICES: 2054 Capitol Building, Sacramento, CA 95814; Phone: (916) 651-4004; Fax: (916) 445-7750; email: senator.aanestad@sen.ca.gov. District: 200 Providence Mine Road, Suite 200, Nevada City, CA 95959; Phone: (530) 470-1846; Fax (530) 470-1847.

COMMITTEES: Appropriations; Business and Professions and Economic Development (vice chair); Environmental Quality; Health (vice chair).

ELECTED: 2002 **TERM LIMIT:** 2010

ELECTION HISTORY: Board of Trustees, Grass Valley School District, 1983–1994; Assembly, 1998–2002.

2002 ELECTION: Aanestad (R) 58%
Smith (D) 37%
Underwood (L) 5%

2006 ELECTION: Aanestad (R*) 61%
Singh (D) 33%
Vizzard (G) 3%
Munroe (L) 3%

RATINGS:

AFL-CIO	CAI	CoC	CLCV	EQCA	CCS	CMTA	FARM	NARAL
14	32	94	4	0	2	80	100	20

RICHARD ACKERMAN (R)
33rd Senate District

Counties: Orange
Cities: Orange, Fullerton, Anaheim, Tustin, Irvine
Ethnicity: 65% White, 20% Latino, 2% Black, 13% Asian
Voter Registration: 27% D - 52% R - 18% DS
President 04: 36% Kerry, 63% Bush

In the political lexicon, the words "Orange County" and "Republican" remain joined at the hip despite huge demographic shifts in the county during the past two decades. One of the reasons is the 33rd District, where registration is two-to-one Re-

Richard Ackerman

publican; GOP general-election victory margins reflect that edge, and Republican primaries rarely involve serious challenges. The district generally is white and upscale and includes a wide swath of the affluent south county, so Senate GOP Leader Richard Ackerman, a tanned, genial lawyer, is a good fit.

The district includes tony Laguna Woods, Laguna Niguel, Mission Viejo, and Rancho Santa Margarita, and even takes a slice out of northeast San Diego County, a conservative GOP bastion. It was the product of a redistricting deal hatched by leaders of both parties, and, by careful design, it skirts Santa Ana, which is heavily Latino and Democratic.

Orange County has provided the core of the Republicans' leadership in the Capitol for decades, and Ackerman has been a familiar figure in the tumult of Orange County politics for 25 years. After 12 years on the Fullerton City Council that included two years as mayor, he headed to the Assembly in a 1995 special election to replace Ross Johnson, who moved to the Senate. In 2000 Ackerman was elected handily in the Senate's 33rd District to replace John Lewis, who was termed out, and Ackerman coasted to an easy re-election victory in 2004. He became Republican leader in 2005.

Ackerman faced tough duty as leader—a notion borne out when an attempted coup almost toppled him after the 2006 elections. First, he succeeded Jim Brulte, who was considered the consummate chieftain as he worked closely with the governor, negotiated assorted budget deals, and played a pivotal role in crafting an incumbent-protection reapportionment plan.

Second, in the absence of any statewide GOP officeholder, Ackerman is the ranking state Republican after Governor Arnold Schwarzenegger, as well as head of the caucus. As such, he is the governor's point man in the Senate, especially on the state budget. More significant, he is the caucus's point man in sessions with the governor, and the perception that he was soft in that role led to the coup. The dual role worked in 2005 when Schwarzenegger was in confrontation mode with Democrats. But when Schwarzenegger made nice-nice with majority Democrats in 2006, Ackerman was caught between his governor and the sharper edge preferred by conservatives in his caucus. Bipartisan appeal did not please the likes of Tom McClintock of Thousand Oaks and Jeff Denham from the Central Valley, who thought Ackerman did not adequately represent the caucus in budget negotiations. Nor did conservatives agree with Ackerman's support for a package of infrastructure bonds on the November 2006 ballot.

The result was a rebellion that sought to replace Ackerman with desert Republican Jim Battin. The attempt failed by a single vote, and Ackerman exacted retribution on the rebels. Denham, one of two Republicans to hold a committee chairmanship, lost his post to Republican Abel Maldonado, whose vote saved Ackerman. Freshman Mark Wyland, who backed Ackerman, was made chairman of the Veterans Affairs Committee, a position previously held by Republican Bill Morrow, who was termed out in 2006.

An attack from the right was uncharacteristic for Ackerman whose natural political bearing is as an anti-tax, anti-spending, just-say-no crusader. As a member of the legislature's budget-writing committee, Ackerman often made his voice heard in ways that should have pleased conservatives. He once earned the wrath of teachers and other educators for suggesting that school-funding guarantees codified in Proposition 98 were bad for the state and ought to be done away with.

Ackerman got into trouble with colleagues because, like many leaders these days, his position as head of the caucus forced him to moderate—at least temporarily. He is not immune to another attack, however, and after subduing the coup, Ackerman promised to hew more closely to conservative values during the 2007-2008 session.

His survival as leader only postponed the inevitable, for Ackerman is termed out when the session ends. A campaign to replace him likely will continue, as will pressure on him to step aside for a leader who can carry on beyond 2008.

BIOGRAPHY: Born: Long Beach, December 5, 1942. Home: Irvine. Education: AB, UC Berkeley; JD, Hastings School of Law. Military: None. Family: wife Linda, three children. Religion: Protestant. Occupation: Attorney.

OFFICES: 305 Capitol Building, Sacramento, CA 95814; Phone: (916) 651-4033; Fax: (916) 445-9754; email: senator.ackerman@sen.ca.gov. District: 17821 East 17th Street, Suite 180, Tustin, CA 92780; Phone: (714) 573-1853; Fax: (714) 573-1859.

COMMITTEES: Senate Republican Leader; Ethics (vice chair); Judiciary; Labor and Industrial Relations.

ELECTED: 2000 **TERM LIMIT:** 2008

ELECTION HISTORY: Assembly, 1995-2000

2000 ELECTION: Ackerman (R) 65%
            Roberts (D) 29%
            Chacon (L) 4%
            Verkamp (NL) 2%

2004 ELECTION: Ackerman (R*) 69%
            Daugherty (D) 31%

RATINGS:	AFL-CIO	CAI	CoC	CLCV	EQCA	CCS	CMTA	FARM	NARAL
	11	28	94	4	0	20	90	100	20

ELAINE ALQUIST (D)
13th Senate District

Counties: Santa Clara
Cities: San Jose, Santa Clara, Mountain View, Sunnyvale, Gilroy
Ethnicity: 33% White, 35% Latino, 4% Black, 28% Asian
Voter Registration: 49% D – 22% R – 25% DS
President 04: 67% Kerry, 31% Bush

Presidents Pro Tempore of the Senate					
Name	**P***	**Year(s)**	**Name**	**P***	**Year(s)**
E. Kirby Chamberlain	—	1849	Stephen M. Whitte	D	1887-89
Elcan Haydenfeldt	W	1851	Thomas Fraser	R	1891
Benjamin F. Keene	D	1852-54	R. B. Carpenter	R	1893
Roy T. Sprague	D	1855	Thomas Flint, Jr.	R	1895-03
Delos R. Ashley	A	1856	Edward I. Wolfe	R	1905-09
Samuel H. Dosh	D	1857	A. E. Boyton	R	1911-13
Samuel A. Merritt	D	1858	N. W. Thompson	R	1915
W. B. Dickenson	D	1859	Arthur H. Breed	R	1917-33
Issaac N. Quinn	D	1860	William P. Rich	R	1935-37
Richard Irwin	DD	1861	Jerrold L. Seawell	R	1939
James Safter	R	1862	William P. Rich	R	1941
A. M. Crane	U	1863	Jerrold L. Seawell	R	1943-45
R. Burnell	U	1864	Harold J. Powers	R	1947-53
S. P. Wright	U	1866	Clarence C. Ward	R	1954-55
Lansing B. Misner	U	1868	Ben Hulse	R	1955-56
Edward J. Lewis	D	1870	Hugh M. Burns	D	1957-69
James T. Farley	D	1872	Howard Way	R	1969-70
William Irwin	D	1874	Jack Schrade	R	1970
Benjamin F. Tuttle	D	1876	James R. Mills	D	1971-80
Edward J. Lewis	D	1878	David Roberti	D	1980-94
George F. Baker	R	1880	William Lockyer	D	1994-98
William Johnston	R	1881	John Burton	D	1998-04
R. F. Del Valle	D	1883	Don Perata	D	2004-
Benjamin Knight, Jr.	D	1885			

*Key to parties: A=American, D=Democrat, DD=Douglas Democrat, I=Independent, P=Progressive, R=Republican, U=Union, — denotes no party.

Elaine Alquist

The 13th, centered on downtown San Jose, stretches northwest toward Santa Clara, Sunnyvale, and Mountain View, replicating the previous version of the district. New territory was added in 2001 east of Highway 101 and Morgan Hill, extending all the way to the Stanislaus County border before eventually rejoining 101 at Gilroy. The 13th now has the second-largest Asian population in the Senate. Democrats dominate its politics, although nearly a quarter of its registered voters are decline-to-state.

Until 2004, the 13th was represented by the dean of the California Legislature—Democrat John Vasconcellos, whose legislative tenure began in the Assembly in 1966. Vasconcellos was termed out in 2004, precipitating a Democratic primary brawl between former Assemblywoman Elaine Alquist and Assemblyman Manny Diaz. Alquist capitalized on a well-known last name and larger home base to defeat Diaz in a close and expensive race marred by sleazy and misleading ads from both campaigns. The two camps were aided by generous independent expenditure campaigns—prison guards and realtors for Alquist, Indian gaming tribes for Diaz.

Alquist's biggest advantage was location: There were more voters in her 21st Assembly District than in Diaz's 22nd District, and he was unable to gain traction in the area she had served from 1996 until termed out in 2002. Nor could Diaz overcome the advantage provided by his opponent's last name, which she shared with her husband, former state Senator Al Alquist. Al Alquist, who died in 2006, was one of the most popular legislators ever to represent the San Jose area, serving in the Assembly and state Senate from 1963 to 1996.

Democratic registration meant the seat would be won in the primary, and as the contest intensified, so did the negative rhetoric and accusations. In one memorable incident, the Diaz camp sent out a mailer that made a *San Jose Mercury News* editorial look as though it had been put through a Vega-matic. The mailer suggested that the paper criticized Alquist when it actually had endorsed her. The editorial reserved its main criticism for Diaz, but that piece was excised in the mailer. Alquist eventually won by little more than 2,000 votes out of 55,000 cast—a margin of 4%—and obliterated her Republican opponent in November.

As a senator, Alquist chaired the always-entertaining Public Safety Committee during her first two years, taking over the Human Services Committee in 2007. She also chairs the Budget subcommittee on health and human services, giving her a prominent voice in the looming debate over health care coverage. As a member of the Health Committee, she previously sponsored bills on the Healthy Families Program, the cost of prescription drugs, long-term health care, and Alzheimer's disease. She has been a vocal opponent of privatizing retirement plans for public employees. Before entering politics, she was a teacher and businesswoman who served as a financial analyst for Stanford University.

BIOGRAPHY: Born: Chicago, IL, August 21, 1944. Home: Santa Clara. Education: BA, MacMurray College; MA, Washington University (St. Louis). Military:

None. Family: widowed, two children. Religion: Greek Orthodox. Occupation: Educator.

OFFICES: 4088 Capitol Building, Sacramento, CA 95814; Phone: (916) 651-4013; Fax: (916) 324-0283; email: senator.alquist@sen.ca.gov. District: 100 Paseo de San Antonio, Suite 209, San Jose, CA 95113; Phone: (408) 286-8318; Fax: (408) 286-2338.

COMMITTEES: Budget and Fiscal Review; Budget Subcommittee 3 on Health and Human Services (chair); Education; Health; Human Services (chair); Revenue and Taxation.

ELECTED: 2004 **TERM LIMIT:** 2012

ELECTION HISTORY: Cupertino Union School District Board, 1983-1991; Assembly, 1996-2002.

2004 ELECTION: Alquist (D) 69%
Connolly (R) 27%
Laursen (L) 4%

RATINGS:

AFL-CIO	CAI	CoC	CLCV	EQCA	CCS	CMTA	FARM	NARAL
100	96	31	100	100	100	0	17	100

ROY ASHBURN (R)
18th Senate District

Counties: Kern, San Bernardino, Tulare, Inyo
Cities: Bakersfield, Tulare, Visalia, Bishop, Needles, Twentynine Palms, Barstow, Tehachapi
Ethnicity: 64% White, 27% Latino, 5% Black, 4% Asian
Voter Registration: 31% D – 50% R – 15% DS
President 04: 69% Bush, 30% Kerry

Roy Ashburn

Not one precinct of the pre-redistricting 18th District remains in the version created in 2001. The old district was coastal and extended from San Luis Obispo County in the north through Santa Barbara County to take in the northern half of Ventura County. The careful reader will note that not one of those counties is included in the new district.

The reason: when Republican and Democratic dealmakers divided the state among themselves, districts along the central coast—from Monterey to Port Hueneme—were put through a Cuisinart. The old 18th was whacked in two, much to the chagrin of its termed-out Democratic incumbent, Jack O'Connell, who was subsequently elected superintendent of public instruction. The northern portion was attached to a new 15th District, and the southern part riveted to the 19th District, leaving nothing behind but the number. Designated as GOP territory, the 18th moved east—way east—where it now glides along the Nevada border from Bishop in the north to south of Needles. Vast stretches of the district are populated by rattlesnakes and jackrabbits and given over to the military in such places as China Basin Naval Weapons Center, Fort Irwin, and Edwards Air Force Base. A large portion of the population resides in and around Bakersfield and in Central Valley communities such as Visalia and Tulare.

The district is reliably conservative and Republican, and most of what passes for competitive politics takes place in the Central Valley, especially Bakersfield and Kern County, where Republican feuds often dictate the tenor of campaigns. Although the incumbent Republican senator, Roy Ashburn, represents one faction of Kern County Republican politics, his election to the Senate in 2002—the first held in the new district—was more of a coronation than a contest. Despite the fact that the seat was open, Ashburn drew nary an opponent, either in the primary or general election. It was a testament to his political prowess after having served a dozen years on the Kern County Board of Supervisors and three terms in the state Assembly that no one—not even another Republican—bothered to oppose Ashburn once he declared for the Senate.

But all is not goodness and light for Ashburn. In the turmoil of Kern County Republican politics, he is identified with a faction that feuds with one of the most powerful Republicans in the nation—Bill Thomas, the now-retired congressman who chaired the House Ways and Means Committee. Thirty years ago, Thomas, then a community college professor, helped wrench the Kern County Republican Central Committee away from conservatives, and the following year he knocked off an incumbent Democrat to win a seat in the state Assembly. He was elected to Congress in 1978 but never let go of his grip on local affairs. That continued control—from 3,000 miles away—rankled many in the local party.

At one time, Ashburn was a Thomas protégé, serving as his field representative during the 1980s. According to local sources, the two broke in 1998, not long after Ashburn was elected to the legislature. It is said that Ashburn chafed under Thomas's long reach from Washington and publicly criticized his former boss in the press. Backed by more conservative allies, a GOP faction grew up around Ashburn, and the two sides began running candidates against each other in selective Republican primaries. The most ferocious of those battles took place in 2004 in the 32nd Assembly District between another Thomas protégé, Kevin McCarthy, and Ashburn ally Dave Maggard. McCarthy won convincingly and went on to become Republican leader of the state Assembly before replacing Thomas in Congress in 2006.

Ashburn, meanwhile, took on another electoral challenge in 2004 that had nothing to do with Thomas—except that he hoped to join Thomas in Washington. Ashburn ran for the congressional seat vacated by the retirement of Democrat Cal Dooley. His opponent was Democrat Jim Costa, a former state lawmaker who had served in both houses of the legislature from 1978 to 2002 and was a former president of the National Council of State Legislators. On paper, the district heavily favored Democrats, but Central Valley voters rarely stick to party labels, and—aided by $1.5 million from congressional Republicans—Ashburn made a contest out of what had been considered a slam dunk for Costa. Vice President Dick Cheney campaigned for Ashburn in the district, as did Governor Arnold Schwarzenegger. Democrats rallied for Costa, strafing the district with TV ads and mailers that singled out Ashburn as the only legislator to vote against a state tax check-off for breast cancer research. Costa eventually won by 6 percent, but Ashburn ran 10 points ahead of Republican registration—a decent showing that reinforced his image as a tenacious and focused campaigner.

After the election Ashburn returned to the Senate where he breezed though his 2006 re-election. As a legislator, he remains fiercely conservative on all issues—gay rights, taxes, abortion, gun control, and limited government. He serves on the Rules Committee thanks to his ties to Republican leader Dick Ackerman, an alliance that put Ashburn in a tough spot following the 2006 election. Some Senate conservatives tried to topple Ackerman because they considered him untrue to his conservative roots in dealing with Governor Schwarzenegger and majority Democrats. Ashburn, one of the legislature's most solid conservatives, stuck with Ackerman and preserved his leadership role.

BIOGRAPHY: Born: Long Beach, March 21, 1954; Home: Bakersfield. Education: BS, CSU Bakersfield. Military: None. Family: Four children. Religion: Catholic. Occupation: Legislator.

OFFICES: 5094 Capitol Building, Sacramento, CA 95814; Phone: (916) 651-4018; Fax: (916) 322-3304; email: senator.ashburn@sen.ca.gov. District: 5001 California Avenue, Suite 105, Bakersfield, CA 93309; Phone: (661) 323-0443; Fax: (661) 323-0446.

COMMITTEES: Appropriations; Public Employment and Retirement; Rules (vice chair); Transportation and Housing.

ELECTED: 2002 **TERM LIMIT:** 2010

ELECTION HISTORY: Kern County Board of Supervisors, 1984–1996; Assembly, 1996–2002.

2002 ELECTION: Ashburn (R) 100%

2006 ELECTION: Ashburn (R*) 70%
　　　　　　　　　Davis (D) 28%
　　　　　　　　　Rick (G) 2%

RATINGS:	AFL-CIO	CAI	CoC	CLCV	EQCA	CCS	CMTA	FARM	NARAL
	7	24	100	4	0	25	80	100	60

JIM BATTIN (R)
37th Senate District

Counties: Riverside
Cities: Corona, Moreno Valley, La Quinta
Ethnicity: 56% White, 31% Latino, 8% Black, 5% Asian
Voter Registration: 34% D – 46% R – 16% DS
President 04: 58% Bush, 41% Kerry

There are many faces to the 37th Senate District, the southern Inland Empire seat that includes such posh spots as Palm Springs and Rancho Mirage and economically depressed areas such as Moreno Valley and Romoland—where more than a fifth of the

Jim Battin

families live below the poverty level. The district, much of it arid, dusty desert, includes a high proportion of affluent retirees attracted by the dry climate, low-income agricultural and service-industry workers, and homeowners with lengthy commutes to coastal communities. More than a third of the population is Latino, although they aren't necessarily reflected in voter registration, where Republicans outweigh Democrats. George Bush won here easily in 2004, 58 percent to 41 percent, and in 2000 by almost as much.

Jim Battin, a former assemblyman with three terms under his belt, won here handily in November 2000 with better than 60 percent of the vote, losing only in the then–Imperial County section of his district, a heavily Latino area that went for his Democratic rival. But the other Republican areas in the district's heavily populated Riverside County portion came in strongly for Battin, ensuring an easy victory. Any angst that Battin or Republicans might have had regarding Imperial and its Democratic proclivities evaporated after the 2001 redistricting scheme when the county was removed.

Battin, with an unusual background, was born and bred for politics. He served for 10 years as an executive at a Palm Desert TV station, and his late father, five-term Congressman James F. Battin of Montana, was appointed a U.S. District Court judge by President Richard Nixon in 1969—the president's first judicial appointment. After his father's death, the federal courthouse in Billings, Montana, was named for him. The younger Battin spent much of his youth in Washington, D.C., where, according to his official biography, he "often played in then-Congressman Gerald Ford's backyard, and knew Bob Dole as one of his father's congressional freshman classmates."

As a state lawmaker, Battin has focused on tax and crime issues, including his authorship of a law preventing sex offenders from being paroled near elementary schools. He won attention for negotiating additional education funding for his district, including $4 million in equalization funds and money for a local library. But while effective for his district and generally surefooted politically, Battin stumbled badly when he set up a private consulting firm that solicited business from casino-owning Indian tribes at the same time he sat on a legislative committee overseeing gambling issues. A day after the story broke in the *Los Angeles Times*, Battin said he would not pursue efforts to get tribal business. Perceptions aside, Battin and his staff said the arrangement was perfectly legal—which it was, to the surprise of many—and the firm had been doing business for some time.

Legal or not, the appearance of conflict added to Battin's reputation as the tribes' best friend in the legislature. Democrats tried their best to keep the issue alive, but the fallout was temporary. In November 2004, he did nearly as well as four years earlier, easily defeating Democrat Pat Johansen with nearly 60 percent of the vote. The loss of Imperial County helped.

Battin displayed his regional influence in 2002 when he helped engineer an Assembly victory for an ally and former aide, Republican Bonnie Garcia, in the 80th District. Although the district had been crafted for a Democrat, Battin used his connections and campaign savvy to push Garcia through three tough challenges between

2002 and 2006. She is termed out and may try to succeed her mentor when he terms out in 2008.

Internally, Battin was the focus of a coup attempt against Senate Republican leader Dick Ackerman following the 2006 elections. Battin and other conservatives considered Ackerman too soft when dealing with newly moderate Gov. Arnold Schwarzenegger, who was repairing his image by making nice with majority Democrats prior to the 2006 elections. They also didn't like the fact that Ackerman went along with the governor and Democrats to back an infrastructure bond package for the November 2006 ballot opposed by many in the GOP caucus.

Emboldened by Assembly Republicans, who ousted their leader after the election for precisely the same reasons, Battin made a run at Ackerman, only to lose by a single vote. Following the vote, Battin said the coup accomplished one goal—to make Ackerman realize that the caucus wanted him to more aggressively push a Republican agenda in dealings with the governor and Democrats. Battin, on the other hand, is likely to spend the remaining two years of his term occupying the far back bench.

BIOGRAPHY: Born: Billings, MT, July 28, 1962. Home: La Quinta. Education: BA, University of Oregon. Military: None. Family: wife Mary, three children. Religion: Presbyterian. Occupation: Businessman.

OFFICES: 3067 Capitol Building, Sacramento, CA 95814; Phone: (916) 651-4037; Fax: (916) 327-2187; email: senator.battin@sen.ca.gov. District: 73-710 Fred Waring Drive, Suite 112, Palm Desert, CA 92260; Phone: (760) 568-0408; Fax: (760) 568-1501; 13800 Heacock, Suite C-112, Moreno Valley, CA 92553; Phone: (951) 653-9502; Fax: (951) 653-9524.

COMMITTEES: Appropriations; Elections, Reapportionment and Constitutional Amendments (vice chair); Energy, Utilities and Commerce; Government Organization.

ELECTED: 2000 **TERM LIMIT:** 2008

ELECTION HISTORY: Assembly, 1994–2000.

2000 ELECTION: Battin (R) 62%
Sanders (D) 34%
Tello (L) 5%

2004 ELECTION: Battin (R*) 59%
Johansen (D) 41%

RATINGS:	AFL-CIO	CAI	CoC	CLCV	EQCA	CCS	CMTA	FARM	NARAL
	11	24	94	0	0	15	80	100	20

RON CALDERON (D)
30th Senate District

Counties: Los Angeles

Cities: Norwalk, Huntington Park, Whittier, Bell Gardens, Cudahy, Bell, Santa Fe Springs, La Mirada

Ethnicity: 16% White, 75% Latino, 2% Black, 6% Asian

Voter Registration: 55% D – 25% R – 16% DS
President 04: 62% Kerry, 37% Bush

Ron Calderon

The 30th District is the most Latino district in the state Senate. Interstate 605 cleaves it lengthwise, from just east of South El Monte through Pico Rivera and skirting the western edge of Norwalk. Highway 72 divides its width, from Whittier to Montebello. The area is solidly Democratic.

From 1998 to 2006, the district was represented by one of the most powerful members of the Senate, Democrat Martha Escutia, who came within one vote of becoming pro tem back in 2004. She lost to Oakland's Don Perata. Despite that failure, Escutia had an influential legislative career that included becoming the first woman to chair the Assembly Judiciary Committee, a post she also held in the Senate. Over the years, Escutia sponsored legislation to protect older workers from age discrimination in the workplace, implement class-size reduction, restructure trial courts, and provide remedial education for students who struggle with regular curricula.

The campaign to replace Escutia was confined to the June 2006 Democratic primary, where Assembly members Rudy Bermudez and Ron Calderon very nearly finished in a dead heat. More than $3 million fueled the brawl, with the candidates spending close to $1.5 million and independent expenditure campaigns adding another $1.6 million. Calderon was backed by longtime allies in the insurance industry, while Bermudez drew on his connection to the California Correctional Peace Officers Association. In one sense, the primary was one of several that pitted a business-oriented moderate (Calderon) against a labor liberal (Bermudez), and as expected, the pair savaged each other for coziness to a well-heeled and influential special interest. Calderon had the added advantage of his name, which provided just enough edge in an election won by 305 votes out of more than 44,000 cast. The result was confirmed only after a recount.

In this section of Los Angeles, clan Calderon has maintained its grip on the area's Assembly seat for better than two decades. Charles Calderon first won it in 1982 and served until 1990 when he moved to the state Senate. Brother Tom Calderon redeemed the Assembly seat in 1998, leaving to make a futile run for insurance commissioner in 2002. Brother Ron Calderon, with nary a day in elective office, stepped up to claim the family fief in 2002. When he ran for the Senate in 2006, Ron passed the Assembly torch back to Charles. Both brothers now represent the area.

Not everyone is enamored of the idea that representation in the Senate and Assembly has evolved into divine right of succession rather than the elective process, and a sizeable number of local officials and legislators lined up to oppose Ron Calderon when he first sought a seat in the Assembly in 2002. But no opponent can easily offset a Calderon's two main assets: last name and a very large campaign treasury supplied by every facet of the insurance industry—long-time benefactors of Clan Calderon. Ron's lawn signs, for instance, never had to mention his first name.

Although it didn't rise to the level of Captain Renault's discovery of gambling in Rick's Café American, Calderon's Assembly agenda focused on insurance, much of it sponsored by the industry itself. Although Calderon held a seat on the Assembly Insurance Committee, his path to the chairmanship was blocked by another industry maven, Democrat Juan Vargas of San Diego. Calderon does not chair the Senate version either, but his bill package in the upper house likely will mirror his priorities in the Assembly.

BIOGRAPHY: Born: Montebello, August 12, 1957. Home: Montebello. Education: BA, UCLA. Military: None. Family: wife Ana, two children. Religion: Decline to state. Occupation: Small Business Owner.

OFFICES: 5080 Capitol Building, Sacramento, CA 95814; Phone: (916) 651-4030; Fax: (916) 327-8755; email: senator.calderon@sen.ca.gov. District: 400 North Montebello Blvd., Suite 100, Montebello, CA 90640; Phone: (323) 890-2790; Fax: (323) 890-2795.

COMMITTEES: Appropriations; Elections, Reapportionment and Constitutional Amendments (chair); Energy, Utilities and Communications;

ELECTED: 2006 **TERM LIMIT:** 2014

ELECTION HISTORY: Assembly, 2002-2006.

2006 ELECTION: R.Calderon (D) 71%
           Minerd (R) 29%

RATINGS:	AFL-CIO	CAI	CoC	CLCV	EQCA	CCS	CMTA	FARM	NARAL
	90	84	65	50	93	90	30	50	60

GIL CEDILLO (D)
22nd Senate District

Counties: Los Angeles
Cities: Los Angeles, Alhambra, Maywood, South Pasadena, San Marino
Ethnicity: 8% White, 73% Latino, 6% Black, 14% Asian
Voter Registration: 58% D – 18% R – 21% DS
President 04: 74% Kerry, 25% Bush

The previous version of the 22nd District sat in a compact chunk atop East Los Angeles between Glendale in the north and Vernon in the south, bounded by Monterey Park, South Pasadena, and Alhambra in the east. Now it looks like something Jackson Pollock might splatter onto a canvas. The district has moved south to include both Vernon and Maywood, while a finger surrounds Huntington Park to pick up Walnut Park on the border with South Gate. At the top, the 22nd trickles north and east into South Pasadena, San Marino, and Alhambra.

Incumbent Gil Cedillo is a legislative veteran who first won a seat in the Assembly in a special election in 1997. He served two terms and moved to the Senate when Democrat Richard Polanco was termed out in 2002. Cedillo's stature is such that when Polanco left, no other Democrat (or Republican, for that matter) bothered to file for

Gil Cedillo

the seat. Cedillo ran unopposed in both the primary and general elections.

Cedillo's first foray into legislative politics wasn't quite so smooth. In 1997 President Bill Clinton appointed then-Assemblyman Louis Caldera, a West Point graduate, as Secretary of the Army. Caldera's departure set off a free-for-all between Cedillo and seven other rivals—the most significant of whom was Vicki Castro, a member of the Los Angeles Unified School Board. Cedillo, at the time general manager of a large public-employee union, was blessed with the backing of labor and Sacramento connections fostered by an old friend, Speaker-in-waiting Antonio Villaraigosa. His campaign targeted union households and thousands of newly franchised Latino voters. The campaign took a nasty turn at the end, but Cedillo prevailed.

Cedillo's personal connection to Villaraigosa—they had been boyhood chums—gave the newly elected lawmaker instant access to Assembly leadership, and he became assistant majority leader not long after his arrival. He was on the short list of potential speakers once Villaraigosa's tenure ended, but personal problems, stemming from his wife's long battle with terminal cancer, took Cedillo out of the picture. She died in 2002.

In Sacramento, both as an assemblyman and senator, Cedillo's chief cause has been driver's licenses for illegal immigrants. His bill to that effect passed the legislature in 2002 only to be vetoed by Governor Gray Davis. A year later, Cedillo again won passage of the legislation, and Davis—embroiled in a recall election and anxious to restore his standing with Latino voters—signed the bill. But his signature proved to be yet another nail in the governor's coffin as the recall campaign and Republican Arnold Schwarzenegger made it a lynchpin of their efforts to oust Davis. After Schwarzenegger became governor, he and Cedillo reached a compromise that resulted in repeal of the law Davis had signed. Schwarzenegger promised to work with Cedillo to fashion similar legislation acceptable to the new governor, an effort that has yet to bear fruit.

Closer to his Los Angeles home, Cedillo has proved to be something of a gadfly. He was the only significant Latino politician to endorse incumbent Mayor James Hahn when Hahn sought re-election in 2005 against Cedillo's old friend, Villaraigosa. It was not altogether unexpected, given Cedillo's close connection to labor and the fact that the Los Angeles Federation of Labor and its powerful executive director—the late Miguel Contreras—endorsed Hahn. But Villaraigosa won, and the already frayed relationship between Cedillo and the new mayor suffered a new strain.

Cedillo's re-election to a final Senate term drew a Republican opponent but not much of a challenge. His political future depends largely on the game of musical chairs. A seat on the Los Angeles City Council opened up in 2007, thanks to Alex Padilla's election to the state Senate, but newly elected Assemblyman Richard Alarcon put his clamps on that election by declaring early and clearing the field.

BIOGRAPHY: Born: Barstow, March 25, 1954. Home: Los Angeles. Education: BA, UCLA; JD, People's College of Law. Military: None. Family: Widowed, one child. Religion: No affiliation. Occupation: Director, Community organization.

OFFICES: 5100 Capitol Building, Sacramento, CA 95814; Phone: (916) 651-4022; Fax: (916) 327-8817; email: senator.cedillo@sen.ca.gov. District: 617 Olive Street, Suite 710, Los Angeles, CA 90014; Phone: (213) 612-9566; Fax: (213) 612-9591.

COMMITTEES: Appropriations; Health; Public Safety; Rules; Transportation and Housing.

ELECTED: 2002 **TERM LIMIT:** 2010

ELECTION HISTORY: Assembly, 1998–2002.

2002 ELECTION: Cedillo (D) 100%

2006 ELECTION: Cedillo (D*) 71%

Ten (R) 20%

Levy (L) 4%

RATINGS:	AFL-CIO	CAI	CoC	CLCV	EQCA	CCS	CMTA	FARM	NARAL
	85	80	50	70	100	85	50	50	100

DAVE COGDILL (R)
14th Senate District

Counties: Fresno, Madera, Mariposa, San Joaquin, Stanislaus, Tuolomne
Cities: Fresno, Modesto, Clovis
Ethnicity: 65% White, 25% Latino, 4% Black, 6% Asian
Voter Registration: 33% D – 50% R – 13% DS
President 04: 64% Bush, 35% Kerry

Dave Cogdill

Viewed sequentially, 14th District maps from 1982, 1991, and 2001 expand and contract across middle California like the flowing goop inside a lava lamp. In the 1980s the district was an enormous blob that sprawled over territory from Yosemite in the east, down through Fresno, and onto the Pacific Ocean where it slopped along a stretch of coastline from Monterey to San Luis Obispo counties. Although Democrats enjoyed nearly a 20 percent registration edge, they never represented it thanks to the popularity of the late Ken Maddy—a moderate Republican from Fresno.

The 1990s brought a significant change as the district ceded all of its coastal territory and contracted instead into an elongated swath of the Central Valley. Centered on Fresno in the north, it oozed down I-5 to Bakersfield. Registration, too, changed with Republicans gaining a slight edge. Maddy held forth for most of the decade before term limits ousted him in 1998. Republican Chuck Poochigian succeeded him.

The current district changed substantially once again, Republican registration ballooning to an 18-point bulge. And like hot lava, the 14th oozed out. The southern portion dropped off, and the district bubbled north and west to take in Lodi and GOP precincts surrounding Modesto and Stockton. Fresno, previously the district's northern anchor, now sits near its southern tip.

Poochigian, termed out in 2006, made an unsuccessful stab at statewide office, losing the race for attorney general to yet another incarnation of Jerry Brown. His place was taken—without much effort—by termed-out Republican Assemblyman Dave Cogdill. Usually, an open legislative seat draws a battalion of candidates, but Cogdill's reputation was such that he cleared the field in the GOP primary, where election in such a strong Republican district is won or lost. It was thought that Fresno Assemblyman Mike Villines might challenge Cogdill, but Villines was a rookie and, it turned out, had other ideas. He was elected Assembly Republican leader following the November 2006 election. Meanwhile, Cogdill's November election was a formality.

Clearing the field is a habit with Cogdill. Before his election to the Assembly in 2000, he served on the Modesto City Council and managed to win an open seat without much struggle. He coupled strong support among Assembly Republicans with a hefty bag of campaign money to score an impressive victory over a former FBI agent who entered the contest late and failed to raise much money. The only controversy arose when Cogdill denied accepting money from Indian gambling interests when in fact he had pocketed $50,000 from a political action committee sponsored by tribes and prison guards. Cogdill claimed the contribution was prison-guard money, but it gave his opponent a slim opening. Too slim, as Cogdill breezed to victory in both the primary and general elections. He has not had a serious challenge since.

In Sacramento, Cogdill has been a diligent and thoughtful—if unspectacular—legislator. Democrats see him as a problem-solver in the GOP caucus despite his conservative philosophy. He has been active on rural health care—a problem in his far-flung Assembly district—and environmental issues relating to agriculture. As befitting his conservative outlook, Cogdill is a staunch opponent of same-sex marriage. He held a post in GOP leadership as minority floor leader in the Assembly and has been given an enormous committee load in the Senate. Not only does he serve on the Budget Committee, but Cogdill also is vice chairman of both the Public Safety and Revenue and Taxation committees. Moreover, he has a seat on two other significant panels—Human Services and Transportation and Housing.

BIOGRAPHY: Born: Long Beach, December 31, 1950. Home: Modesto. Education: High School Diploma. Military: Air National Guard. Family: wife Stephanie, two children, two grandchildren. Religion: Christian. Occupation: Real Estate Appraiser.

OFFICES: 3048 Capitol Building, Sacramento, CA 95814; Phone: (916) 651-4014; Fax: (916) 327-3523; email: senator.cogdill@sen.ca.gov. District: 4974 East Clinton Way, Suite 100, Fresno, CA 93727; Phone: (559) 253-7122; Fax: (559) 253-7127; 1308 Main Street, Suite B, Ripon, CA 95366; Phone: (209) 599-8540.

COMMITTEES: Budget and Fiscal Review; Budget Subcommittee 3 on Health and Human Services; Elections, Reapportionment and Constitutional Amendments;

Human Services; Public Safety (vice chair); Revenue and Taxation (vice chair); Transportation and Housing.

ELECTED: 2006 **TERM LIMIT:** 2014

ELECTION HISTORY: Modesto City Council, 1991–1996; Assembly, 2000–2006..

2006 ELECTION: Cogdill (R) 67%
　　　　　　　　　 Firch (D) 33%

RATINGS: AFL-CIO　CAI　CoC　CLCV　EQCA　CCS　CMTA　FARM　NARAL
　　　　　　　7　　　40　　94　　　4　　　0　　　15　　90　　100　　20

ELLEN CORBETT (D)
10th Senate District

Counties: Alameda, Santa Clara
Cities: Fremont, Hayward, San Leandro, Pleasanton, Union City, Newark
Ethnicity: 39% White, 21% Latino, 7% Black, 33% Asian
Voter Registration: 50% D – 22% R – 24% DS
President 04: 67% Kerry, 32% Bush

Ellen Corbett

The 10th District stretches from the southern edge of Oakland to nearly the heart of San Jose. At the economic center is Fremont, the fourth-largest city in the Bay Area. Fremont boasts more than 1,000 high-tech and bio-tech businesses and a strong retail economy that produces $1 billion in sales each year. The dot-com boom brought investors eager to build offices in Fremont and ex-residents from Silicon Valley who had been priced out of the area. Three freeways, I-880, I-680, and I-238, intersect the district for commuters and residents traveling to and from San Francisco, the East Bay, the San Joaquin Valley, San Jose, and Silicon Valley.

Prior to the arrival of thousands of city dwellers after World War II, the area's fertile land supported fruit crops like cherries and apricots. Agricultural tracts soon turned into housing developments and office space. The area's proximity to San Francisco, Oakland, and San Jose made it a prime destination for another group of settlers—immigrants.

The last 10 years have seen major growth among the patchwork of ethnic communities in cities like Fremont, Milpitas, and Hayward. The Asian community has increased by 10 percent or more since the 1990 Census, with significant additions among Filipinos and Indians. Hispanics have a sizable presence, particularly in Hayward and San Lorenzo. Fremont's Arab population—in the thousands and the largest concentration in the United States—has gained both local and national attention since September 11.

While most families are middle and working class, there are pockets of wealth in Pleasanton, Milpitas, and Fremont despite median household incomes that range from $75,000 to $90,000. In many district households, English is not the first language, and many residents are foreign born.

The last round of redistricting frustrated local Asian-American advocacy groups and leaders who felt that Asians were being taken out of the district. The heavily Asian community of Berryessa was exchanged for more of Republican and predominantly white Pleasanton. Given the composition of the district, though, adding more Republicans is unlikely to endanger a Democratic incumbent. San Jose Airport was added, giving the district an important economic center.

The district once was the province of Democrat Bill Lockyer, the former Senate pro tem and attorney general who was elected state treasurer in 2006. Since Lockyer left in 1998, the area has seen a brutal Democratic primary each time the district has come vacant. In 1998 Assemblywoman Liz Figueroa prevailed over Assemblyman Michael Sweeney. Figueroa's departure in 2006 precipitated yet another knock-about primary, this time featuring three current or former lawmakers: Johan Klehs, John Dutra, and Ellen Corbett.

All three candidates had extensive service in elective office. Klehs was the grizzled veteran, having served three terms in the Assembly and two on the state Board of Equalization. Dutra and Corbett both served in the Assembly from 1998 to 2004. All three had been in local government prior to their legislative careers. In essence, the campaign was one of several statewide where moderates and liberals went head-to-head in Democratic primaries. In this case, Dutra staked out the pro-business middle, while Corbett and Klehs operated from the left.

The candidates touted "effectiveness" as a general theme, promoting their various achievements as legislators, but the money flowed along ideological lines. Business interests, including doctors and realtors, supported Dutra, who donated $500,000 from his own pocket. Teachers, firefighters, and nurses came in for Corbett, as did trial lawyers. Klehs had backing from former Senate pro Tem John Burton and some labor organizations, among others.

As expected from three veterans, the campaign was intense, but Corbett benefited from the fact that she was the only woman on the ballot in a district that had been represented by a woman for eight years. Klehs and Dutra ran almost dead even, both finishing about 6,000 votes behind Corbett. Ironically, Corbett first worked in Sacramento in the 1980s as an intern in Klehs's Assembly office.

As a senator, Corbett's legislative experience staked her to a key assignment for a rookie senator—chair of the Judiciary Committee. As such, she will be in the thick of fights over health care, the environment, and public safety.

BIOGRAPHY: Born: Oakland, December 31, 1954. Home: San Leandro. Education: BS, UC Davis; JD, McGeorge School of Law. Military: None. Family: single, one child. Religion: Catholic. Occupation: Attorney, community college professor.

OFFICES: 4061 Capitol Building, Sacramento, CA 95814; Phone: (916) 651-4010; Fax: (916) 327-2433; email: senator.corbett@sen.ca.gov. District: 43801 Mission Boulevard, Suite 103, Fremont, CA 94539; Phone: (510) 413-5960; Fax: (510) 413-5965.

COMMITTEES: Appropriations; Business, Professions and Economic Development; Ethics; Judiciary (chair); Transportation and Housing.
ELECTED: 2006 **TERM LIMIT:** 2014
ELECTION HISTORY: Assembly, 1998–2004; Mayor, San Leandro, 1998.
2006 ELECTION: Corbett (D) 73%
Filipovich (R) 27%
RATINGS: Newly elected.

LOU CORREA (D)
34th Senate District

Counties: Orange
Cities: Santa Ana, Anaheim, Garden Grove
Ethnicity: 22% White, 59% Latino, 3% Black, 17% Asian
Voter Registration: 41% D – 38% R – 17% DS
President 04: 52% Bush, 47% Kerry

Lou Correa

Orange County's 34th Senate District, once the fiefdom of Republicans and the home of a former Senate GOP leader, is now marginally Democratic, shaped by the twin forces of reapportionment and immigration that have transformed the political landscape in the heart of this Republican-dominated county. The 34th District includes relatively small chunks of Westminster and Fullerton, but the key is Santa Ana where more than 90 percent of the city's 350,000 residents are folded into the district. Latinos account for more than 80 percent of the population—a figure that some believe may be too low because of illegal immigration—and registered Democratic voters outnumber Republicans by nearly two-to-one. More than 16 percent of the families in Santa Ana live below the poverty line. The district was artfully drawn to include some 85 percent of Garden Grove, where Republicans and Democrats each share about 40 percent of the registration and where George Bush and John Kerry each polled 48.2 percent in the 2004 presidential election. Similarly, more than 71 percent of Anaheim is included in the district, with Democrats slightly outnumbering Republicans. Districtwide, Bush won by five points, however, reflecting the fact that this is still Orange County.

For the past eight years, the state senator from the 34th District embodied its transition from GOP stronghold to Democratic toehold. Democrat Joe Dunn, an attorney and pro-consumer litigator, first won the seat in 1998 defeating Rob Hurtt, who had been Senate minority leader. Termed out in 2006, Dunn lost the Democratic primary for state controller, and the election to succeed him produced not one but two intense campaigns.

The first took place in the Democratic primary where Orange County Supervisor Lou Correa defeated Assemblyman Tom Umberg. Both were well-known and well-funded, but Correa had the advantage of being Latino in a district where six out of 10 residents are Hispanic. It helped Correa that local Latinos still simmered over events two years earlier. In 2004, Latinos resented the fact that Umberg—out of office for nearly a decade—won an Assembly primary by using Sacramento connections to bully past Santa Ana Councilwoman Claudia Alvarez. Umberg won that primary by 365 votes, and it was argued at the time that he cared little for the Assembly and only wanted to position himself to run for the Senate in 2006. Correa also was aided by excess cargo attached to the Umberg campaign—an extramarital affair that surfaced after the 2004 election.

The Correa-Umberg campaign itself was, as the *Orange County Register* noted, "shaped by outside forces." One significant force was Senate pro Tem Don Perata, who endorsed Correa and helped funnel resources in his direction. Another was a group called Californians United, funded in part by Perata allies and members of the legislature's Latino Caucus. In all, some $900,000 worth of independent expenditures were dumped into the effort to elect Correa and helped him pile up 60 percent of the primary vote.

The defeat of Umberg was prelude to a bruising general election campaign against Assemblywoman Lynn Daucher, a moderate pro-choice Republican with solid credentials as a lawmaker. The contest marked the Republicans' one chance to pick up a Senate seat, so money was not an issue for either candidate. But the race was complicated by the late appearance of a write-in candidate, Otto Bade, who had undertaken an interesting political odyssey between 2004 and 2006. In 2004 Bade was the Republican who ran against Umberg in the 69th Assembly District. In 2006 he had transformed into an independent write-in for state Senate. But Bade was not so much a candidate as a creature of Californians United, the same group that heavily backed Correa in the primary.

In other words, Bade was a ploy, designed by Democrats to siphon votes away from Daucher. Californians United sank some $92,000 into Bade, touting him to Republican households as the true conservative. Bade wasn't the only shenanigan to infect the campaign; it was fraught with accusations of dirty play, from lies spewed by phone banks to misleading mailers and advertising.

It went to the wire—and beyond. Daucher held a slim lead when polls closed on Election Day, but the fate of both candidates rested with some 80,000 absentee and provisional ballots yet to be counted. Democrats expressed confidence that the uncounted tallies would turn the tide, and they proved correct as the lead slowly shifted from Daucher to Correa. The Democrat won by 1,400 votes out of more than 111,000 cast in the election. Bade polled 911 votes, less than Correa's margin of victory.

Correa's Assembly career was marked by moderation, and he comes to the Senate as part of a new cadre of pro-business Democrats that includes Ron Calderon, Alex Padilla, and Gloria Negrete McLeod. Correa is the only member of that group who was not given a committee chairmanship or a seat on the Rules Committee.

BIOGRAPHY: Born: East Los Angeles, January 24, 1958. Home: Santa Ana. Education: BA, CSU Fullerton; joint law and business degrees, UCLA. Military: None.

Family: wife Esther Correa, four children. Religion: Catholic. Occupation: Investment banker, realtor.

OFFICES: 2080 Capitol Building, Sacramento, CA 95814; Phone: (916) 651-4034; Fax: (916) 323-2323; email: senator.correa@sen.ca.gov. District: 12397 Lewis Street, Suite 2080, Garden Grove, CA 92840; Phone: (714) 705-1580; Fax: (714) 705-1586.

COMMITTEES: Appropriations; Banking, Finance and Insurance; Veterans Affairs.

ELECTED: 2006 **TERM LIMIT:** 2014

ELECTION HISTORY: Assembly, 1998–2004; Orange County Board of Supervisors, 2005–2006.

1998 ELECTION: Correa (D) 50%
　　　　　　　　 Daucher (R) 49%
　　　　　　　　 Bade (I) 1%

RATINGS: Newly elected.

DAVE COX (R)
1st Senate District

Counties: Alpine, Amador, Calaveras, El Dorado, Lassen, Modoc, Mono, Nevada, Placer, Plumas, Sacramento, Sierra

Cities: Truckee, Folsom, Roseville, Auburn, Susanville, Galt, Placerville, Jackson, Ione, Sacramento, Elk Grove

Ethnicity: 82% White, 10% Latino, 3% Black, 5% Asian

Voter Registration: 33% D – 50% R – 17% DS

President 04: 60% Bush, 39% Kerry

Dave Cox

Straddling the Sierra spine nearly halfway down the state, this heavily Republican district includes a lot of cliffs, fossils, and trees in the far north and along the Nevada border from Oregon to Inyo County. But it stretches a finger into the Central Valley and Sierra foothills to take in some of the state's fastest growing suburbs, including communities east and south of Sacramento and the I-80 and U.S. 50 corridors between the capital and Lake Tahoe. White and conservative, it includes burbs that look like Orange County transplants rather than home-grown northern California. It also provides a home to three major prisons—Folsom, Ione, and Susanville.

Politically, the 1st District is where Democratic dreams go to die. Republican Tim Leslie represented it for most of the 1990s before term limits drove him to the Assembly. Fellow Republican Rico Oller took over in 2000, but he left after one term to run—unsuccessfully—for Congress, losing the 2004 GOP primary to former Attorney General Dan Lungren. Oller was replaced by Dave Cox, who moved across the Capitol from the Assembly, where he once served as minority leader. Cox, who has long been involved in Sacramento-area Republican politics, first sought a seat in the legislature back in 1988 when he challenged then-Democratic Senator Leroy Greene. Although Cox lost that race, he subsequently was elected to the Sacramento County Board of Supervisors. He first ran for the Assembly in 1998, easily brushing aside his primary and general election foes by raising and spending what was—for the time—a huge campaign treasury.

Once in the Assembly, Cox made a crusade out of welfare reform in the days before that cause became fashionable, often clashing with liberal Democrats in his efforts to tighten eligibility requirements. He was an early and vocal opponent of increases to the state's vehicle license fee, dubbed the "car tax." In 2001 he was elected Republican Caucus leader and helped keep GOP members in line on budget and other policy matters. He relinquished the role to Bakersfield's Kevin McCarthy in the fall of 2003.

As minority leader, Cox suffered the same fate as his Democratic counterparts—playing second fiddle to the Senate caucus chief; in Cox's case, Jim Brulte of Rancho Cucamonga, seen as the legislature's chief Republican strategist, spokesperson, and disciplinarian. It was Brulte who intervened in the Assembly caucus to warn members of the consequences of cooperating with Democrats during the protracted 2002 budget fight.

As a senator, Cox has been something of an ethics nanny, demanding an investigation of actor Rob Reiner and the California Children and Families Commission for misusing taxpayer money, and calling for a continuing investigation of former Secretary of State Kevin Shelly's alleged misuse of federal voter-registration funds. A frequent and vocal critic of government regulation, he is author of a bill granting hospitals extra time to complete earthquake retrofits. The fiscally conservative Cox denounced a 2006 increase in the minimum wage backed by Governor Arnold Schwarzenegger.

BIOGRAPHY: Born: Holdenville, OK, February 20, 1938. Home: Fair Oaks. Education: BA, University of San Diego; MS, Golden Gate University. Military: None. Family: wife Maggie, three daughters. Religion: Episcopal. Occupation: Businessman.

OFFICES: 2068 Capitol Building, Sacramento, CA 95814; Phone: (916) 651-4001; Fax: (916) 324-2680; email: senator.cox@sen.ca.gov. District: 2140 Professional Drive, Suite 140, Roseville, CA 95661; Phone: (916) 783-8232; Fax: (916) 783-5487; 33 C Broadway, Jackson, CA 95642; Phone: (209) 223-9140.

COMMITTEES: Appropriations (vice chair); Banking, Finance and Insurance; Energy, Utilities and Communications; Health; Local Government (vice chair).

ELECTED: 2004 **TERM LIMIT:** 2012

ELECTION HISTORY: Sacramento County Board of Supervisors, 1992–1998; Assembly, 1998–2004.

2004 ELECTION: Cox (R) 63%
McDonald (D) 34%
Liebman (L) 3%

RATINGS:	AFL-CIO	CAI	CoC	CLCV	EQCA	CCS	CMTA	FARM	NARAL
	11	32	94	4	0	20	90	100	20

JEFF DENHAM (R)
12th Senate District

Counties: Madera, Merced, Monterey, San Benito, Stanislaus
Cities: Salinas, Modesto, Turlock, Madera
Ethnicity: 41% White, 49% Latino, 4% Black, 6% Asian
Voter Registration: 46% D – 38% R – 13% DS
President 04: 51% Bush, 48% Kerry

Jeff Denham

When mapmakers applied their chainsaws to the state Senate in 2001, they ripped apart the old 15th District along the central coast—dedicating that territory for a Republican. In exchange, they retooled the Central Valley's GOP-leaning 12th District to suit a Democrat. Tuolumne and Mariposa counties were stripped out and the district was shoved west to include farm towns along Highway 101 from Salinas to King City. Registration didn't change all that much, but the character of that registration was supposed to bring more loyal and high-propensity voting Democrats into the mix.

It almost worked.

In the deals and machinations surrounding the 12th and 15th districts, Democrats made a choice between two of their own—Assembly members Fred Keeley and Dennis Cardoza. For whatever reason, they accommodated Cardoza, stiffing Keeley in the process. Keeley's natural constituency in Santa Cruz and Monterey counties was divided among three districts and the bulk of it sacrificed to the Republican-leaning 15th District. The 12th then was drawn for Cardoza, regarded as a shoo-in to capture it for Democrats. But a scandal 3,000 miles away in Washington, D.C., laid waste to the plans of all concerned—much to the eventual chagrin of Democrats and delight of Republicans. The area's very popular Democratic congressman, Gary Condit, saw his political career implode after the disappearance of a former intern with whom he had been having an affair.

Cardoza, sensing that Condit had been wounded beyond healing, challenged him in the Democratic primary for Congress, leaving the Senate seat to a small army of Democrats. The most notable was Rusty Areias, a former assemblyman and director of the parks department under Governor Gray Davis. Areias, however, did not have the primary to himself. Among those who entered was Chad Condit, son of Gary, who eventually withdrew, as did a tough Merced County prosecutor named Larry Morse. Areias captured the nomination, beating an unknown Modesto attorney, but the campaign was spiced with a ton of negative publicity, most of it aimed at Areias, whose personal finances were a shambles and who suffered the loss of the family farm in a disputed bankruptcy.

Republicans, too, grasped the possibilities in Cardoza's departure, and their primary featured a pair of candidates with a history, businessman Jeff Denham, who lost an Assembly race in 2000, and Peter Frusetta, the termed-out assemblyman Denham had sought to succeed that year. Adding another layer of coziness, the man Frusetta replaced in the Assembly was Rusty Areias. Denham beat Frusetta easily, winning by a large margin in the piece of the Senate district Frusetta did not represent in the Assembly. Denham and Areias then went after each other in the only state Senate race of any consequence in 2002—which meant big bucks and political tools not designed for home use.

Throughout the campaign Denham focused on one issue, and one issue only: Areias. Areias had spent a dozen years in the Assembly during the 1980s and 1990s, where he was the legislature's *bon vivant*, its hale fellow well met. He also accumulated enough political and personal baggage to weigh down the *Hindenburg*. As a member of rebellious Democrats known as the "Gang of Five," he was a crony of Gary Condit. He finished near the bottom of "integrity" in *California Journal*'s ranking of lawmakers in 1992 and 1994—a fact that the Denham campaign trumpeted about with no small degree of inaccuracy. Areias failed to file reports and fees in a timely manner and was fined by the Fair Political Practices Commission, and he neglected to vote in the 2000 election. On the personal side, he was embroiled in a nasty fight with Bank of America over loss of the family farm. The sheer volume of his cargo led the *Modesto Bee* to question his character and subsequently endorse Denham.

Not surprisingly, the campaign went straight from primary to gutter—and stayed there from March to November, with Denham exposing *ad nauseam* every wart and carbuncle ever associated with his opponent. At one point, Denham accused Areias of being fined by the FPPC a whopping 31 times—an accusation as spectacular as it was false. Areias threatened to sue Denham, but the damage had been done.

Both contenders rode a sea of cash to the finish line; Areias spent more than $4 million, with Denham forking out about $2 million. Denham was particularly effective in funding an aggressive absentee ballot program targeted at occasional Republican voters—a tactic both prescient and fortuitous in an election year where voters who failed to show up outnumbered those who did.

Election Day ended in a virtual dead heat. As expected, Areias carried the district's slice of Monterey County and San Benito County, while Denham prevailed in vote-heavy Merced and Stanislaus counties. But the final result hinged on some 25,000 absentee and provisional ballots that were not tallied until more than a week after the election. As the results trickled in, the lead bounced back and forth between the two camps. Areias clung to a razor-thin lead until Stanislaus dumped nearly all of its absentees into the hopper at one time, creating a Denham tidal wave that swamped Areias's fragile lead. Denham was helped by dismal Democratic voter turnout.

Many observers thought that Democrats would make a serious run at Denham in 2006, provided they could keep Areias on the sidelines. Areias, partner in a successful consulting firm, wanted no part of a rematch. Neither, it appeared, did Democrats. Denham used his first term to build a good-sized treasury and was helped—oddly—when Democrat Don Perata, the Senate pro tem, named him chairman of the Senate Agriculture Committee, not a bad gig for someone who represents so many rural voters. Most name Democrats took a pass on the campaign, including Keeley, now treasurer of Santa Cruz County, and Assemblyman Simon Salinas, who ran successfully for the Monterey County Board of Supervisors. Denham drew attorney Wiley Nickel and won by 25,000 votes.

Unfortunately, Denham's easy re-election campaign left him time for other endeavors, and he turned his attention to playing the role of Servilius Casca, conspiring with other conservative Republicans to topple GOP floor leader Dick Ackerman after the 2006 elections. The coup failed by one vote, and Denham immediately lost his agricultural chairmanship to the person who cast it—Abel Maldonado of Santa Maria.

BIOGRAPHY: Born: Hawthorne, July 29, 1967. Home: Salinas. Education: BA, Cal Poly, San Luis Obispo. Military: U.S. Air Force (Desert Storm). Family: wife Sonia, two children. Religion: Presbyterian. Occupation: Legislator.

OFFICES: 3076 Capitol Building, Sacramento, CA 95814; Phone: (916) 651-4012; Fax: (916) 445-0773; email: senator.denham@sen.ca.gov. District: 1231 8th Street, Suite 175, Modesto, CA 95354; Phone: (209) 577-6592; Fax: (209) 577-4963; 1640 N Street, Suite 210, Merced, CA 95340; Phone: (209) 726-5495; Fax: (209) 726-5498; 369 Main Street, Suite 208, Salinas, CA 93901; Phone: (831) 769-8040.

COMMITTEES: Agriculture; Business, Professions and Economic Development; Education; Governmental Organization (vice chair); Veterans Affairs.

ELECTED: 2002 **TERM LIMIT:** 2010

ELECTION HISTORY: None.

2002 ELECTION: Denham (R) 49%
Areias (D) 47%
Eaton (L) 2%

2006 ELECTION: Denham (R*) 58%
Nickel (D) 42%

RATINGS:	AFL-CIO	CAI	CoC	CLCV	EQCA	CCS	CMTA	FARM	NARAL
	14	56	94	13	0	25	90	100	60

DENISE MORENO DUCHENY (D)
40th Senate District

Counties: Imperial, Riverside, San Diego
Cities: San Diego, Chula Vista, Imperial, El Centro, Calexico, Calipatria, Coachella, Indio, Blythe
Ethnicity: 24% White, 60% Latino, 7% Black, 9% Asian
Voter Registration: 46% D – 32% R – 18% DS
President 04: 53% Kerry, 46% Bush

The 40th is evidence of what steroids can do to a legislative district. Prior to 2001, the district was a tiny sliver of noncoastal San Diego to the Mexican border, plus La Mesa and Lemon Grove. Today, it is a robust swath of largely empty territory that touches the Pacific at Coronado and Imperial Beach and then sweeps east to take in all Imperial County and north to pick up desert regions of Riverside County. It is the only Senate district to touch the Mexican border and is heavily Latino and strongly Democratic, although George Bush fared well here in 2004.

Denise Moreno Ducheny

From 1993 until he was termed out in 2002, the district was represented by Democrat Steve Peace—one of the most intelligent, energetic, and irascible lawmakers ever to grace Sacramento. Peace, creator of the cult film "Attack of the Killer Tomatoes," was the major domo behind nearly every significant piece of legislation during his final term in the Senate—including tough budget negotiations and the disaster that became energy deregulation. When he was termed out, the only Democrat to file was Denise Ducheny, a former member of the Assembly who had been termed out herself in 2000 and spent the intervening two years laying the groundwork to succeed Peace.

In the Assembly, Ducheny was the first woman to chair the Budget Committee when then-Speaker Cruz Bustamante tapped her for the post in 1996—after only one term in office. It was a heady experience for Ducheny and infused her with ambitions for the speakership itself. She made a try for it in 1998, challenging the heir apparent, Majority Leader Antonio Villaraigosa. Despite the quixotic nature of her quest, Ducheny hung in, at one point reportedly talking with Republicans about a coalition speakership. Despite her challenge and the fact she was the last contender to endorse Villaraigosa, the new speaker kept Ducheny on as budget chair where she earned praise for the even-handed and professional way she handled her committee, and for her detailed knowledge of the budget process and the complex laws that govern state spending.

As a rookie senator in 2002, her Assembly experience gained her a seat on the Senate Budget and Fiscal Review Committee and chair of its subcommittee on health and human services. For her second term, she was named to chair the full committee.

Ducheny's legislative agenda has included welfare reform (the CAL Works program) and a rollback of student fees for all higher education. As befitting her district, she is active in issues involving the border with Mexico and was quick to take a healthy swat at Governor Arnold Schwarzenegger's praise for the "Minutemen"—the volunteers who patrol desert regions where illegal aliens cross into California. She called the governor's suggestion that the California-Mexico border be closed a fundamental misunderstanding of how important immigrants are to California's economy. She has been active in ensuring that state funds for border projects are not reduced because of federal funding.

An attorney and former community college trustee, Ducheny is married to Al Ducheny—a San Diego–based political consultant.

BIOGRAPHY: Born: Los Angeles, March 21, 1952. Home: San Diego. Education: University of Lund, Sweden; JD, Southwestern University School of Law. Military: None. Family: husband Al. Religion: Decline to state. Occupation: Attorney.

OFFICES: 5035 Capitol Building, Sacramento, CA 95814; Phone: (916) 651-4040; Fax: (916) 327-3522; email: senator.ducheny@sen.ca.gov. District: 1224 State Street, Suite D, El Centro, CA 92243; Phone: (760) 335-3442; Fax: (760) 335-

3444; 637 3rd Street, Suite C, Chula Vista, CA 91910; Phone: (619) 409-7690; Fax: (619) 409-7688; 53990 Enterprise Way, Suite 14, Coachella, CA 92236; Phone (760) 398-6442; Fax: (760) 398-6470.

COMMITTEES: Agriculture (vice chair); Budget and Fiscal Review (chair).
ELECTED: 2002 **TERM LIMIT:** 2010
ELECTION HISTORY: Assembly, 1994–2000.
2002 ELECTION: Ducheny (D) 57%
　　　　　　　　　Giorgino (R) 40%
　　　　　　　　　Miranda (L) 4%
2006 ELECTION: Ducheny (D*) 62%
　　　　　　　　　Walden (R) 35%
　　　　　　　　　Thomas (L) 3%

RATINGS:	AFL-CIO	CAI	CoC	CLCV	EQCA	CCS	CMTA	FARM	NARAL
	85	84	27	70	93	90	0	17	100

BOB DUTTON (R)
31st Senate District

Counties: Riverside, San Bernardino
Cities: Riverside, Rancho Cucamonga
Ethnicity: 55% White, 31% Latino, 7% Black, 7% Asian
Voter Registration: 34% D – 45% R – 16% DS
President 04: 58% Bush, 42% Kerry

Bob Dutton

When Republican Pooh-Bah Jim Brulte held this seat during the 1990s and early 2000s, it extended well north into San Bernardino County's desert regions and south into Moreno Valley and Hemet. And although Republicans enjoyed a 7 percent edge in voter registration, mapmakers sought to strengthen it during the 2001 redistricting. The desert regions were sliced off, as was Hemet and Moreno Valley. Instead, the 31st pushed west into Riverside, ballooning the GOP advantage to 11 percent and turning a reasonably safe Republican seat into a lock. On a map, the district looks like a predatory Republican sea monster from the Jurassic period about to engulf Democratic precincts in San Bernardino, Rialto, Colton, and Fontana—which it surrounds but does not include.

Brulte held forth here for 14 years—six in the Assembly and eight in the Senate—during which time he was the most influential Republican legislator in California. In 1994 he helped engineer a brief GOP takeover of the Assembly, although circumstances and a key defection prevented him from attaining the speakership. During his tenure, he served as GOP leader in both the Assembly and Senate, bringing much clout to his district and region—one of the fastest growing areas of California.

The 31st District sits in the heart of the Inland Empire and embodies all that is both significant and flawed about this region. The district includes affluent communities such as Redlands, Upland, and Rancho Cucamonga and has harbored some of the intense development that has changed the character of once quiet towns. In Yucaipa, for instance, the last of the town's substantial reservoir of orange groves was uprooted not long ago, replaced by a golf course, strip mall, and tracts of oversized homes. Traffic congestion, bad air quality, and a growing shortage of affordable housing plague the region.

Brulte was replaced in 2004 by Republican Bob Dutton, a former Rancho Cucamonga councilman who served one term in the Assembly before stepping up to the Senate. It was a bit of good timing for Dutton since no other candidate appeared on the horizon, and, surprisingly for an open seat, he had the GOP primary to himself in 2004.

Dutton is typical of the Republican lawmakers who represent the Inland Empire. A fiscal conservative, he touts his opposition to tax increases and his efforts to fix the state's workers' compensation system. He was generally supportive of Governor Arnold Schwarzenegger when the governor was in confrontation mode with majority Democrats and so backed the governor's call for a November 2005 special election. He is not so enamored of Schwarzenegger's recent conciliatory mode, however. A former city councilman, Dutton has been supportive of local government and was named "legislator of the year" for 2006 by the League of California Cities.

BIOGRAPHY: Born: Lincoln, NE, October 13, 1950. Home: Rancho Cucamonga. Education: AA, Los Angeles Valley College. Military: U.S. Army Reserve/California Air National Guard. Family: wife Andrea, one child. Religion: Catholic. Occupation: Legislator.

OFFICES: 3056 Capitol Building, Sacramento, CA 95814; Phone: (916) 651-4031; Fax: (916) 327-2272; email: senator.dutton@sen.ca.gov. District: 8577 Haven Avenue, Suite 210, Rancho Cucamonga, CA 91370; Phone: (909) 466-4180; Fax: (909) 466-4185.

COMMITTEES: Appropriations; Budget and Fiscal Review; Budget Subcommittee 4 on State Administration, General Government, Judicial and Transportation; Energy, Utilities and Communications (vice chair); Rules; Transportation and Housing.

ELECTED: 2004 **TERM LIMIT:** 2012

ELECTION HISTORY: Rancho Cucamonga City Council, 1998–2002; Assembly 2002–2004.

2004 ELECTION: Dutton (R) 60%
  Mikels (D) 40%

RATINGS:

AFL-CIO	CAI	CoC	CLCV	EQCA	CCS	CMTA	FARM	NARAL
11	32	100	9	0	25	90	100	20

DEAN FLOREZ (D)
16th Senate District

Counties: Fresno, Kern, Kings, Tulare
Cities: Fresno, Coalinga
Ethnicity: 23% White, 63% Latino, 7% Black, 7% Asian
Voter Registration: 50% D – 35% R – 12% DS
President 04: 49.6% Bush, 49.5% Kerry

Dean Florez

The 16th District sits almost smack in the middle of the state and is split down the middle by I-5. It is a near-perfect replica of its former self, with the only change marked by tinkering along its southern rim at Bakersfield. Thanks to registration trends in this part of the Central Valley, Democratic strength has eroded—bringing Republicans five points closer to parity than when the district was drawn in 2001. George Bush and John Kerry ran dead even here in 2004 after Bush lost the district by 11 points to Democrat Al Gore in 2000.

Bush's performance notwithstanding, Republicans made no—zero—attempt to pry the district away from Democrats in 2006. That's because the incumbent, Dean Florez, remains one of the most effective elected officials in this part of the Central Valley. He is the picture of a moderate, pro-business Democrat and only term limits will bring an end to his Senate career.

The 16th has been in Democratic hands since 1994 when Jim Costa wrenched a redrawn district away from Republican Phil Wyman. Costa, now a member of Congress, served eight years before term limits forced him out in 2002. He was replaced by Florez, who won without working up a sweat in 2002 and ran unopposed four years later.

Although his independent ways and sometimes abrasive demeanor tend to isolate Florez in the legislature, he has become a politician of consequence in the southern San Joaquin Valley. In 2004, he engineered the demise of his nemesis—Kern County Supervisor Pete Parra, who lost a bid for re-election to Florez's aide Michael Rubio. It was the culmination of a power struggle between two dynamic and well-connected Democrats that mirrored internal party warfare plaguing Kern County Republicans. At one time, Florez and Parra were allies, but their relationship soured during the 1990s, dissolving into a feud with medieval overtones. It affected not only Florez's relationship with Pete Parra but with his daughter, Assemblywoman Nicole Parra. Like many rivalries, reasons for the Florez-Parra grudge have drifted into myth, with the exact explanation lost to time, memory, and the reluctance of either party to elaborate.

Florez first came to the legislature in 1998 after serving as chief of staff to then-Senator Art Torres, now the chairman of the California Democratic Party. In his initial election, Florez defeated a one-term incumbent Republican, Robert Prenter, who was connected to the GOP's conservative wing. Florez was able to capitalize on the fact that Prenter was relatively new to the area, having migrated from Los Angeles just prior to running for office. Florez, on the other hand, was born-and-bred in the district. Florez beat Prenter by a comfortable margin, easily won re-election in 2000, and left the Assembly one term early to secure a seat in the Senate.

An ambitious moderate, Florez often clashes with Democratic colleagues over both issues and procedures. A notable clash occurred in 2002, when Florez was still in the Assembly and serving as chairman of the Joint Legislative Audit Committee. Florez used his post to launch an investigation of Oracle, which had secured a $95 million software contract with the state after making substantial contributions to Governor Gray Davis's re-election campaign, as well as to Attorney General Bill Lockyer. Both subsequently returned the donations, but not until Florez's probing turned the money toxic. Florez's investigation came at a sticky time for the Davis administration, which was buffeted by a deteriorating economy, and Davis's fund-raising was coming under increasing scrutiny as he faced re-election. Among the Oracle employees caught up in the imbroglio was the son of Democratic state Senator Richard Polanco of Los Angeles.

Although Florez earned praise for his investigations, much of it came from Republicans and the media. Democrats loyal to Davis complained privately about Florez's aggressive handling of the Oracle hearings, which zeroed in on administration officials close to the governor. At one point, Speaker Herb Wesson—a Davis ally—added another loyalist, Assemblyman Fred Keeley, to the audit committee, ostensibly to help channel the focus away from the governor. The committee eventually issued a report critical of the administration's contracting procedures.

But Florez wasn't finished. He announced that his committee would look into how the state treats veterans when handing out contracts for state business, which could prove embarrassing to Democrats in the administration. That was enough for Wesson, who in July 2002 fired Florez as committee chair, replacing him with Keeley.

Prior to running for re-election in 2006, Florez considered playing on a bigger stage. He started to raise money for a statewide run for treasurer but eventually changed his mind, helped by the fact that he would have had to tackle Attorney General Bill Lockyer in the Democratic primary. Lockyer won the office, and Florez returned to the Senate where he chairs one of the legislature's most significant committees—Governmental Organization.

It was thought that Nicole Parra might challenge Florez for re-election but she opted to run for a third Assembly term. Parra is gearing up to run for the seat in 2010, when Florez is termed out. Parra is termed out of the Assembly two years earlier, and Florez's mother is considering a run for Parra's Assembly seat in 2008.

On the personal side, Florez's health was a concern in 2005 when he showed up in the Capitol having lost a considerable amount of weight and being pushed around in a wheelchair. The rumor mill had Florez dying of cancer, but the explanation was—although a bit bizarre—far less draconian. Florez claimed he had been on a severe running regimen and broken his pelvis.

BIOGRAPHY: Born: Shafter, April 15, 1963. Home: Shafter. Education: BS, UCLA; MBA, Harvard. Military: None. Family: wife Elsa, two children. Religion: Catholic. Occupation: Investment Banker.

OFFICES: 5061 Capitol Building, Sacramento, CA 95814; Phone: (916) 651-4016; Fax: (916) 327-5989; email: senator.florez@sen.ca.gov. District: 1800 30th Street, Suite 350, Bakersfield, CA 93301; Phone: (661) 395-2620; Fax: (661) 395-2622; 2550 Mariposa Mall, Suite 2016, Fresno, CA 93271; Phone: (559) 264-3070; Fax: (559) 445-6506.

COMMITTEES: Agriculture; Appropriations; Banking, Finance and Insurance; Business, Professions and Economic Development; Environmental Quality; Governmental Organization (chair).

ELECTED: 2002 **TERM LIMIT:** 2010
ELECTION HISTORY: Assembly, 1998–2002.
2002 ELECTION: Florez (D) 70%
                  Knox (R) 30%
2006 ELECTION: Florez (D*) 100%

RATINGS:	AFL-CIO	CAI	CoC	CLCV	EQCA	CCS	CMTA	FARM	NARAL
	86	88	50	70	27	65	30	50	80

TOM HARMAN (R)
35th Senate District

Counties: Orange
Cities: Huntington Beach, Irvine
Ethnicity: 66% White, 15% Latino, 2% Black, 18% Asian
Voter Registration: 29% D – 48% R – 19% DS
President 04: 58% Bush, 40% Kerry

Tom Harman

In compact, densely populated Orange County, "sprawling" doesn't often apply to political jurisdictions, but it does to the 35th Senate District, which touches 18 cities. It includes all of Costa Mesa, Cypress, Dana Point, Fountain Valley, Huntington Beach, Laguna Beach, La Palma, Los Alamitos, Newport Beach, Seal Beach, Newport Coast, Rossmoor, and San Joaquin Hills, about two-thirds of Westminster, and small pieces of Santa Ana and Garden Grove.

Not surprisingly, the district is strongly Republican, with a 20-point GOP registration edge. It also is highly affluent, especially in the coastal areas. One observer once said that Orange County is "diverse but segregated," and the 35th offers some evidence of that: About two-thirds of the district is white, followed by 18 percent Asian and 15 percent Latino. Blacks account for less than 2 percent of the population. George Bush did well here in 2000 and 2004, capturing 55 percent of the vote in 2000 and 58 percent four years later. The area was the long-time political base of Ross Johnson, the tart-tongued, venerable lawmaker who seemed to be at or near the center of every major political fight in the Capitol. Johnson, known as one of the Republican Cavemen, came to Sacramento in 1978 as one of the GOP's crop of Proposition 13 Babies and later moved to the Senate, where he was termed out in 2004.

In stepped John Campbell.

Agreeable and handsome, Campbell is a wealthy businessman, an accountant by training, who made his pile in the automobile dealership business. He came to the Assembly in 2000, handily winning his first election in the 70th Assembly District and winning two re-election campaigns with similar ease. He rose to vice chairman of the Assembly Budget Committee, a key position in the Assembly GOP hierarchy that ensures a position on the six-member, two-house conference committee that actually writes the state budget.

Termed out, he set his sights on the Senate in 2004 and captured Johnson's seat after a nasty primary against fellow Republican Ken Maddox. But Campbell did not stay long in the Senate. When in 2005 President George Bush appointed Orange County Congressman Chris Cox as chairman of the Securities and Exchange Commission, Campbell quickly announced his intention to run for Cox's seat. Such was Campbell's political heft—and ability to self fund—that he chased virtually every other Republican wannabe out of the contest, including Senate minority leader Dick Ackerman.

Campbell's departure left yet another open seat, and soon to be termed-out Assemblyman Tom Harman jumped into the fray. Other Republican legislators considered it, including Todd Spitzer, but none made the move. One elected official who did move was conservative Diane Harkey, a member of the Dana Point City Council, and she and Harman soon hooked up in an intense and nasty primary in April 2006.

At one point, Harkey accused Harman of fleecing taxpayers because he used the car allowance granted to him by the legislature. Harkey donned the conservative cloak and savaged Harman for support he received from public-employee unions, including teachers, firefighters, and prison guards, dubbing him "Take a Hike Tom." Labor support, and backing from a local Indian gaming tribe, meant $300,000 to Harman's coffers. Harkey received backing from conservative forces and pumped $700,000 of her own money into the campaign. She was endorsed by Campbell and most of Orange County's GOP establishment.

Harman relied on his wider name recognition, built during three Assembly campaigns and his years as a Huntington Beach councilman. He ran on his record, both local and legislative, and attacked Harkey as too inexperienced to be effective in Sacramento. Harkey's money and the negative tenor of the campaign made the result close—precariously close—but Harman beat her by 236 votes out of more than 75,000 cast for a Republican candidate. Harman defeated Democrat Larry Caballero in the June runoff; and Harkey returned to the Dana Point council.

Avuncular and generally sure-footed, Harman has walked a political tightrope for years, balancing rock-ribbed fiscal conservatism—the first staple of any Orange County Republican—with his own brand of modest environmentalism that includes his authorship or support of bills to protect native trout (he's an avid fly fisherman) and coastal waters, finance protections for Bolsa Chica lagoon and guard against Killer Algae. By Orange County standards, he is a moderate Republican.

As a legislator, Harman stumbled once, badly, for his apparent support of Democrat-authored legislation to curb greenhouse-gas emissions in vehicles. After a barrage of local criticism, he avoided lasting political damage by ultimately coming out against the bill. The combination of deft maneuvering—nearly three decades as a practicing lawyer helped—and his ability to maintain a soothing low profile proved, once again, that Harman is a survivor.

Harman's triumph in the Senate war was offset by the failure of his wife, Dianne, to succeed him in the Assembly. She tried but was defeated by Orange County Supervisor Jim Silva in the Republican primary. Silva won the seat in November.

In the Senate, Harman was given two significant vice chairmanships—Judiciary and Human Services—as well as a seat on the Revenue and Taxation Committee.

BIOGRAPHY: Born: Pasadena, May 30, 1941. Home: Huntington Beach. Education: BS, Kansas State; JD, Loyola. Military: U.S. Army. Family: wife Dianne, two children. Religion: Decline to state. Occupation: Attorney.

OFFICES: 2052 Capitol Building, Sacramento, CA 95814; Phone: (916) 651-4035; Fax: (916) 445-9263; email: senator.harman@sen.ca.gov. District: 950 South Coast Drive, Suite 240, Costa Mesa, CA 92626; Phone: (949) 863-7070; Fax: (949) 863-9337.

COMMITTEES: Business, Professions and Economic Development; Human Services (vice chair); Judiciary (vice chair); Local Government; Revenue and Taxation.

ELECTED: 2006 **TERM LIMIT:** 2012

ELECTION HISTORY: Huntington Beach City Council, 1995–2000; Assembly, 2000–2006.

2006 PRIMARY: Harman (R) 39%
Harkey (R) 39%
Caballero (D) 22%

2006 RUNOFF: Harman (R) 68%
Caballero (D) 32%

RATINGS:

AFL-CIO	CAI	CoC	CLCV	EQCA	CCS	CMTA	FARM	NARAL
7	40	93	10	0	50	40	100	20

DENNIS HOLLINGSWORTH (R)
36th Senate District

Counties: San Diego, Riverside
Cities: San Diego, Temecula, El Cajon
Ethnicity: 74% White, 16% Latino, 4% Black, 7% Asian
Voter Registration: 27% D – 49% R – 19% DS
President 04: 65% Bush, 35% Kerry

The 36th Senate District, tweaked over the years through reapportionment, now meanders from southern Riverside County into the mountains and suburbs north and east of San Diego. It's an area that was once pastoral and delightfully rural but in recent years has suffered dramatic population growth—not only from newcomers to Califor-

Dennis Hollingsworth

nia but from refugees fleeing coastal areas in search of affordable housing. The district includes 32 communities on both sides of the county line, including such high-growth areas as Temecula and Murrieta in Riverside County, and Fallbrook, Poway, El Cajon, La Mesa, Santee, Ramona, and Julian in San Diego County. Republicans dominate handily here, there is a strain of Christian fundamentalism throughout the district, and the roots of many older locals go back to the exodus from the Dust Bowl in the 1930s. Registered Republicans overwhelmingly outnumber Democrats, the population is about three-fourths white and 16 percent Latino, and the entire district is a mixture of pockets of affluence and low income. Earlier in the decade, the median household income in Murrieta was $66,000, in Poway, $71,000, and in the Jamul area, $87,000—all far higher than the California average of $48,000.

George Bush trounced John Kerry here two to one in 2004 and beat Al Gore 55 percent to 41 percent four years earlier. The 36th District's latest incarnation is one of the best examples of a reapportionment deal in which both Democrats and Republicans sought to protect incumbents. One result of the incumbent-protection reapportionment negotiations was to make conservative districts even more conservative, a result that suits incumbent Republican Dennis Hollingsworth perfectly.

Hollingsworth, of Murrieta, served a term in the Assembly before being elected to the Senate in 2002. He hates traffic and taxes, which is just fine with his constituents, who twice have elected him by large margins over his Democratic challengers. Hollingsworth is an avid hunter—a member and past chairman of Quail Unlimited—and he has long had the support of the California Republican Assembly, a group that is especially strong in the Inland Empire and views the mainstream state Republican Party as slightly to the left of Che Guevara. He enjoys a 90 percent rating from the California Manufacturers and Technology Association for his support of pro-business legislation, has been praised by law enforcement groups for his support of legislation to crack down on sex offenders, and is backed by property-rights groups. After portions of his district were charred by wildfires, Hollingsworth supported legislation allowing homeowners to clear brush and timber from around their dwellings without being subject to penalties under the Endangered Species Act. That position allowed him to combine two of his favorite issues—opposition to the ESA and support of property rights. His first legislation of 2007 dealt with sex offenders, a bill to prevent convicted violent sex offenders from registering as transients and forcing them to wear a GPS device for life.

Hollingsworth's first campaign for the Senate in 2002 featured the kind of all-out civil war that often marks competition between moderates and conservatives in San Diego and Riverside counties. His opponent was Assemblywoman Charlene Zettel, a moderate who hailed from Poway. Although Zettel and Hollingsworth were seen as straight arrows, the campaign devolved into a ferocious, mud-slinging brawl in which Zettel's camp raked up past allegations of Hollingsworth's marital infidelity and failure to pay past business taxes. He accused Zettel of supporting the financing of illegal aliens and education programs for convicted killers, among numerous other misdeeds. In the end, Hollingsworth won with nearly 54 percent of the vote, but the mud never seemed to dry completely.

BIOGRAPHY: Born: San Jacinto, January 12, 1967. Home: Murrieta. Education: Cal Poly, San Luis Obispo; Cornell. Military: None. Family: wife Natalie, two sons. Religion: Christian. Occupation: Farmers' Representative.

OFFICES: 5064 Capitol Building, Sacramento, CA 95814; Phone: (916) 651-4036; Fax: (916) 447-9008; email: senator.hollingsworth@sen.ca.gov. District: 27555 Ynez Road, Suite 204, Temecula, CA 92591; Phone: (951) 676-1020; Fax: (951) 676-1030; 1870 Cordell Court, Suite 107, El Cajon, CA 92020; Phone: (619) 596-3136; Fax: (619) 596-3140.

COMMITTEES: Banking, Finance and Insurance; Budget and Fiscal Review (vice chair); Natural Resources and Water.

ELECTED: 2002 **TERM LIMIT:** 2010

ELECTION HISTORY: Assembly, 2000–2002.

2002 ELECTION: Hollingsworth (R) 70%
Westall (D) 24%
Metti (L) 6%

2006 ELECTION: Hollingsworth (R*) 63%
Hanson (D) 33%
Shea (L) 3%

RATINGS:	AFL-CIO	CAI	CoC	CLCV	EQCA	CCS	CMTA	FARM	NARAL
	11	32	88	4	0	5	90	100	20

CHRISTINE KEHOE (D)
39th Senate District

Counties: San Diego
Cities: San Diego
Ethnicity: 63% White, 19% Latino, 10% Black, 15% Asian
Voter Registration: 40% D – 31% R – 24% DS
President 04: 58% Kerry, 41% Bush

This is a coastal San Diego district that once voted Republican but has been drifting away from the GOP for more than a decade. In December 2000, Democrats held just a 2 percent registration edge, yet a Democrat won the election by 17 points. In fact, Democrats regularly win area elections, mostly by appealing to the large contingent of decline-to-state voters. Redistricting only enhanced the Democrats' margin.

Between 1992 and 2000, the district was represented by Democrat Deirdre Alpert, one of the most respected members of the legislature and *California Journal*'s "Senator of the Year" for the 2003-2004 legislative session. Alpert, who chaired the Senate Appropriations Committee until the end of her tenure, survived for 14 years in districts considered competitive—yet she rarely had a close call on Election Day.

Christine Kehoe

Alpert's departure did not set off a free-for-all to re-place her among either Republicans or Democrats. Demo-cratic Assemblywoman Christine Kehoe and former GOP state Senator Larry Stirling both declared early and cleared the field, and their subsequent contest gave district voters a clear choice between contenders who agreed on almost nothing. Kehoe is a liberal who as a legislator focused on matters parochial to San Diego. Stirling, a retired judge appointed to the bench by Governor George Deukmejian, is a conservative who lost badly to Alpert in 2000. He tried to make an issue of Kehoe's support for gay marriage but did not have the resources to hammer home his message or to paint Kehoe as an anti-business lefty. The race was supposed to be competitive, but Kehoe won by a wider margin than Alpert did in 2000.

Kehoe began her political career in 1993 when she won a seat on the San Di-ego City Council, representing the Third District. She served until 2000 when she succeeded Democrat Susan Davis in the Assembly. But she laid the groundwork for that election in 1998 when she challenged incumbent Republican Brian Bilbray in San Diego's 49th Congressional District. Kehoe's candidacy drew national attention because she was the first openly gay woman to seek election to the U.S. House. The resources and cash focused on Kehoe by gays and Democrats across the country put Bilbray among the three most vulnerable Republicans in Congress. The campaign was nasty on both sides, but Bilbray squeaked through with a two-point victory (49 percent to 47 percent). The Bilbray challenge elevated Kehoe's profile, and she had the Democratic primary to herself when she sought an Assembly seat two years later. The general election was considered one of the more competitive races of 2000—until Election Day when Kehoe won handily.

Circumstances kept Kehoe's legislative focus close to home. The state's energy shortage began in San Diego while Kehoe was a member of the city council, and she saw firsthand how it impacted her community. In Sacramento, she wrote bills to ex-pand energy supplies. In 2003 her San Diego district was devastated by wildfires, and Kehoe sponsored legislation to protect homeowners from the problems of being un-derinsured. She has sponsored legislation to mandate water metering—bills that affect her occasional home in Sacramento to the benefit of water-starved San Diego.

As a first-year senator, she was given chairmanship of the Local Government Committee, which put her in a position to help her hometown, beset by fiscal and po-litical turmoil stemming from public pension liability that threatens it with bankruptcy and the 2005 resignation of Mayor Dick Murphy. Her committee also dealt with is-sues such as eminent domain and homeland security. She relinquished the position in 2007–2008, moving to chair the Energy, Utilities and Communications Committee.

BIOGRAPHY: Born: Troy, NY, October 3, 1950. Home: San Diego. Education: BA, SUNY. Military: None. Family: partner Julie. Religion: No preference. Occupa-tion: Legislator.

OFFICES: 3086 Capitol Building, Sacramento, CA 95814; Phone: (916) 651-4039; Fax: (916) 327-2188; email: senator.kehoe@sen.ca.gov. District: 1010 University Avenue, Suite C207, San Diego, CA 92103; Phone: (619) 294-7600; Fax: (619) 294-2348.

COMMITTEES: Budget and Fiscal Review; Budget Subcommittee 4 on State Administration, General Government, Judicial and Transportation; Energy, Utilities and Communications (chair); Local Government; Natural Resources and Water; Transportation and Housing.

ELECTED: 2004 **TERM LIMIT:** 2012

ELECTION HISTORY: San Diego City Council, 1993–2000; Assembly, 2000–2004.

2004 ELECTION: Kehoe (D) 60%
                Stirling (R) 35%
                Murphy (L) 5%

RATINGS:	AFL-CIO	CAI	CoC	CLCV	EQCA	CCS	CMTA	FARM	NARAL
	100	92	25	87	100	90	0	17	100

SHEILA KUEHL (D)
23rd Senate District

Counties: Los Angeles, Ventura
Cities: Los Angeles, Beverly Hills, Santa Monica, West Hollywood, Oxnard, Port Hueneme, Malibu
Ethnicity: 66% White, 21% Latino, 4% Black, 9% Asian
Voter Registration: 50% D – 26% R – 20% DS
President 04: 65% Kerry, 34% Bush

Sheila Kuehl

Sunshine, ocean waves, coastal bluffs, and bundles of wealth dominate the 23rd District, which stretches along the Pacific Ocean from Santa Monica to Port Hueneme. It is mostly a clone of the 1991 district, with the exception of a spit of coastal territory connecting the old boundary at Mulholland Highway with its new northern enclave at Oxnard. Registration remained about the same.

Until he was termed out in 2000, the district was represented by Democrat Tom Hayden, and his departure set off a primary tussle between Sheila Kuehl and Wally Knox—a pair of Democratic Assembly members with strong liberal credentials. It turned out to be no contest as Kuehl won by nearly 40,000 votes. Each candidate had major endorsements and plenty of cash, so the election turned on name identification, hustle, and get-out-the-vote efforts. Kuehl was especially effective at capitalizing on her past career as a child actress, notably her role as the love-struck Zelda Gilroy on the classic 1950s TV show "The Many Lives of Dobie Gillis."

Kuehl's initial election to the Assembly in 1994 made history: She was the first openly gay woman ever to serve in the legislature. Known for her pioneering work as a women's rights attorney and her early days as an actress, Kuehl helped chart a strategic path for gays and lesbians who aspire to elective office: openly acknowledge your sexual orientation but do not let it define you—either as a candidate or as an elected official. That attitude, plus a natural sense of humor and warmth and a soaring intelligence, has allowed Kuehl to transcend the fact that she is gay—on most matters.

On one point, however, the fact that she is gay likely prevented her from attaining posts for which most observers felt she was supremely suited: president pro tem of the Senate and speaker of the Assembly. At one point, Kuehl launched a brief and unsuccessful campaign for the speakership. Although she didn't lose out simply because she was a lesbian, it was a contributing factor that led to much backstage hand-wringing among Democrats in competitive districts. The same problem plagued her in 2004 when she sought to replace John Burton as pro tem.

In the Assembly, she served as speaker pro tem—the post that runs Assembly floor sessions—and as chair of the Judiciary Committee, where she was able to wield great influence on issues of social justice that lay at the heart of her legislative agenda.

Although unable to attain a leadership post, Kuehl remains one of the most influential Democrats in the legislature, and she has used her clout to head the "Progressive PAC," recruiting and supporting liberal candidates in competitive Democratic primaries—with mixed results. She is regarded as the brightest and most articulate member of either house—a notion reinforced in *California Journal* and *Capitol Weekly* surveys, which regularly placed her at the top when ranking the Capitol's most intelligent members. Her great personal charm helped her to win over colleagues on both sides of the aisle and to forge alliances with conservative Republicans on issues such as domestic violence.

Kuehl has run her last legislative race. In 2008 she faces her final term limit—forced out of the Senate after being termed out of the Assembly in 2000. Her legislative legacy will include paid family leave, improved nurse-patient ratios, protection for victims of domestic violence, and bans on discrimination based on gender, disability, and sexual orientation.

BIOGRAPHY: Born: Tulsa, OK, February 9, 1941. Home: Santa Monica. Education: BA, UCLA; JD, Harvard. Military: None. Family: Single. Religion: No affiliation. Occupation: Legislator.

OFFICES: 5108 Capitol Building, Sacramento, CA 95814; Phone: (916) 651-4023; Fax: (916) 324-4823; email: senator.kuehl@sen.ca.gov. District: 10951 West Pico Boulevard, Suite 202, Los Angeles, CA 90064; Phone: (310) 441-9084; Fax: (310) 441-7024.

COMMITTEES: Agriculture; Appropriations; Environmental Quality; Health (chair); Judiciary; Labor and Industrial Relations; Natural Resources and Water.

ELECTED: 2000 **TERM LIMIT:** 2008

ELECTION HISTORY: Assembly, 1994–2000.

2000 ELECTION: Kuehl (D) 71%
                 Rego (R) 25%
                 Black (L) 5%

2004 ELECTION: Kuehl (D*) 66%
Lanzi (R) 29%
Goldman (L) 5%

RATINGS: AFL-CIO CAI CoC CLCV EQCA CCS CMTA FARM NARAL
100   96   25   100   100   95   0   17   100

ALAN LOWENTHAL (D)
27th Senate District

Counties: Los Angeles
Cities: Long Beach, Downey, Bellflower, Paramount
Ethnicity: 31% White, 45% Latino, 11% Black, 13% Asian
Voter Registration: 48% D – 29% R – 18% DS
President 04: 60% Kerry, 39% Bush

Alan Lowenthal

The artwork that fashioned the 25th Senate District was done for a reason—removal of upscale Republican areas along the coast to make this district safer for Democrats. So Rancho Palos Verdes, Rolling Hills, and adjacent "estates" for each were dropped from the 27th and stitched to the 25th's black-dominated precincts in Compton, Gardena, Inglewood, and Hawthorne—where they could do no harm come Election Day. Friendly Democratic territory in Paramount was added, *et viola!*—a sometimes worrisome 14-point Democratic edge improved to a 19-point bulge.

Not everyone was happy with the result. Republicans along the coast, for instance, had trouble identifying how they formed a "community of interest" with Compton and Inglewood. More significant, Latinos complained that predominately Latino precincts in Bell Gardens, Florence-Graham, and Huntington Park were omitted from the 27th—making it more difficult for a Latino candidate to compete. As a result, the 27th was one of districts included in a MALDEF lawsuit challenging the entire 2001 redistricting plan. The lawsuit itself exposed rifts within the Latino political community when state Senators Gloria Romero and Martha Escutia publicly thrashed MALDEF's lawsuit as "divisive." The suit asked that the 2002 election be postponed—a request that was denied.

Democrat Betty Karnette represented the district from 1996 to 2004. Termed out, she ran for the Assembly in 2004, seeking to replace another Democrat who had been termed out. That Democrat, Alan Lowenthal, swapped seats with Karnette, winning her district. Lowenthal's election was surprisingly easy; he had no opponent in the Democratic primary and only token opposition in the general election.

Lowenthal's only real electoral challenge occurred in his very first race for the Assembly in 1998 against Republican Julie Alban—a wealthy Long Beach prosecutor who was wheelchair-bound after being the victim of a brutal crime. That campaign was relatively clean, if fierce. The Lowenthal matched Alban's personal resources with a strong fund-raising effort of his own and countered her compelling personal story by reminding voters of his experience on the Long Beach City Council. Together, the two candidates spent $3.3 million, with Lowenthal squeaking past Alban by some 3,000 votes.

During his Sacramento career, Lowenthal has come to be regarded as intelligent and hard-working if not consistently effective. An unreconstructed liberal, his focus has been education, local government, the environment, and gun control. He was able to pass legislation in 2001 that limited idle time for truckers servicing ports—a key issue for his district, which includes the Port of Long Beach. He is a leading opponent of efforts to build a liquid natural gas facility in Southern California.

In 2006, Lowenthal's most significant challenge centered on reform of the process for drawing legislative districts, and he ran afoul of legislative leadership for his troubles. Not that Assembly Speaker Fabian Nunez or Senate pro Tem Don Perata publicly thrashed Lowenthal or his bill, SCA 3. Rather, they used legislative sleight-of-hand and backstage maneuvers to accomplish the unusual feat of simultaneously passing and killing the proposal. Both houses approved it in the waning hours of the 2005–2006 session, but the Senate had trouble "transmitting it back to the Assembly" for final consent of technical amendments, and—alas—it expired somewhere in the hallway that connects the two chambers. The bill, backed by most good-government reform groups and a majority of voters, would have removed redistricting from the legislature and vested it in an independent commission. After legislative leaders agreed to revisit the issue in 2007, Lowenthal vowed to revive his bill.

An academic, Lowenthal holds a PhD from Ohio State University and is on leave from the faculty at CSU Long Beach, where he taught community psychology.

BIOGRAPHY: Born: New York City, NY, March 8, 1941; Home: Long Beach. Education: BA, Hobart College; MA, PhD, Ohio State. Military: None. Family: wife Deborah, two sons, one grandchild. Religion: Jewish. Occupation: Psychology Professor.

OFFICES: 3048 Capitol Building, Sacramento, CA 95814; Phone: (916) 651-4027; Fax: (916) 327-9113; email: senator.lowenthal@sen.ca.gov. District: 115 Pine Avenue, Suite 430, Long Beach, CA 90802; Phone: (562) 495-4766; Fax: (562) 495-1876; 16401 Paramount Boulevard, Paramount, CA 90723.

COMMITTEES: Banking, Finance and Insurance; Budget and Fiscal Review; Budget Subcommittee 2 on Resources, Environmental Protection and Energy (chair); Environmental Quality; Ethics (chair); Transportation and Housing (chair).

ELECTED: 2004 **TERM LIMIT:** 2012

ELECTION HISTORY: Long Beach City Council, 1992–1998; Assembly 1998–2004.

2004 ELECTION: Lowenthal (D) 63%
Castellanos (R) 37%

RATINGS:	AFL-CIO	CAI	CoC	CLCV	EQCA	CCS	CMTA	FARM	NARAL
	100	88	31	87	93	90	31	33	100

MICHAEL MACHADO (D)
5th Senate District

Counties: Sacramento, San Joaquin, Solano, Yolo
Cities: Stockton, Davis, Tracy, Vacaville, Fairfield
Ethnicity: 50% White, 27% Latino, 9% Black, 14% Asian
Voter Registration: 46% D – 33% R – 17% DS
President 04: 54% Kerry, 45% Bush

Michael Machado

The 2001 redistricting plan saved the Democrats' bacon in this Central Valley district. After moderate Democratic Assemblyman Mike Machado struggled to capture the old 5th District in 2000, his party sought to spare future Democrats similar angst. Mapmakers axed GOP-friendly precincts in San Joaquin and Sacramento counties while adding left-leaning Yolo County, with the college town of Davis, and cities in eastern Solano County like Fairfield that tend to identify more with the Bay Area than the Central Valley. The effort gave Democrats a nine-point edge in voter registration by 2004, up from four percent in 2000. By 2006, the edge had grown to 13 percent.

Republicans refused to concede Machado's re-election in 2004, however. With few other Senate contests generating much competition, the GOP and its allies poured copious amounts of cash and sweat into the effort to unseat the incumbent, using Stockton Mayor Gary Podesto as their lever. That forced Democrats to crank open their wallets for the incumbent, and the campaign evolved into one of the most expensive legislative races in history.

The contest fired up during the March primary, where both candidates ran unopposed. Podesto actually ran two campaigns. The first was a traditional slash-and-burn attack on Machado, hitting the incumbent on, among other issues, a $61,000 fine from the Fair Political Practices Commission linked to his campaign financing and shreds of distortion that accused Machado of giving Central Valley road money to pave streets in San Francisco. The second was a quirky television campaign in which the mayor played a Marshal Matt Dillon–type character, throwing stingy land developers out of an 1890's era Stockton.

Machado and his allies hit back hard, crowning Podesto "the king of sprawl" and suggesting that he wanted to sell Delta water to Las Vegas—another bit of mythology that played well in mailers and on television but bore little relationship to the truth. By Election Day, Podesto had outspent Machado, laying out $4.3 million to Machado's $3.7 million (nearly a third of which came from the state Democratic coffers). Podesto countered with appearances from Governor Arnold Schwarzenegger. The contest was close, but Machado held his seat, winning 53 percent to 47 percent. As predicted, he did well in Yolo County and even captured Stockton—Podesto's home turf.

It was the second time Machado had been confronted with a rugged Senate election. In 2000 he beat conservative Lodi Mayor Alan Nakanishi by fewer than 1,400 votes. Nakanishi now serves in the Assembly. A farmer, Machado had tough elections during his Assembly days, requiring him to tack to the center as a legislator. Nor has he been immune to personal tragedy. In 1998, his adult son, Christopher, was killed in a tractor accident while working the family farm in Linden.

The district that prompted the 2004 electoral dust-up sweeps southeast from Yolo County's hilly ranges through its agricultural flatlands, stretching from the Central Valley to the outer reaches of the Bay Area, where it juts west into the heart of Solano County. It bridges the Sacramento River Delta to draw in Democratic chunks of Stockton before meandering off to Tracy and Manteca at its southernmost reach.

Flat basins and plains encompass vast expanses of richly productive Central Valley soil throughout most of the district. Tomatoes, wine grapes, fruits, and nuts thrive in the lowlands, while grains are harvested in the northwestern hills, amid cattle range. Much of the district's farmland is irrigated, keeping water issues at the forefront of political discussions. Controversy often centers on policies conceived by the California Bay-Delta Program, which is charged with balancing the needs of farmers, urban users, and environmentalists. Rapid housing development and urban sprawl put further pressure on district water resources. New homes compete for the same water supporting the Valley's bumper harvests.

A growing influx of Bay Area refugees, seeking the good life at modest prices, have found to their dismay that the problems they sought to leave behind have dogged their move. Traffic congestion clogs the concrete arteries that connect Tracy with Livermore and the South and East Bay, and many residents daily inch along crowded Interstate 680 while commuting to jobs whence they came. Homes, while less expensive than in the Bay Area, are not cheap. In Davis, the median home price has climbed to $425,000.

These problems and more provide the focus of Machado's legislative agenda, as they did when he served in the Assembly between 1994 and 2000. In the Senate, he chaired the Agricultural and Water Resources Committee during his first term but left that post in 2004 when he was made chair of one of the Senate's most powerful panels—the Revenue and Tax Committee. He ceded that committee to rookie Senator Jenny Oropeza in 2007, taking over as chair of the Banking, Finance and Insurance Committee instead. He serves on the budget committee and chairs one of its subcommittees.

Machado faced an intriguing choice midway through his second and final term in the Senate. He had a free ride in 2006 and is termed out in 2008. But he gave some thought to taking on Republican Congressman Richard Pombo, a conservative who heads the House Resources Committee but was considered vulnerable in a retooled congressional district. Machado decided to stay put and may rue the choice, given that neophyte Democrat Jerry McNerney ousted Pombo in November.

Machado's impending departure will set up dual primary battles in 2008. Democrats such as Assemblywoman Lois Wolk and her predecessor, Helen Thomson, both are said to be interested, as is Nakanishi.

BIOGRAPHY: Born: Stockton, March 12, 1948. Home: Linden. Education: BA, Stanford; MS, UC Davis. Military: U.S. Navy. Family: wife Diana, three children. Religion: Catholic. Occupation: Farmer/Businessman.

OFFICES: 5066 Capitol Building, Sacramento, CA 95814; Phone: (916) 651-4005; Fax: (916) 323-2304; email: senator.machado@sen.ca.gov. District: 31 East Channel Street, Suite 440, Stockton, CA 95202; Phone: (202) 948-7930; Fax: (209) 948-7993; 1010 Nut Tree Road, Suite 185, Vacaville, CA 95687; Phone: (707) 454-3808; Fax: (707) 454-3811; 1020 N Street, Suite 506, Sacramento, CA 95814; Phone: (916) 232-4306; Fax: (916) 323-2596.

COMMITTEES: Banking, Finance and Insurance (chair); Budget and Fiscal Review; Budget Subcommittee 4 on State Administration, General Government, Judicial and Transportation (chair); Local Government; Natural Resources and Water; Revenue and Taxation.

ELECTED: 2000 **TERM LIMIT:** 2008

ELECTION HISTORY: Assembly, 1994–2000.

2000 ELECTION: Machado (D) 48%
Nakanishi (R) 48%
Brow (L) 3%
Nicolas (NL) 1%

2004 ELECTION: Machado (D*) 53%
Podesto (R) 47%

RATINGS:	AFL-CIO	CAI	CoC	CLCV	EQCA	CCS	CMTA	FARM	NARAL
	61	88	47	74	87	75	40	33	100

ABEL MALDONADO (R)
15th Senate District

Counties: Monterey, San Luis Obispo, Santa Barbara, Santa Clara, Santa Cruz
Cities: San Jose, Watsonville, Monterey, Santa Maria
Ethnicity: 64% White, 24% Latino, 3% Black, 9% Asian
Voter Registration: 40% D – 37% R – 19% DS
President 04: 53% Kerry, 46% Bush

Abel Maldonado

Beyond the rugged beauty of California's coast, the unifying feature of this district is the presence of Highway 101, which flows along the course of the old El Camino Real, the King's Highway the Franciscan missionaries established in 1769. Geographically, the district spans nearly 200 miles of central California's coastline and some of the most exquisite scenery in the state. The district stretches from the southernmost tip of Silicon Valley in Los Gatos and Saratoga down through Santa Cruz and Monterey counties and takes in the rolling mountains of Santa Maria in northern Santa Barbara County. Among the district's many attractions are the opulent 165-room Hearst Castle and Monterey's Cannery Row, which John Steinbeck's 1945 novel turned into a symbol of post-Depression poverty. Cannery Row today is all the more representative of the district, with its sanitized and branded façade luring tourists from around the world to visit the Monterey Bay Aquarium and eat at Bubba Gump's Shrimp Company.

With the exception of the Santa Maria region, every county in the 15th District has a major university, from Cal Poly, San Luis Obispo to California State University, Monterey Bay to the University of California at Santa Cruz and Santa Clara University. These universities supply the region with immense economic benefits from research, jobs, and students. The district has strongly favored education in elections, although voters in its southern end tend to be less enthusiastic about footing the bill.

Land-use issues are always part of the political agenda, with everything from farms to offshore oil drilling motivating voters. San Luis Obispo is a heavily agricultural county, but creeping development from the city of San Luis Obispo to the rural regions beyond has driven up land prices and devoured farmland. Similarly, coastal development has been a flash point in the past, with voters opposed to offshore oil platforms. Any elected official here must be committed to protecting the coastal environment.

Although the 15th was carved as a safe Republican district when lawmakers drew its lines in 2001, the kind of Republican they had in mind was its veteran senator, Bruce McPherson, a respected moderate whose views neatly matched the environmentally sensitive social liberals of the coastal counties. The most conservative, agribusiness-heavy eastern side of Monterey County was cleaved from the district, leaving the more traditionally Republican and rural San Luis Obispo and northern Santa Barbara counties with left-leaning coastal areas of Monterey and Santa Cruz counties.

The region has a history of electing moderates. In addition to McPherson, Democrat Leon Panetta served part of the area in Congress from 1977 to 1993 before joining the Clinton administration. McPherson, who served the northern portion of the area for 11 years in both the Assembly and Senate, was appointed secretary of state by Governor Arnold Schwarzenegger in 2005, after Democrat Kevin Shelly resigned. He ran for the office on his own in 2006 but lost to Democrat Debra Bowen.

With McPherson gone, the district has proven less of a reach for conservative Republicans than Democrats had hoped. Termed-out Republican Assemblyman Abel Maldonado beat Democratic challenger Peg Pinard for the Senate seat in 2004, although Pinard, a San Luis Obispo County supervisor, gave Maldonado and Republicans some uneasy moments during the campaign—mostly because the Democratic Party lavished several million dollars on her campaign, enough to make her competitive. Democrats didn't think Pinard would win, but they invested in her effort to pin down Maldonado's resources, which otherwise could have been used to help fund other GOP contests.

With a free ride in the Senate, Maldonado tried to move up the political ladder in 2006 by running in the Republican primary for state controller. His main GOP opponent was former Assemblyman Tony Strickland, an ultra conservative Southern California lawmaker backed by traditional conservative groups such as the California Republican Assembly. Strickland won by 3 percent, or about 60,000 votes, receiving a substantial electoral boost from Orange and Ventura counties and offsetting Maldonado's strength elsewhere. Strickland was defeated by Democrat John Chiang, like Strickland and Maldonado a political unknown despite his years on the state Board of Equalization. During the campaign, Chiang was able to paint Strickland's brand of conservatism as too far removed from mainstream California, a message that could not be applied to Maldonado.

Following the election, Maldonado became embroiled in machinations inside the Senate GOP caucus where conservatives tried to replace minority leader Dick Ackerman with Jim Battin. Maldonado remained loyal to Ackerman, casting what became the deciding vote that killed the coup, and he was rewarded with a committee chairmanship—Agriculture. One of only two Republicans to hold a chairmanship in the legislature, he replaced Republican Jeff Denham, who helped orchestrate the coup.

BIOGRAPHY: Born: Santa Maria, August 21, 1967. Home: Santa Maria. Education: Cal Poly, San Luis Obispo. Military: None. Family: wife Laura, four children. Religion: Catholic. Occupation: Business Owner.

OFFICES: 4082 Capitol Building, Sacramento, CA 95814; Phone: (916) 651-4015; Fax: (916) 445-8081; email: senator.maldonado@sen.ca.gov. District: 100 Paseo de San Antonio, Suite 206, San Jose, CA 95113; Phone: (408) 277-9461; Fax: (408) 277-9464; 1356 Marsh Street, San Luis Obispo, CA 93401; Phone: (805) 549-3784; Fax: (805) 549-3779.

COMMITTEES: Agriculture (chair); Education; Government Organization; Health.

ELECTED: 2004 **TERM LIMIT:** 2012

ELECTION HISTORY: Santa Maria City Council, 1996–1998; Mayor, 1996; Assembly, 1998–2004.

2004 ELECTION: Maldonado (R) 53%
Pinard (D) 43%
Madsen (G) 4%

RATINGS:	AFL-CIO	CAI	CoC	CLCV	EQCA	CCS	CMTA	FARM	NARAL
	18	60	94	17	0	25	80	83	60

BOB MARGETT (R)
29th Senate District

Counties: Los Angeles, Orange, San Bernardino

Cities: Arcadia, Glendora, La Habra, Yorba Linda, Chino, Diamond Bar, Anaheim, City of Industry, Chino Hills, La Verne, Monrovia, Placentia, San Dimas, Walnut, East Pasadena, Hacienda Heights, Tujunga.

Ethnicity: 49% White, 26% Latino, 4% Black, 21% Asian

Voter Registration: 32% D – 45% R – 19% DS

President 04: 57% Bush, 42% Kerry

The 29th District has a curious and significant electoral history. In November 1994, it was the scene of a special election to replace Republican Frank Hill, who was en route to prison after a conviction for political corruption. Although Republican Assemblyman Richard Mountjoy won the special, a quirk in the law allowed Mountjoy to run simultaneously for the Senate and re-election to the Assembly. That

Bob Margett

was the same 1994 election where Republicans captured a majority of seats in the Assembly, and the same election aftermath where maverick Republican Paul Horcher voted for Democrat Willie Brown as speaker, rather than for his own caucus leader—throwing the Assembly into a year of turmoil. Mountjoy, by virtue of his dual election, postponed his swearing-in ceremony for the Senate to remain in the Assembly and support efforts of Republicans to capture the speakership after Horcher's defection. But a few parliamentary feints by Democrats convinced Mountjoy to accelerate his move to the Senate, and his departure from the Assembly allowed Brown to remain in power.

The Mountjoy saga did not end there. In 2000 a dispute arose over his Senate tenure. The incumbent argued that he had taken office more than halfway through Hill's first term and so was entitled to two full terms of his own. Everyone else this side of Jupiter disagreed, pointing out that the special election had occurred less than halfway through Hill's tenure. Thus, Mountjoy could only run for one additional term before term limits bounced him from the legislature. Mountjoy eventually gave up the quest, and the district came open in the 2000 election that set the stage for, among other things, the way the district was redrawn in 2001.

The 29th District was considered Republican territory, even though voter registration was virtually dead even between the two major parties by the end of the 20th century. Mountjoy, and Hill before him, rarely worked up a sweat while holding the district during the 1990s. But 2000 proved the exception, and it was a warning signal to Republicans who cut a redistricting deal with Democrats to shore up the 29th.

Part of the problem in 2000 was the choice of a Republican candidate. Bob Margett had served in the Assembly since winning yet another special election in 1995 called after Mountjoy moved to the Senate. Margett, the former mayor of Arcadia, won in the fine GOP tradition of the day—easily, firmly, and without much opposition.

After that election, the genial Republican lawmaker entered a political Bermuda Triangle—he virtually disappeared despite winning two more terms. Termed out in 2000, Margett chose to run for Mountjoy's Senate seat, and it became readily apparent to both Republicans and, more significantly, to Democrats that Margett had left nary a paw mark on the political landscape after nearly six years in Sacramento. Republican operatives openly groused how anyone could represent an Assembly district for six years and be virtually unknown to district voters. They were not happy about it, for it meant that the GOP caucus would have to spend a fortune to keep what they regarded as a safe district.

And spend they did—more than $1 million to secure a supposedly safe seat. Democrats forced their hand with West Covina City Councilman Richard Melendez, whose day job was as a Los Angeles cop. Margett was particularly stung when a TV ad purported to show him lecturing police officers, only to have the "police" turn out to be GOP campaign workers playing dress-up. Democrats pumped $1.5 million into the effort to wrest the district away and came perilously close. Margett won by 2,000 votes out of 239,000-plus cast—a margin of less than 1 percent.

The result was too perilous for Republicans. When it came time to cut deals for the next set of districts, GOP strength was bolstered with the addition of Yorba Linda and Brea, as well as foothill communities near Pasadena. The southwest corner was pushed west to capture La Mirada as well. The result is clear in Margett's 2004 victory margin—28 points—and the fact that Democrats didn't much support their candidate.

Margett's Senate years have mirrored his Assembly tenure and now, in his final term, he is not likely to produce a lasting legislative legacy. Outside the legislature, Margett has been active in efforts to help at-risk youth, founding an organization that provides vocational and technical training.

BIOGRAPHY: Born: Los Angeles, May 8, 1929. Home: Arcadia. Education: BA, UC Berkeley. Military: None. Family: wife Beverly, seven children. Religion: Catholic. Occupation: Engineering Contractor.

OFFICES: 3082 Capitol Building, Sacramento, CA 95814; Phone: (916) 651-4029; Fax: (916) 324-0922; email: senator.margett@sen.ca.gov. District: 23355 East Golden Springs Drive, Diamond Bar, CA 91765; Phone: (909) 860-6402; Fax: (909) 860-6519.

COMMITTEES: Banking, Finance and Insurance; Budget and Fiscal Review; Budget Subcommittee 1 on Education; Governmental Organization; Natural Resources and Water (vice chair); Public Safety.

ELECTED: 2000 **TERM LIMIT:** 2008

ELECTION HISTORY: Assembly, 1995–2000.

2000 ELECTION: Margett (R) 49%
Melendez (D) 48%
Faegre (L) 3%

2004 ELECTION: Margett (R*) 61%
Bautista (D) 33%
Fernandes (L) 5%

RATINGS:

AFL-CIO	CAI	CoC	CLCV	EQCA	CCS	CMTA	FARM	NARAL
8	36	94	9	0	20	90	83	20

TOM McCLINTOCK (R)
19th Senate District

Counties: Los Angeles, Santa Barbara, Ventura
Cities: Santa Barbara, Lompoc, Carpinteria, Buellton, Solvang, Thousand Oaks, Simi Valley, Mira Monte
Ethnicity: 70% White, 22% Latino, 2% Black, 6% Asian
Voter Registration: 36% D – 41% R – 18% DS
President 04: 50% Bush, 48% Kerry

In the blink of the 2003 recall election, Republican Tom McClintock went from an unknown legislative gadfly to a respected political celebrity. It was McClintock—rath-

Tom McClintock

er than the eventual Republican victor, Arnold Schwarzenegger—who in a series of televised debates best articulated the low-tax, less-government issues near and dear to Republican hearts. And it was McClintock—along with his ideological counterpart, Green Party nominee Peter Camejo—who emerged from the recall free-for-all as symbols of reasoned debate.

It was an intriguing twist for McClintock, whose off-again, on-again legislative career has spanned nearly a quarter century. Throughout that time, in both the Assembly and Senate, McClintock has been known both as a picker of nits and debater of grand notions, a lone champion of causes dear only to him—the anti-pragmatist. It is not surprising, then, that his role model is Winston Churchill, who labored in the political wilderness for a decade before events resurrected his career in 1939. A libertarian Republican, McClintock has never completely been at home in either his party or the legislature, where he has been a vocal critic of governors both Democratic and Republican.

McClintock was first elected to the Assembly in 1982 at age 26, and from Day One he established himself as the body's parliamentarian and budget scold. In 1991 and 1992 he was the loudest of budget critics, taking on Governor Pete Wilson, a fellow Republican, with particular relish. His tactic: to indicate the impact of every fiscal maneuver on a family of four—especially tax increases Wilson proposed as a way to deal with deficits. His first go-around in the Assembly ended in 1992 when he unsuccessfully tried to unseat Democratic U.S. Representative Tony Beilenson.

Two years later, McClintock surprised the political world by winning the Republican nomination for state controller. Although short of funds, his campaign invented the year's most memorable political character—Angus McClintock, a fictitious relative who talked up his "cousin's" tightfisted ways. The McClintock camp produced a poster that poked gentle fun at its candidate, claiming he was the cheapest man in California and thus the ideal person to guard the state's bank accounts. Humor aside, McClintock did not gain much help from fellow Republicans, and he lost to a well-funded Democrat, Kathleen Connell.

The loss didn't hurt him on his home turf, however, and he returned to the Assembly in 1996—even helping his chief aide, Tony Strickland, win a seat in an adjoining district. Once back in office, McClintock continued to nanny the legislature on fiscal matters, latching on to an issue that would balloon as the years passed—eventually becoming a symbolic cornerstone of the Gray Davis recall election six years later: the vehicle license fee, or "car tax." Pointing out the high cost of registering a car in California, McClintock was the first to call for repeal of the VLF. This time, Republican colleagues jumped aboard, as did Wilson. Eventually, the fee was part of a budget compromise, with Democrats signing on to a graduated rollback. It was that rollback that became an issue during the 2003 recall—after dire economic conditions in 2002 and 2003 had triggered a return to higher fees.

McClintock's Assembly career finally ended with term limits in 2000, but he immediately won a seat in the Senate. In 2002, with a free ride in the upper house, the ever-ambitious lawmaker again sought statewide office, making his second bid for controller. He dispatched former Assemblyman and Board of Equalization member Dean Andal in the primary despite the fact that Andal had been endorsed by, among others, former Governors Pete Wilson and George Deukmejian and the Howard Jarvis Taxpayers' Association. But McClintock out-hustled Andal, raising some $600,000 for the primary, collecting endorsements from a wide range of GOP groups, and using his resources for limited but effective television buys in just three media markets—Fresno, Sacramento, and San Diego. He won by 11 points. Unfortunately, his general-election opponent had enough cash in his personal bank account to fill Lake Havasu.

Democrat Steve Westly, who made a fortune as an eBay executive, was making his first foray into elective politics, and he had the resources to overwhelm any opponent. Although calling McClintock a credit to the legislature, Westly bashed the Republican lawmaker on social issues, especially abortion and gun control—criticism the *San Francisco Chronicle* called irrelevant in endorsing McClintock. McClintock again ran a sparse but effective campaign, forcing the race beyond the wire. Westly won by less than 20,000 votes out of more than six million cast in the election.

But the controller's race was mere prelude to McClintock's finest hour—the 2003 recall election. McClintock declared early that he would be a candidate to replace Davis, and he was undaunted when Schwarzenegger joined him at the eleventh hour. Republicans, sensing that the wounded Davis would lose his job, wanted to unite behind Schwarzenegger and put considerable pressure on McClintock and other prominent Republicans to drop out. One, former baseball commissioner Peter Ueberroth, did, although his name remained on the ballot. McClintock refused to knuckle under, even when conservative allies such as Senator Ray Haynes endorsed Schwarzenegger. The pressure peaked at a mid-campaign Republican convention in Los Angeles, addressed by both candidates. Schwarzenegger's speech was a dud. McClintock brought the house to its feet with a defiant call to the party to adhere to its principles.

McClintock, of course, did not win the election, finishing third behind Schwarzenegger (48.7 percent) and Lieutenant Governor Cruz Bustamante (31.7 percent), the most prominent Democrat on the ballot. But McClintock polled a respectable 13 percent in a field of 135 candidates. More significant, his exposure to a wider audience through televised debates brought him the kind of broad respect that 21 years in the legislature and two statewide runs had not.

McClintock easily won re-election to the Senate in 2004 and made yet another stab at statewide office in 2006, this time for lieutenant governor. He had no significant Republican opposition in the primary and squared off against Insurance Commissioner John Garamendi in the fall. He received little help from the GOP, or from its gubernatorial candidate who chose bipartisanship as his theme and campaigned as though Republican was a cuss word.

Schwarzenegger's approach did not fit McClintock well, for cooperation with even moderate Democrats has never been part of his shtick. Not that it mattered much, because attempts to run as a team with Schwarzenegger were politely rebuffed by the governor. Underfunded again, he ran another credible race, buoyed by residual goodwill from his recall campaign. Garamendi won by a narrow, four-point margin.

Once back in Sacramento, McClintock took up the role of warning bell for a governor bent on governing from the center and fashioning a bipartisan agenda with

Democrats. When Schwarzenegger proposed universal health care for all California children, including those of illegal immigrants, McClintock was quick to caution the governor that he would proceed along that path without any cooperation from legislative Republicans.

Termed out in 2008, McClintock's political future is cloudy. Despite a quarter century in elective office, he is just 50—young by political standards—and, like Churchill, likely will seek out another opportunity.

BIOGRAPHY: Born: White Plains, NY, July 10, 1956. Home: Thousand Oaks. Education: BA, UCLA. Military: None. Family: wife Lori, two children. Religion: Baptist. Occupation: Taxpayer Advocate.

OFFICES: 3070 Capitol Building, Sacramento, CA 95814; Phone: (916) 651-4019; Fax: (916) 324-7544; email: tom.mcclintock@sen.ca.gov. District: 223 East Thousand Oaks Boulevard, Suite 326, Thousand Oaks, CA 91360; Phone: (805) 494-8808; Fax: (805) 494-8812.

COMMITTEES: Ethics; Public Employment and Retirement; Transportation and Housing (vice chair).

ELECTED: 2000 **TERM LIMIT:** 2008

ELECTION HISTORY: Assembly, 1982–1992, 1996–2000.

2000 ELECTION: McClintock (R) 57%
Gonzalez (D) 43%

2004 ELECTION: McClintock (R*) 61%
Graber (D) 39%

RATINGS:

AFL-CIO	CAI	CoC	CLCV	EQCA	CCS	CMTA	FARM	NARAL
7	36	94	0	0	10	90	100	0

GLORIA NEGRETE McLEOD (D)
32nd Senate District

Counties: Los Angeles, San Bernardino
Cities: Ontario, San Bernardino, Fontana
Ethnicity: 23% White, 59% Latino, 13% Black, 5% Asian
Voter Registration: 48% D – 33% R – 15% DS
President 04: 59% Kerry, 40% Bush

Sitting south of the San Gabriel Mountains, this district was once a sun-drenched land of dairy farms and agriculture. Now, as Californians take their quest for affordable housing east of Los Angeles and north of Orange County, fields of single-family homes have replaced the green pastures. The district's narrow western tip starts in Los Angeles County, in a sliver of the city of Pomona. As it spreads east into San Bernardino County, it grows wide to encompass Montclair and Ontario. Then it shifts northward, covering Rialto and Fontana. The district's eastern tail is a section of the city of San Bernardino. Redistricting was so precise that the boundary runs through the middle of California State University at San Bernardino.

Gloria Negrete McLeod

In late summer and fall, the San Gabriel Mountains often ignite in wildfires filling the air with smoke and threatening neighboring towns. In winter, heavy rains flood the cities, and mudslides race into the foothills. Drinkable water is in short supply, a problem made worse by the recent discovery that perchlorate, a chemical from rocket fuel, pollutes area water sources. West Nile virus hit the area hard in the summer of 2004.

As a whole, San Bernardino County may be the largest bedroom community on the map. Few people who live here work here. Each morning and evening the district is smothered with smog from commuters waiting in a 50-mile-long traffic snarl on Interstate 10, the main artery to Los Angeles. Drivers also jam Interstates 215 and 15 as they crawl south to work in Orange County. Billboards advertising hamburgers at a local restaurant chain, Baker's, can't entice weary travelers off the five-lane roads. In this area, people have given up complaining about hour-long drives to work.

The freeways bring life to the local economy, as shipping is the district's main industry. Because trailer trucks add to rush hour congestion, Sacramento legislators are trying to lessen shipping traffic with the Alameda Corridor East project. When finished, the project will have a special track for a two-mile train running through the county to the Los Angeles docks.

National companies are eyeing the San Bernardino International Airport's renovated buildings and soon-to-be-modernized runway for shipping and storage. The airport already houses distribution centers for Kohl's, Mattel, and Pep Boys. Stater Brothers, a supermarket chain founded in the region, projects its building there will create 2,500 jobs. At one time, the airport was the Norton Air Force Base. The Ontario Airport, which handles passengers and cargo, employs 6,000 people.

Economically, the district is relatively poor. In Pomona, Ontario, Montclair, Rialto, and Fontana, the percentage of families living in poverty was greater than the national average in the 2000 Census. In San Bernardino, that percentage was more than double the national average. Downtown San Bernardino is a wasteland of closed-down shops and empty streets. In 2004 its city council issued a nine-month moratorium on opening stores that created a bad image, including check-cashing services and tattoo parlors. Gangs roam the entire district. They don't split neatly into two sides, such as the Bloods and the Crips of Los Angeles. About 20 gangs operate in San Bernardino alone. Between 1999 and 2004, there were 52 gang-related homicides in Rialto and 63 in Pomona.

Frightening warnings about "La Migra," or immigration police, resounded on Spanish radio stations in the summer of 2004, announcing a new wrinkle in the struggles of the working-class district. The Border Patrol opened an office nearby and began stopping Pomona and Ontario residents who looked like illegal immigrants, arresting more than 150. Tensions over immigration have increased since then. Angry American citizens protested the presence of undocumented workers picking up day jobs at San Bernardino's Home Depot a few months later. On KFI-AM, talk show hosts attack politicians whom they deem soft on illegal immigration. The local chapter of the Mexican American Political Association, along with *Libreria del Pueblo* and San Bernardino Community Services, all represent immigrants in this battle.

Because of its large African-American community, the area bounded by Inter-states 215, 15, and 10 is called the "Ebony Triangle." African Americans are politically active in the cities of Rialto and Fontana, supporting local civil rights organizations such as the Westside Action Group and the San Bernardino Black Culture Foundation. Redistricting threatened to split the triangle, but community leaders, especially from black churches, fought to keep it together. While African Americans exercise the most civic power, Hispanics make up more than half of the population of those cities.

Politically, the influx of suburban refugees has pushed up the median home price and threatened to diminish the supply of affordable housing. At the same time, it's changing a region that was solidly Democratic. The new young residents tend to vote Republican. For now, the district remains a Democratic island in a Republican sea.

Democrat Gloria Negrete McLeod represents the district, having swapped seats with Democrat Nell Soto; both were termed out of their respective houses in 2006 and ran for the other's seat. McLeod did not draw a Republican opponent but that does not mean she had an easy road from the Assembly to the Senate. She had a primary campaign to wage against what passes for a dynastic machine in this part of the Inland Empire. Her opponent was Joe Baca Jr., an Assembly colleague and the son of the lo-cal Democratic congressman, Joe Baca Sr.

It was expected to be a close race, but McLeod ran away with it, beating Baca 61 percent to 39 percent and winning convincingly in both the Los Angeles and San Ber-nardino portions of the district. Along the way, she outspent him three to one, includ-ing more than $1 million in independent expenditures. Baca's loss marked a bad day for the family. Although papa Joe won his primary for Congress, brother Jeremy was defeated by Wilmer Carter in his attempt to succeed Joe Jr. in the Assembly.

McLeod is financially conservative and socially liberal. As an Assembly member, she introduced four of Governor Arnold Schwarzenegger's bills in 2003, which gave her some political cover heading into what was supposed to be a tough 2004 re-election campaign against Ontario City Councilman Alan Wapner. Although Schwarzenegger endorsed Wapner, the Republican nominee had more flaws than a cheap suit and was cut loose by his party well before Election Day. McLeod first won the seat in 2000 in an expensive general election brawl with Chino Hills Councilman Dennis Yates. Their contest stood atop both parties' priority list, and McLeod's victory did not firm up until the final week when her campaign dropped one final mailer and Republicans failed to respond.

McLeod has been criticized for supporting gay marriage and driver's licenses for immigrants, but she refused to vote for a bill to legalize same-sex marriages in 2005. A mother of 10, workers' rights and health care for the working poor are her cornerstone issues. In the Senate, she chairs the Local Government Committee and serves as vice chair of the Veterans Affairs Committee, one of two panels chaired by a Republican.

BIOGRAPHY: Born: Los Angeles, September 6, 1941. Home: Chino. Education: AA, Chaffey College. Military: None. Family: husband Gil, 10 children, 27 grandchil-dren. Religion: Decline to state. Occupation: Legislator.

OFFICES: 4074 Capitol Building, Sacramento, CA 95814; Phone: (916) 651-4032; Fax: (916) 445-0128; email: senator.soto@sen.ca.gov. District: 822 North Euclid Avenue, Ontario, CA 91762; Phone: (909) 984-7741; Fax: (909) 984-6695; 505 South Garey Avenue, 2nd Floor, Pomona, CA 91766; Phone: (909) 469-9935; Fax: (909) 469-9206; 247 West 2nd Street, Suite 1, San Bernardino, CA 92401; Phone: (909) 381-3832; Fax: (909) 381-9739.

COMMITTEES: Government Organization; Health; Local Government (chair); Public Employment and Retirement; Veterans Affairs (vice chair).

ELECTED: 2006 **TERM LIMIT:** 2014

ELECTION HISTORY: Chaffey Community College Board of Trustees, 1995–2000, Assembly, 2000–2006.

2006 ELECTION: McLeod (D) 100%

RATINGS:

AFL-CIO	CAI	CoC	CLCV	EQCA	CCS	CMTA	FARM	NARAL
97	96	38	48	100	85	20	60	100

CAROLE MIGDEN (D)
3rd Senate District

Counties: Marin, San Francisco, Sonoma
Cities: San Francisco, Petaluma, Sausalito, San Rafael, Mill Valley, Rohnert Park
Ethnicity: 62% White, 15% Latino, 8% Black, 15% Asian
Voter Registration: 53% D – 17% R – 24% DS
President 04: 78% Kerry, 21% Bush

Carole Migden

Spaniards sailed the Pacific coastline for two centuries without noticing the Golden Gate and the vast bay beyond. It wasn't until 1769 that members of a Spanish military expedition who walked north from San Diego became the first Europeans to see what they later named the Bay of St. Francis.

Today, the eponymous orange bridge looming over the Golden Gate's churning waters is an international icon for the Golden State. Secondarily, the span nearly evenly divides the residents of the 3rd District into two very different parts. The district stretches from San Francisco's densely populated Mission and North Beach neighborhoods to Marin County's leafy, upscale suburbs and isolated beaches and southern Sonoma County's world-famous wineries and neat rows of vines that march over hills and valleys reminiscent of Tuscany or Avignon. It takes in disparate topography that seems as if it could be hundreds of miles—or years—apart. Yet constituents from San Francisco's Cow Hollow district to Sonoma's sprawling dairy farms do have one thing in common: Most live within a few miles of U.S. Highway 101, the north-south link that forms the district's 75-mile spine.

Of these different worlds, there is little doubt about which one wields clout. Political power rests in San Francisco; Marin and Sonoma amount to a big, beautiful appendage that's mostly along for the ride. To some political players from the northern counties, it feels as if their San Francisco leaders are like those Spanish sailors who didn't see anything on the other side of the Golden Gate.

For eight years, the district belonged to Senator John Burton, the liberal icon from San Francisco. Burton was first elected to the Assembly in 1964, went to Congress in 1974, then gave up his seat to enter drug rehab in 1982. After sitting out for a few years, he returned to the Assembly and later moved up to the Senate, where he locked up the votes to become president pro tem in 1998.

In 2004 the seat passed unceremoniously to Democrat Carole Migden, a former San Francisco supervisor who cooled her heels for two years on the Board of Equalization after she was termed out of the Assembly in 2002. Migden, who has waged high-profile gay rights battles at the city and state levels, will likely hold the district until the 2012 legislative session gavels to a close.

Burton, busy running the upper house, did not earn a reputation for dedicating himself to district issues in the North Bay. And while Migden did spend time campaigning there even though she ran essentially unopposed, her Marin and Sonoma constituents don't expect her to be much different from her predecessor.

San Francisco, which includes 55 percent of the district's population, is, of course, heavily Democratic, at 57 percent, but the party's registration is almost equally high in the northern regions. The district lines changed little in the 2001 reapportionment, but there was one notable tweaking in San Francisco, where Senate cartographers working under Burton's control stretched the line a few blocks east to Castro Street.

Gay rights backers were so livid when they saw the new district lines that they threatened to sue. They saw the adjustment as a Burton move designed to dilute the influence of the Castro District, the city's gay Mecca, to make it easier for his old pal Willie Brown to fight off a primary challenge should he run for the Senate seat after his mayoral term ended. Burton dismissed the charge, and the lines became law without a fight. Brown, who had been rumored to be thinking about swapping jobs with Burton, stayed out of the race and left Migden a clear path to becoming the Senate's second openly lesbian member.

As a legislator, Migden is a perpetual high—high intelligence, high energy, high motion, and, especially, high maintenance. When this native New Yorker was elected to the Assembly in 1996 (replacing Brown), she was named chairman of the most demanding committee in the house, Appropriations, her first week in office. From that perch, Migden held sway over every spending bill this side of the budget. She was given the same committee chairmanship in her first term in the Senate.

But she did not hold it long, and the experience prompted some in Democratic leadership circles to proclaim that no rookie would ever again chair such an important committee. That blanket prohibition perhaps is unfair to future rookies, for the problem lay with Migden, not her status.

Migden's downfall from Appropriations began in the frenzied final week of the 2005 legislative session when she cast a floor vote for one of her own bills. The difficulty with this seemingly obvious act was twofold: The floor upon which she cast the vote was the Assembly and, more significant, she cast it by pushing the "yes" button at the desk of a Republican who opposed her bill. This mind-boggling breech of protocol and common sense outraged Republicans and embarrassed Democrats from both houses, and Migden soon was relieved of her committee chairmanship.

The peripatetic lawmaker also ran into problems managing her staff. Yelling and fuming, it turns out, was not a good technique, and the Senate Rules Committee reportedly had to step in to help her cope with rapid turnover and revolt. In its survey of the legislature, for instance, *Capitol Weekly* named Migden the "toughest boss."

As though she did not have enough troubles internal to the legislature, Migden ran afoul of the Fair Political Practices Commission in December 2006. The political watchdog fined her nearly $100,000 for over 40 violations of state rules on reporting campaign contributions between 2002 and 2004. Migden claimed the violations were technical in nature and made by campaign volunteers.

Her troubles aside, Migden remains one of the legislature's most effective and hardest-working members. Democratic leadership recognized this fact by giving her another committee chairmanship for 2007—Labor and Industrial Relations. She has a keen political mind and remains a powerhouse fund raiser who generously shares her loot with other members. As such, she will remain a force in the legislature.

BIOGRAPHY: Born: New York City, NY, August 14, 1948. Home: San Francisco. Education: BA, Adelphi University; MA, CSU Sonoma. Military: None. Family: partner Cristina Arguedas. Religion: Jewish. Occupation: Legislator.

OFFICES: 2059 Capitol Building, Sacramento, CA 95814; Phone: (916) 651-4003; Fax: (916) 445-4722; email: senator.migden@sen.ca.gov. District: 455 Golden Gate Avenue, Suite 14800, San Francisco, CA 94102; Phone: (415) 557-1300; Fax: (916) 445-4722; Marin Civic Center, 3501 Civic Center Drive, Room 425, San Rafael, CA 94903; Phone: (415) 479-6612; Fax: (415) 479-1146.

COMMITTEES: Democratic Caucus Chair; Elections, Reapportionment and Constitutional Amendments; Labor and Industrial Relations (chair); Natural Resources and Water; Public Employment and Retirement; Revenue and Taxation.

ELECTED: 2004 **TERM LIMIT:** 2012

ELECTION HISTORY: San Francisco Board of Supervisors, 1990–1996; Assembly, 1996–2002.

2004 ELECTION: Migden (D) 68%
                 Felder (R) 26%
                 Rhodes (L) 3%
                 Grimes (PF) 3%

RATINGS:

AFL-CIO	CAI	CoC	CLCV	EQCA	CCS	CMTA	FARM	NARAL
96	88	25	100	100	95	0	17	80

JENNY OROPEZA (D)
28th Senate District

Counties: Los Angeles
Cities: Los Angeles, Carson, Torrance, Long Beach, Marina del Rey, El Segundo,
   Redondo Beach, Manhattan Beach, Lomita
Ethnicity: 46% White, 30% Latino, 8% Black, 16% Asian
Voter Registration: 47% D – 28% R – 21% DS
President 04: 62% Kerry, 32% Bush

Jenny Oropeza

A stretch of coastal Los Angeles County, the 28th takes in beach communities from Marina del Rey to Redondo Beach and includes Torrance, Lomita, and a snippet of Long Beach. Republicans don't usually fare well here, although former Insurance Commissioner Chuck Quackenbush managed a slight win in the old version of the district back in 1998. The new version wasn't changed much in 2001.

Until the late 1990s, the area was represented by Democrat Ralph Dills—an octogenarian who had served in the legislature off and on since Franklin Roosevelt sat in the White House. When finally termed out in 1998, Dills was replaced by Democrat Debra Bowen, and the change caused cultural whiplash among both constituents and the Capitol community. While Dills had been a good ol' boy who legislated and made deals in Sacramento watering holes, Bowen was a good-government maverick whose major claim to fame during her early years was a successful effort to put legislative information—including the text of bills—online. She was in the thick of campaign reform and efforts to protect the coast.

Bowen was termed out in 2006 and elected secretary of state, a job that fits perfectly with her interest in everything online. Her departure prompted a tense Democratic primary between Assemblywoman Jenny Oropeza and former Assemblyman George Nakano. Although Nakano and Oropeza agreed on most subjects, Nakano received substantial backing from the business community and moderates, who pumped nearly $500,000 into his campaign. Nakano also had the advantage of geography—most of his old Assembly district fit inside the 28th Senate District while only a small portion of Oropeza's district overlapped. Oropeza pushed her role in Assembly leadership; Nakano touted his coalition-building skills.

As with many Los Angeles–based districts, the contest was fought in mailboxes, and the tone was mostly negative. Nakano pushed the notion that his children attended public schools but presented the information in such a way as to indicate that Oropeza's did not. The reason Oropeza's children do not attend public schools is clear: She and her husband do not have children, a fact missing in the Nakano mailer. Nakano also touted the fact that he voted for three education-related bills, hinting broadly that Oropeza did not. Again, the votes in question were taken before Oropeza was elected to the legislature. Oropeza mailers provided misleading information about Nakano as well.

The result was close, but Oropeza prevailed 53 percent to 47 percent and easily dispatched her Republican opponent in November.

Oropeza came to the legislature in 2000 after serving on the Long Beach City Council, and her three terms in the Assembly included a run at the speakership. In 2003 Oropeza, then chair of the Assembly Budget Committee, was involved in a three-way slugfest to seize the job after soon-to-be-termed-out Speaker Herb Wesson announced that he would relinquish the post once another member had secured the 41 votes needed to replace him. Oropeza, Fabian Nunez, and Dario Frommer were the leading contenders—southern Californians and Latinos all. Nunez, the only freshman among them, had Wesson's blessing, which gave him an edge. Oropeza was handicapped by health problems that kept her away from the Capitol for long stretches. Frommer, the long shot, was first to fall by the wayside, leaving Oropeza and Nunez to battle for support inside the caucus in what turned out to be an interminably long and complicated effort. Eventually, Nunez put together the necessary votes but not before some confusion arose between him and Oropeza over who had committed to whom—confusion that caused bad feelings as well.

The speakership tussle was not Oropeza's toughest battle of 2004. During the summer, she was diagnosed with liver cancer, a malignancy that required surgery and extensive chemotherapy. Although cancer-free, she missed nearly a month of the legislative session.

Oropeza first ran for the seat in a crowded 2000 Democratic primary where her main opponents were a self-funded lawyer named Eddie Tabash and former pro football player Keith McDonald, son of area Congresswoman Juanita Millender-McDonald. Although the district had originally been drawn to enhance the chances of black representation, black candidates had not fared well. Prior to Oropeza, an Anglo, Democrat Dick Floyd, represented the district. In 2000, Oropeza replaced Floyd with backing from the legislative Latino Caucus and labor, as well as support from Bowen and former Los Angeles Mayor Richard Riordan.

Oropeza's legislative agenda has included bills to improve port security, give neighborhoods and cities more control over the sale of alcohol, help businesses owned by disabled veterans, and regulate the use of cameras designed to nab motorists who run red lights. In the Senate, she chairs the important Revenue and Taxation Committee.

BIOGRAPHY: Born: Montebello, September 27, 1957. Home: Long Beach. Education: BS, CSU Long Beach. Military: None. Family: husband Tom Mullins. Religion: Catholic. Occupation: Legislator.

OFFICES: 4074 Capitol Building, Sacramento, CA 95814; Phone: (916) 651-4028; Fax: (916) 323-6056; email: senator.oropeza@sen.ca.gov. District: 2512 Artesia Boulevard, Suite 200, Redondo Beach, CA 90278; Phone: (310) 318-6994; Fax: (310) 318-6733.

COMMITTEES: Appropriations; Elections, Reapportionment and Constitutional Amendments; Revenue and Taxation (chair); Transportation and Housing.

ELECTED: 2006 **TERM LIMIT:** 2014

ELECTION HISTORY: Long Beach City Council, 1994–2000; Assembly, 2000–2006.

2006 ELECTION: Oropeza (D) 62%
Liddle (R) 35%
DeBaets (L) 4%

RATINGS: AFL-CIO CAI CoC CLCV EQCA CCS CMTA FARM NARAL
96   92   13   100   100   94   0   20   40

ALEX PADILLA (D)
20th Senate District

Counties: Los Angeles
Cities: Los Angeles, San Fernando
Ethnicity: 24% White, 61% Latino, 6% Black, 9% Asian
Voter Registration: 53% D – 23% R – 20% DS
President 04: 65% Kerry, 33% Bush

Alex Padilla

The 20th District is a predominately Latino enclave in the San Fernando Valley that has grown more diverse and more Democratic over the past decade, even though it is not much changed from its pre-redistricting self.

From 1998 to 2006, the district was represented by Richard Alarcon, a former Los Angeles councilman who came to the legislature after a divisive primary campaign against former Assemblyman Richard Katz. Alarcon was termed out in 2006 and ran successfully for the Assembly. His place in the Senate was taken by Alex Padilla, the former president of the Los Angeles City Council who survived two crises in 2006—a tense primary against Assemblywoman Cindy Montanez and brain surgery.

The primary, which Padilla won 56 percent to 44 percent, was one of the most expensive and heated of 2006. Padilla and Montanez are both young (33 and 32, respectively), and both rose to positions of prominence early in life. Padilla won a seat on the Los Angeles Council at 26; Montanez was mayor of San Fernando before elected to the Assembly in 2004. In Sacramento, her close alliance with Speaker Fabian Nunez landed her the chairmanship of the Assembly's powerful Rules Committee.

Padilla, a former staff aide to Dianne Feinstein, was endorsed by both of California's U.S. senators and labor groups. Montanez had strong backing from Nunez and Alarcon, plus her own labor cadre, notably firefighters and nurses.

The campaign was laced with bad blood between the two, prompted in part by personality and by what Montanez considered a betrayal by Padilla, who had just been elected to another term on the city council. Montanez had worked for his re-election and felt blindsided when he announced for the Senate—more than a year after Montanez herself made public her plans to run for the same job. She carped throughout the campaign about Padilla's fickleness and grumped that he ought to finish his term on the council before seeking another job.

Although the result was close, Padilla was aided by broader name recognition, built during his half decade on the council and the fact that he served as its president. That gig gave Padilla wide publicity in the wake of the September 11, 2001, terrorist attacks because then-Mayor James Hahn was trapped in Washington, D.C., making Padilla "mayor for a day."

Padilla's introduction to Sacramento was delayed when, shortly after the election, he was diagnosed with a malformation in the outer lining of his brain. Although not life-threatening, the problem required surgery, which Padilla underwent in mid December 2006. He fully recovered by the time the legislature began activity in earnest in January.

Meanwhile, Padilla did not let his rookie status deter his dreams of glory. Before the ink had dried on his certificate of election, Padilla made it known that he wanted to succeed Oakland's Don Perata as Senate president pro tem—the top job in the upper house and one of the most powerful positions in Sacramento. It was said Padilla wasn't much interested in waiting for Perata to step down but was contemplating a coup. Although Padilla denied any revolt, he did not deny the goal, which had veteran legislators and staff grumbling about overly ambitious tyros. There seems little doubt that Padilla will reach for the post, but other Democrats—with far more experience than Padilla—also are interested.

For his part, Padilla's overt ambitions did not hinder his accumulation of significant committee assignments. Perata gave him seats on the Budget and Senate Rules committees—a ploy meant to keep him close, and under observation. But he also gave him a spot on the Education Committee.

BIOGRAPHY: Born: Panorama City, CA, March 22, 1973. Home: Pacoima. Education: BA, MIT. Military: None. Family: Single. Religion: Catholic. Occupation: Legislator.

OFFICES: 4035 Capitol Building, Sacramento, CA 95814; Phone: (916) 651-4020; Fax: (916) 445-6645; email: senator.padilla@sen.ca.gov. District: 6150 Van Nuys Boulevard, Suite 400, Van Nuys, CA 91401; Phone: (818) 901-5588; Fax: (818) 901-5562.

COMMITTEES: Budget and Fiscal Review; Budget Subcommittee 3 on Health and Human Services; Education; Energy, Utilities and Communications; Labor and Industrial Relations; Rules.

ELECTED: 2006 **TERM LIMIT:** 2014

ELECTION HISTORY: Los Angeles City Council, 1999-2006.

2006 ELECTION: Padilla (D) 75%
                   Brown (L) 25%

RATINGS: Newly elected

DON PERATA (D)
9th Senate District

Counties: Alameda, Contra Costa
Cities: Oakland, Berkeley, Alameda, Livermore, Castro Valley
Ethnicity: 39% White, 19% Latino, 25% Black, 17% Asian
Voter Registration: 59% D – 14% R – 21% DS
President 04: 81% Kerry, 18% Bush

Don Perata

Politics has given shape to the many jagged edges, dips, and turns that form the 9th Senate District. One of the most oddly shaped districts in the East Bay (spindly and crooked in the east, squared and robust in the west, with a skinny mid-section), the district begins with 32 miles of shoreline along the peninsula of Richmond, which juts between the San Francisco and San Pablo bays. From there, the district traces the waterfront down to the Berkeley Marina and meanders along I-580 through Oakland before it squeezes through Castro Valley on its way to the vineyards of Livermore—California's original wine country.

From the intersection of I-580 and Park Boulevard in Oakland, it is possible to see the district's two faces. To the northeast, mansion-like homes stand against a backdrop of the Oakland hills. To the southwest, low-income housing and below-market-rate apartments occupy the flatlands. Farther south along the city's shoreline is one of the district's most notable and most economically important features: the Port of Oakland, northern California's primary facility for global trade.

But the port is just one of the district's many standout features. The district is home to Sproul Plaza, birthplace of the Free Speech Movement in 1964 at the University of California, Berkeley, portions of a 2,700-year-old Ohlone Indian burial ground, and Don Perata—the East Bay's political machine and Senate president pro tempore.

Despite his lofty perch, Perata arrived at the top job with some cumbersome political baggage: He has been investigated by the FBI, which reportedly looked into allegations that Perata exchanged political favors for campaign contributions. In December 2004, federal agents raided the residence of Perata's son, Nick, who runs a political direct mail firm affiliated with his father. Numerous newspaper reports said the FBI was checking Perata's actions on behalf of a billboard company, card rooms, and Lily Hu, an Oakland lobbyist and former Perata staffer.

Perata won the pro tem spot in a nail-biting, neck-and-neck race with Democrat Martha Escutia of Whittier. He walked away with a close 13-11 victory after three rounds of votes by fellow Democratic senators. Perata's colleagues chose him over Escutia because of his reputation as a dealmaker and because he will remain in the Senate until 2008; Escutia was termed out in 2006.

Perata moved up from the Assembly to the Senate in a special election in 1998 after Barbara Lee was elected to Congress. He won his first full term in November

2000 with a landslide 84 percent. A native of Alameda, Perata has been winning elective offices in the East Bay for three decades. He served two terms on the Alameda County Board of Supervisors and spent 16 years teaching English, civics, and religion to high school students.

Passionate about education reform, mental health, and gun control, Perata has made some of his biggest legislative strides in these areas. He secured a $100 million bail-out loan to help save the Oakland Unified School District from bankruptcy, co-drafted a law that expanded insurance coverage for the mentally ill, and wrote the toughest assault weapons ban in the nation. Yet, for each achievement, Perata has a blemish to match. Although a heavyweight behind the push toward gun control, Perata himself has a concealed-weapon permit. In a deal that wasn't supposed to cost taxpayers a dime, Perata helped bring the National Football League's Raiders back to Oakland from Los Angeles in 1995. But the real cost to the public is now $200 million and growing. Not only that, but the deal with the Raiders meant that the Oakland Coliseum had to be renovated, and the cost to the stadium's other tenant—baseball's Oakland Athletics—was substantial. A once pristine stadium, with center field open to the Oakland Hills, was retooled and a huge, ugly grandstand looms where the views once were. Watching baseball in the Coliseum now is akin to sitting in the bottom of a wok, and the Athletics have announced plans to relocate to Fremont.

Perata has procured $27 million from the state for ovarian and prostate cancer research, but he also knows how to raise money for himself; sometimes questionably. On multiple occasions, Perata has failed to fully disclose his political donations. He and his political minions are not averse to political shenanigans either. In a heated 2006 state Senate race in Orange County, Perata's political operatives, including his chief political consultant, Sandy Polka, helped orchestrate and fund a write-in campaign on behalf of a second Republican—designed to siphon votes away from the ordained GOP candidate, Assemblywoman Lynn Daucher. She lost by a whisker to Democrat Lou Correa in District 34. Perata's operatives denied any involvement.

Perata is adept at legislative sleight-of-hand, his most significant example being the death of redistricting reform in the waning days of the 2006 session. A bill to take redistricting out of the legislature and vest it in an independent commission passed both houses but mysteriously died after the Assembly made technical amendments and then failed to transmit the bill back to the Senate for concurrence until after the Senate—at Perata's insistence—had adjourned. Each house blamed the other for the snafu.

Closer to home, Perata began the 2007 session with a rumored coup attempt at his front door, led by a senator with one day of legislative experience. Alex Padilla, the ambitious former president of the Los Angeles City Council, was said to arrive in Sacramento with visions of grandeur—fast-tracking to pro tem chief among them. Padilla, who became council president before his 30th birthday, did not quibble with allegations that he wanted the Senate's top job, but he assured Perata that he would not stage a coup. Perata, who is termed out in 2008, must set the stage for his departure as pro tem sometime during the next two years but has said he would like to retain the post for most of the two years remaining in his term.

As pro tem, he and Assembly Speaker Fabian Nunez give voice to Democratic ambitions on policy issues and work with Governor Arnold Schwarzenegger to help realize those ambitions. Their partnership with Schwarzenegger worked well in 2006, with an election looming in the background, and it produced, among other works of art, a $47 billion package of infrastructure bonds passed by voters in November 2006, an increase in the minimum wage, and a landmark bill to address global warming.

The governor promised to continue that spirit of cooperation in 2007, and Perata called him to task in December 2006 by outlining, among other things, an ambitious plan to provide health care coverage for all Californians. In a pre-emptive strike, Perata went public with Democratic plans before the governor could announce his own proposal.

BIOGRAPHY: Born: Alameda, April 30, 1945. Home: Oakland. Education: BA, St. Mary's College. Military: None. Family: Two children. Religion: Catholic. Occupation: Public School Teacher,

OFFICES: 205 Capitol Building, Sacramento, CA 95814; Phone: (916) 651-4009; Fax: (916) 327-1997; email: senator.perata@sen.ca.gov. District: 1515 Clay Street, Suite 2202, Oakland, CA 94612; Phone: (510) 286-1333; Fax: (510) 286-3885.

COMMITTEES: Senate President pro Tempore; Rules (chair).

ELECTED: 1998 **TERM LIMIT:** 2008

ELECTION HISTORY: Alameda County Board of Supervisors, 1986–1994; Assembly, 1996–1998.

1998 ELECTION: Perata (D) 77%
Wright (R) 16%
Feinland (PF) 7%

2000 ELECTION: Perata (D*) 84%
Marshall (R) 11%
Eyer (L) 5%

2004 ELECTION: Perata (D*) 77%
Deutsche (R) 17%
Von Pinnon (L) 2%
Condit (PF) 5%

RATINGS:	AFL-CIO	CAI	CoC	CLCV	EQCA	CCS	CMTA	FARM	NARAL
	86	92	25	87	100	90	10	17	100

MARK RIDLEY-THOMAS (D)
26th Senate District

Counties: Los Angeles
Cities: Los Angeles, Culver City,
Ethnicity: 22% White, 37% Latino, 30% Black, 12% Asian
Voter Registration: 64% D – 13% R – 19% DS
President 04: 82% Kerry, 17% Bush

Mark Ridley-Thomas

One of the most diverse in the state, this Senate district meanders all over central Los Angeles absorbing various communities. Latinos account for 37 percent of the population, blacks 30 percent, whites 22 percent, and Asians 12 percent, although Latinos account for only 15 percent of registered voters and Asians 6 percent.

This has always been an African American–dominated district, represented by now-U.S. Representative Dianne Watson from 1978 to 1998. Prior to redistricting, it was located in south and west Los Angeles, but as more Latinos moved into south L.A., these areas were dropped off to secure the election of a black senator. In their place, white areas to the north were added, including portions of Silver Lake, Los Feliz, Hollywood Hills, Hancock Park, Century City, Westwood, and Bel Air. The district is politically homogeneous and culturally diverse. Areas within the 26th are heavily Democratic, yet their residents rarely mix. Voters in South Los Angeles seldom set foot in West Los Angeles, and vice versa. Anchoring the district both before and after redistricting are Baldwin Hills and Ladera Heights, the center of Los Angeles's affluent African-American community, Crenshaw, which is run down but redeveloping, and historically Jewish, now ethnically diverse, Culver City.

Until 2007, the district was represented by Kevin Murray, scion of a political dynasty who once served in the Assembly alongside his father Willard Murray—the first father and son team in the legislature.

Murray was succeeded in 2007 by Mark Ridley-Thomas, who moved over from the Assembly without much of a challenge, either in the primary or general election. Ridley-Thomas came to the legislature in 2002 after winning a close primary election against Mike Davis, who has since been elected to the Assembly. Ridley-Thomas, an 11-year veteran of the Los Angeles City Council, entered that race as the walk-over favorite. But Davis had backing from two of the area's most powerful forces—U.S. Representative Maxine Waters and former basketball great Magic Johnson, who provided the resources and oomph to bring Davis within a whisker of an upset. Ridley-Thomas won, 49 percent to 43 percent, and then easily won the general election in a district where decline-to-state voters outnumber Republicans.

In Sacramento, Ridley-Thomas has proven himself to be effective and smart. A member of leadership, he chaired the Assembly Democratic Caucus. Some of his successful legislation includes renewing development in the Exposition and University Parks area, which are sites for a major football team. Ever since the Raiders returned to Oakland in the 1990s, America's second-largest city has been without an NFL team. The neighborhood already is home to the University of Southern California, the Shrine Auditorium, and the Los Angeles Memorial Coliseum (home of the 1984 Olympics).

Prior to serving on the Los Angeles City Council, Ridley-Thomas was executive director of the Southern Christian Leadership Conference, the local affiliate of the national civil and human rights organization founded by Martin Luther King, Jr.

BIOGRAPHY: Born: Los Angeles, November 6, 1954. Home: Leimert Park. Education: BA, MA, Immaculate Heart College; PhD, USC. Military: None. Family: wife Avis, two children. Religion: Christian. Occupation: Legislator.

OFFICES: 5050 Capitol Building, Sacramento, CA 95814; Phone: (916) 651-4026; Fax: (916) 445-8899; email: senator.ridley.thomas@sen.ca.gov. District: 600 Corporate Point, Suite 1020, Culver City, CA 90230; Phone: (310) 641-4391; Fax: (310) 641-4395.

COMMITTEES: Business, Professions and Economic Development (chair); Energy, Utilities and Communications; Health; Public Safety.

ELECTED: 2006 **TERM LIMIT:** 2014

ELECTION HISTORY: Los Angeles City Council, 1991–2002; Assembly, 2002–2006.

2006 ELECTION: Ridley-Thomas (D) 89%
Raymond (L) 11%

RATINGS:

AFL-CIO	CAI	CoC	CLCV	EQCA	CCS	CMTA	FARM	NARAL
100	96	19	89	100	100	0	10	100

GLORIA ROMERO (D)
24th Senate District

Counties: Los Angeles
Cities: West Covina, El Monte, Baldwin Park, Los Angeles, Rosemead
Ethnicity: 13% White, 65% Latino, 3% Black, 19% Asian
Voter Registration: 52% D – 24% R – 20% DS
President 04: 64% Kerry, 35% Bush

Gloria Romero

The 24th District has straddled I-10 for two decades, with Irwindale to the north and La Puente to the south, then proceeding through El Monte, Rosemead, and Los Angeles. It is heavily Latino but has a strong, concentrated Asian community in the western San Gabriel Valley.

Incumbent Gloria Romero, the Senate majority leader, came to the upper house in a special 2001 election to replace Democrat Hilda Solis, who vacated the seat after her election to Congress the previous November. In that election, she stomped an Assembly colleague, Marty Gallegos.

Romero has been part of leadership almost from her first days as a legislator. In the Assembly, where she served slightly more than one term, she was named majority whip in her freshman year. Her benefactor, Speaker Antonio Villaraigosa, gave her plum assignments on the Appropriations and Revenue and Taxation committees. In the Senate, newly installed President pro Tempore Don Perata named her majority leader in 2004. That made her the highest-ranking woman in the legislature and the first woman to hold the post. It is an odd ascension for someone who, although bright and hard working, is not considered a tenacious infighter or political schmoozer. Because of her position as majority leader, she was considered a potential successor to Perata, but Romero would have to be considered a long shot for reasons of personality and interest. A policy wonk rather than a political operative, she is notoriously hard on staff.

Romero first came to Sacramento in 1998, her road marked by a tough Democratic primary against Judy Chu, a Monterey Park councilwoman who had narrowly lost the 1996 primary to incumbent Diane Martinez. The contest pitted the district's Asian community against the rising tide of Latino voters. Romero won by 9 percent over Chu, thanks to strong backing from Villaraigosa, the legislature's Latino Caucus, and Los Angeles Mayor Richard Riordan. Chu won the district in 2002 after Romero moved to the Senate.

In the Senate, Romero has made prison reform her special crusade, taking on not only the Davis and Schwarzenegger administrations' handling of the vast system of incarceration, but tackling the influence of the California Correctional Peace Officers Association—one of the most powerful political players in California. In 2005 she authored a bill, signed by Governor Arnold Schwarzenegger, that reorganized the California Youth and Adult Correctional Agency. Among its most significant provisions is the elimination of legislative approval for appointment of wardens, making them accountable to the agency and not the legislature.

Romero's leadership position was threatened after the 2006 elections, not by a coup but by the independence that streaks her personality. In late December, she attended a press conference with the governor, who was discussing prison reform. It was rumored that she participated in the event in defiance of Senate leadership. That same day, Senate pro Tem Don Perata released his choice for committee chairmanships for 2007. Romero was supposed to be named head of the Public Safety Committee, but her name—and that of the committee—were conspicuously omitted from Perata's list.

Romero eventually secured her chairmanship, but her committee load was lighter overall. Conspicuous among the committees where she no longer served was the Budget and Fiscal Review panel.

BIOGRAPHY: Born: Barstow, July 10, 1955. Home: Los Angeles. Education: BA, CSU Long Beach; PhD, UC Riverside. Military: None. Family: One daughter. Religion: Catholic. Occupation: University professor.

OFFICES: 313 Capitol Building, Sacramento, CA 95814; Phone: (916) 651-4024; Fax: (916) 445-0485; email: senator.romero@sen.ca.gov. District: 149 South Mednik, Suite 202, Los Angeles, CA 90022; Phone: (323) 881-0100; Fax: (323) 881-0101.

COMMITTEES: Senate Majority Leader; Banking, Finance and Insurance; Education; Human Services; Public Safety (chair).

ELECTED: 2001 **TERM LIMIT:** 2010

ELECTION HISTORY: Los Angeles Community College Board of Trustees, 1995–1998; Los Angeles Elected Charter Reform Commission, 1997–1998; Assembly, 1998–2001.

2001 ELECTION: Romero (D) 53%
                   Gallegos (D) 27%

House (R) 15%
Swinney (L) 5%
2002 ELECTION: Romero (D*) 71%
House (R) 26%
Swinney (L) 2%
2006 ELECTION: Romero (D*) 74%
Carver (R) 26%
RATINGS:

AFL-CIO	CAI	CoC	CLCV	EQCA	CCS	CMTA	FARM	NARAL
96	96	25	96	93	100	0	17	100

GEORGE RUNNER (R)
17th Senate District

Counties: Los Angeles, San Bernardino, Ventura
Cities: Los Angeles, Lancaster, Palmdale, Santa Clarita, Apple Valley, Hesperia, Victorville
Ethnicity: 58% White, 27% Latino, 9% Black, 6% Asian
Voter Registration: 35% D – 44% R – 17% DS
President 04: 59% Bush, 40% Kerry

George Runner

From the desert to the sea, the 17th District reaches from the dry lakebeds north of Los Angeles to the coastal hills in Ventura County. Along the way, it picks up a bit of the northern Los Angeles sprawl and shoots east into San Bernardino County to take in Victorville, Apple Valley, and Hesperia. But the most significant feature of the newly constituted 17th District is the fact that it bears no resemblance whatsoever to its sprawling predecessor, which took up nearly half the California-Nevada border and included Inyo and Kern counties and the unpopulated east and northern portions of San Bernardino County. That district had been represented by the late Pete Knight, a Republican from Palmdale who died in 2004, just before the end of his second and final term.

Knight's replacement—elected from the new district—is Republican George Runner, who spent six years in the Assembly between 1996 and 2002 and then twiddled his thumbs on the outside for two years before moving to the upper house. Runner was the ordained choice to succeed Knight and had no Republican opposition in the March 2004 primary. Democrats are irrelevant here, so Runner coasted to victory in the fall. Once elected, he became half of the legislature's first husband-and-wife team. His spouse, Sharon Runner, serves in the Assembly, making the Runners something of a Sacramento power couple—if the word power can be applied to Republicans.

During his years in the Assembly, Runner was regarded as a conservatives' conservative: pro-gun, pro–education vouchers, and anti-abortion. Founder of an interdenominational private school, he took an active, if unsuccessful, role in efforts to kill the state's CLAS standardized assessment test for K-12 students. He made an unsuccessful run for minority leader in 1998, losing to Riverside's Rod Pacheco. Ironically, Democrats were rooting for Runner, even though he was considerably to the right of Pacheco. Democrats considered him a pragmatist who was, they said, absolutely true to his word and who had shown a willingness to work toward solutions rather than be a knee-jerk obstructionist. He was the Republicans' go-to guy on budget matters while in the Assembly, serving as vice chair of the Budget Committee. That led to a seat on the Budget and Fiscal Review Committee in the Senate. After the 2006 elections, he was named Republican Caucus chairman.

The Runners' biggest splash of late came not in the legislature but on the ballot where they sponsored Prop. 83—the so-called "Jessica's Law" named for a nine-year-old Florida girl killed by a convicted sex offender. The measure, which passed in November 2006, restricts where convicted offenders can live and requires that they wear a GPS monitoring device for life. Although the Runners protested, a court subsequently struck down provisions making the law retroactive. Runner put the measure on the ballot as an initiative after the legislature failed to pass a similar proposal.

Runner first dipped into politics in 1992 when he was elected to the Lancaster City Council. He was elected mayor three years later, which gave him some expertise and interest in local government issues. As founder and CEO of Desert Christian Schools, he has been involved in education, authoring bills on charter schools and a proposed constitutional amendment to reward teachers for performance rather than tenure.

BIOGRAPHY: Born: New York City, NY, March 25, 1952. Home: Lancaster. Education: BS, University of Redlands. Military: None. Family: wife Sharon, two children. Religion: Baptist. Occupation: Businessman/Educator.

OFFICES: 4066 Capitol Building, Sacramento, CA 95814; Phone: (916) 651-4017; Fax: (916) 445-4662; email: senator.runner@sen.ca.gov. District: 848 West Lancaster Boulevard, Suite 101, Lancaster, CA 93534; Phone: (661) 729-6232; Fax: (661) 729-1683; Victorville City Hall, 14343 Civic Drive, First Floor, Victorville, CA 92392; Phone: (760) 843-8414; Fax: (760) 843-8348; Santa Clarita City Hall, 23920 Valencia Boulevard, Suite 250, Santa Clarita, CA 91355; Phone: (661) 286-1471; Fax: (661) 286-2543.

COMMITTEES: Appropriations; Banking, Finance and Insurance (vice chair); Environmental Quality (vice chair); Revenue and Taxation.

ELECTED: 2004 **TERM LIMIT:** 2012

ELECTION HISTORY: Lancaster City Council, 1992–1996; Mayor, 1995; Assembly, 1996–2002.

2004 ELECTION: G.Runner (R) 60%
                Kraut (D) 36%
                Ballard (L) 4%

RATINGS:	AFL-CIO	CAI	CoC	CLCV	EQCA	CCS	CMTA	FARM	NARAL
	11	24	100	4	0	15	80	100	20

JACK SCOTT (D)
21st Senate District

Counties: Los Angeles
Cities: Los Angeles, Burbank, Glendale, Pasadena, San Gabriel, La Canada Flintridge, Temple City
Ethnicity: 49% White, 26% Latino, 7% Black, 18% Asian
Voter Registration: 46% D – 29% R – 21% DS
President 04: 63% Kerry, 35% Bush

Jack Scott

Democrats took this district away from Republicans during the 1990s, and mapmakers made sure the transition would stick when they redrew it in 2001. The 21st now reaches south into Los Angeles to pick up areas around the downtown warehouses, as well as stretches a finger west from Burbank along Burbank Boulevard and east into Temple City. Less than half the district is white.

Incumbent Democrat Jack Scott is nearing the end of his final term in the Senate and has reached the point in his political career where Republicans didn't bother to field an opponent in 2004. A native Texan, Scott still sports a southern drawl and has a genial disposition that makes him popular with colleagues from both parties.

Scott first arrived in the legislature in 1996 by knocking off nondescript Republican incumbent Bill Hoge. At the time, Scott was widely known in the area as president of Pasadena City College. Articulate and well versed in education issues, Scott had a compelling personal story, having lost an adult son in an accident involving a handgun. Republicans tried to paint Scott as a typical Democratic liberal, but he was too well known for the label to stick. In the end, he was the only challenger in the Assembly to unseat an incumbent, defeating Hoge by 9 percent. He won re-election in 1998 by an even greater margin.

When Democrat Adam Schiff decided to run for Congress in 2000, Scott sought to replace him, passing up his final term in the Assembly. He was opposed in the Democratic primary by Assembly colleague Scott Wildman. The contest matched Scott's money with Wildman's tenacity. Money won. By the end of the campaign, Scott had amassed $1.2 million, with heavy support from insurance, business, and law enforcement. Wildman had half of Scott's bankroll, with the bulk of his support coming from labor, including the hugely influential Los Angeles County Federation of Labor. Wildman hit Scott on his ties to the insurance industry, hinting that it was a major conflict for someone who chaired the Assembly Insurance Committee. The National Rifle Association came to Scott's aid with a ham-handed attempt to help his opponent. Scott prevailed by some 7,000 votes out of 100,000 cast in the Democratic primary. That fall, he defeated South Pasadena City Councilman Paul Zee, a Hong Kong–born Republican, in another expensive showdown.

As a legislator, Scott has focused on education and gun control—with occasional forays into insurance issues. In the Senate, he chairs the Education Committee, which oversees K-12 and higher education. He received his greatest notoriety in 2000 when the Assembly Insurance Committee, with Scott as chairman, held hearings on the scandals plaguing the Department of Insurance and its embattled commissioner, Republican Charles Quackenbush. Although other members of the committee, notably Democrats Darrell Steinberg and Fred Keeley, carried much of the investigative load, Scott's calm, even-handed demeanor defused the often-tense atmosphere. In some ways, the Quackenbush hearings were California's version of the 1973-74 congressional probe into the Watergate scandal, with Scott assuming the role of North Carolina Senator Sam Ervin. The hearings flattened Quackenbush's career, and he resigned in July 2000.

Scott is termed out of the Senate in 2008 but could seek one additional term in the Assembly. His Altadena home is in the 44th Assembly District, however, where a new incumbent, Democrat Anthony Portantino, was elected in 2006 and could serve until 2012. Scott could run for the Assembly seat should Portantino run for Scott's Senate district in 2008.

BIOGRAPHY: Born: Sweetwater, TX, August 24, 1933. Home: Altadena. Education: BA, Abilene Christian; Master of Divinity, Yale; PhD, Claremont. Military: None. Family: wife Lacreta, five children. Religion: Christian. Occupation: Teacher/Administrator.

OFFICES: 2082 Capitol Building, Sacramento, CA 95814; Phone: (916) 651-4021; Fax: (916) 324-7543; email: senator.scott@sen.ca.gov. District: 215 North Marengo Avenue, Suite 185, Pasadena, CA 91101; Phone: (626) 683-0282; Fax: (626) 793-5803.

COMMITTEES: Banking, Finance and Insurance; Budget and Fiscal Review; Budget Subcommittee 1 on Education (chair); Education (chair); Revenue and Taxation.

ELECTED: 2000 **TERM LIMIT:** 2008

ELECTION HISTORY: Assembly, 1996–2000.

2000 ELECTION: Scott (D) 59%
                  Zee (R) 38%
                  New (L) 4%

2004 ELECTION: Scott (D*) 78%
                  New (L) 22%

RATINGS:	AFL-CIO	CAI	CoC	CLCV	EQCA	CCS	CMTA	FARM	NARAL
	96	92	25	100	93	95	0	17	100

JOE SIMITIAN (D)
11th Senate District

Counties: San Mateo, Santa Clara, Santa Cruz
Cities: San Jose, Cupertino, Santa Cruz, Atherton, East Palo Alto, Menlo Park, Redwood City, San Carlos, Campbell, Los Altos, Palo Alto, Capitola
Ethnicity: 63% White, 17% Latino, 4% Black, 16% Asian
Voter Registration: 47% D – 26% R – 22% DS
President 04: 68% Kerry, 30% Bush

Joe Simitian

The 2001 redistricting seriously altered this district by moving it off most of the San Francisco Peninsula and extending it south through Santa Cruz. That had a dual effect: on one hand, it strengthened Democratic registration, giving Democrats a 20-point edge. On the other, it seriously screwed former Assembly Speaker pro Tem Fred Keeley, a termed-out legislator who had designs on running for the Senate but drew the short straw when new districts were parsed out. Keeley's home district had been the 15th, centered in Santa Cruz and Monterey counties. But that district was shattered, with a chunk of the Democrats—including his home—attached to the 11th District. The district's political base remained in the South Bay and Silicon Valley—foreign territory for Keeley.

The new 11th District is a hodgepodge including 18,000 acres of old-growth redwoods in California's first state park, miles of undeveloped coastline, and vast areas of open space separating several densely populated urban zones. Poor families rent small apartments in East Palo Alto, miles of tract homes fill San Jose's suburbs, and $2 million mansions are not uncommon in San Mateo County.

About a third of the voters in the 11th District live in San Jose with the rest spread out over Santa Clara, Santa Cruz, and San Mateo counties. Residents of Santa Clara County, home of the high-tech boom of the '80s and '90s, make up more than half the voters in this district and are influential in dictating political concerns, which tend to be socially progressive and economically conservative. This district is home to large numbers of Asians, Latinos, and Caucasians, as well as a significant population of African Americans.

Some residents of Santa Clara County can still remember walking through fragrant apple, pear, peach, and plum orchards in the spring; those orchards have been replaced by mile after mile of tract homes, small retail shopping centers, and parking lots. After World War II many GIs who had passed through the South Bay on their way to the Pacific put down roots in the loamy soil, attracted by cheap rents and abundant jobs. San Jose, a sleepy town of 50,000 in the 1950s, grew to a quarter of a million in 20 years. It is now the third-largest city in California and the tenth largest in the country with almost one million residents. Despite early aspirations to be the next Los

Angeles, San Jose now has a defined boundary and a growing desire to preserve its remaining open space.

The district has always been a bedroom community for other cities that had jobs, but as the South Bay transitioned from an agricultural and manufacturing base to computers, jobs opened up in San Jose. The coastal areas of San Mateo County are still largely bedroom communities for Silicon Valley, and about a third of the workers in Santa Cruz County commute over Highway 17 and what is known as "the hill."

The computer boom started here in the 1970s with Hewlett Packard. Soaring land costs have prompted companies to base production elsewhere, but many, like Apple, have kept their headquarters and research labs in Silicon Valley.

Twenty years ago this district was a Republican stronghold, but it has tended to be more Democratic with every election and is now firmly in the hands of Democrats. People here favor education and have raised taxes to improve schools. Lack of affordable housing, particularly in San Mateo County, has been a flash point for years.

The presidential election of 1992 had a domino effect on representatives of this region after Bill Clinton invited long-time Representative Norman Mineta to be his secretary of transportation; he served in the same capacity in President George Bush's cabinet before retiring in 2006. Then–State Senator Tom Campbell, a moderate Republican, replaced Mineta in Congress, and Democratic Assemblyman Bryon Sher of Palo Alto won the Senate district in a special election. Joe Simitan won the 2004 election to replace the term-limited Sher.

Simitian's decision to leave the Assembly a term early and run for Sher's seat was not universally popular among members of his caucus, for it created a vacancy in the 21st Assembly District. An expensive brawl ensued that cost Assembly Democrats a fortune. That was the race that featured Republican gazillionaire Steve Poizner, who spent $7 million of his own money and forced Democrats and their allies to open their wallets. Democrat Ira Ruskin's victory over Poizner tempered resentment aimed at Simitian but did not entirely eradicate it.

A former mayor of Palo Alto and Santa Clara County supervisor, Simitian was elected to the Assembly in 2000 and is popular, even though many voters, particularly those in Santa Cruz County, had never heard of him. During his first term in the Assembly, frustrated by lack of citizen participation in the legislative process, he began a yearly contest called "There Oughta Be a Law" where constituents are invited to submit legislative ideas. During the first year, Simitan picked three submissions out of 100 and each was signed into law.

The diversity and sheer physical size of this enormous district provide a serious challenge for Simitan. Representing more than 20 cities separated by so much open space, each with its own Chamber of Commerce and transportation agency and competing concerns, will be a labor-intensive job.

Simitian chaired the Human Resources Committee during his first two years in the Senate, moving over to head the Environmental Quality Committee in 2007. His bill package included attempts to regulate the environmental impact of cruise ships and efforts to force utility companies to include more renewables in their portfolio of energy sources. He is widely regarded as a tenacious and effective lawmaker, as evidenced by his strong showing in *Capitol Weekly*'s survey of the legislature's best and brightest.

BIOGRAPHY: Born: Hackensack, NJ, February 1, 1953. Home: Palo Alto. Education: BA, Colorado College; MA, Stanford; JD, MCP, UC Berkeley. Military: None. Family: wife Mary Hughes. Religion: Decline to state. Occupation: Legislator.

OFFICES: 4062 Capitol Building, Sacramento, CA 95814; Phone: (916) 651-4011; Fax: (916) 323-4529; email: senator.simitian@sen.ca.gov. District: 160 Town and Country Village, Palo Alto, CA 94301; Phone: (650) 688-6384; Fax: (650) 688-6370; 701 Ocean Street, Room 318A, Santa Cruz, CA 95060; Phone: (831) 425-0401; Fax: (831) 425-5124.

COMMITTEES: Budget and Fiscal Review; Budget Subcommittee 1 on Education; Business, Professions and Economic Development; Education; Energy, Utilities and Communications; Environmental Quality (chair); Transportation and Housing.

ELECTED: 2004 **TERM LIMIT:** 2012

ELECTION HISTORY: Palo Alto School Board, 1983–1991; Palo Alto City Council, 1992–1996; Santa Clara County Board of Supervisors, 1997-2000; Assembly, 2000-2006.

2004 ELECTION: Simitian (D) 67%
　　　　　　　　　Zellhoefer (R) 29%
　　　　　　　　　Rice (L) 4%

RATINGS:	AFL-CIO	CAI	CoC	CLCV	EQCA	CCS	CMTA	FARM	NARAL
	100	68	38	100	100	100	0	17	100

DARRELL STEINBERG (D)
6th Senate District

Counties: Sacramento
Cities: Sacramento, Citrus Heights
Ethnicity: 53% White, 18% Latino, 14% Black, 15% Asian
Voter Registration: 47% D – 29% R – 19% DS
President 04: 56% Kerry, 43% Bush

Darrell Steinberg

The 6th Senate District, surrounding downtown Sacramento and its northern suburbs, is solid Democratic territory. For years, it was the province of Democrat Leroy Greene, who was termed out in 1998. He was replaced by fellow Democrat Deborah Ortiz, who had served one term in the Assembly before moving to the Senate. Termed out in 2006, Ortiz ran for secretary of state but lost the Democratic primary to colleague Debra Bowen.

Unlike other open districts, where primary brawls dotted the landscape, Ortiz's replacement had been a foregone conclusion for several years. Democrat Darrell Steinberg had been termed out of the Assembly in 2004 and made very public his intention to succeed Ortiz in 2006. Although he drew a nominal primary opponent, no Democrat of consequence bothered to challenge Steinberg, and he waltzed through the primary and general elections.

The liberal Steinberg is a tour de force as a legislator—highly intelligent, ethical to a fault, and a creature of such hard work that he sometimes exasperates colleagues and staff. In the Assembly, he regularly scored at the top of *California Journal* rankings of the legislature's best and brightest. The *Journal* named him the legislature's "Rookie of the Year" in 2000 and "Assembly Member of the Year" in 2004. He earned these honors because he regularly was found in the middle of the state's thorniest issues and, at one time or another, chaired the Budget, Judiciary and Appropriations committees.

In 2004 he sponsored Proposition 63, the initiative that generates more than $1 billion a year for community mental-health programs. For years, Steinberg had tried to push a similar proposal through the legislature, only to have it stymied by Republican and Democratic governors alike. In his final year in the Assembly, he took it to the ballot, where voters passed it overwhelmingly in November.

During his two years out of the legislature, Steinberg practiced law and involved himself in efforts to build a new multi-purpose sports arena in downtown Sacramento. Hired by the Maloof family, owners of the Sacramento Kings professional basketball team, Steinberg brokered what he thought was a deal between the Kings and Sacramento officials to finance the arena with a quarter-cent increase in the county sales tax. The arrangement went before Sacramento County voters in November 2006 as Measures Q and R but blew up a few weeks before the election when the Maloofs publicly trashed it. An embarrassed Steinberg withdrew from the ensuing mess as both measures failed miserably at the polls.

Steinberg has ambitions for Senate leadership and has made no secret of his desire to succeed Oakland's Don Perata as President pro Tem when Perata, who is termed out in 2008, relinquishes the job. Steinberg had hoped to be named chair of the Appropriations Committee, but that job went to Democrat Tom Torlakson, also termed out in 2008. Instead, Steinberg was named chair of the Natural Resources and Water Committee, which will give him a significant role in allocating infrastructure bond money earmarked for flood protection. He also landed spots on the budget and judiciary committees.

At the same time, he must begin—quietly—to campaign for pro tem, for other ambitious Democrats already are staking out territory. Steinberg almost certainly will be among the top contenders and has as an advantage not only his reputation as a lawmaker but the fact that he comes from Northern California. With the Assembly speakership firmly in the hands of a southern Californian, it is said that the pro-tem ought to remain in the north. That puts Steinberg on the very short list of candidates, given that his fiercest competition likely will come from Alex Padilla, a rookie lawmaker from Los Angeles.

BIOGRAPHY: Born: San Francisco, October 15, 1959. Home: Sacramento. Education: BA, UCLA; JD, UC Davis. Military: None. Family: wife Julie, two children. Religion: Jewish. Occupation: Attorney.

OFFICES: 4035 Capitol Building, Sacramento, CA 95814; Phone: (916) 651-4006; Fax: (916) 323-2263; email: senator.steinberg@sen.ca.gov. District: 1020 N Street, Suite 576, Sacramento, CA 95814; Phone: (916) 651-1529; Fax: (916) 327-8754.

COMMITTEES: Budget and Fiscal Review; Budget Subcommittee 2 on Resources, Environmental Protection and Energy; Environmental Quality; Judiciary; Natural Resources and Water (chair).

ELECTED: 2006 **TERM LIMIT:** 2014

ELECTION HISTORY: Sacramento City Council, 1992–1998; Assembly, 1998–2004.

2006 ELECTION: Steinberg (D) 59%
                   Green (R) 36%
                   Garberoglio (L) 2%
                   Weber (PF) 3%

RATINGS: Newly elected.

TOM TORLAKSON (D)
7th Senate District

Counties: Contra Costa
Cities: Concord, Antioch, Walnut Creek, Pittsburg, Martinez
Ethnicity: 65% White, 15% Latino, 7% Black, 13% Asian
Voter Registration: 47% D – 31% R – 18% DS
President 04: 61% Kerry, 38% Bush

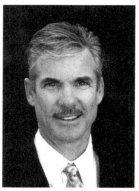

Tom Torlakson

The sun-kissed terrain of eastern Contra Costa County forms the heart of the 7th District. With dramatic views of Mount Diablo, cities like Walnut Creek, Concord, and Alamo comprise affluent, highly educated, largely white voters who repeatedly demonstrate a commitment to public schools by raising thousands of dollars to supplement state and local support.

The district borders the Carquinez Strait and San Francisco Bay to include Martinez, the county seat and birthplace of the Martini, and the northern stretches of Richmond, a city of refineries, railroads, and perpetual financial and political turmoil. At the eastern edge are the fast-growing communities of Brentwood and Oakley, whose residents struggle each day along Highway 4.

The chief issues on voters' minds in this largely affluent district are transportation, housing, education, and urban growth. In November 2004 voters passed a half-cent transportation sales tax that would expand highways and transit systems. One of the district's sore points has been the Caldecott Tunnel, a three-bore system on Highway 24 that carries thousands of commuters from the bedroom communities of Contra

Costa County to jobs in the Easy Bay and San Francisco. The sales tax will help pay for a long-planned fourth bore that will improve traffic flow considerably.

Given the importance of cars, freeways, and real estate in the 7th District, it seems fitting that the district is represented by Tom Torlakson, who, as chair of the Senate Transportation and Housing Committee, reorganized the panel to include both subjects.

In 2000 Torlakson unseated Republican incumbent Richard Rainey in one of the state's most hotly contested races of that election season. He spent a then-record $4 million in the campaign and beat Rainey, the former county sheriff, 55 percent to 42 percent. Torlakson's win was widely attributed to his high level of spending, tireless campaigning, and pro-gun-control stance.

Torlakson is a social and fiscal liberal, championing issues involving abortion and gay rights, labor, and the environment, and rarely advocating government cutbacks. His ties to labor help him in Richmond and Martinez with refinery and port workers. A high school science teacher and cross-country and fitness coach for over 25 years, Torlakson is an avid promoter of physical fitness and healthier living for children and adults.

His legislative experience includes two years on the Antioch City Council, 16 years on the Contra Costa County Board of Supervisors, and four years in the state Assembly. His chief support and source of campaign money comes from affluent central Contra Costa towns like Concord and Pleasant Hill.

Redistricting in 2001 strengthened the Democratic hold on the district, and Torlakson ran unopposed in 2004. His district lost a few cities in Alameda County and gained a few in Contra Costa, including El Cerrito, Kensington, and parts of El Sobrante, adding about 35,000 more residents and enhancing the Democratic registration.

Torlakson has carried legislation to ease traffic congestion and increase public transportation. His policies in favor of housing construction, affordable homes, and highway and transportation expansion have been motivated by the desire to alleviate the long commute times faced by many of his constituents, including those close to his hometown of Antioch.

Torlakson favors incentives for communities that build affordable housing alongside growing business districts and withholding transportation dollars from communities that don't increase housing along with jobs. He says the state should spearhead such efforts, a move that has put him at odds with some local legislators.

Termed out in 2008, Torlakson plans to run for his old Assembly seat, where he has a term remaining. That gig will take him through 2010 when he has expressed a desire to run statewide for superintendent of public instruction. But to accomplish this goal, he had to help orchestrate a game of musical districts with an ally—former Contra Costa County Supervisor Mark DeSaulnier. DeSaulnier won an open Assembly seat in 2006, along the way defeating the wife of Democrat Joe Canciamilla, the termed-out incumbent in that district. DeSaulnier's victory was essential if Torlakson is to run for the Assembly in 2008; had Laura Canciamilla won, Torlakson would have had to take her on. DeSaulnier, on the other hand, plans to vacate the Assembly in 2008 and seek Torlakson's Senate seat against, in all likelihood, Joe Canciamilla.

Meanwhile, Torlakson landed a plum assignment for his final two years in the Senate: chair of the Appropriations Committee. That will allow him to build a tidy nest egg to run statewide.

BIOGRAPHY: Born: San Francisco, July 19, 1949. Home: Antioch. Education: BA, MA, Life Secondary Teaching Credential, UC Berkeley. Military: Merchant Marine. Family: wife Diana, two children. Religion: Catholic. Occupation: Educator.

OFFICES: 5050 Capitol Building, Sacramento, CA 95814; Phone: (916) 651-4007; Fax: (916) 445-2527; email: senator.torlakson@sen.ca.gov. District: 2801 Concord Boulevard, Concord, CA 94519; Phone: (925) 602-6593; Fax: (925) 602-6598; 111 Civic Drive, Hercules, CA 94547; (800) 859-9900; 420 West 3rd Street, Antioch, CA 94509; Phone: (925) 754-1461; Fax: (925) 778-5174.

COMMITTEES: Appropriations (chair); Education; Transportation and Housing.
ELECTED: 2000 **TERM LIMIT:** 2008
ELECTION HISTORY: Assembly, 1996-2000.
2000 ELECTION: Torlakson (D) 55%
                Rainey (R*) 43%
                Billings (NL) 3%
2004 ELECTION: Torlakson (D*) 100%

RATINGS:	AFL-CIO	CAI	CoC	CLCV	EQCA	CCS	CMTA	FARM	NARAL
	96	96	20	100	100	95	0	17	100

ED VINCENT (D)
25th Senate District

Counties: Los Angeles
Cities: Los Angeles, Long Beach, Compton, Inglewood, Gardena, Lawndale, Rolling Hills Estates, Rancho Palos Verdes, Rolling Hills
Ethnicity: 17% White, 41% Latino, 33% Black, 9% Asian
Voter Registration: 59% D – 22% R – 16% DS
President 04: 64% Kerry, 35% Bush

A close look at a map of the 25th District reveals the ghost of the previous district lurking around Hawthorne, Inglewood, and Gardena. Lynwood and Paramount are gone, replaced by a strand of territory bracketing I-710 to Long Beach. From there, the district swoops west along the harbor and coast to snare wealthy Rancho Palos Verdes, Rolling Hills, and the "estates" that accompany each. The artwork required to make this district could be hung in a gallery, representing as it does a backwards "C." The demographics, too, are special, lumping coastal wealth with black inner-city voters who dominate district politics.

Incumbent Ed Vincent spent two terms in the Assembly before winning the Senate seat vacated by termed-out Democrat Teresa Hughes. A former All America–football player at the University of Iowa during the 1950s, Vincent first won a seat in the As-

Ed Vincent

sembly in a heated 1996 Democratic primary that featured the area's most successful political machines, U.S. Representative Maxine Waters versus former Congressman, state Senator, and Lieutenant Governor Mervyn Dymally. Waters backed Vincent, then the mayor of Inglewood, while Dymally forces, with behind-the-scenes help from Latinos in the legislature, backed Mervyn's son, Mark. Vincent easily won the primary and general elections, serving four years before leaving one term early for the Senate.

To reach the Senate, Vincent took on a termed-out Democratic colleague, the irrepressible Dick Floyd, in the 2000 primary. Floyd had several notable disadvantages. First, he is white, and the district, both the old and new versions, is a stronghold for black politicians. Second, Floyd didn't live in the district until he decided to run for the Senate, when he moved into Inglewood. Still, Floyd had early backing from some labor organizations, although the service workers' union eventually weighed in for Vincent. His SEIU endorsement prompted the powerful Los Angeles Federation of Labor to take a pass on the race despite the veteran Floyd's long connection to labor. Latinos, too, weighed in for Vincent, who trounced Floyd with 70 percent of the primary vote.

As a legislator in the Senate and Assembly, Vincent has made a specialty of horseracing legislation and chaired select committees on the horseracing industry in both houses. He missed a good portion of the 2003-2004 legislative session due to his wife's illness. Termed out in 2008, he is eligible for one more term in the Assembly. When he departs, Vincent will not leave much of a legislative legacy despite a dozen years in Sacramento. In 2007, for instance, he has the lightest work load in the legislature—one committee, Government Organization. Prior to his political career, Vincent briefly played football with the Los Angeles Rams and spent more than 35 years as a Los Angeles county probation officer.

BIOGRAPHY: Born: Steubenville, OH, June 23, 1934. Home: Inglewood. Education: BA, CSU Los Angeles. Military: U.S. Army. Family: wife Marilyn, two daughters, three grandchildren. Religion: Christian. Occupation: Legislator

OFFICES: 5052 Capitol Building, Sacramento, CA 95814; Phone: (916) 651-4025; Fax: (916) 445-3712; email: senator.vincent@sen.ca.gov. District: 1 Manchester Boulevard, Suite, 600, Inglewood, CA 90301; Phone: (310) 412-0393; Fax: (310) 412-0996.

COMMITTEES: Governmental Organization.

ELECTED: 2000 **TERM LIMIT:** 2008

ELECTION HISTORY: Assembly, 1996–2000.

2000 ELECTION: Vincent (D) 82%
                McClain (R) 18%

2004 ELECTION: Vincent (D*) 73%
                Spencer (R) 24%
                Ogden (L) 3%

RATINGS: AFL-CIO CAI CoC CLCV EQCA CCS CMTA FARM NARAL
              100   92   25   100   100   100   0   17   40

PAT WIGGINS (D)
2nd Senate District

Counties: Humboldt, Lake, Mendocino, Napa, Solano, Sonoma
Cities: Vallejo, Santa Rosa, Arcata, Ukiah, Napa, Solano, Clearlake, Sebastapol, St. Helena
Ethnicity: 73% White, 16% Latino, 5% Black, 7% Asian
Voter Registration: 48% D – 27% R – 18% DS
President 04: 63% Kerry, 35% Bush

Pat Wiggins

The 2nd District extends along the Pacific coast, touching San Francisco Bay at Vallejo and skimming north to the border between Humboldt and Del Norte counties. Del Norte had been included in the district prior to 2001, but mapmakers instead attached it to a revamped 4th District. Removal of Del Norte excised the state's most infamous prison at Pelican Bay near Crescent City.

Historically, the 2nd District has been a venue for battles between timber companies and environmentalists over logging—the most notable of which occurred over the Headwaters Forest, one of the last remaining stands of old-growth redwoods. It is legendary for its unusual environmental activism, such as tree-sittings by the likes of Julia Butterfly Hill, who lived in a redwood tree for 738 days in 1998 and 1999. The timber industry, once an economic anchor, is fast disappearing, replaced by tourists who frequent the quaint bed-and-breakfast inns that dot the Mendocino and Humboldt County coast, attracting hikers, campers, and whale watchers. The southern half of the district includes some of the state's premier wine-growing regions in Sonoma and Napa counties. The district's largest cash crop, however, is marijuana, which is grown in abundance in some of the more remote climes of Humboldt and Mendocino counties and provides another kind of battleground—between growers, poachers, and law-enforcement officials. The district is home to one of the state's more entertaining newspapers—the weekly *Arcata Eye*, with its eclectic and unusual police log.

A generation ago, the north coast voted Republican—a dynamic that morphed with changing fortunes in the timber industry and the arrival of counterculture refugees from San Francisco and Berkeley during the late 1960s and early 1970s. By the onset of the 21st century, the 2nd District had become a safe and comfortable home for Democrats, with the last real rumble occurring in 1998, when Democrat Wes Chesbro defeated the heir to the Jordan winery fortune, Republican John Jordan. Chesbro won despite Jordan's deep pockets, and the district has been safe ever since. Newly elected incumbent Pat Wiggins, a former Assembly member, took two-thirds of the vote in 2006 to succeed the termed-out Chesbro.

Wiggins, who was born with a congenital hearing problem and wears a special headset on the floor, surprisingly drew no opposition in the Democratic primary for an open seat as potential contenders, such as Assemblywoman Patti Berg and former Assemblywoman Valerie Brown, opted not to challenge Wiggins.

In the Assembly, she focused on land-use and growth issues, founding the Smart Growth Caucus in 2000. In the Senate, she chairs the Public Employee and Retirement Committee where she will be at the center of raging debates over the potential impact of retirement benefits owed to public employees by local governments. Maneuvering through that thicket will require high-wire balancing, for which Wiggins might be ideally suited. Her father was a movie stunt man and her mother one of the first women to parachute from an airplane.

BIOGRAPHY: Born: Pasadena, April 19, 1940. Home: Santa Rosa. Education: BA, UCLA. Military: None. Family: husband Guy Connor, two stepsons, three grandchildren. Religion: Jewish. Occupation: Legislator.

OFFICES: 4081 Capitol Building, Sacramento, CA 95814; Phone: (916) 651-4002; Fax: (916) 323-6958; email: senator.wiggins@sen.ca.gov. District: 710 E Street, Suite 150, Eureka, CA 95501; Phone: (707) 445-6508; Fax: (707) 445-6511; 1040 Main Street, Suite 205, Napa, CA 94559; Phone: (707) 224-1990; Fax: (707) 224-1992; 50 D Street, Suite 120A, Santa Rosa, CA 95404; Phone: (707) 576-2771; Fax: (707) 576-2773; P.O. Box 785, Ukiah, CA 95482; Phone: (707) 468-8914; Fax: (707) 468-8931; 444 Georgia Street, Vallejo, CA 94590; Phone: (707) 648-5312.

COMMITTEES: Banking, Finance and Insurance; Energy, Utilities and Communications; Government Organization; Public Employment and Retirement (chair); Veterans Affairs.

ELECTED: 2006 **TERM LIMIT:** 2014

ELECTION HISTORY: Santa Rosa City Council, 1994–1998; Assembly, 1998-2004.

2006 ELECTION: Wiggins (D) 66%
　　　　　　　　Wiesner (R) 34%

RATINGS: Newly elected.

MARK WYLAND (R)
38th Senate District

Counties: San Diego, Orange
Cities: Oceanside, Escondido, San Clemente, Encinitas, Carlsbad, San Marcos, Solana Beach, Rancho Santa Fe, Vista, San Juan Capistrano.
Ethnicity: 63% White, 26% Latino, 4% Black, 7% Asian
Voter Registration: 28% D – 47% R – 21% DS
President 04: 59% Bush, 40% Kerry

Mark Wyland

If it wasn't for the Camp Pendleton Marine Corps Base, the Los Angeles and San Diego metropolitan areas may just blur into one. But the base—situated on prime real estate along the Southern California coast—creates a break between the two metropolitan areas and provides an only-in-southern-California beachfront view for drivers along I-5.

As coastal southern California crumbles to Democrats, this district and coastal Orange County to the north remain solidly Republican, a unique area where conservatism still goes hand-in-hand with California coastal communities. North of Camp Pendleton the two Orange County cities of San Clemente and San Juan Capistrano provide 10 percent of the district's population. The rest lies south of Camp Pendleton in a swath of northern San Diego County communities. Prior to redistricting, a larger portion of the district was located in Orange County, but the loss of these areas all but ensures that the senator will be from San Diego County. The city of Del Mar was lopped off in the southern portion of the district, replaced with additional inland San Diego County communities that tend to be more conservative.

The coastal portion of the district—from both Orange and San Diego counties—is affluent, while inland communities such as Vista, San Marcos, and Escondido tend to be middle class. Oceanside, with its prime beachfront, bears a burden as the stomping ground for marines from Camp Pendleton but is trying to take advantage of its location to raise its profile and economy.

Republican Bill Morrow was termed out in 2006 and replaced by Mark Wyland, another conservative Republican who came out of the Assembly. Like Morrow, Wyland gained a rare Republican committee chairmanship—in his case, the same committee chaired by Morrow, Veterans Affairs.

Wyland, a Fulbright scholar born and raised in Escondido, was elected to the 74th Assembly District in 2000, replacing Carlsbad conservative Howard Kaloogian, who later went on to play a limited role in the 2003 recall effort against Gray Davis. Wyland served on the Escondido Unified School District board and is a trustee of Pomona College—his alma mater. Wyland, who co-owns the family business that his grandfather founded two generations ago, easily won election in 2002 and 2004 then cleared the field for his Senate run in 2006. It was a curious turn of events, given the open district, because Wyland could have had serious competition from the likes of Assemblyman George Plescia from the 75th District. At the time, Plescia was Assembly Republican floor leader. He was dumped from that post after the 2006 elections and may have regretted not taking on Wyland.

In the Senate, Wyland has one of the largest committee loads of any member. He is one of two Republicans to chair a committee; in his case, Veterans Affairs. But he also serves on five other panels, including the budget committee and as vice chairman of the Education Committee. Finally, he has a seat on the always-lucrative Government Organization Committee, which is a font for fund raising and has jurisdiction over such special interests as alcohol, tobacco, and horse racing.

BIOGRAPHY: Born: San Diego, October 27, 1946. Home: Del Mar. Education: BA, Pomona College; MA, Columbia; Fulbright Scholar. Military: None. Family: one daughter. Religion: Protestant. Occupation: Small Business Owner.

OFFICES: 4066 Capitol Building, Sacramento, CA 95814; Phone: (916) 651-4038; Fax: (916) 445-7382; email: senator.wyland@sen.ca.gov. District: 2755 Jefferson Street, Suite 101, Carlsbad, CA 92008; Phone (760) 434-7930; Fax: (760) 434-8223; 27126-A Paseo Espada, Suite 1621, San Juan Capistrano, CA 92675; Phone: (949) 489-9838; Fax: (949) 489-8354.

COMMITTEES: Budget and Fiscal Review; Budget Subcommittee 2 on Resources, Environmental Protection and Energy; Education (vice chair); Government Organization; Health; Labor and Industrial Relations; Veterans Affairs (chair).

ELECTED: 2006 **TERM LIMIT:** 2014

ELECTION HISTORY: Escondido Union School Board, 1998–2000; Assembly, 2000–2006.

2006 ELECTION: Wyland (R) 74%
Klea (L) 26%

RATINGS:	AFL-CIO	CAI	CoC	CLCV	EQCA	CCS	CMTA	FARM	NARAL
	7	44	94	7	0	15	90	100	20

LELAND YEE (D)
8th Senate District

Counties: San Francisco, San Mateo
Cities: San Francisco, Burlingame, Daly City, South San Francisco, Pacifica
Ethnicity: 45% White, 16% Latino, 4% Black, 35% Asian
Voter Registration: 51% D – 18% R – 26% DS
President 04: 74% Kerry, 25% Bush

Leland Yee

Meandering through the San Francisco peninsula and dividing the predominantly gay Castro District in two, the northwestern boundary of the 8th District is a work of political artistry. This district includes much of the half of San Francisco west of Interstate 280, a busy artery that becomes its centerline as the district lines widen to encompass the entire South Bay until Foster City just south of the San Mateo Bridge. Farther south the district narrows again, including only the central swath of the peninsula, leaving Palo Alto and unincorporated San Mateo County to the neighboring 11th District.

Reshaped in 2001 to include more of liberal San Francisco to balance out acquisition of affluent, Republican, central South Bay, the district remains decidedly progressive, although less so than the 3rd District, its eastern neighbor that represents the remainder of San Francisco.

For 12 years, the district was represented by Quentin Kopp, a former San Francisco supervisor with a powerful vocabulary, who parlayed his independent status to become chairman of the Transportation Committee and was later appointed to the Superior Court bench in San Mateo County by Governor Pete Wilson. The task of representing industrial, working-class South San Francisco, the horsy community of well-to-do Woodside, and incomes in-between then fell to one of the legislature's most tenacious and focused lawmakers, Democrat Jackie Speier.

Never one to shrink from political battle, Speier's mettle has hardened through more personal misfortune than seems possible. In 1978 she accompanied her boss, U.S. Representative Leo Ryan, to Guyana for a fact-finding mission into the activities of cult leader Jim Jones. Jones's gunmen killed Ryan and left Speier for dead on a landing strip in Jonestown. She survived, and ten operations later some bullets remain inside her. After becoming the first legislator to give birth while in office, she suffered several miscarriages and lost her husband to a negligent driver while she was pregnant with her second child. That life experience gave Speier the kind of steel that her successor, former Assemblyman Leland Yee, likely won't match.

Yee comes to the Senate after a tough primary election against San Mateo County Supervisor Mike Nevin and former Assemblyman Lou Papan. Papan, now 77, was a legend in the Assembly back in the 1980s when San Franciscan Willie Brown, Jr., ruled the place as speaker, serving as Brown's enforcer while chair of the Rules Committee. Many thought he got into the race as a spoiler whose candidacy was designed to ruin Nevin's chances. Four years ago, when Papan was termed out of his second go-around as a legislator, he tried to pass the baton to his daughter, Gina. But she lost the primary to Gene Mullin, the mayor of South San Francisco. During that campaign, Nevin endorsed Mullin, and Papan sought revenge.

Whether that mattered or not, the real campaign was between Yee and Nevin, and it was not for the faint of heart. Yee spent nearly $1 million, Nevin slightly less, and the main issue was whether the opponent belonged in prison rather than the legislature. Yee, a former member of the San Francisco Board of Supervisors, had the bigger electoral base and greater name recognition—as well as the biggest bank account. He won with 50 percent of the vote, some 14 percent ahead of Nevin.

In the Assembly, Yee ascended to leadership as assistant speaker pro tempore during his first term. "Assistant" was removed in 2004 when he became speaker pro tem, a job that Yee's Web site billed as the "number two position" in the Assembly. Technically, it is, but the post is more ceremonial than powerful, providing its occupant with visibility rather than clout. The speaker pro tem usually runs Assembly floor sessions, which earns Yee air time on the California Channel if not much sway inside the Democratic caucus.

Yee first won the seat in the 2002 Democratic primary, defeating San Francisco School Board member Dan Kelly. Yee, then a member of the Board of Supervisors, was considered the moderate. Kelly had backing from the teachers' union and the city's liberal establishment, including Board of Supervisors President Tom Ammiano. Yee built up a huge campaign treasury that, coupled with his Asian pedigree and years of service on the board, carried him to a comfortable victory over Kelly. The general election was a formality. He was not required to exert much effort on behalf of his

2004 re-election, although he continued to raise copious amounts of campaign cash—more than $300,000 in 2004.

Once in Sacramento, Yee focused on mental health as befitting someone with a doctorate in child psychology. He led a crusade against violent video games, culminating in legislation, signed by Governor Arnold Schwarzenegger in 2004, that requires retailers to display information about game-rating systems.

BIOGRAPHY: Born: China, November 20,1948. Home: San Francisco. Education: BA, UC Berkeley; MA, CSU San Francisco; PhD, University of Hawaii. Military: None. Family: wife Maxine, four children. Religion: Decline to state. Occupation: Educator, Child Psychologist.

OFFICES: 4048 Capitol Building, Sacramento, CA 95814; Phone: (916) 651-4008; Fax: (916) 327-2186; email: senator.yee@sen.ca.gov. District: 400 South El Camino Real, Suite 630, San Mateo, CA 94402; Phone: (650) 340-8840; Fax: (650) 340-1661; 455 Golden Gate Avenue, Suite 14200, San Francisco, CA 94102; Phone: (415) 557-7857; Fax: (415) 557-7864.

COMMITTEES: Appropriations; Business, Professions and Economic Development; Government Organization; Human Services.

ELECTED: 2006 **TERM LIMIT:** 2014

ELECTION HISTORY: San Francisco Board of Education, 1988–1996; San Francisco Board of Supervisors, 1996–2002; Assembly, 2000-2006.

2006 ELECTION: Yee (D) 78%
                 Skipakevich (R) 22%

RATINGS:

AFL-CIO	CAI	CoC	CLCV	EQCA	CCS	CMTA	FARM	NARAL
100	96	24	86	100	100	10	30	100

Assembly Districts

See Bay Area Map

See Los Angeles Area Map

Bay Area Assembly Districts

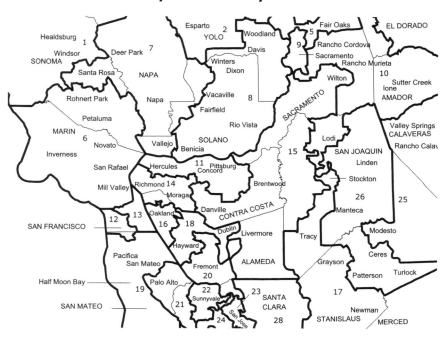

Los Angeles Assembly Districts

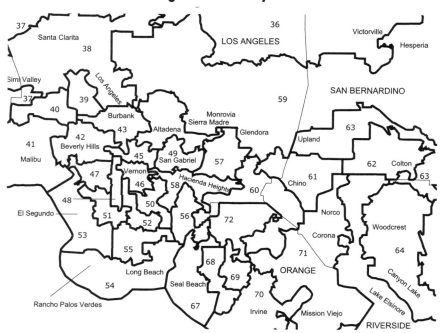

Assembly Members and District Numbers

1	Patty Berg D-Eureka	32	Jean Fuller R-Bakersfield
2	Doug LaMalfa R-Richvale	33	Sam Blakeslee R-San Luis Obispo
3	Rick Keene R-Chico	34	Bill Maze R-Visalia
4	Ted Gaines R-Roseville	35	Pedro Nava D-Santa Barbara
5	Roger Niello R-Fair Oaks	36	Sharon Runner R-Lancaster
6	Jared Huffman D-San Rafael	37	Audra Strickland R-Moorpark
7	Noreen Evans D-Santa Rosa	38	Cameron Smyth R-Santa Clarita
8	Lois Wolk D-Davis	39	Richard Alarcon D-Sun Valley
9	Dave Jones D-Sacramento	40	Lloyd Levine D-San Fernando Valley
10	Alan Nakanishi R-Lodi	41	Julia Brownley D-Santa Monica
11	Mark DeSaulnier D-Livermore	42	Mike Feuer D-Los Angeles
12	Fiona Ma D-San Francisco	43	Paul Krekorian D-Burbank
13	Mark Leno D-San Francisco	44	Anthony Portantino D-La Canada
14	Loni Hancock D-Berkeley	45	Kevin DeLeón D-Los Angeles
15	Guy Houston R-Livermore	46	Fabian Nunez D-Los Angeles
16	Sandre Swanson D-Oakland	47	Karen Bass D-Baldwin Vista
17	Cathleen Galgiani D-Elk Grove	48	Mike Davis D-Los Angeles
18	Mary Hayashi D-Newark	49	Mike Eng D-Monterey Park
19	Gene Mullin D-South San Francisco	50	Hector De La Torre D-South Gate
20	Alberto Torrico D-Newark	51	Curren Price D-Inglewood
21	Ira Ruskin D-Redwood City	52	Mervyn Dymally D-Compton
22	Sally Lieber D-Mountain View	53	Ted Lieu D-Torrance
23	Joe Coto D-San Jose	54	Betty Karnette D-Long Beach
24	Jim Beall D-San Jose	55	Laura Richardson D-Long Beach
25	Tom Berryhill R-Modesto	56	Tony Mendoza D-Artesia
26	Greg Aghazarian R-Stockton	57	Ed Hernandez D-West Covina
27	John Laird D-Santa Cruz	58	Charles Calderon D-Montebello
28	Anna Marie Caballero D-Salinas	59	Anthony Adams
29	Mike Villines R-Clovis	60	Bob Huff R-Diamond Bar
30	Nicole Parra D-Hanford	61	Nell Soto D-Pomona
31	Juan Arambula D-Fresno	62	Wilmer Carter D-Rialto

Assembly Members and District Numbers cont.

63	Bill Emmerson R-Redlands	72	Mike Duvall R-Yorba Linda
64	John Benoit R-Palm Desert	73	Mimi Walters R-Laguna Niguel
65	Paul Cook R-Yucaipa	74	Martin Garrick R-Vista
66	Kevin Jeffries R-Temecula	75	George Plescia R-San Diego
67	Jim Silva R-Huntington Beach	76	Lori Saldana D-San Diego
68	Van Tran R-Garden Grove	77	Joel Anderson R-Santee
69	Jose Solorio D-Santa Ana	78	Shirley Horton R-Bonita
70	Chuck DeVore R-Orange County	79	Mary Salas D-San Diego
71	Todd Spitzer R-Orange	80	Bonnie Garcia R-Cathedral City

ANTHONY ADAMS (R)
59th Assembly District

Counties: Los Angeles, San Bernardino
Cities: Hesperia, Apple Valley, Glendora, Claremont, San Dimas, La Verne, Monrovia, San Bernardino
Ethnicity: 65% White, 21% Latino, 5% Black, 7% Asian
Voter Registration: 33% D – 47% R – 16% DS
President 04: 63% Bush, 36% Kerry

Anthony Adams

In its previous incarnation, the 59th District sat entirely within Los Angeles County. But as the county drifted left, it became increasingly difficult for Republicans to hold the territory. The previous incumbent, Republican Dennis Mountjoy, first occupied the seat in 2000, prior to redistricting. Despite his political pedigree—he is the son of Richard Mountjoy, a former Republican state senator and candidate for U.S. Senate in 2006—he barely won that contest over labor official Meline Hall. Republicans were unexpectedly forced to spend some $300,000 to rescue Mountjoy in a seat that should have been theirs.

The close result set off an alarm bell, and in 2001, redistricting mapmakers moved the district east and north into the high desert of San Bernardino County, making it safely Republican. As a result, the district became substantially less Latino. The district includes some of Los Angeles County's wealthier suburbs, high desert communities as well as snowcapped mountains in San Bernardino County, creating a geographically diverse district. It could be a target for neutral mapmakers in the next redistricting, especially if the task is taken out of the hands of the legislature.

In Los Angeles County, the district pushes up against the Angeles National Forest along the I-210 freeway. Republicans generally represent the area, although voters tend to be more moderate, especially on social and environmental issues. Smog is a potent issue given the way it clings to the foothill communities that make up one edge of the district. The district's conservative bent comes from the east, in San Bernardino County, where voters tend to be to the right economically and socially. Hesperia and Apple Valley in San Bernardino's high desert are the largest cities in the district and are still growing.

With Mountjoy termed out in 2006, a sharp, five-way Republican primary unfolded, but most of the area's GOP power structure united behind Anthony Adams, a former aide to San Bernardino County Supervisor Bill Postmus. Adams gained the nomination with a comfortable 10-point margin despite a bruising primary, in part because those backing him were Inland Empire luminaries Jim Brulte, George Runner, Kevin McCarthy, Gary Ovitt, Ray Haynes, and others in the area's legislative delegation. Even Los Angeles County Sheriff Lee Baca lent his name to Adams's effort.

Adams easily dispatched Democrat Elliott Barkan in November 2006 to win his ticket to Sacramento. In succeeding Mountjoy, the 34-year-old Adams replaces one of the Legislature's more colorful members, an outspoken conservative who occasionally bucked his party's caucus to hand a vote to Democrats. Prior to running for the Assembly, Adams served as director of legislative affairs for San Bernardino County, where he worked to obtain transportation funding for an area stricken with growth and gridlock. He lists transportation funding as his top district priority and touts his youth, intending to use his office to connect the young to politics and government.

Born into a military family, Adams spent part of his childhood in Southern California while his father was stationed at George Air Force Base near Bellflower. His teenage years were spent abroad, notably in England. His interest in politics dates from 1996, when he interned for then-Republican Assemblyman Keith Olberg. Characterized by an associate as passionate to the point of rashness, Adams seems unafraid to voice his views. Befitting someone who hosted a radio talk show in Hesperia, for instance, Adams signed on to blog for the *Flash Report*, Jon Fleischman's Republican stream-of-consciousness Web site.

He landed in a legislative thicket when the Assembly's Republican leadership named him vice chairman of the Elections and Redistricting Committee—the battleground over proposals to reform the drawing of legislative and congressional districts. Currently, the legislature itself draws the districts after each decennial U.S. census, but reformers—including the governor and most Republicans—consider it a conflict of interest and want to place the process in the hands of an independent commission. Democrats, who control redistricting by virtue of their majority status, resist any change. So Adams will carry Republican water—uphill, in this case.

BIOGRAPHY: Born: Los Angeles, February 27, 1972. Home: Hesperia. Education: BA, CSU San Bernardino; JD, Western State University College of Law. Military: None. Family: Wife Deanna. Religion: Protestant. Occupation: Legislator.

OFFICES: 4015 Capitol Building, Sacramento, CA 95814, Phone: (916) 319-2059, Fax: (916) 319-2159, email: assemblymember.adams@assembly.ca.gov. District:

135 West Lemon Avenue, Suite A, Monrovia, CA 91016, Phone: (626) 359-8305, (888) 377-2212, Fax: (626) 358-5826.
COMMITTEES: Elections and Redistricting (vice chair); Judiciary; Rules
ELECTED: 2006 **TERM LIMIT:** 2012
ELECTION HISTORY: None.
2006 ELECTION: Adams (R) 56%
                   Barkan (D) 38%
                   Stone (L) 6%

GREG AGHAZARIAN (R)
26th Assembly District

Counties: San Joaquin, Stanislaus
Cities: Stockton, Manteca, Ceres, Turlock, Modesto
Ethnicity: 52% White, 33% Latino, 4% Black, 8% Asian
Voter Registration: 41% D – 42% R – 13% DS
President 04: 57% Bush, 42% Kerry

Greg Aghazarian

In California's San Joaquin Valley, Highway 99 wanders through the fertile California farmlands that drew Okies like John Steinbeck's fictional Joad family west in "The Grapes of Wrath." Though agriculture remains a large part of the picture in the 26th District's economy, its newest wave of fortune seekers are often traveling east, out of the increasingly expensive Bay Area, seeking affordable rural plots and new tract homes in the Valley, one of the strongest housing markets in the state.

Along with the 17th District to the south and west, the region is a crucial gateway to central California, through which nearly all the products that sustain the Valley travel, by rail, boat, or truck. Between the northernmost reach in Stockton and the foot in Turlock, the 26th boasts wineries and orchards, fruit stands, and antique shops. It includes outer parts of Modesto and all of Manteca, Ripon, Escalon, Ceres, and Patterson, with Highway 99 delineating much of its western border. It includes roughly 40% of San Joaquin and Stanislaus counties, which together hold about 200,000 registered voters. Many constituents live in unincorporated areas of the district's two counties. The majority of district residents are white, with large numbers of Latinos. Over the next 50 years demographers in the California Department of Finance expect those numbers to flip-flop, establishing a Hispanic and Latino majority.

Both San Joaquin and Stanislaus are agriculturally rich, ranking in the top 10 agricultural producers for the state. San Joaquin is the sixth-largest producer. Stanislaus is eighth. Top products include milk—almost $625 million worth in 2000—almonds, grapes, chickens, and cattle.

Increasing acreage in the district is given over to housing its booming population. Large stocks of affordable housing have drawn people from more expensive regions, like the Bay Area, contributing in part to the region's steady growth. Local populations grew nearly 3% between 2002 and 2003 alone. Growth hotspots include Modesto, Turlock, and Manteca. But, even in Manteca, homes priced under $300,000 have become scarce, according to the *Manteca Bulletin*.

Food and service sector businesses have fared well, serving the growing population. The district's unemployment rate has slowly headed toward 8% during the past few years, while incomes of those with jobs have grown modestly. Like other Central Valley districts, the 26th struggles with air pollution. Over a quarter of respondents rated air quality as the Valley's most pressing issue in a 2004 survey by the Public Policy Institute of California. Some have compared it to Los Angeles's fabled smog. Many locals blame the Bay Area's airborne pollution for exacerbating the Valley's woes, making regional air quality legislation a hot political issue. Tension over water rights also marks the district. While most district constituents favor retaining as much of their San Joaquin Delta water as possible, northerners in the district sometimes find themselves fighting southern constituents seeking more water to sustain their crops.

When Assemblyman Democrat Dennis A. Cardoza was termed out in 2002, he left a district completely reshaped by reapportionment. Much of the old 17th District was drawn into the new 26th. What had been a marginal if winnable Democratic district became more evenly split between Democrats and Republicans. Democrats have been losing ground ever since; they had a 3% edge when the district was first unveiled in 2001 but now trail by 2%.

Sensing that trend in 2002, Republican heavyweights lined up behind Greg Aghazarian, a prominent local businessman and school trustee whose family's apparel business is universally known throughout the region. He had given Democrat Barbara Matthews a run for her money in 2000 in the old 17th District, and the redrawn 26th included his hometown of Stockton. Hoping to retain the district in 2002, Democrats countered with criminal prosecutor Tom Hallinan, funding his candidacy with $500,000, but it wasn't enough to change the tide. Aghazarian trounced Hallinan by 14 points, the seat changed hands, and it is not likely to change back any time soon.

As a legislator, Aghazarian is known as the Republicans' energizer bunny for the non-stop, high velocity pace he sets for himself and his staff. A conservative, it is said he nonetheless chafes at restraints placed on members by the conservative-dominated GOP caucus. Capitol insiders consider him a good Republican soldier, albeit one who will listen to arguments if not cough up a vote. There was some talk that Democrats might take advantage of a favorable tide to make a run at Aghazarian in 2006, but the challenge never materialized. He breezed to victory over Democrat Ken Goeken, a special ed teacher from Ceres.

BIOGRAPHY: Born: Stockton, September 10, 1964. Home: Stockton. Education: BS, USC; JD, McGeorge School of Law. Military: None. Family: wife Esther, two children. Religion: Catholic. Occupation: Businessman.

OFFICES: 4167 Capitol Building, Sacramento, CA 95814, Phone (916) 319-2026, Fax: (916) 319-2126, email: assemblymember.aghazarian@assembly.ca.gov. District: 4557 Quail Lakes Drive, Suite C-3, Stockton, CA 95207, Phone: (209)

Speakers of the Assembly

Name	P*	Year(s)	Name	P*	Year(s)
Thomas J. White	—	1849	Cornelius W. Pendleton	R	1901
John Bigler	D	1849–51	A. H. Hewitt	R	1911
Richard P. Hammond	D	1852	C. C. Young	R-P	1913–17
Isaac B. Wall	D	1853	Henry W. Wright	R	1919–21
Charles S. Fairfax	D	1854	Frank Merriam	R	1923–25
William C. Stratton	D	1859	Edgar C. Levey	R	1927–31
Phillip Moore	D	1860	Walter J. Little	R	1933
R. N. Burnell	DD	1861	F. C. Clowdsley	R-P	1934
George Barstow	R	1862	Edward Craig	R	1935
Tim Machin	U	1863	William Moseley Jones	D	1937
William H. Sears	U	1864	Paul Peek	D	1939
John Yule	U	1866	Gordon H. Garland	R	1940–41
Caisas T. Ryland	D	1868	Charles W. Lyon	R	1943–45
George H. Rogers	D	1870	Sam L. Collins	R	1947–52
Thomas B. Shannon	R	1872	James W. Silliman	R	1953–54
Morris M. Estee	I	1874	Luther H. Lincoln	R	1955–58
G. J. Carpenter	D	1876	Ralph M. Brown	D	1958–1961
Campbell P. Berry	D	1878	Jesse M. Unruh	D	1961–68
Jabez F. Cowdery	R	1880	Robert T. Monagan	R	1969–70
Williams H. Parks	R	1881	Bob Moretti	D	1971–74
Hugh M. Larue	D	1881	Leo T. McCarthy	D	1974–1980
William H. Parks	R	1883	Willie Brown, Jr.	D	1980–1995
William H. Jordan	D	1885	Doris Allen	R	1995
Robert Howe	D	1889	Brian Setencich	R	1995
Frank L. Coombs	R	1891	Curt Pringle	R	1996
F. H. Gould	D	1893	Cruz Bustamante	D	1996–98
John C. Lynch	R	1895	Antonio Villaraigosa	D	1998–2000
Frank Coombs	R	1897	Robert Hertzberg	D	2000–02
Howard E. Wright	R	1899	Herb Wesson	D	2002–04
Alden Anderson	R	1899	Fabian Nunez	D	2004–

*Key to parties: A=American, D=Democrat, DD=Douglas Democrat, I=Independent, P=Progressive, R=Republican, U=Union, — denotes no party.

473-6972, Fax: (209) 473-6977; 222 South Thor Street, Suite 21C, Turlock, CA 95380, Phone: (209) 634-1426, Fax: (209) 634-2128.
COMMITTEES: Natural Resources; Public Safety (vice chair); Rules
ELECTED: 2002 **TERM LIMIT:** 2008
ELECTION HISTORY: Lincoln Unified School District, 1998–2002.
2002 ELECTION: Aghazarian (R) 57%
Hallinan (D) 43%
2004 ELECTION: Aghazarian (R*) 63%
Weintz (D) 37%
2006 ELECTION: Aghazarian (R*) 59%
Goeken (D) 41%

RATINGS:	AFL-CIO	CAI	CoC	CLCV	EQCA	CCS	CMTA	FARM	NARAL
	7	48	100	4	0	30	90	100	20

RICHARD ALARCON (D)
39th Assembly District

Counties: Los Angeles
Cities: Los Angeles, San Fernando, Sylmar, Pacoima, Panorama City, Mission Hills, Sun Valley, Arleta.
Ethnicity: 13% White, 74% Latino, 4% Black, 7% Asian
Voter Registration: 58% D – 19% R – 19% DS
President 04: 70% Kerry, 29% Bush

Richard Alarcon

A pair of freeways—I-405 and I-210—brackets this San Fernando Valley district, while a third, I-5, splits it in two. Nearly three-fourths of the population is Latino, as are half the registered voters.

Democrat Cindy Montanez left the district one term early to make an unsuccessful bid for the state Senate, losing the Democratic primary to Alex Padilla, president of the Los Angeles City Council. Her place in the Assembly was taken by a familiar name—Richard Alarcon, who sought to extend his legislative career after serving two terms in the state Senate. Alarcon is a rare breed, having been elected to the upper house in 1998 without having first served in the Assembly. Thus, he is eligible for three terms—six years—in the Assembly.

Chances are Alarcon will not fill out that run. His election to the lower house had yet to be officially certified when the 53-year-old legislator announced he would run for his old seat on the Los Angeles City Council—the seat vacated by Padilla's election to Alarcon's Senate seat.

The council seat became attractive to Alarcon when, in November 2006, Los Angeles voters passed Proposition R, which allowed council members to serve a third, four-year term. He had served only one term on the council prior to his election to the state Legislature so is eligible for an eight-year run on the council. He also is in line for a substantial pay raise; legislators make $110,800 a year while council members are paid $171,168. The special election to replace Padilla is set for March 2007.

Alarcon's decision set off another game of toppling dominoes, for among those big-footed by his desire to return to local politics was Montanez, giving the game of musical offices a cozy sense of closure. She withdrew her candidacy, mumbling about the realities of facing Alarcon.

He first came to the Legislature after one of the most controversial and bruising primaries in California history—his 1998 dust-up with then-Assemblyman Richard Katz. The campaign produced a bitter divide between Latinos and the local Jewish community, as both sides produced mailers their opponents viewed as "race baiting." Alarcon won by a scant 29 votes out of more than 94,000 cast, and it took years to smooth over rifts widened during the contest.

Alarcon's association with state Senator Richard Polanco, a power in the Senate and Latino caucus, allowed him to gain key assignments in Sacramento. He served as majority whip and chair of the Labor and Industrial Relations Committee. A former teacher, he often carried education bills, especially those related to teacher-training programs, and championed health access for the poor and affordable housing.

In 2005, his political ambitions were channeled into a run for mayor of Los Angeles, where he clashed with incumbent mayor James Hahn and two former Assembly speakers, Robert Hertzberg and Antonio Villaraigosa. Hertzberg cut into Alarcon's political base in the San Fernando Valley, while Villaraigosa ripped away huge chunks of the Latino vote. As a result, Alarcon never gained much traction and finished a dismal fifth in the March 2005 primary. He stood on the sidelines as Villaraigosa whipped Hahn in the runoff to become the city's first Latino mayor since pioneer days.

BIOGRAPHY: Born: Glendale, November 24, 1953; Home: Sylmar; Education: BA, CSU Northridge; Military: None. Family: Four children; Religion: Catholic. Occupation: Legislator.

OFFICES: 5119 Capitol Building, Sacramento, CA 95814, Phone: (916) 319-2039, Fax: (916) 319-2139, email: assemblymember.montanez@assembly.ca.gov. District: 120 North Maclay, Suite E, San Fernando, CA 91340, Phone: (818) 838-3939, Fax: (818) 838-3931.

COMMITTEES: Arts, Entertainment, Sports, Tourism and Internet Media; Natural Resources; Rules.

ELECTED: 2006 **TERM LIMIT:** 2012

ELECTION HISTORY: Los Angeles City Council, 1993–1998; state Senate, 1998–2006

2006 ELECTION: Alarcon (D) 100%

RATINGS:

AFL-CIO	CAI	CoC	CLCV	EQCA	CCS	CMTA	FARM	NARAL
93	92	25	91	87	85	11	17	100

JOEL ANDERSON (R)
77th Assembly District

Counties: San Diego
Cities: El Cajon, La Mesa, Santee, San Diego
Ethnicity: 75% White, 15% Latino, 3% Black, 4% Asian
Voter Registration: 29% D – 47% R – 19% DS
President 04: 63% Bush, 36% Kerry

Joel Anderson

The 77th once was a compact urban district that stretched from El Cajon in the north down through La Mesa to Chula Vista. It was marginally competitive between Republicans and Democrats, with both parties representing it in the 1990s. After mapmakers finished with it in 2001, any competitiveness had been wrung from it, and it became a desert district migrating eastward from El Cajon and fleeing across I-8 to the Imperial County border, then north to take in Borrego Springs. Most of its population is still concentrated in the same area, now the district's southwest corner.

The elective history of the old 77th lends context to the effort to rearrange it in 2001. For a brief time in the 1990s, a Democrat, Tom Connolly, held forth. A moderate, Connolly won in 1992 by defeating uber-conservative Republican Steve Baldwin and spent most of his only term trying to put a happy face on his past drug addictions and fending off allegations that he sexually harassed female employees. That led to a 1994 re-match with Baldwin, who thumped him in a good year for Republicans across the nation. Baldwin held the seat until termed out in 2000, but he never quite outran a reputation as a character from "The Far Side," engendered by a remark he made during his 1992 campaign against Connolly—that the U.S. Air Force employed an official witch.

Jay La Suer replaced Baldwin in 2000, winning a hard-fought primary that was a metaphor for philosophical schisms that fracture the Republican Party. At the time, the conservative La Suer was vice mayor of La Mesa and a 31-year veteran of law enforcement. His opponent was a pro-choice moderate and a school trustee who eschewed philosophy, instead attacking La Suer's fiscal acumen as a San Diego County undersheriff and accusing him of using county employees as campaign workers. La Suer weathered the sludge-filled onslaught and a marginally competitive general election, eventually serving three terms in the Assembly before being termed out in 2006. Redistricting fixed any notions of future competitiveness.

La Suer's replacement is Joel Anderson, a water expert who emerged from a five-way June primary that featured a pair of well-connected challengers—charter school founder Debbie Beyer and long-time Santee City Councilman Jack Dale. Beyer ran from the far right, with La Suer's endorsement, and touted her experience in education. Dale pointed to a record of public service that dates back to his 1986 election to the Santee council, where he also served eight years as mayor. He was endorsed by Charlene Zettel, a moderate Republican who once represented a neighboring Assembly district. Among Zettel's GOP primary opponents when she first ran for the Legislature in 1998 was Joel Anderson.

Anderson pulled endorsements from significant conservatives such as the California Republican Assembly, the Howard Jarvis Taxpayers Association, and state Senator Tom McClintock, the party's nominee for lieutenant governor. President of the Padre Dam Municipal Water District and a veteran political activist, Anderson was a known commodity in Santee, which helped him make inroads into Dale's natural constituency. Anderson was aided by conservatives who questioned Dale's stance on abortion, labeling him a "liberal" because he once had been pro-choice. Anderson touted his willingness to tighten border security and pledged to work against tax increases, calling attention to Dale's fee increases in the city of Santee and questioning his pledge not to raise taxes in Sacramento. Anderson won a squeaker, besting Dale 32 percent to 30 percent, with Meyer polling 18 percent. As expected for a Republican in this district, he easily brushed aside Democrat Chris Larkin in November. Larkin had lost to La Suer in 2004 as well.

Anderson has made water his issue, telling *Capitol Weekly* that he planned to help revive several local water projects that Democrats had kept out of the infrastructure bond approved by voters in November 2006. He was named vice chairman of the Aging and Long-Term Care Committee.

BIOGRAPHY: Born: Detroit, MI, February 11, 1960. Home: Alpine. Education: BS, California Polytechnic Pomona. Military: None. Family: wife Kate, two children. Religion: Decline to state. Occupation: Businessman.

OFFICES: 2111 Capitol Building, Sacramento, CA 95814, Phone: (916) 319-2077, Fax: (916) 319-2177, email: assemblymember.anderson@assembly.ca.gov. District: 5360 Jackson Drive, Suite 120, La Mesa, CA 91942, Phone: (619) 465-7723, Fax: (619) 465-7765.

COMMITTEES: Aging and Long-Term Care (vice chair); Public Employees, Retirement and Social Security; Rules (alternate); Water, Parks and Wildlife.

ELECTED: 2006 **TERM LIMIT:** 2012

ELECTION HISTORY: Padre Dam Municipal Water District, 2002–2006.

2006 ELECTION:　　Anderson (R) 61%
　　　　　　　　　　　Larkin (D)　36%
　　　　　　　　　　　Belitz (L)　3%

JUAN ARAMBULA (D)
31st Assembly District

Counties: Fresno, Tulare
Cities: Fresno, Reedly, Selma, Sanger, Dinuba
Ethnicity: 22% White, 62% Latino, 6% Black, 9% Asian

Voter Registration: 49% D – 36% R – 11% DS
President 04: 53% Kerry, 46% Bush

Juan Arambula

The 31st District is another heavily Latino Central Valley district that was reshaped during the 2001 redistricting. Instead of north-south, it now runs east-west, with everything south of Selma and Dinuba having been lopped off. More than half the population lives in the southern half of Fresno.

Democrat Juan Arambula represents the district, having run unopposed for a second term in 2006. That cakewalk stands in marked contrast with Arambula's first election in 2004. A former Fresno County supervisor, Arambula is the son of immigrant migrant farmworkers and brings an impressive political and educational pedigree to his legislative career. When he first announced for the seat in 2004, he cleared the Democratic field and ran unopposed in the primary. The seat was open because incumbent Democrat Sarah Reyes was termed out. At the time, few thought the 2004 general election would produce much of a contest, even though the GOP nominee was Paul Betancourt, a respected community leader and former president of the California Farm Bureau.

But Republicans, encouraged by President George Bush's strong showing in local polls, decided to play heavily in the district. They pumped a small fortune into Betancourt's campaign, forcing Democrats to respond with resources that could have been spent elsewhere. Governor Arnold Schwarzenegger lent his political gravitas to Betancourt as well, as did the Chamber of Commerce–sponsored JOBSPAC, which rolled an independent expenditure campaign into the district.

The 2004 campaign itself traveled the high road for most of the fall, although Betancourt spent the last week on a tour of the local political sewer. A Republican Party mailer, sent on his behalf, criticized Arambula for backing driver's licenses for illegal immigrants, and a flyer with an unflattering photo of the Democratic nominee called attention to his membership in a group that lobbies on behalf of Mexican immigrants. The mailer was a thinly disguised attempt to exploit the Republicans' self-confessed belief that racial bias influences Anglo voters in this part of the Central Valley, regardless of party label. The mailer earned Betancourt a rebuke in an op-ed piece in *The Fresno Bee*. It also made little difference.

In Sacramento, Arambula was given several plum assignments, including a seat on the Budget Committee and chair of the Jobs, Economic Development and the Economy Committee. He served as vice chair of the Legislative Rural Caucus, while his bill package focused on housing for farmworkers and education issues. Arambula pushed to bolster state intervention in the battle to clean up Central Valley air, now considered among the most harmful in California, and to increase the number of doctors who practice in rural areas of his district.

BIOGRAPHY: Born: Brownsville, TX, January 29, 1952. Home: Fresno. Education: BA, Harvard; MA, Stanford; JD, Boalt Law School, UC Berkeley. Military:

None. Family: wife Amy, four children. Religion: Decline to state. Occupation: Attorney.

OFFICES: 2141 Capitol Building, Sacramento, CA 95814, Phone: (916) 319-2031, Fax: (916) 319-2131, email: assemblymember.arambula@assembly.ca.gov. District: Hugh Burns State Building, 2550 Mariposa Mall, Suite 5031, Fresno, CA 93721, Phone: (559) 445-5532, Fax: (559) 445-6006.

COMMITTEES: Budget; Budget Subcommittee 4 on State Administration (chair); Higher Education; Jobs, Economic Development and the Economy (chair); Revenue and Taxation.

ELECTED: 2004 **TERM LIMIT:** 2010

ELECTION HISTORY: Fresno Unified School Board, 1987–1996; Fresno County Board of Supervisors, 1997–2004.

2004 ELECTION: Arambula (D) 57%
Betancourt (R) 43%

2006 ELECTION: Arambula (D*) 100%

RATINGS:

AFL-CIO	CAI	CoC	CLCV	EQCA	CCS	CMTA	FARM	NARAL
76	92	55	67	67	95	0	50	100

KAREN BASS (D)
47th Assembly District

Counties: Los Angeles
Cities: Los Angeles, Culver City
Ethnicity: 29% White, 26% Latino, 31% Black, 12% Asian
Voter Registration: 64% D – 13% R – 19% DS
President 04: 81% Kerry, 18% Bush

Karen Bass

The 47th District, an ethnically balanced territory dominated politically by African Americans, is mostly unchanged from its pre-redistricting self. The only alteration came in the form of a small bulge in the northwest corner that includes UCLA, a bit of plastic surgery to accommodate then-Speaker Herb Wesson who represented the district from 1998 to 2004.

When Wesson departed, a crowd of Democratic hopefuls jumped into the primary to replace him, led by Wesson's handpicked successor, entertainment attorney Rickey Ivie, former City Councilman and state Senator Nate Holden, and community activist Karen Bass. In some ways, the primary contest was a battle between a pair of political factions within the African-American community, led by U.S. Representative Diane Watson and Los Angeles County Supervisor Yvonne Braithwaite Burke.

Bass, backed by Watson, brought more than a decade's worth of grassroots organizing and community activism to the race. She is the founder of the Community

Coalition, a 3,500-strong group battling drug dealing and the proliferation of liquor stores in South Central. A well-known figure in this part of inner Los Angeles, Bass had support from Assembly Speaker Fabian Nunez and former Speaker, now Mayor Antonio Villaraigosa. More significant, she was backed by the late Miguel Contreras and the Los Angeles Federation of Labor, which made her election a priority.

Bass won a resounding primary victory that was an ode to grassroots activism and the value of community involvement, allowing her to reach out to the district's diverse ethnic groups. Labor poured more than $330,000 in independent expenditures into the district on her behalf, helping her coast to an easy victory.

Once in Sacramento, Bass quickly established herself as a hard-working and savvy legislator, and her first legislative effort produced bills to help parolees ease back into mainstream life and expand Cal Grant eligibility. Her most significant work has been in the area of foster care, where she teamed with Republican Bill Maze to create a bipartisan approach to improving the lives of children caught up in a near-dysfunctional system of care.

Bass was easily re-elected to a second term in November 2006, an event marred by the death of her daughter and son-in-law in a late-October traffic accident. When the Legislature convened in December 2006, Bass became part of Assembly leadership when Speaker Fabian Nunez tapped her as majority floor leader for the 2007–2008 legislative session, a nod that put her in contention as a possible successor to Nunez, who is termed out in 2008.

BIOGRAPHY: Born: Los Angeles, October 3, 1953. Home: Los Angeles. Education: BS, CSU Dominguez Hills; PA, USC. Military: None. Family: one child (deceased). Religion: Decline to state. Occupation: Legislator.

OFFICES: 319 Capitol Building, Sacramento, CA 95814, Phone: (916) 319-2047, Fax: (916) 319-2147, email: assemblymember.bass@assembly.ca.gov. District: 5750 Wilshire Boulevard, Suite 565, Los Angeles, CA 90036, Phone: (323) 937-4747, Fax: (323) 937-3466.

COMMITTEES: Business and Professions; Health; Housing and Community Development; Utilities and Commerce.

ELECTED: 2004 **TERM LIMIT:** 2010

ELECTION HISTORY: None.

2004 ELECTION: Bass (D) 81%
Everett (R) 15%
DeBaets (L) 4%

2006 ELECTION: Bass (D*) 85%
Dodge (R) 15%

RATINGS:

AFL-CIO	CAI	CoC	CLCV	EQCA	CCS	CMTA	FARM	NARAL
100	92	24	96	100	100	0	10	100

JIM BEALL, JR. (D)
24th Assembly District

Counties: Santa Clara
Cities: San Jose, Campbell, Saratoga, Santa Clara
Ethnicity: 56% White, 18% Latino, 3% Black, 20% Asian
Voter Registration: 45% D – 29% R – 22% DS
President 04: 62% Kerry, 37% Bush

Jim Beall, Jr.

Democrats didn't much care for the way this San Jose–area district came together during the 1992 redistricting because, although nominally competitive, its voters had the gall to elect moderate Republicans such as Charles Quackenbush and Jim Cunneen. Even after Democrat Rebecca Cohn wrested it away in 2000, Democrats sought to remove it from GOP target lists by performing surgery during the 2001 redistricting. They used a chainsaw. Cupertino and the Santa Clara County communities of Los Gatos and Monte Serrano were removed, while district boundaries were pushed northeast to take in the Fruitdale, Burbank, and Midtown areas north of San Jose. Another finger was extended into neighborhoods west of Alum Rock.

The result was dramatic. In 2000, Cohn won a taut general election against Monte Serrano Mayor Suzanne Jackson. Two years and one chainsaw later, Cohn ran unopposed for re-election. In 2004, she easily dispatched Republican Ernie Konnyu, a former assemblyman and former member of Congress.

Cohn was termed out in 2006, but the effort to replace her did not produce the typical multi-player brawl among Democrats because the territory was staked out early by Jim Beall, who spent more than a quarter century in Santa Clara politics before running for the legislature. Elected to the San Jose City Council in 1980, he moved to the Santa Clara County Board of Supervisors in 1994—a position he held when elected to the Assembly. During that time, he focused on public transportation and the delivery of human services, including a stint as chair of the Metropolitan Transportation Commission. Upon arrival in Sacramento, Beall was named chair of the Human Services Committee. He also received significant assignments to the Budget and Higher Education committees.

BIOGRAPHY: Born: San Jose, December 7, 1951. Home: San Jose. Education: BA, San Jose State. Military: None. Family: wife Pat, two step-sons. Religion: Catholic. Occupation: Legislator.

OFFICES: 5016 Capitol Building, Sacramento, CA 95814, Phone (916) 319-2024, Fax: (916) 319-2124, email: assemblymember.beall@assembly.ca.gov. District: 100 Paseo De San Antonio, Suite 319, San Jose, CA 95113, Phone: (408) 282-8920, Fax: (408) 282-8927.

COMMITTEES: Budget; Budget Subcommittee 1 on Health and Human Services; Higher Education; Human Services (chair); Veterans Affairs.
ELECTED: 2006 **TERM LIMIT:** 2012
ELECTION HISTORY: San Jose City Council, 1980–1994; Santa Clara Board of Supervisors, 1994–2006.
2006 ELECTION: Beall (D) 65%
                 Hileman (R) 31%
                 Silva (L) 4%

JOHN BENOIT (R)
64th Assembly District

Counties: Riverside
Cities: Riverside, Moreno Valley, Palm Desert
Ethnicity: 55% White, 29% Latino, 9% Black, 5% Asian
Voter Registration: 34% D – 46% R – 16% DS
President 04: 58% Bush, 41% Kerry

John Benoit

Every once in a while, legislative mapmakers demonstrate a sentimental streak, and so it was with the 64th District in 2001. The northwest corner of the old district—represented by small patches of the city of Riverside—was retained in the new district, an heirloom framed and set on the mantle. The rest of the district—new territory all—booms south along I-15 to skirt Lake Elsinore and sprawls east across the desert to anchor on Palm Desert, Indian Wells, and Rancho Mirage. It is a bit less Democratic than the old version, as though that matters politically in this part of the Inland Empire.

Given that the district is so solidly Republican, battles for supremacy and power take place in the GOP primary, usually between moderates and conservatives. The intrigues that brought incumbent John Benoit to office in 2002 were worthy of a Venetian doge. In Republican politics, 2002 was the "year of the conservative," yet the most conservative candidate in the 64th did not win due to a small technicality: He was thrown off the ballot.

That candidate, Ray Horspool, was backed by every significant conservative in the region. Unfortunately, Horspool lived in Yucaipa, which is in the 65th District. Horspool argued that he was registered to vote in Riverside, in the 64th, where he did business as a CPA. A court disagreed and, citing such nominal Yucaipa activities as maintaining a residence complete with family, dog, and backyard barbeque, ordered Horspool's name removed from consideration.

The Horspool incident was just one in a series of squabbles between conservative and moderate factions of the Inland Empire Republican Party and reduced the field of contenders to two. It was thought at the time that the prime beneficiary of Horspool's demise would be 29-year-old public relations executive Lou Monville, who was endorsed by the *Riverside Press Enterprise* and aligned with area moderates such as departing incumbent Rod Pacheco. Instead, Horspool's fate galvanized conservatives behind Benoit, a retired Highway Patrol captain from the district's desert region. Horspool and his allies—including state legislators Dennis Hollingsworth and Ray Haynes—rallied their troops for Benoit, who scored a 12-point victory in the primary and barely raised a sweat winning the general.

As a legislator, Benoit has focused on education, transportation, and law-and-order issues, although his special pet has been an effort to make per-student community college funding more equitable across the state. Annually, he introduces a bill to seek federal money for housing illegal immigrants in California jails and prisons—a symbolic gesture that is annually ignored by majority Democrats and the federal government. He has been more successful at securing money to help local governments upgrade and improve grade crossings, improving child safety at day-care facilities, and increasing penalties for illegal street racing. One of the Assembly's more conservative Republicans, Benoit was given a 100 percent rating by the California Farm Bureau in 2004–2005. Gays and environmentalists, on the other hand, gave him zeroes. As befitting the district's Republican nature, Benoit has not been seriously challenged for election, clearing 60 percent of the vote in 2004 and 2006. He is termed out in 2008.

BIOGRAPHY: Born: Kankakee, IL, December 27, 1951. Home: Palm Desert. Education: AA, Riverside City College; BA, CSU Los Angeles; MA, CSU San Bernardino; FBI National Academy. Military: None. Family: wife Sheryl, two children. Religion: Catholic. Occupation: Law Enforcement Officer.

OFFICES: 4144 Capitol Building, Sacramento, CA 95814, Phone: (916) 319-2064, Fax: (916) 319-2164, email: assemblymember.benoit@assembly.ca.gov. District: 1223 University Avenue, Suite 230, Riverside, CA 92507, Phone: (951) 369-6644, Fax: (951) 369-0366; 73-710 Fred Waring Drive, Suite 108, Palm Desert, CA 92260, Phone: (760) 674-0164, Fax: (760) 674-0184.

COMMITTEES: Budget; Budget Subcommittee 5 on Information Technology and Transportation; Insurance (vice chair); Rules.

ELECTED: 2002 **TERM LIMIT:** 2008

ELECTION HISTORY: Desert Sands Unified School District, 1999–2002.

2002 ELECTION: Benoit (R) 63%
                     Melsh (D) 37%
2004 ELECTION: Benoit (R*) 61%
                     Melsh (D) 39%
2006 ELECTION: Benoit (R*) 62%
                     Rasso (D) 39%

RATINGS:	AFL-CIO	CAI	CoC	CLCV	EQCA	CCS	CMTA	FARM	NARAL
	3	30	94	0	0	15	90	100	20

PATTY BERG (D)
1st Assembly District

Counties: Del Norte, Humboldt, Lake, Mendocino, Sonoma, Trinity
Cities: Eureka, Arcata, McKinleyville, Clearlake, Healdsburg, Ukiah
Ethnicity: 78% White, 12% Hispanic, 1% Black, 2% Asian
Voter Registration: 45% D – 29% R – 19% DS
President 04: 60% Kerry, 38% Bush

Patty Berg

California's north coast is a region of contrasts, including Redwood National Park, Clearlake, ruggedly beautiful coastal resorts at Mendocino and Bodega Bay, Sonoma County wine country, hidden marijuana farms, and the state's most notorious prison at Pelican Bay. It takes in communities such as Willits, Ukiah, Lakeport, Healdsburg, McKinleyville, and Eureka. Physical beauty aside, the iconoclastic character of the district is exemplified by an irreverently witty police log published each week by the *Arcata Eye*.

The district was left largely unchanged in the 2001 redistricting, with only sparsely populated areas in Trinity County (Weaverville, Lewiston, and Hayfork) laser-burned onto the previous version. Environmentalists and timber interests jostle for emotional control of the region—with marijuana farmers tossed into the mix. The economy, such as it is, depends on agriculture and tourism.

Politically, the district has been safe Democratic territory for more than two decades, although registration for both Republicans and Democrats has slipped in recent years as voters opt for the Green Party or Decline to State. The political contrasts across the district are highlighted by the vote on Proposition 69, the 2004 initiative that expanded the use of DNA testing in criminal cases. Humboldt earned the distinction as the only county in California to vote against 69, opposing it nearly two-to-one, while the same ratio of voters in neighboring Del Norte supported the measure.

The district is represented by Democrat Patty Berg, a party activist whose most notable victory prior to election to the legislature was a successful 1999 campaign to keep WalMart from replacing a large swath of coastal trees with a concrete barn. Berg won the seat in 2002 by capturing the Democratic primary against three opponents—one of whom had signed an agreement with the Green Party to champion its causes. Berg prevailed with backing from the area's popular state senator, Wes Chesbro, and with financial support from labor, trial lawyers, and realtors. In the 2002 general election, Berg won by a comfortable, if not stunning, 10,000-vote margin, as her Republican opponent ran more than 10 points ahead of registration, giving the impression that the district's growing number of decline-to-state voters tilted toward the GOP. Berg put that notion to rest in 2004, winning by more than 50,000 votes and wracking up 62% of the vote.

As a legislator, Berg sits on Assembly Appropriations and focused on issues involving the elderly and problems that loom as baby boomers get older. In 2004, she headed a legislative advisory committee that published a report on aging boomers. Berg chairs the standing Committee on Aging and Long-Term Care and the Joint Committee on Fisheries and Aquaculture—befitting a district that maintains some semblance of a fishing industry.

As her middle term began, Berg had yet to compile much of a track record, was rarely mentioned in *California Journal*'s 2004 survey of the legislature's best and brightest, and managed not a single vote for *Journal* Rookie-of-the-Year. In the 2004–2005 session, however, Berg emerged as the legislative champion of "death with dignity," pushing controversial bills that would allow terminally ill patients to control the end their lives. She based her legislation on the experiences of Oregon, which has endured court challenges to its 1997 assisted suicide laws, and her efforts coincided with the inflammatory case of Terry Schiavo, a comatose Florida woman who gradually starved to death as advocates on both sides—including President George Bush—debated the issue in the courts and media. Her bill eventually failed, and it is unclear whether she plans to spend political capital to revive it in 2007.

With health care high on just about everyone's agenda for 2007, Berg could find herself in the middle of legislative brawls as head of "sub-one," the Assembly Budget Committee's subcommittee on Health and Human Services. She retains her chair of the Aging and Long-Term Care Committee, which is trying to prepare the state for the influx of baby boomers into the ranks of the retired.

BIOGRAPHY: Born: Seattle, WA, June 6, 1942. Home: Eureka. Education: BA, CSU Los Angeles. Military: None. Family: widowed, two step-children. Religion: decline to state. Occupation: Social Worker.

OFFICES: 4146 Capitol Building, Sacramento, CA 95814, Phone: (916) 319-2001, Fax: (916) 319-2101, email: assemblymemberberg@assembly.ca.gov. Districts: 235 Fourth St., Suite C, Eureka, CA 95501, Phone: (707) 445-7014, Fax (707) 445-6607; 104 W. Church St., Ukiah, CA 95482, Phone: (707) 463-5770, Fax: (707) 463-5773; 50 D St., Suite 450, Santa Rosa, CA 95404, Phone: (707) 576-2526, Fax: (707) 576-2297.

COMMITTEES: Aging and Long-Term Care (chair); Budget; Budget Subcommittee 1 on Health and Human Services (chair); Health; Insurance.

ELECTED: 2002; **TERM LIMIT:** 2008.

ELECTION HISTORY: None

2002 ELECTION: Berg (D) 48%
Brown (R) 40%

2004 ELECTION: Berg (D*) 62%
Tyrone (R) 33%

2006 ELECTION: Berg (D*) 65%
Tyrone (R) 31%
Reed (L) 5%

RATINGS:

AFL-CIO	CAI	CoC	CLCV	EQCA	CCS	CMTA	FARM	NARAL
100	96	18	100	100	100	0	20	100

TOM BERRYHILL (R)
25th Assembly District

Counties: Calaveras, Madera, Mariposa, Mono, Stanislaus, Tuolumne
Cities: Modesto, Oakdale, Riverbank, Chowchilla
Ethnicity: 71% White, 19% Latino, 3% Black, 3% Asian
Voter Registration: 36% D – 45% R – 14% DS
President 04: 61% Bush, 38% Kerry

Tom Berryhill

A lesson in not-so-ancient history: In 1994, a version of this Central Valley district rested in the hands of Democrat Margaret Snyder, one of the few Democrats ever to earn a solid rating from the National Rifle Association. It helped her not at all; in 1996, Snyder was ousted by Republican George House. That tidbit of political lore shows how far across the political spectrum this slice of the Central Valley has traveled. Democrats, truth-seekers to the core, acknowledged reality when they agreed to sod over any semblance of competitiveness during the 2001 redistricting compromise. The district straddles the central Sierra and slops into the Valley just enough to snare most of Modesto. Mono County was surgically attached when the seat was redrawn in 2001, as was a slice of Calaveras County gold country.

Republican Dave Cogdill succeeded House and served three terms, terming out of the Assembly in 2006. Cogdill is now ensconced in the state Senate, and his departure created an open seat that was filled after one of the more bizarre primary campaigns of the 2006 election season. The antagonists were Tom Berryhill and Bill Conrad. Berryhill had most of the advantages, given that he is the son of the late Clare Berryhill, former legislator and director of the state Department of Agriculture under Gov. George Deukmejian. Needing some way to cut his opponent down to size, Conrad ran an attack ad that generated no end of negative publicity—for himself—and no end of sympathy for Berryhill. In a burst of bad judgment, Conrad focused on his opponent's health; specifically, the fact that Berryhill had undergone a heart transplant some years before. In a mailer, Conrad suggested, in ascending waves of bad taste, that the legislature is a stressful place, that stress kills transplant patients, and that Berryhill, if elected, likely would die in office. The tag line: "Berryhill doesn't have the heart for State Assembly." When stunned observers finally regained their composure, most characterized the attack as the foulest piece of campaign mail ever dispatched.

Berryhill won the primary with 70% of the vote, then breezed to victory in November over Democrat James Bufford, who had the good sense not to refer to Berryhill's health history. A rancher by trade, the new legislator is expected to focus on water and agricultural issues. Republican leadership named him vice chairman of the Human Services Committee, but he also landed spots on the Agriculture and Water, Parks and Wildlife committees—two significant panels for his district.

BIOGRAPHY: Born: Ceres, August 27, 1957. Home: Modesto. Education: BA, Cal Poly, San Luis Obispo. Military: None. Family: wife Loretta, two children. Religion: Presbyterian. Occupation: Farmer.

OFFICES: 4116 Capitol Building, Sacramento, CA 95814, Phone (916) 319-2025, Fax: (916) 319-2125, email: assemblymember.berryhill@assembly.ca.gov. District: 1912 Staniford Avenue, Suite 4, Modesto, CA 95350, Phone: (209) 576-6425, Fax: (209) 576-6426.

COMMITTEES: Agriculture; Human Services (vice chair); Water, Parks and Wildlife.

ELECTED: 2006 **TERM LIMIT:** 2012

ELECTION HISTORY: None.

2006 ELECTION: Berryhill (R) 62%
  Bufford (D) 33%
  Dell'Orto (L) 5%

SAM BLAKESLEE (R)
33rd Assembly District

Counties: San Luis Obispo, Santa Barbara
Cities: Santa Maria, Lompoc, San Luis Obispo, Atascadero, Paso Robles
Ethnicity: 64% White, 27% Latino, 3% Black, 4% Asian
Voter Registration: 35% D – 42% R – 17% DS
President 04: 55% Bush, 43% Kerry

Sam Blakeslee

A coastal enclave, the 33rd District includes some of the most scenic territory in California. Centered on the city of San Luis Obispo, it includes the western half of Santa Barbara County. The Latino population is growing, although political power remains in the hands of Anglo voters, and the district is solidly Republican.

Incumbent Sam Blakeslee had to win a tough, three-way primary to inherit the district from termed-out Republican Abel Maldonado, who was elected to the state Senate. Blakeslee was a trustee of Cuesta Community College when he announced for the seat and quickly became the front-runner thanks to a bevy of local and state endorsements. He pumped $132,000 of his own money into the campaign, just to demonstrate his sincerity, and piled up an early lead in most polls.

But both of Blakeslee's opponents—Matt Kokkonen and Mike Zimmerman—ran aggressive campaigns that whittled his lead. Eventually, all three candidates brought in at least 30% of the GOP primary vote, with Blakeslee's 39% giving him the brass ring. He easily defeated his Democratic opponent and won re-election in 2006 by a two-to-one margin.

Blakeslee was made vice chair of the Retirement and Social Security Committee, which allowed him to sit on the keg of dynamite known as the governor's attempt to revamp state-run retirement programs for state workers and teachers. He also sat on the Budget Committee and the Utilities and Commerce Committee, where he carried the governor's water on financing renewable energy. For his sophomore term, Blakeslee was made vice chairman of the powerful Rules Committee.

For a rookie Republican, Blakeslee was relatively successful at moving legislation, having 20 bills signed into law. Among his legislative package were bills promoting renewable energy, reducing greenhouse gases, and allowing leave and vacation time to be donated to co-workers hit by catastrophic illness or injury.

Blakeslee brings an unusual pedigree to his job as a legislator. He worked in construction after graduation from San Luis Obispo High School and before attending Cuesta Community College. He went on to the University of California, Berkeley, where he earned degrees in geophysics. He earned a Ph.D. from UC Santa Barbara for research in seismic scattering and micro-earthquake studies and is published in a number of scientific journals. Blakeslee worked as a research scientist for Exxon in Texas, where he patented a technique for creating images of geologic formations using medical cat-scan technology. On his return to California, he forsook earthquakes and the oil industry to enter the family investment business.

BIOGRAPHY: Born: San Luis Obispo, June 25, 1955. Home: San Luis Obispo. Education: BA, MA, UC Berkeley; PhD, UC Santa Barbara. Military: None. Family: wife Kara, three children. Religion: Decline to state. Occupation: Research scientist, businessman.

OFFICES: 4117 Capitol Building, Sacramento, CA 95814, Phone: (916) 319-2033, Fax: (916) 319-2133, email: assemblymember.blakeslee@assembly.ca.gov. District: 1302 Marsh Street, San Luis Obispo, CA 93401, Phone: (805) 549-3381, Fax: (805) 549-3400.

COMMITTEES: Budget; Budget Subcommittee 3 on Resources; Rules (vice chair); Utilities and Commerce.

ELECTED: 2004 **TERM LIMIT:** 2010

ELECTION HISTORY: Cuesta Community College Board of Trustees.

2004 ELECTION: Blakeslee (R) 56%
Jenkins (D) 33%
Hutchings (G) 6%
Kirkland (L) 5%

2006 ELECTION: Blakeslee (R*) 67%
Cuthbert (D) 33%

RATINGS:	AFL-CIO	CAI	CoC	CLCV	EQCA	CCS	CMTA	FARM	NARAL
	7	56	94	21	0	20	80	100	20

JULIA BROWNLEY (D)
41st Assembly District

Counties: Los Angeles, Ventura
Cities: Los Angeles, Santa Monica, Oxnard, Port Hueneme, Calabasas, Tarzana, Malibu, Pacific Palisades, Encino
Ethnicity: 67% White, 20% Latino, 3% Black, 8% Asian
Voter Registration: 48% D – 29% R – 19% DS
President 04: 62% Kerry, 37% Bush

Julia Brownley

District 41 stretches along the Pacific coast from newly acquired Oxnard and Port Hueneme in Ventura County to Santa Monica in Los Angeles County. It is relatively safe Democratic territory represented for the past six years by Democrat Fran Pavley who made the environment her specialty. By all accounts, Pavley will be a hard act to follow. Her quiet, unassuming demeanor belied an inner toughness that saw her shepherd cutting-edge environmental measures through the Legislature, including the "greenhouse gas emissions bill" of 2002.

Her replacement, Julia Brownley, is a three-term member of the Santa Monica–Malibu School Board whose number-one priority is education. Brownley came to Sacramento on the heels of a hotly contested Democratic primary and a no-contest November election. The cast of characters for the primary was as varied as the district itself, and their list of endorsements highlighted the often-fractured nature of coastal politics. Brownley came from education and had backing from the two women who previously represented the area—state Sen. Sheila Kuehl and Pavley. Calabasas Mayor Barry Groveman was endorsed by U.S. Sen. Dianne Feinstein and Supt. of Public Instruction Jack O'Connell. Anti-war activist Kelly Hayes-Raitt, a former aide to then-Lt. Gov. Leo McCarthy, drew support from actor Martin Sheen, U.S. Rep. Maxine Waters, and Lt. Gov. Cruz Bustamante. Attorney Jonathan Levey had former U.S. Rep. Mel Levine, state Sen. Jack Scott from Pasadena, and the San Fernando Valley Young Democrats. He was endorsed by the *Los Angeles Times,* which cited his pragmatic approach to solving problems, and the alternative *LA Weekly*. Although four viable candidates graced the ticket, Groveman and Levey remained frontrunners throughout the campaign, mostly on the strength of their treasuries; both raised in excess of $300,000. But the two also went after each other, with Groveman drawing late blood with a mailer that linked Levey with tobacco giant Philip Morris—a former client of Levey's law firm and a toxic bit of baggage in any Democratic primary. The Levey-Groveman brawl proved a murder-suicide, allowing Brownley to slip through with 35% of the vote. Groveman took 27%, Levey 20%. Brownley's biggest margin came from Los Angeles County, although she also finished first in Ventura County, aided in part by a strong push from Hayes-Raitt that sapped votes from Groveman and Levey.

Brownley plans to make education her priority, and Assembly leaders gave her a good pulpit for that effort—chair of "sub two," the Budget Subcommittee on Education Finance. As president of a school board, Brownley is well versed on the subject. Among her other educational notions are early intervention to identify and help at-risk students, greater incentives to lure talent into the teacher pool, extension of class-size reduction beyond third grade, and better training and accountability for principals. In other areas, she plans to push for extension of the Exposition Corridor light rail project into Santa Monica to relieve congestion on I-10 and opposes building a liquid natural gas facility off the Southern California coast.

BIOGRAPHY: Born: Aiken, SC, August 28, 1952. Home: Santa Monica. Education: BA, George Washington University; MBA, American University. Military: None. Family: two children. Religion: Protestant. Occupation: educator.

OFFICES: 6011 Capitol Building, Sacramento, CA 95814, Phone: (916) 319-2041, Fax: (916) 319-2141, email: assemblymember.brownley@assembly.ca.gov. District: 6355 Topanga Canyon Boulevard, Suite 205, Woodland Hills, CA 91367, Phone: (818) 596-4141, Fax: (818) 596-4150.

COMMITTEES: Aging and Long Term Care; Budget; Budget Subcommittee 2 on Education Finance (chair); Education; Natural Resources.

ELECTED: 2006 **TERM LIMIT:** 2012

ELECTION HISTORY: Santa Monica-Malibu School Board, 1994–2006.

2006 ELECTION: Brownley (D) 62%
                       Dolz (R) 35%
                       Frankowski (L) 3%

ANNA MARIE CABALLERO (D)
28th Assembly District

Counties: Monterey, San Benito, Santa Clara, Santa Cruz
Cities: Salinas, Watsonville, Gilroy, Hollister, San Jose
Ethnicity: 28% White, 59% Latino, 2% Black, 9% Asian
Voter Registration: 51% D – 28% R – 18% DS
President 04: 60% Kerry, 39% Bush

The 2001 redistricting rearranged some territory in the 28th District but did little to disturb the relative position of dominant Democrats and underdog Republicans. The district itself is an odd mix of rapidly growing suburbs south of San Jose and inland Monterey County farm towns along Highway 101. Latinos dominate the political landscape with nearly 40% of registered voters.

Incumbent Simon Salinas was termed out in 2006, and given the district's registration tilt, his replacement was chosen in the Democratic primary. That campaign featured a pair of Latinas, each of whom was mayor of one of the district's larger burgs—Anna Marie Caballero of Salinas and Ana Ventura Phares of Watsonville. The candidates had remarkably similar histories. Both are attorneys who once worked

Anna Marie Caballero

for the California Rural Legal Assistance program. Both came from modest circumstances; Caballero from a mining family, Phares from migrant farm workers.

At the outset, Phares had the gaudier list of endorsements, including the National Organization of Women, both teachers' unions, the United Farm Workers, school employees, teamsters, the California Federation of Labor, state employees and the California Faculty Association —to name but a few labor groups in her camp. She drew support from Dolores Huerta of the Farmworkers, U.S. Rep. Loretta Sanchez, and a significant group of state legislators—Hispanic and non-Hispanic alike. Caballero had business, agricultural, and developer groups in her corner, which helped her outspend Phares. Caballero also benefited from more than $300,000 in independent expenditures from insurance companies and the California Farm Bureau. At least one significant labor group, hotel workers, jumped on for Caballero as well, and that helped blunt Phares' lock-step labor support.

In the end, Caballero won convincingly, carrying all four counties in the district and defeating Phares 61% to 39%. The difference may have been the size and voting tendencies of their respective constituencies. Salinas offered Caballero a bigger electoral base, and her more affluent core of backers tends to turn up at the polls more frequently. Phares was dependent on rural and poor voters, who do not vote in great numbers.

Caballero easily defeated Republican Ignacio Velazquez in November, running on her record as mayor of a city whose tottering finances required tough choices during the early 2000s. In Sacramento, that experience helped gain Caballero chairmanship of the Local Government Committee. It is the same committee chaired by her predecessor Simon Salinas.

BIOGRAPHY: Born: (Member declined to provide). Home: Salinas. Education: BS, UC San Diego; JD, UCLA. Military: None. Family: husband Juan Uranga, three children, one grandchild. Religion: Decline to state. Occupation: Attorney.

OFFICES: 3132 Capitol Building, Sacramento, CA 95814, Phone: (916) 319-2028, Fax: (916) 319-2128, email: assemblymember.caballero@assembly.ca.gov. Districts: 100 West Alisal Street, Salinas, CA 93901, Phone: (831) 759-8676, Fax: (831) 759-2961; 354-A Fourth Street, Hollister, CA 95023, Phone: (831) 638-3228, Fax: (831) 638-3226; 250 Main Street, Watsonville, CA 95076, Phone: (831) 761-7428, Fax: (831) 761-7426.

COMMITTEES: Appropriations; Jobs, Economic Development and the Economy; Local Government (chair); Water, Parks and Wildlife.

ELECTED: 2006 **TERM LIMIT:** 2012

ELECTION HISTORY: Salinas City Council, 1991–1998; Mayor, 1998–2006.

2006 ELECTION: Caballero (D) 58%
                 Velazquez (R) 42%

CHARLES CALDERON (D)
58th Assembly District

Counties: Los Angeles
Cities: Downey, Montebello, Pico Rivera, Whittier
Ethnicity: 18% White, 67% Latino, 1% Black, 12% Asian
Voter Registration: 52% D – 27% R – 17% DS
President 04: 61% Kerry, 38% Bush

Charles Calderon

Like other districts in this area, the 58th was recast on the mapmaker's forge, extending southwest to gather in Downey but giving up Norwalk in the south and South El Monte in the north. Hacienda Heights was added, as was the bulk of East Los Angeles. As a result, the voter-registration spread between Democrats and Republicans narrowed considerably—although not nearly enough to make elections uncomfortable for the majority party.

As for the assemblyman's name, it is Calderon, as it has been since the early days when George Deukmejian was settling into the governor's chair. It is always nice to keep a precious possession in the family, and the Calderon clan has maintained its grip on the area's Assembly seat for better than two decades. The new incumbent, Charles, is making his second appearance in the Assembly, having first been elected from this area in 1982. He served until 1990 when he won a seat in the state Senate. Although the district languished in the Democratic Party's political pawnshop for eight years, brother Tom Calderon came along to redeem it in 1998, leaving after two terms to make a futile run for insurance commissioner in 2002. Not that there was any danger the tribe would lose its grip on the fiefdom; brother Ron Calderon, with nary a day in elective office, stepped up to lay claim to the family fief in 2002. He served for two terms before he, too, moved on to the state Senate in 2006.

Re-enter Charles, who is eligible for three additional Assembly terms because he departed the lower house before the term limits clock began to tick with the passage of Prop. 140 in 1990.

Not everyone was enamored of the idea that representation in the 58th had become divine right of succession rather than the elective process, prompting three other Democrats to vie for the seat in the June primary. But the bigger field aided Calderon, who came away with 37% of the vote and the nomination, which is tantamount to victory in November.

Calderon enters the Assembly as a rookie in name only. Although his most recent day as a legislator occurred in 1998, before the century turned, he has 16 years as a legislator under his belt. In a house burdened with 35 other freshmen, Calderon's experience landed him a plum chairmanship, the Revenue and Taxation Committee, as well as a seat on the always-juiced Governmental Organization panel with its jurisdiction over horse racing, tobacco, and alcohol. And, of course, what session of the legislature would be complete without a Calderon sitting on the Insurance Committee. During his previous go-around in the Assembly and Senate, Calderon focused on insurance and banking issues and was regarded as one of those industries' most trusted allies.

But Calderon's enduring Capitol reputation comes as a member of what was known in the late 1980s as the "Gang of Five." That was a group of renegade Democratic assemblymen who tried to join forces with Republicans to topple the speakership of Willie Brown. The attempt failed for a variety of reasons, and the "Gang" suffered obligatory punishment at the hands of Brown and his leadership team. Each was stripped of prime committee assignments and relegated to small offices with limited staff until such time as penance was done. Gary Condit never reconciled with Brown, while Steve Peace, Rusty Areias, and Jerry Eaves eventually earned their way back into Brown's good graces. For his part, Calderon soon left the Assembly for the Senate where the stigma of a failed coup was less of a problem.

Calderon prospered in the Senate, becoming majority leader during his final term. Termed out in 1998, he made a run at attorney general, finishing a distant third in the Democratic primary won by Bill Lockyer. He has been a practicing attorney while out of office.

BIOGRAPHY: Born: Montebello, March 12, 1950. Home: Whittier. Education: BA, CSU Los Angeles; JD, UC Davis School of Law. Military: None. Family: wife Lisa, three children. Religion: Christian. Occupation: Attorney.

OFFICES: 2117 Capitol Building, Sacramento, CA 95814, Phone: (916) 319-2058, Fax: (916) 319-2158, email: assemblymember.calderon@assembly.ca.gov. District: 400 North Montebello Boulevard, Suite 100, Montebello, CA 90640, Phone: (323) 838-5858, Fax: (323) 838-0677.

COMMITTEES: Governmental Organization; Insurance; Revenue and Taxation (chair); Water, Parks and Wildlife.

ELECTED: 2006 **TERM LIMIT:** 2012

ELECTION HISTORY: Montebello School Board, 1979–1982; Assembly, 1982–1990; State Senate, 1990–1998.

2006 ELECTION: Calderon (D) 69%
                    Kleinpell (R) 31%

WILMER AMINA CARTER (D)
62nd Assembly District

Counties: San Bernardino
Cities: Rialto, Fontana, San Bernardino, Colton
Ethnicity: 21% White, 60% Latino, 14% Black, 3% Asian
Voter Registration: 49% D – 32% R – 15% DS
President 04: 62% Kerry, 37% Bush

Creeping into the foothills of San Bernardino County, this district is the last of the Wild West. Modern-day cowboys speed along in muscle trucks. The major road,

Wilmer Amina Carter

Highland Avenue, is a dusty highway that might have inspired Hank Williams to strum a tune about loneliness. In Fontana crowds gather at the California Speedway, one of the rodeo re-inventions known as a NASCAR racetrack. Staying in character, the district features a high-noon political duel.

Democrats from this part of the Inland Empire have long engaged in civil war. On one side sits U.S. Rep. Joe Baca, Sr., on the other, those who don't like Baca. The latter group is an often disparate mishmash of folks, many of whom once backed the legendary man Baca replaced in Congress—the late George Brown, Jr. This civil war plays out on various battlefields, this Assembly district included. Two years ago, Baca's son—Joe Junior—captured the seat by defeating a candidate associated with the old Brown camp. Instead of running for re-election, however, Junior sought to move up to a state Senate seat vacated by termed-out Democrat Nell Soto. In turn, the Bacas attempted to pass this seat to brother Jeremy. But their path was blocked by Wilmer Amina Carter, a 16-year veteran of the Rialto School Board. More significant, Carter had been George Brown's district director.

It proved a bad move all around for Clan Baca. Although dad easily won another term in Congress, both Joe Junior and Jeremy saw their dynastic reveries melt away in the June Democratic primary. Joe lost to fellow Assembly member Gloria Negrete McLeod. Jeremy was bounced by Carter, perhaps a victim of the family's aggressive reach. Woefully short of experience, Jeremy Baca had the advantage of family name—and a war chest in excess of $300,000. Carter ran outside the local Democratic Party machinery and raised only a quarter of Baca's treasury. But she, too, had name recognition, "tied to accomplishments," she told a local newspaper. Long involved in education, Carter is the only sitting member of the Legislature with a school named after her—Wilmer Amina Carter High School in Rialto. Baca gained some unwanted publicity when it was revealed that a DUI conviction forced him to participate in alcohol-treatment classes. During the campaign, the district's main newspapers, the *San Bernardino Sun* and *Riverside Press-Enterprise*, both endorsed Carter.

Carter won the primary 58% to 42%, then coasted past her November opponent, Republican Marge Mendoza-Ware, who Joe Baca, Jr., had defeated in 2004.

Carter, who is African American, inherits a diverse district. The "Ebony Triangle," with a large African-American community, has swayed politics for decades. In the cities of Fontana and Rialto, residents support local civil rights organizations such as the Westside Action Group and the San Bernardino Black Culture Foundation. In each of those cities, however, Hispanics outnumber African Americans.

As in the old West, danger comes in many forms—man made and natural. About 20 gangs operate in San Bernardino, which has the highest crime rate in the county. Between 1982 and 2002, the number of violent crimes reported annually tripled in Fontana and Rialto. In the summer of 2004, West Nile Virus broke out and spread rapidly. Perchlorate, a chemical found in rocket fuel, contaminates the drinking water wells. The hospital Community Care of San Bernardino has been sinking into debt over the last year and threatening to close its 291-bed facility and emergency room. The mountains above the district often ignite in wildfires that threaten the foothills, fill the air with smoke, and create a risk of winter mudslides that damage neighborhoods below. In the fall of 2004, rainstorms cut the fire season short, but then flooded the area and turned San Bernardino's streets into creeks.

San Bernardino County has exploded with housing development, but that hasn't lifted the district's economy. In 2000, the percentage of individuals and families living in poverty in Rialto, Colton, and Fontana was far higher than the national average. That percentage was nearly double the national average in San Bernardino, and more than double in Bloomington.

The major industry here is shipping and distribution. Since the former Norton Air Force Base has been transformed into the San Bernardino Airport, the industry has grown stronger, with national retailers opening distribution centers in the airport's warehouses. Still, in the district's major city and the seat of county government, San Bernardino, speed addicts and Jehovah's Witnesses walk the streets by day, passing the deserted Carousel Mall and empty storefronts. Panhandlers circle the gas stations, selling stories about their broken cars. The city council recently put a nine-month moratorium on opening pawnshops, 99-cent stores, and tattoo parlors downtown. The county's newspaper, *The San Bernardino Sun,* has begun building new digs on the outskirts of town. Restaurant Row, along the edge of the city, promises to lure dollars back with national restaurants and chains, from Starbucks to Home Depot. The effects remain to be seen.

BIOGRAPHY: Born: Neshoba County, MS, July 12 (declined to provide year). Home: Rialto. Education: BA, MA, CSU San Bernardino. Military: None. Family: husband Ratibu Jacocks, three daughters, six grandchildren. Religion: Baptist. Occupation: Businesswoman.

OFFICES: 2175 Capitol Building, Sacramento, CA 95814, Phone: (916) 319-2062, Fax: (916) 319-2162, email: assemblymember.carter@assembly.ca.gov. District: 201 North E Street, Suite 205, San Bernardino, CA 92401, Phone: (909) 388-1413, Fax: (909) 388-1176.

COMMITTEES: Aging and Long-Term Care; Business and Professions; Rules; Transportation; Veterans Affairs.

ELECTED: 2006 **TERM LIMIT:** 2012

ELECTION HISTORY: Rialto Unified School District Board of Education, 1983–1999

2006 ELECTION: Carter (D) 68%
                    Mendoza-Ware (R) 32%

PAUL COOK (R)
65th Assembly District

Counties: Riverside, San Bernardino
Cities: Moreno Valley, Hemet, Yucaipa, Perris, Banning, Beaumont, San Jacinto

Ethnicity: 61% White, 27% Latino, 6% Black, 3% Asian
Voter Registration: 35% D – 47% R – 13% DS
President 04: 60% Bush, 39% Kerry

Paul Cook

In 2001, the mapmakers who oversaw redistricting performed major surgery on the 65th District while maintaining its essential Republican character. An enormous wedge of unpopulated San Bernardino County north of Twentynine Palms was removed, as was half of heavily populated Moreno Valley in the west. Hemet and Perris were added as the district was pushed south along the crowded I-215 corridor. The district now looks like an odd undersea creature peering over a ledge. Contained within that creature, however, is some of the fastest growing territory in California where once-sleepy communities such as Yucaipa have seen miles of orange groves give way to golf courses, shopping malls, and big houses squeezed onto small parcels and breeding traffic congestion, bad air, and overcrowded schools.

The district was represented for the first half of the decade by Republican Russ Bogh, a descendent of San Bernardino's first mayor. Termed out in 2006, Bogh's major legislative accomplishment was the formation of an Inland Empire Caucus to focus on issues close to home. His replacement, Paul Cook, is in the conservative mold required of local Republicans. A Marine who did two tours of duty in Vietnam and retired as a colonel, he is a cancer survivor and *Capitol Weekly* newspaper named him honorary chair of the "Assembly Toughness Committee." Prior to his election, Cook taught anti-terrorism courses at UC Riverside. He survived a very competitive five-way GOP primary in June 2006, with four of the candidates gaining at least 20% of the vote.

During the campaign, Cook was involved in a testy argument over military credentials with another Republican candidate, Jim Ayers. Ayers, a San Jacinto councilman and retired Air Force reservist, objected that Cook listed himself as a "retired Marine colonel," even though that accurately described the 62-year-old Cook. Ayers protested to the courts, which refused to order a change. Ayers, meanwhile, was accused of misrepresenting his own military career and had to alter claims on his Web site that he had received a combat award during the Gulf War. Ayers had received a certificate available to anyone who participated in that action—not a medal.

Republican leadership recognized Cook's credentials with the military when he arrived in Sacramento by appointing him vice chair of the Veterans Affairs Committee.

BIOGRAPHY: Born: Meriden, CT, March 3, 1943. Home: Yucca Valley. Education: BS, Southern Connecticut State; MA, UC Riverside; MPA, CSU San Bernardino. Military: U.S. Marine Corps, retired colonel. Family: wife Jeanne, two children. Religion: Catholic. Occupation: Retired military, college professor.
OFFICES: 5126 Capitol Building, Sacramento, CA 95814, Phone: (916) 319-2065, Fax: (916) 319-2165, email: assemblymember.cook@assembly.ca.gov. District:

34932 Yucaipa Boulevard, Yucapia, CA 92399, Phone: (909) 790-4196, Fax: (909) 790-0479.

COMMITTEES: Budget; Budget Subcommittee 4 on State Administration; Higher Education; Veterans Affairs (vice chair).

ELECTED: 2006 **TERM LIMIT:** 2012

ELECTION HISTORY: Yucca Valley City Council, 1998–2006; Mayor, 2001, 2006.

2006 ELECTION: Cook (R) 60%
Ramirez-Dean (D) 37%
Taleb (PF) 3%

JOE COTO (D)
23rd Assembly District

Counties: Santa Clara
Cities: San Jose
Ethnicity: 19% White, 47% Latino, 4% Black, 27% Asian
Voter Registration: 51% D – 22% R – 23% DS
President 04: 66% Kerry, 33% Bush

Joe Coto

For years and years and years, the constituents of this section of San Jose grew accustomed to significant clout in the halls of the Capitol. Democrat John Vasconcellos, whose legislative career began in 1966 and included long stints as chair of the Assembly Budget Committee (and Ways and Means before that committee was split in two), represented part of the district, as did former state Senator Al Alquist, another local lion whose career ended in the 1990s.

But Vasconcellos's career finally came to an end in 2004 when he was termed out of the Senate, and Alquist has been gone from elective office for a decade. So, the reality of term limits finally has come home to the denizens of San Jose, most of whom live within the confines of the 23rd District.

An elongated district cut in two by Highway 101, the 23rd has an 80% ethnic population, with Latinos and Asians contributing equal numbers of registered voters. The district wasn't changed much from the previous version, although it lost some of its western territory, adding some to the south. The most dramatic changes occurred a decade ago, in the 1992 redistricting, when Democratic registration was strengthened, making what had been a marginal district into solid Democratic territory.

Democrat Manny Diaz held the district from 2000 to 2004 but left one term early to seek an open state Senate seat. It turned out to be a bad choice, given that he lost the Democratic primary to former Assemblywoman Elaine Alquist.

Diaz's departure set the stage for a four-way Democratic primary. The anointed candidate was Joe Coto. Although he had never been elected to office, Coto had the backing of Diaz, moderates in the Assembly Democratic Caucus, the Latino Caucus, firefighters and other labor groups, and a bevy of local elected officials. More significant, Coto, former superintendent of the Eastside Union High School District, was backed by teacher unions, which made him the "education candidate."

His principal opponent was San Jose businesswoman Kathy Chavez Napoli, who loaned her campaign $100,000 for the primary. That allowed her to hire Sacramento-based political guru Richie Ross to run her campaign. She had backing from Assemblymember Sally Lieber, a liberal Democrat who represents a neighboring district.

Although Napoli's seed money gave her temporary parity, Coto benefited from a number of independent expenditure campaigns, especially from the South Bay Labor Council and Moderate Democrats for California. Coto scored a comfortable primary victory and won big in the fall.

Once settled in Sacramento, Coto was given significant committee assignments, including seats on Rules, Budget, Education and Governmental Organization. Nearly all of the 21 bills introduced by Coto dealt with education. For the 2007 session, Coto was named to chair one of the Assembly's top juice committees—Insurance—but was dropped from both Rules and Budget.

But Coto's first term was marked by controversy stemming from another leadership post—that of vice chairman of the Latino Caucus, which found itself embroiled in several heated primary campaigns. In two instances, independent expenditure efforts funded by the caucus were denounced as racist. One mailer accused a Democratic candidate of supporting Armenian terrorists; a second mailer hit on a candidate's Asian heritage. In both instances, the targeted candidates were running against Latinos for open seats in safe Democratic districts. As caucus vice chair, Coto was in charge of raising money and doling it out to various IE campaigns.

BIOGRAPHY: Born: Miami, AZ, September 4, 1939. Home: San Jose. Education: BA, California Western Univ.; MA, Univ. of Phoenix. Military: None. Family: wife Camille. Religion: Decline to state. Occupation: Educator.

OFFICES: 2013 Capitol Building, Sacramento, CA 95814, Phone: (916) 319-2023, Fax: (916) 319-2123, email: assemblymember.coto@assembly.ca.gov. District: 100 Paseo De San Antonio, Suite 300, San Jose, CA 95113, Phone: (408) 277-1220, Fax: (408) 277-1036.

COMMITTEES: Arts, Entertainment, Sports, Tourism and Internet Media; Banking and Finance; Education; Insurance (chair).

ELECTED: 2004 **TERM LIMIT:** 2101

ELECTION HISTORY: None.

2004 ELECTION: Coto (D) 68%
                    Patrosso (R) 28%
                    Bloomberg (G) 5%

2006 ELECTION: Coto (D*) 74%
                    Patrosso (R) 26%

RATINGS:	AFL-CIO	CAI	CoC	CLCV	EQCA	CCS	CMTA	FARM	NARAL
	100	92	24	93	100	100	0	20	100

MIKE DAVIS (D)
48th Assembly District

Counties: Los Angeles
Cities: Los Angeles
Ethnicity: 5% White, 52% Latino, 30% Black, 12% Asian
Voter Registration: 69% D – 11% R – 16% DS
President 04: 86% Kerry, 13% Bush

Mike Davis

For most of the past half century, "South Central" has been synonymous with Los Angeles's African-American community, rap music, and gangs. This is the area that the 1991 film "Boyz 'n the Hood" put on the map and provides a comfort zone for rap artists like Snoop Doggy Dog. But the demographics of South Central are changing as Latino immigrants move into the area and blacks disperse to the west and other suburban areas, such as the high desert and Inland Empire. Asians have moved in, especially to a northern-district area known as "Koreatown." Currently, Latinos are more than half the population, although less than half that number have registered to vote. Until Latino voter registration improves, the political district—as opposed to the demographic district—will remain African-American.

A rectangle, this uniquely shaped district measures just three miles east to west, with its eastern boundary anchored on the I-110 freeway. North-south, it runs for nearly 11 miles, from Beverly Boulevard in the north to El Segundo Boulevard in the south. Redistricting shored up the black vote by lopping off Watts, which is increasingly Latino, and adding areas in the north and the south.

The new incumbent, Mike Davis, captured the seat in his second attempt, having lost a close primary in 2002 to then-Los Angeles City Councilman Mark Ridley-Thomas. Davis then had to twiddle his thumbs for four years until Ridley-Thomas ran for a state Senate district left vacant when Democrat Kevin Murray was termed out in 2006. Ridley-Thomas was elected to the Senate in 2006.

When he first ran for the legislature in 2002, no one gave Davis much of a chance against the well-known Ridley-Thomas. But Davis, an aide to Los Angeles Supervisor Yvonne Braithwaite-Burke, had backing from two of the area's most powerful forces—U.S. Representative Maxine Waters and former basketball great Magic Johnson, who provided the resources and oomph to bring Davis within a whisker of upsetting Ridley-Thomas. That campaign laid the groundwork for Davis's 2006 effort, but he did not come easily to the seat thanks to a tough, three-way primary. His main opponent was Anthony Willoughby, a Guatemalan-born civil-rights attorney backed by, among others, labor and Ridley-Thomas. Willoughby seeded his campaign with $80,000 and gained endorsements from both the *Los Angeles Times* and the alternative *LA Weekly*. With the exception of Ridley-Thomas, however, Davis rallied support from the area's African-American power structure, and that proved decisive. Davis won the primary with 53.5% of the vote, compared to 33.5% for Willoughby. A third candidate, community activist Ed Turner, took 13%.

In Sacramento, Davis is expected to hone in on transportation and labor, issues of interest to his former boss, Braithwaite-Burke. Unlike many of his freshman colleagues, Davis received no committee chairmanships, nor was he given a minor leadership post.

BIOGRAPHY: Born: Charlotte, NC, April 2, (declined to reveal year). Home: Los Angeles. Education: BA, University of North Carolina; MPA, CSU Northridge; MA, CSU Dominiguez Hills. Military: None. Family: wife Avis, two children. Religion: Baptist. Occupation: Legislator.
OFFICES: 2160 Capitol Building, Sacramento, CA 95814, Phone: (916) 319-2048, Fax: (916) 319-2148, email: assemblymember.davis@assembly.ca.gov. District: Administrative Offices East, 700 State Drive, Los Angeles, CA 90037, Phone: (213) 745-6656, Fax: (213) 745-6722.
COMMITTEES: Appropriations; Arts, Entertainment, Sports, Tourism and Internet Media; Human Services; Rules; Utilities and Commerce.
ELECTED: 2006 **TERM LIMIT:** 2012
ELECTION HISTORY: None.
2006 ELECTION: Davis (D) 89%
Green (R) 11%

HECTOR DE LA TORRE (D)
50th Assembly District

Counties: Los Angeles
Cities: South Gate, Lynwood, Bellflower, Bell Gardens, Downey, Bell
Ethnicity: 11% White, 79% Latino, 5% Black, 3% Asian
Voter Registration: 59% D – 19% R – 17% DS
President 04: 71% Kerry, 28% Bush

Hector De La Torre

The 50th District was reconfigured in the 2001 redistricting, with Lynwood and Bellflower added after Maywood and Huntington Park were stripped away. It is heavily Latino, but that hasn't prevented it from being an occasional battleground in Democratic primaries.

Rookie Assemblyman Hector De La Torre easily won the seat by capturing the 2004 Democratic primary, succeeding the late Marco Firebaugh who represented the area from 1998 to 2004. At the time, De La Torre was the mayor of South Gate and had been among a cadre of reformers trying to clean up a city plagued by scandal in recent years. His efforts resulted in a string of indictments.

As a freshman legislator, De La Torre was named to the Budget Committee and a key chairmanship—the subcommittee on health and human services. After his easy 2006 re-election, De La Torre was given one of the legislature's most significant assignments—chairman of the Assembly Rules Committee. That chairmanship embroiled him in an investigation soon after the 2006–2007 session began that fostered a nasty brawl with a Democratic colleague—Mervyn Dymally, the 80-year-old dean of the legislature. The probe centered on the practice of giving badges to donors and other favored constituents, badges that resemble those carried by members of the Assembly. Dymally had given one to a constituent who subsequently flashed it at a police officer in an attempt to avoid an arrest for drunk driving. The incident hit the papers, and Speaker Fabian Nunez ordered an investigation, to be headed up by De La Torre.

Dymally reacted badly. During a television interview, he called De La Torre "the most racist legislator I have encountered in over 40 years"—no mean statement from someone whose elective career began in 1963 and who has served as a legislator, congressman, and lieutenant governor. The bad blood between the two did not develop over fake badges, however. As several news outlets noted, Dymally and De La Torre clashed during the effort to clean up South Gate. Dymally later issued an apology that fell short of retracting his views of De La Torre.

BIOGRAPHY: Born: Los Angeles, May 29, 1967. Home: South Gate. Education: BA, Occidental College. Military: None. Family: wife Christine, three children. Religion: Decline to state. Occupation: Legislator.

OFFICES: 3173 Capitol Building, Sacramento, CA 95814, Phone: (916) 319-2050, Fax: (916) 319-2151, email: assemblymember.delatorre@assembly.ca.gov. District: 8724 Garfield Avenue, Suite 104, South Gate, CA 90208, Phone: (562) 927-1200, Fax: (562) 927-6670.

COMMITTEES: Budget; Budget Subcommittee 3 on Resources; Health; Local Government; Public Safety; Rules (chair);.

ELECTED: 2004 **TERM LIMIT:** 2010

ELECTION HISTORY: South Gate City Council, 1997–2004.

2004 ELECTION: De La Torre (D) 75%
　　　　　　　 Miller (R) 25%

2006 ELECTION: De La Torre (D*) 78%
　　　　　　　 Miller (R) 22%

RATINGS:	AFL-CIO	CAI	CoC	CLCV	EQCA	CCS	CMTA	FARM	NARAL
	100	96	24	90	100	100	0	20	100

KEVIN DE LEON (D)
45th Assembly District

Counties: Los Angeles
Cities: Los Angeles
Ethnicity: 12% White, 68% Latino, 2% Black, 16% Asian

Voter Registration: 57% D – 15% R – 23% DS
President 04: 79% Kerry, 20% Bush

Kevin De Leon

At the beginning of the decade, the 45th was home base to the speaker of the Assembly, Antonio Villaraigosa. Villaraigosa was elected mayor of Los Angeles in 2005, but his old district remains essentially the same—a mid–Los Angeles enclave centered on Elysian Park and Dodger Stadium and anchored on the south by a newly added chunk of East Los Angeles. Although more than half the registered voters are Latino, the district was represented for six years by an Anglo—former Los Angeles City Councilwoman Jackie Goldberg.

Goldberg was termed out in 2006, and the campaign to replace her created a fierce Democratic primary that featured the granddaughter of Cesar Chavez pitted against a close boyhood pal of Speaker Fabian Nunez—with three other candidates tossed into the salad.

Despite the allure of Christine Chavez's pedigree, Nunez's chum Kevin De Leon had all the advantages. An employee of the California Teachers Association, he was backed by Nunez, of course, but also by Mayor Villaraigosa and the county labor federation. That provided big bucks, but the scope of labor's involvement also led to second guessing. The Los Angeles federation made De Leon its top priority, and it poured resources into the effort at the expense of other candidates in Democratic primaries for open Assembly and Senate seats. Only De Leon emerged on top; the others lost, and some observers wondered if labor had diverted resources from those races in response to De Leon's persistent cries for help. Those cries proved misleading, as De Leon defeated Chavez by nearly 20 points.

The De Leon–Chavez primary provided a local venue for a power struggle playing out in Sacramento between Nunez and Sacramento-based political consultant Richie Ross, whose influence inside the legislature waned with Nunez's ascendancy. Ross's connection to the Chavez family goes back decades, to his work with Cesar Chavez and the embryonic United Farm Workers. But Ross is a political consultant and registered lobbyist who cannot contribute to political campaigns. That became an issue during the primary when *The Sacramento Bee* revealed that Ross had paid for substantial amounts of Chavez's campaign materials—in apparent violation of the law. The donation, which some characterized as a loan, prompted a complaint to the Fair Political Practices Commission. In the end, none of it mattered. Chavez's ancestry wasn't enough to overcome the local institutional firepower mustered on behalf of De Leon. He won convincingly over Chavez and three others; among them, tenants' rights lawyer Elena Popp, a Goldberg ally who had been endorsed by *La Opinion* and the *Los Angeles Times*.

De Leon secured a minor leadership post after the November election, that of assistant floor leader. But it was rumored that Nunez and his principal political guru—consultant Gale Kaufman—had visions of De Leon succeeding to the speakership once Nunez steps aside.

BIOGRAPHY: Born: San Diego, December 10, 1966. Home: Los Angeles. Education: BA, Pitzer College. Military: None. Family: Divorced, one daughter. Religion: Catholic. Occupation: Senior official, California Teachers Association.

OFFICES: 4140 Capitol Building, Sacramento, CA 95814, Phone: (916) 319-2045, Fax: (916) 319-2145, email: assemblymember.deleon@assembly.ca.gov. District: 106 North Avenue 56, Los Angeles, CA 90042, Phone: (323) 258-0450, Fax: (323) 258-3807.

COMMITTEES: Arts, Entertainment, Sports, Tourism and Internet Media; Governmental Organization; Health; Insurance.

ELECTED: 2006 **TERM LIMIT:** 2012

ELECTION HISTORY: None.

2006 ELECTION: De Leon (D) 83%
                    Allen-Newman (R) 17%

MARK DeSAULNIER (D)
11th Assembly District

Counties: Contra Costa
Cities: Concord, Antioch, Pittsburg, Martinez, Pinole
Ethnicity: 54% White, 21% Latino, 9% Black, 12% Asian
Voter Registration: 52% D – 25% R – 19% DS
President 04: 64% Kerry, 35% Bush

Mark DeSaulnier

Historically blue-collar and working-class, District 11 now flanks three bodies of water—San Pablo Bay, the Carquinez Strait, and Suisun Bay from Pinole to Antioch. It is solidly Democratic, even though the home-team margin was reduced with the removal of Richmond as part of the 2001 redistricting.

Physically, the district resembles a rectangle running across northern Contra Costa County. Two bridges connect Contra Costa County with Solano County, and one of them is a testament to the area's union roots—the newly constructed Al Zampa Memorial Bridge spanning Carquinez Strait from Crockett to Vallejo. The first major suspension bridge opened in the United States in the last 30 years, it is named for an ironworker who survived a fall while helping build the Golden Gate Bridge in the 1930s.

Unlike other Contra Costa districts, AD 11 isn't affluent. Rodeo, Pinole, and Crockett anchor it in the west, with their heavy Italian and Portuguese influence. Concord is the largest city in Contra Costa County and one of the Bay Area's older suburban communities. Ethnically diverse Pittsburg and Antioch lie along the eastern portion.

Democrat Mark DeSaulnier represents the area. A former Contra Costa County supervisor, DeSaulnier won the seat in 2006 after one easy and one tough election. The easy contest came in November against Republican Arne Simonsen, an Antioch city councilman who had Gov. Arnold Schwarzenegger stump for him but couldn't overcome a 27-point deficit in voter registration.

DeSaulnier's tough election was the June primary against three other Democrats, only one of whom was able to crack 5% of the vote. That would be Laura Canciamilla, a member of the Pittsburg school board and, more significantly, the wife of Joe Canciamilla, the termed-out iconoclastic Democratic lawmaker who held this seat from 2000 to 2006. During his six-year run, Joe Canciamilla showed a penchant for crossing party lines to work with Republicans on a myriad of issues, especially the budget where he formed a partnership with Keith Richman, a San Fernando Valley Republican known to buck his caucus. With Richmond, Canciamilla formed the Bi-Partisan Caucus, which tried to affect cooperation in an era marked by ear-blasting partisanship. He convened the Moderate Democrats Caucus as an attempt to balance the Assembly Democrats' noticeable shift to the left. Canciamilla further endeared himself to colleagues in the 2005–2006 legislative session by introducing a measure to take redistricting out of the hands of the legislature—a notion pursued by Schwarzenegger.

Joe Canciamilla's efforts did not go unnoticed by Democratic leadership, which rewarded him with zero committee chairmanships and by heavily backing DeSaulnier in the 2006 primary.

The 11th Assembly District was not the only brass ring at the heart of maneuvering by both DeSaulnier and the Canciamillas. Also in play is an East Bay Senate district (SD 7) now held by Democrat Tom Torlakson. Torlakson is termed out in 2008 and would like to run for statewide office in 2010, preferably superintendent of public instruction. But he faces a two-year gap between the end of his Senate career and the campaign for superintendent—a gap he would like to fill by moving to the Assembly; namely, to this district. To do that, he needs a handshake agreement to swap seats with the holder of this district. He could shake hands with an ally such as DeSaulnier, who is expected to run for the Senate in 2008. He could not shake hands with Laura Canciamilla for the simple reason that her husband plans to run for that very same Senate seat.

Against that backdrop, among others, did this Democratic primary take shape. It featured forces of moderation (for Canciamilla) against forces of liberalism (for DeSaulnier), both of which poured about $600,000 worth of independent expenditures into the campaign. The Chamber of Commerce weighed in for Canciamilla through JOBSPAC. Labor, developers, and environmentalists came through for DeSaulnier. The campaign was heavily negative, with Canciamilla calling attention to the support DeSaulnier has received over the years from developers to hint that he was for sale. Political extortion was evident as well. At one point, the *Contra Costa Times* reported that a local elected official had been pressured to withdraw an endorsement for Canciamilla by none other than Torlakson. DeSaulnier won by 13 points, with local observers citing as reasons low turnout and Canciamilla's negative campaign.

Unlike other rookies, DeSaulnier did not receive a committee chairmanship or leadership post once he hit Sacramento, but he did get a spot on the Rules and Appropriations committees. He also was named to the Transportation panel, which will give him a platform for his efforts to curb urban sprawl and gain funding to widen Highway 4—one of the East Bay's most congested transportation corridors. He also plans to lay the groundwork for a Senate bid in 2008, most likely against Joe Canciamilla.

BIOGRAPHY: Born: Lowell, MA, March 31, 1952. Home: Concord. Education: BA, College of Holy Cross. Military: None. Family: Two sons. Religion: Catholic. Occupation: Restaurant owner.

OFFICES: 4162 Capitol Building, Sacramento, CA 95814, Phone: (916) 319-2011, Fax: (916) 319-2111, email: assemblymember.desaulnier@assembly.ca.gov. Districts: 815 Estudillo Street, Martinez, CA 94553, Phone: (925) 372-7990, Fax: (925) 372-0934.

COMMITTEES: Appropriations; Human Services; Labor and Employment; Rules; Transportation.

ELECTED: 2006 **TERM LIMIT:** 2012

ELECTION HISTORY: Concord City Council, 1991–1993; Concord Mayor, 1994; Contra Costa County Board of Supervisors, 1994–2006.

2006 ELECTION: DeSaulnier (D) 67%
                    Simonsen (R) 30%
                    Nott (L) 4%

CHUCK DeVORE (R)
70th Assembly District

Counties: Orange
Cities: Newport Beach, Irvine, Tustin, Lake Forest
Ethnicity: 66% White, 13% Latino, 2% Black, 17% Asian
Voter Registration: 28% D – 48% R – 20% DS
President 04: 57% Bush, 42% Kerry

Chuck DeVore

With all the talk about Orange County's political and ethnic diversity, it may come as a surprise that there's an Assembly district that actually reflects the county's classic stereotype—white, rich, and Republican. Welcome to the 70th Assembly District, home turf of Assemblyman Chuck DeVore, where whites outnumber Latinos better than six to one, Asians four to one, and there are nearly twice as many registered Republicans as Democrats. The affluent communities of Irvine, Laguna Beach, Laguna Woods, Newport Coast, Portola Hills, Lake Forest, and Foothill Ranch are entirely within the district, as are some 90% of Newport Beach and Tustin. This is Republican Country, where Democratic candidates for state and federal elective office, from president on down, are sent scurrying, although an occasional local Democrat such as Irvine's Mayor Larry Agran manages to break cover.

The well-connected DeVore, an aerospace executive and major in the Army National Guard, was an aide to former U.S. Representative Chris Cox of Newport Beach, who left Congress in June 2005 after Pres. George Bush appointed him chairman of the Securities and Exchange Commission.

DeVore makes no bones about his partisan bent. In one League of Women Voters' profile for the March 2002 election, when DeVore was running for re-election to the Orange County Republican Central Committee, he listed his priorities as "build and motivate the Republican volunteer base, get out the vote, and help elect more Republicans." Clearly in sync with his base, DeVore was elected five times to the Central Committee. In the legislature, his chief priorities have been to cut taxes and provide funding to fight traffic congestion—he serves on the Budget and Revenue and Taxation committees and co-authored legislation, with Democrat Joe Canciamilla of Martinez, to provide $1.3 billion for transportation projects. DeVore was an early and ardent backer of Gov. Arnold Schwarzenegger, one of the governor's key allies in the Assembly budget machinery, and a voluble, articulate proponent of the GOP's tax-cutting, strong-defense mantra. That ardor cooled in 2006 when the governor cozied up to legislative Democrats as his re-election approached.

DeVore is an author, having penned "China Attacks," a 415-page paperback fictional account of a military move by China against Taiwan. That there were mixed reviews is an understatement: The 2001 paperback was described by some as an intriguing political drama and a must-read page-turner, and by others as the poorly crafted product of a "right-wing Clinton-hater." The book was not a bestseller.

DeVore is ambitious and has made no secret of his desire to eventually serve in Congress. Midway through 2005, an opportunity arose when Cox vacated his congressional seat en route to the SEC. DeVore was prominently mentioned as a candidate to succeed Cox, and given that the vacancy was to be filled in a special election, DeVore and others risked only ego and electoral reputation by entering the fray. DeVore opted out, persuaded by the large campaign treasury of the eventual winner—state Sen. John Campbell. DeVore also passed on running in the special election to replace Campbell, deferring to Diane Harkey, a conservative councilwoman from Dana Point. She lost the all-important GOP primary by only a few hundred votes to moderate Republican Assm. Tom Harman.

DeVore easily won a second term in 2006 and returns to Sacramento as vice chair of the Revenue and Taxation Committee and assistant floor whip.

BIOGRAPHY: Born: Seattle, WA, May 20, 1962. Home: Irvine. Education: BS, Claremont McKenna College; U.S. Army Command and General Staff College; Combined Arms Staff Services School. Military: U.S. Army, major, Desert Storm. Family: wife Diane, two daughters. Religion: Decline to state. Occupation: Business Executive.

OFFICES: 4102 Capitol Building, Sacramento, CA 95814, Phone: (916) 319-2070, Fax: (916) 319-2170, email: assemblymember.devore@assembly.ca.gov. District: 3 Park Plaza, Suite 275, Irvine, CA 92614, Phone: (949) 863-7070, Fax: (949) 863-9337.

COMMITTEES: Budget; Budget Subcommittee 4 on State Administration; Revenue and Taxation (vice chair); Veterans Affairs.
ELECTED: 2004 **TERM LIMIT:** 2010
ELECTION HISTORY: None.
2004 ELECTION: DeVore (R) 61%
                 Mariz (D) 36%
                 Baldwin (L) 4%
2006 ELECTION: DeVore (R*) 61%
                 Glover (D) 41%

RATINGS:

AFL-CIO	CAI	CoC	CLCV	EQCA	CCS	CMTA	FARM	NARAL
3	36	94	0	0	10	100	100	20

MIKE DUVALL (R)
72nd Assembly District

Counties: Orange
Cities: Fullerton, Anaheim, Placentia, Orange, Brea, Yorba Linda
Ethnicity: 46% White, 38% Latino, 2% Black, 11% Asian
Voter Registration: 32% D – 48% R – 17% DS
President 04: 60% Bush, 38% Kerry

Mike Duvall

The 72nd Assembly District includes northern inland Orange County, traditionally fertile Republican ground that, like much of the county, has seen shifting demographics in the past decade. Nearly half of Yorba Linda and all of Fullerton, Placentia, and Brea are in the district, plus pieces of Anaheim, La Habra, and Orange. Nearly 39% of the population is now Latino, up nearly 10% since the 1990 census, but fewer than one in five are registered voters—which works to the advantage of the largely white Republicans who have controlled the district for years. Nearly half the registered voters are Republicans, and overall the GOP has a 48% to 32% edge over Democrats, whose first political priority here is to tap into the large, unregistered Latino population. Thus far, they've had mixed results in a district that has somewhat a blue-collar flavor, pockets of income below Orange County's household average, and a turnout that went three-to-two for Bush in 2004.

For the past six years, the district was represented by moderate Republican Lynn Daucher, a former teacher who was capable, collegial, energetic, and low-profile. Daucher tried to move to the state Senate in 2006, but she was narrowly defeated by Democrat Lou Correa, an Orange County supervisor.

The campaign to replace Daucher in the Assembly was all about the Republican primary, which was intense but not nearly as close as some predicted. The winner was Mike Duvall, a businessman and member of the Yorba Linda City Council, who defeated Brea Councilman Marty Simonoff. Duvall clearly was the power establishment's preferred candidate, having racked up endorsements from the area's congressional delegation and most conservative members of the Assembly. He was backed by Anaheim Mayor Curt Pringle, a former Assembly speaker, the conservative California Republican Assembly, and the more moderate New Majority. Duvall and Simonoff tried to get to the right of each other on the issue of eminent domain, trading barbs over who most disliked the practice of government taking private property. The endorsements, and the cash and independent expenditure support they generate, provided Duvall with a comfortable leg up, and he defeated Simonoff two-to-one. Surprisingly, Duvall failed to crack 60% of the vote against Democrat John MacMurray, but that could be attributed to the overlapping Senate race between Daucher and Correa, which helped energize Democratic turnout.

Transportation is a key issue in this district, and GOP leaders put Duvall in a position to influence transportation policy—as much as any Republican can influence policy in the Democrat-dominated legislature by naming him vice chair of the Transportation Committee.

BIOGRAPHY: Born: Castro Valley, June 14, 1955. Home: Yorba Linda. Education: High School degree. Military: None. Family: wife Susan, two children. Religion: Catholic. Occupation: Insurance agency owner.

OFFICES: 4177 Capitol Building, Sacramento, CA 95814, Phone: (916) 319-2072, Fax: (916) 319-2172, email: assemblymember.duvall@assembly.ca.gov. District: 210 West Burch Street, Suite 202, Brea, CA 92821, Phone: (714) 672-4734, Fax: (714) 672-4737.

COMMITTEES: Budget; Budget Subcommittee 2 on Education Finance; Insurance; Transportation (vice chair).

ELECTED: 2006 **TERM LIMIT:** 2012

ELECTION HISTORY: Yorba Linda City Council, 2000–2006.

2006 ELECTION: Duvall (R) 59%
 MacMurray (D) 38%
 Cross (L) 3%

MERVYN DYMALLY (D)
52nd Assembly District

Counties: Los Angeles
Cities: Los Angeles, Compton, Paramount, Long Beach
Ethnicity: 3% White, 65% Latino, 29% Black, 1% Asian
Voter Registration: 67% D – 15% R – 14% DS
President 04: 86% Kerry, 13% Bush

One of the state's least Republican districts, the 52nd is dominated politically by blacks despite the fact that 65% of its population is Latino. The old district stopped at

Mervyn Dymally

Firestone Boulevard on the north, but the overhauled version extends to Martin Luther King Jr. Boulevard, taking in neighborhoods east of I-110 near Memorial Coliseum. Lynwood was dropped and a sliver of Long Beach tacked on in the south.

The lawmaker who represents the area—Democrat Mervyn Dymally—has been involved in more comeback tours than the Rolling Stones. This is the same Mervyn Dymally who first won election to the Assembly 42 years ago, staying for two terms before winning a pair of elections to the state Senate. It is the same Mervyn Dymally who served as Jerry Brown's lieutenant governor from 1975 to 1979 and who was defeated for re-election by Republican Mike Curb in 1978. Although nothing was ever proven, that loss was partially blamed on 11th-hour allegations, carried in the *Los Angeles Times*, that Dymally was involved in corruption of the state's Medi-Cal system.

In 1980, Dymally engineered the first of his comebacks by winning a dramatic Democratic primary for a seat in Congress. In that election, Dymally challenged nine-term incumbent Charlie Wilson, who had been caught up in an influence-peddling scandal known as "Koreagate." Also in the hunt was a former Democratic congressman named Mark Hannaford. Dymally blitzed the field, winning the primary with nearly 50% of the vote. He served six terms in the House of Representatives and then abruptly announced his retirement just before the filing deadline for the 1992 elections. Dymally timed his departure to give best advantage to his chosen successor, who happened to be his daughter, Lynn, a member of the Compton school board. Despite the best efforts of her father, Lynn Dymally lost the Democratic primary to Compton Mayor Walter Tucker, whose brief career in Congress ended in 1996 with a conviction for political corruption stemming from his days as mayor. While in Washington, Dymally had a reputation as one of the Congress's most accomplished junketeers, taking many trips to foreign lands, often at the behest of special interests that paid his tab.

Dymally fashioned his most recent comeback tour in 2002 when, at age 75, he ran for an open seat in the Assembly. Because all of his previous legislative service predates term limits, Dymally is eligible for a full 14-year ride—six in the Assembly and eight in the Senate. Given the district's overwhelming Democratic registration, Dymally's only hurdle came in the Democratic primary where his most formidable opponent was Paramount City Councilwoman Diane Martinez. But Dymally had the backing of then-Speaker Herb Wesson, former Speaker Bob Hertzberg, and then-Senate pro Tem John Burton—as well as financial support from several large independent expenditure campaigns. An effort to derail Dymally (dubbed "ABM," or "anybody but Mervyn") went nowhere as the veteran politician swept 52% of the primary vote against three challengers. He has used his second legislative go-around to champion community colleges and access to higher education for students from ethnic communities.

Dymally's election to the Assembly put his government pension on a serious escalator. Although the same initiative that imposed term limits (Proposition 140 in 1990) eliminated the legislative pension system, it grandfathered in those who already had qualified—Dymally among them. Before his current election, his pension was pegged to his highest salary as a state official, or the $42,500 he made as lieutenant governor in 1979. After raises granted in 2005, his salary as a legislator is $110,880.

Dymally's third and final term in the Assembly got off to a rocky start after the 2006 election when his office was in the middle of a controversy over the issuance of fake Assembly badges. Lawmakers are issued police-like badges as a means of identification, and several legislators have produced a variant of those badges as mementos for close associates, campaign volunteers, and contributors. One Dymally recipient flashed his souvenir at a Malibu police officer in an attempt to wiggle out of an arrest for drunk driving. The incident hit the papers, and an embarrassed Assembly Speaker Fabian Nunez ordered an investigation, headed by Democrat Hector De La Torre, chair of the Assembly Rules Committee. Dymally and De La Torre have a long and contentious history, which prompted Dymally to attach racial motives to the investigation. At one point, he called De La Torre "the most racist legislator I have encountered in over 40 years." Dymally later apologized for the remark. On a brighter note, Dymally was given a significant committee chairmanship, that of the Health Committee. Health care is expected to be one of the legislature's hottest issues in 2007 and 2008, placing Dymally at the forefront of efforts to reduce costs and to expand care to millions of Californians who do not carry health insurance.

Termed out of the Assembly in 2008, Dymally has already announced plans to run for the state Senate in District 25, now held by Democrat Ed Vincent. Vincent, too, is termed out in 2008, and Dymally likely will face stiff competition in the Democratic primary from a pair of former Assembly members: Carl Washington and Rod Wright.

BIOGRAPHY: Born: Trinidad, West Indies, May 12, 1926. Home: Compton. Education: BA, CSU Los Angeles; MA, CSU Sacramento; PhD, US International University. Military: None. Family: wife Alice, two children. Religion: Episcopalian. Occupation: Legislator.

OFFICES: 6005 Capitol Building, Sacramento, CA 95814, Phone: (916) 319-2052, Fax: (916) 319-2152, email: assemblymember.dymally@assembly.ca.gov. District: 322 West Compton Boulevard, Suite 100, Compton, CA 90220, Phone: (310) 223-1201, Fax: (310) 223-1202.

COMMITTEES: Agriculture; Budget; Budget Subcommittee 2 on Education Finance; Health (chair); Utilities and Commerce.

ELECTED: 2002 **TERM LIMIT:** 2008

ELECTION HISTORY: Assembly, 1963–1966, state Senate, 1967–1974; Lieutenant Governor, 1975–1979; U.S. House, 1981–1992.

2002 ELECTION: Dymally (D) 90%
Iles (R) 10%

2004 ELECTION: Dymally (D*) 100%

2006 ELECTION: Dymally (D*) 100%

RATINGS:

AFL-CIO	CAI	CoC	CLCV	EQCA	CCS	CMTA	FARM	NARAL
100	96	18	100	100	95	0	30	100

BILL EMMERSON (R)
63rd Assembly District

Counties: Riverside, San Bernardino
Cities: Rancho Cucamonga, Redlands, Upland, San Bernardino, Highland
Ethnicity: 51% White, 30% Latino, 9% Black, 7% Asian
Voter Registration: 35% D – 45% R – 16% DS
President 04: 56% Bush, 43% Kerry

Bill Emmerson

This Republican stronghold just east of Los Angeles takes on the shape of a partially eaten donut as it coils around the Democratic 62nd District. It starts at the western border of San Bernardino County in the suburban towns Rancho Cucamonga and Upland, then sweeps east along the edge of the San Bernardino Mountains, scoops up parts of the cities of San Bernardino and Highland, dips south through Redlands and Loma Linda into Riverside County, and finally curls west through Grand Terrace. Although its political orientation did not change with redistricting, its geography was altered with the loss of territory north of I-215 including Crestline.

Water is a crucial issue. It has always been scarce and now perchlorate, a rocket fuel component, has been found polluting area water sources. In addition, Mother Nature can be irritable. In the dry summer and fall, the mountains often erupt into devastating fires, and in winter, when the floods saturate the ravaged earth, the foothills are prey to landslides. Smog is thick, and commuting times on the area's spider web of freeways are long, as many residents work in nearby Los Angeles and Orange counties.

None of those downsides has stopped people from buying houses here with a fire-sale frenzy. Between 1996 and 2006, the median home price in San Bernardino County more than tripled to above $360,000, and the price in Riverside County quadrupled to over $415,000. Those amounts are attractively lower than anywhere else in southern California, and both counties still have an abundance of old farming land to transform into housing.

Two cities act as the district's power bases. In Rancho Cucamonga, near Los Angeles, white stucco houses and strip malls stretch through a barren landscape. This is the epicenter of San Bernardino County's housing development, and residents are primarily affluent white homeowners. Commuters have endured headache-inducing traffic jams thanks to construction work extending the 210 Freeway, Rancho Cucamonga's main road, which finished in 2006. Picturesque Redlands, on the east, has a similar population, although its median family income is slightly lower. Redlands is more established than its western sister, with wooden homes and boutiques on tree-lined streets. This is one of few cities in San Bernardino County where a person can dine at an independently owned restaurant rather than another link in some gastronomic chain.

In most of the district's other cities, the numbers are similar. Whites dominate and the percentage of people living in poverty is lower or equal to the rest of the country. The city of San Bernardino is the exception, with the percentage of those living in poverty twice the national rate—although the section that falls in this district isn't considered the "bad" part of the city.

One of the biggest tensions in both counties is illegal immigration. In the summer of 2004, the U.S. Border Patrol opened a new office in Temecula, a town in Riverside County far from the typical immigration hotspots of San Diego.

The freeway system has turned shipping and distribution into the area's main economic engine. United Parcel Service is one of the largest employers in the area, as is Environmental Systems Research Institute, an international software company that's leading the charge in Geographic Information Systems, or computer-based mapmaking. It employs 1,400 people at its Redlands headquarters. Private education helps the local economy as well. Run by the Seventh-Day Adventist Church, Loma Linda University has medical, nursing, and dental schools and a children's hospital and special cancer treatment center. There are 4,150 students enrolled in the University of Redlands, many in graduate programs for working adults.

Bill Emmerson, a dentist, won this seat in 2004 with 59% of the vote. But as in most safe districts, the real contest took place in the Republican primary. And because 2004 produced an open seat, the GOP primary brawl was as expensive as it was ugly. The incumbent, Bob Dutton, had served all of one term before moving on to the Senate seat vacated by termed-out Republican Jim Brulte.

Six Republicans filed for the race, and two of them—Emmerson and realtor Elia Pirozzi—went at each other with instruments not intended for home use. At issue was integrity, and each side sacrificed its own to prove that its opponent had none at all. Emmerson's team won overall election honors for "stupid pet trick of the year" when some of his operatives placed a crank call to Pirozzi headquarters, then forgot to hang up while discussing a plot to send out a fake labor endorsement of their opponent. Emmerson confessed after being confronted with a tape of the conversation, prompting several local officials to ask him to withdraw. He refused—and the campaign progressed in a concentric downward spiral right through to Election Night where a fistfight nearly broke out between campaign staffs gathered around a computer at the county registrar's office. A third candidate, businessman Mike Morrell, mostly watched the carnage from the sidelines. Underspent by his two hyper rivals, Morrell nonetheless polled well, in part due to voter disgust with the way Emmerson and Pirozzi conducted themselves.

The California Dental Association and California Medical Association created Emmerson's viability as a candidate out of whole cloth, spending $700,000 on him, or $68 for every vote Emmerson received on Election Day. With other cash and considerations, Emmerson forked out more than $1 million—about 10 times what Pirozzi spent. All that huff and huzzah bought Emmerson a victory margin the width of dental floss—he won by about 200 votes out of 35,000 cast and had to wait several weeks for the final results.

The general election was a walkover, but even so, Emmerson raised another half million dollars from dentists, dental supply companies, and dental associations and their employees. In the early 1970s, Emmerson cut his political teeth assisting Representative Jerry L. Pettis and Assemblyman Craig Piddle. After Sacramento, he returned home to Riverside County and joined his father's dentistry practice. This is his first elected office. Emmerson's ideology falls in line with Republican colleagues. Balancing the budget? He says cut spending without increasing taxes. Creating jobs? Cut business taxes. Driver's licenses for undocumented immigrants? No. Gay marriage? He prefers civil unions.

In Sacramento, some regard Emmerson as a bridge builder who wants to solve problems. But every politician arrives in the Capitol bearing plaudits or scars earned in previous jobs and campaigns. That reputation either serves as a foundation or is in need of repair. In Emmerson's case, his campaign shenanigans speak directly to his integrity and the sense of trust others must confide in him. At the outset, his reputation was something to overcome, but a generally gregarious nature and a knack for politics honed during the 1970s served him well. After an easy 2006 re-election, he was named vice chair of the Business and Professions Committee and made an assistant floor leader—a minor leadership post.

BIOGRAPHY: Born: Oakland, October 28, 1945. Home: Redlands. Education: BA, La Sierra University; MS, DDS, Loma Linda School of Dentistry. Military: None. Family: wife Nan, two daughters. Religion: Decline to state. Occupation: Orthodontist.

OFFICES: 4158 Capitol Building, Sacramento, CA 95814, Phone: (916) 319-2063, Fax: (916) 319-2163, email: assemblymember.emmerson@assembly.ca.gov. District: 10681 Foothill Boulevard, Suite 325, Rancho Cucamonga, CA 91730, Phone: (909) 466-9096, Fax: (909) 466-9892.

COMMITTEES: Appropriations; Business and Professions (vice chair); Health.
ELECTED: 2004 **TERM LIMIT:** 2010
ELECTION HISTORY: None.
2004 ELECTION: Emmerson (R) 59%
               McNamee (D) 35%
               Keedy (L) 7%
2006 ELECTION: Emmerson (R*) 60%
               Westwood (D) 40%

RATINGS:

AFL-CIO	CAI	CoC	CLCV	EQCA	CCS	CMTA	FARM	NARAL
7	44	100	4	0	25	90	100	20

MIKE ENG (D)
49th Assembly District

Counties: Los Angeles
Cities: El Monte, Alhambra, Monterey Park, Rosemead, San Gabriel
Ethnicity: 12% White, 47% Latino, 1% Black, 39% Asian
Voter Registration: 45% D – 26% R – 25% DS
President 04: 61% Kerry, 38% Bush

Mike Eng

Bisected by the I-10 freeway, this central San Gabriel Valley district is represented by Chinese-American Mike Eng, who was elected in November 2006 to replace his wife, Judy Chu, who had won the seat in 2001 after a special election that was something of an ironic victory. The special election was necessary because then-incumbent Gloria Romero had jumped to the state Senate. In 1998 Chu lost a Democratic primary to Romero, a tussle that symbolized district competition for power between Asians and Latinos. Termed out in 2006, Chu won a seat on the state Board of Equalization.

During the 1990s, Latinos usually won those battles, but redistricting increased the number of Asians and Republicans while slicing into the Latino and Democratic vote. East L.A., the most historic Latino community in California, was removed and replaced with El Monte and affluent San Marino to the north, home to the Huntington Library and Botanical Gardens. It is half Asian and votes Republican, although Democrats still enjoy a commanding lead in voter registration and the district isn't likely to fall into the GOP column any time soon.

The district has the highest percentage of Asian registered voters in southern California, mostly concentrated in the west and north in communities such as Monterey Park (Eng's home), Alhambra, San Gabriel, Rosemead, and San Marino. Latinos live in the east around El Monte. Monterey Park is the first city in the United States to have a majority Chinese-American City Council. Chu and Eng both have been on that council, and both served as mayor. Chu's brother Dean made a mark as mayor of Sunnyvale in 2004–2005 and is reportedly interested in an Assembly career as well.

Eng comes to the Assembly after a bruising June primary against Daniel Arguello, a city councilman from Alhambra who lost an Assembly primary to Chu in 2001. The contest split the Asian and Latino communities and divided loyalties within the Latino power structure. While Arguello corralled support from area lawmakers such as Sens. Gil Cedillo and Martha Escutia and Assm. Ed Chavez and Dario Frommer, Eng brought home the heavyweights—Los Angeles Supervisor Gloria Molina and Mayor Antonio Villaraigosa. He also had labor in his corner with an endorsement from the influential Los Angeles Federation of Labor and the California Teachers Association.

The campaign had negative racial overtones, with Eng the target. A last-minute mailer slammed Chu's attempt to hand the district to her husband and proclaimed that the seat "belongs to our community." It singled out Eng, warning that "he's not like us." The "us" in question was the Latino community, and the mailer was produced by an independent expenditure committee with close ties to the Assembly's Latino Caucus. The broadside generated anger among all ethnic groups for its blatant attempt to drive a wedge between two ethnic communities that have long worked to ease political and communal tensions.

In the end, it didn't matter. Eng, bolstered by a sizeable campaign treasury and endorsements from the *Los Angeles Times* and the alternative *LA Weekly*, cruised to a 17-point victory over Arguello. A third candidate, Dave Siegrist, took 11% of the vote.

Siegrist himself provided an entertaining side story: His daughter, Esthela Siegrist, was the Republican candidate who lost to Eng in November.

In Sacramento, Eng immediately secured a committee chairmanship—Business and Professions.

BIOGRAPHY: Born: Oakland, September 14, 1946. Home: Monterey Park. Education: BA, MA, JD, University of Hawaii. Military: None. Family: wife Judy Chu. Religion: Decline to state. Occupation: Immigration attorney.

OFFICES: 6025 Capitol Building, Sacramento, CA 95814, Phone: (916) 319-2049, Fax: (916) 319-2149, email: assemblymember.eng@assembly.ca.gov. District: 1255 Corporate Center Drive, Suite PH9, Monterey Park, CA 91754, Phone (323) 981-3426, Fax: (323) 981-3436; 10505 Valley Boulevard, Suite 306, El Monte, CA 91731, Phone: (626) 450-6116, Fax: (626) 450-6119.

COMMITTEES: Business and Professions (chair); Education; Environmental Safety and Toxic Materials; Joint Legislative Budget; Revenue and Taxation.

ELECTED: 2006 **TERM LIMIT:** 2012

ELECTION HISTORY: Monterey Park City Council, 2003–2006; Mayor, 2004–2005.

2006 ELECTION: Eng (D) 63%
Siegrist (R) 29%
Brown (L) 8%

NOREEN EVANS (D)
7th Assembly Distrtict

Counties: Napa, Sonoma, Solano
Cities: Santa Rosa, Vallejo, Napa, Calistoga
Ethnicity: 59% White, 20% Hispanic, 8% Black, 10% Asian
Voter Registration: 51% D – 27% R – 18% DS
President 04: 65% Kerry, 34% Bush

Noreen Evans

In its previous incarnation, this district encompassed the two primary wine valleys north of San Francisco—Napa and Sonoma. But in 2001, mapmakers sought to re-unify the cities of Santa Rosa and Vallejo, so the 7th District ceded Sonoma to the neighboring 6th District. The more famous Napa Valley remained, as did the Highway 29 wine tour that extends from Calistoga in the north to Napa in the south, with stops along the way at St. Helena and Yountville. The district has three main population centers—Santa Rosa in the west, Vallejo in the south, and Napa between them.

The district economy is mixed, although heavily dependant on—what else?—grapes and whatever is extracted from them. Vallejo is still recovering from the 1996 closure of the Mare Island Naval Base, although the Six Flags Marine World amusement park attracts tourists from all over northern California.

Redistricting did not change the district's political character; it remains Democratic and most of the action takes place in Democratic primaries. That is where Santa Rosa City Councilwoman Noreen Evans essentially won the right to succeed termed-out Democrat Pat Wiggins in 2004. Evans's opponent was Santa Rosa School Board member Jim Leddy, who served as district director for the area's Democratic state senator, Wes Chesbro.

Evans's victory came after a spirited primary that saw heavyweight Democrats weigh in on each side. Evans earned the endorsement of Assembly Speaker Fabian Nunez and then-San Francisco Mayor Willie Brown, Jr., while Leddy was backed by the area's powerful congresswoman, then-House Minority Leader Nancy Pelosi, state Senate pro Tem John Burton, state schools chief Jack O'Connell, and the teachers' and school employees' unions.

The district was a battleground for independent expenditures. Trial lawyers, firefighters, and nurses weighed in for Evans; doctors and realtors spent heavily for Leddy. Each campaign raised and spent about $300,000 exclusive of independent expenditures. Total primary expenditures exceeded $900,000, making it one of the most expensive legislative races in north coast history, according to the *Santa Rosa Press Democrat*.

In the end, Evans won by more than 10%—something of a landslide given the political dollars and heft committed to each side. She capitalized on the fact that her tenure on the Santa Rosa Council had lasted nine years longer than Leddy's on the school board, and many more voters knew her in their shared elective base. Her general election victory was a cakewalk.

Once in Sacramento, Evans—as a candidate backed by the speaker—landed a chairmanship (Human Services) and coveted spots on the Budget and Judiciary committees. She proved a loyal soldier during that first tour, and her credentials were bolstered when, in 2006, she ran unopposed for a second term—allowing her to share whatever money she raised.

Evans lost her chairmanship following the 2006 elections, but it was not a demotion. She was named Democratic Caucus chair—a prominent position on Nunez' leadership team.

BIOGRAPHY: Born: San Diego, April 22, 1955. Home: Santa Rosa. Education: BA, CSU Sacramento; JD, McGeorge School of Law. Military: None. Family: husband Mark Fudem, three children. Religion: Decline to state. Occupation: Attorney.

OFFICES: 3152 Capitol Building, Sacramento, CA 95814, Phone: (916) 319-2007, Fax: (916) 319-2107, email: assemblymember.evans@assembly.ca.gov. Districts: 50 D Street, Suite 301, Santa Rosa, CA 95404, Phone: (707) 546-4500, Fax: (707) 546-9301; 640 Tuolumne Street, Suite B, Vallejo, CA 94590, Phone: (707) 649-2307, Fax: (707) 649-2311.

COMMITTEES: Environmental Safety and Toxic Materials; Governmental Organization; Insurance; Judiciary.

ELECTED: 2004 **TERM LIMIT:** 2010
ELECTION HISTORY: Santa Rosa City Council, 1996–2004.
2004 ELECTION: Evans (D) 60%
                   Kreuger (R) 37%
                   Smith (L) 3%
2006 ELECTION: Evans (D*) 100%
RATINGS: AFL-CIO CAI CoC CLCV EQCA CCS CMTA FARM NARAL
             96   96   24   100   100 100   10   20   100

MIKE FEUER (D)
42nd Assembly District

Counties: Los Angeles
Cities: Los Angeles, Beverly Hills, West Hollywood
Ethnicity: 75% White, 10% Latino, 4% Black, 8% Asian
Voter Registration: 53% D – 21% R – 22% DS
President 04: 72% Kerry, 27% Bush

Mike Feuer

Money, money, money. And more money. This is California's most affluent Assembly district and one of its most liberal. It also happens to be the home of California's two most recent governors—Gray Davis and Arnold Schwarzenegger. Davis began his elective career in this district when he fleetingly represented it in the Assembly during the early 1980s. Although neither Davis nor Schwarzenegger is Jewish, the district touts the highest percentage of Jewish voters in the state.

The 42nd District personifies what is commonly known as the "Westside." And while Hollywood and neighborhoods to the east have become more bohemian, the 42nd maintains its aura of affluence, style, and pizzazz.

A Democratic district surrounded by more Democratic districts did not leave much room for tinkering and trade-offs during the 2001 redistricting. Basically, the old district was pushed north toward Burbank Boulevard, while the southern end, including UCLA, was donated to then-Speaker Herb Wesson. The eastern part of the district is home to the Hollywood Hills and Hancock Park, while in the middle lie West Hollywood, with its large gay and Russian populations, and Beverly Hills. The district takes in Brentwood, Bel Air, and portions of the San Fernando Valley, including Sherman Oaks, Studio City, and Universal City (home to Universal Studios).

District representatives are reliably liberal and have to be lest they suffer a challenge from the left. Paul Koretz represented the area from 2000 to 2006, and the campaign to replace him attracted five Democrats, a pair of Republicans, and a Libertarian. Of those eight pretenders, only two mattered, Democrats both: Los Angeles

City Councilman Mike Feuer and West Hollywood Councilwoman Abbe Land. The primary was expensive and highly competitive, with the two contenders spending over $800,000. Feuer, however, had several advantages. A former executive director of Bet Tzedek Legal Services, which provides free legal aid to the poor, Feuer raised more money than Land, though not by much, and was better known thanks to his council seat and previous campaigns. In 2001, for instance, he was the putative frontrunner for Los Angeles city attorney but fell victim to an upset fashioned by Rocky Delgadillo. Feuer originally won his city council seat by defeating Barbara Yaroslavsky, the wife of Los Angeles County Supe. Zev Yaroslavsky. In this campaign, he was endorsed by Koretz and other legislators, as well as the *Los Angeles Times,* which cited his "pragmatism, candor and coalition-building skills." Land had backing from state Sen. Sheila Kuehl, among others.

The campaign went heavily negative at the end, with Feuer accusing Land of casting votes on behalf of contributors while a member of the West Hollywood Council. Land's allies rallied to her defense, with Kuehl especially calling Feuer "ill prepared" for the Assembly. In the end, Feuer won convincingly despite wide respect for Land, piling up 52% of the vote to her 36%.

Known as a consensus builder, Feuer earned a reputation as a budget expert during his five years on the LA Council, and that experience landed him a seat on the Assembly Budget Committee and chairmanship of its subcommittee on technology and transportation. He also was named to two other significant panels—Judiciary and Revenue and Taxation. He said he would work to reduce class sizes and provide universal health care for children.

BIOGRAPHY: Born: San Bernardino, May 14, 1958. Home: Los Angeles. Education: BA, JD, Harvard. Military: None. Family: wife Gail, two children. Religion: Jewish. Occupation: Attorney.

OFFICES: 4005 Capitol Building, Sacramento, CA 95814, Phone: (916) 319-2042, Fax: (916) 319-2142, email: assemblymember.feuer@assembly.ca.gov. District: 9200 Sunset Boulevard, PH-15, West Hollywood, CA 90069, Phone: (310) 285-5490, Fax: (310) 285-5499.

COMMITTEES: Budget; Budget Subcommittee 5 on Information Technology and Transportation (chair); Environmental Safety and Toxic Materials; Judiciary; Revenue and Taxation.

ELECTED: 2006 **TERM LIMIT:** 2012

ELECTION HISTORY: Los Angeles City Council, 1995–2000.

2006 ELECTION: Feuer (D) 74%
Sion (R) 22%
Goldman (L) 5%

JEAN FULLER (R)
32nd Assembly District

Counties: Kern, San Bernardino

Cities: Bakersfield, Ridgecrest, Tehachapi
Ethnicity: 65% White, 24% Latino, 5% Black, 3% Asian
Voter Registration: 30% D – 52% R – 14% DS
President 04: 70% Bush, 29% Kerry

Jean Fuller

The most difficult job in a term-limited legislature is that of a rookie. Mastering Sacramento's learning curve is akin to scaling Mt. Everest, where the summit is shrouded in a fog of policy and politics and the climb must begin even before one is sworn into office. It must be made with a minimum of missteps, and there are few if any veterans to help show the way.

The previous incumbent from this district, Republican Kevin McCarthy, mastered the basics. Chosen in 2004 as *California Journal*'s Rookie of the Year, McCarthy's swift rise to power exceeded all expectations. He did not linger long in the legislature. When the retirement of the region's powerful congressman Bill Thomas opened up a House seat, McCarthy seized it, leaving his Assembly seat vacant.

The vacancy stirred up long-held grudges among Republicans in this part of the southern Central Valley. On one side stood Thomas and his allies, including McCarthy; on the other, conservatives and those who chafe under what they consider Thomas's dictatorial political machine. In this race, the Thomas forces backed Jean Fuller, the former superintendent of schools for Bakersfield. Thomas's foes, led by state Sen. Roy Ashburn, weighed in for Stan Ellis, a wealthy businessman from Bakersfield.

As Republican campaigns in this area are wont to be, the GOP primary was expensive and tense, with the various camps trading charges and countercharges to promote their conservative credentials and with more than $1.5 million thrown into the fray from all sides. Ellis held an advantage in money, having seeded his campaign with more than $500,000 in personal funds, and then raised another $100,000 from other donors. Fuller raised close to $300,000, adding a $160,000 loan to herself.

There was a third Republican of note—former Assm. and state Sen. Phil Wyman, an old political warhorse first elected to the legislature in the 1970s. Wyman, who has been out of office for nearly a decade, raised short of $200,000. But he felt the brunt of a negative independent expenditure from an old political foe—the California Correctional Peace Officers Association—which dumped $386,000 in an effort to keep Wyman from returning to office.

Ultimately, the Thomas machine prevailed, although the campaign was not without its amusing moments. At one point, the Ellis forces distributed a mailer that implied endorsements from both Thomas and McCarthy. The pair, of course, backed Fuller, who captured 42% of the primary vote, with Ellis snagging 36% and Wyman a distant third with 22%. Fuller easily defeated the Democrat in November.

Fuller represents a southern San Joaquin Valley district that includes the bulk of Bakersfield but pushes east into the Mojave Desert and south to the I-5 Grapevine. Republican leadership named her vice chair of the Assembly Natural Resources Committee, and she serves as an assistant floor whip. Given her background and work experience, Fuller likely will focus on education issues as well.

BIOGRAPHY: Born: Kern County, April 16, 1950. Home: Bakersfield. Education: AA, CSU Fresno; BA, CSU Los Angeles; MPA, UC Santa Barbara; PhD, USC. Military: None. Family: husband Russell. Religion: Decline to state. Occupation: School superintendent.

OFFICES: 3098 Capitol Building, Sacramento, CA 95814, Phone: (916) 319-2032, Fax: (916) 319-2132, email: assemblymember.fuller@assembly.ca.gov. District: 4900 California Avenue, Suite 140A, Bakersfield, CA 93309, Phone: (661) 395-2995, Fax: (661) 395-3883.

COMMITTEES: Agriculture; Budget; Budget Subcommittee 2 on Education Finance; Natural Resources (vice chair).

ELECTED: 2006 **TERM LIMIT:** 2012

ELECTION HISTORY: None.

2006 ELECTION: Fuller (R) 72%
Vega (D) 28%

TED GAINES (R)
4th Assembly District

Counties: Alpine, El Dorado, Placer, Sacramento
Cities: Roseville, Rocklin, South Lake Tahoe, Auburn, Placerville, Folsom, Rio Linda
Ethnicity: 79% White, 11% Hispanic, 3% Black, 4% Asian
Voter Registration: 31% D – 47% R – 17% DS
President 04: 61% Bush, 38% Kerry

Ted Gaines

In terms of land mass, the 4th District was given liposuction during the 2001 redistricting, shrinking considerably with the loss of Mono County and mountainous chunks of Amador and Calaveras counties. The surgery was necessary to offset population growth in suburban areas north and east of Sacramento, including the newly attached Rio Linda—talk-show host Rush Limbaugh's favorite California punching bag. Although most of California's famed Mother Lode has been excised, the Lake Tahoe resort area remains, as do most of northern California's best ski areas. But the loss of territory did not change the district's political character. It was solid Republican before surgery and solid Republican after mapmakers finished with it.

Republican Tim Leslie represented the area in one house or the other for 18 years. A former lobbyist and legislative aide, Leslie never let defeat—personal or political—get him down. After several unsuccessful tries for public office, he finally captured an Assembly seat in 1986, and although a rookie, Leslie arrived with plenty of Capitol experience, having served as a Republican consultant to the old Ways and Means Committee and as a lobbyist for the counties. He eventually was elected to the state Senate in 1990, and in 2000 returned for three more terms in the Assembly after being termed out of the upper house in 1998. In the two-year gap, he ran unsuccessfully for lieutenant governor (losing to Cruz Bustamante in 1998) and battled a rare form of bone cancer.

Termed out of the legislature for good, Leslie left a vacant chair to be filled in 2006. Like all districts where voter registration is lopsided in favor of one party, Leslie's was captured in the Republican primary. Unlike such districts, this one did not produce much of a primary tussle. Placer County Supe. Ted Gaines declared early, raised a lot of money, pulled in any endorsement worth having, and ran away with 81% of the vote. He thumped Democrat Robert Haswell in the November general election and can look forward to a six-year career in the Assembly. A conservative, Gaines introduced his first bill on the first day of the legislative session, a measure that restricts increases in state spending to inflation and population growth. Although a rookie, he was given a committee vice chairmanship—Banking and Finance.

BIOGRAPHY: Born: Sacramento, April 25, 1958. Home: Roseville. Education: BA, Lewis and Clark College. Military: None. Family: wife Beth, six children. Religion: Christian. Occupation: Owner, insurance agency.

OFFICES: 2002 Capitol Building, Sacramento, CA 95814, Phone: (916) 319-2004, Fax: (916) 319-2104, email: assemblymember.gaines@assembly.ca.gov. District: 1700 Eureka Road, #160, Roseville, CA 95661, Phone: (916) 774-4430, Fax: (916) 774-4433.

COMMITTEES: Banking and Finance (vice chair); Health; Labor and Employment.

ELECTED: 2006 **TERM LIMIT:** 2012

ELECTION HISTORY: Placer County Board of Supervisors, 2000–2006.

2006 ELECTION: Gaines (R) 58%
              Haswell (D) 36%
              Fritts (G) 3%
              Murphy (L) 3%

CATHLEEN GALGIANI (D)
17th Assembly District

Counties: Merced, San Joaquin, Stanislaus
Cities: Stockton, Tracy, Merced, Los Banos, Atwater
Ethnicity: 37% White, 43% Latino, 6% Black, 10% Asian
Voter Registration: 47% D – 37% R – 13% DS
President 04: 49.7% Kerry, 49.3% Bush

Cathleen Galgiani

The reconstruction of Central Valley Assembly districts in 2001 reinforced the notion that the Valley is in political flux, with Republican gains more noticeable here than anywhere else in California. Prior to redistricting, two Democratic districts lay across this area. But because of the conservative nature of the San Joaquin Valley, the 26th District was rebuilt to strengthen Republicans. In exchange, Democrats shored up their dwindling majority in the 17th District. The machinations did not remove the 17th from GOP target lists, however, because Republicans running statewide continue to do well here. In 2004, George Bush and John Kerry ran dead even, highlighting the district's competitive nature.

The old version of AD 17 was compact and fully contained within San Joaquin County, anchored by Stockton. The new version resembles Italy with gout as it slices the heart out of Stockton, then sprawls south and east to capture a pair of Central Valley anchors—Los Banos and the city of Merced. The Merced County portion of the district will vote Republican, as evidenced by the fact that George Bush received 57% of the Merced vote in 2004 despite a three-point Democratic registration edge. Arnold Schwarzenegger did even better in 2006, capturing 63% of Merced's vote.

Those trends foretold all-out war for this district in 2006, when incumbent Democrat Barbara Matthews termed out and the seat became vacant. Matthews weathered repeated GOP targeting in her three campaigns for the Assembly, but Republicans came close only in 2000—before the district was revamped. Matthews was the ideal Democrat for the area. A moderate who often bucked her caucus on issues involving business, agriculture, and the environment, she tacked far enough right to mollify such district powerhouses as the farm bureau and local chambers of commerce.

The Democrat chosen to carry the flag in 2006 was in the Matthews mold. In fact, she was Matthews' chief of staff—Cathleen Galgiani, a veteran legislative aide with her own strong ties to the district. Moderate like her former boss, Galgiani had little trouble with Winton businessman William Sweet in the Democratic primary. Backed with substantial resources from Assembly Democrats and their allies, Galgiani brushed Sweet aside with 77 percent of the primary vote, girding herself for what promised to be a nail-tough campaign against Republican Gerry Machado, president of the Tracy Unified School District board.

Although from different parties, little separated the two candidates on seminal issues such as illegal immigration, health care, and education, so the campaign focused on peripherals—experience and family values. Machado touted his work on the school board; Galgiani cited her role in Matthews' legislative operations and her history of working for area legislators such as John Garamendi and Patrick Johnston. Machado's allies used family values to club Galgiani for being single and childless, and although the candidate distanced himself from remarks made by others, they added a negative tone to the campaign's final days.

The contest proved expensive. Like her former boss, Galgiani was backed by the California Farm Bureau Federation and other political action committees, and by

Democratic Party operations around the state. These contributions totaled well over $1.4 million and were the source of controversy as campaign-finance reformers such as Common Cause claimed that Democrats were gaming the system to fund Galgiani and others far beyond what the law allowed from a single source.

When polls closed, Galgiani's margin of victory exactly mirrored Matthews in 2004—60% to 40%. Galgiani's money was one reason, but another was the swirl created throughout the district by an overlapping election campaign—the Democrats' successful effort to defeat incumbent U.S. Rep. Richard Pombo. That campaign generated national interest as Republicans and Democrats vied for control of the Congress, and millions of dollars worth of resources—not to mention top political talent—poured into this part of the San Joaquin Valley. Democrats were energized to vote, and that energy helped Galgiani.

Given her rhetoric during the campaign and her political pedigree as Matthews' chief aide, Galgiani is expected to be one of the more moderate members of the Assembly Democratic Caucus. She was initially overlooked when Democratic leaders passed out committee chairmanships, 13 of which went to Galgiani's fellow rookies. She does sit on two committees of vital importance to her district, however—Agriculture and Transportation.

BIOGRAPHY: Born: Stockton, January 4, 1964. Home: Stockton. Education: BA, CSU Sacramento. Military: None. Family: Single. Religion: Decline to state. Occupation: Legislative chief of staff.
OFFICES: 2170 Capitol Building, Sacramento, CA 95814, Phone: (916) 319-2017, Fax: (916) 319-2117, email: assemblymember.galgiani@assembly.ca.gov. Districts: 31 East Channel Street, Suite 306, Stockton, CA, 95202, Phone: (209) 948-7479, Fax: (209) 465-5058; 806 West 18th Street, Merced, CA 95340, Phone (209) 726-5465, Fax: (209) 726-5469.
COMMITTEES: Agriculture; Higher Education; Labor and Employment; Transportation.
ELECTED: 2006 **TERM LIMIT:** 2012
ELECTION HISTORY: None.
2006 ELECTION: Gagliani (D) 60%
                   Machado (R) 40%

BONNY GARCIA (R)
80th Assembly District

Counties: San Diego, Imperial
Cities: Indio, Cathedral City, El Centro
Ethnicity: 33% White, 60% Latino, 4% Black, 2% Asian
Voter Registration: 46% D – 37% R – 14% DS
President 04: 52% Kerry, 47% Bush

Bonny Garcia

Tinkering around the edges of this large desert district so changed its political character that Republican Dave Kelley, a 23-year veteran of the legislature, retired despite having two Assembly punches left on his Capitol ticket. Rancho Mirage, La Quinta, and Indian Wells were removed, as were parts of Hemet and Valle Vista. Although registration didn't change much (Democrats went from a 3% to an 8% advantage), a third of registered voters were now Latino, and the dual hit was enough for Kelley—whose pre-redistricting margin of victory in 2000 had been 8%.

With Kelley gone for 2002, Republicans coalesced around Bonnie Garcia—legislative aide to the area's state senator, Jim Battin. Garcia reaped support from legislative Republicans, insurance interests, prison guards, and the area's influential gaming tribes to capture her first victory over Democrat Joey Acuna, Jr., who had lost to Kelley in 2000 in the old district. With her victory, Garcia became the first Puerto Rican American elected to the California Legislature.

Thus began a wild ride through the annals of California elective and legislative history. Garcia has proven to be ebullient, voluble, and colorful, infusing her legislative tenure with passion and controversy. In 2004, she won re-election over Democrat Mary Ann Andreas, former head of the Morongo Band of Mission Indians, one of California's most powerful gaming tribes. That connection alone was supposed to play havoc with Battin, Garcia's political benefactor and a close tribal ally. The havoc never materialized, and Garcia rang up an impressive win. For instance, she won Democrat-leaning Imperial County with 60% of the vote—the exact percentage Imperial gave to U.S. Senator Barbara Boxer.

In 2005, Garcia sponsored a controversial initiative—backed by the governor—to increase from two to five years the period required before a public school teacher can gain tenure. Called the "Put Kids First Act," the proposal has made Garcia the bane of the California Teachers Association and put her—once again—at the top of Democratic target lists come 2006. The candidate chosen to wage that war was Steve Clute, a former legislator who had served in the Assembly during the 1980s and 1990s but who had been out of elective politics for more than a decade. Democrats poured money into Clute's campaign, seeing it as one of the few opportunities to gain a seat.

As in previous elections, Garcia had strong support from Gov. Arnold Schwarzenegger—some of it controversial. In a broadside fired in the campaign for governor, Democrats leaked a supposedly private—and highly embarrassing—audio tape purloined from Schwarzenegger's Web site, during which the governor was heard describing Garcia as "hot." Garcia shrugged off the comment, but during her campaign, she told a high school class she wouldn't kick the governor out of bed. The comment was typical of Garcia, whose often earthy language spices her floor debates. Garcia apologized, but the comment affected her campaign, especially among conservative retirees who populate parts of her district. Clute immediately seized on the remark, questioning Garcia's ethics and propriety. With each side shelling out over $1 million, the desert became saturated with mailers and low-budget TV and radio ads.

In the waning days, Clute tried to make Garcia the sole issue, accusing her of self-promotion at the expense of district needs. Garcia responded by branding Clute a career politician in search of a district, a fact that Clute's campaign seemed to verify when it conceded that although his legal residence was inside the 80th District, his primary home for years had been Palm Desert—in another Assembly district.

The election was too close to call on Election Day and did not resolve itself until nearly three weeks later, after more than 100,000 absentee ballots had been counted. Garcia survived, but barely, aided in part by her having captured—once again—Imperial County. She returned to Sacramento, where she resumed her post as vice chair of the Housing and Community Development Committee, and her role as one of the legislature's entertainment centers.

BIOGRAPHY: Born: New York City, NY, August 13, 1962. Home: Cathedral City. Education: BS, Southern Illinois University. Military: None. Family: husband Javier, two children. Religion: Christian. Occupation: Businesswoman.

OFFICES: 4009 Capitol Building, Sacramento, CA 95814, Phone: (916) 319-2080, Fax: (916) 319-2180, email: assemblymember.garcia@assembly.ca.gov. District: 1430 Broadway, Suite 8, El Centro, CA 92243, Phone: (760) 336-8912, Fax: (760) 336-8914.

COMMITTEES: Governmental Organization; Housing and Community Development (vice chair); Jobs, Economic Development and the Economy.

ELECTED: 2002 **TERM LIMIT:** 2008

ELECTION HISTORY: None.

2002 ELECTION: Garcia (R) 51%
                     Acuna (D) 49%

2004 ELECTION: Garcia (R*) 58%
                     Andreas (D) 42%

2006 ELECTION: Garcia (R*) 52%
                     Clute (D) 48%

RATINGS:

AFL-CIO	CAI	CoC	CLCV	EQCA	CCS	CMTA	FARM	NARAL
10	52	100	11	7	21	80	90	20

MARTIN GARRICK (R)
74th Assembly District

Counties: San Diego
Cities: Carlsbad, Escondido, Encinitas, San Marcos
Ethnicity: 65% White, 26% Latino, 2% Black, 5% Asian
Voter Registration: 29% D – 45% R – 21% DS
President 04: 57% Bush, 42% Kerry

The inland region of northern San Diego County is rock-ribbed Republican, marked by pell-mell growth that in little more than two decades has transformed a largely rural, agricultural area into sprawling suburbia laced with crowded highways

Martin Garrick

and subdivisions. In the heart of the region is the 74th Assembly District, which ranges from Escondido in the east to Del Mar, Carlsbad, and Solana Beach in the west, and all of Vista in the middle. The entire district, especially the Lake San Marcos, Vista, and inland areas, are havens for retirees who are attracted to the genial climate, and the elderly have been the fast-growing portion of the population for years. Voter registration runs 45% Republican to 29% Democrat, two-thirds of the population is white, and just over a quarter is Latino, although only about 8.6% of the Latino population is registered to vote. As in other political districts with sizeable Latino communities, the Latinos' lack of registration has cost them considerably.

Median household income is about $50,000, and housing prices in the north county—as in the rest of San Diego—are spiraling out of sight, far outstripping the purchasing power of most first-time home buyers. One 2005 study put the average cost of a new detached home in San Diego at $781,000, a resold single family home at $530,000, and a new condominium at $490,000—a third above the national average and a crimp in the area's attempt to attract a new, younger workforce. Those prices may not shock those in Orange, Ventura, Monterey, or San Francisco counties, but they are higher than most of the rest of California. At those prices, one used to be able to get a nice place in La Jolla or Del Mar. Now, it buys you 1,200 square feet far inland—maybe. In return for all the money, you get a legendary climate, miserable traffic along Highway 78, the Oceanside-Escondido corridor; an overabundance of shopping malls, and crowds everywhere. Bush took nearly 57% of the vote here in 2004, and nearly as much in 2000, and few Democrats have any realistic expectation of making headway.

Mark Wyland, a Fulbright scholar born and raised in Escondido, served three terms representing this area in the Assembly, and a nifty brawl erupted to replace him. The three GOP contenders (the lone Democrat mattered not at all) were Escondido City Councilwoman Marie Waldron, former Vista Councilman Scott Packard, the son of former U.S. Rep. Ron Packard, and Martin Garrick, who had worked for Pres. Ronald Reagan but had never held elective office.

It was not a pretty campaign. Garrick especially went negative, at one point referring to Packard as a "shady contractor" because he had once been the target of a lawsuit in Nevada. The same mailer tried to link Packard, a Mormon, with the Las Vegas gaming industry because of his previous Nevada connections. Packard fired back, questioning Garrick's integrity because Garrick claimed never to have run for public office. In fact, he had run unsuccessfully for the Solana Beach City Council in the early 1990s. Garrick later clarified his claim, saying he had never run for partisan office.

Waldron used her position on the Escondido council to drive home her credentials as a foe of illegal immigration. She proposed a controversial ordinance that would have forced landlords to verify the residency status of anyone who wanted to rent an apartment. The ordinance passed, but courts later shot it down. With immigration the hot topic, Waldron picked up a significant endorsement from the San Diego Minutemen, the local vigilante group that helps patrol border areas. She got significant local endorsements from Assm. George Plescia and Mimi Walters, state Sen. Dennis Hollingsworth, and former Assm. and state Sen. Ray Haynes.

Garrick, however, was able to outspend both opponents and used his considerable war chest to hammer home his staunch stance against illegal immigration, plus the usual conservative mantras on low taxes and less bureaucratic interference for small business. He gave or loaned his primary campaign some $300,000. His allies included U.S. Rep. Darrell Issa, former U.S. Atty. Gen. Ed Meese, state Sen. Tom McClintock and San Diego Sherriff Bill Kolender. In winning, he captured 43% of the vote. Waldron was second with 32%, and Packard third with 25%. In November, Garrick defeated Democrat Roxana Folescu.

In Sacramento, Garrick was given one of the Assembly's plum assignments for a Republican—vice chairman of the Education Committee. That will put him in the middle of key fights over testing, accountability, teacher tenure, and education funding—as well as in the crosshairs of the California Teachers Association.

BIOGRAPHY: Born: Glendale, March 24, 1953. Home: Solana Beach. Education: BS, California Western University, U.S. International University. Military: None. Family: wife Jane, four children. Religion: Episcopalian. Occupation: Small business owner.

OFFICES: 2016 Capitol Building, Sacramento, CA 95814, Phone: (916) 319-2074, Fax: (916) 319-2174, email: assemblymember.garrick@assembly.ca.gov. District: 1800 Thibodo Road, Suite 300, Vista, CA 92081, Phone: (760) 599-1641, Fax: (760) 599-1650.

COMMITTEES: Education (vice chair); Insurance; Transportation.
ELECTED: 2006 **TERM LIMIT:** 2012
ELECTION HISTORY: None.
2006 ELECTION: Garrick (R) 58%
                    Folescu (D) 42%

LONI HANCOCK (D)
14th Assembly District

Counties: Alameda, Contra Costa
Cities: Berkeley, Richmond, Oakland, San Pablo, Pleasant Hill, Lafayette, El Cerrito, Orinda, Moraga
Ethnicity: 51% White, 15% Latino, 16% Black, 15% Asian
Voter Registration: 59% D – 16% R – 20% DS
President 04: 81% Kerry, 18% Bush

The 14th District is a place of contrasts. It connects the gritty streets of Richmond, the birthplace of the Free Speech movement in Berkeley, and ritzy suburban hillside homes in Lafayette, Orinda, and Moraga.

Loni Hancock

But behind its reputation as one of the state's most liberal Democratic strongholds, the 14th District is a mixed bag. Democratic? Yes—even after the 2001 redistricting doubled Republican Party registration. John Kerry took 81% of its vote in the 2004 presidential sweepstakes. In 2003 over three-fourths of district voters opposed recalling Gray Davis.

But uniform? No. After the 2001 redistricting, the 14th lost portions of Oakland and its boundaries shifted east. It picked up wealthy sections of Contra Costa County, leaving the district with the richest of the rich and the poorest of the poor. In Lafayette, 30% of households have an income of $150,000 or greater. In Berkeley, only 10% of households fall under that income bracket, while 21% make less than $15,000. Redistricting also created racial disparities. Moraga is 90% white, 9% Asian, and less than half a percent black. San Pablo is 32% white, 18% black, and 16% Asian.

The district's center of political gravity is Berkeley, a remarkable jumble of a city, where Jamaican Soul, Indian Fashion, Lee Wah Restaurant, and Lanesplitter Pub, a biker bar, are neighbors at the corner of San Pablo and University avenues. An Indian clothing store offers shoppers "saree & more" while next door the window displays a camouflage shirt with a portrait of Tupac Shakur.

And few places can match Berkeley for the richness of its political history. The atomic bombs dropped on Japan at the end of World War II had their origins in Le Conte Hall on the campus of the University of California, Berkeley in a seminar conducted by J. Robert Oppenheimer. In October 1964 the Free Speech Movement began a few hundred yards away in Sproul Plaza when a protest erupted over the arrest of a student who violated a campus directive against political organizing on campus. The rise of Ronald Reagan as governor of California and the anti–Vietnam War movement each has roots in Sproul Plaza.

The district is remarkable for the close ties of the last three members of the Assembly. The incumbent is Loni Hancock, elected in 2002 after serving two terms as mayor of Berkeley, a job now held by her husband, Tom Bates, who represented the district in the Assembly for two decades before being termed out in 1996. Bates unsuccessfully challenged the term limits law in court. Dion Aroner, who occupied the seat from 1996–2002, was a longtime Bates aide.

Hancock and Bates have lived in Berkeley since 1964. Hancock earned her stripes with local citizens when she forged a historic agreement in 1989, temporarily putting to rest a 20-year battle between the university, which wanted to develop People's Park, and the city, whose liberal constituents opposed the plans. Known for her progressive politics, financial know-how, and ability to build coalitions, Hancock clinched her first Assembly win in 2002 with 98% of the vote and secured a second in 2004 with 86%.

Hancock, who served as western region chief of the Department of Education under President Bill Clinton, has championed legislation on education, the environment, and the economy—the "three Es" she used to launch her campaign. In 2002 Hancock led an effort to enable the bankrupt West Contra Costa County School District, mostly in the impoverished city of Richmond, to reduce its bailout loan interest rate. She chairs the Natural Resources Committee, which has broad jurisdiction over environmental legislation, a big issue in her district.

Hancock was the first state legislator with her own blog, which she uses to denounce the expansion of Indian casinos in the East Bay. Termed out in 2008, she already has opened a committee for the Oakland-based state Senate seat currently held by Senate President pro Tem Don Perata, who, like Hancock, is termed out in 2008. Among those who have their eyes on that seat are Democrat Wilma Chan, an Assembly colleague from Oakland who was termed out in 2006, and Aroner.

BIOGRAPHY: Born: Chicago, IL, April 10, 1940. Home: Berkeley. Education: BA, Ithaca College; MA, Wright Institute. Military: None. Family: husband Tom Bates, four children. Religion: Decline to state. Occupation: Legislator.

OFFICES: 4126 Capitol Building, Sacramento, CA 95814, Phone: (916) 319-2014, Fax: (916) 319-2114, email: assemblymember.hancock@assembly.ca.gov. District: 712 El Cerrito Plaza, El Cerrito, CA 94530, Phone: (510) 559-1406, Fax: (510) 559-1478.

COMMITTEES: Education; Health; Housing and Community Development; Joint Legislative Budget Committee; Natural Resources (chair); Rules (alternate).

ELECTED: 2002 **TERM LIMIT:** 2008

ELECTION HISTORY: Berkeley City Council, 1971–1979; Mayor, 1986–1994.

2002 ELECTION: Hancock (D) 100%

2004 ELECTION: Hancock (D*) 76%
Montauk (R) 19%
O'Neal (L) 5%

2006 ELECTION: Hancock (D*) 82%
Wolf (R) 18%

RATINGS:	AFL-CIO	CAI	CoC	CLCV	EQCA	CCS	CMTA	FARM	NARAL
	100	92	18	100	100	100	0	10	100

MARY HAYASHI (D)
18th Assembly District

Counties: Alameda
Cities: Hayward, San Leandro, Pleasanton, Dublin, Oakland
Ethnicity: 42% White, 24% Latino, 13% Black, 17% Asian
Voter Registration: 55% D – 21% R – 20% DS
President 04: 70% Kerry, 29% Bush

Mapmakers tinkered with this East Bay district in 2001, but the result was treading water for Republicans and Democrats. The new version added a small chunk of Oakland, more of Pleasanton, and all of Dublin while dropping Union City. The consequence of this chiseling was an overwhelmingly Democratic district that is less white, more Latino, and more black than its previous incarnation.

Mary Hayashi

Veteran lawmaker Johan Klehs was termed out in 2006, and his departure precipitated a taut Democratic primary between Alameda County Fire Chief Bill McCammon and Mary Hayashi, president of a nonprofit health foundation and an appointed member of the state Board of Registered Nursing. Neither candidate had run for office, but both spent more than a year stumping the district. Carpet-bagging became an issue in the campaign as the 52-year-old McCammon stressed a lifetime of public service in the district while pointing out that Hayashi only moved into the district late in 2004. Prior to that, she had lived in the Central Valley. Her husband, attorney Dennis Hayashi, ran unsuccessfully for the Assembly in 2004 against Alberto Torrico in District 20.

Both candidates had significant political support and big enough treasuries to wage an effective campaign, as the results proved. Hayashi won by 1,000 votes out of more than 42,000 cast in the election.

November proved bittersweet for the Hayashis, however. While Mary brushed aside Republican Jill Buck, her husband lost his bid for a judgeship. The general election campaign was entertaining, if not suspenseful, given the district's lopsided Democratic registration. Republicans called in some guns on behalf of the moderate Buck, including former New Jersey Gov. Christine Todd Whitman. Buck even wiggled an endorsement out of Dublin Mayor Jane Lockhart, a self-described "life-long Democrat."

The help went for naught, however, as Hayashi won convincingly. The first Korean American elected to the Assembly, she was named to a minor leadership post as assistant floor whip. She also gained seats on the Budget, Health and Revenue and Taxation committees—significant panels all. Hayashi likely will focus on health care and can be expected to be a staunch ally for the politically active nurses association.

BIOGRAPHY: Born: South Korea, August 13, 1967. Home: Castro Valley. Education: BS, University of San Francisco; MBA, Golden Gate University. Military: None. Family: husband Dennis. Religion: Decline to state. Occupation: Health foundation executive.

OFFICES: 2188 Capitol Building, Sacramento, CA 95814, Phone (916) 319-2018, Fax: (916) 319-2118, email: assemblymember.hayashi@assembly.ca.gov. District: 22320 Foothill Boulevard, Suite 540, Hayward, CA 94541, Phone (510) 583-8818, Fax: (510) 583-8800.

COMMITTEES: Budget; Budget Subcommittee 4 on State Administration; Business and Professions; Health; Revenue and Taxation.

ELECTED: 2006 **TERM LIMIT:** 2012

ELECTION HISTORY: None.

2006 ELECTION: Hayashi (D) 68%
                   Buck (R) 32%

ED HERNANDEZ (D)
57th Assembly District

Counties: Los Angeles
Cities: West Covina, Baldwin Park, Azusa, Covina, La Puente
Ethnicity: 19% White, 63% Latino, 4% Black, 12% Asian
Voter Registration: 50% D – 29% R – 18% DS
President 04: 59% Kerry, 40% Bush

Ed Hernandez

This district once was centered on El Monte, but in 2001 it was loaded on a freight car and transported east along I-10 to West Covina and its smaller sister—Covina. El Monte and Hacienda Heights were removed altogether. The shift enhanced Republican registration by a few percentage points but not by enough to make the GOP even remotely competitive.

Incumbent Ed Chavez represented both the old and new districts but was termed out in 2006. He tried to keep the seat in the family by supporting his wife, Renee, as his successor, but that effort sputtered during a competitive Democratic primary. The primary winner was optometrist Ed Hernandez, a client of Sacramento consultant Richie Ross who benefited from nearly $400,000 in independent expenditures tossed in by Hernandez's fellow eye docs. The Chavez campaign was run by Leo Briones, a Los Angeles–based consultant and husband of former state Sen. Martha Escutia.

Although never elected to public office, Hernandez has political experience gained during a stint as president of the California Optometric Association—a politically active group that often lobbies in Sacramento and engages in occasional turf wars with ophthalmologists. Organized labor backed him, and that was enough to gain the nod of the California Democratic Party. A third candidate, former West Covina Councilman Bradley McFadden, muddied the waters a bit. Hernandez won the primary with 41% of the vote, compared with Chavez's 34% and McFadden's 17%. A fourth Democrat pulled 8% to round out the field. The November result was anti-climactic.

Hernandez was given a committee chairmanship—Public Employees, Retirement and Social Security—that could put the rookie lawmaker under a microscope as the legislature and governor attempt to deal with the impact of pension liability on both state and local governments. It is a potentially sensitive position, given the influence public-employee unions exert with Democrats. Gov. Arnold Schwarzenegger learned painfully about that power when he attempted to rein in pensions in 2005, claiming they could bankrupt cities and counties. His effort proved politically disastrous, and the governor since has softened both his rhetoric and ambitions for pension reform. As chairman, Hernandez likely will be asked to brick over Republican attempts to revive those efforts.

BIOGRAPHY: Born: Montebello, October 17, 1957. Home: West Covina. Education: BS, CSU Fullerton; OD, Indiana University. Military: None. Family: wife Diane, two daughters, three grandchildren. Religion: Catholic. Occupation: Doctor of Optometry.

OFFICES: 4112 Capitol Building, Sacramento, CA 95814, Phone: (916) 319-2057, Fax: (916) 319-2157, email: assemblymember.hernandez@assembly.ca.gov. District: 13181 Crossroads Parkway North, Suite 160, Industry, CA 91746, Phone: (626) 961-8492, Fax: (562) 695-8319.

COMMITTEES: Budget; Budget Subcommittee 1 on Health and Human Services; Business and Professions; Health; Public Employees, Retirement and Social Security (chair); .

ELECTED: 2006 **TERM LIMIT:** 2012
ELECTION HISTORY: None.
2006 ELECTION: Hernandez (D) 63%
                   Carver (R) 37%

SHIRLEY HORTON (R)
78th Assembly District

Counties: San Diego
Cities: San Diego, Chula Vista, Lemon Grove
Ethnicity: 39% White, 28% Latino, 13% Black, 17% Asian
Voter Registration: 41% D – 35% R – 20% DS
President 04: 51% Kerry, 48% Bush

Shirley Horton

The 78th District has a notable distinction among the 80 Assembly districts: it is the only district to contain not one precinct of its former self. The 78th had proved a troublesome battleground throughout the 1990s, and Democrats—who controlled the redistricting process in 2001—simply obliterated the old version, shifting the number inland. Previously, it had sliced along the coast from Del Mar and La Jolla in the north to the Mexican border. Now, it sits east of I-805 from Mission Trails Park in the north to Chula Vista in the south. Still competitive, Democrats tried to make it more comfortable for their candidates.

They made it a tad safer for John Kerry in 2004, but it hasn't turned out quite the way Democrats envisioned in legislative races. The trouble began with the district's debut in 2002 when Democrats anointed what turned out to be a less-than-impressive candidate. Vince Hall, a former staff director for Governor Gray Davis, won a five-way primary thanks to generous support from Assembly Democrats and their allies in labor. Republicans pinned their hopes on Shirley Horton, then the mayor of Chula Vista and a former president of the San Diego County board of realtors.

The final result was an irony of sorts. While Democrats had constructed the district to be friendlier, their candidate was undone because, in 2002, Democrats stayed out of the voting booth in droves, and nothing about Hall inspired them to show up. Horton had to wait nearly a week to declare victory and won by less than 1%, but she accomplished what no Republican candidate had been able to do for more than a decade—add the 78th to the GOP column.

Not that victory made Horton secure. Democrats returned in 2004 with another heavily funded campaign in an effort to oust her. Their contender was a Shirley Horton clone—a blonde woman who served on the Chula Vista City Council and had been past president of the county board of realtors. Horton didn't help her own cause by compiling what could charitably be called a "spotty record" in Sacramento. During her first term, Horton was absent for nearly 400 votes in committee and on the floor—a lapse that Democrats force-fed into district mailboxes. They noted that she received low ratings from environmental groups—which in coastal sensitive San Diego is akin to being scolded by Mother Teresa. Finally, Democrats caught Horton in a bit of media hypocrisy during that summer's long budget stalemate; she noisily insisted that she would not accept her legislative salary during the impasse then quietly sought to have it restored once the budget was approved.

As expected, the campaign was noisy and grime-filled, with Horton reminding voters that her opponent once had her real estate license suspended. Gov. Arnold Schwarzenegger came to Horton's rescue with an 11th-hour campaign swing through her district. Election Night proved *déjà vu* for Horton, who had to sweat through the counting of absentee ballots before learning that she had been returned to Sacramento for a second term by the same 1% margin as during her first go-around in 2002.

By those standards, Horton's third re-election was a landslide; she won by 5% over Democrat Maxine Sherard, a retired university professor. Horton's ratings from various groups—liberal and conservative—display her balancing act. While not by any means a lefty, she scores better than any GOP colleague with groups such as NARAL, a pro-choice advocacy group. Her 22 from environmentalists was the highest score given to any Republican and only four points lower than that given to Democrat Nicole Parra. In fact, her scores overall mirror Parra's—a moderate Democrat who must perform the same kind of balancing act in her Central Valley district to mollify Republican voters.

Termed out in 2008, Horton leaves a competitive district where the parties likely will wage all-out war.

BIOGRAPHY: Born: San Diego, July 17, 1952. Home: Chula Vista. Education: BA, San Diego State. Military: None. Family: husband Luther. Religion: Decline to state. Occupation: Legislator.
OFFICES: 2174 Capitol Building, Sacramento, CA 95814, Phone: (916) 319-2078, Fax: (916) 319-2178, email: assemblymember.shirley.horton@assembly.ca.gov. District: 7144 Broadway, Lemon Grove, CA 91945, Phone: (619) 462-7878, Fax: (619) 462-0078.
COMMITTEES: Business and Professions; Higher Education (vice chair); Transportation.
ELECTED: 2002 **TERM LIMIT:** 2008

ELECTION HISTORY: Mayor, Chula Vista, 1994–2002.
2002 ELECTION: Horton (R) 49%
      Hall (D) 48%
      Menanno (L) 3%
2004 ELECTION: Horton (R*) 49%
      Davis (D) 48%
      Hale (L) 3%
2006 ELECTION: Horton (R*) 51%
      Sherard (D) 46%
      Gibson (L) 3%

RATINGS:

AFL-CIO	CAI	CoC	CLCV	EQCA	CCS	CMTA	FARM	NARAL
11	64	88	22	0	55	70	80	60

GUY HOUSTON (R)
15th Assembly District

Counties: Alameda, Contra Costa, Sacramento, San Joaquin
Cities: Livermore, Walnut Creek, Danville, San Ramon, Elk Grove, Oakley
Ethnicity: 73% White, 14% Latino, 2% Black, 9% Asian
Voter Registration: 38% D – 40% R – 18% DS
President 04: 49.6% Kerry, 49.5% Bush

Guy Houston

This sprawling East Bay district, which encompasses one of the fastest growing regions in California, has the distinction of being the only Republican territory in the Bay Area. While that has been the case for decades, legislative mapmakers had to do a little creative re-carving in 2001 to keep it that way. At the top of the district, in Sacramento County, lie the agricultural towns of Elk Grove and Galt. Along the Highway 680 corridor, the district takes in slices of Pleasanton and Stockton, and at the district's center in Alameda County sits the mushrooming city of Livermore. To the west are the established, wealthy, and increasingly Democratic Contra Costa County towns of Walnut Creek, San Ramon, and Danville. On the district's eastern edge is the booming Sacramento–San Joaquin Delta region, including the fast-developing commuter town of Brentwood.

In the suburban and urban areas of the 15th District, traffic and the equalization of funding for schools are major issues. Due to the high growth rate, the district's schools on average get some of the lowest amounts of funding per student in the state, and residents complain about the often-snarled roadways. The growth of the biotechnology sector is a major reason for traffic problems. Biotech companies are spilling out of Silicon Valley, and employees who don't want a long commute find themselves buying homes in the cities along the 680 freeway. As a result, housing prices are increasing.

Those who can no longer afford homes along 680 are moving over the Altamont Pass to Brentwood. A major point of contention is Vasco Road, the heavily traveled commute route between Brentwood and Livermore. Seventy-three car crashes occurred on the 15-mile stretch last year, and locals frequently clash on the best way to make it safer. Incumbent Republican Guy Houston is actively involved in such matters.

Houston, formerly the mayor of Dublin, won this Assembly seat in a hotly contested race in 2002, replacing Republican Lynne Leach who was termed out. A former mortgage broker with an MBA from St. Mary's College, Houston is a fiscally conservative, pro-growth, anti-tax businessman whose voter base is business owners and conservative farmers. During redistricting, legislative mapmakers took the cities of Lafayette, Orinda, Moraga, and Dublin out of the district, so Houston had to move from Dublin to San Ramon so he could qualify to run. He eventually moved his family to Livermore.

Legislators expanded the district to include a rural piece of southern Sacramento County, a decided plus for Houston. Although registered Republicans narrowly outnumber registered Democrats in the district as a whole, the reason for Houston's victory over Contra Costa County Supervisor Donna Gerber in 2002 was widely attributed to a larger Republican voter turnout.

Regardless of a registration edge, Houston found himself a target again in 2004, with Democrat Elaine Shaw the participant in what became a particularly vicious campaign. At the last minute, sensing possible victory, Shaw released a slew of TV ads and mailers that attacked Houston on several fronts, including his involvement in a bankruptcy scandal involving his father's investment company, and a lawsuit accusing Houston of elder abuse. Despite the mailers and ads, and a flurry of fundraising by Shaw, Houston won by a slightly bigger margin than in 2002. The issues raised during the campaign, however, returned to haunt him in future elections.

In 2006, he ran against consumer attorney Terry Coleman. The scandals involving the Houston family surfaced again, and Houston had to obtain a gag order from a court to prevent his testimony in the case from being made public until the election was over. District voters seemed weary of the *déjà vu*-like negativity, returning Houston for a third term by exactly the same margin as in 2004. He will be termed out in 2008, but his legislative future seems doubtful. In years past, he talked about taking on state Sen. Tom Torlakson in SD 7 but passed in 2006. The seat is open in 2010 but is solidly Democratic, and the putative frontrunner is newly elected Assm. Mark DeSaulnier, a former Contra Costa County supervisor.

Houston suggested he might try for a congressional seat, and the opportunity might present itself in 2008 in the district recently taken away from Republican incumbent Richard Pombo. Democrat Jerry McNerney, who upset the scandal-ridden Pombo in 2006, will have to defend a very competitive 11th Congressional District without the benefit of an opponent suffering from numerous self-inflicted wounds.

BIOGRAPHY: Born: Walnut Creek, October 20, 1960. Home: Livermore. Education: BS, MBA, St. Mary's College. Military: None. Family: wife Inge, three children. Religion: Decline to state. Occupation: Businessman.

OFFICES: 2130 Capitol Building, Sacramento, CA 95814, Phone (916) 319-2015, Fax (916) 319-2115, email: assemblymember.houston@assembly.ca.gov. Districts: 1666 North Main, Walnut Creek, CA 94596, Phone: (925) 988-6915, Fax: (925) 988-6918; 1635-A Chestnut Street, Livermore, CA 94551, Phone: (925) 606-4990, Fax: (925) 606-4488.

COMMITTEES: Banking and Finance; Local Government (vice chair); Transportation.

ELECTED: 2002 **TERM LIMIT:** 2008
ELECTION HISTORY: Mayor, Dublin, 1994–2001.
2002 ELECTION: Houston (R) 54%
Gerber (D) 46%
2004 ELECTION: Houston (R) 55%
Shaw (D) 45%
2006 ELECTION: Houston (R*) 55%
Coleman (D) 45%

RATINGS:

AFL-CIO	CAI	CoC	CLCV	EQCA	CCS	CMTA	FARM	NARAL
3	40	94	4	0	25	90	100	20

BOB HUFF (R)
60th Assembly District

Counties: Los Angeles, Orange, San Bernardino
Cities: Chino Hills, Diamond Bar, Anaheim, La Mirada, Orange, Yorba Linda, La Habra
Ethnicity: 47% White, 24% Latino, 3% Black, 24% Asian
Voter Registration: 30% D – 48% R – 19% DS
President 04: 61% Bush, 38% Kerry

Bob Huff

It wasn't as though Democrats actually won this seat in the previous decade, despite a voter-registration edge of 5% or more (depending on the hour of the day). But they kept Republican candidates and officeholders light on their feet because the district was anything but safe. Just ask Republican Robert Pacheco, who spent three Assembly terms looking behind every rock for some Democratic Liberty Valance to shout "stand and deliver." Pacheco, who was termed out in 2004, never caught a serious challenge, but the threat always was present.

So when it came time to make deals in the 2001 redistricting, Republicans had the 60th high on their list of places to strengthen. As a result, the only resemblance between the previous version of the 60th District and the current one is the number. The old district was obliterated. Once confined to Los Angeles County, mapmakers blew away West Covina, Hacienda Heights, and most of Whittier while sliding the 60th into San Bernardino County to pick up the GOP stronghold of Chino Hills. As though that wasn't enough to hold back Democratic ambitions, they dipped into Orange County for half of Yorba Linda and a tidy slice of Anaheim. The result: a 5% Democratic registration edge became a 17-point deficit.

The paucity of Democratic voters meant that Pacheco would be replaced in the 2004 GOP primary, and the Pachecos tried to keep the seat in the family, but Gayle Pacheco lost the primary to Diamond Bar Mayor Bob Huff. A community college trustee, Pacheco had the backing of many Republican legislators, including then-Minority Leader Kevin McCarthy and the GOP's main legislative poobah, state Senator Jim Brulte. Huff beat Pacheco handily despite her familial connections and long list of endorsements. Most district voters live in Orange and Los Angeles counties, and that is where Huff concentrated his resources and where he prevailed. A third candidate from Orange County did well there, while Pacheco's only success came in San Bernardino County, with the smallest chunk of voters.

As a legislator, Huff introduced an eclectic series of bills, ranging from political reform to zip codes to peace-officer training. His first bill was, if nothing else, ambitious. Meant to ban legislative fund raising during the budget process, it was held without recommendation in the Assembly Elections and Reapportionment Committee where it eventually died a muffled death.

A conservative, Huff maneuvered successfully through leadership fights that engulfed the Republican Caucus after McCarthy stepped down to run for Congress. After the election, he was given the significant post of caucus chairman, where he will help Minority Leader Michael Villines keep the caucus together during critical budget negotiations. Villines sounded the partisan trumpet following the 2006 elections, and Huff is seen as his chief lieutenant and enforcer. Keeping caucus members from straying on key issues will be no mean trick if Gov. Arnold Schwarzenegger follows through with his pledge to operate in a bipartisan fashion because much of the pressure to stray will come not from Democrats but from the charismatic Republican governor.

BIOGRAPHY: Born: Calexico, May 6, 1953. Home: Diamond Bar. Education: BA, Westmont College. Military: None. Family: wife Mei Mei, four children. Religion: Decline to state. Occupation: Businessman.

OFFICES: 4098 Capitol Building, Sacramento, CA 95814, Phone: (916) 319-2060, Fax: (916) 319-2160, email: assemblymember.huff@assembly.ca.gov. District: 17800 Castleton Street, Suite 125, City of Industry, CA 91748, Phone: (626) 839-2000, Fax: (626) 839-2005.

COMMITTEES: Education; Transportation; Veterans Affairs.

ELECTED: 2004 **TERM LIMIT:** 2010

ELECTION HISTORY: Diamond Bar City Council, 1995–2004; Mayor, 1997, 2001.

2004 ELECTION: Huff (R) 66%
Martinez (D) 34%

2006 ELECTION: Huff (R*) 70%
Tamom (D) 30%

RATINGS:

	AFL-CIO	CAI	CoC	CLCV	EQCA	CCS	CMTA	FARM	NARAL
	7	40	94	0	0	15	90	100	20

JARED HUFFMAN (D)
6th Assembly District

Counties: Marin, Sonoma
Cities: San Rafael, Novato, Petaluma, Rohnert Park, Mill Valley, Larkspur, Sausalito
Ethnicity: 78% White, 13% Hispanic, 2% Black, 5% Asian
Voter Registration: 51% D – 24% R – 20% DS
President 04: 71% Kerry, 28% Bush

Jared Huffman

The symbol of California's reputation as an international kook fest is a chic, scenic, well-heeled district north of San Francisco. Here sits Marin County—hot tubs, houseboats, Buck Trust, rugged shoreline and all. The district includes the Sonoma County wine country, Point Reyes National Seashore, and seaside communities at Stinson Beach, Bolinas, and Dillon Beach.

Sonoma is a new addition, tacked onto the district in 2001 when the northern boundary was flattened to strip out Sebastopol and parts of Santa Rosa. Not that the district's political character changed much; it still is decidedly Democratic as befits the home of California's junior United States senator, Barbara Boxer.

The district was represented for three terms by moderate Democrat Joe Nation, who was termed out in 2006 and subsequently lost a congressional primary to incumbent Democrat Lynn Woolsey. Nation's departure set the stage for a six-way Democratic primary where, given the Democrats' edge in voter registration, the final outcome would be decided as well.

Going into the primary, two women—elected officials both—led the pack. Pam Torliatt was a Petaluma city councilwoman backed by Woolsey and the only candidate from Sonoma County. She was endorsed by the Service Employees International Union, two teacher unions, and the area's termed-out state senator, Wes Chesbro. Cynthia Murray was a Marin County supervisor and, like Nation, a moderate supported by the business community and some law-enforcement groups. Both candidates were ambushed by Jared Huffman, a member of the Marin Municipal Water District, a job that did not provide Huffman with his most serious credential. His credibility and viability as a candidate came from his paying job—senior attorney for the Natural Resource Defense Council, as powerful an environmental group as exists anywhere in the country. In that capacity, Huffman was responsible for writing and lobbying some far-reaching and critical legislation in Sacramento. Not surprisingly, he was backed by the League of Conservation Voters but also by the politically active California Nurses Association.

In some ways, the result could be classified as a murder-suicide between Torliatt and Murray who clobbered one another with highly negative mailers in the last days of the campaign. That may have had voters scrambling for an alternative. Huffman was helped by his environmental pedigree at a time when the debate over global warming was reaching a crescendo. Although a plethora of absentee ballots kept the issue in doubt for several days after the election, Huffman eventually prevailed by some 3,000 votes over Torliatt, with Murray a distant third in a million-dollar contest fueled in large measure by outside interests.

The November election, as anticipated, provided little suspense as Huffman rolled over Republican Michael Hartnett and two minor-party candidates. With such a large edge in registration, Huffman was able to devote most of his energies to another item on that November ballot—Measure R, or the Sonoma-Marin Rail Transit project. Huffman chaired the "Yes" campaign. It would have levied a quarter-cent on the sales tax in those two counties to build what became known as the "Smart Train," connecting the towns of Cloverdale and Larkspur. The train was meant to ease the commute and was heavily backed by the business community in both counties. As a tax increase, it required a two-thirds majority but fell just short, garnering 65% of the vote. Proponents, including the newly elected Assm. Huffman, vowed to put the train on the ballot again.

In Sacramento, Huffman is expected to be the legislature's strongest environmental voice since the 2004 departure of veteran Byron Sher. Huffman was named chairman of the Environmental Safety and Toxic Materials Committee, which has jurisdiction over, among other issues, drinking water.

BIOGRAPHY: Born: Independence, MO, February 2, 1964. Home: San Rafael. Education: BA, UC Santa Barbara; JD, Boston College. Military: None. Family: wife Susan, two children. Religion: Decline to state. Occupation: Environmental attorney.

OFFICES: 4139 Capitol Building, Sacramento, CA 95814, Phone: (916) 319-2006, Fax (916) 319-2106, email: assemblymember.huffman@assembly.ca.gov. Districts: 50 D Street, Suite 305, Santa Rosa, CA 95404, Phone: (707) 576-2631, Fax: (707) 576-2735; 3501 Civic Center Drive, Suite 412, San Rafael, CA 94903, Phone: (415) 479-4920, Fax: (415) 479-2123.

COMMITTEES: Appropriations; Environmental Safety and Toxic Materials (chair); Utilities and Commerce; Water, Parks and Wildlife.

ELECTED: 2006 **TERM LIMIT:** 2012

ELECTION HISTORY: None.

2006 ELECTION: Huffman (D) 65%
　　　　　　　　　Hartnett (R) 28%
　　　　　　　　　Woods (G) 4%
　　　　　　　　　Olmstead (L) 3%

KEVIN JEFFRIES (R)
66th Assembly District

Counties: Riverside, San Diego
Cities: Riverside, Temecula, Murrieta, Lake Elsinore
Ethnicity: 56% White, 33% Latino, 4% Black, 4% Asian

Voter Registration: 28% D – 50% R – 18% DS
President 04: 65% Bush, 34% Kerry

Kevin Jeffries

In the rearranging of Inland Empire Republican districts, the 66th retreated from desert communities between Lake Elsinore and La Quinta, then slid north to take in about a third of the city of Riverside and all of Rubidoux. All the shifting sands didn't affect its stature; the 66th was and remains as Republican as any district in the state.

Republican Ray Haynes represented the area for 14 years in the Assembly and Senate, but the conservative lawmaker was termed out of the legislature for good in 2006 and subsequently lost a primary bid for state Board of Equalization.

The vacancy set off a scramble for his Assembly seat that featured four area Republicans. Chief among them was Kevin Jeffries, a member of the Western Municipal Water District Board endorsed by Haynes. Jeffries ran for this same seat in 1994, losing another four-way GOP primary to Bruce Thompson. Since then, he had built chits inside the Republican Party, serving seven years as Riverside County chairman. His opponents were Riverside City Councilman and retired police officer Steve Adams, attorney and former Lakewood City Councilman Dan Branstine, and Nancy Knight, publisher of a community newspaper called *The Bugle*. Jeffries wielded the biggest wallet, raising over $300,000 on the primary. Adams and Branstine raised $200,000 and $125,000 respectively.

All four candidates focused on issues of significance to a district whose prime concerns are population growth and its attendant problems: traffic congestion, housing, illegal immigration, and the use of eminent domain to foster development. While Knight ran a grassroots campaign and raised little money or endorsements, the other three were backed by various local politicos. Along with Haynes backing, Jeffries solidified his conservative credentials with endorsements from state Sen. Dennis Hollingsworth, U.S. Rep. Darrell Issa, and most of the local political establishment. Adams had two prominent county supervisors in his corner, Jeff Stone from Riverside and Bill Horn from San Diego. Branstine, a former Democrat, was backed by state Sen. Bill Morrow.

If Adams and Jeffries had one major dispute, it came over the issue of bipartisanship. Adams, borrowing a page from the Schwarzenegger campaign, expressed a willingness to work with Democrats in Sacramento. Jeffries said he would not cooperate if it meant co-opting his core beliefs.

At the bell, issues didn't matter—name ID did, and among local Republicans, the clear advantage lay with Jeffries. He rolled to victory with 49% of the vote; neither Adams nor Branstine cracked 20%. Knight, in her seventh run for office, finished with 12%. In Sacramento, Jeffries landed a vice chairmanship on the Public Employees, Retirement and Social Security Committee, a post that should put him in the vanguard of Republican attempts to reform public-employee pension systems at the state and local level. It is an issue of growing importance to cities and counties saddled with enormous pension liabilities. It is also is an issue that Schwarzenegger tried unsuccessfully to tackle in 2005, and one he has shied away from ever since.

BIOGRAPHY: Born: Downey, November 24, 1960. Home: Lake Elsinore. Education: High School degree. Military: None. Family: wife Chris, two children. Religion: Christian. Occupation: Small business owner.

OFFICES: 5128 Capitol Building, Sacramento, CA 95814, Phone: (916) 319-2066, Fax: (916) 319-2166, email: assemblymember.jeffries@assembly.ca.gov. District: 27555 Ynez Road, Suite 205, Temecula, CA 92591; Phone: (951) 699-1113, Fax: (951) 694-1039.

COMMITTEES: Environmental Safety and Toxic Materials; Governmental Organization; Public Employees, Retirement and Social Security (vice chair).

ELECTED: 2006 **TERM LIMIT:** 2012

ELECTION HISTORY: Western Municipal Water District; Elsinore Valley Municipal Water District.

2006 ELECTION: Jeffries (R) 62%
                   Nicholson (D) 38%

DAVE JONES (D)
9th Assembly District

Counties: Sacramento
Cities: Sacramento
Ethnicity: 37% White, 23% Latino, 17% Black, 18% Asian
Voter Registration: 54% D – 21% R – 19% DS
President 04: 66% Kerry, 33% Bush

Dave Jones

Sacramento, with the state Capitol anchoring a reviving core, is one of the most diverse cities in America according to a 2002 survey by *Time* magazine. Its Asian, Latino, African-American, and white communities are politically active, and any legislative district that takes in Sacramento will lean left, be reliably Democratic, and be subject to multi-ethnic brawls come election time.

Sacramento has seen significant growth over the past decade, but civic identity remains confused. The bankrupt symphony is silent, while a raging debate continues over whether to use public money for yet another arena for the city's NBA franchise—the Sacramento Kings. Restaurants, cafes, and coffee bars abound in the downtown area, creating a sense of a hip, urban, inner city social community, while the suburbs that ring the city have become ever more white and conservative. The center of the city features high-rise office buildings, the state Capitol, and the Hyatt Regency, which has been the *de facto* governor's mansion since mega-celebrity Arnold Schwarzenegger occupied the office and became Sacramento's number-one tourist attraction.

Over half of the population of Sacramento resides in the southern part of the city, living in older enclaves such as upper-income Land Park, Curtis Park, and Oak Park, which is a mix of Latino and African American. The southern reaches are home to a significant number of whites, African Americans, and Asians.

Bureaucrats, young professionals, and an expanding class of service personnel make up the district's constituency. Consistently progressive, they vote for Democrats and favor bond and tax measures to support social services, from housing and emergency shelters to after-school programs. Although district voters disapproved the 2003 recall election against Gray Davis, they only narrowly backed the Democratic candidate to succeed Davis—Lieutenant Governor Cruz Bustamante—over Republican Arnold Schwarzenegger (40% to 39%).

Liberal Democrats have represented the area in the Assembly for most of the past two decades, and all of them have come out of local government. Phil Isenberg served as mayor of Sacramento before his 1982 election to the Assembly, where he became one of the chief architects of Democratic policy under Speaker Willie Brown, Jr. Isenberg was succeeded in 1996 by Deborah Ortiz, a Sacramento councilwoman who held the seat for one term before being elected to the state Senate. Ortiz, in turn, was replaced by former Sacramento City Councilman Darrell Steinberg, who eventually chaired both the Budget and Appropriations committees during his six years in the lower house. After two years out of office, he returned to the Capitol as a senator, replacing the termed-out Ortiz in 2006.

The current placeholder is Dave Jones, another migrant from the Sacramento City Council. In 2004, he emerged from a six-way Democratic primary that featured enough direct mail to denude a medium-sized forest. Mail, in this case, was the love child of money, and the top three contenders—Jones, Councilmember Lauren Hammond, and Sacramento County Supervisor Roger Dickinson—had sizeable fund-raising operations and targeted independent expenditure campaigns. A fourth prominent contender, school board member Manny Hernandez, had decent name recognition but was chronically short of cash.

Jones took the brass ring with substantial help from labor, especially service workers, firefighters, teachers, and nurses. He was helped by a last-second $94,000 television buy that tipped the balance, allowing the 42-year-old progressive to win handily on Election Day. During his rookie term, he chaired the Assembly Judiciary Committee and mulled over whether to challenge Steinberg for Ortiz's vacant Senate district come 2006. He opted to remain in the Assembly where *Capitol Weekly*'s survey of legislative talent named him the legislature's most effective non-leadership member.

Jones 2006 re-election was a cakewalk, not that he snoozed through the campaign season. Jones was a prime mover in efforts to defeat two local measures—Measures Q and R—that would have raised the sales tax in Sacramento County by a quarter cent to finance a new multi-purpose sports and entertainment complex not far from the state Capitol. Jones and others objected to spending more than $500 million on a new arena for the NBA Kings while other city and county needs went begging. The arena campaign fractured the local political establishment, with many elected officials backing the proposals, including Sacramento Mayor Heather Fargo, City Councilman Rob

Fong and Jones's old foe Roger Dickenson. Steinberg, too, was on board on behalf of Q and R, but both measures lost by huge margins thanks in main to boorish behavior on the part of the Kings' owners, Joe and Gavin Maloof. The outcome put Jones on the winning side of the 2006 arena campaign. If the Kings move elsewhere (as has been rumored), the 2006 victory over Q and R could prove pyrrhic for any politician seen as having helped drive the team away.

BIOGRAPHY: Born: Philadelphia, PA, January 4, 1962. Home: Sacramento. Education: BA, Depauw University; JD, Harvard/Kennedy School of Government. Military: None. Family: wife Kim Flores, two children. Religion: Decline to state. Occupation: Attorney.

OFFICES: 3146 Capitol Building, Sacramento, CA 95814, Phone (916) 319-2009, Fax: (916) 319-2109, email: assemblymember.jones@assembly.ca.gov. District: 915 L Street, Suite 110, Sacramento, CA 95814, Phone: (916) 324-4676, Fax: (916) 327-3338.

COMMITTEES: Agriculture; Budget; Budget Subcommittee 3 on Resources; Judiciary (chair); Utilities and Commerce.

ELECTED: 2004 **TERM LIMIT:** 2010

ELECTION HISTORY: Sacramento City Council, 1999–2004.

2004 ELECTION: Jones (D) 67%
Garcia (R) 28%
Morgan (L) 5%

2006 ELECTION: Jones (D*) 70%
Chan (R) 30%

RATINGS:

	AFL-CIO	CAI	CoC	CLCV	EQCA	CCS	CMTA	FARM	NARAL
	100	96	24	100	100	100	0	20	100

BETTY KARNETTE (D)
54th Assembly District

Counties: Los Angeles
Cities: Long Beach, Los Angeles, Rancho Palos Verdes
Ethnicity: 50% White, 26% Latino, 9% Black, 12% Asian
Voter Registration: 43% D – 35% R – 18% DS
President 04: 57% Kerry, 42% Bush

One of the legislature's few competitive districts, the 54th is a coastal enclave centered on the port of Long Beach. The district is mostly unchanged from the previous version and remains a fertile and often expensive political battleground—as the 2004 elections demonstrated once again.

The district was open in 2004 after termed-out Democrat Alan Lowenthal ran for the state Senate. And if the contest to replace Lowenthal looked like *déjà vu* all over again—it was. The first showdown between Democrat Betty Karnette and Republican Steve Kuykendall took place a decade before. At the time, Karnette was a one-term

Betty Karnette

incumbent who had won the seat in 1992 by knocking off a longtime Republican legislator named Gerald Felando. Kuykendall recaptured the district for the GOP in 1994 when a last-minute, $125,000 campaign contribution from tobacco giant Philip Morris allowed the Republican to unleash an attack on Karnette in what turned out to be a Republican year. Kuykendall narrowly defeated Karnette, but the price was lasting and high. Tobacco money is as toxic in politics as smoke in a healthy lung, and Kuykendall has been dogged by the 1994 contribution ever since, despite some political successes.

Karnette and Kuykendall went separate ways after 1994. He barely survived re-election in 1996, then captured an open seat in Congress in 1998 by defeating Democrat Janice Hahn—sister of former Los Angeles Mayor James Hahn. Kuykendall's congressional career was short-lived, however; he was knocked off by Democrat Jane Harman two years later and was out of elective office before trying for the Assembly in 2004. Karnette, meanwhile, was elected to two terms in the state Senate (1996 and 2000). Although termed out of the upper house, she had two terms remaining in the Assembly before making the run in 2004 that put her up against Kuykendall for the second time.

The Karnette-Kuykendall contest posed the question: How long does the memory of tobacco money linger? Answer: Forever. The donation has hung around Kuykendall's neck like rotting meat for a decade, and even Republicans claimed that 2004 was no exception. The campaign itself centered on Long Beach, which is home turf for Karnette and where the electorate tends to be parochial in its voting patterns. Teachers, especially, gave substantial support to Karnette—a former teacher who has championed education and teacher-related issues for her entire legislative career. As legislative elections go these days, the results were somewhat close as Karnette won with 53% of the vote.

In addition to education, Karnette has focused on transportation issues, especially ports—not surprising for a lawmaker whose district includes Long Beach and San Pedro. From 2004 to 2006, she chaired the Assembly Select Committee on Ports. She authored legislation in the current session to protect whistleblowers in the California State University system.

Karnette's 2006 election—her last for the legislature under term limits—was a breeze. She returned to Sacramento as chair of the Arts, Entertainment, Sports, Tourism, and Internet Media Committee. When she finally leaves office in 2008, another two-party brawl likely will erupt over control of the district.

BIOGRAPHY: Born: Paducah, KY, September 13, 1931. Home: Long Beach. Education: BA, MA, CSU Long Beach. Military: None. Family: husband Richard, one child. Religion: Decline to state. Occupation: Teacher and Education Consultant.

OFFICES: 2136 Capitol Building, Sacramento, CA 95814, Phone: (916) 319-2054, Fax: (916) 319-2154, email: assemblymember.karnette@assembly.ca.gov. District: 3711 Long Beach Boulevard, Suite 801, Long Beach, CA 90807, Phone:

(562) 997-0794, Fax: (562) 997-0799; 461 West 6th Street, Suite 306, San Pedro, CA 90371, Phone: (310) 548-6420, Fax: (310) 548-4160.
COMMITTEES: Appropriations; Arts, Entertainment, Sports, Tourism, and Internet Media (chair); Education; Transportation.
ELECTED: 2004 **TERM LIMIT:** 2008
ELECTION HISTORY: Assembly, 1992–1994; state Senate, 1996–2004.
2004 ELECTION: Karnette (D) 53%
Kuykendall (R) 45%
Sterne (L) 3%
2006 ELECTION: Karnette (D*) 61%
Jackson (R) 39%

RATINGS:

AFL-CIO	CAI	CoC	CLCV	EQCA	CCS	CMTA	FARM	NARAL
96	88	24	89	100	100	0	20	100

RICK KEENE (R)
3rd Assembly District

Counties: Butte, Lassen, Nevada, Placer, Plumas, Sierra, Yuba
Cities: Chico, Paradise, Truckee, Susanville, Grass Valley, Marysville, Oroville, Nevada City, Colfax
Ethnicity: 81% White, 10% Hispanic, 2% Black, 3% Asian
Voter Registration: 33% D – 42% R – 18% DS
President 04: 57% Bush, 42% Kerry

Rick Keene

The 2001 version of the 3rd Assembly District demonstrates how Republicans are distributed in northern California. The previous edition, crafted in 1991 by the courts, encompassed all 4,203 square miles of Modoc County but stopped at the Placer-Nevada county line. When mapmakers redrew the district, they included not one inch of Modoc, replacing it with a sliver of Placer County along Interstate 80 between North Auburn and Truckee. The population, and Republican registration, remained the same. Hardly anyone lives in Modoc County (population: 9,449), while the I-80 corridor is booming with suburban development—and Republicans.

The district has several population centers separated by miles of empty if scenic landscape, including the spine of the Sierras. Susanville, with its pair of state prisons, lies on the eastern slope, isolated from most of the district. Chico and Paradise sit on the district's western boundary, while Marysville and Oroville occupy the approaches to metropolitan Sacramento.

Politically, the district is heavily Republican despite the presence of Chico with its marginal Democratic edge in registration. Since 2002, the district has been represented by Republican Rick Keene, who parlayed seven years on the Chico City Council into a seat in the legislature. Keene's only significant opposition came in the 2002 GOP primary where he butted heads with Dan Ostrander, a local author and political neophyte. The seat was open because incumbent Republican Sam Aanestad ran for state Senate. Keene's advantage was his base in vote-heavy Chico, which proved enough to offset the fact that Ostrander loaned himself enough money to service the national debt of Peru. The pro-choice Ostrander suffered from being on the wrong side of the philosophical boundary in a year when "moderate" was a Republican cuss word. Endorsements from area lawmakers such as Assemblyman Tim Leslie and state Senator Rico Oller solidified Keene's conservative credentials in the district's second-largest voting bloc—Nevada County. He easily won the general election and breezed to re-election in 2004 and 2006.

Once in Sacramento, Keene became a player in GOP caucus politics and earned a reputation as a thoughtful lawmaker willing to consider opposing views and take a bipartisan approach to legislating. In 2004 he was given a prominent role in fiscal affairs by being named vice chairman of the Budget Committee, where he enhanced his bipartisan credentials. Two years later, a new GOP leadership team, bent on a more partisan approach, replaced Keene with Roger Niello at the Budget Committee. Keene moved to vice chair of the Utilities and Commerce Committee.

While Keene the legislator was earning kudos in Sacramento, Keene's lawyering back in Chico was subjected to a sound public thrashing by the 9th U.S. Circuit Court of Appeals. The 1997 conviction of a Keene client on a murder charge was overturned by the court, which cited Keene's inept defense as the reason for reversal.

BIOGRAPHY: Born: Hayfork, November 16, 1957. Home: Chico. Education: BA, CSU Chico; JD, California Northern Law School. Military: None. Family: wife Janice, five children. Religion: Christian. Occupation: Attorney.

OFFICES: 2158 Capitol Building, Sacramento, CA 95814, Phone: (916) 319-2003, Fax (916) 319-2103, email: assemblymember.keene@assembly.ca.gov. District: 1550 Humboldt Road, #4, Chico, CA 95928, Phone: (530) 895-4217, Fax: (530) 895-4219.

COMMITTEES: Judiciary; Natural Resources; Utilities and Commerce (vice chair).

ELECTED: 2002 **TERM LIMIT:** 2008

ELECTION HISTORY: Chico City Council, 1994–2001.

2002 ELECTION: King (D) 34%
Keene (R) 61%
Peterson (L) 5%

2004 ELECTION: Woods (D) 37%
Keene (R*) 60%
Burk (L) 3%

2006 ELECTION: Harrington (D) 39%
Keene (R*) 61%

RATINGS:	AFL-CIO	CAI	CoC	CLCV	EQCA	CCS	CMTA	FARM	NARAL
	3	44	94	4	0	20	80	100	20

PAUL KREKORIAN (D)
43rd Assembly District

Counties: Los Angeles
Cities: Glendale, Los Angeles, Burbank
Ethnicity: 50% White, 29% Latino, 3% Black, 12% Asian
Voter Registration: 44% D – 29% R – 22% DS
President 04: 64% Kerry, 35% Bush

Paul Krekorian

At one time during the 1980s, the 43rd District was regarded as safe Republican territory, producing the likes of former GOP Leader Pat Nolan and Congressman Jim Rogan. But even then, Nolan complained that the region's demographics and political profile were skidding out from Republican control.

In the 1990s, the district was mildly competitive. Congressman Adam Schiff never felt entirely at ease here in the early part of the decade, and Democratic Assemblyman Scott Wildman first won it in 1996 by a few hundred votes, then survived two years later because his GOP opponent had more flaws than a cheap diamond. Despite winning easily in 2000, Democrats sought to reinforce their hold in redistricting by extending a finger west of Vineland Avenue to pick up Democratic precincts while dropping neighborhoods between Forest Lawn and Occidental College. Latinos and Asians are 41% of the district's residents but only 22% of registered voters. A large, politically active Armenian community flexed its muscle in 2006. The tinkering did not increase Democratic registration as much as it produced a decline for Republicans and a dramatic increase in the number of those registering decline-to-state.

With Democrat Dario Frommer termed out in 2006, Latinos sought to continue their hold on the district with Frank Quintero, a city councilman from Glendale. He was opposed in the primary by Paul Krekorian, an attorney and former school board member from Burbank. A third potential candidate was Wildman, who sought a return to the legislature after more than a decade on the sidelines. But he dropped out early, leaving the field to Quintero and Krekorian.

It became, over the course of the campaign, a messy field, spiked with negative campaigning and racial overtones. In the final week of the campaign, Democratic households were hit with a mailer that linked Krekorian with an alleged Armenian terrorist. The mailer was followed up with a phone call that reinforced the same message. Both the call and mailer were funded by an independent expenditure, financed in part by the California Latino Leadership Fund, which received some of its money from the legislature's Latino caucus. A similar mailer, also rife with racial overtones, landed in a neighboring district and slammed an Asian candidate. A consultant who helped create the Krekorian mailer dismissed any racial intent, but several members of the Latino caucus joined a chorus that denounced both broadsides.

If nothing else, the mailer may have backfired on Quintero. Krekorian, bolstered by endorsements from the *Los Angeles Times* and *LA Weekly* and backed by the likes of the California Teachers Association, defeated Quintero 58% to 42%. It remains to be seen how his primary battle with Quintero affects Krekorian's legislative career under a Latino speaker, but Krekorian was not one of the 16 Democratic freshmen rewarded with a committee chairmanship or leadership post.

Prior to his election, Krekorian was an attorney specializing in entertainment and intellectual property law. Back in the early 1990s, he served as special counsel to the Webster Commission, organized to investigate police behavior during the 1992 Los Angeles riots.

Krekorian was shut out of a committee chairmanship in his rookie term, but he did land a boatload of significant committee assignments, including Appropriations, Judiciary and Rules.

BIOGRAPHY: Born: San Fernando Valley, March 24, 1960. Home: Burbank. Education: BA, USC; JD, Boalt Hall, UC Berkeley. Military: None. Family: wife Tamar, two children. Religion: Methodist. Occupation: Attorney.

OFFICES: 5135 Capitol Building, Sacramento, CA 95814, Phone: (916) 319-2043, Fax: (916) 319-2143, email: assemblymember.krekorian@assembly.ca.gov. District: 620 North Brand Boulevard, Suite 403, Glendale, CA 91203, Phone: (818) 240-6330, Fax: (818) 240-4632.

COMMITTEES: Appropriations; Human Services; Judiciary; Rules; Utilities and Commerce.

ELECTED: 2006 **TERM LIMIT:** 2012

ELECTION HISTORY: Burbank Board of Education, 2003–2006.

2006 ELECTION: Krekorian (D) 63%
Agbaba (R) 30%
Myers (L) 7%

DOUG LaMALFA (R)
2nd Assembly District

Counties: Butte, Colusa, Glenn, Modoc, Shasta, Siskiyou, Sutter, Tehama, Yolo
Cities: Redding, Red Bluff, Williams, Willows, Yuba City,
Ethnicity: 76% White, 15% Hispanic, 1% Black, 4% Asian
Voter Registration: 32% D – 48% R – 15% DS
President 04: 66% Bush, 32% Kerry

On a map, the Assembly's 2nd District looks like a large T-bone steak splayed across the northern third of California. Its head rests on the Oregon border and takes in Siskiyou and Modoc counties, while its tail forms the meat around the bone of Interstate 5 as it runs south from Mt. Shasta to the edge of metropolitan Sacramento. The district is similar to its predecessor, although Modoc was added along with a chunk of Republican precincts in Yolo County, while portions of Trinity County were removed and tacked to the neighboring 1st District. Mt. Shasta and Mt. Lassen are in

Doug LaMalfa

the district, while the cities of Yreka, Redding, Red Bluff, Willows, and Winters lay strung out along I-5.

The rural, agricultural district suffers from developmental pressures caused by the relentless expansion of Sacramento County north along Highway 113 towards Yuba City. Politically conservative, the district gives its votes almost exclusively to Republicans. President George W. Bush did as well here as anywhere in the state in 2000 and 2004.

Republican Doug LaMalfa was elected in 2002 after a surprisingly easy primary that featured three other Republicans—the most formidable of whom was Pat Kight, the mayor of Redding. LaMalfa, a fourth-generation rice farmer from Richvale, benefited from a fractious GOP gubernatorial primary between conservative businessman Bill Simon and the moderate former mayor of Los Angeles, Richard Riordan. That election helped rally conservatives to the polls, and LaMalfa's conservative credentials were reinforced by endorsements from the Howard Jarvis Taxpayers' Association and Mike Reynolds, author of the state's "three strikes" law. Largely self-funded, LaMalfa touted his "real world experience" in agriculture—a message that resonated in a rural district and provided a stark contrast with the city-dwelling Kight. As a result, rural counties gave LaMalfa 70% of their votes, he won Kight's home base in Shasta County, and he breezed to victory in the 2002 general election.

In 2004, LaMalfa drew a spirited Democratic opponent in Barbara McIver, who conducted an energetic campaign and even drew a glimmer of interest from Assembly Democrats. She earned endorsements from several area newspapers, including the *Redding Record Searchlight*. But all the spirit in the world couldn't overcome a 15% registration deficit, and LaMalfa scored another convincing victory. He won his third and final term in 2006, again convincingly.

As a legislator, LaMalfa earned high marks for his willingness to consider all sides of an issue, although his voting record was strictly conservative. As expected of someone who has spent his life tending the land, LaMalfa sought to ease environmental regulations that he considers a bane to farming—especially the Endangered Species Act. He opposed any efforts to raise taxes to resolve the state's budget crisis. In his final term, he was named vice chair of the Agriculture Committee.

BIOGRAPHY: Born: Oroville, July 2, 1960. Home: Richvale. Education: BS, Cal-Poly, San Luis Obispo. Military: None. Family: wife Jill, two children. Religion: Christian. Occupation: Rice farmer.

OFFICES: 4164 Capitol Building, Sacramento, CA 95814, Phone: (916) 319-2002, Fax: (916) 319-2102, email: assemblymember.lamalfa@assembly.ca.gov. Districts: 2865 Churn Creek Blvd., Suite B, Redding, CA 96002, Phone: (530) 223-6300, Fax: (530) 223-6737; 1527 Starr Drive, Suite U, Yuba City, CA 95993, Phone: (530) 751-8351, Fax: (530) 751-8379.

COMMITTEES: Agriculture (vice chair); Appropriations; Water, Parks and Wildlife.

ELECTED: 2002 **TERM LIMIT:** 2008
ELECTION HISTORY: None.
2002 ELECTION: Kinyon (D) 30%
　　　　　　　　　LaMalfa (R) 67%
　　　　　　　　　Bret (L) 3%
2004 ELECTION: McIver (D) 35%
　　　　　　　　　LaMalfa (R*) 65%
2006 ELECTION: Smith (D) 29%
　　　　　　　　　LaMalfa (R*) 68%
　　　　　　　　　Dynan (L) 2%

RATINGS:	AFL-CIO	CAI	CoC	CLCV	EQCA	CCS	CMTA	FARM	NARAL
	7	36	94	0	0	15	100	100	20

JOHN LAIRD (D)
27th Assembly District

Counties: Monterey, Santa Clara, Santa Cruz
Cities: Santa Cruz, Morgan Hill, Seaside, Monterey, Marina, Pacific Grove
Ethnicity: 69% White, 18% Latino, 3% Black, 6% Asian
Voter Registration: 48% D – 27% R – 19% DS
President 04: 67% Kerry, 32% Bush

John Laird

From the stunning cliffs of Big Sur to the gaudy beaches of Santa Cruz, the coast and environmental concerns for years defined the politics of the 27th District. But with the latest redistricting, a portion of Santa Clara County, some 50,000 voters in and around Morgan Hill (12% of the district), is now attached to this liberal coastal district. While Santa Cruz is known as a sleepy beach and university town and Monterey, Seaside, and Carmel-by-the-Sea house mostly affluent people, the new voters from Santa Clara County are a mix of those involved in high-tech industries, agriculture, and commuting. Though residents of Santa Cruz have long commuted "over the hill" on Highway 17, they tend to view San Jose and its suburbs with scorn.

Elections here are won and lost in the liberal county of Santa Cruz, which holds a little less than half of the voters. Students and the faculty of UC Santa Cruz sway the political climate in favor of progressive environmental and social policies. For every two registered Republicans in this district there are about three Democrats; more than 19% of the district is not affiliated with any party, but these people often vote Democratic.

This district consists of three densely populated areas—around Monterey, Santa Cruz, and Morgan Hill—separated by long stretches of undeveloped coast and open space. The fight to preserve the coastal areas north of the city of Santa Cruz, prevent offshore oil drilling, and protect Monterey Bay National Marine Sanctuary have all been pivotal in the shaping of this district, both politically and geographically. Growth and water are key issues.

Few districts contain a University of California and a California State University campus and as many community colleges as the 27th, so education is a critical issue. People involved with higher education tend to vote more progressively, and their concerns lately revolve around budget cuts and enrollment caps.

Assemblyman John Laird is one of the first openly gay male legislators in California. In his first term, Laird co-authored a landmark civil rights bill, which extended the rights and responsibilities of marriage to registered domestic partners. Traditional liberal issues are almost taken for granted in Laird's district. Even the area's most recent Republican Assembly member, Bruce McPherson, appointed by Schwarzenegger as secretary of state in 2005, supported abortion rights.

Laird was elected in his second attempt. More than a decade before, he ran in a special Assembly election made necessary when incumbent Democrat Sam Farr won a seat in Congress, replacing Democrat Leon Panetta, who had been named to President Bill Clinton's cabinet. Laird lost the Democratic primary to Santa Cruz County Supervisor Gary Patton, who then lost the runoff to McPherson, whose family owned the *Santa Cruz Sentinel*. When McPherson moved to the state Senate in 1996, he was replaced by Democrat Fred Keeley, a former county supervisor who was forced out of the legislature by term limits in 2002. Finally, the time was right for Laird, and he won easily with 61% of the vote.

Laird served two terms on the Santa Cruz City Council, two terms as mayor, and eight years as a trustee of Cabrillo College, and has worked for the county in various capacities since 1974. With his deep roots in the community and long years of building contacts, he took Santa Cruz County by force in 2002, had a strong showing in Monterey, and barely squeezed a victory out of Santa Clara County.

Laird was one of five freshman Assembly members named chair of a committee; Environmental Safety and Toxic Materials—a good spot for a member whose district is filled with environmentalists.

Laird did well in 2004 when Capitol insiders evaluated lawmakers for *California Journal*'s biennial "Minnie Awards," given to the legislature's best and brightest. He scored well in all categories and received several votes for Legislator of the Year. Although the "Rookie of the Year" award went to Republican Leader Kevin McCarthy, Laird was singled out as the Democrats' top freshman—besting Speaker Fabian Nunez—because of his intelligence and the respect accorded him by other members. In *Capitol Weekly*'s survey of the legislature's top talent, Laird was runner up to state Sen. Sheila Kuehl as the Capitol's smartest lawmaker. He was named "legislator you'd most like to have a drink with."

Laird's talents were recognized in his second term when Nunez handed him one of the Assembly's most challenging and prestigious jobs—chairman of the Budget Committee. That role puts Laird at the fulcrum of Democratic policymaking and makes the Santa Cruz lawmaker a prominent voice in negotiations—or verbal warfare—with Republicans and the Schwarzenegger administration. He retained that chairmanship after a resounding 2006 re-election to a third and final term.

BIOGRAPHY: Born: Santa Rosa, March 29, 1950. Home: Santa Cruz. Education: AB, UC Santa Cruz. Military: None. Family: partner John Flores. Religion: Decline to state. Occupation: Legislator.

OFFICES: 6026 Capitol Building, Sacramento, CA 95814, Phone: (916) 319-2027, Fax: (916) 319-2127, email: assemblymember.laird@assembly.ca.gov. Districts: 701 Ocean Street, Suite 318-B, Santa Cruz, CA 95060, Phone: (831) 425-1503, Fax: (831) 425-2570; 99 Pacific Street, Suite 555D, Monterey, CA 93940, Phone: (831) 649-2832, Fax: (831) 649-2935.

COMMITTEES: Budget (chair); Joint Legislative Budget; Judiciary; Labor and Employment; Natural Resources.

ELECTED: 2002 **TERM LIMIT:** 2008

ELECTION HISTORY: Santa Cruz City Council, 1981–1990; Mayor, 1983–1984, 1987–1988.

2002 ELECTION: Laird (D) 60%
Carter (R) 36%
Sachtjen (L) 4%

2004 ELECTION: Laird (D*) 69%
Barlich (R) 31%

2006 ELECTION: Laird (D*) 70%
Morrison (R) 30%

RATINGS:	AFL-CIO	CAI	CoC	CLCV	EQCA	CCS	CMTA	FARM	NARAL
	100	96	24	100	100	100	0	20	100

MARK LENO (D)
13th Assembly District

Counties: San Francisco
Cities: San Francisco
Ethnicity: 49% White, 16% Latino, 10% Black, 21% Asian
Voter Registration: 56% D – 10% R – 28% DS
President 04: 86% Kerry, 12% Bush

The 13th District that takes in San Francisco's eastern half is generally less fog-bound and more politically explosive than its sleepier west side neighbor, the 12th District. Perhaps, then, it is fitting that Assemblyman Mark Leno always has a great tan and is one of the more dependable rabble-rousers in the lower house.

The district stretches from the foot of the Golden Gate Bridge in the north to the stadium still known by most as Candlestick in the south. Between those extremes are several distinct neighborhoods that make up some of the most liberal, most gay, most diverse territory anywhere in California—or even the country.

In the first half of the last century, the docks along the eastern waterfront formed the city's working-class economic backbone and turned young wharf rat Harry Bridges of the ILWU into one of labor's fabled leaders. But all that started to dissolve in the 1970s as container ships turned east to unload at the Port of Oakland's modern docks.

Mark Leno

The city shifted over the next couple decades from punch clocks and heavy lifting to dot-coms and gene sequencing.

No matter how profound the economic changes, San Francisco remains a labor town, and the dot-com boom only served to provoke local progressives outraged with soaring rents and burgeoning gentrification of old neighborhoods like the Mission District. That anger played a big role in the 2000 supervisorial elections, where solid left candidates defeated Mayor Willie Brown's picks for the board, including several incumbents.

District voters are 56% Democratic, 10% Republican, and 28% decline-to-state. In spite of the favorable numbers, there's a Green Party bull in the city's Democratic china shop. In the 2004 race to succeed Brown as mayor, unkempt Green Supervisor Matt Gonzales terrified the Democratic establishment by closing in on hunky Democrat Gavin Newsom, Brown's chosen successor. Democrats brought in Clinton, Gore, and a ton of campaign cash that helped them fend off the challenge by a scant six points.

Leno was elected in 2002, after a punishing four-way Democratic primary that amounted to the first real fight for the seat in almost 40 years. Brown owned the seat for 32 years starting with his 1964 victory over an aging incumbent who'd barely held off Brown's first challenge two years earlier. When term limits forced Brown from office in 1996, San Francisco Supe. Carole Migden essentially ran unopposed after scaring off potential challengers by waving around bags of money and endorsements long before the primary.

Leno's primary contest pitted him against three other candidates, including another gay man, former ally Harry Britt, who had labor's backing. In one of those twists of San Francisco politics, the liberal Leno played the centrist to Britt's pure progressive and prevailed by 1,929 votes.

As a freshman Leno landed on the Public Safety Committee and quickly established himself as one of the top Democratic cash machines in Sacramento by raking in six-figure sums for the party. In the final days before the 2003 recall of Governor Gray Davis, Leno fired a very public shot across the bow of contender Arnold Schwarzenegger, who was accused of groping women on movie sets, by promising to introduce legislation increasing penalties for sexual battery. But Leno abandoned the bill, which he called "Arnold's Law," after the recall dust settled and never spoke of it again.

Personable and hard working, Leno scored well in *California Journal*'s ranking of the legislature's best and brightest—the 2004 "Minnie Awards." Capitol insiders considered him among the elite in the large freshman class, and although he was not named "Rookie of the Year"—that honor went to Republican Kevin McCarthy—he and Santa Cruz Democrat John Laird were thought to be at the top of the Democrats' list.

Leno made his most significant legislative push with gay marriage bills. In 2004, when Democrats were already preparing to lose a few seats in the election, Leno got the blessing of party leaders and went ahead, but Speaker Fabian Nunez later had the bill euthanized in committee. In 2005, Leno's bill progressed to the floor, where it was defeated by four votes in June, with a number of his fellow Democrats either voting "no" or sitting on their hands. But it did mark one victory for Leno and his backers: It was the first time any legislature in the nation had directly debated whether to issue marriage licenses to gays. The bill passed in 2006, only to be vetoed by Gov. Arnold Schwarzenegger.

After his third and final Assembly election in 2006, Leno secured one of the Assembly's key chairmanships—Appropriations. That should allow him to continue to raise copious amounts of cash. And he may also have an eye on how to spend that money. After the 2006 elections, Leno commissioned a poll to see if a particular political effort might be viable two years down the road. That effort, should he proceed, would be startling although not unprecedented in an era of term limits, for Leno is considering a run against a sitting incumbent from his own party in the 2008 primary; in this case, state Sen. Carole Migden.

Migden is no slouch when it comes to fund raising and would be a very tough target. She is a lioness of Bay Area politics. But Leno's poll apparently indicated that she might be vulnerable to the right kind of challenge from the right kind of challenger, and Leno is contemplating whether he is that person. Migden has negatives, prompted in part by erratic and irascible behavior. She lost the chairmanship of Appropriations in 2006 after she attempted to ghost vote for a Republican on the floor of the Assembly (don't ask). A *Capitol Weekly* survey named her the legislature's "toughest boss", a polite euphemism for "worst boss" that was verified when the Senate Rules Committee took over management of her staff in spring 2006. She has had trouble with political gendarmes such as the Fair Political Practices Commission, which fined her $94,600 in 2006 for failing to properly disclose donations in previous election cycles.

Others beside Migden would be less than pleased with the challenge. It would split San Francisco's politically active gay community and give Senate Democrats an awkward choice: circle the wagons around a loose cannon who happens to be one of their own, or allow a savvy and polished alternative to exercise the only option afforded him by term limits. In that case, their only choice would be to back Migden, if for no other reason than to discourage future attempts by other ambitious members of the lower house.

BIOGRAPHY: Born: Milwaukee, WI, September 24, 1951. Home: San Francisco. Education: BA, American College of Jerusalem; attended University of Colorado; attended Hebrew Union. Military: None. Family: Single. Religion: Jewish. Occupation: Small Business Owner.

OFFICES: 2114 Capitol Building, Sacramento, CA 95814, Phone (916) 319-2013, Fax: (916) 319-2113, email: assemblymember.leno@assembly.ca.gov. District: 455 Golden Gate Avenue, Suite 14300, San Francisco, CA 94102, Phone: (415) 557-3013, Fax: (415) 557-3015.

COMMITTEES: Appropriations (chair); Elections and Redistricting; Labor and Employment; Public Safety.

ELECTED: 2002 **TERM LIMIT:** 2008

ELECTION HISTORY: San Francisco Board of Supervisors, 1998–2002.

2002 ELECTION: Leno (D) 82%
                   Neira (R) 14%
                   Maden (L) 5%
2004 ELECTION: Leno (D*) 82%
                   Neira (R) 13%
                   Marvin (L) 5%
2006 ELECTION: Leno (D*) 87%
                   Maldonado (R) 13%

RATINGS: AFL-CIO CAI CoC CLCV EQCA CCS CMTA FARM NARAL
             100   96   24 100 100 100   10   10   100

LLOYD LEVINE (D)
40th Assembly District

Counties: Los Angeles
Cities: Los Angeles
Ethnicity: 42% White, 39% Latino, 5% Black, 12% Asian
Voter Registration: 48% D – 29% R – 19% DS
President 04: 60% Kerry, 38% Bush

Lloyd Levine

Redistricting allowed Republicans to gain some registration in the 40th District as it shifted west, losing territory between I-405 and the Hollywood Freeway and pushing north of Roscoe Boulevard around the California State University campus at Northridge, then west and south of Topanga Canyon Road. Not that the GOP gains promised an election victory any day soon.

This district once was the province of the speaker of the Assembly, Democrat Robert Hertzberg. It also is the scene of Hertzberg's somewhat ignoble departure—an attempted torch-passing that went awry in the mud-filled debris of the 2002 Democratic primary. Hertzberg's chosen recipient was a *wunderkind* named Andrei Cherny whose list of preprimary endorsements began with Al Gore and included John Emerson, Melrose Larry Green, Al Checchi, the Los Angeles Dodgers, then-Speaker Herb Wesson, the entire Latino legislative caucus, Congressman Howard Berman, and Ed Begley, Jr. All that was missing was Lassie, Trigger, and the Mormon Tabernacle Choir. All these folks had clamored aboard the Cherny bandwagon because the 26-year-old candidate was regarded as the golden boy of the New Democratic movement, a founding editor of its magazine, *Blueprint*, the author of a "visionary" book on the future of public life, and a speechwriter for Gore and—according to Cherny's Web site—Bill Clinton and Dick Gephardt. At the time, his Web site raised self-aggrandizement to an art form by revealing that CNN and the *New York Times* identified Cherny as a superstar. This was too much dazzle for Hertzberg to ignore, and he anointed him as his successor.

Unfortunately for Cherny and Hertzberg, not everyone was awestruck. Although Hertzberg was able to stiff arm his district director out of the race, another Democrat stayed in—Lloyd Levine, a legislative staff aide and the son of local political activist and campaign consultant Larry Levine. And Levine had plenty of support where it counted—in the bank and on the ground.

In truth, neither Levine nor Cherny had much recent connection with the district. Both were raised in this part of the San Fernando Valley, but both had long since departed, muting any charges of carpetbagging. Differences between them on issues were not muted, however. Cherny was handicapped by his association with New Democrats in a district where old-fashioned Democratic liberals provided the largest voting bloc. He had set down his centrist philosophy in his book and backed school vouchers and tort reform, which brought teachers and trial lawyers streaming into Levine's camp, armed with lavish independent expenditures and plenty of Election Day volunteers. Trial lawyers saw the Levine-Cherny race as a chance to poke Hertzberg who, as a pro-business legislator, often crossed swords with trial lawyers. More significant, Cherny's book promoted privatization of Social Security, a notion praised by Republicans but considered traitorous among liberal Democrats.

The campaign became increasingly turbulent as Election Day approached, the low point reached when Cherny accused Levine forces of stealing a mailer. Levine, in turn, called several Cherny mailers slanderous and threatened to sue. Cherny accused Levine of being squishy on the issue of choice; Levine knocked Cherny over a donation funded with tobacco money. Levine was helped by—of all people—Hertzberg, who caused resentment among longtime supporters for the way he brushed aside his own district aide in favor of Cherny. As the election neared, Levine began pulling away in polls and eventually won the two-man contest by more than 10 points. Hertzberg abandoned Cherny's sinking ship early, spending Election Night in the Central Valley.

Levine worked as legislative director for Assm. John Longville prior to moving back to Los Angeles, and did not need much coaching. He secured a first-term seat on the Budget Committee and a second-term chairmanship of the Utilities and Commerce Committee, a position he continued to hold in his third term. In that capacity, Levine was the author of one of the legislature's most contentious bills of 2006, a cable competition measure designed to allow telephone companies to provide cable TV service without obtaining approval from local governments. Cable operators, forced to secure that approval, fought the bill until a compromise removed them from the approval process as well. Then, only local governments were grumpy, but the bill passed and was signed by Gov. Arnold Schwarzenegger.

Levine is regarded the Democrats' most partisan advocate, a role recognized in *Capitol Weekly*'s annual survey of legislative talent. He also was named "most likely to call a press conference."

BIOGRAPHY: Born: Burbank, July 3, 1969. Home: San Fernando Valley. Education: BA, UC Riverside; MA, CSU Sacramento. Military: None. Family: Single. Religion: Jewish. Occupation: Legislator.

OFFICES: 5136 Capitol Building, Sacramento, CA 95814, Phone: (916) 319-2040, Fax: (916) 319-2140, email: assemblymember.levine@assembly.ca.gov. District:

Van Nuys State Building, 6150 Van Nuys Boulevard, Suite 300, Van Nuys, CA 91401, Phone: (818) 904-3840, Fax: (818) 902-0764.
COMMITTEES: Aging and Long-Term Care; Appropriations; Elections and Redistricting; Governmental Organization; Joint Legislative Audit; Utilities and Commerce (chair).
ELECTED: 2002 **TERM LIMIT:** 2008
ELECTION HISTORY: None.
2002 ELECTION: Levine (D) 57%
                 Friedman (R) 43%
2004 ELECTION: Levine (D*) 58%
                 Isler (R) 42%
2006 ELECTION: Levine (D*) 63%
                 Montaine (R) 37%

RATINGS:

AFL-CIO	CAI	CoC	CLCV	EQCA	CCS	CMTA	FARM	NARAL
100	96	24	100	100	100	0	10	100

SALLY LIEBER (D)
22nd Assembly District

Counties: Santa Clara
Cities: Sunnyvale, San Jose, Santa Clara, Mountain View, Cupertino
Ethnicity: 47% White, 14% Latino, 2% Black, 34% Asian
Voter Registration: 43% D – 25% R – 28% DS
President 04: 67% Kerry, 31% Bush

Sally Lieber

Democrats who look at a map of the 22nd District could be excused if they come away believing it is some hallucinogenic-induced image of a ponytailed Arnold Schwarzenegger in full body building pose. The heavily muscled right arm is Mountain View; the left is a chunk of Santa Clara. The massive chest is Cupertino. The head juts up toward Fremont, while the ponytail slices east, just below Milpitas.

This jarring image is in stark contrast to the quiet legislator who has represented the area since 2002—Democrat Sally Lieber. In some ways, Lieber's trip to Sacramento was an accident made possible by the improbable implosion of her 2002 primary opponent, former Santa Clara City Councilman Rod Diridon, Jr.

Diridon had just about everything a candidate could want when he announced for the Assembly seat being vacated by Democrat Elaine Alquist. He had an elective record, more than $500,000 in the bank, and a list of endorsements that included two former San Jose mayors, state Senator John Vasconcellos, influential Assemblyman Fred Keeley, and U.S. Transportation Secretary Norm Mineta, himself a former mayor of San Jose. He had labor. And he had a wealth of name identification, thanks to his father—a popular Santa Clara County supervisor. Moreover, his two primary opponents shared an elective base in Mountain View, where both served on the City Council.

All this made the seat Diridon's to lose—on paper. And lose he did—on the ground in the nitty gritty of a hotly contested campaign.

The general feeling was that Diridon fell victim to the siren song of polling, which showed him comfortably ahead a week before the primary. As a result, he committed a cardinal sin: he finished the campaign in second place despite having more than $100,000 in the bank that he failed to spend for extensive mail over the final eight days, an iffy tactic in a contested election. This was especially so in 2002, where other polls revealed that a large chunk of the electorate was undecided only a week before Election Day. When the votes began to move, they shifted away from Diridon, motivated by money and independent expenditures from trial lawyers on behalf of Lieber. With Diridon virtually dark, the money allowed Lieber and her allies to blanket the district with last-minute mail, some of which savaged Diridon for accepting money from tobacco interests. The late hits were orchestrated by Lieber's campaign guru Richie Ross, a Sacramento consultant known for his eleventh-hour blitz campaigns. That alone should have alerted Diridon to a potential roughing he chose to ignore.

In the end, Lieber won the primary by a couple thousand votes and Diridon became a poster boy for that fatal blend of overconfidence and incompetence. Lieber coasted to victory in November 2002, winning re-election in 2004 and 2006 by over 40,000 votes.

Lieber's most notable legislative effort has been her attempt to raise the minimum wage, which for some time pit her squarely against the Schwarzenegger administration and its allies in the business community. She failed in that effort in 2004 but revived it in 2006 and reached agreement with the governor to boost the minimum wage to $8 an hour, up from $6.35.

For the 2007–2008 session, her last in the Assembly, Lieber will serve as speaker pro tem, meaning that she will run Assembly floor sessions in the absence of the speaker—which is most of the time. That gives Lieber a lot of exposure on the California Channel, which broadcasts floor sessions statewide. Among her bills are those to reform the parole system and vaccinate California school girls against the sexually transmitted HPV virus. The latter effort puts her in conflict with conservative religious groups that argue such a program would encourage girls to be sexually active at an early age.

BIOGRAPHY: Born: Detroit, MI, April 24, 1961. Home: Mountain View. Education: BA, Stanford. Military: None. Family: husband Dave. Religion: Decline to state. Occupation: Legislator.

OFFICES: 3013 Capitol Building, Sacramento, CA 95814, Phone: (916) 319-2022, Fax: (916) 319-2122, email: assemblymember.lieber@assembly.ca.gov. District: 274 Castro Street, Suite 202, Mountain View, CA 94041, Phone: (408) 277-2003, Fax: (408) 277-2084.

COMMITTEES: Assembly Speaker pro Tempore; Health; Insurance; Judiciary; Local Government.

ELECTED: 2002 **TERM LIMIT:** 2008

ELECTION HISTORY: Mountain View City Council, 1998–2002; served as vice mayor.
2002 ELECTION: Lieber (D) 58%
Kawczynski (R) 37%
Watson (L) 5%
2004 ELECTION: Lieber (D*) 70%
Dominguez-Gasson (R) 30%
2006 ELECTION: Lieber (D*) 69%
Riffenburgh (R) 31%

RATINGS: AFL-CIO CAI CoC CLCV EQCA CCS CMTA FARM NARAL
100 96 24 100 100 100 0 10 100

TED LIEU (D)
53rd Assembly District

Counties: Los Angeles
Cities: Torrance, Los Angeles, Redondo Beach, Lomita, El Segundo
Ethnicity: 61% White, 17% Latino, 3% Black, 17% Asian
Voter Registration: 41% D – 35% R – 19% DS
President 04: 57% Kerry, 42% Bush

Ted Lieu

Of the 26 Assembly districts that lie wholly or partially in Los Angeles County, only three touch the Pacific Ocean, and only one contains the glitz associated with the county's beach communities—the 53rd, also known as the "Baywatch district." The district is moderately Democratic today but was mostly Republican territory until 1992, when Democrat Debra Bowen planted her party's flag. It was not changed much by the 2001 redistricting, although a tiny portion of West Los Angeles was stitched to it, increasing the Democrats' advantage.

Democratic strength lies in the north, centered on West L.A., Venice, Mar Vista, Marina del Rey, and Westchester. The south—El Segundo, Manhattan Beach, Hermosa Beach, Redondo Beach, Lomita, and Torrance—is split between Democrats and Republicans.

That's not to say that Republicans have walked away without a fight. Bowen never felt safe here, nor did her immediate successor, Democrat George Nakano. But Bowen and Nakano never experienced the kind of brawl that took place in 2004 between Democrat Mike Gordon, the former mayor of El Segundo, and Republican Greg Hill, the mayor of Redondo Beach. Gordon acquired a new first name—"Telemarketer"—courtesy of the Hill camp, while Hill was "whacky Greg Hill" according to the Gordon campaign.

Gordon and Hill differed along party lines on education funding, affirmative action, stem cell research, taxes, and the environment, battling out their differences in candidate forums and in the mail. Democrats maintained a simple campaign strategy, one that worked in a number of contested legislative districts. They reminded voters that Hill was a Republican—as was the unpopular incumbent at the top of the ticket, Pres. George W. Bush. Hill recognized the value of that argument, distancing himself from the president.

Gordon won, but his tenure was short. He died in June 2005 at age 47, having been diagnosed with a malignant brain tumor not long after taking office in January. A September 2005 special election to replace him saw Torrance Councilman Ted Lieu poll 60% of the vote against five other candidates. Fortunately for Lieu, four of the others were Republicans. By gaining more than half the vote, Lieu avoided a runoff.

Despite his late start, Lieu became one of the Assembly's more accomplished freshmen, scoring runner-up status as "rookie of the year" in *Capitol Weekly*'s survey of legislative talent. His most notable piece of legislation linked him with superstar Tom Cruise and came in response to Cruise's statement that he had bought an ultrasound machine for home use after his fiancée became pregnant. Lieu's bill, which passed the legislature, would have banned the purchase, but Gov. Arnold Schwarzenegger vetoed it. Another bill, signed by the governor, expanded the number of permits that allow hybrid cars to use carpool lanes. In the new session, where Lieu will chair the Banking and Finance Committee, he plans to introduce legislation to expand membership in the South Coast Air Quality Management District, giving South Bay cities more say in board policy.

BIOGRAPHY: Born: Taipei, Taiwan, March 29, 1969. Home: Torrance. Education: BS, BA, Stanford; JD, Georgetown. Military: U.S. Air Force; USAF Reserves. Family: wife Betty, two sons. Religion: Catholic. Occupation: Attorney.

OFFICES: 4016 Capitol Building, Sacramento, CA 95814, Phone: (916) 319-2053, Fax: (916) 319-2153, email: assemblymember.lieu@assembly.ca.gov. District: 1700 East Walnut Avenue, #601, El Segundo, CA 90245, Phone: (310) 615-3515, Fax: (310) 615-3520.

COMMITTEES: Appropriations; Banking and Finance (chair); Veterans Affairs; Water, Parks and Wildlife.

ELECTED: 2005 **TERM LIMIT:** 2010

ELECTION HISTORY: Torrance City Council, 2002–2006.

2005 ELECTION: Lieu (D) 60%
Ford (R) 19%
Hill (R) 5%
Nowatka (R) 12%
Whitehead (R) 2%
Smith (PF) 2%

2006 ELECTION: Lieu (D*) 59%
Ford (R) 37%
Thottam (G) 2%
Abrams (PF) 2%

RATINGS: AFL-CIO CAI CoC CLCV EQCA CCS CMTA FARM NARAL
                    NA   96   24   96   100   100   10   11   NA

FIONA MA (D)
12th Assembly District

Counties: San Francisco, San Mateo
Cities: San Francisco, Daly City
Ethnicity: 34% White, 14% Latino, 5% Black, 44% Asian
Voter Registration: 53% D – 13% R – 30% DS
President 04: 79% Kerry, 19% Bush

Fiona Ma

The question to ask about this San Francisco–Daly City legislative seat is not whether a Republican might score an upset, but will a Republican candidate ever crack 20% of the vote? Thus far, the answer is "no," which is what one might expect when decline-to-state registrants outnumber Republicans more than two-to-one in what has become one of the state's most reliable Democratic strongholds.

The 2001 redistricting did not much change district geography. It still occupies the western portion of San Francisco, although it picked up another slice of Daly City, plus Colma and Broadmoor, while losing a wedge of voters who live east of Highway 101. The 12th is home to the Assembly's largest Asian voting bloc and the largest percentage of decline-to-state voters. Prior to redistricting, the area was represented by Democrat Kevin Shelley, who went on to fame—and infamy—as secretary of state. Shelley, who won that statewide post in 2002, was forced to resign in 2004 following a scandal that involved several constituents from the district's large and influential Chinese-American population.

Democrat Leland Yee represented the district from 2002 to 2006 but left the Assembly one term early to run for and win the 8th Senate District vacated by Democrat Jackie Speier. Yee left an open seat in his wake, as well, and that set up one of the year's most expensive and brutal primary elections. The contenders were San Francisco Supe. Fiona Ma and former television reporter Janet Reilly, a member of the Golden Gate Bridge District board. Reilly was best known as the wife of Clint Reilly, the one-time slash-and-burn political consultant and mayoral candidate who became immensely wealthy as an investor in real estate.

Despite Reilly's wealth, Ma was the favorite, having gained her political experience as a protégé of former Senate pro Tem John Burton and been endorsed by most of the city's political establishment. The race was fabulously expensive, with the two sides raising and spending more than $3 million. Reilly spent $400,000 of her own money, while Ma benefited from $1.2 million in fund raising—not to mention the nearly $650,000 worth of independent expenditures dumped into the campaign on her behalf by interests close to Burton and Assm. Spkr. Fabian Nunez. Sacramento-based political consultant Gale Kaufman hovered over the Ma campaign, and Senator Barbara Boxer weighed in on her behalf, as did former Lt. Gov. Leo McCarthy and Supe. Tom Ammiano. Mayor Gavin Newsom was neutral.

The ground war was waged over experience more than issues—Ma touted her work with Burton and on the board; Reilly claimed it was time for new blood and new ideas. The two clashed over issues as well. Ma supported the death penalty; Reilly was opposed. Reilly backed the high school exit exam; Ma was skeptical of it.

On Election Day, Ma won big, gaining 60% of the vote and a 10,500-vote bulge over Reilly. In Sacramento, Nunez made her part of his leadership team, naming her to the position of majority whip.

BIOGRAPHY: Born: New York City, NY, March 4, 1967. Home: San Francisco. Education: BS, Rochester Institute of Technology; MS, Golden Gate University; MBA, Pepperdine. Military: None. Family: Single. Religion: Presbyterian. Occupation: CPA.

OFFICES: 2176 Capitol Building, Sacramento, CA 95814, Phone: (916) 319-2012, Fax: (916) 319-2112, email: assemblymember.ma@assembly.ca.gov. District: 455 Golden Gate Avenue, #14600, San Francisco, CA 94102, Phone: (415) 557-2312, Fax: (415) 557-1178.

COMMITTEES: Appropriations; Health; Joint Legislative Audit; Public Safety; Revenue and Taxation.

ELECTED: 2006 **TERM LIMIT:** 2012

ELECTION HISTORY: San Francisco Board of Supervisors, 2002–2006.

2006 ELECTION: Ma (D) 71%
Epstein (R) 16%
Hermanson (G) 13%

BILL MAZE (R)
34th Assembly District

Counties: Inyo, Kern, San Bernardino, Tulare
Cities: Visalia, Tulare, Porterville, Barstow, Bishop, Needles
Ethnicity: 52% White, 38% Latino, 4% Black, 3% Asian
Voter Registration: 33% D – 47% R – 16% DS
President 04: 66% Bush, 33% Kerry

The huge 34th District extends along the Nevada border from Bishop in the north to Twentynine Palms in the south and thrusts west from Highway 395 to pick up Visalia and Tulare in the heart of the Central Valley. Along the way, it takes in some of the most beautiful and rugged territory in California, including Sequoia, Death Valley, and Rainbow Basin national parks and Inyo National Forest. Much of the geography is home to more bears than people, with voters concentrated in the Central Valley and

Bill Maze

around Barstow. Because it is so vast, the district boasts a multifaceted economy tailored to its varied geographic areas. Tourism plays a role in the north and east and along the spine of Route 395, which bisects the district north to south. Agriculture dominates the western district, while a portion of the district plays host to various military installations, including Edwards Air Force Base and the Marine Corps Logistics Base at Barstow.

Before redistricting came along in 2001, the population base extended south in the valley to Bakersfield and Tehachapi in Kern County, and to the San Bernardino County communities of Hesperia and Victorville. But mapmakers dropped those areas, pushing the district north to take in Tulare County. The reigning incumbent's home was erased from the district, and he chose to run elsewhere. All the territorial changes did not alter the district's political sympathies, however; it remains strongly Republican.

In 2002, Republican Bill Maze pulled off a surprising coup by running unopposed for an open seat. At the time, Maze was a popular 10-year veteran of the Tulare County Board of Supervisors, but open seats in safe districts usually draw hordes of candidates. Maze's walkover was all the more surprising because the 34th had a GOP incumbent entitled to yet another term in the legislature—Phil Wyman. But Wyman opted to run in the neighboring 36th District, which included his home in Victorville, where he lost the GOP primary to Sharon Runner. It was an odd decision for Wyman, who had been something of a political nomad during his 20 years in elective office, because Runner was the wife of the termed-out 36th District incumbent. Wyman could have moved a few miles north to Barstow and run in the 34th as the incumbent against Maze. He did not, and Maze became one of the few freshmen ever to arrive in Sacramento having not attracted a challenger in the primary for an open seat. He had only nominal opposition in the general elections of 2002, 2004, and 2006.

A businessman and farmer, Maze is vice chairman of the Water, Parks and Wildlife Committee, having held that position previously with the Agriculture Committee. He also sat on the Budget Committee in 2005–2006. The conservative lawmaker has made a crusade out of his opposition to same-sex marriage, joining with the Traditional Values Coalition to hold rallies in his district in "celebration of marriage."

He is a strong proponent of removing the districting process from the hands of the legislature and vesting it in a panel of retired judges—an effort backed by, among others, Common Cause, the Voices of Reform Project, and Gov. Arnold Schwarzenegger. He has been a crusader to reform the foster care system and authored at least one bill—to help prevent identity theft among children in that system—signed into law by the governor. Maze is termed out in 2008.

BIOGRAPHY: Born: Woodlake, April 9, 1946. Home: Visalia. Education: BS, Cal Poly San Luis Obispo. Military: U.S. Army, Vietnam era. Family: wife Becky, five children. Religion: Christian. Occupation: Building Contractor.

OFFICES: 5160 Capitol Building, Sacramento, CA 95814, Phone: (916) 319-2034, Fax: (916) 319-2134, email: assemblymember.maze@assembly.ca.gov. District: 5959 South Mooney Boulevard, Visalia, CA 93277, Phone (559) 636-3440, Fax: (559) 636-4484.

COMMITTEES: Budget; Budget Subcommittee 1 on Health and Human Services; Business and Professions; Water, Parks and Wildlife (vice chair).

ELECTED: 2002 **TERM LIMIT:** 2008

ELECTION HISTORY: Tulare County Board of Supervisors, 1992–2002. Chairman, 1997–2002.

2002 ELECTION: Maze (R) 65%
                            Gurrola (D) 35%

2004 ELECTION: Maze (R*) 69%
                            Florez (D) 31%

2006 ELECTION: Maze (R*) 68%
                            Farrelly (D) 29%
                            Silva (G) 3%

RATINGS:

AFL-CIO	CAI	CoC	CLCV	EQCA	CCS	CMTA	FARM	NARAL
4	44	100	0	0	20	90	100	20

TONY MENDOZA (D)
56th Assembly District

Counties: Los Angeles, Orange
Cities: Norwalk, Buena Park, Cerritos, Whittier
Ethnicity: 24% White, 52% Latino, 4% Black, 18% Asian
Voter Registration: 48% D – 31% R – 18% DS
President 04: 55% Kerry, 44% Bush

Tony Mendoza

Throughout the latter half of the 1990s, the 56th was a political battleground that forced majority Democrats to sink ever-increasing amounts of campaign cash into their candidates. The 17-point registration edge that Democrats enjoyed through most of that time belied the district's true character. At the time, it took in northern Long Beach and communities such as Bellflower, Cerritos and Downey—an area once solidly white, working class, and Republican. By 2000, the area had become multi-ethnic, working class, and marginally Democratic. But mostly, it was conservative and voted more like an inland district than a coastal one, which is why Republicans thought that enough money and a bit of good luck could wrest it away. The focus of their efforts in three elections from 1996 to 2000 was incumbent Democrat Sally Havice.

By the time redistricting came along in 2001, Democrats had seen enough of these struggles and dismantled the 56th—shoving it east, north, and south and creating a two-piece Mutt and Jeff that straddles the Los Angeles–Orange county line. Artesia, once the eastern anchor, now sits in the west. Bellflower, once the heart of the district, has been removed, as have Downey and most of Lakewood. Santa Fe Springs and South Whittier were added to the top, while at the bottom, the district dips into Orange County to capture Buena Park.

The immediate beneficiary of this surgery was Democrat Rudy Bermudez, a state parole officer and Norwalk city councilman, who sought to replace Havice when she was termed out in 2002. Bermudez parlayed strong labor support in outspending Sally Zuniga Flowers two-to-one and outpolling her by some 20%. He dispatched his Republican opponent that November to win a spot in Sacramento.

Bermudez had a term remaining to him when he ran for a vacant Senate seat in 2006, but he fell short in the primary to colleague Ron Calderon. His decision opened the seat, and three Democrats jumped in, including Flowers. She was joined by Artesia Councilman Tony Mendoza and policeman Rick Ramirez. Money flowed liberally to Mendoza and Ramirez, less so to Flowers who hoped to capitalize on the name ID built during her previous run. Mendoza corralled most of the key area endorsements, including Bermudez, state Sen. Richard Alarcon, Sheriff Lee Baca, and other area lawmakers. He had most of labor in his corner, as well as the California Medical Association, League of Conservation Voters, and the grocers' association. Flowers boasted an endorsement from Baca and Orange Co. Supe. Chris Norby. Ramirez had backing from Sen. Martha Escutia and many law-enforcement groups. Among his major donors were Indian gaming tribes.

Mendoza's connections, especially the ground troops supplied by labor for phone banking and GOTV efforts, proved decisive as he captured 46% of the primary vote. Flowers and Ramirez split the rest nearly evenly.

The fall election proved more taxing than Democrats expected, thanks to a well-financed campaign on behalf of the Republican nominee, former Cerritos City Councilwoman Grace Hu. She raised and spent more than $500,000 on the contest—enough to give Democrats pause. Mendoza took nothing for granted, hitting Hu hard on a $40,000 judgment against her real estate business from the state Dept. of Corporations. Mendoza made trust a key issue, while Hu touted her business experience.

Despite the money, Hu was unable to make much of a dent in the Democrats' registration edge, and Mendoza won by more than 11,000 votes. Once in Sacramento, Mendoza was shut out of a committee chairmanship or leadership post, perhaps due to his relationship with Richie Ross—a rival of Spkr. Fabian Nunez and his political guru, consultant Gale Kaufman.

BIOGRAPHY: Born: Los Angeles, April 22, 1971. Home: Artesia. Education: BA, CSU Long Beach; Teaching Credential, CSU Los Angeles. Military: None. Family: wife Letty, three daughters. Religion: Catholic. Occupation: Teacher.

OFFICES: 5144 Capitol Building, Sacramento, CA 95814, Phone: (916) 319-2056, Fax: (916) 319-2156, email: assemblymember.mendoza@assembly.ca.gov. Dis-

trict: 12501 East Imperial Highway, Suite 210, Norwalk, CA 90650, Phone: (562) 864-5600, Fax: (562) 863-7466.
COMMITTEES: Agriculture; Banking and Finance; Elections and Redistricting; Governmental Organization; Rules.
ELECTED: 2006 **TERM LIMIT:** 2012
ELECTION HISTORY: Artesia City Council, 1997–2006; Mayor, 1998–1999.
2006 ELECTION: Mendoza (D) 58%
Hu (R) 42%

GENE MULLIN (D)
19th Assembly District

Counties: San Mateo
Cities: San Mateo, South San Francisco, San Bruno, Pacifica, Daly City, Burlingame, Foster City
Ethnicity: 52% White, 18% Latino, 3% Black, 24% Asian
Voter Registration: 50% D – 23% R – 23% DS
President 04: 69% Kerry, 30% Bush

Gene Mullin

At one time not long ago—like, in the 1992 redistricting—the 19th District formed a tight wishbone between San Francisco Bay and the Pacific Ocean south of the city of San Francisco. Its voters never saw a Democrat they didn't like and over the years were represented by some of the most powerful legislators in Sacramento. But the 2001 redistricting altered the shape and scope of the district, trading dense urban precincts in Broadmoor and Daly City for large empty mountain tracts between Pacifica and the Santa Cruz County line due west of Boulder Creek. The geographic swap affected the district's political character not at all.

For many years, the area was the province of Democrat Lou Papan—a brusque yet highly effective lawmaker who served as one of Speaker Willie Brown's top lieutenants during the 1980s. Papan chaired the Rules Committee and was known around the Capitol as "the enforcer." He tried and failed to win a state Senate seat in 1986, losing out to San Francisco County Supe. Quentin Kopp, who ran as an independent. Papan was out of elective politics for a decade before returning in 1996 to an Assembly culture dramatically altered by term limits.

When his second legislative career ended in 2002, Papan tried to toss the brass ring to his daughter Gina, an attorney and deputy attorney general. It might have worked had the very name Papan not prompted others to enter the Democratic fray—one of whom was Gene Mullin, a South San Francisco city councilman and retired schoolteacher backed by the area's state senator and longtime Papan foe, Jackie Speier.

At times during a rugged primary campaign, it was difficult to realize that the Papan on the ballot was *not* Lou but his daughter. Mullin and two other Democratic contenders pummeled clan Papan, invoking the father's name at every opportunity, mostly in the negative. Lou Papan was accused of funneling campaign contributions to his daughter's coffers, of having accepted money from Enron, and Enron's accountant, and big tobacco companies—all of which he bestowed on Gina in the days before Proposition 34 banned such transfers. He was accused of strong-arming other contributors into donating to his daughter and of attempting to bully mapmakers into drawing the 19th District to exclude a San Mateo supervisor seen as a threat to Gina. And on and on.

Mullin was the chief beneficiary of the mud balls. Speier provided generous help as well, lining up endorsements and even appearing in his TV ads. Trial lawyers— never friendly to Papan despite his Democratic pedigree—went to bat for Mullin with independent expenditures, as did labor. A third candidate, high-tech executive David Pine, self-funded to the tune of $500,000—using some of the money to give out pine-scented air fresheners.

Gina Papan fought back, trying to remind voters that she had an independent track record of community service, but all her efforts could not prevent the election from becoming a referendum on her father. Nor could she get to the left of Mullin—an important factor in what became a ho-hum election that mostly attracted the party's hard-core liberal voters. In the end, Mullin won with 42% of the vote; Papan came in second with 35%, and Pine, who spent $70 a vote, finished third with 19%.

Once in Sacramento, the unassuming Mullin appeared invisible at times, gaining little mention from Capitol insiders asked to choose the outstanding rookies from the legislature's class of 2002. He was regarded as thoughtful, if a bit of a lefty, and a good Democratic soldier if not much of an original thinker. In his second term, Mullin was given chairmanship of the Housing and Community Development Committee as well as a seat on the Budget Committee, both of which elevate him to the Assembly's middle bench. He focused on issues involving airports, including noise abatement and security—not surprising for a lawmaker whose district includes San Francisco International.

In his third term, he was handed the Education Committee, always a spotlight for glory and trouble in this era of exit exams, teacher tenure, administrative accountability, and test scores. A teacher and administrator himself, he won't rabble rouse in the post.

Mullin's legislative future beyond 2008 currently is cut off. Speier was termed out in 2006 and her place taken by Democrat Leland Yee, thus shutting off that step on the ladder until 2014—an eternity in the political life of a new-age legislator.

BIOGRAPHY: Born: San Francisco, April 21, 1937. Home: South San Francisco. Education: BA, Teaching Credential, University of San Francisco. Military: U.S. Army, 1959–1960. Family: wife Terri, two children. Religion: Catholic. Occupation: Educator.

OFFICES: 2163 Capitol Building, Sacramento, CA 95814, Phone: (916) 319-2019, Fax: (916) 319-2119, email: assemblymember.mullin@assembly.ca.gov. District:

1528 South El Camino Real, Suite 302, San Mateo, CA 94402, Phone: (650) 341-4319, Fax: (650) 341-4676.

COMMITTEES: Budget; Budget Subcommittee 2 on Education Finance; Education (chair); Housing and Community Development; Public Employees, Retirement and Social Security; Water, Parks and Wildlife.

ELECTED: 2002 **TERM LIMIT:** 2008

ELECTION HISTORY: South San Francisco City Council, 1995–2002; Mayor, 1998, 2001–2002.

2002 ELECTION: Mullin (D) 63%
Kawas (R) 26%
Chamberlain (G) 10%
Giedt (L) 2%

2004 ELECTION: Mullin (D*) 71%
Brinkman (R) 26%
Glister (L) 3%

2006 ELECTION: Mullin (D*) 74%
Gufler (R) 26%

RATINGS:

AFL-CIO	CAI	CoC	CLCV	EQCA	CCS	CMTA	FARM	NARAL
100	96	18	100	100	95	0	20	100

ALAN NAKANISHI (R)
10th Assembly District

Counties: Amador, El Dorado, Sacramento, San Joaquin
Cities: Lodi, Elk Grove, Stockton, Rancho Cordova, Ione, Jackson
Ethnicity: 64% White, 15% Latino, 7% Black, 11% Asian
Voter Registration: 38% D – 42% R – 16% DS
President 04: 57% Bush, 43% Kerry

Alan Nakanishi

The 10th District is testament to the power of how drawing district lines can make a difference. Before 2001, the 10th covered southern Sacramento and northern San Joaquin counties, was Republican-leaning and considered one of the more competitive in the state. In the 1998 election, for example, Republican Anthony Pescetti defeated his Democratic challenger by fewer than 300 votes out of more than 139,000 cast.

Ever mindful of that narrow victory, Pescetti spent four years cooperating with majority Democrats, in the process angering fellow Republicans by supporting Democratic Gov. Gray Davis's 2001 budget in return for $7.5 million in projects for his district. Punishment for Pescetti's indiscretion came that same year when his district was significantly altered by a redistricting deal struck between legislative Republicans and

Democrats. Amador County and El Dorado Hills were added, while Galt, Wilton, and sections of Elk Grove and the city of Sacramento were dropped.

As a result, four of every 10 voters were new to the district, which now covers all of Amador County and parts of Sacramento, El Dorado, and San Joaquin counties. Pescetti chose not to seek re-election in 2002 rather than run in the newly drawn district. He denied that party leaders forced him out, saying the newly drawn district needed an Assembly member who wouldn't be termed out of office so soon.

His successor was party loyalist Alan Nakanishi, the former mayor of Lodi, a conservative and a formidable vote-getter who turned the 10th into safe Republican territory. Since 1971, Nakanishi, an eye surgeon, has practiced medicine in Stockton and is the cofounder of Delta Eye Medical Group. Nakanishi came to the attention of the Republican state hierarchy in 2000 when he nearly pulled off a spectacular political upset in a race for an open seat in the state Senate, coming within a few hundred votes of defeating Democratic Assemblyman Mike Machado. Nakanishi had been given little chance of defeating the better-known and well-financed Machado, but he ran a slash-and-burn campaign that attacked Machado's record and his ties to then-San Francisco Mayor and former Assembly Speaker Willie Brown.

The race produced excellent name identification for Nakanishi, who benefited from the fact that the redistricting deal made Lodi the district's biggest bloc of voters. Several Republicans wanted to succeed Pescetti in 2002, but party leaders lined up behind Nakanishi, who won both the primary and general elections. In 2004 the Democrats didn't even bother to run a candidate, although a Libertarian opponent managed 25% of the vote. Nakanishi drew three opponents in 2006, including a Libertarian and a Peace and Freedom candidate. That, plus a Democrat, dropped Nakanishi's vote to 61%.

As an assemblyman, Nakanishi opposed assisted-suicide legislation that would allow doctors to prescribe lethal medication to terminally ill patients. That legislation was narrowly defeated in 2006 and promises to be reintroduced, lending significance to Nakanishi's new position as vice chair of the Health Committee. He has supported the notion of a part-time legislature and toed the conservative line in opposition to gay marriage and driver's licenses for illegal immigrants.

If he has ambitions beyond the Assembly, Nakanishi has options, although not good ones. His 10th District includes parts of three Senate districts, but only one offers any immediate opportunities—the 5th now occupied by his old nemesis, Mike Machado, who also is termed out in 2008. Machado's district leans Democratic but is considered competitive, and Nakanishi could give it another whirl. The other two Senate districts are sealed off. The 1st is the most Republican, but incumbent Dave Cox is still in his first term and is not termed out until 2012. The 6th is solidly Democratic and occupied by Darrell Steinberg, who is not termed out until well after the next redistricting.

BIOGRAPHY: Born: Sacramento, March 21, 1940. Home: Lodi. Education: BA, Pacific Union; MA, Virginia Commonwealth; MD, Loma Linda. Military: U.S. Army, Vietnam service. Family: wife Sue, three children, eight grandchildren. Religion: Seventh Day Adventist. Occupation: Physician.

OFFICES: 5175 Capitol Building, Sacramento, CA 95814, Phone: (916) 319-2010, Fax: (916) 319-2110, email: assemblymember.nakanishi@assembly.ca.gov. District: 218 West Pine Street, Lodi, CA 95241, Phone: (209) 333-5330, Fax: (209) 333-5333.

COMMITTEES: Appropriations; Education; Health (vice chair); Joint Legislative Audit.

ELECTED: 2002 **TERM LIMIT:** 2008

ELECTION HISTORY: Lodi City Council, 1998–2002; Mayor, 2001–2002.

2002 ELECTION: Nakanishi (R) 60%
　　　　　　　　 Maestas (D) 40%

2004 ELECTION: Nakanishi (R) 76%
　　　　　　　　 Lang (L) 24%

2006 ELECTION: Nakanishi (R*) 61%
　　　　　　　　 Cook (D) 34%
　　　　　　　　 Bonser (L) 3%
　　　　　　　　 Troyer (PF) 1%

RATINGS:

AFL-CIO	CAI	CoC	CLCV	EQCA	CCS	CMTA	FARM	NARAL
4	52	100	4	0	10	90	90	20

PEDRO NAVA (D)
35th Assembly District

Counties: Santa Barbara, Ventura
Cities: Ventura, Santa Barbara, Oxnard, Carpinteria
Ethnicity: 54% White, 38% Latino, 2% Black, 4% Asian
Voter Registration: 45% D – 31% R – 19% DS
President 04: 60% Kerry, 39% Bush

Pedro Nava

The 35th District runs from Los Padres National Forest in the north of Santa Barbara County to the central coastal towns of Santa Barbara, Isla Vista, Goleta, Montecito, and Carpinteria, and into Ventura County, including Ventura and half of Oxnard. People along the coast are socially liberal and pro-environment thanks, in part, to a 1969 oil spill at a drilling platform off the Santa Barbara coast that many consider the birth of the environmental movement. Coastal residents have been anti–oil rig ever since, though water quality issues occupy more of peoples' minds these days. Santa Barbara—with its million-dollar homes, magnificent white mission, liberal values, and university—is the focal point for the county that bears its name.

Northwest of Santa Barbara, in the rural Santa Inez Valley, political attitudes run more socially conservative and anti-growth. Residents here have a farming and cattle-raising heritage that sometimes clashes with the environmental views on the coast.

The district once ran from the Santa Ynez Valley eastward to Santa Paula, but artful redistricting carved off Los Alamos, Ojai, and Santa Paula and added half of Oxnard to make it more comfy for Democrats, who now enjoy a 10-percent bulge over Republicans.

Highway 101 plays an important role for the estimated one-third of Santa Barbara's south coast workers who commute from outside the region. With home prices soaring above $1 million in Santa Barbara's south coast, and a shrinking supply of large land parcels for affordable housing within the city, the middle class, including teachers and law enforcement, are fleeing farther south to places like Ventura or north out of the district. As a result, businesses struggle to attract employees discouraged by the high cost of housing and high tech industry in Goleta is expanding. Feeling the pressure, voters in Ventura County adopted a series of anti-sprawl measures called S.O.A.R. (Save Open Space and Agricultural Resources) that other counties look to as a model.

Latinos, the largest minority group, make up about 38% of the population but only about 18% of registered voters. Oxnard has the largest concentration of Latinos between the Bay Area and Los Angeles, but the landscape is changing. Democrat Pedro Nava, a Latino civil litigator, beat Republican Bob Pohl in November 2004, replacing Democrat Hanna-Beth Jackson, who was termed out. The contest featured a pair of well-regarded candidates backed by a diverse set of political allies. Pohl had strong support from JOBSPAC, the Chamber of Commerce-sponsored amalgam that promoted business candidates. Nava drew support from prison guards, firefighters, teachers, and card clubs, and his campaign made an issue of Pohl's financial support—pointing out to environmentally sensitive voters that much of JOBSPAC's money came from large oil and energy companies. Gov. Schwarzenegger campaigned for Pohl—an indication that Republicans thought the district winnable. It wasn't.

Nava was appointed to the California Coastal Commission in 1997 and reappointed three times, which caused him some headaches during the campaign when his opponent pointed out that Nava's wife once lobbied the commission. Nava was president of the Santa Barbara County Action Network and the Hispanic Chamber of Commerce and a trustee of the Santa Barbara Museum of Art. His wife, Susan Jordan, is a Santa Barbara County planning commissioner.

After his relatively easy re-election in 2006, Nava was made chair of the Transportation Committee, which will help decide how to spend billions in transportation bond money authorized by voters in November 2006. Among his current package of legislation is a bill to consolidate disaster and emergency response entities, placing the Office of Emergency Services and Homeland Security in the same agency. It follows his 2006 legislation that reorganized the Emergency Response Council.

BIOGRAPHY: Born: Monterrey, Mexico, February 6, 1948. Home: Santa Barbara. Education: BA, San Bernardino State; JD, UC Davis. Military: None. Family: wife Susan, one child. Religion: Decline to State. Occupation: Attorney.

OFFICES: 2148 Capitol Building, Sacramento, CA 95814, Phone: (916) 319-2035, Fax: (916) 319-2135, email: assemblymember.nava@assembly.ca.gov. District: 101 West Anapamu Street, Suite A, Santa Barbara, CA 93101, Phone: (805) 564-1649, Fax: (805) 564-1651.

COMMITTEES: Appropriations; Environmental Safety and Toxic Materials; Transportation (chair); Water, Parks and Wildlife.
ELECTED: 2004 **TERM LIMIT:** 2010
ELECTION HISTORY: None
2004 ELECTION: Nava (D) 53%
                     Pohl (R) 47%
2006 ELECTION: Nava (D*) 63%
                     Martin (R) 37%

RATINGS:	AFL-CIO	CAI	CoC	CLCV	EQCA	CCS	CMTA	FARM	NARAL
	100	96	29	93	100	100	0	20	100

ROGER NIELLO (R)
5th Assembly District

Counties: Placer, Sacramento
Cities: Citrus Heights, Folsom, Sacramento
Ethnicity: 75% White, 10% Hispanic, 5% Black, 5% Asian
Voter Registration: 36% D – 42% R – 18% DS
President 04: 57% Bush, 42% Kerry

Roger Niello

The old 5th District looked like a buffalo pointed east toward the Sierra, with its horns butting against El Dorado County, its body taking in suburban Sacramento and its rump due west in Yolo County. The new version has developed a sway back with the removal of Rio Linda and territory north of McClellan Air Force Base. The poor creature seems to be protesting his sudden deformity because the addition of Granite Bay looks like a wide-open mouth about to swallow Folsom Lake.

Politically, the district is homogenous Republican. But in terms of demographics and economics, it includes wealthy and not-so-wealthy clumps of metropolitan Sacramento as Arden Arcade, Folsom, and Granite Bay coexist with North Highlands.

From 1998 to 2004, the area was represented by Republican Dave Cox, a former Sacramento County supervisor who rose to become minority leader of the Assembly before being elected to the state Senate in 2004. Prior to Cox, the area sent Republicans Tim Leslie and the flamboyant B.T. Collins to the Assembly.

The Sacramento Board of Supervisors once again served as a conduit to this seat as Supervisor Roger Niello replaced Cox. A conservative whose name recognition is built on the fact that he and his family own one of the region's most successful auto dealerships, Niello served on many local boards and commissions, including a stint as president of the Sacramento Chamber of Commerce.

His rookie season in the legislature was marked by a legislative package that included bills to limit unfunded state mandates to local government and prevent local government from using taxpayer dollars to lobby for or against ballot measures.

Niello's second term was marked by a significant appointment—vice chairman of the Assembly Budget Committee. The new GOP leadership team, led by Minority Leader Mike Villines, is expected to snub Gov. Arnold Schwarzenegger's call for bipartisanship and return instead to the days of hard-line Republican opposition to Democratic initiatives and overtures. The centerpiece of that opposition is the state budget, and as the chief caucus voice on budgetary matters, Niello will toe that hard line, making his second term potentially contentious. It also should endear him to his conservative suburban constituency.

BIOGRAPHY: Born: San Francisco, June 2, 1948. Home: Fair Oaks. Education: BA, UC Berkeley; MA, UCLA. Military: None. Family: wife Mary, five children. Religion: Decline to state. Occupation: Auto dealer.

OFFICES: 6027 Capitol Building, Sacramento, CA 95814, Phone (916) 319-2005, Fax: (916) 319-2105, email: assemblymember.niello@assembly.ca.gov. District: 4811 Chippendale Drive, Suite 501, Sacramento, CA 95841, Phone: (916) 349-1995, Fax: (916) 349-1999.

COMMITTEES: Budget (vice chair); Budget Subcommittee 1 on Health and Human Services; Elections and Redistricting.

ELECTED: 2004 **TERM LIMIT:** 2010

ELECTION HISTORY: Sacramento County Board of Supervisors, 1999–2004

2004 ELECTION: Carey (D) 36%
                     Niello (R) 60%
                     Manfre (L) 4%

2006 ELECTION: Bell (D) 36%
                     Niello (R*) 62%
                     Lopez (PF) 3%

RATINGS:

AFL-CIO	CAI	CoC	CLCV	EQCA	CCS	CMTA	FARM	NARAL
7	48	100	4	0	10	90	100	20

FABIAN NUNEZ (D)
46th Assembly District

Counties: Los Angeles
Cities: Los Angeles, Huntington Park, Maywood
Ethnicity: 4% White, 85% Latino, 6% Black, 4% Asian
Voter Registration: 63% D – 14% R – 19% DS
President 04: 81% Kerry, 18% Bush

For nearly three decades, between 1964 and 1994, the California speakership was marked by relative stability and orderly transitions. The only exception was a brawl between Democrats Leo McCarthy of San Francisco and Howard Berman of Los An-

Fabian Nunez

geles that extended through 1979 and 1980 and led to the rise and ultimate demise of the speakership as a power center. The result of the Berman-McCarthy fight was the ascension of Assemblyman Willie L. Brown, Jr., of San Francisco following the 1980 elections.

During his record 15-plus years as speaker, the charismatic, quick-witted, and keenly intelligent Brown was arguably the most powerful legislator in California, his political influence second only to that of the governor. Brown and his Democratic minions ran the Assembly as a closely held corporation, with a budget beyond the scrutiny of the public or even of rival Republicans. The term "imperial speakership" was coined especially for Brown who, for most of his time in office, maintained personal control over the dispensing of legislative perks and pork—everything from committee assignments and office space to budgets and staffing.

But the often high-handed way that Brown conducted the speakership provided the motivation for Proposition 140—the 1990 initiative that imposed term limits on the legislature and ended Brown's tenure and the speakership as a repository of power. In the era of term limits, the speakership lost most of its luster. First, the speaker has little opportunity to consolidate his or her power over a long period of time. Most speakers gain the post midway through their second terms and from the outset are lame ducks facing pressure from those who want to succeed the incumbent. Second, with Assembly membership constantly turning over, legislative power has migrated to the Senate.

Finally, the speakership was severely tarnished by Brown's shenanigans in the wake of the 1994 elections when he maneuvered to retain the position despite the fact that Republicans had gained a 41–39 majority. His manipulations spawned nearly a year of turmoil and destroyed the inherent stability of the speakership.

In 1994 and 1995, Brown held unto the speakership by playing on divisions and distrust among Assembly Republicans. First, he gained the support of a disgruntled Republican (Paul Horcher of Diamond Bar) and used suspect parliamentary maneuvering to oust another Republican (Richard Mountjoy of Monrovia) who had been elected to the Assembly and Senate in the same election. The result was a 40-39 vote for speaker in Brown's favor.

Having kept his job, Brown engineered his departure on terms favorable to his caucus. In the summer of 1995 he passed the speakership to yet another disgruntled Republican, Doris Allen of Cypress, who won the post with only one GOP vote—her own. She subsequently gained an ally in Republican freshman Brian Sentencich of Fresno.

But Allen's tenure was a legislative joke. Ill-equipped to handle the job despite her years in the legislature, and completely ostracized from her own caucus, she was besieged from the beginning by outraged Republicans who eventually succeeded in having her recalled by her Orange County constituents in December 1995. She handed the speakership to Sentencich, who held it only until January 1996 when Republicans finally mustered the strength to install their choice for speaker—Orange County's Curt

Pringle. He held the job until December when, in the aftermath of the 1996 elections, Democrats again gained a majority of the house and elected Cruz Bustamante as speaker. Brown went on to serve two terms as mayor of San Francisco.

The instability of the speakership is noted in the number of people who have held the title. One person—Brown—held it for 15 years between 1980 and 1995. In the decade since 1995, however, the post has dropped in and out of the hands of eight others (Allen, Sentencich, Pringle, Bustamante, Antonio Villaraigosa, Robert Hertzberg, Herb Wesson, and the current incumbent, Fabian Nunez of Los Angeles).

With Speaker Wesson's help, Nunez became speaker in his first term in the legislature, affording him at least three years in power and returning stability and clout to the speakership. Unlike his four immediate Democratic predecessors, however, Nunez did not have an easy road to the top or a seamless transition into the job. Bustamante, Villaraigosa, Hertzberg, and Wesson all avoided a public fight; Nunez did not—despite the fact he was Wesson's hand-picked successor.

As Wesson's Assembly career wound down late in 2003, he made it known that he would relinquish the speakership once a successor had gathered the 41 votes needed to be elected to the post—votes that had to come from the 48-member Democratic caucus. Three Democrats were in contention: Nunez, Jenny Oropeza of Long Beach, and Dario Frommer of Los Feliz. Of the three, only Nunez was a freshman.

Nunez, Frommer, and Oropeza stalked votes for three months—from September to November 2003—before Nunez emerged with the requisite majority. Even then, the final result was accompanied by confusion and mystery. At one point, Oropeza claimed that Nunez had agreed to withdraw in favor of her. But when Frommer bowed out in late November, Nunez denied the claim. After meeting with members who backed Frommer, a disgruntled and disappointed Oropeza realized she did not have the votes and withdrew, leaving the field to Nunez. It was an inauspicious beginning for Nunez who took three months to nail down 41 votes despite active support from the incumbent speaker and his leadership team. Nunez assumed the post in February 2004, halfway through his first term in the Assembly.

Nunez is a survivor. One of a dozen children of Mexican immigrants, he grew up poor in San Diego where his father was a gardener and his mother a maid. He cut his teeth as political director for the powerful Los Angeles Federation of Labor and served as government-relations director for the huge Los Angeles Unified School District.

Nunez was first elected to the Assembly in 2002, winning the Democratic primary to succeed Democrat Gil Cedillo, who was running for the Senate. His main opponent was Pedro Carrillo, a staff aide to Congresswoman Lucille Roybal-Allard. His standing as labor's number-one legislative priority gave Nunez an edge Carrillo could not overcome, and Nunez won handily.

Once installed as speaker, Nunez sought to impose his imprint on the institution and to assert his authority. He successfully reduced both the number and size of standing committees and revamped the Speaker's Office of Majority Services, the large operation that provides Democratic members with advice and serves as a holding tank for political operatives who go off the state payroll during election years to help run Democratic campaigns.

At first, Nunez was unable to build the bipartisan support he called for during his acceptance speech. Unlike Wesson, who cultivated a relationship with the newly elected Gov. Schwarzenegger, Nunez became an especially vocal critic of Schwarzenegger and his policies. Nunez's criticisms of the governor helped harden relations between the administration and Democrats and led, in part, to Schwarzenegger's disastrous decision to bypass the legislature in 2005 and take his case for change to voters via a special election.

Despite winning the speakership during his freshman year, Nunez did not fare especially well during interviews for *California Journal*'s 2004 "Minnie Awards"—which identify the legislature's best and brightest. He was not considered "Rookie of the Year" (that went to his GOP counterpart, Kevin McCarthy), nor was he considered the top rookie in his own caucus (bested by both John Laird of Santa Cruz and Mark Leno of San Francisco).

But Nunez warmed to the job as he gained experience as a lawmaker, so much so that by the time *Capitol Weekly* conducted its survey of the best and brightest in late 2006, Nunez was deemed the Assembly's "most effective member" and the "hardest working" in the entire legislature.

Over time, Nunez reclaimed the speakership as the primary voice of the legislature. More significant, he came to a rapprochement with the governor that led to a moderately productive session in 2006. Schwarzenegger was politically wounded after voters rejected all of his proposals during the 2005 special election and needed to repair his reputation on the eve of a re-election campaign. That required working with the legislature, and Nunez seized the chance to advance the Democrats' agenda.

The bipartisan love fest produced bills that raised the minimum wage, addressed global warming, allowed for the "safe surrender" of infants without penalty, lowered the cost of prescription drugs, imposed accountability standards on the child welfare system, and established a border council with Mexico. The administration and legislature cooperated to put a significant infrastructure bond package on the November 2006 ballot. Nunez was politically invested in the success of the package, which would, by the way, be on the same ballot as the governor's re-election. Schwarzenegger and his campaign team so intertwined their effort with the bond campaign that it became impossible to promote one without appearing to promote the other. That put Nunez and other legislative leaders in something of a pickle.

Not that they seemed to mind. As the November campaign unfolded, Nunez and other legislative Democrats were criticized for their less-than-enthusiastic support of Schwarzenegger's Democratic opponent, state Treas. Phil Angelides. Although Nunez endorsed Angelides and served as his state co-chair, he did little campaigning for him. And there was widespread speculation that Nunez and other Democrats would prefer Schwarzenegger to Angelides, for political and legislative reasons. The governor's continued call for bipartisan cooperation stoked their preference.

More Machiavellian was the notion that some Democrats would benefit politically from the governor's re-election—Nunez among them. Should Angelides become governor, he likely would serve two terms, thus occupying the governor's horseshoe suite of offices until 2014 and shutting down the ambitions of other Democrats who see themselves running for governor when Schwarzenegger is termed out in 2010. Chief among those other Democrats is Los Angeles Mayor Antonio Villaraigosa, an ally of Nunez. And among those seen as succeeding Villaraigosa as mayor is none other than Nunez.

Regardless of whether the plot thickened in quite this way, Nunez is poised to lead the Assembly through most of the 2007–2008 session. At some point, he must time his departure as speaker, for he, too, is now termed out. In the meantime, he began the current session by outlining an ambitious effort to make health care accessible and affordable to all Californians, what he called the "fair share health care proposal." The governor, too, has made health care coverage a centerpiece of his agenda for 2007.

The devil will be in the details.

BIOGRAPHY: Born: San Diego, December 27, 1966. Home: Los Angeles. Education: BA, Claremont College. Military: None. Family: three children. Religion: No preference. Occupation: Legislator.

OFFICES: 219 Capitol Building, Sacramento, CA 95814, Phone: (916) 319-2046, Fax: (916) 319-2146, email: assemblymember.nunez@assembly.ca.gov. District: 320 West 4th Street, Room 1050, Los Angeles, CA 90013, Phone: (213) 620-4646, Fax: (213) 620-6319.

COMMITTEES: Speaker of the Assembly.

ELECTED: 2002 **TERM LIMIT:** 2008

ELECTION HISTORY: None.

2002 ELECTION: Nunez (D) 86%

Aldana (R) 14%

2004 ELECTION: Nunez (D*) 86%

Aldana (R) 14%

2006 ELECTION: Nunez (D*) 100%

RATINGS:

AFL-CIO	CAI	CoC	CLCV	EQCA	CCS	CMTA	FARM	NARAL
100	96	24	96	100	100	0	40	100

NICOLE PARRA (D)
30th Assembly District

Counties: Fresno, Kern, Kings, Tulare

Cities: Hanford, Delano, Bakersfield, Wasco, Coalinga

Ethnicity: 26% White, 61% Latino, 7% Black, 4% Asian

Voter Registration: 47% D – 38% R – 11% DS

President 04: 57% Bush, 42% Kerry

A heavily Latino district in the lower Central Valley, the 30th was retooled slightly in the 2001 redistricting. Voters are concentrated along I-5 in the west and Highway 99 in the east, but the southern portion of the old district was shaved off and replaced with territory east of Corcoran. As a result, the district now approaches Bakersfield from the north rather than from the south. A decade ago, it was solid Democratic territory, with nearly 60% of voters registered as Democrats. But Democratic support has been eroding here, as it has in most of the Central Valley, so that now the district is considered competitive between the two parties. Pres. George Bush carried the district by 1% in 2000 but by 15% four years later.

Nicole Parra

The 30th District has been dubbed "Earthquake Alley" because the region around Coalinga is periodically rocked by serious tremors. But the reputation could apply to district politics. The elections of 2002 and 2004 made a shambles of the political landscape and left voters wondering about the region's stability, let alone the sanity of those who seek to represent them in the Capitol halls. The 2006 election was hotly contested once again but far more sane and restrained, although mayhem could return in 2008 when the current incumbent—Democrat Nicole Parra—is termed out.

The troubles began in 2002 when incumbent Democrat Dean Florez opted to run for the state Senate, leaving an open seat. Into the breech stepped five Democratic contenders, two of whom brawled for the nomination. The winner was Parra, daughter of Kern County Supervisor Pete Parra and an aide to the area's Democratic congressman, Cal Dooley. Strongly backed by the United Farm Workers and nearly every liberal this side of Sheila Kuehl, Parra was the candidate from the left, which should have signaled trouble down the road in a district where Democrats consider themselves moderates and less than loyal to party labels once safely inside the confines of a voting booth. Moreover, Parra defeated a moderate backed by Florez—an old enemy of the Parra clan. That, too, should have flashed a red light to Democratic kingmakers in Sacramento. But Democrats and Parra appeared to draw the long straw, for the GOP nominee was a political neophyte, businessman Dean Gardner from Bakersfield, who became a poster boy for abandoned causes after Assembly Republicans dismissed him as a viable candidate.

At first, the campaign evolved along predictable lines. Parra, a Latina in a majority Hispanic district, outspent Gardner nearly ten-to-one and touted her connections to the UFW and her deep political roots in the district. Just two weeks before the election, a poll by *The Bakersfield Californian* showed Parra ahead by nearly 20 points. But the potential for disaster was evident in that poll, which indicated that nearly half the voters had yet to make up their minds, although the undecideds leaned toward Parra. The poll gave Democrats a false sense of security, which led to a decision to shift resources from the 30th District to contests elsewhere in the state.

At that very moment, Gardner was given two nickels, which he rubbed together to create a series of attack ads. His campaign was buoyed not by the newspaper's poll but by the suspicion among Republicans (later confirmed by Democrats) that Anglos in this part of the Central Valley will vote against any candidate with a Latino surname, regardless of party label. Gardner thumped Parra for having been fired as a teacher, and for wanting to raise taxes on farmers. Parra responded in kind, sinking the campaign into the mud. In the end, Parra won, but only by a few hundred votes, her bacon saved in Kern County where she took 70% of the vote in her father's supervisorial district.

Tense and testy, 2002 was merely prelude to Parra's re-election in 2004. Gardner's strong showing blinded Republicans to some of his monumental faults—the details of which Democrats would gleefully recite to voters. For her part, Parra tried hard during the intervening two years to shed her liberal tag, so much so that the UFW abandoned her in 2004 and her ratings by the manufacturers' association and state Chamber of Commerce are among the highest given to a Democrat.

It is difficult to adequately evaluate or describe the district's 2004 election because so little of it made sense. Republicans, still sifting through the debris of 2002, considered Parra the most vulnerable Democratic incumbent west of the Mississippi River, and they laid plans to wage the kind of high-priced campaign that buys lavish homes, vacation cabins, and expensive SUVs for an army of consultants, pollsters, and fundraisers.

But rather than conduct a districtwide search for a viable candidate to oppose Parra, Republicans went dumpster diving. After a few half-hearted attempts to recruit an alternative, they turned again to Gardner, with the subsequent explanation that his close call in 2002 earned him another shot. That Gardner was burdened with enough political baggage to outfit Paris Hilton did not faze GOP poobahs, or, worse, they didn't know about it.

Democrats working for Parra quickly enlightened the GOP—and anyone else with a Web address—about Gardner's qualifications for office, which did not extend beyond the fact that he had a pulse. Democrats rolled out, in excruciating detail, a long, soiled, and well-documented history of his bankruptcies, tax liens, name changes, and litigation. By the time they finished with him, Gardner looked more like a candidate for San Quentin than Sacramento.

Undaunted, Republicans remained committed—financially, at least—to the race. They dumped money into Gardner's campaign in $100,000 packets all through the fall, emboldened by Bush's strong showing in the district and an endorsement from Gov. Schwarzenegger, who helped Gardner raise money. They used their resources in an attempt to expose Parra as the consummate liberal. It is only a slight exaggeration to say they blamed her for single-handily raising the car tax, building a monument to homosexual veterans, abusing her Capitol staff, and personally setting fire to at least a dozen kittens. There was a malicious little whispering campaign about Parra's "alternative lifestyle," suggesting she might be gay.

More than $2 million flowed into the district on each side, and Parra's swing to the middle as a rookie legislator helped her immensely. Although the UFW took a walk, she was aided with money, ground support, and independent expenditures by the prison guards' union, corporate agriculture, Indian casinos, and others. Gardner received substantial backing from the Republican Party and conservative groups such as the Club for Growth. After the last sludge ball was flung, Parra was re-elected with a much more comfortable margin than in 2002, the victory settled by another strong showing in Kern County (which, ironically, had turned her father out of office in March thanks to a challenge engineered by his old nemesis, Dean Florez).

Not that Parra could rest. Her victory was comfortable but nowhere near the margin she should have built up against a candidate as flawed as Gardner. That alone emboldened Republicans to come at her again in 2006.

Parra helped Republicans when her second term did not start well. She was named to chair the Joint Legislative Audit Committee, which immediately found itself in the midst of a firestorm called Kevin Shelley. Parra's committee, called on to investigate a series of scandals that embroiled the Democratic secretary of state, was under heavy pressure to subpoena him. Parra delayed putting Shelley himself under a public microscope, so much so that Republicans and others began to accuse her of trying to shelter the embattled officeholder. Shelley eventually resigned, but Parra seemed unable to extract herself from a dicey political dilemma: her duty to investigate and her loyalty to a mortally wounded Democrat. Her performance was less than heroic.

Around the Capitol, Parra built a reputation as a difficult boss, one who wilts staff faster than an August day in Bakersfield. Parra's staff turnover was documented in her hometown paper, *The Bakersfield Californian,* which reported in May 2005 that she had lost yet another chief of staff—the fourth to work for her in two-plus years in office. Even as her chief of staff was quitting, Parra was advertising for two other staff. Capitol insiders call her "the little princess" and say she has too much ego resting on too little ability.

That said, she continued to walk fine lines politically. Her ratings from liberal and conservative advocacy groups (see below) mark her as the consummate moderate. Her 94 from the Chamber of Commerce is highest among Democrats and exactly the same as for conservative Republicans such as Doug La Malfa and Minority Leader Mike Villines. The 70 received from the Farm Bureau is the highest given to a Democrat, as is the 40 from the manufacturer's association.

Those rankings didn't keep Republicans from mounting yet another tough challenge in 2006, this time from a candidate vetted long and hard by GOP kingmakers: Danny Gilmore, an ex-Marine and 31-year veteran of the California Highway Patrol who retired as a district commander in 2003. The campaign was mostly negative, although tame compared with Parra's previous brawls. Democrats paid heavily to save her seat, with Parra and her allies spending $1.4 million, twice what Gilmore spent. She won by some 1,600 votes, and the narrow result surprised many observers who thought she would have an easier time with a political neophyte such as Gilmore. Once again, she was saved by Kern County, which backed her nearly two-to-one.

Parra returns to Sacramento as chair of the Assembly Agriculture Committee. Termed out in 2008, she is eyeing Florez's Senate seat when it comes up in 2010. Among those looking to replace Parra is Florez's mother, Fran, a situation that could put the two women on a collision course for the Senate two years later.

BIOGRAPHY: Born: Bakersfield, February 3, 1970. Home: Hanford. Education: BA, UC Berkeley; JD, Catholic University. Military: None. Family: single. Religion: Catholic. Occupation: Legislator.

OFFICES: 5155 Capitol Building, Sacramento, CA 95814, Phone: (916) 319-2030, Fax: (916) 319-2130, email: assemblymember.parra@assembly.ca.gov. District: 601 24th Street, Suite A, Bakersfield, CA 93301, Phone: (661) 334-3745, Fax: (661) 334-3796; 321 North Douty. Suite B, Hanford, CA 93230, Phone: (559) 585-7170, Fax: (559) 585-7175.

COMMITTEES: Agriculture (chair); Banking and Finance; Insurance; Water, Parks and Wildlife.

ELECTED: 2002 **TERM LIMIT:** 2008
ELECTION HISTORY: None.
2002 ELECTION: Parra (D) 50%
Gardner (R) 50%

2004 ELECTION: Parra (D*) 55%
                Gardner (R) 45%
2006 ELECTION: Parra (D*) 52%
                Gilmore (R) 48%
RATINGS: AFL-CIO CAI CoC CLCV EQCA CCS CMTA FARM NARAL
             69   96   94   26   73   85   40   70   100

GEORGE PLESCIA (R)
75th Assembly District

Counties: San Diego
Cities: San Diego, Escondido, Poway
Ethnicity: 64% White, 13% Latino, 2% Black, 18% Asian
Voter Registration: 29% D – 44% R – 24% DS
President 04: 56% Bush, 43% Kerry

George Plescia

The 75th is one of San Diego's inland districts that barely grazes the Pacific Ocean at La Jolla near the campus of the University of California. Solidly Republican and mostly Anglo, it includes some of San Diego's most notable landmarks, including the zoo's Wild Animal Park and Torrey Pines Golf Course.

Incumbent George Plescia was elected in 2002, thanks in part to state and local battles between moderate and conservative factions of the Republican Party. Statewide, conservative Bill Simon and moderate Richard Riordan were engaged in an intense primary for governor, while locally a pair of Assembly members—the 75th's moderate incumbent, Charlene Zettel, and conservative Dennis Hollingsworth from the neighboring 76th District—fought for a seat in the state Senate. Those contests galvanized conservative GOP voters and brought them to the polls, giving a boost to identified conservatives in other races. In the 75th District, that meant Plescia, who needed all the aid and comfort he could secure.

At the start of the 2002 campaign, Plescia was far from the most well-known GOP candidate. That honor belonged to Jim Roache, the former sheriff of San Diego County. Another candidate (among five Republicans in the race) was Escondido Mayor Lori Pfeiler. But Plescia, a staff aide to area Sen. Bill Morrow, was able to stake out the right, thanks to endorsements from Morrow and state Sen. Ross Johnson. That backing, plus a generous campaign treasury, helped Plescia offset the name ID enjoyed by his two principal opponents. Plescia captured 30% of the Republican vote, but that was good enough for a three-point victory over Pfeiler, with Roache another point back in third place.

Once in Sacramento, Plescia carried a modest bill load and kept a relatively low profile, serving as vice chairman of the Governmental Organization Committee, one of the Assembly's most lucrative "juice committees" and one that oversees gaming, horse racing, alcohol, and tobacco. He held a modest leadership post as chief whip. It was something of a surprise when Plescia put together the votes in caucus to become minority leader in April 2006. The job was up for grabs because leader Kevin McCarthy had declared for Congress.

Plescia's tenure as minority leader didn't last long; by November, he was out, replaced in a swift coup by Mike Villines, a fiscal conservative from Clovis in the Central Valley. His undoing could be laid at the feet of Gov. Schwarzenegger. First, Plescia happened to be GOP leader at a time when the governor was resurrecting his shattered political reputation by going bipartisan, and that relegated legislative Republicans to doormat status during negotiations over the 2006–2007 budget and key pieces of legislation. Second, the governor's chief of staff, Susan Kennedy, was heard referring to Plescia as a "deer in the headlights" on what was supposed to be a private tape downloaded from the governor's Web site and released to the press. Villines immediately pledged to take a tougher stand with both Democrats and Schwarzenegger in 2007.

Plescia was returned to his vice chairmanship of Governmental Organization but is termed out in 2008. He could have run for Morrow's Senate seat in 2006 but decided to forgo what would have been a tough race against fellow Republican Mark Wyland, who won the seat. The next opportunity to advance won't arise until 2010 when Hollingsworth is termed out of the 36th District.

BIOGRAPHY: Born: Sacramento, August 19, 1966. Home: San Diego. Education: BA, CSU Sacramento. Military: None. Family: wife Melissa. Religion: Decline to state. Occupation: Legislator.

OFFICES: 3141 Capitol Building, Sacramento, CA 95814, Phone: (916) 319-2075, Fax: (916) 319-2175, email: assemblymember.plescia@assembly.ca.gov. District: 9909 Mira Mesa Boulevard, Suite 130, San Diego, CA 92131, Phone: (858) 689-6290, Fax: (858) 689-6296.

COMMITTEES: Arts, Entertainment, Sports, Tourism and Internet Media; Governmental Organization (vice chair); Joint Legislative Audit; Revenue and Taxation.

ELECTED: 2002 **TERM LIMIT:** 2008

ELECTION HISTORY: None.

2002 ELECTION: Plescia (R) 59%
Witt (D) 39%
Senecal (L) 3%

2004 ELECTION: Plescia (R*) 60%
Heumann (D) 38%
Senecal (L) 2%

2006 ELECTION: Plescia (R*) 58%
Meyer (D) 39%
Teyssier (L) 3%

RATINGS:

AFL-CIO	CAI	CoC	CLCV	EQCA	CCS	CMTA	FARM	NARAL
7	44	94	7	0	25	90	100	20

ANTHONY PORTANTINO (D)
44th Assembly District

Counties: Los Angeles
Cities: Pasadena, Los Angeles, Arcadia, Temple City, Monrovia, Duarte
Ethnicity: 38% White, 30% Latino, 10% Black, 20% Asian
Voter Registration: 45% D – 31% R – 20% DS
President 04: 61% Kerry, 38% Bush

Anthony Portantino

An ethnically diverse district, the 44th stretches along I-210 from La Canada–Flintridge on the west to Duarte on the east and is anchored in the south by Pasadena. The addition of Arcadia and Los Angeles neighborhoods around Occidental College give a slight boost to Democratic registration. The real gains are in "decline-to-state," which climbed 4% between 2001 and 2005.

Incumbent Anthony Portantino begins his legislative career after winning a competitive 2006 primary to replace Democrat Carol Liu. Portantino is an independent filmmaker and art director whose screen credits include "Unsolved Mysteries" and "Grizzly Adams." A two-term councilman and former mayor of La Canada Flintridge, Portantino faced off against three Democrats in the primary, including self-funded attorney Adam Murray and Gloria Molina staffer Brian Center. His most notable foe was Diana Peterson-More, a Pasadena planning commissioner backed by most women's groups.

Portantino had backing from Liu and the area's state senator, Democrat Jack Scott, and received substantial support from the gay community thanks to his brother, Michael Portantino, publisher of the San Diego-based *Gay & Lesbian Times*. A member of the Santa Monica Mountains Advisory Committee, Portantino received support from environmental groups. Most significant, however, were endorsements and help he received from Mayor Antonio Villaraigosa and the Los Angeles County Federation of Labor. That brought resources and ground troops none of the other candidates could match.

The only ding in Portantino's otherwise solid portfolio came from the *Los Angeles Times*, which endorsed Murray and questioned Portantino's ability to distance himself from labor. The newspaper's concerns notwithstanding, Portantino won the primary with 43% of the vote. Murray, with 26%, was second. That victory was the ballgame, as Portantino easily defeated his Republican opponent in November.

In Sacramento, Portantino is expected to hone in on environmental issues, although he was named to chair the Higher Education Committee. Given recent administrative troubles at both the University of California and California State University, his committee could be the focus of legislative efforts to more closely control spending at both institutions. Portantino will have to battle for that turf with the state Senate, which thus far has taken the lead in providing oversight for both universities.

BIOGRAPHY: Born: Long Branch, NJ, January 29, 1961. Home: La Canada. Education: BS, Albright College, Pennsylvania. Military: None. Family: wife Ellen, two daughters. Religion: Catholic. Occupation: Independent filmmaker.

OFFICES: 2003 Capitol Building, Sacramento, CA 95814, Phone: (916) 319-2044, Fax: (916) 319-2144, email: assemblymember.portantino@assembly.ca.gov. District: 215 North Marengo Avenue, Suite 115, Pasadena, CA 91101, Phone: (626) 577-9944, Fax: (626) 577-2868.

COMMITTEES: Governmental Organization; Higher Education (chair); Public Safety; Transportation.

ELECTED: 2006 **TERM LIMIT:** 2012

ELECTION HISTORY: La Canada Flintridge City Council, 1999–2006; Mayor, 2001, 2005.

2006 ELECTION: Portantino (D) 58%
      Carwile (R) 33%
      Costa (G) 4%
      Yanaga (L) 4%

CURREN PRICE (D)
51st Assembly District

Counties: Los Angeles
Cities: Inglewood, Hawthorne, Los Angeles, Gardena, Lawndale
Ethnicity: 14% White, 44% Latino, 32% Black, 8% Asian
Voter Registration: 62% D – 18% R – 17% DS
President 04: 76% Kerry, 24% Bush

Curren Price

The city of Inglewood is the political heavyweight in a district that borders Los Angeles International Airport. The Latino population is rising in this area, as it is in many parts of urban Los Angeles, but the biggest voting bloc is black.

Incumbent Curren Price replaces Democrat Jerome Horton, who termed out in 2006. An Inglewood councilman, Price comes to this overwhelmingly Democratic seat after a razor-thin primary victory over Gardena City Councilman Steve Bradford, district director for U.S. Rep. Juanita Millender-McDonald. Price, Horton's choice to succeed him, won by 113 votes out of more than 26,000 cast.

Price and Bradford differed little on issues, so the campaign focused on personality. In other words, it went negative from the opening bell and stayed that way until polls closed on Election Day. Bradford hit Price for being absent too often from official meetings and for voting himself (and other city officials) a pay raise. Price reminded voters that Bradford had been arrested in 2002 for attempting to horn in on an accident scene and attacked Bradford for supporting a Republican candidate for mayor of Gardena. The two disagreed on one immigration issue: sending National Guard troops to help patrol the Mexican border. Bradford opposed it; Price said it was necessary.

In the end, Price's win could be an accident of geography. His Inglewood constituency provides far more voters than does Gardena, and that advantage was critical in so narrow a win.

As he did as a local official, Price plans to push for smart growth, or urban development that emphasizes in-fill rather than sprawl. But his main focus may be diverted after he was named chairman of the Assembly Elections and Redistricting Committee. Gov. Schwarzenegger and interest groups such as Voices of Reform and California Common Cause have made redistricting reform a key issue for the 2007–2008 session. Reformers want to take the process of drawing legislative and congressional districts out of the hands of the legislature and vest it in a more neutral entity—either an independent commission or panel of retired judges. A bill to that effect nearly made its way out of the legislature in 2006, but it fell victim at the final hour to procedural maneuvering by Senate and Assembly leaders designed to keep it from passing. The governor was poised to sign it.

Lawmakers are loathe to give up a privilege, and Democrats especially see the drawing of favorable districts—gerrymandering—as a divine right, one that allows them to dictate the process that determines control of the legislature. Republicans, who routinely suffer under the current system, want change and reform. So, too, does the public. Price will be under great pressure to conduct his committee in such a way as to protect Democratic prerogatives and turf. He will have to give the impression that change is on the way without actually delivering reform.

BIOGRAPHY: Born: Los Angeles, December 16, 1950. Home: Inglewood. Education: BA, Stanford; JD, Santa Clara. Military: None. Family: Single. Religion: Christian Methodist Episcopal. Occupation: Professor.

OFFICES: 2179 Capitol Building, Sacramento, CA 95814, Phone: (916) 319-2051, Fax: (916) 319-2151, email: assemblymember.price@assembly.ca.gov. District: One Manchester Boulevard, Inglewood, CA 90301, Phone: (310) 412-6400, Fax: (310) 412-6354.

COMMITTEES: Business and Professions; Elections and Redistricting (chair); Governmental Organization; Jobs, Economic Development and the Economy.

ELECTED: 2006 **TERM LIMIT:** 2012

ELECTION HISTORY: Inglewood City Council, 1993–1997, 2001–2006.

2006 ELECTION: Price (D) 74%
Moen (R) 23%
Swinney (L) 3%

LAURA RICHARDSON (D)
55th Assembly District

Counties: Los Angeles
Cities: Long Beach, Los Angeles, Carson, Lakewood
Ethnicity: 21% White, 45% Latino, 15% Black, 15% Asian
Voter Registration: 53% D – 25% R – 18% DS
President 04: 63% Kerry, 36% Bush

Laura Richardson

The 55th was retooled during redistricting to help Democrats in the neighboring 56th District. The eastern boundary was pushed into Lakewood and a chunk of Compton was removed. Still, it remains solidly Democratic.

Incumbent Jenny Oropeza was termed out in 2006 and won a seat in the state Senate, and the campaign to replace her produced a competitive primary between Long Beach Councilwoman Laura Richardson and Los Angeles Community College Trustee Warren Furutani. Each candidate had a long history of public service, with Richardson's first run for the Assembly made 10 years ago. She lost a Democratic primary back then to Gerry Schipskie, who subsequently lost the general election to Republican Steve Kuykendall. She served as a field rep for U.S. Rep. Juanita Millender-McDonald as well. Furutani has been a member of the Los Angeles Board of Education and an education advisor to several Assembly speakers, including Fabian Nunez. He raised more money than Richardson and was endorsed by Nunez, the Labor Federation, and Mayor Antonio Villaraigosa. But the district is centered on Long Beach, and the local mayor—Betty O'Neill—backed Richardson, as did Millender-McDonald.

Richardson, 44, also received substantial help from the Legislative Black Caucus, led by veteran Democrat Mervyn Dymally. He helped channel some independent expenditures from Indian tribes to aid Richardson's effort and offset Furutani's advantage. Richardson won 54% to 46% and credited Dymally's assistance as critical to her victory.

In Sacramento, she plans to focus on transportation and port issues, not surprising for someone who now represents the ports of Long Beach and Los Angeles. She received no committee chairmanship but did secure a minor leadership position—assistant speaker pro tempore. It carries no power whatsoever but does afford a chance to appear regularly on television, running floor sessions when the speaker and speaker pro tem are absent.

BIOGRAPHY: Born: Los Angeles, April 14, 1962. Home: Long Beach. Education: BA, UCLA; MBA, USC. Military: None. Family: Single. Religion: Christian. Occupation: Legislator.

OFFICES: 3126 Capitol Building, Sacramento, CA 95814, Phone: (916) 319-2055, Fax: (916) 319-2155, email: assemblymember.richardson@assembly.ca.gov. District: 1 Civic Plaza, Suite 460, Carson, CA 90745, Phone (310) 518-3324, Fax: (310) 518-3508.

COMMITTEES: Assistant Speaker pro Tempore; Budget; Budget Subcommittee 5 on Information Technology and Transportation; Governmental Organization; Human Services; Utilities and Commerce.

ELECTED: 2006 **TERM LIMIT:** 2012

ELECTION HISTORY: Long Beach City Council, 2000–2006.

2006 ELECTION: Richardson (D) 68%
Underhill (R) 32%

SHARON RUNNER (R)
36th Assembly District

Counties: Los Angeles, San Bernardino
Cities: Lancaster, Palmdale, Victorville, Adelanto
Ethnicity: 52% White, 30% Latino, 12% Black, 4% Asian
Voter Registration: 36% D – 44% R – 16% DS
President 04: 60% Bush, 38% Kerry

Sharon Runner

The legislature has entertained a Republican named Runner since 1996, when George Runner was first elected to the Assembly from the previous version of District 36. Runner was termed out in 2002 and replaced by another Republican named Runner; in this case Sharon Runner, who happens to be George's wife. In 2004, George was elected to the state Senate, making the Runners the first husband-wife team to serve simultaneously in the California Legislature.

Sharon Runner's road to Sacramento was paved by one of the most inexplicable political judgments in legislative history—the 2002 decision by then-GOP Assemblyman Phil Wyman to run here after his old 34th District was shattered into three parts by the 2001 redistricting. Wyman could have run in any of the three (32, 34, or 36). In a political career that had spanned more than two decades, Wyman never showed much regard for geography. First elected to the Assembly in 1978 from Tehachapi in Kern County, he served until 1992 when he moved into Los Angeles County's Antelope Valley to run for Congress. He lost the GOP primary to Buck McKeon but moved back to Bakersfield in 1993, winning a special election to the state Senate—a seat he held for less than a year before losing to Democrat Jim Costa. Still entitled to two terms in the Assembly, Wyman moved again to his ancestral home to run in the old 34th District after the incumbent was termed out in 2000.

In 2002, Wyman could have run as the 34th District incumbent but chose to slide west to challenge Runner in the 36th District—a decision that qualifies for the Bad Political Choices Hall of Fame. Not only had Runner's husband represented the area for six years, Sharon Runner was an accomplished political consultant and businesswoman in her own right. Thus did Wyman enter the lion's den, where he was quickly consumed as an outsider. He tried to stake out the right and brought an impressive array of conservative endorsements with him, including former Governor George Deukmejian. Unfortunately, it is difficult to out-right the Runners, and the primary campaign did not turn on endorsements. Nasty and distanced from real issues of consequence, it steadily dissolved into a personal feud between Runner and Wyman, with an occasional grenade lobbed by one of two other GOP candidates.

The campaign meaninglessly turned ugly almost from day one, with Wyman questioning Runner's integrity and accusing her of lying about the funding source for a poll. It continued along that low road to the end when Wyman accused Runner of hiring a private detective, alleging that the man broke into Wyman's apartment to gather evidence that he did not actually live in the district. Runner denied the allegation, but it generated a ton of negative press on the eve of the March election.

Ultimately, Wyman was undone by charges of carpet bagging, which had some legitimacy among voters in a Los Angeles–San Bernardino district when applied to a candidate who spent the bulk of his career representing Kern County. Runner won the primary by 10 points over Wyman, then breezed past her Democratic opponent in November.

After George Runner's election to the Senate in 2004, the Runners became the Sacramento version of a power couple, if that term can be applied to a pair of Republicans operating in a Democratic state, Democratic town, and Democratic legislature. Sharon Runner gained a significant committee assignment in 2004 when she was named vice chair of Appropriations. Her bill load focused on families and children.

In 2006, the Runners became godparents for Prop. 83—an initiative to restrict where convicted sex offenders can live. They originally tried to work the notion through the legislature, and some staff argued that Democratic lawmakers ought to pass it, if for no other reason than its restrictive nature would force offenders to move to rural parts of the state—such as those represented by, say, the Runners. But the proposal went nowhere in the legislature, so the Runners spearheaded a signature drive and qualified it for the November 2006 ballot. Law enforcement and others opposed arguing that it was overly expensive and impossible to administer, but it passed. As is the case with many controversial initiatives, the courts immediately began to shred portions of it—focusing initially on whether its mandates were retroactive and applied to those who had long paid their dues to society. The fate of the measure as a whole is still pending.

The Runners' district once resembled Oklahoma, but after redistricting finished with it in 2001, it looks like Ohio—the panhandle having been lopped off. More than half the population lives in a western bulge around Palmdale and Lancaster, with another 20% situated in Victorville and Adelanto to the east. It is the scene of heavy suburban growth as Los Angelenos push away from the central city.

BIOGRAPHY: Born: Los Angeles, May 17, 1954. Home: Antelope Valley. Education: Antelope Valley College. Military: None. Family: husband George, two children. Religion: Christian. Occupation: Legislator.

OFFICES: 5158 Capitol Building, Sacramento, CA 95814, Phone: (916) 319-2036, Fax: (916) 319-2136, email: assemblymember.runner@assembly.ca.gov. District: 14343 Civic Drive, First Floor, Victorville, CA 92392, Phone: (760) 843-8045, Fax: (760) 843-8396; 747 West Lancaster Boulevard, Lancaster, CA 93534, Phone: (661) 723-3368, Fax: (661) 723- 6307.

COMMITTEES: Appropriations; Arts, Entertainment, Sports, Tourism and Internet Media (vice chair); Housing and Community Development.

ELECTED: 2002 **TERM LIMIT:** 2008

ELECTION HISTORY: None.

2002 ELECTION: Runner (R) 64%
Davenport (D) 36%

2004 ELECTION: Runner (R*) 67%
Scioneaux (D) 33%

2006 ELECTION: Runner (R*) 62%
Bynum (D) 39%

RATINGS:

AFL-CIO	CAI	CoC	CLCV	EQCA	CCS	CMTA	FARM	NARAL
7	48	94	4	0	20	90	100	20

IRA RUSKIN (D)
21st Assembly District

Counties: San Mateo, Santa Clara

Cities: Redwood City, San Jose, Palo Alto, Menlo Park, Los Altos, Los Gatos, San Carlos

Ethnicity: 64% White, 17% Latino, 4% Black, 12% Asian

Voter Registration: 45% D – 31% R – 21% DS

President 04: 67% Kerry, 32% Bush

Ira Ruskin

While its reputation as "the Mensa Highway" may have been more deserved during the dot-com boom, Highway 280 still shuttles millions of high-achievers from the lush peninsula in the 21st District north to San Francisco and south to San Jose every day. Along the route lie Sand Hill Road, famous as the epicenter of Silicon Valley venture capital, and Stanford University, the alma mater of current and former high-tech luminaries Steve Ballmer of Microsoft, William Hewlett and David Packard of Hewlett-Packard, and the leaders in web portals, Yahoo!'s Jerry Yang and Google's Sergey Brin and Lawrence Page.

On the southern end of the district, the lush wooded hills of the Santa Cruz Mountains are home to a lower-profile but no less affluent clientele. Here lie the enclaves of Woodside, Los Altos Hills, and Los Gatos, all nestled against huge expanses of open space, natural reserves, and state and regional parks. The district's western and southern edges also abut vast stretches of open space and natural reserves, most notably the 23,000-acre Crystal Springs Reservoir, which supplies San Francisco's water. This combination of money and natural beauty makes the peninsular region similar to wealthier (and more liberal) Marin County in its politics, though the predominance of Silicon Valley business concerns, as well as the South Bay's farming and industrial history, brings the area closer to the center.

In keeping with the Democratic nature of the Bay Area, the 21st District has long been a safe Democratic seat, and the 2001 redistricting changed it very little. The Almaden Valley along the southern edge was lopped off, but registration still comfortably favors Democrats.

In recent elections, Gray Davis received about 10% more support in the area in 2002 than his tepid 47% statewide. And in the 2003 recall election, San Mateo and Santa Clara were two of 10 counties where Arnold Schwarzenegger received less than 40% of the vote. Despite that pedigree, Republicans have captured seats here in the past, and in 2004, the 21st produced one of the most expensive legislative races in history.

All of the South Bay, but especially the district's peninsular region, relies heavily on high-tech to sustain its affluence. Voters in the district know that the industry similarly relies on a highly educated workforce to remain competitive globally, so education is always a motivating issue for the region.

The South Bay in general and this district in particular have elected Republicans to office, but they usually are moderate and reform-minded. Ed Zschau and his protégé, Tom Campbell, are prime examples. Campbell, who has served in the legislature and Congress, was director of the Department of Finance under Gov. Arnold Schwarzenegger.

Befitting its affluence, the district produced one of the more unusual—and costlier—elections in Assembly history in 2004. The Democrats had a sharply contested primary, made so because incumbent Democrat Joe Simitian left one term early to run for the state Senate. The candidate who emerged—Ira Ruskin—then squared off against Republican entrepreneur Steve Poizner, who had the GOP primary to himself.

The two candidates presented stark differences. Ruskin had an electoral base, having served on the Redwood City Council for nearly a decade, including a stint as mayor. Poizner was a political newcomer, but one with an unusual and important asset: a vast personal fortune. Eventually, Poizner spent $7 million of his own money on the campaign, setting a new record for self-funding for an Assembly election and outspending Ruskin of his Democratic allies by about three to one.

The district has a 14-point Democratic registration advantage, a basic fact of the local political topography that augured well for Ruskin. Poizner's one hope of leveling the playing field was to spend his money, and that he did. He spent $500,000 in the primary, signaling his intentions, and then kept right on going once he got the Republican nomination. Building up his name recognition, his campaign was the single biggest advertiser on Bay Area television through the summer. In one sense, all the commercials worked, for Poizner's estimated name ID eventually shot up to the 80 percent range, an astonishing figure. But in the meantime Ruskin was telling voters about Poizner too, emphasizing the fact that Poizner was a Republican (given the district, Poizner did no bragging about this point) who had contributed to George Bush's re-election campaign. Traditional Democratic allies such as labor unions and teachers helped Ruskin to spread the word about Poizner's partisan allegiance.

On election day, the Democrats' big registration edge made it impossible for Poizner to win. He actually took a very respectable 48 percent of the vote, topping Bush in the district and running 17 percent ahead of his party's registration. But it makes a difference whether a candidate's name is followed by an "R" or a "D," and Ruskin rode a wave of Democratic loyalty all the way to victory.

As a legislator, Ruskin authored bills to regulate hazardous waste sites, assist charitable foundations, and protect and monitor drinking water. At the beginning of his second term, he was named to the Budget Committee and given chairmanship of its subcommittee on resources—a key environmental post.

BIOGRAPHY: Born: New York, NY, November 12, 1943. Home: Redwood City. Education: BA, UC Berkeley; MA, Stanford. Military: None. Family: wife Cheryl. Religion: Jewish. Occupation: Communications Consultant.

OFFICES: 3123 Capitol Building, Sacramento, CA 95814, Phone: (916) 319-2021, Fax: (916) 319-2121, email: assemblymember.Ruskin@assembly.ca.gov. District: 5050 El Camino Real, Suite 117, Los Altos, CA 94022, Phone (650) 691-2121, Fax: (650) 691-2120.

COMMITTEES: Budget; Budget Subcommittee 3 on Resources (chair); Higher Education; Labor and Employment; Transportation.

ELECTED: 2004 **TERM LIMIT:** 2010

ELECTION HISTORY: Redwood City Council, Mayor, 1995–2004.

2004 ELECTION: Ruskin (D) 52%
                    Poizner (R) 48%

2006 ELECTION: Ruskin (D*) 68%
                    Kiraly (R) 32%

RATINGS:	AFL-CIO	CAI	CoC	CLCV	EQCA	CCS	CMTA	FARM	NARAL
	100	96	18	100	100	100	0	10	100

MARY SALAS (D)
79th Assembly District

Counties: San Diego
Cities: San Diego, Chula Vista, National City, Imperial Beach, Coronado
Ethnicity: 24% White, 57% Latino, 8% Black, 9% Asian
Voter Registration: 46% D – 29% R – 21% DS
President 04: 56% Kerry, 43% Bush

Mary Salas

The 79th became a donor district for Democrats during the 2001 redistricting by ceding about a third of Chula Vista and a chunk of inland San Diego to the always-troubled 78th District. As compensation, it added a coastal swath from North Island to Imperial Beach and the Mexican border. Although Democratic registration dropped 10 points after the revamp, the district remains solidly Democratic. Latinos are 40% of registered voters.

For the previous six years, the district was represented by Democrat Juan Vargas, an ambitious and highly regarded attorney who has run for a number of posts around San Diego. Most recently, he tried to take out incumbent U.S. Rep. Bob Filner in the 2006 Democratic primary, but lost.

That same primary produced Vargas's successor in the Assembly; in this case, Mary Salas. Salas did not enter the campaign as the favorite, even though she scored an impressive victory over a pair of opponents. Instead, the early favorite was National City Mayor Nick Inzunza, who was backed by Vargas. Before the parties even approached the starting line, Inzunza was crippled by allegations that he was a slumlord. The *San Diego Union-Tribune* ran a series of articles highlighting the run-down condition of Inzunza's property and explaining how he and his partner/wife regularly evicted tenants who complained. Inzunza also had to weather a fine from the San Diego Ethics Commission for fund-raising violations and watch as his brother Ralph, a member of the San Diego City Council, was sentenced to 21 months in jail during a corruption scandal. It was all too much, and Inzunza withdrew.

That left the field to Salas. She was endorsed by two former state senators—Lucy Killea and Dede Alpert—as well as by Filner. That, plus her record on the Chula Vista Council, was more than enough as she took 63% of the vote in both the primary and general elections. She takes over as chairwoman of the Veterans Affairs Committee, a key post for a San Diegan where the military has a strong presence and many veterans choose to settle once their military careers are over.

BIOGRAPHY: Born: Chula Vista, March 17, 1948. Home: Chula Vista. Education: BSW, San Diego State. Military: None. Family: husband Sal, two daughters. Religion: Catholic. Occupation: Business owner.

OFFICES: 2137 Capitol Building, Sacramento, CA 95814, Phone: (916) 319-2079, Fax: (916) 319-2179, email: assemblymember.salas@assembly.ca.gov. District: 678 3rd Avenue, Suite 105, Chula Vista, CA 91910, Phone: (619) 409-7979, Fax: (619) 409-9270.

COMMITTEES: Health; Jobs, Economic Development and the Economy; Veterans Affairs (chair); Water, Parks and Wildlife.

ELECTED: 2006 **TERM LIMIT:** 2012

ELECTION HISTORY: Chula Vista City Council, 1996–2004.

2006 ELECTION: Salas (D) 63%
Roesch (R) 37%

LORI SALDANA (D)
76th Assembly District

Counties: San Diego
Cities: San Diego
Ethnicity: 62% White, 21% Latino, 6% Black, 8% Asian
Voter Registration: 40% D – 30% R – 25% DS
President 04: 60% Kerry, 39% Bush

Lori Saldana

San Diego was the scene of unconventional politics in 2004. Although the mayoral candidacy of Donna Frye (who, as a write-in, nearly beat incumbent Dick Murphy) was the grand show, events in the 76th Assembly District, both in the primary and general elections, proved a worthy second show. The 76th includes downtown San Diego, Hillcrest, Balboa Park, Clairemont, Mission Valley, Point Loma, Mission Beach, and Pacific Beach. In an effort to make the district more Democratic, redistricting mapmakers removed some of the suburban areas to the north and east of downtown, adding downtown and a few coastal neighborhoods. Little did mapmakers know what would transpire inside those new lines.

The first eruption took place in the Democratic primary. Nearly every indicator available before Election Day pointed to a close contest between former Gray Davis aide Vince Hall and pollster Heidi von Szeliski. The indicators were correct; Hall and Szeliski finished within 1,000 votes of each other. Unfortunately for them, both finished at least 5,000 votes behind the winner—a community college professor, environmental activist, and novice politician named Lori Saldana. Saldana had polled well early on but was dismissed because Democratic power brokers did not believe she had the resources to keep up with either Hall or Szeliski, both of whom touted backing from legislative Democrats and the support of well-heeled interest groups.

The Hall-Szeliski dust up resembled a murder-suicide as the two candidates savaged each other with heavy attack ads best described as "variations on a theme"—the theme being "truth." Saldana dispatched her share of negativity as well, but Hall and Szeliski were so focused on each other that the winner skipped past them, well under their radar. Saldana even received scant attention when some of her mailers featured prominent local officials who had endorsed other candidates.

Saldana credited her victory to shoe leather and grassroots organizing. She was ridiculously outspent by her opponents. The California Teachers Association alone dumped a $100,000 independent expenditure into the district on behalf of Szeliski—an amount four times Saldana's entire treasury. And it in turn was dwarfed by the $330,000-plus worth of IE messages for Hall spray-painted throughout the district by a variety of backers that included moderate Democrats, prison guards, and EdVoice.

Republicans greeted Saldana's victory as a mixed blessing. On one hand, they actively rooted for Hall, who they believed was a deeply flawed candidate (not only was he a former chief of staff to Gray Davis, he had lost an Assembly bid in 2000 in the old 78th District). But they considered the novice Saldana vulnerable, especially given that their candidate was a former legislator.

Unfortunately, Republicans failed to notice that their own nominee, Tricia Hunter, also was a deeply flawed candidate. Hunter was trying to make a comeback after a 12-year absence from the legislature. And what had she been doing during those dozen years? Earning a living as a lobbyist. Lobbyists have clients, and the significant question for Hunter and Republicans became: How much distance can you put between yourself and your client list, especially when one of your former clients was named Enron?

Democrats worked overtime to tie Hunter to Enron and just about every energy/oil company this side of Bahrain. Thus did another Assembly race veer away from issues that might concern a voter.

The attack points between Hunter and Saldana were clear. Saldana, fueled by a million dollars from the state Democratic Party, went after Hunter for her past association with Enron. She went after Hunter's financial backers—JOBSPAC, realtors, horseracing interests, and developers—claiming the Republican was a tool of business special interests. For her part, Hunter chose to play the race card, attacking Saldana for supporting driver's licenses for illegal immigrants, allowing illegals to attend community college free of charge, and opposing construction of a border fence. Virtually all of Hunter's TV buys hammered Saldana over immigration, and it backfired. This is a coastal district, and voters tend to be more liberal than elsewhere in San Diego, with the large numbers of decline-to-state voters tacking left as well. Saldana was helped by linking her campaign to Frye, whose near victory in the mayoral race brought her candidacy into the national spotlight.

Despite hefty financial support during the general election campaign, Saldana came to Sacramento with her feelings bruised, thanks mostly to the way she was ignored during the three-way primary with Hall and Szeliski. Those feelings were salved in part when Saldana was made part of the leadership, serving as assistant majority whip, and given a seat on the Appropriations committee.

Her 2006 re-election was much quieter—no primary opponent and not much challenge in November. She returns to Sacramento as chair of the Housing and Community Development Committee, a post that will put her in the thick of debates over how to spend infrastructure bond money meant to help relieve the state's housing crunch. That funding was approved by voters in November as part of a four-bond package.

BIOGRAPHY: Born: San Diego, November 7, 1958. Home: San Diego. Education: BA, MA, San Diego State. Military: None. Family: Single. Religion: Decline to state. Occupation: Educator.

OFFICES: 5150 Capitol Building, Sacramento, CA 95814, Phone: (916) 319-2076, Fax: (916) 319-2176, email: assemblymember.saldana@assembly.ca.gov. District: 1557 Columbia Street, San Diego, CA 92101, Phone: (619) 645-3090, Fax: (619) 645-3094.

COMMITTEES: Elections and Redistricting; Housing and Community Development (chair); Local Government; Natural Resources; Veterans Affairs.

ELECTED: 2004 **TERM LIMIT:** 2010
ELECTION HISTORY: None.
2004 ELECTION: Saldana (D) 55%
Hunter (R) 41%
Osborne (L) 4%
2006 ELECTION: Saldana (D*) 65%
Denney (R) 35%
RATINGS: AFL-CIO CAI CoC CLCV EQCA CCS CMTA FARM NARAL
100 96 24 100 100 100 0 20 100

JIM SILVA (R)
67th Assembly District

Counties: Orange
Cities: Huntington Beach, Anaheim, Cypress, Westminster, Garden Grove
Ethnicity: 62% White, 19% Latino, 2% Black, 15% Asian
Voter Registration: 31% D – 47% R – 18% DS
President 04: 59% Bush, 40% Kerry

Jim Silva

Voters in Orange County's 67th Assembly District are heavily Republican and nearly two-thirds white—the two dominating facts that define its politics. The district spans cities that have become identified in the popular mind as quintessential Orange County—western Anaheim and all or part of Cypress, Garden Grove, Huntington Beach, La Palma, Los Alamitos, Rossmoor, Seal Beach, Stanton, and Westminster—and while the demographics have fluctuated in the past decade, the basic mix here is the same: White Republicans rule. Although there has been an influx of voting-age, Democrat-leaning Latinos—3.6% over the previous decade—only a third of them have actually registered to vote, and while Democrats have gained slightly and Republicans have lost about the same during the past decade, the district remains safely Republican and affluent, marked by soaring property values and a countywide median household income of more than $64,000—some $10,000 higher than the state average.

Republican Tom Harman won this seat in 2000 by taking advantage of the lone election conducted under California's short-lived blanket primary. That permitted any voter to participate in any primary, regardless of party affiliation, and it allowed the moderate Harman to win the GOP nomination with cross-over votes from Democrats. Conservatives chafed about it ever since, even though Harman tacked right after arriving in Sacramento. Termed out in 2006, he won a seat in the state Senate.

The Harmans attempted to keep the seat in the family when the incumbent's wife, Diane, ran in the 2006 GOP primary. She had hoped to capitalize on her pedigree, and the fact that she was the moderate in a three-way contest where the other two contenders would battle fiercely for the conservative vote. It didn't help her cause that the conservatives each had an elective base. Mike McGill was a city councilman from Cypress; Jim Silva was an Orange County supervisor.

As expected, McGill and Silva focused on each other in a tensely negative campaign. McGill accused Silva of going soft on cop killers and illegal immigrants, cozying up to labor unions and spending like a—egad—liberal Democrat. Silva responded by accusing McGill of voting to exercise Cypress's right to take property under the concept of eminent domain—a hot-button issue with conservatives.

Some conservatives fretted over the possibility that McGill and Silva would participate in a murder-suicide and allow the more moderate Harman to win the nomination. But it was misplaced angst. Although the two battled to the wire, the more well-known Silva prevailed with 45% of the vote, compared with 34% for McGill. The spectral Harman was far back in third, with 21%.

Orange County supervisors are powerful political players, and Silva comes to the legislature with heft not usually seen in a rookie. He is vice chairman of the Jobs, Economic Development and Economy Committee and could be seen as a player inside the Republican caucus.

BIOGRAPHY: Born: Fullerton, January 15, 1944. Home: Huntington Beach. Education: BA, San Jose State; MA, Chapman. Military: None. Family: wife Connie, two children. Religion: Lutheran. Occupation: Educator and businessman.

OFFICES: 3149 Capitol Building, Sacramento, CA 95814, Phone: (916) 319-2067, Fax: (916) 319-2167, email: assemblymember.silva@assembly.ca.gov. District: 17011 Beach Boulevard, Suite 570, Huntington Beach, CA 92647, Phone: (714) 843-4966, Fax: (714) 843-6375.

COMMITTEES: Budget; Budget Subcommittee 3 on Resources; Governmental Organization; Jobs, Economic Development and the Economy (vice chair).

ELECTED: 2006 **TERM LIMIT:** 2012

ELECTION HISTORY: Huntington Beach City Council, 1988–1994; Orange County Board of Supervisors, 1994–2006.

2006 ELECTION: Silva (R) 64%
Roberts (D) 36%

CAMERON SMYTH (R)
38th Assembly District

Counties: Los Angeles, Ventura
Cities: Los Angeles, Santa Clarita, Simi Valley
Ethnicity: 65% White, 20% Latino, 3% Black, 9% Asian
Voter Registration: 35% D – 43% R – 18% DS
President 04: 55% Bush, 44% Kerry

Cameron Smyth

The district was seriously retooled in 2001 to bolster the GOP registration edge. It sits in the San Fernando Valley—a hotbed of secessionist sentiment in 2002—and includes Santa Clarita, neighborhoods surrounding (but not including) the city of San Fernando, and two-thirds of the Simi Valley.

For the past six years, the district was represented by Keith Richman, a Republican physician and iconoclast who more often than not bucked his caucus, especially on matters concerning the budget. But Richman is gone, thanks to term limits, and his replacement had little trouble winning the seat either in a contested GOP primary or in the general election.

At 38, Cameron Smyth comes with a long political history that belies his relative youth and conservative credentials that will salve those on the right who often regarded Richman as an open wound. Smyth cut his political teeth working with one of the area's arch-conservative legislators—the late Pete Knight—and serving as a field rep for the state Republican Party before opening a consulting business.

As vice chair of the Environmental Safety and Toxic Materials Committee, he can be expected to push for a balanced approach between the environment and regulation. The chair of that committee is freshman Democrat Jared Huffman—a senior attorney with the Natural Resources Defense Council, one of the more militant and aggressive environmental groups in the country. So, Smyth's likely to be pushing against a steel wall.

BIOGRAPHY: Born: Pasadena, August 19, 1971. Home: Santa Clarita. Education: BA, UC Davis. Military: None. Family: wife Lena, two children. Religion: Christian. Occupation: Small businessman.

OFFICES: 4153 Capitol Building, Sacramento, CA 95814, Phone: (916) 319-2038, Fax: (916) 319-2138, email: assemblymember.smyth@assembly.ca.gov. District: 10727 White Oak Avenue, Suite 124, Granada Hills, CA 91344, Phone: (818) 368-3838, Fax: (818) 885-3307.

COMMITTEES: Environmental Safety and Toxic Materials (vice chair); Local Government; Utilities and Commerce.

ELECTED: 2006 **TERM LIMIT:** 2012

ELECTION HISTORY: Santa Clarita City Council, 2000–2006; Mayor, 2003, 2005.

2006 ELECTION: Smyth (R) 57%
Shaw (D) 38%
Christensen (L) 6%

JOSE SOLORIO (D)
69th Assembly District

Counties: Orange
Cities: Santa Ana, Anaheim, Garden Grove
Ethnicity: 13% White, 74% Latino, 1% Black, 10% Asian
Voter Registration: 46% D – 35% R – 16% DS
President 04: 53% Kerry, 46% Bush

Jose Solorio

Nowhere is the dramatic change in Republican Orange County's ethnic makeup more dramatic than in the 69th Assembly District, where more than two-thirds of the voting population is Latino—there are four times as many Latinos as whites of voting age—and Democrats enjoy an 11-point voter registration edge. The district, artfully drawn by Democrat-controlled reapportionment, includes all of Santa Ana, a sliver of Garden Grove, and a chunk of Anaheim. Santa Ana, the governmental seat of Orange County, is bustling and vibrant but marked by pockets of poverty. Nearly a fifth of the population lives below the federal poverty line, and although the official 2000 census puts the city's population at nearly 338,000, some estimates place the number far higher, over 500,000, driven by a surge in illegal immigration. Per capita income is about half the statewide average. By one estimate, nearly nine out of every 10 people in Santa Ana have Latino roots.

The 69th District is not representative of the county as a whole, which is nearly two-thirds white and among the most affluent in the state. In 2004 it was the scene of one of the strangest legislative campaigns in recent memory. Lawyer Tom Umberg barely survived the March Democratic primary against Santa Ana City Council member Claudia Alvarez, beating her by a razor-thin 365 votes. Umberg then spent the entire fall campaign on active military duty in Cuba to help prosecute enemy combatants held at Guantanamo Bay. A full colonel in the Army Reserves with 25 years in the military, Umberg's presence was felt but never seen during the campaign. The law bars active-duty military personnel from seeking partisan office, but Umberg launched his campaign eight months before he was called up, allowing him to stay in the race. His absence from the campaign proved an advantage: he wasn't around to engage in debates; he wasn't a ready target for attacks; indeed, he wasn't a target at all. Umberg was a sort of political will o' the wisp, a ghost who gave the frustrated Bade fits.

Not every Democrat was pleased with Umberg's return to the legislature. Some Latinos—governed by the notion that one of their own ought to represent a district where three-fourths of the residents are Hispanic—grumped that Umberg had little interest in the Assembly and only ran because he wanted to use the seat as a holding tank until he could seek the 34th state Senate district now held by Democrat Joe Dunn.

Dunn, like Umberg, is termed out in 2006. Umberg did go after that seat in 2006, but fell short, losing the Democratic primary to Orange County Supe. Lou Correa.

The effort to replace Umberg drew three Democrats, all Hispanic. Included in the group was Alvarez, making her second attempt. She was opposed by Santa Ana City Councilman Jose Solorio and businessman Armando de la Libertad. Despite her previous close call against Umberg, Alvarez entered the campaign as the underdog to Solorio, who boasted endorsements from Umberg, U.S. Rep. Loretta Sanchez, Correa, state Sen. Joe Dunn, and the political establishment of Santa Ana. More significant to his campaign, he was backed by labor, which poured some $300,000 into the effort. He won with 52% of the vote and then brushed aside his November opponent, Republican Ryan Williams.

Solorio, who once served as a Senate Fellow in Sacramento, is moderate by Democratic standards. A Catholic, he is pro-life and against issuing driver's licenses to illegal immigrants. As chair of the Public Safety Committee, he jumps into the middle of debates over determinate sentencing and prison reform, the latter an issue of critical importance to the Schwarzenegger administration. As chair, he takes over from San Francisco Democrat Mark Leno, one of the legislature's most liberal members. Although often a hard-liner on illegal immigration, Solorio is sensitive to the plight of immigrants. His first bill was aimed at providing better programs for English-learners.

BIOGRAPHY: Born: Michoacan, Mexico, September 28, 1970. Home: Santa Ana. Education: BA, UC Irvine; MA, Harvard University Kennedy School of Government. Military: None. Family: wife Linn, two sons. Religion: Catholic. Occupation: Marketing administrator

OFFICES: 2196 Capitol Building, Sacramento, CA 95814, Phone: (916) 319-2069, Fax: (916) 319-2169, email: assemblymember.solorio@assembly.ca.gov. District: 2323 North Broadway, Suite 225, Santa Ana, CA 92706, Phone (714) 285-0355, Fax: (714) 285-1301.

COMMITTEES: Appropriations; Education; Public Safety (chair); Transportation.
ELECTED: 2006 **TERM LIMIT:** 2012
ELECTION HISTORY: Santa Ana City Council, 2000–2006.
2006 ELECTION: Solorio (D) 66%
                     Williams (R) 34%

NELL SOTO (D)
61st Assembly District

Counties: Los Angeles, San Bernardino
Cities: Ontario, Pomona, Chino, Montclair
Ethnicity: 25% White, 59% Latino, 8% Black, 6% Asian
Voter Registration: 46% D – 35% R – 16% DS
President 04: 54% Kerry, 44% Bush

Nell Soto

Like California's ubiquitous poison oak, this area grows and grows. It straddles the San Bernardino and Los Angeles counties, a gateway to the Inland Empire, and the growth has brought political instability as Republicans and Democrats battle for the hearts and minds of regional émigrés.

The 61st District was a minor battleground until redistricting took the starch out of its competitive nature in 2001. More often than not, Republicans played the role of frustrated wannabes, but Democrats could never rest comfortably. They enjoyed only a 9% edge in voter registration in December 2000—the last time the old, court-drawn district held an election—and targeted contests tended to be the norm nearly every two years. Democrats sought to end that tradition through creative surgery during the 2001 redistricting, which expanded their margin to 15% by 2004. Mapmakers removed Republican precincts in Chino Hills in the south and Upland in the north, shrinking the GOP share from 36% to 33%.

Area growth has given rise to a pair of major problems: too little water, too much traffic. The increased demand for water for new housing is coupled with the realization that years of farming polluted the area's underground reservoir. Freeways rule the district, and people often give its location by listing the five-lane highways cutting through the land (they're the 10, 15, 210, 60, and 57). Drivers idle through commute traffic slowed near construction to expand the 210, a project that won't end until 2007. Freeways keep the shipping and distribution industries running, and they fuel the local economy. United Parcel Service is the largest employer in Ontario with six times as many employees as the second-largest employer, Mag Instrument, a flashlight maker. The district plays host to busy rail lines that connect the Alameda Corridor in Los Angeles with the Union Pacific's enormous freight hub in Fontana, which connects Southern California with the nation.

The expanding Ontario International Airport brings commerce to the area. In 2003, 6.5 million people passed through the airport, along with half a million tons of freight. About 6,000 people work among the terminals and planes. Mall life dominates area commerce. The Ontario Mills shopping compound has a wide range of outlet and chain stores, 21 restaurants, a 30-screen movie theater, and its own police station. This is where Arnold Schwarzenegger called state legislators "girly-men" while rallying support for his 2004 budget.

The district's population is primarily Latino. According to the 2000 census, the Latino population is far greater than that of whites or African Americans in Pomona, Ontario, and Montclair. In Chino, it's slightly less than that of whites. In the district's dominant cities, Pomona, Ontario and Montclair, the percentage of families living below the poverty line was higher than the national average in 2000. This is changing as more affluent families are lured by homes that sell for much less than in Orange and Riverside counties. And this migration threatens affordable housing. The median home price in Ontario has increased by 98% since 2000, to $248,000. In Chino, the median price is well over $300,000.

Nell Soto is the incumbent, having joined the term-limit-inspired tradition of moving back and forth between the Assembly and Senate as timing and vacancies dictate. Soto, the widow of former Assemblyman Phil Soto, served in the Assembly from 1998 to 2000, when she won a special election to the Senate. Termed out of the Senate in 2006, she moved back to the Assembly where she is good for another two terms.

Politically, she plugs into a network of local Democrats led by U.S. Rep. Joe Baca, who was the senator from this district until 1999 when he won a special election to replace the late George Brown, who died in office. It was Baca's vacancy in the Senate that caused Soto to move to the upper house in the first place. Before her election to the legislature, Soto was a member of the Pomona City Council, and in her first race for Assembly, she captured a seat that had been held by a termed-out Republican—Fred Aguiar, who was for a time secretary of the State and Consumer Services Agency and later cabinet secretary under Gov. Schwarzenegger. She was aided in her quest by the Republican Party, which nominated a candidate far too conservative for the district. According to her press secretary, Soto considers herself "a labor Democrat, a populist Democrat, or even a Bill Clinton Democrat"—a litany of somewhat contradictory labels that could mean anything from liberal to centrist.

As a senator in 2002, Soto formed a perchlorate task force. She sat on the Transportation Committee and, in the 2003–2004 session, authored bills to improve highways, increase pedestrian right of ways, and raise surcharges on vehicle registration fees for smog reduction. To help create jobs nearby, Soto introduced legislation expanding the Los Angeles Fairplex into a one-mile-long horse racetrack.

Soto had little competition once she decided to continue her career by returning to the Assembly to replace Democrat Gloria Negrete McLeod, who termed out. In essence, it was a seat swap as McLeod captured Soto's Senate seat. McLeod's road was a tad more difficult than Soto's, for she had to get by a Democratic colleague in the June primary—Joe Baca, Jr. She easily defeated him and won the Senate seat in November. Soto defeated Paul Avila in he June primary, racking up 70% of the vote. Ironically, McLeod and Soto ran against each other for the Assembly in the 1998 Democratic primary, which Soto won.

As a legislator, Soto rarely carries significant legislation, but she does chair what can be a significant committee—Joint Legislative Audit. That is the panel with investigative power over a range of government activity and which, in the past, has conducted serious probes into the activities of the Department of Insurance and former Governor Gray Davis's fundraising operations.

BIOGRAPHY: Born: Pomona, June 18, 1926. Home: Pomona. Education: Attended San Antonio College. Military: None. Family: widowed, six children, twelve grandchildren. Religion: Catholic. Occupation: Public Affairs Specialist.

OFFICES: 3091 Capitol Building, Sacramento, CA 95814, Phone: (916) 319-2061, Fax: (916) 319-2161, email: assemblymember.soto@assembly.ca.gov. District: 4959 Palo Verde Street, Suite 100B, Montclair, CA 91763, Phone: (909) 621-2783, Fax: (909) 621-7483.

COMMITTEES: Governmental Organization; Joint Legislative Audit (chair); Local Government; Public Employees, Retirement and Social Security; Transportation.

ELECTED: 2006 **TERM LIMIT:** 2010

ELECTION HISTORY: Pomona City Council, 1987–1998; Assembly, 1998–2000.
2006 ELECTION: Soto (D) 63%
               Lopez (R) 37%

RATINGS:

AFL-CIO	CAI	CoC	CLCV	EQCA	CCS	CMTA	FARM	NARAL
100	92	20	96	93	89	0	17	60

TODD SPITZER (R)
71st Assembly District

Counties: Orange, Riverside
Cities: Corona, Mission Viejo, Rancho Santa Margarita, Orange, Norco
Ethnicity: 63% White, 24% Latino, 3% Black, 8% Asian
Voter Registration: 27% D – 53% R – 17% DS
President 04: 65% Bush, 34% Kerry

Todd Spitzer

The 71st Assembly District is typically viewed, rightly so, as an Orange County Republican bastion, but it spills into Riverside County to include all of Norco and Corona—two fast-growing communities that have exploded in recent years with house-hunting suburbanites eager to find increasingly scarce affordable shelter. All of the affluent areas of Coto de Caza, Mission Viejo, Rancho Santa Margarita, and all but a tiny sliver of the Tustin Foothills are in the district, where family income levels generally exceed Orange County's median household income of $58,820 and where voters reflect the two driving sentiments of area politics—anti-crime and anti-tax. The district, not surprisingly, is solidly GOP. Registered Republicans outnumber Democrats here by two to one and Latinos by nearly five to one, even though Latinos in the last census showed a 22% increase. The area went for George Bush by two to one and has sent a long line of GOP officeholders to the state Capitol. The real political struggles here take place in Republican primaries, and the GOP traditionally has had a lock on the general elections—a tradition that continued with the most recent redistricting.

Into this district stepped Todd Spitzer in 2002, an aggressive, rapid-fire attorney, former prosecutor, and twice-elected member of the powerful Orange County Board of Supervisors. Spitzer, who once taught high school English in East Los Angeles and served four years on the Brea-Olinda school board, is a former police officer who has a reputation, well deserved, as a quick political study. He has been named "Legislator of the Year" by assorted business and law-enforcement groups, and he easily won his 2002 and 2004 elections. He had no problem running for a third term in 2006, but he had other options that made the decision difficult. The fast-moving Spitzer has toyed with the notion of running instead against incumbent Orange County District Attorney

Tony Rackauckas in 2006. But Spitzer withdrew from that race in February 2005, opting for a third term in the Assembly. At the time, Spitzer said a Rackauckas challenge would be too hard on the families of both candidates—an explanation sniffed at by a columnist for the *Orange County Register* who characterized Spitzer's attempts to micromanage his image as "Eddie Haskell channeling Machiavelli."

What sets Spitzer apart from many politicians is his unabashed ambition and his ability to capture media attention. He positioned himself, often, to get that attention, including a stint as chairman of the Orange County Transportation Authority, a high-profile job in a county consumed by traffic, highway, and transit issues. Even before he arrived in the state Capitol, he had built a reputation as a man with a quick quote and a talent for corralling reporters for coverage—attributes that served him well in the maelstrom of Orange County Republican politics. Indeed, the phrase, "Spitzer is coming!" resonated through the Capitol corridors among reporters, lawmakers, and political pros familiar with the county. But like other politicians before him, Spitzer clearly sees a quicker path upward than in the Capitol, where term limits have forced an incessant turnover of lawmakers. Spitzer's ultimate goal may be state attorney general or governor, as those close to him have no doubt and a notion reinforced by his giving serious thought to tackling an incumbent district attorney. On the other hand, governors are not made by notions but by actions, and Spitzer's decision not to challenge Rackauckas is a sign that, after a career built on pugnacity, Spitzer may be adding caution to his political character.

Midway through 2005, Spitzer was on the short list of those considering a run for Congress in the district vacated by Republican Chris Cox, who President George Bush appointed chairman of the Securities and Exchange Commission. Spitzer, who has professed a desire to remain in California, opted out once again, and the seat was won by state Sen. John Campbell. Spitzer also passed on running for Campbell's Senate seat, a post taken by another Orange County GOP colleague, Tom Harman.

BIOGRAPHY: Born: Whittier, November 26, 1960. Home: Orange. Education: BA, UCLA; MA, UC Berkeley; JD, Hastings College of Law. Military: None. Family: wife Jamie, one son. Religion: Jewish. Occupation: Attorney.

OFFICES: 5164 Capitol Building, Sacramento, CA 95814, Phone: (916) 319-2071, Fax: (916) 319-2171, email: assemblymember.spitzer@assembly.ca.gov. District: 1940 North Tustin Street, Suite 102, Orange, CA 92865, Phone: (714) 998-0980, (909) 737-1671, Fax: (714) 998-7102.

COMMITTEES: Human Services; Joint Legislative Audit; Public Safety.

ELECTED: 2002 **TERM LIMIT:** 2008

ELECTION HISTORY: Orange County Board of Supervisors, 1996–2002.

2002 ELECTION: Spitzer (R) 73%
　　　　　　　　　Foster (D) 27%

2004 ELECTION: Spitzer (R*) 68%
　　　　　　　　　Foster (D) 32%

2006 ELECTION: Spitzer (R*) 72%
　　　　　　　　　LaChance (D) 28%

RATINGS:	AFL-CIO	CAI	CoC	CLCV	EQCA	CCS	CMTA	FARM	NARAL
	3	52	100	0	0	26	90	100	20

AUDRA STRICKLAND (R)
37th Assembly District

Counties: Los Angeles, Ventura
Cities: Thousand Oaks, Simi Valley, Camarillo, Los Angeles, Moorpark
Ethnicity: 67% White, 23% Latino, 2% Black, 6% Asian
Voter Registration: 34% D – 44% R – 18% DS
President 04: 55% Bush, 44% Kerry

Audra Strickland

Once a coastal enclave, this new version of the 37th District never quite touches the water but skirts inland to encompass Thousand Oaks, wanders north of Santa Clarita, then takes in a chunk of largely unpopulated Los Angeles County, from the I-5 Grapevine south to Castaic Lake. Gone are Oxnard and Port Hueneme. None of the tinkering changed either district demographics or politics; it remains overwhelmingly white and Republican.

From 1998 to 2004, the area was represented by Republican Tony Strickland, who was termed out at the tender age of 33. But the Stricklands kept the job in the family when, in 2004, the incumbent's wife, Audra Strickland, was elected to succeed him.

Because the district is safely Republican, Strickland's fate was determined in the 2004 GOP primary, dubbed the "battle of the Gen Xers" because all three major candidates were younger than the outgoing incumbent. Audra Strickland was 29, legislative aide Mike Robinson 28, and deputy Ventura County DA Jeff Gorell 33.

Audra Strickland began the campaign having locked down most major endorsements, including the Senate and Assembly Republican leadership. She even managed to wangle a dual endorsement from local Senate icon Tom McClintock, whose legislative aide—Robinson—was in the hunt. In addition, Indian gaming tribes, conservative Edward Atsinger III, and nearly every member of the Assembly GOP Caucus supported Strickland.

And she needed every bit of that help to offset the large checks that Robinson kept writing to himself. Independently wealthy, he pumped six-figure lumps of money into his treasury on a regular basis to keep himself competitive. While Strickland was able to match Robinson's spending, Gorell came from the other side of the financial tracks, and his lack of resources hampered his ability to mount an extensive absentee-ballot program. That cost him votes in both Los Angeles and Ventura counties and prevented him from capitalizing on the fact that he was a moderate. Robinson tacked far to the right, while the conservative Strickland staked out what passes for the center in a GOP primary. A long list of prominent Republicans backed Gorell, including former Governor Pete Wilson, former Los Angeles Mayor Richard Riordan, and local Ventura officials.

The contest was close to the end, with all three Republicans topping 30% of the vote. Strickland edged ahead with 36%, some 1,400 votes ahead of Gorell. In Sacramento, she was made vice chair of a committee—Arts, Entertainment, Sports, Tourism and Internet Media—with more sound than substance attached to it, unless one considers steroid use in baseball as "substance." She also sat on the Health Committee.

A former junior high school teacher, Strickland got her elective feet wet as a member of her local school board and was a legislative aide to former Assembly Speaker Curt Pringle, now mayor of Anaheim.

While her re-election to a second term in 2006 raised nary a concern, the Stricklands were embroiled in a tough election year. Husband Tony was the Republican nominee for state controller, facing off against Democrat John Chiang, chairman of the state Board of Equalization. It was not a good year for Republicans generally across the country, but Strickland gained notoriety when two interests—Indian gaming tribes and software giant Intuit—each pumped $1 million worth of independent expenditures in support of his candidacy. It made him more viable, if not ultimately successful, and he lost.

For her second term, Strickland has been named vice chair of the Labor and Employment Committee. Her bill load has been modest to date, and except for parochial bills of interest only to her district, or bills that make small technical changes in law, most of her legislation dies peacefully in committee. She made illegal immigration a focus and was named to co-chair a task force on the subject late in her rookie year.

BIOGRAPHY: Born: Newport Beach, July 10, 1974. Home: Moorpark. Education: BA, UC Irvine. Military: None. Family: husband Tony. Religion: decline to state. Occupation: Teacher.

OFFICES: 4208 Capitol Building, Sacramento, CA 95814, Phone: (916) 319-2037, Fax: (916) 319-2137, email: assemblymember.strickland@assembly.ca.gov. District: 2659 Townsgate Road, Suite 236, Westlake Village, CA 91361, Phone: (805) 230-9167, Fax: (805) 230-9183.

COMMITTEES: Arts, Entertainment, Sports, Tourism and Internet Media; Health; Labor and Employment (vice chair).

ELECTED: 2004 **TERM LIMIT:** 2010

ELECTION HISTORY: None.

2004 ELECTION: Strickland (R) 55%
Masry (D) 42%
Prince (G) 4%

2006 ELECTION: Strickland (R*) 58%
Masry (D) 43%

RATINGS:

AFL-CIO	CAI	CoC	CLCV	EQCA	CCS	CMTA	FARM	NARAL
3	40	94	0	0	15	90	100	0

SANDRE SWANSON (D)
16th Assembly District

Counties: Alameda
Cities: Oakland, Piedmont, Alameda

Ethnicity: 27% White, 21% Latino, 30% Black, 19% Asian
Voter Registration: 62% D – 10% R – 22% DS
President 04: 86% Kerry, 13% Bush

Sandre Swanson

The 16th District marries two disparate sections of Oakland—downtown with its waterfront and tony Piedmont. One would think this a tumultuous relationship, but elections here were quiet during the first half of the decade. The 2006 Democratic primary, where four contenders vied to replace the termed-out Wilma Chan, provided some fireworks, but nothing like the kind of raucous, unpredictable scuffles of the late 1990s.

Back then, a chain reaction of overlapping resignations, retirements, and special elections roiled the waters from 1998 to 2000 and produced one of the most improbable upsets in California legislative history. And all this in a district where Republicans have about as much chance of winning as Osama bin Laden has of capturing the Nobel Peace Prize. Longtime Congressman Ron Dellums set the chain in motion when, in 1998, he decided to retire. State Senator Barbara Lee won Dellums's seat, vacating her Senate district, which was subsequently captured by then-Assemblyman Don Perata. Thus was Perata's Assembly seat left open, to be filled in a 1999 special election.

Into that breach stepped Democrat Elihu Harris, a former legislator who had just ended eight lackluster years as mayor of Oakland. Nonetheless, Harris had backing from Bay Area establishment Democrats, including his old ally—San Francisco Mayor and former Assembly Speaker Willie Brown, Jr. But Harris had a challenger in the Democratic primary, Oakland attorney John Russo who gathered support from liberals in the legislature and bashed Harris over his tenure in Oakland. With no Republican on the ballot, Harris won the primary, but not by a big enough margin to avoid a runoff.

Enter Audie Bock, a Green Party candidate who joined Harris in the runoff. Although outspent nearly 20 to 1, Bock pounded the pavements and knocked on countless doors in a classic David-and-Goliath campaign. Brown and then-Speaker Antonio Villaraigosa backed Harris with money and manpower, but he proved a curiously inept and overconfident candidate who eventually lost to Bock by 327 votes. Thus did this district produce the first third-party candidate to take a seat in the legislature in 82 years.

Bock's tenure was short. From Day One, she dwelt in Democratic crosshairs, and the candidate anointed to take her out was Chan, then an Alameda County supervisor. Bock seemed to realize the vulnerability of her situation, for she abandoned the Greens not long after arriving in Sacramento, opting to run for re-election as an independent.

It mattered not at all. Chan, who began campaigning for the seat before Bock took office, ran a vigorous, well-funded campaign that crushed Bock by a three-to-one margin and made Chan the first Asian-American woman to serve in the legislature since the late 1960s.

Chan's departure in 2006 set the stage for the primary, where only two of the four Democrats were viable. The first was the same Russo, by now the Oakland city attorney and a former councilman. The second was Sandre Swanson, former chief of staff to U.S. Rep. Barbara Lee. Ex Piedmont school board member Ronnie Caplane and Alameda City Councilman Tony Daysog rounded out the field, but neither had the support or cash to compete with Russo and Swanson.

Russo had lots of cash and name ID due to allies in the legal community and his elective track record. Swanson, on the other hand, had three decades of attention to district needs as congressional staffer, first for Dellums and later for Lee. He had been involved in everything from education to port dredging. Plus, he had a network of contacts at every level of district life and commerce. He had competed in two unsuccessful campaigns for county supervisor in the 1980s, including in 1986 against Don Perata, now pro tem of the Senate. Dellums, who was running successfully for mayor of Oakland, endorsed Swanson, and labor weighed in with resources, money, and ground troops.

Russo, who once served as president of the League of California Cities, ran on his record as county attorney, touting efforts to deal with troubled liquor stores and prodding CalTrans to clean up some of its slumlord-like property. But he could not overcome 30 years of goodwill accorded to Swanson, who beat him by 4,500 votes, or 8%. In November, Swanson's lone opponent came from the Peace and Freedom Party.

Swanson landed a committee chairmanship in his rookie term, the Labor and Employment Committee, but said education would be his top priority. In addition to his chairmanship, he serves on the Budget, Banking and Finance and Housing committees.

BIOGRAPHY: Born: Oakland, November 28, 1948. Home: Alameda. Education: AA, Laney College; BA, San Francisco State. Military: None. Family: wife, four children. Religion: Baptist. Occupation: Congressional staff.

OFFICES: 6012 Capitol Building, Sacramento, CA 95814, Phone: (916) 319-2016, Fax: (916) 319-2116, email: assemblymember.swanson@assembly.ca.gov. District: 1515 Clay Street, Suite 2204, Oakland, CA 94612, Phone: (510) 286-1670, Fax: (510) 286-1888.

COMMITTEES: Arts, Entertainment, Sports, Tourism and Internet Media; Banking and Finance; Budget; Budget Subcommittee 4 on State Administration; Housing and Community Development; Labor and Employment (chair).

ELECTED: 2006 **TERM LIMIT:** 2012
ELECTION HISTORY: None.
2006 ELECTION: Swanson (D) 90%
 Ytuarte (PF) 10%

ALBERTO TORRICO (D)
20th Assembly District

Counties: Alameda, Santa Clara
Cities: Fremont, Milpitas, Newark, Union City
Ethnicity: 38% White, 17% Latino, 4% Black, 37% Asian

Voter Registration: 47% D – 23% R – 25% DS
President 04: 66% Kerry, 33% Bush

Alberto Torrico

Before the 2001 redistricting, the 20th District took in a slice of San Jose that was subsequently removed, with Union City added as compensation. The district is centered on Fremont and has a diverse ethnic makeup, with Asians and whites the largest groups. Less than half the Asian population is registered to vote, however, making whites the most potent voting bloc.

Democrat John Dutra represented the 20th for three terms from 1998 to 2004, and his departure set up a five-way Democratic primary battle that was not for the faint of heart. Dutra's personal choice as successor, Newark Councilman Alberto Torrico, won the primary—tantamount to winning it all in such a lopsided Democratic district—but not before learning the nuances of political brawls and the pitfalls of independent expenditure campaigns. Dutra helped Torrico line up an impressive array of supporters, including Assembly Speaker Fabian Nunez and many members of his caucus. Torrico's chief opponents were former Pleasanton Mayor Tom Pico, former Milpitas Mayor Henry Manayan, and political novice Dennis Hayashi, whose wife would win an Assembly seat in 2006. The contest exposed schisms among local Democrats as Dutra backed Torrico while the local state senator, Tom Torlakson, backed Pico.

The contest itself became a jousting ground for special interests that poured in money and resources on behalf of Pico (developers, builders), Hayashi (trial lawyers), Manayan (realtors and EdVoice), and Torrico (Indian gaming tribes, insurance interests, and labor). By the time the mud stopped flowing, Torrico had scored a narrow victory over Pico, with Hayashi third and Manayan a distant fourth.

Along the way, Torrico had to repudiate an independent mailer sent on his behalf by the Moderate Democrats for California. The piece, which dropped just before the primary, accused Pico of junketing on the taxpayers' dime to, among other exotic locales, Dublin, Ireland. Pico admitted visiting Dublin, but, unfortunately for Torrico and his allies, it was Dublin, California. Although the MDC apologized, the damage was done.

Torrico allies—notably the Chamber-sponsored JOBSPAC—pumped more than $100,000 into an anti-Hayashi campaign, which itself was buoyed by nearly $200,000 in independent expenditures (IEs) from trial lawyers. Torrico tried to distance himself from the IE campaigns, insisting that his effort was above board, but a sour aroma lingered over the field nonetheless.

In Sacramento, Torrico was made chair of a firestorm operating under the name "Retirement and Social Security Committee" at the legislative epicenter of battles with the Schwarzenegger administration over pension reform and the Bush administration over efforts to overhaul the federal Social Security system. He authored a number of bills dealing with public-employment retirement systems and procedures and pushed a bill to provide safe havens for the surrender of unwanted infants.

Following the 2006 elections, Torrico landed one of the legislature's plum assign-ments—chairman of the Assembly Governmental Organization Committee. The panel has jurisdiction over horse racing, the liquor industry, gambling, and tobacco. In other words, it can be a font for special-interest money, and its chair often is expected to raise copious amounts for caucus coffers.

BIOGRAPHY: Born: San Francisco, March 18, 1969. Home: Newark. Education: BA, Santa Clara; JD, Hastings. Military: None. Family: wife Raquel, two chil-dren. Religion: Decline to state. Occupation: Attorney.
OFFICES: 3160 Capitol Building, Sacramento, CA 95814, Phone: (916) 319-2020, Fax: (916) 319-2120, email: assemblymember.torrico@assembly.ca.gov. District: 39510 Paseo Padre Parkway, Suite 280, Fremont, CA 94538; Phone: (510) 440-90430; Fax: (510) 440 9035.
COMMITTEES: Banking and Finance; Business and Professions; Governmental Organization (chair); Joint Legislative Audit; Public Employees, Retirement and Social Security.
ELECTED: 2004 **TERM LIMIT:** 2010
ELECTION HISTORY: Newark City Council, 2001–2004.
2004 ELECTION: Torrico (D) 69%
　　　　　　　　　Williams (R) 31%
2006 ELECTION: Torrico (D*) 65%
　　　　　　　　　Nishimura (R) 35%

RATINGS:	AFL-CIO	CAI	CoC	CLCV	EQCA	CCS	CMTA	FARM	NARAL
	96	96	47	70	93	100	10	40	100

VAN TRAN (R)
68th Assembly District

Counties: Orange
Cities: Costa Mesa, Garden Grove, Westminster, Fountain Valley, Anaheim
Ethnicity: 42% White, 29% Latino, 1% Black, 25% Asian
Voter Registration: 31% D – 45% R – 19% DS
President 04: 60% Bush, 38% Kerry

At the heart of Orange County is the 68th Assembly District, and at the heart of the 68th is Little Saigon, that complex, densely populated hive bridging Garden Grove and Westminster that by most estimates includes some 85,000 voters of Vietnamese descent—the largest and oldest Vietnamese enclave in the U.S. Deeply conservative, the Vietnamese here fled from Vietnam in 1975 when American forces pulled out, ar-riving first at Camp Pendleton 30 miles to the south, then settling in Orange County to pick up the pieces of their lives. Three decades later, they are potent, well-organized, tightly knit, on the move, and a good fit in the affluent, racially diverse, Republi-can-dominated county that has backed every Republican presidential contender for decades. Despite a steadily developing Democratic presence fueled by a burgeoning

Van Tran

Latino population, it maintains a three-to-two Republican edge in voter registration and routinely sends GOP majorities to the state Capitol and Congress.

To outsiders, Vietnamese-American political influence may appear to be an exotic phenomenon; in Orange County it is not unusual: four out of every 10 county residents speak a language other than English at home, and countywide more than three dozen languages are routinely heard. Orange County is more complex than the popular TV image of blond-haired surfers and right-wing white Republicans.

The spearhead of this emerging political clout is Van Tran, who came to the U.S. when he was 10 years old. A former Garden Grove councilman and former aide to U.S. Representatives Bob Dornan and Ed Royce, Tran is the first Vietnamese American elected to a state legislature in the nation. Political handicappers immediately saw that his election was only the tip of the iceberg: Three other Vietnamese-American candidates won local offices in November 2004—one to Tran's former city council seat and two others to the Garden Grove Unified School District, where Vietnamese Americans captured a majority.

Van's only real challenge was in the March 2004 primary, when he faced fellow city council member Mark Leyes, who was favored and who had built up heavy name recognition from an earlier run for supervisor. But Tran beat Reyes by a 15-point margin, nearly 6,000 votes, following a fierce and nasty campaign in which Tran fended off racial attacks and presented himself as a true conservative by exploiting Leyes's background as a former Democrat. Tran mounted exhaustive fund-raising, voter-registration, and get-out-the-vote efforts in the Vietnamese community, not only in Garden Grove and Westminster, but in Fountain Valley and Santa Ana, as well. His campaign staff said they registered 10,000 new Vietnamese-American voters. He collected some $800,000 for his campaign treasury, and nearly two-thirds of the donations came from Vietnamese Americans. In the general election, Tran beat Democrat Al Snook in a near landslide, 61% to 39%, a clear indication that Tran was able to reach across racial lines to capture support.

Tran, a savvy lawyer, is well aware of the landmark nature of his election, and the fact that he broke new political ground. He also is sensitive to racial tensions afoot in his home county. During the 2006 election, a Vietnamese Republican congressional candidate was linked to a letter sent to Latino households warning them about penalties for illegally attempting to vote. The letter was universally denounced, but it is significant that the first bill Tran introduced for the 2007–2008 legislative session stiffens penalties for acts of voter intimidation, making the violation a felony rather than a misdemeanor. It is co-authored by Assm. Jose Solorio, a newly elected Democrat from Orange County. It is also in keeping with Tran's new job—vice chair of the Assembly Judiciary Committee, a significant post for a Republican.

BIOGRAPHY: Born: Saigon, Vietnam, October 19, 1964. Home: Garden Grove. Education: BA, UC Irvine; MA, JD, Hamline University. Military: None. Family: wife Cindy Nguyen. Religion: Decline to state. Occupation: Attorney.

OFFICES: 4130 Capitol Building, Sacramento, CA 95814, Phone: (916) 319-2068, Fax: (916) 319-2168, email: assemblymember.tran@assembly.ca.gov. District: 1503 South Coast Drive, Suite 205, Costa Mesa, CA 92626, Phone: (714) 668-2100, Fax: (714) 668-2104.
COMMITTEES: Governmental Organization; Judiciary (vice chair); Utilities and Commerce.
ELECTED: 2004 **TERM LIMIT:** 2010
ELECTION HISTORY: Garden Grove City Council, 2000–2004.
2004 ELECTION: Tran (R) 58%
              Snook (D) 42%
2006 ELECTION: Tran (R*) 62%
              Lucas (D) 38%

RATINGS:

AFL-CIO	CAI	CoC	CLCV	EQCA	CCS	CMTA	FARM	NARAL
10	52	100	11	0	20	89	100	20

MIKE VILLINES (R)
29th Assembly District

Counties: Fresno, Madera, Tulare
Cities: Fresno, Clovis, Madera
Ethnicity: 55% White, 30% Latino, 4% Black, 7% Asian
Voter Registration: 34% D – 51% R – 12% DS
President 04: 63% Bush, 36% Kerry

Mike Villines

A Republican fortress, the 29th District takes in the Sierras, Kings Canyon National Park, and Sequoia National Forest. That's a lot of natural beauty for one legislative district. Good thing that the constituents—living mostly in the northern half of Fresno and Madera—have something in their favor because GOP politics in the 29th have displayed about as much beauty—and decorum—as a twelve-car crash.

Perhaps it's the water. Or something in the air. Whatever the reason, this area has sent some quirky Republicans to Sacramento in recent years. First, there was Mike Briggs who once pled no contest to a charge of statutory rape. Briggs was elected in 1998 and subsequently lost a 2002 congressional primary because he had cooperated with Assembly Democrats to provide a key budget vote. After leaving office, he was rewarded for that vote with a controversial "thank you" contract from Democratic Speaker Herb Wesson. Briggs has one term remaining before his Assembly carriage turns into a term-limit-induced pumpkin, but he has about as much chance of cashing in that chit as Donald Trump does of becoming "Mr. Conviviality."

Briggs was succeeded in 2002 by Steve Samuelian, whose own pumpkin broke apart before ever becoming a carriage. After surviving a gutterball primary against Larry Willey in 2002, Samuelian's Assembly career was destroyed in 2003 when Fresno police stopped him for loitering in a section of town known for prostitution. Although no charges were filed, the publicity—and Samuelian's less-than-adequate explanation—angered supporters, who dropped him like a stone in local polls. When two other Republicans filed to run against him in the primary, Samuelian dropped out.

And then came the 2004 primary to succeed the disgraced Samuelian. A food fight masquerading as a primary, it featured three candidates—including, of all people, the legislator formerly known as Mike Briggs. As in 2002, the 2004 version quickly slipped into the fetid muck of charge and countercharge, albeit with a different cast of characters. Ironically, Briggs—a political target the size of Arnold Schwarzenegger's ego—was neither the thrower nor the target of much muck. The real mudballs flew at and from his opponents: former Fresno City Councilman and uber-conservative Mike Mathys and former Pete Wilson aide Mike Villines.

Villines was the clear choice of the GOP establishment, having earned backing from former governors Wilson and George Deukmejian, Assembly Republican Leader Kevin McCarthy, former Secretary of State Bill Jones (a Fresnan), most members of the Assembly Republican Caucus, most Republican state senators, and most area congressmen. Mathys countered that endorsement edge with a whack-and-whomp campaign that tried to paint Villines as—egad—a moderate, accusing him of being soft on every issue from abortion to zookeeper safety. Villines grumped that Mathys's billboards and signs were misleading and placed without permission from property owners.

As though the two didn't have enough material to hurl at each other, both Mathys and Villines turned on Briggs for his past sins on behalf of Democrats. The final blow for Briggs, however, came in the form of an endorsement from *The Fresno Bee*, which backed his candidacy because, it reminded voters, he had a history of working with Democrats. In this district, *The Bee*'s attempt to favor Briggs was lighting the way by setting fire to the candidate. If the hapless Briggs took any solace from the election, it was the fact that he took over a quarter of the vote despite being outspent nearly ten to one over the final two months of the campaign.

In the end, Villines scored an impressive victory over Mathys and Briggs, then walloped his Democratic opponent in November. As a former legislative aide to state Senator Chuck Poochigian, Villines arrived in Sacramento with few rookie jitters and was given a seat on the Budget Committee and vice chairmanship of the Water, Parks and Wildlife Committee.

But Villines, the son of Oklahoma migrants, had grander ambitions. Shortly after the 2006 elections, Villines staged a successful coup against Assembly GOP Leader George Plescia and seized the job for himself. It was said at the time that Republicans wanted stability and so chose someone with two terms left; Plescia is termed out in 2008, Villines not until 2010. But the real reason had more to do with spine than time. Plescia was considered no match for Assembly Democrats or Gov. Arnold Schwarzenegger when it came to budget negotiations during the 2005–2006 session, and Villines immediately promised to take a firmer stand in the negotiations. Some observers equated that with a return to partisan rancor, given Villines's often combative nature and staunch fiscal conservatism. Villines, for instance, was one of the few Republicans willing to stand against Schwarzenegger's effort to pass four infrastructure bonds on the November 2006 ballot.

Now, he is the face and voice of the Assembly Republican Caucus, and his relationship with Schwarzenegger could define the tone and tenor of the 2007–2008 legislative session. The governor and Democrats need six Republican votes for the budget, and it will be Villines's job to keep the caucus together, to broker those votes for the best leverage possible.

His GOP colleagues thought Villines had the tenacity to do just that kind of job.

BIOGRAPHY: Born: Fresno, March 30, 1967. Home: Fresno. Education: BA, CSU Fresno. Military: None. Family: wife Christina, three children. Religion: Christian. Occupation: Public relations executive.

OFFICES: 3104 Capitol Building, Sacramento, CA 95814, Phone: (916) 319-2029, Fax: (916) 319-2129, email: assemblymember.villines@assembly.ca.gov. District: 83 East Shaw Avenue, Suite 202, Fresno, CA 93710, Phone: (559) 243-4192, Fax: (559) 243-4196.

COMMITTEES: Assembly Republican Leader.

ELECTED: 2004 **TERM LIMIT:** 2010

ELECTION HISTORY: None.

2004 ELECTION: Villines (R) 63%
Macias (D) 34%
Crockford (G) 3%

2006 ELECTION: Villines (R*) 66%
Avila (D) 30%
Zwickel (L) 1%
Crockford (PF) 3%

RATINGS:

	AFL-CIO	CAI	CoC	CLCV	EQCA	CCS	CMTA	FARM	NARAL
	3	44	94	4	0	10	90	100	20

MIMI WALTERS (R)
73rd Assembly District

Counties: Orange, San Diego
Cities: Oceanside, Laguna Niguel, San Clemente, San Juan Capistrano, Dana Point, Laguna Hills
Ethnicity: 65% White, 22% Latino, 4% Black, 6% Asian
Voter Registration: 27% D – 50% R – 20% DS
President 04: 60% Bush, 39% Kerry

Much of Orange County's fabled coastline is within the 73rd Assembly District, which includes all of San Juan Capistrano, San Clemente, Dana Point, Camp Pendleton, Laguna Hills and Laguna Niguel, and almost all of Oceanside in San Diego County. More than half of this affluent district's registered voters are Republicans,

Mimi Walters

while Democrats account for fewer than 28%. Democrats here are nearly irrelevant at the polls, although they frequently tap the area's wealthy business interests for fund raising. And while Latinos account for more than 22% of the population, only about 9% are registered to vote. The Latino population surge that has transformed much of the rest of Orange County has been quiescent here, growing only slightly during the past two decades, and two out of three residents are white. Bush took 60% of the vote in 2004 and 57% in 2000, and there is no indication that Republican domination is likely to change, although Democrat Barbara Boxer and Republican Bill Jones closely divided the U.S. Senate vote in the district's San Diego County section in 2004.

But if the easy-going, surfer lifestyle permeates much of this district, the politics are strictly Orange County conventional, with a touch of northern San Diego County's far right and the heavy military presence of the sprawling Camp Pendleton Marine Corps base thrown in. Republicans thrive in a district where money talks, and the only political contests of note are in the primaries when the Republicans' moderate and conservative wings clash.

In March 2004, Mimi Walters, backed by the county's New Majority Republican social moderates and looking to succeed termed-out incumbent Pat Bates (who endorsed Walters), got through a tough GOP primary, capturing some 15,000 votes—41% of the total. Her two Republican challengers, Vista School Board member Jim Gibson and Orange County Supervisor Tom Wilson, split the vote with 29% each. After the bruising primary, it was clear sailing for Walters.

Walters is strong on fiscal issues and knows how to use money to make money. She was an investment executive with Drexel, Burnham & Lambert, later worked for Kidder Peabody, and served on the board of the National Association of Women Business Owners. She served on the Laguna Niguel City Council, was elected mayor in 2000, and raised her political profile when she took a leading role in efforts to block the transformation of the El Toro Marine Air Base into a commercial airport, serving as chairman of the El Toro Reuse Planning Authority. The issue dominated endless local media coverage, and Walters developed into a major player in the political fight. Walters was a county leader in the successful 2003 effort to recall Democratic Governor Gray Davis, an effort that began and was strongest in Orange County.

Midway through 2005, Walters was one of a handful of Orange County legislators suddenly faced with a life decision: Do I run for Congress or do I sit tight? The catalyst for this angst was the sudden decision by President George Bush to nominate Orange County Congressman Chris Cox as chairman of the Securities and Exchange Commission. Open congressional districts, offering as they do lifetime employment, are rare, and the chance to seize one is difficult to pass up—especially when the contest is a free ride for all contenders. The opposition promised to be formidable; Senator John Campbell quickly announced, for instance, hoping his stature and money would clear the field for a special election. Walters gave the matter considerable thought, demonstrating that her ambitions run deep, but eventually opted out of a race that Campbell ultimately won.

Walters begins her second term with a key position, vice chair of the Assembly Appropriations Committee. The chair of that committee, San Francisco Democrat Mark Leno, is among the Assembly's most liberal members, so the contrast with Walters will be stark. As her first action of the new session, she introduced a constitutional amendment to restrict the use of eminent domain by local jurisdictions—the same notion voters defeated as Prop. 90 during the November 2006 elections.

BIOGRAPHY: Born: Pasadena, May 14, 1962. Home: Laguna Niguel. Education: BA, UCLA. Military: None. Family: husband David, four children. Religion: Occupation: Businesswoman.

OFFICES: 6031 Capitol Building, Sacramento, CA 95814, Phone: (916) 319-2073, Fax: (916) 319-2173, email: assemblymember.walters@assembly.ca.gov. District: 302 North Coast Highway, Oceanside, CA 92054, Phone: (760) 757-8084, Fax: (760) 757-8087.

COMMITTEES: Aging and Long-Term Care; Appropriations (vice chair); Banking and Finance.

ELECTED: 2004 **TERM LIMIT:** 2010

ELECTION HISTORY: Laguna Niguel City Council, 1996–2004; Mayor, 2000.

2004 ELECTION: Walters (R) 62%
                    Calzada (D) 32%
                    Favor (L) 5%

2006 ELECTION: Walters (R*) 73%
                    Favor (L) 27%

RATINGS: AFL-CIO CAI CoC CLCV EQCA CCS CMTA FARM NARAL
              7   36   94   0   0   15   90   100   0

LOIS WOLK (D)
8th Assembly District

Counties: Solano, Yolo
Cities: Fairfield, Vacaville, Davis, Woodland, West Sacramento, Benicia, Winters, Suisun
Ethnicity: 57% White, 21% Latino, 8% Black, 10% Asian
Voter Registration: 46% D – 30% R – 20% DS
President 04: 56% Kerry, 43% Bush

A vast rolling expanse of farms, vineyards, and orchards that stretches from the San Francisco Bay Area to the Sacramento Valley, the 8th District includes huge chunks of Yolo and Solano counties. Nearly all of Yolo is in the district, including 615,000 rural acres of walnut groves and tomato fields, but most of the county's 150,000 residents live in just four cities—West Sacramento, Davis, Winters, and Woodland, the county seat. Some 70% of Solano County's population, or about 260,000 people, lives in

Lois Wolk

the district, mostly in five major cities—Benicia, Dixon, Fairfield, Suisun, and Vacaville. Although the percentage of registered Democrats in the district has declined since 2002, it still remains high at 45% compared with 32% Republican. The district did not change much in the 2001 redistricting, although it no longer crosses the Sacramento River west of Elk Grove.

Only once since 1928 has Yolo County voted for a Republican president, Dwight Eisenhower in 1952. The most liberal of California's land-locked counties, Yolo's politics are influenced in large part by the University of California campus in Davis, a city known for whizzing bicycles and a tunnel to protect toads.

Still, the district shows signs of sliding gradually to the right. Of the 14 counties that voted against the governor's recall, Yolo led by the smallest margin, a mere 158 votes. Moreover, Democratic registration has slipped slightly in recent years, while the number of registered Republicans and decline-to-state voters has grown as suburban housing tracts along the Interstate 80 corridor have blossomed. The demographics are slowly changing with the influx of families from the Bay Area, but most communities are white, with percentages reaching into the 70s and 80s. The percentage of Asians in Fairfield and Davis breaks double digits, as do the numbers of Hispanics in Vacaville, Dixon, and West Sacramento.

In the gubernatorial recall, 58% of the district voted "no." In the replacement election, Republican Arnold Schwarzenegger made a surprisingly strong showing, winning 44% of the vote. Democrat Cruz Bustamante, the lieutenant governor, came in second with 33%, followed by Green Party nominee Peter Camejo with 4%.

Perhaps indicative of the district's change is Assemblywoman Lois Wolk, a Democrat who says she is committed to working across party lines. Wolk, now serving her third and final term, is a founding member of the Bipartisan Working Group—a group of legislators trying to resolve the state budget deficit. The need for compromise in the polarized Assembly is a recurring theme in Wolk's speeches, and she credits her ability to get along with both parties for her success in the negotiations over Propositions 57, a bond measure to pay off the deficit, and 58, a measure requiring the state to enact balanced budgets. Wolk started as a councilwoman in Davis, whose young politically active population makes it a formidable power base. Her eventual Republican opponent in 2004 was a familiar face; California Department of Forestry and Fire Protection soil scientist John Munn had run against Wolk in the 2002 race to replace term-limited Assemblywoman Helen Thomson. Wolk won easily, enhancing her margin in 2004. Munn gave up in 2006, ceding sacrificial honors to John Gould.

In the hurry-up world of term limits, Wolk is an experienced lawmaker with a list of legislative achievements, including bills to allow the Fairfield Suisun School District to use a year-round single-track calendar year, equip commuter buses with bicycle racks, and require cities receiving state money for solar energy systems to comply with the Solar Rights Act. She also maintains one of the more hectic committee loads, sitting on five panels that include Budget and Banking and Finance. She also chairs the Water, Parks and Wildlife Committee.

Wolk will be searching for some other job now, likely the state Senate seat now held by Democrat Mike Machado—whose term ends in 2008. Among her potential opponents is Helen Thompson, the Davis Democrat who preceded Wolk in the Assembly. Among those already casting an eye on Wolk's district is West Sacramento Mayor Chris Cabaldon.

BIOGRAPHY: Born: Philadelphia, PA, May 12, 1946. Home: Davis. Education: BA, Antioch College; MA, Johns Hopkins School of Advanced International Studies. Military: None. Family: husband Bruce, two children. Religion: No preference. Occupation: Legislator, former teacher.

OFFICES: 3120 Capitol Building, Sacramento, CA 95814, Phone: (916) 319-2008, Fax: (916) 319-2108, email: assemblymember.wolk@assembly.ca.gov. District: 555 Mason Street, Suite 275, Vacaville, CA 95688, Phone: (707) 455-8025, Fax: (707) 455-4090.

COMMITTEES: Banking and Finance; Budget; Budget Subcommittee 5 on Information Technology and Transportation; Natural Resources; Veterans Affairs; Water, Parks and Wildlife (chair).

ELECTED: 2002 **TERM LIMIT:** 2008

ELECTION HISTORY: Davis City Council, 1990–1998; Mayor, 1992–1994; Yolo County Board of Supervisors, 1998–2002.

2002 ELECTION: Wolk (D) 58%'
Munn (R) 42%

2004 ELECTION: Wolk (D*) 64%
Munn (R) 36%

2006 ELECTION: Wolk (D*) 66%
Gould (R) 34%

RATINGS:	AFL-CIO	CAI	CoC	CLCV	EQCA	CCS	CMTA	FARM	NARAL
	89	92	35	35	100	100	20	20	100

7

The Congressional Delegation:
Less Than Meets the Eye

History properly will credit Nancy Pelosi for leading her party to victory in the 2006 congressional elections and cracking the marble ceiling to become the first female Speaker of the House of Representatives. But the bigger achievement by far was getting there in spite of being a Californian, and somewhere in that great smoke-filled room beyond, her mentor, San Francisco's legendary congressman Phil Burton, must be tossing back the Stolis. Burton lost a race for House Majority Leader in 1976 by one vote—and with it the chance to be Speaker. No Californian since, in either party, made it to the top rungs of the House leadership ladder until Pelosi became Minority Whip in 2001.

Pelosi's inner circle of advisers includes three of California's most senior Democrats: Howard Berman of Van Nuys, a consummate insider player who holds the number two post on both the House Judiciary and the International Relations Committee; Henry Waxman, who as chairman of the Government Reform Committee has the lead authority on House oversight investigations; and George Miller, a close friend who chairs the Education and Labor Committee and co-chairs the Democratic Steering and Policy Committee, the panel that oversees legislative strategy and committee appointments for Democrats. One of Pelosi's first moves as Speaker was to beef up California's representation on the Appropriations Committee with new seats for Democrats Barbara Lee of Oakland, Adam Schiff of Pasadena, and Mike Honda of Campbell.

Delegation watchers were quick to note that these additions barely made the state's share of Democratic seats on the money panel (5 of 37) equal to its proportion of Democratic members in the House, 34 of 233. Nonetheless, they held their collective breath lest the move be seen as too preferential to California and ultimately backfire.

Superior size does have advantages in the House where California's 53-member delegation dwarfs those from all the other states and will for the foreseeable future. But even with senior members on almost every major committee, something always seems to work against California when it comes to congressional clout, regardless of which party occupies the White House, the Speaker's chair, or the governor's desk in Sacramento.

The stories of California's lost opportunities and botched or thwarted legislative efforts during the decades the Democrats previously ruled Congress are legendary: the failure to be even a finalist for the site of the superconducting supercollider; the contract for an earthquake engineering center that went, of all places, to Buffalo; the difficulty in getting disaster relief money after the 1989 Loma Prieta earthquake; the inability to forestall or ameliorate four economically devastating rounds of military base closures in the late 1980s and early 1990s.

In the twelve years that Republicans ruled, from 1995–2007, Californians ascended to the chairmanships of six full committees, including the powerful Appropriations, Armed Services, Rules, and Ways and Means panels. California Democrats held positions as ranking minority members on four other full committees, and Pelosi, of course, moved up to the post of House Minority Leader in 2002. But even with that extraordinary reach, delivering on behalf of the state was problematic for reasons that became institutional as well as simply peculiar to an unwieldy, undisciplined delegation. No matter that Californians ran important committees. Under the Republicans, the powers of committee chairmen were significantly diminished. Their chairmanships were term limited, not guaranteed by strict seniority, and more subject to the direction of the House leadership than they had been in 40 years. No matter that Californians were senior minority members of committees and subcommittees. Washington was an evermore partisan town.

Against the backdrop of a GOP-controlled House, Senate, and White House, the dwindling number of members with moderate inclinations in either party had little incentive to work across partisan lines. And as Governor Arnold Schwarzenegger, who campaigned on promises that he would be "the Collectinator" for California, discovered, even GOP star status doesn't really help wrest money from Washington when funding formulas favor poorer states and the federal budget deficit is soaring.

With Democrats now in control, Californians have lost the chairmanships on Appropriations, where Jerry Lewis of Redlands became the ranking Republican; Ways and Means, where Bill Thomas of Bakersfield retired; Rules, where David Dreier became the top Republican, and Armed Services, where Duncan Hunter of San Diego also moved over to be the ranking GOP member. The defeat of Rep. Richard Pombo (R-Tracy), the sole Californian to lose his seat in 2006, also meant the loss of a chairmanship on the Resources Committee. Californians hold eight seats—six Democratic and two Republican—on the panel, to which Democrats have restored the name *Natural* Resources. New chairmanships on the Government Reform, International Relations, Education and Labor, Administration, and Veterans' Affairs panels may be plums for individual California Democrats but are more likely to translate to national policy platforms for the party than economic muscle for the state. That is particularly true for master legislators like Waxman, whose talents will be applied to ferreting out corruption in the Bush administration, and for staunch liberals like Miller at Education and Labor and Pete Stark of Fremont, who chairs the Ways and Means Subcommittee on Health.

In the Senate Barbara Boxer will chair the Environment and Public Works Committee, and Dianne Feinstein, in addition to chairing the largely administrative Senate Rules Committee, will head the Interior Subcommittee of Appropriations, a post of much more direct importance to California.

Californians in both parties acknowledge the delegation's problems translating numbers and seniority to legislative muscle, even on nonformula-driven federal programs and on what should be "no-brainer" policy issues with major California implications, like Medicaid reimbursement, transportation, and homeland security funding and, of course, immigration. The delegation's performance suffers by comparison to the next largest in the House, the 32-member contingent from Texas. Long before the presidencies of either George Bush, or the rise of former House Majority Leader Tom Delay, members from the Lone Star State were known for being able to put aside their differences and battle together, with the cooperation of their two U.S. senators, when Texas interests were on the line.

The Californians did manage a victory in 2005 when Texas and California were pitted directly against each other for a renewal of the lucrative contract to run the Los Alamos National Weapons Laboratory in New Mexico. The federal lab had been managed by the University of California since it opened in 1943. UC collaborated with Bechtel National and other industrial partners in a struggle to retain the contract after a series of security, safety, and accounting problems prompted DOE to put it up for competitive bidding in 2002. In December 2005 the contract was awarded to California.

But the Californians, riven by regional and personal conflicts as well as extremes of ideology, can't even manage to hold regular, bipartisan meetings. That's partly a hangover from a delegation gathering way back in the 1970s that ended in partisan fisticuffs, but it also reflects the sheer logistical difficulty of getting a critical mass of the 53 members together, on the same page, in the same place, at the same time. The Democrats and Republicans gather separately each week; Senators Dianne Feinstein and Barbara Boxer are often not part of delegation efforts and, according to lobbyists and House members, are so compartmentalized in their areas of interest that they rarely collaborate either with each other or with their Bay Area colleague, Pelosi.

The ideological divisions within the delegation would be almost comical if they weren't so often paralyzing. Out of 34 Democrats, eight are part of the 44-member Blue Dog Coalition, an organization of moderate and conservative Democrats built on the remnants of the party's once powerful Dixie wing. Founded in 1994, the organization tends to be more rural and socially conservative than the New Democratic Coalition, founded in 1997 to represent the interests of moderates from more suburban and wealthy districts. Seven California Democrats, including Ellen Tauscher of Walnut Creek, who was elected chairman of the NDC in 2007, belong to both. Another 13 California Democrats belong to the 62-member Congressional Progressive Caucus, a liberal group co-chaired by Bay Area representatives Barbara Lee and Lynn Woolsey.

On the Republican side, 11 Californians belong to the conservative Republican Study Committee, a 100-member organization co-founded by John Doolittle.

The noteworthy exception to the delegation's fractious tendencies was a hold harmless redistricting bargain in 2001 engineered by Democrats and blessed by the Bush White House as well as the chairman of the National Republican Congressional Committee. Under the plan designed to protect incumbents in both parties, California Republicans got 19 of the 20 congressional districts they won in 2000. The 20th, occupied by Steve Horn of Long Beach and long trending Democratic anyway, was collapsed and reconfigured to produce a Democratic district with a Latino voting majority. Horn retired, and Linda Sanchez, the sister of Rep. Loretta Sanchez of Garden Grove, won the seat in 2002. In exchange for Horn's lost seat, Democratic mapmakers drew a new, safely Republican seat in the Central Valley (won by Devin Nunes of Visalia in 2002). The final piece of the bargain was agreement by House Republicans and national GOP officials to persuade Assembly Republicans in Sacramento to vote for the plan, thus ensuring its passage with a two-thirds majority and avoiding a ballot initiative fight later.

If the incumbent protection plan engendered any spirit of bipartisan cooperation in the delegation, it evaporated when Rep. Darrell Issa of Temecula began funding the campaign to recall Governor Gray Davis in 2003. Relations soured further in February 2004 when newly sworn-in governor Arnold Schwarzenegger made a visit to Washington, D.C., and met only with Republican members of the delegation. By early 2005, his relationship with GOP delegation members had frayed as well over his proposal to end the legislature's responsibility for redistricting and turn it over to a panel of retired judges. Republicans were not pleased with a plan that would eliminate the congressional delegation's traditional bargaining role in the process of redrawing political boundaries, but they were especially unhappy about the proposal's stipulation that lines be altered before the 2006 election. It now seems unlikely, however, that any change in political boundaries will occur before the new census in 2010.

Schwarzenegger has also found that it's easy to get caught in the delegation's political cross currents. A five-year deal with the Bush administration to secure Medicaid funds for California hospitals that he announced in summer 2005 drew fire from delegation Democrats and the California Association of Public Hospitals as well as leaders of the California State Association of Counties. While the governor said the deal was better than any other state got in view of administration plans to cut Medicaid funding, the governor's critics said he should have done more to persuade the administration against the cuts in the first place. They said the agreement lacked assurances on the amount of and access to the federal funding, on the adequacy of state funding, and the ability to transfer poor patients to managed care health programs.

The bipartisan California Institute for Federal Policy Research, a Washington think tank aimed at helping the delegation identify and coalesce around issues and legislation important to the state, has had some success in the first part of its mission. Established in the early 1990s, as the California economy reeled under the impact of recession and military restructuring, the Institute is funded by a collection of the state's universities, major private industries, and public policy organizations. But coordinating and communicating policy research can only go so far in a delegation that continues to lack any real center of political gravity.

At the beginning of 2005, the delegation lost one of its most senior and most respected and well-liked members, Democrat Robert Matsui of Sacramento who died on January 1 of a rare bone marrow disease. Matsui, a fiscal moderate who became increasingly liberal once the Republicans gained control of Congress, was Pelosi's hand-picked chairman of the Democratic Congressional Campaign Committee. He was the third most senior Democrat on Ways and Means and the ranking member of its Social Security subcommittee. He was replaced in Congress by his wife, Doris, a former aide to President Bill Clinton, in a special election three months later. She is one of three delegation members—along with Democrat Lois Capps of Santa Barbara and Republican Mary Bono of Palm Springs—who took the seats of their deceased husbands.

—Susan Rasky

U.S. Senate

BARBARA BOXER (D)

Barbara Boxer

The election of 2006 provided an enormous bonus for California's senior United States senator, Barbara Boxer, even though she was not on the ballot. The liberal lawmaker, who has dwelt for most of her elective career as the focus of Republican angst and desire, returned to the nation's capital in January 2007 no longer a member of a frustrated minority. With Democrats taking control of the Senate, she returned as chairwoman of the Senate Environment and Public Works Committee, and it signaled the dawn of a new era in Washington.

"The days of rollbacks on environmental protection" are over, she declared in *The Sacramento Bee*, adding that her first act would be to convene hearings on global warming and climate change—two notions that the previous Republican majority considered mythological nonsense. That said, she also hopes to take partisan sting out of the environment. It is the only way she can move her agenda forward in a house where a handful of determined senators can cripple intent and 59 of her colleagues are needed to end a filibuster.

Still, the new Congress provides heady days for Boxer, generally considered California's luckiest politician, a reputation reinforced only a scant two years ago in the election of 2004.

Long known as one of the most liberal members of Congress, the 64-year-old Boxer has run for the U.S. Senate three times now and, in each instance, circumstances—and the Republican Party—have conspired to grease her path to Washington.

Unlike previous years, the 2004 edition of Barbara Boxer no longer was considered the most vulnerable member of the U.S. Senate. Her 1998 re-election had put a dent in that reputation, despite the fact that she continued to tack strongly to the left. But in 2004, the Republican strategists and their allies who bankroll attacks against targets of opportunity left Boxer mostly alone. They had other ships to sink—Senate Democratic Leader Tom Daschle of South Dakota, for instance—in states where Democrats are not so strongly hulled. As a result, she sailed blithely to a third term, her 20-point re-election victory made all the more remarkable by the fact that her challenger, former Secretary of State Bill Jones, was the most qualified and distinguished opponent she had yet to face.

The year did not start in quite so sanguine a fashion. Looking back to the March 2004 primary, it is difficult to remember that 10 Republicans vied for the right to take on Boxer, and the field included, in addition to Jones, former U.S. Treasurer Rosario Marin and former state Senator Howard Kaloogian—one of the prime motivators behind the successful 2003 recall of Governor Gray Davis. Jones overwhelmed the field, capturing 45% of the vote, more than twice that of Marin.

It was Jones's high-water mark.

When it came to the fall campaign against Boxer, Jones disappeared into a political landscape alive with the pulse-pounding rhythms of presidential debates, Indian gambling, stem cell research, three strikes, and health care reform. Ignored even by his own party, he became the invisible man.

No metaphor, Jones's invisibility was imposed by the lack of money and resources to mount even a minimal statewide campaign. At the finish, Jones's financial misery resulted in an unprecedented and embarrassing state of affairs—he was the first major party U.S. Senate candidate in four decades not to air a single television ad.

Boxer raised $16 million with ease, spent a nickel on the primary, and cruised into the final week of the general election with $1.5 million in the bank—having already paid for TV buys. She spent the entire campaign running positive spots, traveling the state, and meeting with voters.

From the beginning, Jones was dismissed as a viable candidate because he could not replicate the two criteria that have proved to be essential for successful statewide Republican candidates: movie-star celebrity and a personal fortune. He was, in a nutshell, not Arnold Schwarzenegger. Jones, in fact, was the anti-Arnold, and his financing was determined by two questions: (1) Who else is asking for money? and (2) Where can it be better spent? In 2004, that meant: (1) Just about everyone, and (2) Just about anywhere.

In the end, Jones prevailed in many California counties. But, with the exception of Orange and Riverside, his catch mostly included places where nobody lives. Boxer took the population centers, in some cases by astronomical majorities. She won Los Angeles County, for instance, by a million votes.

Boxer's run of luck began in 1992—an unusually active political year in California. Not only did then-Congresswoman Boxer seek a Senate seat opened by the retirement of Democrat Alan Cranston, fellow Bay Area Democrat Dianne Feinstein was on the ballot as well, running for the seat vacated when Republican Pete Wilson left the U.S. Senate to become governor in 1991. Feinstein drew a weak GOP opponent, John Seymour, who had been appointed by the new governor and had to run to fill out the remainder of Wilson's six-year term. Seymour, although nominally the incumbent, was no match for Feinstein who had narrowly lost the governorship to Wilson in 1990. Her stature allowed her freedom of movement, and she stumped as much for Boxer as for herself. In fact, it could be said that Feinstein won two Senate seats—her own and Boxer's.

Boxer was helped by the dynamic of the Republican Party primary, which featured seven candidates—three of whom were serious contenders. The most dangerous for Boxer was U.S. Representative Tom Campbell, a pro-choice moderate and Stanford law professor with an academic pedigree longer than the California coastline. But moderates have trouble winning GOP primaries, and the quirky Campbell was challenged from the right by Los Angeles commentator Bruce Herschensohn, who was bankrolled by conservatives. Campbell also was saddled with a third Republican contender who pitched to the same centrist community—Palm Springs Mayor

Sonny Bono. The combination proved too much, and Campbell narrowly lost to Herschensohn.

His victory set up a classic liberal-conservative brawl with Boxer, who led by 22 points shortly after Labor Day. But her lead evaporated by mid October, thanks to a Republican media blitz that defined Boxer on GOP terms: bouncer of 143 checks at the House bank, a big-spending liberal who rode in limousines, a shrill feminist with a poor voting record, and a peacenik who beat up the military while 200,000 defense jobs disappeared from California. Boxer's campaign failed to respond to the attacks, husbanding its resources for a final TV effort that actually reinforced the strident image created for her by Herschensohn.

Feinstein came to the rescue, stumping the state with Boxer in tow, devoting most of her speeches to praise for Boxer who took what had to be a humbling experience with equanimity. The two campaigned as a team and, once elected, promised to work as a team on behalf of California. If nothing else, Feinstein's effort kept voters' minds open, slowing the erosion around Boxer's base and preventing her opponent from solidifying his gains. That proved important during the final week when a political land mine went off under Herschensohn's victory tour—the revelation that the GOP candidate had frequented strip clubs and often shopped for pornography at a local Los Angeles newsstand. Released by Democratic operative Bob Mulholland, the news derailed a campaign that had been predicated in part on family values.

On Election Day, Boxer edged past Herschensohn to win a six-year term. Feinstein also won, but only the two years remaining on Wilson's term. She was forced to run for her six-year stint in 1994, when Feinstein faced a very stiff challenge from Republican Congressman Michael Huffington. Boxer returned Feinstein's favors during that election by raising a maharaja's fortune for the Feinstein campaign.

Boxer's re-election to a second term came around in 1998 and, for the second time, she was blessed. This time, the election was billed as one between an extremist and a moderate—just the kind of election Boxer had feared in 1992—but the final result was no one's view of reality. Boxer was pegged the extremist by no less an authority than *National Journal*, a highly respected weekly magazine that identified her as the most liberal member of the U.S. Senate. But by the time the campaign ended, Boxer had been swept back into office as the centrist, while barely moving a philosophical inch. She accomplished this pirouette-in-place by running an aggressive, well-financed, and well-timed campaign—and by having a clueless Republican opponent, state Treasurer Matt Fong, who at times seemed to be competing on another planet.

The lefty label fortified the notion that Boxer was beatable. Her record on such issues as the death penalty, crime, taxes, and spending for social programs appealed to narrow constituencies and provided so many targets of opportunity that many Republicans considered her fodder for a walkover. History also worked against her, for 1998 was the sixth year of the Clinton presidency—and elections held in the sixth year have been disasters for the president's party. Clinton's impeachment hearings geared up just as the election season got underway, and Democrats fretted that their voters, demoralized by details of his sex scandal with a White House intern, would evaporate on Election Day.

U.S. Senators from California
(Elected by the Legislature prior to 1914)

Seat A			Seat B		
John C. Fremont	D	1849	William M. Gwin	D	1849
John B. Weller	D	1852			
David C. Broderick	D	1857			
Henry P. Haun	D	1859			
Milton S. Latham	D	1860	James A. McDougall	D	1861
John Conness	U	1863	Cornelius Cole	U	1865
Eugene Casserly	D	1869			
John S. Hager	D	1873	Aaron A. Sargent	R	1873
Newton Booth	I-R	1875	James T. Farley	D	1879
John F. Miller	R	1881	Leland Stanford	R	1885
A. P. Williams	R	1886			
George Hearst	D	1887			
Charles N. Fenton	R	1893	George C. Perkins	R	1893
Stephen M. White	D	1893			
Thomas R. Bard	R	1899			
Frank P. Flint	R	1905			
John D. Works	R	1911	James D. Phalen	D	1915
Hiram W. Johnson	R	1917	Samuel M. Shortridge	R	1921
William F. Knowland	R	1945	William G. McAdoo	R	1932
Clair Engle	D	1959	Thomas M. Storke	D	1938
Pierre Salinger	D	1964	Sheridan Downey	D	1939
George Murphy	R	1964	Richard Nixon	R	1951
John V. Tunney	D	1971	Thomas Kuchel	R	1952
S. I. Hayakawa	R	1977	Alan Cranston	D	1969
Pete Wilson	R	1983			
John Seymour	R	1991			
Dianne Feinstein	D	1992	Barbara Boxer	D	1992

*Key to parties: D=Democrat, R=Republican, U=Union, I-R=Independent-Republican

All this fed the notion that Republicans couldn't lose. All they had to do was nominate a decent candidate—preferably a moderate—raise a barrel of cash, and concoct a strategy that made the election a referendum on Boxer.

Republicans managed two out of three. They nominated Fong, son of former Democratic Secretary of State March Fong Eu and an overcautious moderate averse to taking risks. Although outspent by Boxer, they raised enough money to wage a viable effort. What they did not get was anything resembling a coherent campaign. After the primary, Boxer remained silent, hoarding resources and staying out of the Clinton-dominated limelight. But instead of taking advantage of that void by hammering Boxer, Fong ran a series of "soft" ads that never mentioned the incumbent or her record. To Boxer's good fortune, the electorate paid no attention at all, and Boxer and Fong began the real campaign virtually even in the polls.

In October, Boxer went on the attack with a relentless television blitz. There was nothing soft about the effort; no squishy spots designed to tell her story. Boxer wasn't interested in telling her story. She wanted to tell her version of Matt Fong's story. In 1992 Boxer let her opponent define her. This time, she defined her opponent at a time when voters were just waking up to the election and few had an opinion about Fong. At the time, his positive image far outweighed his negatives. By the time Boxer finished with him, Fong stood somewhere to the right of Vlad the Impaler, and his negatives had eclipsed his positives in nearly every poll. Boxer had won the air war—and it proved fatal to Fong's candidacy.

Boxer chose themes that dominated the campaign: gun control, the environment, education, HMO reform, and abortion. Then, she defined Fong on those issues, sometimes inaccurately. But her tenacity and the ferocity of her attacks kept Fong on the defensive and the spotlight away from issues that might have proved harmful to Boxer.

When Fong did respond, he did so in a curious way. He attacked Boxer's record on the stump—where few voters heard him—but remained a charmless talking head on television, where he tried to articulate his core beliefs and where most voters learned about the campaign and its candidates. He failed miserably to hit Boxer where it counted, and to push her image to the left.

As the campaign wound toward Election Day, Fong imploded. Instead of using TV to attack Boxer's record, he put his mother before the cameras where she scolded the incumbent for going negative. And at the very last moment, it was revealed that Fong had given $50,000 to the Traditional Values Coalition—a conservative anti-abortion, anti-gay group. The donation angered gay and pro-choice Republicans; his subsequent explanation ticked off conservatives. Boxer stayed on message and won by 10%. Ironically, the Senate's most liberal member returned for a second term by appealing to the center.

Boxer was a member of the Marin County Board of Supervisors when she first came to Congress in 1982, having won a seat that had been held by Democrat John Burton. In the House, she was elected president of the freshman class and made her focus ineffective government. She exposed the Air Force's infamous purchase of a $7,622 coffee pot and became an expert on government procurement. By her third term, she was on the Armed Services Committee, one of the most exclusive good-old-boy clubs in the House. She simultaneously assaulted and wooed the club, leading a fight for laws that require more competitive contract bidding and protection for whistle-blowers while learning how to negotiate inside an established network. Her most notable moment occurred when she marched to the door of the Senate Judiciary Committee in 1991—while still a member of the House—to protest how the Senate handled the confirmation hearing of Clarence Thomas to the U.S. Supreme Court.

In her first Senate campaign, Boxer drew a bead on the capital's premier good-old-boy network—the cliques that run the upper house—but showed little interest in rocking boats once she was safely ensconced inside the club. Her career has been characterized by a mastery at building coalitions that bring core issues such as abortion, consumer safety, and military accountability to center stage.

Her recent voting record reflects her continued sense of liberal priorities. She opposed the 2002 authorizations for the use of force in both Iraq and Afghanistan and in 2003 voted against allocating $86 billion for operations in those two countries. She has fought against plans to drill for oil in the Arctic National Wildlife Refuge and against efforts to lessen liability for gun manufacturers. She is helping fight a rear-guard action to protect against erosion of Roe v. Wade—the Supreme Court decision guaranteeing a woman's right to choose an abortion. In June 2005 she introduced major legislation designed to protect the oceans, including creation of an independent National Oceanic and Atmospheric Administration—now part of the Commerce Department.

Until she ascended to her current chairmanship, Boxer's most influential post was as a member of the Senate Foreign Relations Committee and its subcommittee on international operations and terrorism. She used that placement to bedevil the Bush administration's conduct of foreign policy. In 2005, for instance, Boxer gained national notoriety when she took on Bush's appointment of Condoleezza Rice as secretary of state, using Rice's confirmation hearings as a platform for a tough, no-quarter grilling that questioned Rice's veracity and integrity. Later that same year, she helped lead the fight against the confirmation of John Bolton as ambassador to the United Nations.

Boxer is not reticent about poking at members of her own party either. In 2004, in the midst of her re-election campaign, she took San Francisco Mayor Gavin Newsom to task for performing gay marriages in violation of state law, calling the law "fair." It was a strong rebuke designed to help defuse a troublesome issue for Democrats in the middle of a tense and narrow campaign for the presidency.

It has been a long, steady climb for the daughter of an uneducated immigrant mother and a father who went to night school to earn a law degree while working days to support his family. Boxer credits her own considerable drive to her father's sense of responsibility. She became a labor lawyer but gave up her career to raise her children, one of whom—daughter Nicole—is married to Tony Rodham, brother of U.S. Senator Hillary Rodham Clinton of New York. Boxer re-entered the work force as a weekly newspaper reporter in Marin County. From there, she spent two years as Burton's field representative, which gave her the experience to deal with the erratic males she often finds in the halls of Congress. In 1976 she won a seat on the Marin County Board of Supervisors, parlaying that into a congressional seat when Burton stepped down in 1982 to deal with his drug and alcohol dependency.

BIOGRAPHY: Born: Brooklyn, NY, November 11, 1940. Home: Greenbrae. Education: BA, Brooklyn College. Military: None. Family: husband Stewart, two children. Religion: Jewish.

OFFICES: Capitol: Hart Senate Office Building 112, Washington, DC 20515, Phone: (202) 224-3553, email: senator@boxer.senate.gov. District: 501 I Street, Suite 7-600, Sacramento, CA 95814, Phone: (916) 448-2787, Fax: (916) 448-2563; 1700 Montgomery Street, Suite 240, San Francisco, CA 94111, Phone: (415) 403-0100, Fax: (415) 956-6701; 312 North Spring Street, Suite 1748; Los Angeles, CA 90012, Phone: (213) 894-5000, Fax: (213) 894-5042; 1130 O Street, Suite 2450, Fresno, CA 93721, Phone: (559) 497-5109, Fax: (559) 497-5111; 600 B Street, Suite 2240, San Diego, CA 92101, Phone: (619) 239-3884, Fax: (619) 239-5719; 201 North E Street, Suite 210, San Bernardino, CA 92401, Phone: (909) 888-8525, Fax: (909) 888-8613.

COMMITTEES: Commerce, Science and Transportation; Foreign Relations; Environment and Public Works (chair).

ELECTED: 1992

ELECTION HISTORY: Marin County Board of Supervisors, 1977–1982; U.S. House, 1982–1992.

1998 ELECTION: Boxer (D*) 53%
Fong (R) 43%

2004 ELECTION: Boxer (D*) 58%
Jones (R) 38%

RATINGS:

ACU	ADA	AFL-CIO	CoC	GO	LCV	NTU	PIRG
12	100	92	24	F-	100	11	95

DIANNE FEINSTEIN (D)

Dianne Feinstein

On June 7, 2005, the United States Senate approved President George Bush's nomination of Janice Rogers Brown to the District of Columbia Court of Appeals—a judicial post considered only a step away from the highest court in the land. Brown, a justice of the California Supreme Court, had been the center of a political firestorm, her confirmation held up for two years by Democrats who considered her too conservative, too inflexible, and far too hostile to traditional Democratic constituencies.

The seminal event associated with the Brown nomination was her appearance before the Senate Judiciary Committee in October 2003 where she was subjected to what LAW.com called a "scathingly hostile hearing." The person who grilled her the hardest, at one point characterizing Brown's judicial opinions as "extraordinarily intemperate," was the senior senator from her home state, Dianne Feinstein.

Although a member of the minority party, Feinstein's stature and unyielding resistance helped forestall Brown's elevation to the federal bench, and she lost out in the end only because the battle over the nomination had escalated to the point where it threatened the very fabric of the Senate itself.

Some consider Feinstein's tenacious opposition to Brown a miscalculation and argue that she should have acquiesced to the nomination in the first place. Doing so, they argue, would have accomplished two things: removed Brown from the California Supreme Court, a notion cherished by many in the state's legal community, including most of her colleagues on the high court; and allowed Democrat Gray Davis—rather than Republican Arnold Schwarzenegger—to appoint a justice to the state Supreme Court. Miscalculation or principled endeavor, Feinstein's role in the confirmation brawl underscores the notion that she is a significant force in the Senate.

It has been a long road up for Feinstein, who has spent nearly four decades in a very public life. From her election to the San Francisco Board of Supervisors in 1969 to her becoming mayor upon the 1978 assassination of her friend George Moscone to her narrow defeat for governor in 1990 to her savage 1994 campaign for re-election to the U.S. Senate to her stature today as chair of the Senate Rules Committee and California's most respected public official, Feinstein is nearing the end of a political journey experienced by few politicians in history. It has been a sometimes painful road, but it has brought her a level of respect accorded to few elected officials.

It has cloaked her in a mantle of electability that makes Democrats salivate but obligates Feinstein to work her way through difficult and personal career decisions. In 1997 and again in 2003, she was the person Democrats wanted as their candidate for governor. This was especially true in 2003 when a recall election against incumbent Democrat Gray Davis qualified for the ballot.

A recall is two elections: a referendum on the sitting governor and a runoff to see who will replace the governor if the recall is successful. Feinstein, it was assumed, would be the strongest candidate to replace Davis regardless of who else entered the race; and that included Arnold Schwarzenegger. At first, Feinstein was vague about her intentions, fueling speculation that she had never quite let go of a long-held ambition to be governor. At the time, Feinstein and other prominent Democrats faced conflicting pressures. On one hand, the party did not want to lose its grip on the governorship and thus needed a strong contender on the ballot should Davis be recalled. But some Democratic tacticians felt that if no prominent Democrat filed, the recall could be characterized as a partisan effort by Republicans to accomplish via a special election what they had failed to do in 2002. The best way for Davis to survive, so the theory went, was to present a united front behind an admittedly unpopular governor.

Feinstein had private reasons for deciding not to offer herself up as a potential replacement for Davis. Two decades earlier, she had beaten back an attempt to recall her as mayor of San Francisco, and she bore a personal distaste for the entire process. In addition, she had gained an elevated stature inside the club of the Senate and could look forward to holding the seat for as long as she chose.

The Davis recall qualified for the ballot on July 23, 2003, but it took Feinstein two weeks to finally announce that she would not run, doing so on August 6. Although she may not have intended it, her decision lit a green light for others. Within hours, Schwarzenegger had opted in. So, too, had Lieutenant Governor Cruz Bustamante, shattering any notion of Democratic solidarity. Many observers believe the Schwarzenegger and Bustamante decisions were predicated on whether Feinstein was a candidate.

The 2003 recall election was not the first time Feinstein had been the Democrats' one best hope. Throughout 1997, Democrats eager to recapture the governorship after 16 years of Republican rule urged Feinstein to enter the 1998 race. Given the ultimate course of events, she undoubtedly would have been elected governor. But that course was not apparent a year before the election, and Feinstein stewed over the decision, torn between her flourishing career in the Senate and her desire to return to California. Ultimately, she opted not to run—just as she did in the recall half a decade later. But she also dithered for months before announcing her decision, creating a period of uncertainty that hampered the efforts of other potential Democratic candidates to raise money.

Feinstein has never expressed regret over her decision not to seek the governorship in 1998, despite the eventual disaster that befell the Democrat who won that year, Gray Davis. Her decision had been based on several factors, not the least of which was her rise to prominence and influence in Washington. To become governor would have required not one but two grueling statewide races, and Feinstein already had endured a pair of such campaigns—for governor in 1990 and re-election to the Senate in 1994. The Democratic primary already was crowded with the likes of Davis and Northwest Airlines co-chairman Al Checchi, a multimillionaire who eventually would spend $40 million of his own money in a failed attempt to win the nomination. Also contemplating the race was Leon Panetta, a former Clinton chief of staff and congressman. It was Feinstein's dithering that eventually blocked Panetta.

Had she survived the primary, Feinstein would have faced Attorney General Dan Lungren in the general election, and no one could foresee how badly Lungren would implode in the campaign. To put her decision in perspective, had she entered the 1998 race for governor, Feinstein would have mounted a difficult and demanding statewide campaign in every election of the decade, save 1996.

In 2000 and again in 2004, Feinstein briefly was considered for an even more exalted post—vice president on Democratic tickets eventually headed by Al Gore and John Kerry. It was not the first time Feinstein had been in contention for the vice-presidency. In 1984, she was on Walter Mondale's short list before he opted for Geraldine Ferraro. Now, once again, she was potentially in a position to become the first woman and first Jew to serve as vice president. Eventually, Gore and Kerry chose senators other than Feinstein.

The Worst of Times

If there was a time in Feinstein's political life when she might have been tempted to cash in her chips, it was the election of 1994 where she sought re-election to a full six-year term in the Senate. Two years earlier, Feinstein had captured her seat by brushing aside incumbent Republican John Seymour, who had been appointed to the job by Pete Wilson after Wilson left the Senate to become governor in 1991. Seymour was simply not a viable opponent, freeing Feinstein to help elect the other Democratic senatorial candidate running that year, Barbara Boxer.

Two years later, the atmospherics had changed, and Feinstein had to fight for her political life. The 1994 campaign proved difficult for Democrats all over the country, and Feinstein was no exception. Some prominent Democrats, such as then-Speaker of the House Tom Foley of Washington, did not survive. Others squeaked through as Republicans, led by Georgia Representative Newt Gingrich, fashioned a "Contract with America" that nationalized every corner of the election.

Feinstein drew a lightly regarded Republican opponent, Michael Huffington who had made little impact representing a Santa Barbara congressional district. But Huffington, then-husband of Arianna and scion of a family that had made a fortune in the oil business, was not light in the wallet. By the time the campaign ended, he had poured $27.5 million of his own money into the fray. Feinstein spent $12.5 million—$2.5 million from her own pocket—and became a convert to campaign finance reform. In part, it was the specter of Huffington, as much as anything else, that helped her decide against the 1998 gubernatorial primary against Checchi.

Most campaigns bend and distort images, but the Feinstein-Huffington race, by dint of its magnitude, was perhaps the most pervasively nasty and dishonest in state history. One ad, later pulled, quoted NBC News saying a Feinstein TV spot was "the year's meanest, sneakiest," a statement NBC never made. Another ad attacked Feinstein for failure to pay federal income taxes in 1978, 1979, and 1985—the information gleaned from the fact that Feinstein had made her tax returns public during her 1990 campaign for governor. They showed that, for the years in question, Feinstein owed no taxes due to financial losses. Huffington, meanwhile, refused to make his returns public yet saw no hypocrisy in his assault on Feinstein. Yet another ad accused Feinstein of appointing judges who were soft on crime, ignoring the fact that, as a mayor and senator, Feinstein never had the power to appoint a judge, and those she recommended were not known to coddle criminals.

And in the most famous incident of the campaign—one that eventually derailed Huffington just as he seemed to have the momentum necessary to defeat Feinstein— the Republican challenger accused Feinstein of a criminal violation for "knowingly employing an alien." This came at a time when anti-immigrant sentiments ran high thanks to the highly inflammatory campaign waged on behalf of Proposition 187—the Wilson-backed initiative that denied social and educational benefits to illegal aliens. Unfortunately for Huffington, it was not a crime in the early 1980s to employ someone who was in the country legally—as Feinstein had done. Even more significant, it was soon revealed that Huffington had employed an illegal alien as a nanny, a situation he at first denied, then lied about, and finally blamed on his wife.

Feinstein flung her share of mud. Once her campaign realized that its once substantial lead had slipped away by mid August, she went negative, at the same time deploring the need for it. But even after all the ballots had been counted, Huffington gracelessly refused to concede defeat, saying he had evidence of massive voter fraud. Asked for the evidence, he offered a few isolated examples, despite substantial spending to discover more. The new Republican leadership of the U.S. Senate obliged him by opening an investigation that eventually discovered nothing and was allowed to die quietly.

Feinstein arrived in Congress in 1992 having easily defeated Seymour and compiled a solid record in her first term. She worked for immigration reform and carried bills for California agriculture—work that earned her a re-election endorsement from the usually conservative and Republican-leaning California Farm Bureau. She ended an eight-year stalemate when she won passage of the California Desert Protection Act—the largest wilderness and park bill in the nation. She also did productive work on the Senate Appropriations Committee, where she demonstrated that women in the Senate cannot be taken for granted.

Feinstein's arrival as a lawmaker of substance came during debate on her successful amendment to ban the sale of 19 different assault weapons. Senator Larry Craig, a conservative from Idaho and board member of the National Rifle Association, called her "typical of those who study the issue" of gun control for the first time and admonished that she should "become a little more familiar with firearms."

Craig's patronizing remark, made on the floor of the Senate, was prelude to the moment that likely will live as a centerpiece of her legacy. "I am quite familiar with firearms," Feinstein told Craig and her colleagues. "I became mayor as a product of an assassination. They found my assassinated colleague, and you could put a finger through the bullet hole."

Her words recalled a grim November day in 1978 when Feinstein, then a San Francisco County supervisor, heard shots and smelled gunpowder. Running down a hallway, she found fellow Supervisor Harvey Milk face down in his blood, dead. Someone else found Mayor George Moscone's body. Minutes later, facing television cameras, Feinstein announced the murders. What the cameras did not show, however, was her personal turmoil. Only hours before the shootings, she had told reporters that she would not seek re-election. Her husband had recently died, and she had tired of petty City Hall intrigues. She had failed twice to become mayor, and it was time to do something else.

All that changed with Moscone's death. The crazed gunman was none other than a former colleague—Dan White, a young political neophyte that Feinstein had taken under wing. As president of the board, Feinstein became mayor, going on to win twice on her own and swamping a 1983 recall attempt.

Accomplishments aside, her first term in the Senate was a difficult time. Feinstein is known as a tough boss and experienced significant staff turnover, caused in part by the sheer volume of work but also exacerbated by Feinstein's penchant for micromanaging. She rankled some senior icons of the Senate, notably West Virginia Democrat Robert Byrd, by giving some very un-Democratic support to proposals for a line-item veto and balanced-budget amendment. Byrd responded by ranking Feinstein last in seniority on Byrd's very prestigious Appropriations Committee—a slight that eventually cost Feinstein a seat on the panel when Republicans took control in 1994.

A Trendsetter

Feinstein is a trendsetter in California politics: First woman on the San Francisco Board of Supervisors and first chairwoman. First San Francisco woman mayor. One of the first politicians to court gay voters and embrace their quest for equality. First woman to make a serious run for governor of California. And first woman to hold a U.S. Senate seat from California (she was sworn in before Barbara Boxer, even though they both won a seat in 1992). First woman on the Senate Judiciary Committee. First woman to chair the powerful Senate Rules Committee.

Feinstein was the eldest of three daughters of Leon and Betty Goldman. Her father was a surgeon, and her mother suffered from an undiagnosed brain disorder that

Congressional Members and District Numbers

#	Name	#	Name	#	Name
1	Mike Thompson - D	19	George Radanovich - R	37	Juanita Millender-McDonald - D
2	Wally Herger - R	20	Jim Costa - D	38	Grace Napolitano - D
3	Dan Lungren - R	21	Devin Nunes - R	39	Linda Sanchez - D
4	John Doolittle - R	22	Kevin McCarthy - R	40	Ed Royce - R
5	Doris Matsui - D	23	Lois Capps - D	41	Jerry Lewis - R
6	Lynn Woolsey - D	24	Elton Gallegly - R	42	Gary Miller - D
7	George Miller - D	25	Howard "Buck" McKeon - R	43	Joe Baca - D
8	Nancy Pelosi - D	26	David Dreier - R	44	Ken Calvert - R
9	Barbara Lee - D	27	Brad Sherman - D	45	Mary Bono - R
10	Ellen Tauscher - D	28	Howard Berman - D	46	Dana Rohrabacher - R
11	Jerry McNerney - R	29	Adam Schiff - D	47	Loretta Sanchez - D
12	Tom Lantos - D	30	Henry Waxman - D	48	John Campbell - R
13	Fortney "Pete" Stark - D	31	Xavier Becerra - D	49	Darrell Issa - R
14	Anna Eshoo - D	32	Hilda Solis - D	50	Brian Bilbray - R
15	Mike Honda - D	33	Diane Watson - D	51	Robert Filner - D
16	Zoe Lofgren - D	34	Lucille Roybal-Allard - D	52	Duncan Hunter - R
17	Sam Farr - D	35	Maxine Waters - D	53	Susan Davis - D
18	Dennis Cardoza - D	36	Jane Harman - D		

manifested itself in fits of rage and alcoholism. After graduating from Stanford with a less-than-distinguished record, she married Jack Berman, who later became a San Francisco Superior Court judge, and they had one daughter, Katherine. The Bermans divorced after Dianne became discontent with the role of homemaker.

At a party, she met neurosurgeon Bert Feinstein. They married, and Dianne Feinstein began to build a career in politics. She was well into her career on the board of supervisors when Bert died of cancer. After a year in the mayor's office, Feinstein married investment banker Richard Blum in 1979.

Multimillionaire Blum has been an ideal mate for Feinstein. In her first U.S. Senate race, for instance, he helped her raise more money in New York than she did in southern California. Nonetheless, Blum's involvement also was the source of her biggest headache in both her senatorial campaigns. Opponents capitalized on her troubles with the state Fair Political Practices Commission, which sued Feinstein for a record $8.5 million in fines for allegedly committing a raft of campaign law violations when she ran for governor against Wilson. Most serious of the allegations was that she did not disclose the actual source of $2.7 million in loans from Bank of America and Sumitomo Bank. Instead, she reported that she was the source of the loans. At the time, Blum owned two million shares of BankAmerica and sat on Sumitomo's board of directors. Six weeks after her election, Feinstein settled with the FPPC for $190,000 as part of an agreement where her campaign admitted the errors but said they were unintentional.

Because Feinstein won her first term in a special election, she was sworn into office in November 1992—two full months ahead of the 11 other freshmen. That puts her ahead of the class in seniority, an advantage she will enjoy as long as she serves in the Senate. At the same time, the Democratic leadership, which ran the Senate in 1992, was aware that Feinstein faced re-election in only two years and thoughtfully positioned her with a high-profile role. Boxer, sworn in with the rest of the freshman class, was equally cooperative in allowing Feinstein to assume a more prominent position.

Neither could foresee that they would begin 1995 in a Republican-controlled Congress. Minority Democrats have few opportunities for legislative innovation, and the reversal of fortunes called for a new game plan based on securing what Democrats had previously won. After losing a seat on Appropriations, Feinstein was named to Rules, Foreign Relations, and Judiciary.

Like many members of Congress, Feinstein became enmeshed in the 1998 scandals that haunted the final years of the Clinton presidency. Although she voted against impeaching President Bill Clinton in the Senate, Feinstein was one of the president's harshest critics, enduring the wrath of the White House and fellow Democrats for introducing a measure to censure Clinton for his behavior after the Senate had acquitted him. The steel in Feinstein's anger stemmed from assurances given to her by Clinton himself that he had never engaged in a sexual relationship with White House intern Monica Lewinsky—which lay at the heart of his impeachment. Clinton's assurances were a lie—and Feinstein never bought the spin that their "sexual relationship" was a matter of semantics. Her willingness to take on Clinton in such a public forum helped raise Feinstein's stature on issues of personal morality and ethical behavior.

Feinstein's third election to the Senate occurred in 2000 when she thumped Republican Congressman Tom Campbell, winning by nearly two million votes. Her fourth, in 2006, was more of a coronation than an election. Republicans nominated an obscure former state senator, Richard Mountjoy, and gave him little or no support. Neither Campbell nor Mountjoy left much of a footprint on the political map.

BIOGRAPHY: Born: San Francisco, June 22, 1933. Home: San Francisco. Education: BA, Stanford. Military: None. Family: husband Sidney Blum, one child, three stepchildren. Religion: Jewish.

OFFICES: Capitol: Hart Senate Office Building 331, Washington, DC 20515, Phone: (202) 224-3341, Fax: (202) 228-3954, email: senator@feinstein.senate.gov. District: One Post Street, Suite 2450, San Francisco, CA 94104, Phone: (415) 393-0707, Fax: (415) 393-0710; 11111 Santa Monica Boulevard, Suite 915, Los Angeles, CA 90025, Phone: (310) 914-7300, Fax: (310) 914-7318; 750 B Street, Suite 1030, San Diego, CA 92101, Phone: (619) 231-9712, Fax: (619) 231-1108; 1130 O Street, Suite 2446, Fresno, CA 93721, Phone: (559) 485-7430, Fax: (559) 485-9689.

COMMITTEES: Judiciary; Appropriations; Energy and Natural Resources; Intelligence; Rules and Administration.

ELECTED: 1992

ELECTION HISTORY: San Francisco Board of Supervisors, 1969–1978; San Francisco mayor, 1978–1988

1994 ELECTION: Feinstein (D*) 47%
Huffington (R) 45%
2000 ELECTION: Feinstein (D*) 56%
Campbell (R) 36%
2006 ELECTION: Feinstein (D*) 60%
Mountjoy (R) 35%
RATINGS: ACU ADA AFL-CIO CoC GO LCV NTU PIRG
12 95 62 50 F- 100 13 84

Congressional Districts

See Bay Area Map

See Los Angeles Area Map

Bay Area Congressional Districts

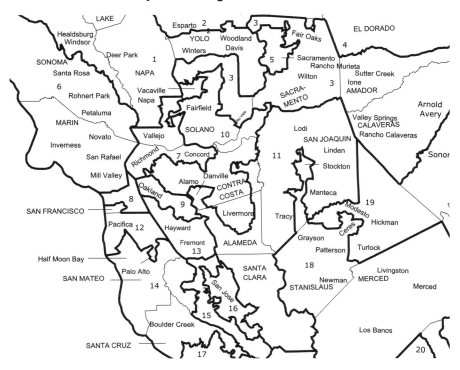

Los Angeles Congressional Districts

U.S. House of Representatives

JOE BACA (D)
43rd Congressional District

Counties: San Bernardino
Cities: Ontario, San Bernardino, Fontana, Colton
Ethnicity: 23% White, 58% Latino, 13% Black, 3% Asian
Voter Registration: 48% D – 34% R – 15% DS
President 04: 58% Kerry, 41% Bush

Joe Baca

The only vaguely Democratic enclave in the Inland Empire, the 43rd District has a rich and storied history as a battleground littered with the bones of Republican pretenders and the tattered ruins of GOP treasuries. Before the 2001 reapportionment, this was the 42nd District, and it included not only Democratic strongholds in San Bernardino County but Republican areas in Rancho Cucamonga and parts of Upland. Mapmakers dumped the latter, creating a safer Democratic district and one that may avoid the primary and general election mêlées that entertained voters in the old version.

At the center of all the previous carnage was Democrat George Brown, Jr., an unreconstructed liberal whose political demise was predicted every two years but who held onto his seat by increasingly slimmer margins all through the 1980s and 1990s. In fact, his most resounding victory—by 15%—came in his final election in 1998 against Republican businessman Elia Pirozzi. The previous election, against an unpredictable but colorful judge named Linda Wilde, had nearly ended in a dead heat, with Brown finally emerging victorious by less than 1%. Among his other prominent opponents were aviator Dick Rutan, creator and pilot of the Voyager aircraft that circumnavigated the globe without refueling in 1986, and Rob Guzman, who came within 2,500 votes of unseating Brown in 1994 despite having just moved into the district from Los Angeles. Brown died in office in 1999, and the district was rebuilt to make his successor a bit more secure come Election Day.

That successor is Democrat Joe Baca, a former state senator and assemblyman and political patriarch whose ambitions to create a mini dynasty in this part of the Inland Empire crashed and burned in 2006. His son, Joe, Jr., served in the Assembly from 2004 to 2006. Another son, Jeremy, tried to win his brother's seat in 2006 when Joe, Jr., ran for the state Senate. Both were mauled in Democratic primaries, temporarily derailing the dynasty, although the family still has allies sprinkled throughout local government in San Bernardino County. Not that Joe Baca, Sr., resembles a legislative heavyweight; in Congress, as in the legislature, he is the very picture of a backbencher.

At one point during his Assembly days, Baca had moved into leadership as speaker pro tem—a ceremonial post but one with high visibility because the pro tem runs Assembly floor sessions. Baca quickly proved unequal to the task and was replaced. In surveys of legislative competence conducted biennially by *California Journal* magazine, Baca routinely was characterized as a nonentity in Sacramento.

For all his perceived shortcomings in places other than the Inland Empire, Baca has consolidated power among Democrats at home. In 2004, for instance, he helped engineer the defeat of an old nemesis, former Assemblyman John Longville, in a race for the San Bernardino County Board of Supervisors.

Baca first gained a seat in the legislature in 1992 on his third try. His first two attempts had failed in the Democratic primary where he tried to unseat incumbent Jerry Eaves. In 1992, Eaves decided to return home and run for the San Bernardino Board of Supervisors. Baca defeated a pair of tough primary candidates to win the nomination and cruised to victory that fall over his Republican challenger. In 1998, he moved on to the state Senate, replacing a local legend that had been termed out, Democrat Ruben Ayala.

Baca's chance at even greater electoral glory came less than a year later when Brown suddenly died in office. The special election to replace him drew two prominent Democrats: Baca and Brown's widow, Marta. At the time, only one of the 35 most recent widows seeking to replace their husbands in Congress had been defeated. But Brown ran a campaign predicated on gun control, which proved to be a mistake in a district where Democrats trend heavily to the middle. Baca defeated Brown by less than 600 votes in a bitter and hard-fought campaign and then cooked his Republican opponent in the runoff. With reapportionment giving him much more breathing room than ever was enjoyed by George Brown, Baca can look forward to a lifetime commute to Washington.

Baca's fortunes, and the fortunes of the region he represents, changed when the Democrats regained control of the Congress. The Inland Empire had brandished clout in the Republican Congress, mainly through Republican Jerry Lewis of Redlands, who served as chairman of the House Appropriations Committee from 2004 to 2006. His influence takes an enormous hit as he cedes that chairmanship to a Democrat. Baca's star will ascend, but not nearly to the lofty heights enjoyed by Lewis. The most he can hope for is a subcommittee chairmanship, likely on Agriculture though more of his legislation might see the light of day now that Democrats are in charge.

Baca represents a district on the wrong side of affluence. The median family income is some 20% below the national average, while nearly 21% of residents live below the federal poverty line. Only 5% of district households earned more than $100,000 a year in 1999. If the Inland Empire has pockets of poverty, they exist here in San Bernardino and the communities along Interstate 10 such as Colton and industrial Fontana.

BIOGRAPHY: Born: Belin, NM, January 23, 1947. Home: Rialto. Education: AA, Barstow Community College; BA, CSU Los Angeles. Military: U.S. Army. Family: wife Barbara, four children. Religion: Catholic.

OFFICES: Capitol, 328 Cannon Office Building, Washington, DC 20515-0542, Phone: (202) 225-6161, Fax: (202) 225-8671, email: joe.baca@mail.house.gov.

District: 201 North E Street, Suite 102, San Bernardino, CA 92401, Phone: (909) 885-2222, Fax: (909) 888-5959.
COMMITTEES: Agriculture; Financial Services.
ELECTED: 1999
ELECTION HISTORY: Assembly, 1992–1998; State Senate, 1998–1999.
2002 ELECTION: Baca (D*) 66%
Neighbor (R) 31%
Mohler (L) 3%
2004 ELECTION: Baca (D*) 67%
Laning (R) 34%
2006 ELECTION: Baca (D*) 65%
Folkens (R) 36%

RATINGS:	ACU	ADA	AFL-CIO	CoC	GO	LCV	NTU	PIRG
	32	90	100	58	B-	75	16	59

XAVIER BECERRA (D)
31st Congressional District

Counties: Los Angeles
Cities: Los Angeles
Ethnicity: 10% White, 70% Latino, 4% Black, 14% Asian
Voter Registration: 58% D – 16% R – 21% DS
President 04: 77% Kerry, 22% Bush

Xavier Becerra

A heavily Latino district that previously bore the number 30, the 31st District endured minor tinkering in the 2001 reapportionment. Where once the district's southern boundary stopped at Pico Boulevard north of I-10, it now crosses the interstate and slides south to Slauson Avenue near Vernon and Huntington Park. It laps over South Alvarado Boulevard, although precincts west and east of Western Avenue were dropped. The district includes Koreatown and Dodger Stadium and surrounds downtown Los Angeles on three sides, gaining part of the city's South Central area in the process. It is a relatively poor area, with the median family income only half the U.S. average. Nearly 28% of the families and 30% of the individuals live below the federal poverty line.

The area once was represented by one of the state's pioneering Latino politicians—Democrat Ed Roybal, who fashioned a 30-year career in Congress. When Roybal retired in 1992, he sparked an inevitable clash between Latino factions eager to add his seat to their political portfolio. At first, Roybal tried to toss the district to his aide, Henry Lozano, but the primary was soon crowded with 10 contestants representing various factions. Lozano eventually withdrew and backed Assembly member Xavier Becerra, as did Roybal.

Becerra had little elective experience—one term in the legislature—but a wealth of connections. A deputy attorney general and aide to former state Senator Art Torres, now chairman of the California Democratic Party, Becerra won his Assembly seat in 1990 when its incumbent, Charles Calderon, moved to the state Senate. At the time, Becerra fashioned political credentials as a crime fighter based on his experience in the attorney general's office.

When Becerra sought Roybal's seat, he gained backing from a Latino faction that included Los Angeles County Supervisor Gloria Molina. Although part of a crowded slate, school board member Leticia Quezada provided Becerra's only real opposition, and she had support from, among others, Torres. Becerra captured 31% of the vote, enough for a comfortable margin over Quezada. It was the last time Becerra even breathed hard during an election. In 2006, he ran unopposed for an eighth term.

Becerra did not hit the ground running in Congress. Although a liberal freshman, Democrats who controlled the House gave him only his second-choice committee assignments, and he failed in efforts to advance his legislative passion, health-care reform. Two years later, Republicans took control of Congress and Becerra became a junior member of the minority. Toward the end of the 1990s, however, his influence began to mature, as he became chair of the Congressional Hispanic Caucus. He later became the first Latino to gain a seat on the House Ways and Means Committee. As a member of the minority, he has not put forward a robust legislative agenda. His current bills include an effort to create an American Latino Community Museum.

That situation will change now that Democrats have regained control of the House. As the only Southern California Democrat on Ways and Means, he is certain to have an influential voice on that committee. In addition, Speaker Nancy Pelosi named Becerra as "assistant to the speaker," a post that puts him in the vanguard of implementing the Democrats' policy agenda—"A New Direction for America."

Becerra has been a frequent and consistent critic of the war in Iraq, voting against the Bush administration–sponsored resolution for war in 2002. He was one of a handful of House members to demand a full explanation of the Bush plan before the U.S. invaded Iraq. At one point, Becerra called for a universal draft, believing it would have prevented the war.

BIOGRAPHY: Born: Sacramento, January 26, 1958. Home: Los Angeles. Education: AB, JD, Stanford; Universidad de Salamanca. Military: None. Family: wife Dr. Carolina Reyes, three daughters. Religion: Catholic.

OFFICES: Capitol, Longworth Building 1119, Washington, DC 20515, Phone: (202) 225-6235, Fax: (202) 225-2202, email: xavier.becerra@mail.house.gov. District: 1910 Sunset Boulevard, Suite 560, Los Angeles, CA 90026, Phone: (213) 483-1425, Fax: (213) 483-1429.

COMMITTEES: Ways and Means.

ELECTED: 1992

ELECTION HISTORY: Assembly, 1990-1992.

2002 ELECTION: Becerra (D*) 81%
                 Vega (R) 19%

2004 ELECTION: Becerra (D*) 81%
Vega (R) 19%
2006 ELECTION: Becerra (D*) 100%
RATINGS: ACU ADA AFL-CIO CoC GO LCV NTU PIRG
0   95   92   37 F- 100 14   85

HOWARD BERMAN (D)
28th Congressional District

Counties: Los Angeles
Cities: Los Angeles, San Fernando
Ethnicity: 31% White, 56% Latino, 4% Black, 6% Asian
Voter Registration: 56% D – 20% R – 20% DS
President 04: 71% Kerry, 28% Bush

Howard Berman

The southern portion of the 28th District covers the San Fernando Valley side of the Hollywood Hills, including the communities of Hollywood Hills, Studio City, Sherman Oaks, and Encino. These neighborhoods are affluent, white, and Jewish—reflecting perfectly their congressman—Howard Berman.

Moving deep into the San Fernando Valley are working class communities of North Hollywood, Van Nuys, Panorama City, Pacoima, Sylmar, and the small city of San Fernando. Today, these places are heavily Latino, a change of character from when the valley was first settled by whites more than half a century ago. The Jewish community long dominated the area's power structure, but times are changing. Although both Jews and Latinos here produce Democratic voters, the two communities sometimes clash—most notably in a 1998 state Senate race between Richard Katz, who represented the area in the Assembly, and then-City Councilman Richard Alarcon. The campaign, which Alarcon won by the width of a gnat's wing, was divisive and nasty, with racial overtones that still simmer below the surface.

Prior to the 2001 reapportionment, the district—then the 26th—mainly included Latino communities in the San Fernando flatlands. But that posed something of a political threat to the incumbent, so the Berman family, which has historically controlled the drawing of districts in southern California, re-crafted it to better suit the incumbent. Chief mapmaker Michael Berman added more white voters. Where once its southern border rested on Highway 101 west of Burbank, it now reaches into the Hollywood Hills almost to Sunset Boulevard.

A generation of voters knows Howard Berman as a congressman. But those with longer memories remember him as the front half of one of southern California's most powerful political machines—the Berman-Waxman operation was legendary for its fund raising and its success at promoting itself and others at the ballot box. Its power began to erode during the mid-1990s, diminished by a series of losses in 1992 and 1994. Term limits ate into its local dominance, as did the rise of Latino machines with deeper voting bases.

Berman served in the Assembly during the 1970s until his election to Congress in 1982. While in Sacramento, he was at the center of one of the legislature's most divisive speakership campaigns, fomenting a 1980 revolt against Speaker Leo McCarthy. The carnival lasted for more than a year and dominated most legislative activity, with the two camps running slates of candidates against each other in the 1980 Democratic primaries—even knocking off a few incumbent loyalists along the way. The brawl was settled in 1981 when a third contender, Willie L. Brown, Jr., captured the speakership with help from Republicans. McCarthy eventually served three terms as lieutenant governor; Brown held the speaker's post until 1995; and Berman left Sacramento for Washington after Brown created a congressional district for him in 1982.

Berman became more of a team player in Congress, championing causes such as the protection of intellectual property and civil liberties. He has become especially adept at forming bipartisan coalitions, so much so that the "Almanac of American Politics" credits him with influencing a wide range of legislation despite the fact that he is in the minority party. He has worked with Republicans to curb trade with nations that support or aid terrorists and to protect against false claims by whistleblowers.

With the new dawn of a Democratic age, Berman takes over as chairman of a Judiciary subcommittee near and dear to the industry that dominates his district, entertainment. Berman will honcho the panel on Courts, Internet and Intellectual Property and is ranking member of the House Ethics Committee. By tradition, that puts Berman in line to be chairman of a sensitive panel often asked to investigate and punish wayward colleagues.

BIOGRAPHY: Born: Los Angeles, April 15, 1941. Home: North Hollywood. Education: BA, LLB, UCLA. Military: None. Family: wife Janis, two daughters. Religion: Jewish.

OFFICES: Capitol, Rayburn Building 2221, Washington, DC 20515, Phone: (202) 225-4695, Fax: (202) 225-3196, email: howard.berman@mail.house.gov. District: 14546 Hamlin Street, Suite 202, Van Nuys, CA 91411, Phone: (818) 994-7200, Fax: (818) 994-1050.

COMMITTEES: International Relations; Judiciary; Ethics.

ELECTED: 1982

ELECTION HISTORY: Assembly, 1973–1982.

2002 ELECTION: Berman (D*) 71%
                    Hernandez (R) 23%
                    Ross (L) 5%

2004 ELECTION: Berman (D*) 71%
                    Hernandez (R) 22%
                    Ross (L) 6%

2006 ELECTION: Berman (D*) 74%

Kesselman (R) 19%
DeLear (G) 4%
Ross (L) 3%

RATINGS:	ACU	ADA	AFL-CIO	CoC	GO	LCV	NTU	PIRG
	4	90	93	41	F-	100	13	86

BRIAN BILBRAY (R)
50th Congressional District

Counties: San Diego
Cities: San Diego, Escondido, Solano Beach, Del Mar, Encinitas, Carlsbad, San Marcos
Ethnicity: 66% White, 19% Latino, 2% Black, 11% Asian
Voter Registration: 30% D – 44% R – 22% DS
President 04: 55% Bush, 44% Kerry

Brian Bilbray

An affluent slice of San Diego County, the 50th District includes oceanfront from Carlsbad to Del Mar, where it jogs inland around La Jolla. It is nearly a clone of the pre-reapportionment 50th District—with one exception. Poway has been cut off and replaced with a knob of San Diego south of La Jolla. Although the district includes a lot of beachfront property, the southern knob stops short of the Pacific, with La Jolla Boulevard and Torrey Pines included in the neighboring 53rd District. The median family income is $67,500—more than a third higher than the national average—while the poverty rate is 5%, a little less than half the national average.

In June 2005, incumbent Republican Randy Cunningham, a former Navy fighter pilot, was midway through his eighth term when his political rocket veered out of control. At issue were Cunningham's financial dealings with a defense contractor—a cozy relationship that drew more than passing interest from a federal grand jury, the U.S. Attorney's Office in Washington, D.C., and the FBI. Cunningham's problems first surfaced during spring 2005 when his hometown newspaper, the *San Diego Union-Tribune*, reported that the lawmaker had sold his Del Mar home to contractor Mitchell Wade, only to have Wade sell it a year later for a $700,000 loss. Once on the scent, the media rolled out other revelations, including the fact that Cunningham lived aboard Wade's yacht in Washington and Wade's firm has received more than $150 million in defense contracts over the past three years with Cunningham's help.

With the scandal mushrooming around him, Cunningham announced in July 2005 that he would not seek a ninth term in 2006. Fate, however, intervened long before Cunningham could ride peacefully into the sunset. By the time the election rolled around, Cunningham was in a federal prison in North Carolina and the district had a new incumbent, Republican Brian Bilbray, elected in a June 2006 special election.

Bilbray's rise was precipitated by Cunningham's resignation in November 2005 after pleading guilty to allegations of bribery that were breathtaking in scope. Cunningham's departure set up an April 2006 special election, a contest that drew 14—count 'em—14 Republicans, two Democrats, a Libertarian and an independent. Despite the profusion of GOP candidates, most attention focused on the Democrat considered most viable—Francine Busby, a suburban school board member who had lost to Cunningham in 2004. Because it was a special election, Busby could get herself elected by capturing 50% of the vote and thus avoid a runoff against whatever Republican emerged from the 14-way free-for-all. It was the Democrats' best chance to secure a seat where the GOP enjoyed such a lopsided registration edge, and the national Democratic Party poured money and resources into the effort, but she earned precisely the share of the district vote given to Democratic presidential hopeful John Kerry two years before—44%, or 6% short of her goal.

Bilbray, meanwhile, received only 15.3% of the vote, but that was enough to finish first among Republicans and qualify for a June 2006 runoff against Busby—a campaign that drew national attention again as a potential precursor to the fall election. Busby made ethics the centerpiece of her campaign, even though Bilbray was not Randy Cunningham. A former member of Congress himself, Bilbray spent most of this bruising contest on the defensive as the national spotlight focused not only on Cunningham but on a laundry list of scandals plaguing the Republican Congress.

At issue was a simple question: Could Democrats capitalize on Republican scandals to unseat a GOP candidate in a strong Republican district? Each side spent $10 million in quest of an answer, and when it was over, the response from voters was, "not quite." Bilbray took just shy of 50% of the vote, Busby came in with 45%. The two squared off again in November 2006, with Bilbray scoring slightly better and Busby resolving another question: What is the ceiling for a Democratic candidate in this district? Answer: 45%.

His election marks Bilbray's second go-around in the House. A member of the San Diego County Board of Supervisors, he was first elected to Congress in the Republican tide of 1994 where he defeated incumbent Democrat Lynn Schenk, and then survived bruising re-elections in 1996 and 1998 against Democrats Peter Navarro and Christine Kehoe. That Bilbray had become the political equivalent of a "Survivor" contestant was not lost on Democrats, who targeted him heavily in 2000. Assemblywoman Susan Davis was their club, and she finally ousted Bilbray in yet another narrow election.

As a local elected official and member of Congress, Bilbray has been independent and outspoken. He tackled welfare reform and environmental laws but also cast a few votes that vexed GOP leadership, especially then-Speaker Newt Gingrich. For instance, he voted against repealing the assault-weapon ban and for raising the federal minimum wage. His political demise, however, may have been linked to another vote where he went lock-step with Gingrich and his fellow Republicans—the vote to impeach then-President Bill Clinton. Davis used that as a grenade during their 2000 campaign.

In 2006, Bilbray returned to Congress as a minority Republican. Although he likely will remain on the Armed Services Committee, his influence will wane substantially under Democratic leadership.

BIOGRAPHY: Born: Coronado, January 28, 1951. Home: Imperial Beach. Education: BA, Southwestern College. Military: None. Family: wife Karen, five children. Religion: Catholic.

OFFICES: Capitol, Cannon Office Building 227, Washington, DC 20515, Phone: (202) 225-5452, Fax: (202) 225-2558, email: brian.bilbray@mail.house.gov. District: 462 Stevens Avenue, Suite 107, Solana Beach, CA 92075, Phone: (858) 350-1150, Fax: (858) 350-0750.

COMMITTEES: Armed Services; Veterans Affairs; Government Reform.

ELECTED: 2005

ELECTION HISTORY: Imperial Beach City Council, 1977–1985; Mayor, 1979–1985; San Diego Board of Supervisors, 1985–1995; U.S. House, 1995–2001.

2006 SPECIAL ELECTION:	Bilbray (R) 50%
	Busby (D) 45%
	King (L) 2%
	Griffith (I) 4%
2006 GENERAL ELECTION:	Bilbray (R*) 53%
	Busby (D) 44%
	King (L) 2%
	Clark (PF) 2%

RATINGS:	ACU	ADA	AFL-CIO	CoC	GO	LCV	NTU	PIRG
	78	NA	NA	95	F	0	NA	NA

MARY BONO (R)
45th Congressional District

Counties: Riverside
Cities: Moreno Valley, Hemet, Palm Springs, Palm Desert
Ethnicity: 50% White, 38% Latino, 7% Black, 3% Asian
Voter Registration: 36% D – 46% R – 15% DS
President 04: 56% Bush, 43% Kerry

Republican Mary Bono rocketed into the world of elective politics in January 1998 when her then-husband—celebrity/entertainer Sonny Bono—died in a skiing accident. Less than two weeks after his funeral, the former cocktail waitress announced that she would carry on his legacy by seeking his seat. Four months later, she was sworn into office. Immediately written off by insiders as a lightweight, she was thrust into a global spotlight, with print and television reporters hanging on her every move.

It was an unexpected and remarkable rise for someone who prepared for public life by attaining an art history degree and working as a personal fitness trainer. But

Mary Bono

Bono proved the insiders wrong by bringing a common sense demeanor and streetwise approach to the job of legislating, sometimes saving her colleagues' bacon in the process.

When she arrived in Washington, Bono enjoyed none of the quiet time often accorded freshman legislators for she became one of the newest members of the House Judiciary Committee. At the time, the committee had just launched the national angst that would become the impeachment of President Bill Clinton. With barely enough time to learn committee etiquette, Bono was matching wits with some of the sharpest legal scholars in the country, including Special Prosecutor Kenneth Starr whose report had sparked the proceedings by accusing Clinton of impeachable offenses. Bono was asking questions, on national television, with only her instincts to guide her. Her lack of Washington sophistication showed as Bono made mistakes and at times appeared to ramble through both questions and remarks.

But her performance also was refreshing and reminiscent of her late husband's self-deprecating take on himself and the world of politics. She was unpretentious, humble, and worldly wise—characteristics that not only served her well during relentless hearings but set her apart from congressional colleagues more inclined to posture than ferret out facts. Bono added a personal touch often missing in congressional hearings, asking, for instance, about the toll the Clinton impeachment had taken on Kenneth Starr's personal life. She flummoxed Clinton attorney Gregory Craig by wondering if he had ever told his children not to lie. At one point, she is credited with saving her GOP colleagues from a miscalculation by advising those who wanted testimony from Clinton intern Monica Lewinsky that they might be considered mean-spirited if they pressed the issue.

The daughter of a Pasadena surgeon, Bono was 24 when she became the fourth wife of the goofier half of "Sonny and Cher." She managed his Italian restaurant and settled into the role of political wife after he was elected mayor of Palm Springs and later to Congress. His death was as unexpected as it was tragic, and the imperatives of elective politics gave her little time to grieve.

Her election presented Bono with challenges not shared by most of her colleagues, and she was candid in discussing the problems faced by a single mom with a 3,000-mile commute to work each week. Although remarried in 2001, Bono nonetheless endured several years where she tried to balance the demands of congressional work with the equally important demands imposed by two growing children a continent away.

The celebrity associated with Bono's arrival in Congress eventually gave way to growth and maturity as a lawmaker. She shed the image of "Sonny's spouse," cutting her long blond hair and wearing tailored suits more befitting a legislator. After four re-elections, she has far outdistanced her late husband's shadow, even as she took up the same issues that occupied his time—foremost among them, efforts to revitalize the Salton Sea. Her current legislative load is modest, although she has carried a bill—with 61 cosponsors—to protect Internet users from unknowingly transmitting personal information through "spyware" programs. A loyal Republican, Bono backed the Bush administration's use of force in Iraq but broke with the president—and with House GOP leadership—on the issue of stem cell research, voting in 2005 to expand federal funding.

One of Bono's most significant pieces of legislation was her last under a Republican Congress—a clarification in law that allowed the families of firefighters killed in the line of duty to receive support from nonprofit agencies. At issue was more than $1 million raised by United Way on behalf of the survivors of five federal firefighters who died in early fall of 2006 while battling an arson-set fire in the Esperanza National Forest, located in Riverside County and in Bono's district. Under the current law, United Way could not raise money for individuals, and its tax-exempt status was put at risk if it tried to distribute the funds. Bono, with help from other members of the California delegation, pushed through a bill that rectified the problem. President George Bush signed the measure in time for the 2006 Christmas holidays.

Bono's district was renumbered in the 2001 reapportionment (from 44 to 45) but little changed in terms of geography. It still stretches through blistering desert from Blythe on the Arizona border to high-growth regions of Riverside County. Although it captures desert communities along Interstate 10 and Highways 74, 86, and 111, the 45th is not the pocket of wealth one might expect in a district that includes some of California's most lavish desert resorts. The median household income is some $1,500 below the national average, and 15% of its citizens live below the federal poverty line—a figure nearly 3% above the national average. Thirty percent of its households have incomes below $25,000 a year. As such, it is a district of contrasts, from the Palm Springs homes of such luminaries as the late former President Gerald Ford to less-well-off retirees living in trailer parks and young families in endless Riverside County subdivisions.

BIOGRAPHY: Born: Cleveland, OH, October 24, 1961. Home: Palm Springs. Education: BA, USC. Military: None. Family: Husband Glenn Baxley, two children. Religion: Presbyterian.

OFFICES: Capitol, Cannon House Office Building 104, Washington, DC 20515, Phone: (202) 225-5330, Fax: (202) 225-2961; email: mary.bono@mail.house. gov. District: 707 East Tahquitz Canyon Way, Suite 9, Palm Springs, CA 92264, Phone: (760) 320-1076, Fax: (760) 320-0596; 1600 E. Florida Avenue, Suite 301, Hemet, CA 92544, Phone: (909) 658-2312, Fax: (909) 652-2562.

COMMITTEES: Energy and Commerce.

ELECTED: 1998

ELECTION HISTORY: None.

2002 ELECTION: Bono (R*) 65%
Kurpiewski (D) 33%
Miller-Boyer (L) 2%

2004 ELECTION: Bono (R*) 67%
Meyer (D) 34%

2006 ELECTION: Bono (R*) 61%
Roth (D) 39%

RATINGS:

	ACU	ADA	AFL-CIO	CoC	GO	LCV	NTU	PIRG
	71	15	20	93	D	25	55	7

KEN CALVERT (R)
44th Congressional District

Counties: Orange, Riverside
Cities: Riverside, San Clemente, Corona, San Juan Capistrano, Norco
Ethnicity: 51% White, 36% Latino, 6% Black, 5% Asian
Voter Registration: 32% D – 47% R – 17% DS
President 04: 59% Bush, 40% Kerry

Ken Calvert

This district (originally numbered 43) was created to provide a congressional voice to hordes of voters streaming into the Inland Empire and, like many court-drawn districts of 1992, was compact, extending from the city of Riverside in the north to Murrieta in the south and taking in Corona, Lake Elsinore, and Perris along the way. Many of its residents were young families seeking affordable housing and enduring brutal commutes to and from jobs in Orange and San Diego counties.

Reapportionment radically altered the district in 2001, changing its number to 44, stripping away territory and voters between Lake Elsinore and Murrieta, and adding a swath of Orange County that touches the Pacific Ocean and links the old version with San Juan Capistrano and San Clemente. No longer compact, the 44th District now looks as though mapmakers poked a hole in the southern boundary that caused it to ooze toward the sea. It is only slightly more Republican than the previous district—but decidedly less Democratic, the percentage of Democratic voters having fallen from 36% to 32% because of reapportionment.

Anglos and Republicans dominate district politics, although the Latino population is growing—as it is everywhere in the Inland Empire. Economically, the 44th is middle class, with a median household income about 20% above the national average but with pockets of poverty in Riverside County. Nearly 9% of families live below the federal poverty line—less than one percent below the national average. More than 65% of the workforce is in white-collar occupations, 14% in service jobs, and 11% in trades, such as construction.

Incumbent Republican Ken Calvert has represented the district since its inception, but his early career was marked by struggle. In 1992 he beat six challengers to nab the GOP nomination and seemed assured of a trip to Congress from a district where Republicans outnumbered Democrats 46% to 42%. But the general election didn't quite go the way Republicans envisioned. With Bill Clinton romping to the presidency and district voters grumpy over base closures and economic malaise, Calvert suffered, actually trailing Democrat Mark Takano on Election Day and only snatching victory from the jaws of defeat after absentee ballots were counted. The campaign was hard-hitting, with the two sides trading half-truths.

But 1992 was merely the prelude to a savage campaign in 1994. With the 1992 result so close, the inevitable rematch played out from the start in the murky confines of the gutter. Calvert's reputation had been stung midway through his first term by an incident involving a prostitute, about which he had initially lied. A realtor, he also was burned by reports that he owed back taxes on property. Takano highlighted Calvert's warts in neon, while Calvert responded with a whispering campaign about Takano's sexuality. Calvert eventually prevailed by a more comfortable margin than in 1992, and then seemed to put his electoral troubles behind him with solid if unspectacular victories through the end of the decade. He had no trouble winning in the new district.

Calvert's early career in Congress was modest, with a small legislative agenda and a presence in the Republican-dominated House that could be characterized as "invisible." He spent a good portion of his time trying to ease the impacts of military downsizing, which took a heavy toll on his Riverside County district during the 1990s.

The Republican Congress helped Calvert expand his influence, especially when he was named chairman of the House Resources Subcommittee on Water and Power, which oversees federal water rights in the West. He served on the Armed Services Committee, which put him in a position to protect what remains of a military presence in his district. In the 2005 round of base closures, however, Calvert batted only .500. March Air Force Base was spared the axe, but the district stands to lose the Naval Surface Warfare Center in Corona.

Considered a moderate, Calvert has been a strong supporter of the war on terrorism, voting with the Bush administration on the use of force in Iraq and Afghanistan. He broke with the administration on one critical issue in 2005, joining 49 other House Republicans in favor of expanding federal support for stem cell research in defiance of the president and House leadership.

Recently, Calvert's experience as a realtor helped him financially but raised some troubling questions about his ethics. A May 2006 article in the *Los Angeles Times* detailed a series of his real-estate transactions on property near March Air Force Base. According to the paper, Calvert and a partner paid $550,000 for a four-acre parcel, which they sold in less than a year for close to $1 million. More significant, the *Times* reported, Calvert used the congressional practice of "earmarking" to gain funding for commercial development and freeway interchanges not far from the property and to support using federal money for transportation projects near other holdings. Earmarks are funding items inserted in legislation at the behest of a lawmaker without the usual review process. Calvert claimed that his critics were "trying to manufacture controversy" where none existed.

BIOGRAPHY: Born: Corona, June 8, 1953. Home: Corona. Education: BA, San Diego State University. Military: None. Family: Divorced. Religion: Episcopal.
OFFICES: Capitol, Rayburn Building 2201, Washington, DC 20515, Phone: (202) 225-1986, Fax: (202) 225-2004, email: ken.calvert@mail.house.gov. District: 3400 Central Avenue, Suite 200, Riverside, CA 92506, Phone: (909) 784-4300, Fax: (909) 784-5255.
COMMITTEES: Armed Services; Resources; Science.
ELECTED: 1992
ELECTION HISTORY: None.

2002 ELECTION: Calvert (R*) 63%
Vandenberg (D) 32%
Courtney (G) 5%
2004 ELECTION: Calvert (R*) 61%
Vandenberg (D) 36%
Akin (PF) 3%
2006 ELECTION: Calvert (R*) 60%
Vandenberg (D) 37%
Akin (PF) 3%

RATINGS:

ACU	ADA	AFL-CIO	CoC	GO	LCV	NTU	PIRG
84	0	13	93	A-	8	55	6

JOHN CAMPBELL (R)
48th Congressional District

Counties: Orange
Cities: Irvine, Newport Beach, Tustin
Ethnicity: 68% White, 15% Latino, 2% Black, 14% Asian
Voter Registration: 27% D – 49% R – 20% DS
President 04: 58% Bush, 40% Kerry

John Campbell

In terms of geography, the 48th District could be the best place to live in Orange County. It includes all of Dana Point at its southern tip, then moves northward to include Laguna Beach, Laguna Niguel, Laguna Coast, and Newport Beach, and swings eastward to encompass El Toro and the Tustin Foothills. The district is solidly Republican, the population two-thirds white, and the median household income level in one enclave, Laguna Coast, is at least $164,000, more than triple the statewide average. When one thinks of "Orange County," this district offers the stereotypes: affluence, beaches, and Republicans.

Until midway through 2005, the congressman who represented this attractive area for 17 years was Newport Beach–based Christopher Cox, a handsome, bright, Harvard-trained lawyer (he has a Harvard MBA as well). But in June 2005 President George W. Bush appointed Cox as chairman of the Securities and Exchange Commission, creating a rare opening in the state's congressional delegation.

And what do open House seats produce in the term-limited world of California politics? A brawl. In the case of the 48th District, the scramble to replace Cox was a closed affair among Republicans; Democrats need not apply in a district where over half of registered voters side with the GOP. At first, the race promised to attract the legislature's entire Orange County Republican delegation, including Senate Minority

Leader Dick Ackerman, Assembly members Chuck DeVore of Irvine, Todd Spitzer of Orange, and Mimi Walters of Laguna Niguel, and former Assemblywomen Pat Bates and Marilyn Brewer. Then another senator dropped in—John Campbell, who only won his Senate seat in 2004. Campbell is a wealthy businessman whose deep pocket gave Ackerman pause, and he dropped out as quickly as he dropped in, citing the disharmony a contested primary might cause just as the legislature was trying to come to grips with a budget. The rest soon followed, leaving Campbell alone with mostly unknown Republicans. The only exception was Brewer, who remained in until the end.

The most formidable opponent, in fact, was not a Republican or Democrat but a member of the American Independent Party—Jim Gilchrist, a founder of The Minutemen Project. That's the group of vigilantes who patrol the U.S.-Mexico border in an effort to stem the tide of illegal immigrants. Although Campbell blew away the opposition in the October 2005 primary, he failed to get the 50% of the vote required to avoid a runoff. More significant, Gilchrist polled 15% of that vote—nearly twice that of the Democratic frontrunner, Steven Young. In the December runoff, Campbell won with 44% to Young's 28%, with Gilchrist polling a respectable 26%.

Prior to his election to the state legislature in 2000, the agreeable and handsome Campbell was a wealthy businessman, an accountant by training, who made his pile as an automobile dealer. He came to the Assembly in 2000, handily winning his first election in the 70th Assembly District and winning two re-election campaigns with similar ease. He rose to become vice chairman of the Assembly Budget Committee, a key position in the Assembly GOP hierarchy that assured a position on the six-member, two-house conference committee that actually writes the state budget.

His election to the state Senate turned on a rough primary with colleague Ken Maddox—an affair that was not for the faint of heart. Campbell accused Maddox's campaign of faxing around a last-minute hit piece that accused Campbell of having an affair with a staff aide. After an initial round of denials by Maddox's chief of staff, Campbell obtained the surveillance tape from a local Kinko's that showed a Maddox campaign aide feeding a fax machine at the same transmission time listed on the offending fax. The document was sent after midnight on February 13, three weeks before the election, and prompted the outraged Campbell, who denied the allegation, to file a $4.25 million libel suit against the offending staffer. The bad blood persisted well after the election. In 2005 Maddox sought a gubernatorial appointment to the board of the Narcotic Addict Evaluation Authority, a $49,848-a-year job that determines parole suitability for convicted drug addicts. Several lawmakers, including Ackerman, endorsed Maddox for the position, but the appointment fell through after Campbell reportedly intervened with the governor's office.

In Washington, Campbell enjoyed majority status only briefly, although he secured a seat on the Budget Committee. He spent much of his time on border security, including support for construction of a border fence. He backed efforts to give the president line-item veto power over the federal budget—a proposal that went nowhere in the 109th Congress and is unlikely to gain much headway in a House dominated by Democrats.

BIOGRAPHY: Born: Los Angeles, July 19, 1955. Home: Irvine. Education: BA, UCLA; MS, USC. Military: None. Family: wife Catherine, two children. Religion: Presbyterian.

OFFICES: Capitol, Rayburn Building 2402, Washington, DC 20515, Phone: (202) 225-5611, Fax: (202) 225-9177, email: john.campbell@mail.house.gov. District: 610 Newport Center Drive, Suite 330, Newport Beach, CA 92660, Phone: (949) 756-2244, Fax: (949) 251-9309.

COMMITTEES: Budget; Financial Affairs; Veterans Affairs.

ELECTED: 2005

ELECTION HISTORY: Assembly, 2000-2004; state Senate, 2005.

2005 ELECTION: Campbell (R) 44%
                     Young (D) 28%
                     Cohen (L) 1%
                     Gilchrist (AI) 26%
                     Tiritilli (G) 1%

2006 ELECTION: Campbell (R*) 60%
                     Young (D) 37%
                     Cohen (L) 3%

RATINGS:

ACU	ADA	AFL-CIO	CoC	GO	LCV	NTU	PIRG
100	0	0	50	A	25	NA	NA

LOIS CAPPS (D)
23rd Congressional District

Counties: San Luis Obispo, Santa Barbara, Ventura
Cities: Oxnard, Santa Barbara, Goleta, Santa Maria
Ethnicity: 49% White, 42% Latino, 2% Black, 5% Asian
Voter Registration: 45% D – 31% R – 19% DS
President 04: 58% Kerry, 40% Bush

Prior to redistricting, the 23rd District encompassed all of San Luis Obispo and Santa Barbara counties, with the exception of the small city of Carpinteria in southern Santa Barbara County. Ten years ago the district was strongly Republican, until Walter Capps captured it for Democrats in 1996. It was the second time that Capps had run for the seat, having lost a close election to Republican Andrea Seastrand during the Republican tide year of 1994. Seastrand had gone into elective office in the late 1980s when her late husband, Eric, died of cancer and she replaced him in the Assembly. She moved to Congress in 1994 after incumbent Republican Michael Huffington ran for the U.S. Senate.

Ironically, Capps himself died in 1997 of a heart attack, prompting his widow, Lois, to run for his seat. The drama of that special election took place on the Republican side, however; not the Democratic side. Some influential Republicans, anxious to regain the seat, persuaded then-Assemblyman Brooks Firestone to run for Congress. Firestone already had announced his intention to run for lieutenant governor in

Lois Capps

1998 but turned his attention instead to the congressional race. Conservative Republicans stepped in with their own candidate, Assemblyman Tom Bordonaro, and the GOP primary turned nasty and divisive. Bordonaro won despite the fact that Speaker of the House Newt Gingrich supported Firestone. It was a pyrrhic victory for the right because Bordonaro proved far too conservative for the district. In the March 1998 special election, Capps beat Bordonaro after another brutally negative campaign, marked by independent expenditure campaigns on issues such as abortion. Capps solidified her hold on the district by beating Bordonaro again in the 1998 general election. Although pressed at times since, she has not had a seriously competitive re-election.

To ensure that Capps remains secure, mapmakers changed the district significantly in 2001. Losing most of its land mass, the district now goes south into Ventura County, absorbing the heavily Latino and Democratic city of Oxnard. At its deepest point, the district only extends 12 miles inland; for with every mile inland, the number of conservative voters increases. From the Monterey–San Luis Obispo county line south to Oxnard, it follows California's Central Coast and includes some of the state's most pristine beachfront communities, with voters who are wealthy and historically Republican. But many of them have been driven to vote Democratic because, as coastal residents, they tend to be liberal on the environment, if conservative on fiscal issues. As such, they vote their scenery not their pocketbooks, making them ripe for the Democratic Party.

Oxnard, an agricultural region in Ventura County, is the largest city in the district, overwhelmingly Democratic and anything but affluent. It is considerably different from its neighbors to the north. Latinos, 42% of the district's population, represent only 21% of its voters.

Capps serves on the Committee on Budget, Committee on Energy & Commerce and its Subcommittees on Energy & Air Quality and Health. She is vice-chair of the Women's Caucus and founder of the bipartisan School Health and Safety Caucus and bi-partisan Nursing Caucus. Her position on the energy committee has given her a platform to fight efforts to revive oil exploration and drilling off her district's coast. She was unable to prevent a bill to that effect from passing the 109th Congress, controlled by Republicans, but likely will attempt to reverse that legislation in the Democrat-controlled 110th Congress.

BIOGRAPHY: Born: Ladysmith, WI, January 10, 1938. Home: Santa Barbara. Education: BA, Pacific Lutheran University; MA, Yale, University of Santa Barbara. Military: None. Family: Widow, two children, three grandchildren. Religion: Lutheran.

OFFICES: Capitol, Longworth Building 1110, Washington, DC 20515, Phone: (202) 225-3601, Fax: (202) 225-5632, email: lois.capps@mail.house.gov. District: 1216 State Street, Suite 403, Santa Barbara, CA 93101, Phone: (805) 730-1710, Fax: (815) 730-9153; 1411 Marsh Street, Suite 205, San Luis Obispo, CA 93401,

Phone: (805) 546-8348, Fax: (805) 546-8368; 141 South A Street, Suite 204, Oxnard, CA 93030, Phone: (805) 385-3440, Fax: (805) 385-3399.
COMMITTEES: Budget; Energy and Commerce.
ELECTED: 1998
ELECTION HISTORY: None.
2002 ELECTION: Capps (D*) 59%
Rogers (R) 39%
Hill (L) 2%
2004 ELECTION: Capps (D*) 64%
Regan (R) 34%
Favorite (L) 3%
2006 ELECTION: Capps (D*) 65%
Tognazzini (R) 35%

RATINGS:

ACU	ADA	AFL-CIO	CoC	GO	LCV	NTU	PIRG
0	95	93	32	F-	100	14	91

DENNIS CARDOZA (D)
18th Congressional District

Counties: Fresno, Merced, Stanislaus, San Joaquin, Madera
Cities: Stockton, Ceres, Modesto, Patterson, Newman, Lathrop
Ethnicity: 39% White, 42% Latino, 6% Black, 9% Asian
Voter Registration: 48% D – 37% R – 12% DS
President 04: 49.6% Bush, 49.3% Kerry

Dennis Cardoza

Prior to the 2001 reapportionment, the 18th District had a nickname—"Condit Country"—reflecting the electoral prowess of the man who held the seat, Democrat Gary Condit of Ceres. Although voter registration slightly favored Democrats, Condit regularly smashed his Republican opposition—when it materialized at all. Such was Condit's reputation as a former state legislator and member of Congress that Democrats never worried about his ability to hold this Central Valley seat.

Then came the Chandra Levy scandal—and Condit's world fell apart.

Levy, a 24-year-old intern in Condit's Washington, D.C., office, disappeared in April 2001, and her remains were found a year later in a Washington park. Condit, it was revealed, had been romantically involved with Levy, and the resulting scandal created a media frenzy that dogged the incumbent for more than a year. Every sordid detail of his life was splashed across newspapers, tabloids, and television, including his reputation as a womanizer during his six years in the Assembly in the 1980s. Although Condit was investigated with regard to Levy's disappearance, no charges were ever filed and his involvement never progressed beyond the status of barroom gossip.

But perception is nine-tenths of political law, and Condit was deeply wounded by the incident. Ironically, Condit first came to Congress in a 1989 special election prompted by another scandal that ended the career of his predecessor—Democrat Tony Coelho. But unlike Coelho, who resigned rather than face either an investigation or the electorate, Condit fought for his career.

His timing was bad because the scandal coincided with reapportionment, and Democrats were no longer confident that Condit could hold a seat where voter registration was slipping more and more toward Republicans. So, Democratic mapmakers sought to bolster the seat—not for Condit, who they hoped would slip quietly into the sunset, but for another Democrat, Assemblyman Dennis Cardoza.

Although Condit's home in Ceres was retained inside the district, mapmakers pushed its northern boundary into Democrat-friendly precincts in Stockton—territory where voters knew Condit only as the focus of a scandal. Other parts of "Condit Country" were deleted, notably Turlock and the foothills of Stanislaus County. Democrats thought Condit would see the new district and opt for retirement. They especially trusted he would avoid what could only be a brutal primary fight with Cardoza.

But Condit had other ideas. Enmeshed in scandal and abandoned by most of his longtime financial backers and party leaders, the beleaguered incumbent sought an eighth term, fighting for his political life with the kind of vigor that had characterized his 30-year career in political life. As expected, the campaign drew national attention as Condit stumped tirelessly in every corner of the district. He confronted voters and detractors alike, including one campaign contributor who asked for her money back. He appeared at candidate forums from Merced to Stockton, waded through feedlots, sipped coffee at rural diners, staked out shopping malls, and mainly raised the anxiety level of his chief primary opponent.

Cardoza, who had been a Condit aide and whom Condit considered a traitor for making the challenge, had planned to run for the state Senate but was persuaded otherwise by Democratic leaders in both Sacramento and Washington, who fed his ambition for a seat in Congress. Chairman of the Assembly Rules Committee and a power in Sacramento, Cardoza brought the kind of stature to the race that Democrats sought. But he brought surprisingly little energy, preferring instead a rose garden campaign that saw him skip most forums until late in the game. Condit's spirited effort so reduced Cardoza's once-formidable lead in polls that, on the eve of the election, a battalion of Cardoza "volunteers" was summoned from the state Capitol to walk precincts and help with get-out-the-vote efforts.

In the end, the Democrats' reapportionment strategy worked. Condit did well in his old territory but carried only a quarter of the vote in newly acquired San Joaquin County. Sixty percent of the new vote went to Cardoza, who won the nomination with 54% of the overall tally in a six-candidate Democratic field.

Not that the district was secure for Democrats. The region has always tilted right despite its Democratic edge, the Republican candidate was a termed-out legislator, state Senator Dick Monteith, and the GOP was encouraged by Cardoza's less-than-vigorous primary endeavor—an effort that prompted *National Journal* analyst Charlie Cook to label Cardoza an "atrocious candidate" and others to brand him as lazy. Monteith represented most of the district in the legislature and benefited from the fact that the race was the only competitive congressional contest in California that fall, promising resources to wage a significant campaign.

The race gained national stature and President George W. Bush traveled to the Central Valley to stump for Monteith, while a host of national Democratic luminaries traipsed in for Cardoza. The campaign was marred by the continued presence of Clan Condit. A month before the election, Condit's grown children mailed a letter to Democrats, accusing Cardoza of trafficking on their father's troubles for political gain. Not that either candidate needed the Condits' help in driving the contest into the gutter. Both sides trotted out every conceivable malfunction of the opponent's ethical machinery in mailer after mailer.

At the final bell, however, Republicans misfired. Although late polls showed the election close, the GOP failed to provide the funding promised Monteith at the outset. That left his campaign stranded without sufficient resources to mount a strong finish, and Cardoza won. Once again, reapportionment had saved the Democrats. Although Monteith captured four of the five counties that make up the district, he took a pasting in San Joaquin County—the Stockton-based precincts added to the district to bolster Democrats and convince Condit to withdraw. That Democratic margin gave Cardoza the victory, and it was the last time he has been seriously challenged. His two subsequent elections have been walkovers.

Regarded as a liberal in Sacramento, Cardoza moved to the center in Congress, chairing the Blue Dog Coalition of moderate and conservative Democrats. Ironically, it is the same coalition that Condit helped found and symbolized during his tenure in Washington. Cardoza helped with the effort to found a new University of California campus at Merced in the Central Valley, gained seats on two committees vital to his district, Agriculture and Resources, and is a senior whip on the Democratic Steering and Policy Committee.

BIOGRAPHY: Born: Merced, March 31, 1959. Home: Atwater. Education: BA, University of Maryland. Military: None. Family: wife Dr. Kathleen McLoughlin, three children. Religion: Catholic.

OFFICES: Capitol: Cannon House Office Building 435, Washington, DC 20515, Phone: (202) 225-6131, Fax: (202) 225-0819, email: dennis.cardoza@mail. house.gov. District: 2222 M Street, Suite 305, Merced, CA 95340, Phone: (209) 383-4455, Fax: (209) 726-1065; 1321 I Street #1, Modesto, CA 95354, Phone: (209) 527-1914, Fax: (209) 527-5748; 445 West Weber Ave., Suite 240, Stockton, CA 95203, Phone: (209) 946-0361, Fax: (209) 946-0347.

COMMITTEES: Agriculture; International Relations; Resources.

ELECTED: 2002

ELECTION HISTORY: Atwater City Council, 1984–1987; appointed Merced City Council, 1994–1995; Assembly, 1996–2002.

2002 ELECTION: Cardoza (D) 51%
Monteith (R) 44%
Cripe (AI) 3%
DeGroat (L) 2%

2004 ELECTION: Cardoza (D*) 68%
　　　　　　　　Pringle (R) 32%
2006 ELECTION: Cardoza (D*) 66%
　　　　　　　　Kanno (R) 35%

RATINGS:	ACU	ADA	AFL-CIO	CoC	GO	LCV	NTU	PIRG
	44	85	100	67	B-	58	25	47

JIM COSTA (D)
20th Congressional District

Counties: Fresno, Kern, Kings
Cities: Fresno, Bakersfield, Hanford
Ethnicity: 21% White, 63% Latino, 7% Black, 6% Asian
Voter Registration: 51% D – 35% R – 11% DS
President 04: 51% Kerry, 49% Bush

Jim Costa

Boundaries in this southern San Joaquin Valley district have changed little since 1990 when it was drawn with an eye toward creating a heavily Latino, strongly Democratic district. Although the rest of the valley has started to trend Republican, it remains the strongest Democratic Valley seat between Los Angeles and Sacramento.

From the northwestern corner of sunny Fresno County, it reaches out to the less affluent neighborhoods of Fresno and Sanger before encompassing all of Kings County and dipping south into Kern County, where it picks up old Bakersfield neighborhoods and Lamont. Republicans hold a bit more sway in the southernmost reaches of the district, where it overlaps the 32nd Assembly district, typically considered as safely Republican.

As in most Valley districts, the economy is heavily dependent on agriculture. The livelihoods of many district voters are linked to harvests of grapes, cotton, tomatoes, nuts, and citrus, as well as the sale of cattle, poultry, and milk. Large swaths of land host some of the nation's largest farming operations. Irrigation and cheap steady water supplies are crucial to the farmers, but both are increasingly threatened by growing demand in southern California and halting but certain state moves toward a freer market for water—a trend that could cost the valley millions in the long run. Other government supports are crucial to the district, including crop price subsidies and immigration law exceptions. A guest worker program has long been politically popular, though it has failed to gain congressional support. For all the agricultural bounty, the local economy still does not generate enough high paying jobs, and the district suffers from fairly steep unemployment and poverty.

Beyond agriculture, food processing dominates in Fresno County, and oil extraction remains important in Kern County, where four of the nation's 10 largest oil fields are found. An aggressive pro-business stance has attracted major businesses such as The Gap in Fresno and State Farm Insurance and Frito-Lay in Kern County. In Kings County, government employs many residents at two state prisons, Avenal and Corcoran, and Lemoore Naval Air Station. Together these facilities provide a quarter of the county's jobs.

Poor air quality plagues the district, which has one of the dirtiest air basins in the nation according to the Great Valley Center. Fresno County alone has taken on more than $300 million in health care costs to combat asthma, and heavily concentrated ozone has been blamed for nearly 15% in reduced crop yields.

Regardless, the district's population continues to grow. Large numbers of Latinos and Asians, especially Hmong, continue to move to the region, seeking work and joining family. The most heavily Latino regions of the district are in Firebaugh, Sanger, Delano, McFarland, Mendota, Avenal, and Lamont. Asians have settled mostly in Fresno, Delano, and unincorporated parts of the district.

Despite heavy Democratic leanings, the district produced a highly competitive congressional race in 2004, prompted by the retirement of Democrat Cal Dooley. The contest pitted a pair of Sacramento veterans—former Democratic state Senator Jim Costa and current state Senator Roy Ashburn, a Republican.

At first glance, Costa seemed a shoe-in. The Fresno native and third-generation family farmer started his legislative career in the state Assembly in 1978 at age 26. He went on to become a state senator in the old 16th District, the footprint of which covered the present congressional district. In Sacramento, he chaired the Senate Agriculture and Water Resources Committee and served on three others, including the Finance, Investment and International Trade, Housing and Community Development, and Transportation committees. During his long tenure, Costa was considered a consummate insider. At one point, he even served a term as president of the National Conference of State Legislatures.

But despite strong local name recognition and legislative credentials, he faced dual hurdles: First, Dooley endorsed his former chief of staff, Lisa Quigley, in the primary. Quigley regurgitated old campaign bromides used against Costa for nearly 20 years—his 1986 arrest for soliciting a prostitute and a 1994 incident in which police found drug paraphernalia in his house. There was nothing new in these charges, which had been fully vetted in previous elections, and Costa went on to win 73% of the primary vote.

Sensing an opportunity for a win, Republicans poured more than $1.5 million into Ashburn, attacking Costa as a liberal allied with recalled Governor Gray Davis and suggesting he would raise taxes on low-income families. Polling by the Costa campaign indicated that voters were far more interested in health care and jobs. Emphasizing his record on farm worker safety and housing, water bond issues and well drilling, Costa responded with an attack on Ashburn, noting that, as a senator, he was the only legislator of either party to vote against a tax check-off for breast cancer research. Costa won with 53% of the vote. With the Ashburn challenge safely behind him, Costa drew nary an opponent in 2006, running unopposed.

In Washington, Costa tacked to the middle, as evidenced by the fact that his rating from the U.S. Chamber of Commerce is 28 points higher than his rating from the League of Conservation Voters, and he landed a B- from Gun Owners of America; most California Democrats received an F-. His bill load mostly consisted of suspending the duty on a variety of pesticides and herbicides, and another measure directed at federal authority over Indian gaming.

BIOGRAPHY: Born: Fresno, April 13, 1952. Home: Fresno. Education: BS, CSU Fresno. Military: None. Family: Single. Religion: Catholic.

OFFICES: Capitol: Longworth Building 1004, Washington, DC 20515, Phone: (202) 225-225-3341, Fax: (202) 225-9308, email: congressmanjimcosta!@mail.house. gov. District: 855 M Street, Suite 940, Fresno, CA 93721, Phone: (559) 495-1620, Fax: (559) 495-1027; 2700 M Street, Suite 225, Bakersfield, CA 93301; Phone: (661) 869-1620; Fax: (661) 669-1027.

COMMITTEES: Science; Agriculture; Resources.

ELECTED: 2004

ELECTION HISTORY: State Assembly, 1978–1994; State Senate, 1994–2002.

2004 ELECTION: Costa (D) 53%
Ashburn (R) 47%

2006 ELECTION: Costa (D*) 100%

RATINGS:

ACU	ADA	AFL-CIO	CoC	GO	LCV	NTU	PIRG
32	80	93	70	B-	42	23	59

SUSAN DAVIS (D)
53rd Congressional District

Counties: San Diego
Cities: San Diego, Lemon Grove, Imperial Beach, Coronado
Ethnicity: 51% White, 29% Latino, 8% Black, 9% Asian
Voter Registration: 41% D – 29% R – 25% DS
President 04: 61% Kerry, 38% Bush

This district was known as the 49th in the previous reapportionment and that incarnation was a little too dicey for Democratic ambitions. Both parties represented it during the 1990s, although the Democratic hold was brief—Lynn Schenk held it from 1992 to 1994 before Brian Bilbray defeated her in a year when Republican fortunes ran supreme. Bilbray held forth until 2000 when Democrats took it back. By then, Democrats had a mere 3% registration edge (39% to 36%, with 18% declined to state), setting the stage for an overhaul in 2001. (The old 49th District began life in 1992 with an unusual twist: Three incumbent Republican congressmen—Randy Cunningham, Bill Lowery, and Duncan Hunter—were tossed into it by that year's nonpartisan, court-ordered reapportionment, and all three fled rather than run there.)

Susan Davis

When mapmakers assaulted the San Diego area in 2001, they took a knob of Republican precincts surrounding La Jolla out of the now-numbered 53rd District and replaced them with friendly territory that dribbles south of Highway 94 to pick up Lemon Grove. That change and other tweaks looked subtle on a map but reduced Republican registration to 30 percent, making the new district safe Democratic territory. Those registering decline-to-state are a growing force in the district and now comprise a quarter of voters.

Economically, the district is not what one thinks about San Diego. Twenty percent of its residents live below the poverty line—well above the 12% national average. The median household income is some $5,000 below the national average. But this is San Diego, and the median price of a home is nearly $100,000 above the national average.

Democrat Susan Davis first captured the district in 2000, ousting three-term incumbent Brian Bilbray in a hard-fought election. A termed-out assemblywoman, Davis benefited from Bilbray's stature atop the Democrats' congressional target list, and the Democratic Congressional Campaign Committee poured or steered millions of dollars in resources into her campaign. Republicans responded in kind as the two parties battled across the national map for control of Congress.

Bilbray found himself in crosshairs because of the region's propensity to elect Democratic women in Republican-leaning districts and because he had barely survived a similar assault two years earlier when registration figures were more favorable for Republicans. Davis was no stranger to tough campaigns in difficult districts, having won and held an Assembly seat for three terms in districts where Democrats never enjoyed much of an edge.

The 2000 campaign attracted some $8 million in special-interest money, much of it spent for television ads that made Davis and Bilbray as ubiquitous on local airwaves as Regis Philbin. President Bill Clinton stumped the district for Davis, motivated in part by Bilbray's vote for impeachment. U.S. Senator John McCain came in for Bilbray. Davis was considered the ideal Democrat for the district. A centrist and former school board member, Davis otherwise had only one flaw—she had been in office and voted for energy deregulation as a state legislator, a fact that Bilbray jumped on with alacrity in a year when San Diego became the first battleground in what would become an explosive statewide issue. Davis was saved, in part, by timing—the crisis, which saw local energy rates triple over the summer, had abated by November. Davis won by 4%. Reapportionment then removed anything that could be considered an electoral threat, and Davis has racked up solid majorities ever since.

Since coming to Congress, Davis has moved away from her centrist tag although she bills herself as a consensus builder. A member of the Armed Services Committee, Davis opposed U.S. intervention in Iraq and has spoken out against Bush administration policies since the overthrow of Sadam Hussein. In 2002 she voted against the Iraq war resolution and since against most appropriations for prosecuting both the war and the occupation—a stance that served her well as the war slipped into the realm of a national disaster. With so large a military presence in and around her district, Davis has worked on issues affecting veterans and military procurement, as well as homeland security issues that affect the U.S.-Mexico border.

BIOGRAPHY: Born: Cambridge, MA, April 13, 1944. Home: Kensington. Education: BA, UC Berkeley; MA, University of North Carolina. Military: None. Family: husband Steve, two children, two grandchildren. Religion: Jewish.
OFFICES: Capitol, Longworth Building 1526, Washington, DC 20515, Phone: (202) 225-2040, Fax: (202) 225-2948, email: susan.davis@mail.house.gov. District: 4305 University Avenue, Suite 515, San Diego, CA 92105, Phone: (619) 280-5353, Fax: (619) 280-5311.
COMMITTEES: Armed Services; Education; Workforce.
ELECTED: 2000
ELECTION HISTORY: San Diego Unified School District Board, 1983–1992; Assembly, 1994–2000.
2002 ELECTION: Davis (D*) 62%
VanDeWeghe (R) 38%
2004 ELECTION: Davis (D*) 67%
Hunzeker (R) 28%
Rockwood (G) 3%
Van Susteren (L) 2%
2006 ELECTION: Davis (D*) 68%
Woodrum (R) 30%
Lippe (L) 2%

RATINGS:	ACU	ADA	AFL-CIO	CoC	GO	LCV	NTU	PIRG
	0	90	93	41	F	92	14	96

JOHN DOOLITTLE (R)
4th Congressional District

Counties: El Dorado, Lassen, Modoc, Nevada, Placer, Plumas, Sierra, Sacramento
Cities: Roseville, Orangevale, Grass Valley, South Lake Tahoe, Auburn, Nevada City, Truckee, Placerville, Susanville, Rocklin
Ethnicity: 84% White, 9% Latino, 1% Black, 3% Asian
Voter Registration: 30% D – 48% R – 17% DS
President 04: 61% Bush, 37% Kerry

Geographically, the 4th District underwent reconstructive surgery in the 2001 reapportionment, with five Sierra Nevada counties slashed away south of El Dorado County. Gone are Amador, Calaveras, Alpine, Tuolumne, and Mono counties. Attached in their stead were five counties—Nevada, Sierra, Plumas, Lassen, and Modoc—that extend the new district north from Placer County all the way to the Oregon border. The change tilted the political landscape not one whit.

John Doolittle

At its core, it is a district of contrasts, from its sparsely populated and remote northeast corner to the southeastern tourist meccas between Truckee and South Lake Tahoe to the booming suburban areas between Roseville and Auburn, and between Sacramento and Placerville. Since the 1960s the district has seen a constant influx of affluent migrants seeking relief from the urban jumbles of Sacramento and the Bay Area. Along the spines of Interstate 80 and U.S. Highway 50, these migrants have created suburban jumbles that more often resemble Orange County than the bucolic valley and foothill communities they have transformed.

Under normal circumstances, the overwhelmingly Republican district is the kind of place that a conservative Republican such as John Doolittle can regard as comfortably secure.

But life has been anything but normal for Doolittle and his beleaguered constituents. The congressional scandals that rocked the Republican Congress for much of 2005 and 2006 created a fault line beneath Doolittle's mountainous little pasture and threatened to end his long career in politics. Those scandals focused on a lobbyist named Jack Abramoff, who eventually pled guilty to a litany of misdeeds, bribes, and influence peddling and agreed to cooperate with federal prosecutors. Among those close to Abramoff over the years was John Doolittle, whose wife, Julia, worked for the disgraced lobbyist.

Abramoff was only the start of Doolittle's troubles. It was revealed that the lawmaker's wife ran his fund-raising operation, taking a 15% cut of every dollar raised for his campaign coffers. In essence, his fund-raising enriched his family income—a controversial practice that tiptoes up to the line marked "bribe." It was rumored that Doolittle was under investigation by several federal agencies, including the FBI, although nothing was confirmed. Still, Doolittle hired a criminal attorney to address the matter.

Republicans and Democrats both seized on the incumbent's troubles in an effort to send him packing. He drew a spirited primary challenge from Auburn Mayor Mike Holmes, who focused on Doolittle's ethical troubles. As is his wont, Doolittle wrapped himself in the flag and his conservative ethos, branded Holmes a liberal too filled with hubris—and beat back the challenge by accumulating two-thirds of the Republican vote. He spent $1 million on the primary, however, a signal that he considered himself highly vulnerable.

The primary merely set the stage for a bruising general election campaign against Democrat Charlie Brown, a retired Air Force colonel and Vietnam combat veteran who savaged Doolittle over the Abramoff scandal and over his support for the Iraq war. Republicans, fearful of losing control of Congress, rallied to Doolittle's defense. President George W. Bush and Vice Pres. Dick Cheney both visited the district, appearing at events and fundraisers for the incumbent. Doolittle tried to paint Brown as soft on terrorism and a war wimp, but the charges rang hollow, given the Democrat's military record. At the buzzer, Doolittle eked out his ninth term in Congress, although he received less than 50% of the vote and won by only 3%. Two years before, he had won by 30%. Brown and Doolittle ran close in all nine counties in the district, but Brown won only in Democrat-leaning Nevada County.

Following the election, Doolittle announced that he would forego any Republican leadership position and concentrate on re-building his reputation and political base. It was an announcement couched in the obvious; with the Abramoff scandals yet to resolve themselves completely, Doolittle was damaged goods in Washington, as well as in the California foothills.

Despite his long career, Doolittle often has skated on the edge of political oblivion. He first arrived on the scene in 1980 when he won a seat in the state Senate at age 29. Early in his political life, Doolittle's career was saved by a bit of creative mapmaking known as the "Doolittle Dip"—the name given to a piece of real estate added to the 1st Senate District in 1982. The same redistricting plan had vaporized Doolittle's existing district even though he had two years remaining on his term. As a result, he faced un-employment in 1984 unless help was forthcoming. In 1982, he tried to run in a nearby Democratic district but was defeated by incumbent Leroy Greene. Senate Republicans fashioned a rescue, aided by a statewide referendum that delayed implementation of a new redistricting plan. Essentially, Republicans tried to persuade veteran Republican state Senator Ray Johnson, who represented the 1st District, to retire by shifting his Butte County base to the 4th District and replacing it with a soupcon of Sacramento County, which just happened to include Doolittle's home. Doolittle immediately de-clared that he would run for the 1st District seat in 1984.

Johnson did not go quietly. Angered by the scheme, he moved back into the 1st District, declared himself an independent to avoid a primary shootout with Doolittle, and waged a spirited fight in the fall. With the election in doubt, Doolittle perpetrated a bit of fraud on the electorate by financing a mailer on behalf of the district's under-funded and virtually nonexistent Democrat. Republicans hoped to siphon potential Democratic votes away from the independent Johnson, who claimed foul. The ploy helped Doolittle eke through by a mere 3%.

That kind of bare-knuckles, anything-goes brawling marked several of Doolittle's early campaigns, which often were characterized by the kind of gross distortions that raised mudslinging to an art form. In his 1994 campaign for re-election to Congress, for instance, he falsely accused his Democratic opponent of having run a business into bankruptcy. That same year the Fair Political Practices Commission fined Doolittle and an aide for laundering money into the 1991 state Senate campaign of Republican Tim Leslie.

After his election to Congress in 1990, Doolittle worked his way up in Republi-can leadership. Unlike other GOP colleagues from California, Doolittle did not hold a glitzy title or chairmanship. But he became secretary of the House Republican Confer-ence, the sixth highest elected office in the House, sat on the Appropriations Commit-tee, and was one of 17 majority whips.

Politically, Doolittle is conservative, a strident opponent of stem cell research, abortion, same-sex marriage, and free-spending liberals; an ardent champion of Min-uteman border patrols, gun rights, the war in Iraq, and school vouchers for parochial schools.

Over the years, Doolittle devoted much of his legislative effort to building the Auburn Dam. He eventually helped negotiate a comprehensive water plan for northern

California with an old adversary, the late Democratic Congressman Robert Matsui—an ardent foe of the dam project. Doolittle has been a strong advocate for creation of a "Hydrogen Highway" to fuel cars and help ease U.S. dependence on foreign oil.

Having fought off both Holmes and Brown, his future now depends on the whims and doggedness of federal prosecutors. Although his attorney stated late in 2006 that Doolittle was not the "target" of a Justice Department investigation, Doolittle himself told the *Sacramento Bee* that he does not know whether he faces criminal liability or is under investigation. Abramoff is singing in Uncle Sam's ear and it is unclear to all but federal attorneys whether Doolittle is part of the lyric. If so, he could face charges of political corruption. And that circumstance would accomplish what no political opponent has yet been able to do—ring down the curtain on Doolittle's long-running career.

BIOGRAPHY: Born: Glendale, October 30, 1950. Home: Rocklin. Education: BA, UC Santa Cruz; JD, McGeorge School of Law. Military: None. Family: wife Julia Harlow, two children. Religion: Mormon.
OFFICES: Capitol: Rayburn Building 2410, Washington, DC 20515, Phone: (202) 225-2511, Fax: (202) 225-5444, email: john.doolittle@mail.house.gov. District: 4230 Douglas Boulevard, Suite 200, Granite Bay, CA 95746, Phone: (916) 786-5560, Fax: (916) 786-6364.
COMMITTEES: Appropriations; House Administration.
ELECTED: 1990
ELECTION HISTORY: State Senate, 1981–1991.
2002 ELECTION: Doolittle (R*) 65%
        Norberg (D) 32%
        Roberts (L) 3%
2004 ELECTION: Doolittle (R*) 65%
        Winters (D) 35%
2006 ELECTION: Doolittle (R*) 49%
        Brown (D) 46%
        Warren (L) 5%

RATINGS:	ACU	ADA	AFL-CIO	CoC	GO	LCV	NTU	PIRG
	92	0	13	85	A	0	55	8

DAVID DREIER (R)
26th Congressional District

Counties: Los Angeles, San Bernardino
Cities: Rancho Cucamonga, Arcadia, Upland, Glendora, San Dimas
Ethnicity: 53% White, 24% Latino, 5% Black, 16% Asian
Voter Registration: 34% D – 44% R – 18% DS
President 04: 55% Bush, 44% Kerry

David Dreier

David Dreier has been in Congress for a quarter century and for most of that time, he toiled as a strident conservative, anti-government foot soldier in the minority. He campaigned for a balanced budget, the transfer of more federal lands and services to private hands, and deregulation of just about any industry that came under the ogling eyes of government. His was an ideological fervor that didn't always sit well with some older GOP colleagues, including get-along moderates such as then-Republican House Leader Bob Michel of Illinois.

But when lightning struck the GOP in the 1994 election, few Republicans benefited as much as Dreier. When it struck Democrats in 2006, few Republicans lost as much as Dreier.

In the early 1990s, he joined with other conservatives to oust fellow Californian Jerry Lewis from his leadership post, then replaced the moderate Lewis on the National Republican Congressional Committee. As a result, Dreier became a chief recruiter of Republican candidates in western states. That, in turn, put Dreier on the inside of Newt Gingrich's leadership team at the precise moment that Republicans seized control of the House in 1994 and the conservative Gingrich became the first Republican Speaker in 40 years. Dreier's proximity to Gingrich earned him chairmanship of the Republicans' standing committee transition team, which set out to overhaul the House after four decades of Democratic rule. His panel axed three full committees and 30 subcommittees while reshaping many others to reflect GOP priorities, and that performance earned Dreier the vice-chairmanship of one of the most significant committees in Washington—Rules.

In 1999 Rules Chairman Gerald Solomon of New York retired, and Dreier took his place. At the time, the San Dimas incumbent had become the most powerful Californian ever to serve in the House—more so than the late Phil Burton who once held the number-three position in the Democratic hierarchy. The Rules Committee, more than any other panel, shapes legislation; it sets the parameters for House debate on bills and holds sway over which amendments will be offered. Dreier held the California slot on the Republican Steering Committee, which decides committee assignments. Clearly, Dreier had become a consummate Washington insider—in the majority party. And in 2001, it became a majority party that controlled the White House.

The 2006 elections reversed Dreier's fortunes and eclipsed his stature as California's most-powerful member of the House. Democratic control of the House cost Dreier his chairmanship. And his historic stature was knocked about when San Franciscan Nancy Pelosi became the first Californian ever to ascend to the very pinnacle of House leadership, the speakership.

Dreier's heady rise in the House retarded what otherwise might have been an even steeper climb up the political ladder. In 1998, for instance, he was on the very short list of potential Republican challengers to Democratic U.S. Senator Barbara Boxer. Having already amassed a sizeable campaign treasury, Dreier would have posed a formidable problem for the liberal Boxer—considered the most vulnerable Democrat in the Senate. Knowing he was about to be named chairman of Rules, Dreier declined an all-or-nothing confrontation that would have seen him defeat Boxer or hit the streets. The nomination went to state Treasurer Matt Fong, who was flattened by Boxer in November.

Dreier also declined to run against Boxer in 2004, making it clear that he would not mull over other options while Republicans controlled the House. He has admitted that he now is a creature of Washington and the House, and he is not motivated to give up what has become a cushy situation. Much of the cush has gone out of his situation for the moment, but Dreier's time as a Senate contender may have passed. Boxer does not stand for election again until 2010, and other younger, more aggressive Republicans are in the queue of potential challengers.

Cushy in Washington did not always mean comfortable at home, and Dreier wanted a more secure district from the 2001 reapportionment. It was not an unreasonable request, given the numbers. By the time he ran his final race in the old district—the 28th—Democrats actually held a 1% edge in voter registration and Dreier was held under 60% of the vote. As chairman of Rules, he could demand a better margin as part of the bipartisan compromise that became the new political map of California.

Dreier got his wish, at least on paper. In the west, a little hook added La Canada Flintridge, while the southern portion pushed west from Arcadia to take in San Marino. West Covina was dropped. Most significant, where the old district had stopped at the Los Angeles County line, the new version invaded San Bernardino County to capture Republican strongholds in Upland and Rancho Cucamonga. By the time mapmakers finished massaging Dreier's new 26th District, registered Republicans outnumbered their Democratic counterparts by 13%.

The result: Dreier did worse. Although he polled 64% of the vote in 2002—the first election in his new district—he suffered something of a meltdown two years later. In 2004 the incumbent powerbroker was Teflon challenged, attracting bad publicity that stuck. In the middle of the summer, he refused to appear on a popular Los Angeles drive-time talk show—KFI radio's "John and Ken Show"—and the two hosts savaged him on air for three months leading up to the election. Then Dreier was subjected to a whispering campaign about his sexuality, the rumors fueled by an article in the alternative LA Weekly newspaper. The paper reported that Dreier was the subject of a Web site that exposes as homosexual those Republicans who promote an anti-gay agenda. The allegations were fanned when they appeared on The Raw Story, a liberal blog. It didn't help that Dreier's 2004 Democratic opponent, Cynthia Matthews, was gay and cited the articles—and whispers—in her campaign.

Whatever the reason, Dreier was held to 54% of the vote, and the message may have seeped through to the candidate. Whether it is coincidence or a matter of conscience, Dreier has inched toward the center in 2005. In May, for instance, he broke with President Bush and his own House leadership team to vote in favor of a bill that extends federal funding for stem cell research—by most polls, a popular idea in California. It was not the conservative position on stem cell, and his vote could signal that Dreier—the creature of Washington—has gazed down from his lofty perch and decided to pay a bit more attention to notions that matter back home.

The change didn't provide much oomph in his 2006 re-election, again against Matthews. He did better than in 2004 but still failed to break 60% of the vote. With his role in Washington diminished, Dreier may be paying more attention to his district, but that has never been his forte. He is not in trouble at home, not from Democrats at least. But he drew two primary opponents in 2006 and, combined, they received more than a third of the Republican vote. Neither of those challengers was considered a major threat, but that doesn't mean such a threat might not materialize down the road. In an era of term limits, primary challenges launched by state legislators against incumbent members of Congress are becoming more frequent. With this in mind, Dreier must keep a sharp eye on the home front, lest some ambitious, termed-out Republican—with nothing to lose—assaults from the right.

BIOGRAPHY: Born: Kansas City, MO, July 5, 1952. Home: San Dimas. Education: BA, Claremont-McKenna College; MA, Claremont Graduate School. Military: None. Family: Single. Religion: Christian.

OFFICES: Capitol, Cannon House Office Building 233, Washington, DC 20515, Phone: (202) 225-2305, Fax: (202) 225-7018, email: david.dreier@mail.house. gov. District: 2220 East Route 66, Suite 225, Glendora, CA 91740, Phone: (626) 852-2626, Fax: (866) 373-6321.

COMMITTEES: Rules (chair).

ELECTED: 1980

ELECTION HISTORY: None.

2002 ELECTION: Dreier (R*) 64%
                    Mikels (D) 34%
                    Weissbach (L) 3%

2004 ELECTION: Dreier (R*) 54%
                    Matthews (D) 43%
                    Weissbach (L) 4%

2006 ELECTION: Dreier (R*) 57%
                    Matthews (D) 38%
                    Graham (AI) 2%
                    Brown (L) 3%

RATINGS:

ACU	ADA	AFL-CIO	CoC	GO	LCV	NTU	PIRG
84	0	13	93	B-	17	55	6

ANNA ESHOO (D)
14th Congressional District

Counties: San Mateo, Santa Clara, Santa Cruz
Cities: Sunnyvale, Palo Alto, Half Moon Bay, Redwood City
Ethnicity: 60% White, 18% Latino, 3% Black, 17% Asian
Voter Registration: 45% D – 27% R – 23% DS
President 04: 68% Kerry, 30% Bush

The San Mateo County town of Redwood City, nestled between Belmont and Palo Alto on the peninsula south of San Francisco, boasts a picturesque downtown with an arch proudly announcing "Climate Best by Government Test." This obscure relic is

Anna Eshoo

based on surveys by the United States and German governments at the beginning of the last century that found Redwood City situated in one of the three most ideal climates worldwide.

Redwood City itself has long since been subsumed into the economic powerhouse collectively labeled "Silicon Valley," and its climate has no doubt suffered from traffic congestion and environmental pollution, but its steady grasp on history is a key element of what defines the region. Many of the cities in the 14th District, which stretches from just south of San Francisco down the peninsula and over the Santa Cruz mountains to embrace Scotts Valley at its southern edge, have cultivated the small-town image that makes them so attractive to transplants.

The peninsula exploded with activity in the 1980s, as the companies that would prime the pump of the dot-com boom laid roots in the region. Many of the past and present leaders of the technological boom learned their trade at Stanford University: William Hewlett and David Packard; Yahoo!'s Jerry Yang; and the founders of Google, Sergey Brin and Lawrence Page. Voters and representatives alike know that the region would not exist as it does today without placing equal emphasis on high-quality education and developing industries.

At the same time, the importance of education and business issues to the district's political interests are complemented by the region's immense natural beauty. The western half of the district is predominantly natural preserves and open space, redwoods, lush valleys, and rugged coastal cliffs.

Politically, the region has long favored centrist candidates, especially Republicans with very moderate politics. Past Republicans such as Ed Zschau, Tom Campbell, and Pete McCloskey have made waves by bucking the national party. Zschau, for instance, raised eyebrows across the district when he campaigned for the 1996 vice-presidential nomination in the Reform Party. And Pete McCloskey, who served as a representative from the area from 1967 to 1983, made waves as an early Republican opponent of the Vietnam War and a high-profile supporter of the Republicans for Kerry campaign in 2004. He re-surfaced in 2006 after a long political hiatus to take on incumbent Republican Richard Pombo in the 11th Congressional District. He lost the primary, and Pombo subsequently lost the general.

Perhaps owing to the passion for open space and natural beauty, representatives here place the same value on protecting the environment as their constituents, and balance it with the ever-present need to ensure good jobs and good education for residents. But the same influx of "cultural creatives" from the late-'80s to the turn of the century tilted regional politics to the left. Many of the newcomers were highly educated tech and business workers who found in the area a perfect mix of natural beauty and economic possibility, and sought to maintain the balance by sending Democrats to Washington.

Democrat Anna Eshoo was first elected in 1992 and overwhelmingly won her eighth term in 2006. The 2001 redistricting has only minimally affected the demographics of the district. It lost a portion of its Democratic edge as Cupertino moved to the 15th District, while Saratoga and Scotts Valley, two of the more conservative towns in the region, returned to the fold.

In Washington, Eshoo serves on the House Committee on Energy and Commerce, whose responsibilities include issues of vital importance to the district—particularly in matters such as telecommunications, the Internet, health-based environmental laws, biotechnology, high technology, water resources, bioterrorism, and homeland security. A close friend of Speaker Nancy Pelosi, Eshoo was given a coveted seat on the House Intelligence Committee in 2003 and is expected to play a role in Pelosi's speakership. In the 109th Congress, she worked across party lines to establish BARDA—the Biomedical Advance Research and Development Authority, which will oversee development of vaccines and other measures to combat bioterrorism and the pandemic spread of diseases such as bird flu.

BIOGRAPHY: Born: New Britain, CT, December 13, 1942. Home: Atherton. Education: AA, Canada College. Military: None. Family: Divorced, two children. Religion: Catholic.

OFFICES: Capitol, Cannon House Office Building 205, Washington, DC 20515, Phone: (202) 225-8104, Fax: (202) 225-8890, email: anna.eshoo@mail.house.gov. District: 698 Emerson Street, Palo Alto, CA 94301, Phone: (650) 323-2984, Fax: (650) 323-3498.

COMMITTEES: Energy and Commerce.

ELECTED: 1992

ELECTION HISTORY: San Mateo County Board of Supervisors, 1982-1992.

2002 ELECTION: Eshoo (D*) 68%
Nixon (R) 28%
Carver (L) 4%

2004 ELECTION: Eshoo (D*) 70%
Haugen (R) 26%
Holtz (L) 4%

2006 ELECTION: Eshoo (D*) 71%
Smith (R) 24%
Brouillet (G) 2%
Holtz (L) 2%

RATINGS:

ACU	ADA	AFL-CIO	CoC	GO	LCV	NTU	PIRG
4	100	93	38	F-	100	14	91

SAM FARR (D)
17th Congressional District

Counties: Monterey, San Benito, Santa Cruz
Cities: Salinas, Watsonville, Hollister, Santa Cruz, Monterey
Ethnicity: 46% White, 43% Latino, 3% Black, 6% Asian
Voter Registration: 51% D – 26% R – 18% DS
President 04: 66% Kerry, 33% Bush

Sam Farr

The 17th District is based largely on the watershed of Monterey Bay. To the north lie the Santa Cruz Mountains, to the east the Diablo range and the five major rivers that flow to Monterey Bay, preserved in 1992 as the nation's largest marine sanctuary. From the towering redwoods of California's first state park at Big Basin, where annual rainfall can reach 48 inches, to yucca plants in the desert of Parkfield, a small town on the move with the San Andreas Fault, this district contains wide biological and geographical diversity.

Vast swaths of public land separate the population centers connected by two main thoroughfares: Santa Cruz, Monterey, Carmel, and Big Sur by Highway 1 and Salinas, Gonzales, Soledad, and King City by U.S. Highway 101. The federal and state land also includes miles of protected seashore, Pinnacles National Monument, several military bases, and Los Padres National Forest, at nearly two million acres one of the largest in the country. The five Spanish missions in the district bear witness to the intense and successful campaign waged to convert the natives to Christianity. Monterey became the first state capital, and the state constitution was written there in 1849.

The population can be roughly divided in two groups: those who live within sight of the ocean—who tend to be whiter, richer, and concerned about the environment and international affairs—and those behind the "Lettuce Curtain" and beyond the ocean's spray—who tend to be Mexican, poorer, and more conservative. Coastal constituents often depend on education and tourism for their paychecks, while their inland neighbors rely heavily on agriculture.

The Salinas and Pajaro valleys are prime farm land, though the entire district enjoys a temperate climate ideal for many crops. The "sunny refrigerator" of the Salinas Valley is home to almost 100 different crops and produces 90% of the iceberg lettuce consumed in the country, as well as nearly all the commercial artichokes and more than half of the strawberries. Total agricultural sales for the region reach $3 billion a year.

Agricultural interests in the district were rocked in 2006 by nationwide outbreaks of E. coli traced to spinach and lettuce grown in the Monterey region. Although the tainted produce came from one farm in San Juan Bautista, the resultant public-relations panic threatened crops grown throughout the district, and Farr introduced the Spinach Research and Recovery Act of 2006 to aid stricken farmers. He is expected to pursue that legislation in the 110th Congress.

The Monterey Bay Aquarium and Santa Cruz Boardwalk draw tourists from around the West, and the Big Sur coastline and abundant outdoor recreation opportunities of the Central Coast make this a popular destination for a variety of travelers. Finally, a University of California campus in Santa Cruz, California State University, Monterey Bay at former Ft. Ord, the Defense Language Institute and Naval Post-Graduate School in Monterey, and a variety of community colleges help produce progressive-minded voters and make education an important part of the economy.

When Democrat Leon Panetta resigned his House seat in 1993 to join the Clinton administration, he forced a special election. Assemblyman Sam Farr, a fifth generation Californian and son of long-time state Senator Fred Farr, was elected to replace Panetta. Peppered with an array of primary and general election opponents through the years, Farr has never been seriously challenged. He drew the wrath of labor for supporting NAFTA, but that wrath never materialized in punishment at the polls, and the AFL-CIO routinely scores him in the high 90s.

Farr served in the Peace Corps in Colombia for two years before returning home to begin his political career. He was an Assembly staffer for 10 years, before becoming a Monterey County supervisor in 1975. Five years later he was elected to the Assembly, where he helped author the California Certified Organic Standards, later to become a model for similar federal standards, and is remembered for writing strict oil spill liability legislation.

Farr has managed to balance the diverse needs and issues of his constituents by appealing to the "three Es"—education, environment, and employment. "This district is so much more than pretty scenery," he is fond of saying. "When you preserve the environment you get more jobs, and more educational opportunities."

BIOGRAPHY: Born: San Francisco, July 4, 1941. Home: Carmel. Education: BS, Willamette University; Military: None. Family: wife Shary, one daughter. Religion: Episcopalian.

OFFICES: Capitol, Longworth Building 1221, Washington, DC 20515, Phone: (202) 225-2861, Fax: (202) 225-8890, email: sam.farr@mail.house.gov. District: 100 West Alisal Street, Salinas, CA 93901, Phone: (831) 424-2229, (800) 340-FARR, Fax: (831) 424-7099; 701 Ocean Street, Room 318, Santa Cruz, CA 95060, Phone: (831) 429-1976, Fax: (831) 424-7099.

COMMITTEES: Appropriations.

ELECTED: 1993

ELECTION HISTORY: Monterey County Board of Supervisors, 1975–1980; State Assembly, 1981–1993.

2002 ELECTION: Farr (D*) 68%
Engler (R) 27%
Glock-Grueneich (G) 3%
Lee (L) 2%

2004 ELECTION: Farr (D*) 67%
Risley (R) 29%
Glock-Grueneich (G) 2%
Smolen (L) 1%
Williams (PF) 1%

2006 ELECTION: Farr (D*) 76%
De Maio (R) 23%
Taylor (I) 2%

RATINGS:

ACU	ADA	AFL-CIO	CoC	GO	LCV	NTU	PIRG
8	100	93	42	F-	100	17	92

ROBERT FILNER (D)
51st Congressional District

Counties: Imperial, San Diego
Cities: San Diego, Chula Vista, Brawley, El Centro, Calexico, National City
Ethnicity: 21% White, 53% Latino, 10% Black, 13% Asian
Voter Registration: 47% D – 30% R – 19% DS
President 04: 53% Kerry, 46% Bush

Robert Filner

In geography alone, the 51st District is one of the most unusual and imposing in the nation: It runs eastward from the water at the southern tip of San Diego County, includes densely populated Chula Vista and National City, part of southern San Diego, then heads east along a narrow corridor until it traverses a portion of the Laguna Mountains, widens, then reaches the fearsome desert of impoverished Imperial County, which it completely enfolds.

The district, a monument to the art of reapportionment, includes California's entire border zone with Mexico. For those raised in San Diego, the district includes the dusty towns that became familiar during the traditional Memorial Day trek to the Colorado River—such as Holtville, Ocotillo, El Centro, Westmorland, and Imperial. Imperial County's average per capita income is less than a third the statewide average, and the average in two towns, Palo Verde and Winterhaven, is less than a fourth of the state average. The economy is largely agricultural, and the county's political clout rests with its strategic position between the Colorado River and San Diego, which increasingly needs precious water from the Colorado to sustain its growth and lifestyle. Three-fourths of the 51st District's Imperial County population is Latino, while overall the district is more than half Latino. For Democrats, this is safe territory: In presidential elections, Democrat Al Gore carried the district by 16 percentage points in 2000, although John Kerry's margin was less half that in 2004. Its design was not popular with all groups; Latinos claim it diminished their ability to elect one of their own despite the fact that more than half of the district residents are Latino. As a result, it was the subject of a court challenge.

Nor did the design please the incumbent who has held the district for 15 years—Democrat Bob Filner, a former San Diego State University history professor and voluble, combative Pennsylvania transplant who has become known as California's Border Congressman. Filner felt it left him too vulnerable to a Latino challenge. As the 2006 primary would prove, Filner's fears were not delusional.

Filner arrived in San Diego in 1970 and got his political start nine years later winning a long-shot race to the San Diego school board and parlaying that into a seat on the city council before winning election to Congress in 1992. He's a scrappy campaigner—one local independent analyst, perhaps prone to hyperbole, described him as "mean and he's ugly, but he's tough." He's also cerebral, with a Ph.D. and a reputation at SDSU as an activist professor. He is a strong advocate for veterans' rights—he serves on the Veterans' Affairs Committee—and is usually engaged in some fight or another to wheedle federal transportation dollars for his vast district. He's a member of the Transportation and Infrastructure Committee, which helps. He's won his last four general election campaigns by 20 percentage points or better and may be able to continue to do so for the foreseeable future.

The political danger for Filner lies in the primary, as 2006 so richly showcased. Filner is unusual in that he is an Anglo representing a solidly Hispanic district. Filner grumped about the possibility of a potential Latino challenge in the Democratic primary, and termed-out Assemblyman Juan Vargas obliged him in 2006. No slouch at waging blistering campaigns, Vargas was regarded as one of the legislature's best and brightest, and political observers predicted a bare-knuckles campaign. Aside from his Latino heritage, Vargas is a Harvard-trained lawyer and one of 10 children of parents who came to California from Mexico in the 1940s.

There has always been a "dancing on the head of a pin" quality to Filner's congressional career, and the 2006 primary proved no exception. Vargas and Filner had gone at it twice before in congressional primaries, but in a pre-reapportionment district with less Latino influence. Filner won both confrontations, but their history gave the 2006 rematch a nasty overtone and led to personal attacks on both sides. At one point, Vargas compared Filner to convicted San Diego congressman Randy Cunningham, accusing Filner of employing his wife as a consultant and paying her with campaign funds. Filner accused Vargas of being in the pocket of the insurance industry. Both sides spent liberally, but the power of incumbency won out. Filner won 51% of the vote, compared with 43% for Vargas. A third Democrat, Danny Ramirez, took 6%. Although Filner now has defeated Vargas in three Democratic primaries for Congress, a rematch in 2008 is not out of the question.

BIOGRAPHY: Born: Pittsburgh, PA, September 4, 1942. Home: San Diego. Education: BA, PhD, Cornell University; MA, University of Delaware. Military: None. Family: wife Jane Merrill, two children, one grandchild. Religion: Jewish.

OFFICES: Capitol, Rayburn Building 2428, Washington, DC 20515, Phone: (202) 225-8045, Fax: (202) 225-9073, email: robert.filner@mail.house.gov. District: 333 F Street, Suite A, Chula Vista, CA 91910, Phone: (619) 422-5963, Fax: (619) 422-7290; 1101 Airport Road, Suite D, Imperial, CA 92251, Phone: (760) 355-8800, Fax: (760) 355-8802.

COMMITTEES: Transportation and Infrastructure; Veterans Affairs.

ELECTED: 1992

ELECTION HISTORY: San Diego School Board, 1979–1983; San Diego City Council, 1987–1992.

2002 ELECTION: Filner (D*) 58%
Garica (R) 39%
Keup (L) 3%

2004 ELECTION: Filner (D*) 62%
Giorgino (R) 35%

Metti (L) 3%
2006 ELECTION: Filner (D*) 68%
Miles (R) 30%
Litwin (L) 2%
RATINGS:　ACU ADA AFL-CIO CoC GO LCV NTU PIRG
　　　　　　 4　 95　　93　　 37　F-　92　 20　　89

ELTON GALLEGLY (R)
24th Congressional District

Counties: Santa Barbara, Ventura
Cities: Simi Valley, Thousand Oaks, Camarillo, Solvang, Lompoc, Buellton, Ojai, Moorpark
Ethnicity: 69% White, 22% Latino, 2% Black, 5% Asian
Voter Registration: 34% D – 44% R – 17% DS
President 04: 56% Bush, 43% Kerry

Elton Gallegly

This district once bore the number 23 and was mostly confined to Ventura County, with just a smidgen of Santa Barbara County and a few precincts of Los Angeles County Republicanism tossed into the mix. As such, it took in the Ventura County coastline, then extended inland to the Kern County line and east to Los Angeles. The 2001 reapportionment gave it a facelift. The district contains only a small swath of Ventura coastline from Port Hueneme to the Los Angeles County line. The rest of the Ventura coast has been removed to the new 23rd District. Added to the district is the bulk of Santa Barbara County, but none of the Santa Barbara coast. That, too, has been tacked onto the 23rd, which is all beach from Morro Bay to Oxnard. The territory remaining to the new 24th District is the high-growth enclaves of the 1960s that saw white-flight refugees from Los Angeles move north into Ventura communities such as Simi Valley.

Incumbent Elton Gallegly has represented the area for nearly two decades. The former mayor of Simi Valley has endured only one sweat since capturing the district in 1986 and that took place in 1992 when the previous reapportionment dumped him into a district with fellow Republican Congressman Bob Lagomarsino. Gallegly avoided a primary fight when Lagomarsino was persuaded to shift north into a Santa Barbara district. It proved an unfortunate move for Lagmarsino who lost the 1992 Republican primary to Michael Huffington.

In Congress, Gallegly has become one of the California delegation's resident experts on terrorism, with a seat on the House Permanent Subcommittee on Intelligence. He chairs the International Relations Subcommittee on Europe and Emerging Threats and previously chaired a subcommittee on international terrorism.

Gallegly made his mark on immigration during the 1990s, proposing enough bills on illegal immigration to denude a small forest, including a constitutional amendment that would have denied citizenship to children born in this country to undocumented mothers. Most of his bills went nowhere when Democrats controlled the Congress, although when the GOP took over after the 1994 election, he was put in charge of a task force on immigration. But even California Republicans rankled at his suggestion—ultimately adopted in law—that federal welfare benefits be curtailed to legal, as well as illegal, immigrants when Congress reformed the welfare system in 1995.

On other matters, Gallegly has been a loyal vote for the Bush administration, including support for the war in Iraq and 2005 efforts to curtail federal funding for stem cell research. His conservative voting record has earned him the not-so-loyal opposition of liberals who maintain a "Gallegly Watch" Web page to track the incumbent's voting record and speechmaking.

As the 2006 elections approached, Gallegly suddenly announced that he would not seek re-election, setting off the salivary glands of every ambitious Republican within hailing distance of the district. The problem surfaced over the timing of his announcement—five days after the filing deadline to replace him. Although Gallegly tried to have the deadline extended, it was unclear that he would succeed, leaving the primary field to an unknown Republican attorney and a pair of Democrats. Gallegly pegged his decision to his health, saying he was battling a problem that had yet to be resolved. Four days later, Gallegly reversed himself and said he would seek an 11th term. It was said at the time that White House advisor Karl Rove, among others, put pressure on Gallegly to serve one more term.

At the same time Gallegly announced for re-election, he insisted this would be his final term and launched the 2008 campaign to replace him. Chief among those said to be interested are state Sen. Tom McClintock, who is termed out in 2008, and former Assm. Tony Strickland. Both lost contests for statewide office in 2006; McClintock for lieutenant governor and Strickland for controller.

BIOGRAPHY: Born: Huntington Park, March 7, 1944. Home: Simi Valley. Education: Attended CSU Los Angeles. Military: None. Family: wife Janice, four children, seven grandchildren. Religion: Protestant.

OFFICES: Capitol: Rayburn Building 2309, Washington, DC 20515, Phone: (202) 225-5811, Fax: (202) 225-1100, email: elton.gallegly@mail.house.gov. District: 2829 Townsgate Road, Suite 315, Thousand Oaks, CA 91361, Phone: (805) 497-2224, (800) 423-0023, Fax: (805) 497-0039; 485 Alisal Road, Suite G-1A, Solvang, CA 93463, Phone: (805) 686-2525, Fax: (805) 686-2566.

COMMITTEES: International Relations; Judiciary; Resources; Permanent Subcommittee on Intelligence.

ELECTED: 1986

ELECTION HISTORY: Simi Valley City Council, 1979–1980; Simi Valley Mayor, 1980–1986.

2002 ELECTION: Gallegly (R*) 65%
                     Rudin (D) 32%
                     Harber (L) 3%

2004 ELECTION: Gallegly (R*) 62%
　　　　　　　　Wagner (D) 34%
　　　　　　　　Bechman (G) 3%
2006 ELECTION: Gallegly (R*) 62%
　　　　　　　　Martinez (D) 38%

RATINGS:	ACU	ADA	AFL-CIO	CoC	GO	LCV	NTU	PIRG
	80	0	13	92	A-	8	54	13

JANE HARMAN (D)
36th Congressional District

Counties: Los Angeles
Cities: Los Angeles, Torrance, Redondo Beach, Lomita, Marina del Rey
Ethnicity: 49% White, 30% Latino, 4% Black, 14% Asian
Voter Registration: 44% D – 31% R – 21% DS
President 04: 59% Kerry, 40% Bush

Jane Harman

The 36th District symbolizes how reapportionment can be used to craft districts that either are or are not competitive. It has been both. Created as a new district in the court-drawn 1992 reapportionment, it hosted a free-for-all in nearly every election of the 1990s. Party registration was relatively even, producing spirited and tense elections with Republican and Democratic winners. Democrat Jane Harman began the carnage when she captured the seat for the first time in 1992, defeating Los Angeles City Councilwoman Joan Milke Flores—who had won the GOP primary against, among others, Maureen Reagan. Harman's 1994 re-election was a squeaker, although she won a bit more comfortably in 1996 before abandoning the seat in 1998 to run for governor.

That same year, the district finally fell to a Republican when Assemblyman Steve Kuykendall fashioned a narrow victory over Democrat Janice Hahn, sister of Los Angeles Mayor James Hahn and daughter of legendary Los Angeles County Supervisor Kenny Hahn. He held it for all of one term before Harman took it back in 2000—again by the slimmest of margins. In five elections governed by the district plan of 1992, margins of victory in the 36th District were less than 1% (Harman, 1992 and 1994), a landslide 9% (Harman, 1996), 2% (Kuykendall, 1998), and 1% (Harman, 2000).

When reapportionment rolled around again in 2001, bipartisan dealmakers had had enough of resource-sapping elections and made the 36th a prime target for overhaul. The new district was designated for Democrats, and to accomplish the transition from competitive to safe, mapmakers removed troublesome Republican precincts in the Palos Verdes Peninsula, trading them for safer Democratic territory along Highway 1 north of the Long Beach harbor. The Democratic registration edge ballooned to 12%, giving Harman a trio of snoozer re-elections.

Although the political trade-offs brought more low-income families into the district, the 36th remains relatively affluent. Median household income is 20% above the national average, while the number of constituents living at or below the poverty level is 12%—almost exactly the national average. The median value of a house is $320,000, nearly three times the national average.

A centrist for most of her political career, Harman's first tenure in Congress was distinguished from the get-go when she gained a seat on the influential House Armed Services Committee—a rare accomplishment for a freshman. She used that position to help protect defense and aerospace resources vital to her district—with mixed success during an era of military downsizing. She joined the Blue Dogs, a faction of moderate Democrats that included, among others, California colleague Gary Condit. Harman arrived in Washington with solid credentials as an insider, having previously served as a Department of Defense lawyer, counsel to former U.S. Senator John Tunney, and deputy cabinet secretary in the Jimmy Carter White House. She also served as chief counsel to Harman Industries—the lucrative electronics firm owned by her husband, Sidney Harman.

In 1998 Harman launched an up-or-out quest to be governor, a decision driven in part by a weak Democratic field and a conservative Republican nominee—Attorney General Dan Lungren—on the wrong side of most issues dear to California voters. Harman's Democratic opponents were millionaire businessman Al Checchi, a political novice, and Lieutenant Governor Gray Davis, a veteran with a considerable load of political baggage. As a moderate and the only woman in the race, Harman was considered ideally positioned to win the nomination.

But Harman entered the race too late, which forced her to spend considerable personal resources in an all-out war on the front-runner, Checchi. He responded in kind, and the campaign devolved into a slash-and-burn inferno that eventually torched both candidates. California Journal, among others, referred to the Harman-Checchi brawl as a murder-suicide, with the prime beneficiary being the eventual winner, Davis.

Harman returned to Congress in 2000 where she has backed, among other initiatives, federal funding for stem cell research. But her most prominent role has come in the areas of terrorism, homeland security, and intelligence. She is ranking Democrat on the Permanent Subcommittee on Intelligence, which put her center stage in post 9/11 hearings on terrorism and the Iraq war. She has been a vocal critic of Bush administration policy, although in 2002 she voted in favor of the resolution authorizing the use of military force in Iraq.

In 2006, Harman was poised to benefit from the Democratic takeover. As ranking member of the House Intelligence Committee, she was—by tradition and position—primed to take over this key committee. But Harman never enjoyed a cordial relationship with the new Speaker, fellow California Democrat Nancy Pelosi of San Francisco who, as House Speaker, would name the committee chair. Instead, Pelosi gave the post to Democrat Silvestre Reyes of Texas. It was a slap at Harman but one most observers expected, given Harman's past support for the war in Iraq and the use of domestic wiretaps without benefit of a warrant.

BIOGRAPHY: Born: New York, NY, June 28, 1945. Home: Marina del Rey. Education: BA, Smith College; JD, Harvard. Military: None. Family: husband Sidney, four children. Religion: Jewish.

OFFICES: Capitol: Rayburn Building 2400, Washington, DC 20515, Phone: (202) 225-8220, Fax: (202) 225-7290, email: jane.harman@mail.house.gov. District: 2321 Rosecrans Boulevard, Suite 3270, El Segundo, CA 90245, Phone: (310) 643-3636, Fax: (310) 643-6445; 544 North Avalon Boulevard, Suite 307, Wilmington, CA 90744, Phone: (310) 549-8282, Fax: (310) 549-8250.

COMMITTEES: Energy and Commerce; Select Committee on Homeland Security; Permanent Subcommittee on Intelligence.

ELECTED: 2000

ELECTION HISTORY: U.S. House, 1992-1998.

2002 ELECTION: Harman (D*) 61%
Johnson (R) 35%
McSpadden (L) 4%

2004 ELECTION: Harman (D*) 62%
Whitehead (R) 34%
Binkley (L) 2%
Stek (PF) 2%

2006 ELECTION: Harman (D*) 63%
Gibson (R) 32%
Binkley (L) 2%
Smith (PF) 3%

RATINGS:

ACU	ADA	AFL-CIO	CoC	GO	LCV	NTU	PIRG
5	70	82	58	F-	100	20	75

WALLY HERGER (R)
2nd Congressional District

Counties: Butte, Colusa, Glenn, Shasta, Siskiyou, Sutter, Tehama, Trinity, Yuba
Cities: Chico, Redding, Paradise, Marysville, Yuba City, Williams, Colusa, Red Bluff, Yreka
Ethnicity: 76% White, 14% Latino, 1% Black, 4% Asian
Voter Registration: 33% D – 45% R – 16% DS
President 04: 62% Bush, 37% Kerry

The 2nd District is split by Interstate 5 from its northern border with Oregon to where its southern boundary bumpers against metropolitan Sacramento. Although reapportionment did not change the Republican edge, the district's physical contours were reshaped. Counties of the northern Sierra—Modoc, Lassen, Nevada, Sierra, and Plumas—were removed as the district shifted west to incorporate newly acquired Tehama, Glenn, Colusa, and parts of Yolo counties. Much of the district is rural, with far-flung hamlets and towns serving farms and high-country ranches. Tourism bolsters the economy, which once sported a robust timber industry now fallen on hard times.

Wally Herger

Changes in district geography don't bother its long-time representative—Republican Wally Herger, who has served the area in one capacity or another for nearly a quarter century. A decade ago, after the 1992 court-drawn reapportionment, Herger found himself living outside the boundaries of his district. While not against the law for a member of Congress, angst caused Herger to move from Sutter County to Marysville, where he handily won re-election without the stigma associated with unintentional carpetbagging. Herger routinely wins elections in a district where a Democrat serves the same function as a tackling dummy.

While his Republican brethren have thrived as part of the GOP majority, becoming chairs of significant committees or advancing through House leadership, Herger has limped along as a middle-bencher, showing little inclination to engage in congressional activism. Like most members with a significant military presence in his or her district, Herger was active—if not instrumental—in efforts to protect Beale Air Force Base during the 2005 round of base closures. He serves on the Ways and Means Committee, chairing its subcommittee on human services. Social Security comes under the purview of his panel, but Herger is not leading the charge on Social Security reform but rather bobbing along on the gravitational pull of forces stronger than he. His position dovetails nicely with the Bush administration, opposing more taxation and backing the ability of younger workers to set up private retirement funds.

As the GOP recedes into minority status, Herger's limited clout will recede along with it.

Herger represents a conservative constituency, which suits this cattle rancher-turned politician. On environmental matters, he favors tinkering with the endangered species act, especially as it applies to the flooding that threatens parts of his district. He would make it easier to suspend the act for construction of flood-control projects and supports construction of the Auburn Dam and a similar dam on the Yuba River.

Politics aside, Herger is one of the more personable members of Congress and won't likely have his electoral feathers ruffled—by a Republican or Democrat—any time soon.

BIOGRAPHY: Born: Yuba City, May 20, 1945. Home: Marysville. Education: AA, American River College; attended CSU Sacramento. Military: None. Family: wife Pamela, eight children. Religion: Mormon.

OFFICES: Capitol: Rayburn Building 2268, Washington, DC 20515, Phone: (202) 225-3076, Fax: (202) 225-0852, email: wally.herger@mail.house.gov. District: 55 Independence Circle, Suite 104, Chico, CA 95973, Phone: (530) 893-8363, Fax: (530) 893-8619; 410 Hemsted Drive, Suite 115, Redding, CA 96002, Phone: (530) 223-5898.

COMMITTEES: Ways and Means
ELECTED: 1986
ELECTION HISTORY: State Assembly, 1981–1986.

2002 ELECTION: Herger (R*) 66%
Johnson (D) 30%
Martin (L) 2%
Thiessen (NL) 3%
2004 ELECTION: Herger (R*) 67%
Johnson (D) 33%
2006 ELECTION: Herger (R*) 64%
Sekhon (D) 33%
Hinesley (L) 3%

RATINGS:

ACU	ADA	AFL-CIO	CoC	GO	LCV	NTU	PIRG
96	0	13	93	A	0	67	5

MIKE HONDA (D)
15th Congressional District

Counties: Santa Clara
Cities: San Jose, Santa Clara, Milpitas, Cupertino, Gilroy, Campbell, Los Gatos
Ethnicity: 47% White, 17% Latino, 3% Black, 30% Asian
Voter Registration: 43% D – 27% R – 25% DS
President 04: 63% Kerry, 36% Bush

The 15th was a true swing district during the 1990s, represented at one time or another by both Republicans and Democrats. But the 2001 reapportionment deal that assigned districts to one party or another put this Silicon Valley enclave in the Democratic column. To accomplish this, mapmakers used a wine press to perform delicate surgery on what had been a tidy district. Saratoga, Monte Serreno, and most everything west of Highway 17 was squeezed off, including every precinct in San Mateo and Santa Cruz counties. Milpitas was added in the north, while the district bled south to include Gilroy. The surgery wrought little change to Democratic registration, which improved not a whit. Republican registration, on the other hand, plunged from 35% in 2000 to 29% in 2004. Decline-to-state registrants increased from 17% to 23%, following a trend in districts with large Asian populations. The 15th boasts the biggest Asian community of any congressional seat in the state. The district now is safely Democratic.

The 15th is rather affluent, as one might suspect for this part of the Silicon Valley. Its median family income is some 60% above the national average, while the median price of a home hovers nearly four times above the national average. Although there are places where wealth is scarce, only 4.4% of district families live below the federal poverty line—less than half the national average.

The district is represented by one of the most liberal members of the House, Mike Honda, who was first elected in 2000. At the time, Honda had one term remaining in the state Assembly, but incumbent Republican Tom Campbell vacated his seat to challenge the re-election of Dianne Feinstein to the U.S. Senate. Honda easily outpaced four other contenders in the 2000 Democratic primary, then squared off against

Mike Honda

Republican Assemblyman Jim Cunneen. It was supposed to be a blisteringly close election featuring two popular elected officials, but Honda won comfortably—helped in part by a visit from President Bill Clinton.

The son of sharecroppers, Honda is a former school principal who helped create a Wireless Task Force in the House to encourage high tech development. In 2003 he worked to pass the 21st Century Nanotechnology Research and Development Act, legislation that authorized $3.7 billion in nanotechnology research, which involves designing devices on the scale of one-billionth of a meter.

Honda, who spent part of his childhood in a relocation camp in Colorado, has been a critic of the government's policy of interning Japanese Americans during World War II. In February 2003, he demanded an apology from North Carolina Representative Howard Coble, who had suggested that the internment was necessary to protect Japanese Americans during a time of national crisis. In 2005 Honda joined with Representatives Bill Thomas of Bakersfield and Doris Matsui of Sacramento to support legislation encouraging the preservation of the camps where Japanese Americans were interned. The bill, opposed by the Bush administration, requires local governments and nonprofit groups to match federal money spent to preserve the camps.

With other Bay area Democrats, Honda has been a vocal critic of the Bush administration's Iraq war policy. In April 2005 he backed legislation that would restrict access of military recruiters to high school campuses. Under the "No Child Left Behind Law," public high schools are required to give recruiters access to the names, addresses, and phone numbers of students unless a parent objects. Honda and other opponents said the policy is an infringement on students' privacy rights and puts some students at risk of sexual abuse. Honda has supported local efforts to get more federal money to extend the Bay Area Rapid Transit (BART) system to San Jose.

Honda chairs the Asian Pacific American Caucus, and when Democrats secured control of the House following the 2006 election he was given a seat on the powerful Appropriations Committee.

BIOGRAPHY: Born: Stockton, June 27, 1941. Home: San Jose. Education: BS, BA, MA, San Jose State University. Military: None. Family: Widower, two children. Religion: Protestant.

OFFICES: Capitol: Longworth Building 1713, Washington, DC 20515, Phone: (202) 225-2631, Fax: (202) 225-2699, email: mike.honda@mail.house.gov. District: 1999 South Bascom Avenue, Suite 815, Campbell, CA 95008, Phone: (408) 558-8085, Fax: (805) 558-8086.

COMMITTEES: Appropriations.

ELECTED: 2000

ELECTION HISTORY: San Jose Unified School Board, 1981–1991; Santa Clara County Board of Supervisors, 1990-1996; State Assembly, 1996–2000.

2002 ELECTION: Honda (D*) 66%

Hermann (R) 31%
Landauer (L) 3%
2004 ELECTION: Honda (D*) 72%
Chukwu (R) 28%
2006 ELECTION: Honda (D*) 72%
Chukwu (R) 28%
RATINGS:

ACU	ADA	AFL-CIO	CoC	GO	LCV	NTU	PIRG
4	100	93	37	F-	100	16	98

DUNCAN HUNTER (R)
52nd Congressional District

Counties: San Diego
Cities: San Diego, El Cajon
Ethnicity: 73% White, 14% Latino, 4% Black, 6% Asian
Voter Registration: 30% D – 46% R – 20% DS
President 04: 61% Bush, 38% Kerry

Duncan Hunter

The 52nd District was treated to a facelift in the 2001 reapportionment in an effort to accommodate its powerful and longtime incumbent—Republican Duncan Hunter, then-chairman of the House Armed Services Committee. Not that Hunter had suffered anything resembling an electoral challenge during his nearly quarter century in Congress. Far from it; in 2000 he had won re-election in his old district two to one, with his Democratic opponent running 5% behind party registration. Still, the old 52nd included pesky Imperial County, with its strong Democratic outlook and growing numbers of Latino residents. So mapmakers dropped Imperial into Democrat Bob Filner's 51st District, essentially replacing it with voters concentrated in and around Poway. Where once the district included the entire border with Mexico, it now touches that border nowhere, staying north of the meandering State Highway 94. It is an upper-middle-class district, with a median family income some 20% above the national average. Although their district no longer touches the border, immigration remains a primary concern to constituents.

Hunter, a former Army Ranger and Vietnam veteran, upset a nine-term Democrat when he first won a seat in Congress in 1980. At the time, he represented a new breed of young, conservative Republicans who often annoyed the House's more moderate GOP leadership. Leadership noted his talents, however, rewarding him with the chairmanship of the Republican Research Committee—a group charged with developing strategies for emerging issues. His committee was abolished in 1994 when Newt Gingrich became the first Republican Speaker in 40 years and bypassed Hunter for bigger assignments, which went to Californians such as David Dreier, Bill Thomas, and Chris Cox.

The 1992 reapportionment was singularly unkind to Hunter, who had to sell his Coronado residence and move into a new district redrawn by a neutral, court-appointed panel with exasperating indifference to the whims of incumbent lawmakers. That, plus his involvement in several minor scandals—bouncing checks on the House bank and more than $1.5 million worth of franked mailers to constituents—made 1992 a minor hell for Hunter, especially when Democrats targeted him. He won, but managed only 52% of the vote. Democrats renewed their efforts in 1994 with the same challenger, but Hunter blew her away, essentially ending his electoral worries.

Hunter is the definitive conservative, consistently casting pro-life, anti-gun-control, anti-immigration, anti-tax, pro-school-voucher and pro-school-prayer votes in Congress. He backed the Bush administration effort to limit funding for stem cell research using human embryos and has supported war efforts in Iraq and Afghanistan. Not surprising for a San Diego lawmaker and a member of Armed Services, he lists his legislative priorities as a strong national defense and protecting the border with Mexico.

In 2005, Hunter generated some unusual publicity by bucking Pentagon policy on women in combat. He proposed an amendment to the 2006 defense authorization bill that would have prevented women from serving in units stationed in forward zones or in proximity to combat units. Hunter tried to head off a confrontation by negotiating with the Defense Department but pushed his agenda via legislation when those talks went nowhere. He claimed he was merely codifying existing Army policy, but Pentagon officials disagreed, saying Hunter's amendment would cause "confusion in the ranks." Hunter eventually withdrew his amendment under pressure from Secretary of Defense Donald Rumsfeld.

Hunter also surprised the administration and GOP colleagues in November 2005 when he introduced a resolution calling for the immediate withdrawal of American troops from Iraq. It failed 403 to three.

When Republicans lost control of the House in the 2006 election, Hunter joined his GOP colleagues as a member of the minority party. Yet all misery is not equal, and few suffered a power outage equal to Hunter. His chairmanship evaporated and materialized in the office of Ike Skelton, a Missouri Democrat. Hunter will continue to work on security and immigration issues, such as co-sponsoring a bill to construct a fence along the Mexican border.

Seeking an outlet for his energies after losing the chairmanship, Hunter took a bold—some might say quixotic—step in November 2006 by launching a campaign for president in 2008. Chances that a congressman from an obscure corner of California might raise enough money to compete, let alone win, the Republican nomination are—at best—remote.

BIOGRAPHY: Born: Riverside, May 31, 1948. Home: Alpine. Education: University of Montana; UC Santa Barbara; BSL, JD, Western State University. Military: U.S. Army (Vietnam era). Family: wife Lynne, two children, two grandchildren. Religion: Baptist.

OFFICES: Capitol: Rayburn Building 2265, Washington, DC 20515, Phone: (202) 225-5672, Fax: (202) 225-0235, email: duncan.hunter@mail.house.gov. District: 1870 Cordell Court, Suite 206, El Cajon, CA 92020, Phone: (619) 448-5201, Fax: (619) 449-5241.
COMMITTEES: Armed Services
ELECTED: 1980
ELECTION HISTORY: None
2002 ELECTION: Hunter (R*) 70%
      Moore-Kochlacs (D) 26%
      Benoit (L) 4%
2004 ELECTION: Hunter (R*) 69%
      Keliher (D) 27%
      Benoit (L) 3%
2006 ELECTION: Hunter (R*) 65%
      Rinaldi (D) 32%
      Benoit (L) 3%

RATINGS:	ACU	ADA	AFL-CIO	CoC	GO	LCV	NTU	PIRG
	92	5	20	88	A	0	56	7

DARRELL ISSA (R)
49th Congressional District

Counties: Riverside, San Diego
Cities: Oceanside, Vista, Temecula
Ethnicity: 58% White, 30% Latino, 5% Black, 4% Asian
Voter Registration: 29% D – 48% R – 19% DS
President 04: 63% Bush, 37% Kerry

Darrell Issa

The 49th Congressional District, which includes pieces of southern Riverside County and northern San Diego County, is solidly Republican, to put it mildly. In the Fallbrook-Bonsall-Hidden Meadows-Valley Center region, George Bush won in 2004 in a landslide over John Kerry. The area includes large pockets of agriculture and ranching, and Latinos overall account for 30% of the population. The mostly affluent district—household incomes in some areas are $15,000 or more above the statewide average—includes all of Oceanside; it is not a coastal district but rather a hilly, inland, fast-growing area swelling with refugees from high-cost cities and with senior citizens in search of space and an agreeable climate. Registered Republicans outnumber Democrats by nearly 20 percentage points. Republicans control the area politically at all levels of state, local, and federal government, making it easy territory for U.S. Representative Darrell Issa, the Vista-based car-alarm magnate who was first elected in 2000 and has won easily here in the past three general elections.

That Issa has been able to be successful here at all is due in part to his wealth—he's reputed to be worth $200 million—and his personal charm and popularity, as well as his ability to weather unsavory episodes from his past life. He won the undying gratitude of many Republicans for bankrolling the 2003 recall initiative that swept former Democratic Governor Gray Davis from office. Clearly, without Issa's money, the recall signature-gathering campaign would have fizzled. Issa and Governor Arnold Schwarzenegger, Davis's successor, remain close friends. Still, Issa's involvement in the recall effort was motivated in part by a desire to become governor himself, and he already had declared his candidacy to succeed Davis when Schwarzenegger announced his intention to run. Issa, a realist if nothing else, soon bowed out of the race during a tear-filled press conference.

Issa's ambitions to run statewide had surfaced before—during his first political campaign, a 1998 GOP primary challenge against Matt Fong for the U.S. Senate. But Issa withered before a scandal that developed in the final weeks of the race, when the *Los Angeles Times* reported details of his early business background, including an episode in which Issa allegedly waved a gun during a confrontation with a former business associate. Issa downplayed the incident—"Shots were never fired," he was quoted as saying, in what became the most memorable comment of the campaign.

Later, the *San Francisco Chronicle* reported an incident in Santa Clara County, in which Issa and his brother allegedly faked the 1980 theft of Issa's Mercedes Benz and sold it to a car dealer for $16,000, according to court records. It was the second car theft incident in Issa's past; eight years earlier, in 1972, then-19-year-old Issa was indicted with his brother William in Ohio on a charge of felony grand theft for allegedly stealing a red Maserati sports car from a car dealership in Cleveland, court records show. The case was dropped.

Perhaps Issa was merely testing the equipment because he built his personal fortune making and marketing anti-theft automobile alarms. In 1994, before he went into politics, Issa received the "Entrepreneur of the Year" Award from *Inc. Magazine* and the *San Diego Union-Tribune.*

Despite his rocky beginnings, Issa has developed into a capable and respected lawmaker. When Republicans controlled the House, he served as chairman of the Subcommittee on Energy and Resources and as a member of the House International Relations Committee, the Judiciary Committee, and the Energy and Commerce Committee. But as his bankroll of the recall election shows, Issa's statewide ambitions continue to percolate just below the surface. After the 2006 elections, Issa flashed his ambitions internally, running for chairman of the House Republican Policy Committee. He was thwarted by Thad McCotter of Michigan but remains a member of the committee.

BIOGRAPHY: Born: Cleveland, OH, November 1, 1953. Education: BA, Sienna Heights University. Military: U.S. Army. Family: wife Kathy, one son. Religion: Eastern Orthodox.

OFFICES: Capitol: Cannon Building 211,Washington, DC 20515, Phone: (202) 225-3906, Fax: (202) 225-3303, email: darrell.issa@mail.house.gov. District: 1800

Thibodo Road, Suite 310, Vista, CA 92081, Phone: (760) 599-5000, Fax: (760) 599-1178.
COMMITTEES: Energy and Commerce
ELECTED: 2000
ELECTION HISTORY: None.
2002 ELECTION: Issa (R*) 78%
                    Dietrich (L) 22%
2004 ELECTION: Issa (R*) 62%
                    Byron (D) 35%
                    Grossmith (L) 3%
2006 ELECTION: Issa (R*) 63%
                    Criscenzo (D) 34%
                    Grossmith (L) 3%
RATINGS: ACU ADA AFL-CIO CoC GO LCV NTU PIRG
               84   0   13   93   A-   0   59   4

TOM LANTOS (D)
12th Congressional District

Counties: San Francisco, San Mateo
Cities: San Francisco, Daly City, South San Francisco, San Mateo, San Carlos, Hillsborough, Millbrae, Burlingame, Foster City, Pacifica
Ethnicity: 48% White, 16% Latino, 3% Black, 30% Asian
Voter Registration: 51% D – 21% R – 24% DS
President 04: 72% Kerry, 27% Bush

Tom Lantos

Not much changed in this district during the 2001 reapportionment. It still straddles the San Francisco Peninsula, starting near the city's Sunset District and reaching south to Redwood City. It includes the uninhabited Farrallon Islands, the state's second-largest Asian population, and the highest number of decline-to-state registrants of any congressional district. Affluent doesn't begin to describe parts of the area such as Hillsborough, which help raise the median family income over 60% higher than the national average. The median value of a home is nearly four times the national average. The unemployment rate was listed as 2% in 2000, while only 5% of district residents live below the federal poverty line. Voters tend to be pro-environment, well educated, and more and more concerned with the traffic congestion that marks their commutes to and from work either in San Francisco or in other parts of the Silicon Valley.

Incumbent Tom Lantos has been in Congress since 1980 and shows no signs of slowing down as he approaches 80. The only holocaust survivor to serve in Congress, Lantos came to the United States in 1947 after spending part of World War II as a member of the Hungarian underground. His experiences during the war were filmed as part of an award-winning documentary, "Last Days," produced by the Shoah Foundation.

After the war, Lantos earned degrees in economics and international affairs, and prior to entering elective office, he was a professor of economics at San Francisco State University. He has spent his congressional career as a champion of the world's have-nots, founding the Congressional Human Rights Caucus more than 20 years ago and continuing to serve as its co-chair. He has been an ardent champion of increased funding for stem cell research and has worked to secure rebates for Californians hurt during the energy crisis of the late 1990s. He maintains a keen interest in foreign affairs and took over as chairman of the influential International Relations Committee when the 110th Congress convened in January 2007. He had been ranking member under Republican leadership.

Lantos, a devoted liberal, often demonstrates independence in Congress, voting his conscience rather than the party line. After a quarter century in office, he has become one of the most respected members of the California delegation—a respect that often is not bounded by party lines. In 2005, when Lantos's granddaughter gave a concert at the Kennedy Center in Washington to raise money for research into a rare blood disease from which she suffers, she was accompanied on the piano by no less than Secretary of State Condoleezza Rice. Among those in the audience was another Lantos family friend, then-United Nations Secretary-General Kofi Annan.

That respect is reflected at home. He tends his district well and has been instrumental in securing funding for many local projects, including extension of the BART system into his district. There likely are many area officials who covet Lantos's safe Democratic seat, but he has given no indication that he plans to retire. Re-election is not a question but a certainty if his name is on the ballot, and 2006 provided him with his biggest margin of victory in years.

BIOGRAPHY: Born: Budapest, Hungary, February 1, 1928. Home: San Mateo. Education: BA, MA, University of Washington; PhD, UC Berkeley. Military: None. Family: wife Annette, two daughters, seventeen grandchildren. Religion: Jewish.

OFFICES: Capitol: Rayburn Building 2413, Washington, DC 20515, Phone: (202) 225-3531, Fax: Not available; email: tom.lantos@mail.house.gov. District: 400 South El Camino Real, Suite 410, San Mateo, CA 94402, Phones: (650) 342-0300, (415) 566-5257, Fax: (650) 375-8270.

COMMITTEES: International Relations (chair); Government Reform.

ELECTED: 1980

ELECTION HISTORY: Millbrae Board of Education, 1958–1966.

2002 ELECTION: Lantos (D*) 68%
  Moloney (R) 25%
  Abu-Ghazalah (L) 7%

2004 ELECTION: Lantos (D*) 68%
  Garza (R) 21%

                        Gray (G) 9%
                        Harrison (L) 2%
2006 ELECTION: Lantos (D*) 76%
                        Moloney (R) 24%
RATINGS: ACU ADA AFL-CIO CoC GO LCV NTU PIRG
                0   95   93   38   F-   92   11   92

BARBARA LEE (D)
9th Congressional District

Counties: Alameda
Cities: Oakland, Berkeley, Castro Valley
Ethnicity: 35% White, 19% Latino, 27% Black, 16% Asian
Voter Registration: 63% D – 10% R – 21% DS
President 04: 86% Kerry, 13% Bush

Barbara Lee

California's 9th District, geographically one of the smallest north of the Central Valley, encompasses just over 130 square miles of land east of the San Francisco Bay. The district includes 44% of Alameda County, beginning in the northwest corner with the mudflats of Albany, moving south through the hills and old-growth redwood forests of Berkeley and Oakland, taking in the rapidly gentrifying, high-tech enclave of Emeryville, the flourishing Port of Oakland, and ending 27 miles southeast of San Francisco in unincorporated Castro Valley.

For such a tiny land mass, the 9th packs a wealth of cultural diversity and history. It is home to the University of California, Berkeley, birthplace of the Free Speech and anti-war movements of the 1960s, and the city of Oakland, where Huey Newton, Bobby Seale, and David Hilliard founded the Black Panther Party. Today, it contains a high percentage of same-sex couples and Asian Pacific Americans. More than a quarter of its population is foreign born, and 35% of its population speaks a language other than English at home. In Albany's school district alone, students speak more than 17 languages, including Korean, Mandarin, and Cantonese.

The district is patchwork of municipalities that often have little in common but a shared boundary. The district takes in Piedmont—one of the state's wealthiest, most educated cities—and Oakland, which tips the scale in the other direction. Spanning 1.8 square miles, Piedmont is the district's second smallest city but its largest concentration of wealth. During the roaring '20s it was nicknamed "City of Millionaires." Today, its per capita income is about $71,000, the highest in the district and more than triple that of Oakland. Nearly 78% of Piedmont's population holds a bachelors degree or higher, compared to 31% in Oakland.

When reapportionment altered the political landscape in 2002, the district gained San Leandro and some unincorporated land south of Oakland, changing its geography but not its political leanings. Democrat Barbara Lee clinched a sixth term in November 2006 with 86% of the vote. The district, a long-time Democratic stronghold, cast almost as many votes for Ralph Nader in 2000 as for George W. Bush. And votes for Al Gore surpassed both by six to one. Nearly nine out of 10 district voters preferred John Kerry over Bush in 2004.

Lee gained her House seat in a 1998 special election following the retirement of Ron Dellums, Lee's former boss and the area's congressman for nearly three decades. Lee, more reticent and less fiery than Dellums, was largely unrecognized outside of the Bay Area until 2001, when she cast the lone vote against authorizing the use of force in retaliation after the September 11 terrorist attacks. In another congressional district, that vote might have cost Lee any possibility of re-election, but it only enhanced her support in the East Bay, where protest and anti-war politics are honored traditions. Locally, Lee is known for her ability to build coalitions and raise funds. Meanwhile, her old boss, Dellums, came out of political retirement in 2006 to become mayor of Oakland.

Among Lee's top legislative priorities are peace issues, the fight against HIV/ AIDS, and affordable housing. Lee has recently secured $5 million in funding for HIV/AIDS services in Alameda County and a $34 million grant from the Department of Housing and Urban Development for Oakland. She procured $50 million for dredging silt from the Port of Oakland, America's fourth largest container port, and she has raised $18 million toward the Ed Roberts campus project—a $35 million endeavor to provide Bay Area disabled persons with a center for independent living.

Lee's congressional clout and fortunes soared when Democrats took control of the House following the 2006 election. Speaker Nancy Pelosi named Lee to a seat on the powerful Appropriations Committee where she joins five other Californians—including two others from the Bay Area.

BIOGRAPHY: Born: El Paso, TX, July 16, 1946. Home: Oakland. Education: BA, Mills College; MSW, UC Berkeley. Military: None. Family: Divorced, two children, two grandchildren. Religion: Baptist.

OFFICES: Capitol: Rayburn Building 2444, Washington, DC 20515, Phone: (202) 225-2661, Fax: (202) 225-9817, email: barbara.lee@mail.house.gov. District: 1301 Clay Street, Suite 1000N, Oakland, CA 94612, Phone: (510) 763-0360, Fax: (510) 763-6538.

COMMITTEES: Appropriations; International Relations; Financial Services.

ELECTED: 1998

ELECTION HISTORY: State Assembly, 1990–1996; State Senate, 1996–1998.

2002 ELECTION: Lee (D*) 82%
                     Udinsky (R) 15%
                     Eyer (L) 3%

2004 ELECTION: Lee (D*) 84%
                     Bermudez (R) 13%
                     Eyer (L) 3%

2006 ELECTION: Lee (D*) 86%
                 denDulk (R) 11%
                 Eyer (L) 3%
RATINGS: ACU ADA AFL-CIO CoC GO LCV NTU PIRG
             4   95   93   31 F- 100 21   97

JERRY LEWIS (R)
41st Congressional District

Counties: San Bernardino, Riverside
Cities: Redlands, Hesperia, San Bernardino, Yucaipa, Apple Valley, Needles, Beaumont, Banning, Calimesa, Yucca Valley, Twentynine Palms, Desert Hot Springs
Ethnicity: 64% White, 23% Latino, 6% Black, 4% Asian
Voter Registration: 32% D – 48% R – 16% DS
President 04: 62% Bush, 37% Kerry

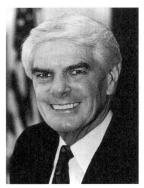

Jerry Lewis

The character of this very solid Republican district did not change much when congressional districts were reapportioned in 2001, but the number (from 40 to 41) and geography were altered. The northern third of San Bernardino County and all of Inyo County were lopped off and the district's southern boundary extended into Riverside County almost to Hemet. The territory is still vast—anything involving most of San Bernardino County would be—but the population center has been expanded into more high-growth areas of the Inland Empire. Traffic congestion, bad air, uncontrolled wildfires, and lack of affordable housing all plague the region—providing grist for issues of concern to voters—as does the continued influx of urban refugees from Orange, San Diego, and Los Angeles counties. Sprawl—with all its variations and ramifications—continues to alter the character of once languid communities such as Yucaipa, Redlands, and San Jacinto. The military maintains a strong presence in the district at such places as Edwards Air Force Base, China Basin Naval Weapons Center, and the Marine Ground Force Training Command. Tourism also is important, especially in the mountainous areas of San Bernardino County, the Mojave Desert, and around Joshua Tree National Monument.

Incumbent Republican Jerry Lewis has represented the area in one place or another for 40 years, having launched his elective career on the San Bernardino School Board when Lyndon Johnson lived in the White House. Lewis was first elected to Congress in 1978 after a decade in the state Assembly, and when the Republicans took control, his seniority gained him one of the most powerful positions in Congress—chairman of the House Appropriations Committee. Accordingly, his tumble was precipitous when Democrats took over the House in the 110th Congress. Although he remains on the Appropriations Committee, his chairmanship passed to Democrat David Obey of Wisconsin.

Lewis's fall from power is the least of his worries as the new Congress convenes. In June 2006 the *Los Angeles Times* revealed Lewis's oh-so-cozy relationship with a defense contractor, who paid thousands of dollars in fees to Lewis's stepdaughter at the same time the contractor was seeking funds from Congress. More significant were Lewis's close ties to a lobbying firm headed by former U.S. Rep. Bill Lowery, a San Diego Republican. One of the firm's clients is yet another defense contractor named as a co-conspirator in the investigation that nabbed San Diego Republican Randy Cunningham, who pled guilty in 2005 to charges of political corruption and now resides in a federal prison in North Carolina. Among other connections, a former Lewis aide went to work for Lowery's firm, which has since dissolved. A federal grand jury is looking into Lewis's use of earmarks, or spending mandates, to benefit specific individuals or companies, and has issued subpoenas to those who may have connections to Lewis and the Lowery firm. Lewis denied any wrongdoing, but he also hired a team of attorneys and a legal spokeswoman.

It is not the first time that Lewis generated his share of controversy, but his past troubles had more to do with ideology than ethics. During the early 1990s, he served as chair of the House Republican Conference and as the California representative on the House committee on committees—a powerful position that oversees committee appointments for individual members. As chair of the Republican Conference, he worked with then-GOP Leader Bob Michel of Illinois to help set the party's legislative agenda.

But a growing number of conservatives in the GOP delegation considered him too much of a moderate, and in 1992 he was bounced as conference chair by Texan Dick Armey, a revolt that presaged a more partisan House under Newt Gingrich who rose to the speakership following the 1994 election. Armey eventually became majority leader. Ironically, California Republicans provided Armey's margin of victory over Lewis, whose fall from grace was greased in some ways by his bipartisan approach to legislating. At one time, he and California Democrat Vic Fazio, who held a position in leadership, were considered the best bipartisan team in Congress—a designation that won Lewis no chits among the GOP's growing army of partisan warriors.

More recently, Lewis broke with Republican leadership and with the George Bush administration to vote in favor of increased federal funding for stem cell research. He was one of only a handful of Republicans who joined with Democrats in 2005 to approve the additional dollars.

BIOGRAPHY: Born: Seattle, WA, October 21, 1934. Home: Redlands. Education: BA, UCLA. Military: None. Family: wife Arlene, seven children. Religion: Presbyterian.

OFFICES: Capitol: Rayburn Building 2112, Washington, DC 20515, Phone: (202) 225-5861, Fax: (202) 225-6498, email: jerry.lewis@mail.house.gov. District: 1150 Brookside Avenue, Suite J5, Redlands, CA 92373, Phone: (909) 862-6030, Fax: (909) 335-9155.

COMMITTEES: Appropriations.

ELECTED: 1978

ELECTION HISTORY: San Bernardino School Board, 1965–1968; State Assembly,
   1969–1979.
2002 ELECTION: Lewis (R*) 67%
                    Johnson (D) 30%
                    Craig (L) 3%
2004 ELECTION: Lewis (R*) 83%
                    Mottahedek (L) 17%
2006 ELECTION: Lewis (R*) 67%
                    Contreras (D) 33%
RATINGS: ACU ADA AFL-CIO CoC GO LCV NTU PIRG
                 76   0   13   93 B-   0   53   7

ZOE LOFGREN (D)
16th Congressional District

Counties: Santa Clara
Cities: San Jose
Ethnicity: 32% White, 38% Latino, 4% Black, 24% Asian
Voter Registration: 48% D – 25% R – 24% DS
President 04: 63% Kerry, 36% Bush

Zoe Lofgren

Stretching along Highway 101 through San Jose, the 16th District was shoved north in the 2001 reapportionment. Gone from the old district are Morgan Hill and Gilroy, while a significant portion of San Jose was added to the northern part of the district. The political character of the district was unaffected by the change, however, and remains solidly Democratic.

Democrat Zoe Lofgren was first elected to the House in 1994, replacing a legendary member of Congress—Democrat Don Edwards, who had held the seat for 32 years and was the dean of the California delegation. Lofgren, despite 13 years on the Santa Clara Board of Supervisors, was an upset winner of the primary to replace Edwards, having defeated former San Jose Mayor Tom McEnery by a slim 3%. Although the McEnery campaign marked Lofgren's last significant electoral challenge, her victory that fall was auspicious, for she was the only newly elected Democrat from west of the Rockies in a year when Republicans finally took control of the Congress after decades of Democratic domination.

A former immigration attorney, Lofgren brought a strong women's agenda to Congress, but her first few years were marked by frustration. As a junior member of a party struggling with sudden and unexpected minority status, she received relatively minor committee assignments and was not in a position to influence legislative policy in her areas of interests—health care, transportation, and the environment.

During her second term, Lofgren co-sponsored the Patients' Bill of Rights and was part of the Clinton administration's congressional effort on education and children's issues. She pushed for wider Internet access in schools and for relief in the cost of prescription drugs for seniors. In the recent session, Lofgren co-sponsored a House resolution to abolish the Electoral College and replace it with a system of direct elections for president and vice president, a notion that went nowhere in the Republican-controlled Congress.

In 2002 Lofgren voted against congressional authorization for the invasion of Iraq, saying that the Bush administration did not provide enough evidence about Iraq's involvement with terrorism and possession of weapons of mass destruction. She subsequently opposed a supplemental budget appropriation for Iraq in 2003 but voted for $78 billion in emergency funds in 2004. Lofgren had one other tangential connection with Iraq; according to *USA Today*, her former press secretary was arrested on charges that she accepted $10,000 to work for Iraqi Intelligence Service prior to the invasion. No connection to Lofgren—or Lofgren's opposition to the invasion—was ever made.

On social issues, Lofgren has compiled a liberal voting record, including opposition to bans on late-term abortions and same-sex marriages. On abortion, she attempted to replace the late-term bill with one that did not confer legal rights on a fetus. It was defeated in the House, although it did garner 196 votes. She has opposed normalizing trade relations with Vietnam because of that country's record on human rights and, closer to home, has been a persistent and vocal critic of domestic surveillance by the National Security Administration.

BIOGRAPHY: Born: Palo Alto, December 21, 1947. Home: San Jose. Education: BA, Stanford; JD, University of Santa Clara. Military: None. Family: husband John Marshall Collins, two children. Religion: Protestant.

OFFICES: Capitol: Cannon Office Building 102, Washington, DC 20515, Phone: (202) 225-3072, Fax: (202) 225-3336, email: zoe.lofgren@mail.house.gov. District: 635 North First Street, Suite 8, San Jose, CA 95112, Phone: (408) 271-8700, Fax: (408) 271-8713.

COMMITTEES: Homeland Security; Judiciary; House Administration.

ELECTED: 1994

ELECTION HISTORY: Santa Clara County Board of Supervisors, 1981-1994.

2002 ELECTION: Lofgren (D*) 67%
McNea (R) 30%
Umphress (L) 3%

2004 ELECTION: Lofgren (D*) 71%
McNea (R) 26%
Welch (L) 3%

2006 ELECTION: Lofgren (D*) 73%
Winston (R) 27%

RATINGS:

ACU	ADA	AFL-CIO	CoC	GO	LCV	NTU	PIRG
4	100	93	37	F-	92	15	91

DAN LUNGREN (R)
3rd Congressional District

Counties: Alpine, Amador, Calaveras, Sacramento, Solano
Cities: Folsom, Citrus Heights, Carmichael, Murphys, Roseville
Ethnicity: 74% White, 11% Latino, 5% Black, 7% Asian
Voter Registration: 36% D – 43% R – 17% DS
President 04: 58% Bush, 41% Kerry

Dan Lungren

The 3rd District is a strangely shaped beast. Its western end splits into two prongs that curl around Sacramento to include its conservative suburbs while excluding the city's more liberal downtown core. The shady, tree-lined streets and towering Victorian homes of inner Sacramento are a sharp political contrast from these sprawling suburbs, where dry prairie grasses still grow on the flat valley expanses between crops of squat, red-roofed single family homes in towns like Folsom, Citrus Heights, and Rancho Cordova. The majority of voters live in these staunchly Republican suburbs, but the district stretches through the Gold Country foothills to touch the Nevada border south of Lake Tahoe. Besides suburban Sacramento, the district encompasses most of the woodsy, mountainous counties of Alpine, Amador, and Calaveras, and a small slice of southern Solano County.

The district, once the province of Democrat Vic Fazio, was made friendlier for Republicans in the 2001 reapportionment. The previous version included parts of eastern Solano and Yolo counties that made the district competitive. Registration numbers have held relatively consistent since 2001, with Republicans firmly in control. According to some observers, it's not possible for a candidate here to be too conservative. The district voted overwhelmingly for Bill Simon in the 2002 governor's race, and two-thirds of voters endorsed the recall of Governor Gray Davis in 2003. In the replacement election, 58% voted for Schwarzenegger, 20% for Democrat Cruz Bustamante, and 16% for conservative Republican Tom McClintock. In November 2004 voters selected Republican Dan Lungren to replace incumbent Republican Doug Ose, who decided not to seek a fourth term.

Politics has been part of Lungren's life since childhood. His father was former President Richard Nixon's personal physician. He walked precincts as a youngster. He graduated from Notre Dame and has often made his Catholicism part of his political profile.

Lungren served in Congress once before—but not from northern California. From 1979 to 1988, he represented Long Beach. In 1988, then-Governor George Deukmejian, a friend and supporter from Long Beach, nominated Lungren to become state treasurer after the death of the incumbent Democrat Jesse Unruh. But the legislature's Democratic majority rejected the nomination. Lungren gained statewide office the old-fashioned way in the next election; he ran for and was elected attorney general in

1990. Following his election, he moved to Roseville and shifted his political base to the north.

Lungren served two terms as attorney general, then tried to follow Deukmejian's route to the top job by running for governor in 1998. As attorney general, Lungren burnished his tough-on-crime, pro–capital punishment credentials and was thought to be a tough candidate for governor. But he ran an inept campaign, focusing on, among other issues, his opposition to abortion—a position that put him out of the mainstream for California voters. He was crushed by Gray Davis and subsequently became a talk show host on the Catholic Radio Network.

In 2004, when Ose decided not to seek re-election, the Republican primary became central to winning the seat. Ironically, Lungren, a self-described Reaganite, was dismissed as the "liberal" underdog to state Senator Rico Oller—an attack-dog conservative who focused his energies on defeating the third GOP candidate of note—Mary Ose, sister of the incumbent. Lungren bided his time until the final weeks of the campaign, then launched an 11th-hour media blitz that took advantage of the fact that voters had soured on both Oller and Ose. He narrowly defeated Oller, with Ose a distant third. He easily brushed aside his Democratic challenger in a district where Democrats are window dressing at best.

Technically a freshman, Lungren was no typical first-termer. Thanks to his previous service in the House, he landed spots on the Budget and Judiciary committees. He lobbied to be named chairman of the Homeland Security Committee after its chairman, Republican Chris Cox of Newport Beach, left the House to head the Securities and Exchange Commission. Lungren got a subcommittee chairmanship instead. Closer to his district home, he joined neighboring Republican John Doolittle to help revive plans to construct a dam across the American River at Auburn—a simmering environmental and flood-control issue that Doolittle has long championed.

When Republicans lost control of the House, Lungren sought a top leadership position in the shakeup that was inevitable after the 2006 election debacle. He ran for chairman of the House Republican Conference, the third-ranking leadership post, and campaigned for the job on a return to conservative principles; namely, smaller government and reduced spending. He finished fourth out of four candidates, quipping to *The Sacramento Bee* that he was "everyone's second choice." Floridian Adam Putnam won the post.

BIOGRAPHY: Born: Long Beach, September 22, 1946. Home: Roseville. Education: BA, Notre Dame; JD, Georgetown. Military: None. Family: wife Bobbi, three children, two grandchildren. Religion: Catholic.

OFFICES: Capitol: Rayburn Building 2448, Washington, DC 20515, Phone: (202) 225-5716, Fax: (202) 226-1298, email: dan.lungren@mail.house.gov. District: 11246 Gold Express Drive, Suite 101, Gold River, CA 95670, Phone: (916) 859-9906, Fax: (916) 859-9976.

COMMITTEES: Budget; Homeland Security; Judiciary.

ELECTED: 2004

ELECTION HISTORY: U.S. House, 1979-1989; California Attorney General, 1990-1998.

2004 ELECTION: Lungren (R) 62%
Castillo (D) 35%
Tuma (L) 3%
2006 ELECTION: Lungren (R*) 60%
Durston (D) 38%
Tuma (L) 2%
Roskey (PF) 1%
RATINGS:

ACU	ADA	AFL-CIO	CoC	GO	LCV	NTU	PIRG
92	0	13	93	F	8	63	0

DORIS MATSUI (D)
5th Congressional District

Counties: Sacramento
Cities: Sacramento
Ethnicity: 43% White, 21% Latino, 15% Black, 16% Asian
Voter Registration: 51% D – 25% R – 19% DS
President 04: 61% Kerry, 38% Bush

Doris Matsui

The 5th Congressional District, the most Democratic in the Central Valley, consists of the city of Sacramento and a few close-in suburbs. The Democratic registration edge includes large numbers of state government workers and many members of unions. Another reason for this edge is the city's ethnically mixed neighborhoods, making Sacramento one of the most diverse cities in the nation. The 5th was designed in the 2001 redistricting to produce a safe seat for veteran Democrat Robert Matsui, with lines only tinkered with from the last redistricting in 1991. Matsui was an easy re-elect in 2002 and 2004.

When the congressman unexpectedly died on New Year's Day 2005 of complications from a rare bone marrow disease, Democratic insiders feared a bruising special election, with veteran politicians such as former Assemblyman Darrell Steinberg and state Senator Deborah Ortiz, among others, vying for a rare congressional opening. But the party was spared an internal bloodbath when Matsui's widow, Doris, sent early signals that she would likely run to succeed her husband. The Democratic establishment quickly united behind Matsui, although the termed-out Ortiz dithered for a few days before finally joining the team. As a result, Doris Matsui breezed to an easy election over a field of 11 lesser-known contenders, capturing 69% of the March 2005 vote.

Her stature as Matsui's spouse—and a Washington, D.C., political force in her own right—did not spare her from sharp attacks by opponents for largely avoiding public debates. She was attacked for being a Washington insider, having been a lobbyist in D.C., and for making a two-year profit of $214,000 from financial partnerships with Sacramento developer Angelo Tsakapoulos, a longtime friend.

Matsui, 62, joins Democrat Lois Capps of Santa Barbara and Republican Mary Bono of Palm Springs in the California congressional delegation as members who took office following the deaths of their husbands. But unlike either Capps or Bono, Matsui is no political neophyte. For years Doris and Robert Matsui, who served on the powerful House tax-bill writing Ways and Means Committee, were among Washington's power couples. Doris served on President Clinton's transition board in 1992, as a special aide to the president during the Clinton administration, and as a Capitol Hill lobbyist.

As a newly elected congresswoman, Matsui was rewarded with a seat on the Rules Committee, a post that gained new significance when Democrats won control of the House. The highly partisan Rules Committee sets the schedule for House floor debate and decides the bills to be heard. In her first term, Matsui used her Washington ties to fight for more federal flood-control and light-rail money and to oppose cuts in Amtrak. She is on record in opposition to President Bush's suggestion that people have the option to set up private accounts under Social Security and in favor of federal stem cell research. She opposed congressional efforts to direct the courts to rehear the case of Terri Schiavo, a disabled Florida woman who died in March 2005 after judges ordered her feeding tube removed.

As the 110th Congress organized under Speaker Nancy Pelosi, Matsui was named to the Democratic Steering and Policy Committee, a 50-member body that recommends committee memberships and chairmanships and helps establish the party's congressional agenda for 2007-2008.

BIOGRAPHY: Born: Poston, AZ, September 25, 1944. Home: Sacramento. Education: BA, UC Berkeley. Military: None. Family: Widow, one child. Religion: Methodist.

OFFICES: Capitol: Cannon Office Building 222, Washington, DC 20515, Phone: (202) 225-7163, Fax: (202) 225-0566, email: doris.matsui@mail.house.gov. District: 501 I Street, Suite 12-800, Sacramento, CA 95814, Phone: (916) 498-5600, Fax: (916) 444-6117.

COMMITTEES: Rules

ELECTED: 2005

ELECTION HISTORY: None.

2005 ELECTION: Matsui (D) 69%
                  J.Padilla (D) 9%
                  Pineda (D) 1%
                  Chernay (R) 4%
                  Flynn (R) 8%
                  O'Brien (R) 3%
                  Singh (R) 2%
                  Stevens (R) 1%
                  Driscoll (G) 1%
                  Morgan (L) 1%
                  Reiger (PF) 0%

                    L.Padilla (I) 1%
2006 ELECTION: Matsui (D*) 71%
                    Yan (R) 24%
                    Kravitz (G) 4%
                    Reiger (PF) 1%
RATINGS: ACU ADA AFL-CIO CoC GO LCV NTU PIRG
              0   100   93   46   F- 100   11   91

KEVIN McCARTHY (R)
22nd Congressional District

Counties: Kern, Los Angeles, San Luis Obispo
Cities: Bakersfield, Paso Robles, Lancaster, Atascadero, Tehachapi, Taft, Morro Bay
Ethnicity: 67% White, 21% Latino, 6% Black, 3% Asian
Voter Registration: 30% D – 51% R – 15% DS
President 04: 68% Bush, 31% Kerry

Kevin McCarthy

If you chair the House Ways and Means Committee and want a safer seat, you get a safer seat—whether you need it or not. And so it was with Republican Bill Thomas when reapportionment time came around after the 2000 Census. Thomas's old district—the 21st—had stretched up the Central Valley from its base in Kern County near Bakersfield to take in parts of Tulare and Madera counties. The district—renumbered 22—now pushes west to the Pacific at Morro Bay and south into Los Angeles County as far as Lancaster. How the district deals with territory adjoining Bakersfield is map drawing at its most creative, however, as it surrounds but does not include a narrow corridor to the south of the city. The corridor, part of the Democratic 20th District, connects the main body of that seat with Democratic precincts in east Bakersfield and another bubble of unfriendly territory to the southeast at Arvin. The result, for Republicans, is an unassailable fortress where GOP registration runs 21% ahead of the Democrats.

Thomas manned this fortress for two elections, but then decided to retire—a prescient decision given that Republicans lost control of the House in 2006, and Thomas would have lost his Ways and Means chairmanship along with it. While he served, Thomas was a hub of power and a wellspring of controversy. He rode a roller coaster since first elected to the House in 1978 after two terms in the state Assembly. He was a rising force in Republican politics when Ronald Reagan lived in the White House, serving as vice chair of the National Republican Congressional Committee and his home state's representative on the GOP policy body that makes House committee assignments. He lost that post to Jerry Lewis when moderates gained clout in the delegation. Not that he was the darling of conservatives either, because Californian David Dreier replaced him on the NRCC, while John Doolittle took over another of his assignments—state expert on reapportionment.

Thomas managed to hold onto one significant job as ranking member of the House Oversight Committee, which made him the only Californian with a chairmanship when Republicans took over Congress after the 1994 election. He soon gained a seat on Ways and Means, ascending eventually to the chairmanship of one of Congress's most visible and powerful panels.

Locally, Thomas exerted control over all things Republican since he helped end conservative dominance of the Kern County Republican Party back in 1973. At the time, Thomas was a community college political science instructor and most local officials were Democrats. But the next year, Thomas won a seat in the legislature by defeating an incumbent Democrat. Four years later, he went to Congress, where he has won re-election by substantial majorities ever since. He expanded his influence by recruiting young Republicans for office, and among his protégés now in elective positions are the man who replaced him, former Assembly Republican Leader Kevin McCarthy, and U.S. Rep. Devin Nunes of the neighboring 21st District.

But to win their seats, both McCarthy and Nunes had to survive contested primaries against a faction that is neither in step with Thomas nor cowed by his exalted position. Those primaries, especially McCarthy's, were expensive and nasty, and the rifts created by the tenor of those campaigns have been slow to heal. Among those who often oppose Thomas at home is state Senator Roy Ashburn of Bakersfield, another former Thomas ally who broke with his former mentor and boss in 1998.

McCarthy's ride to Washington was substantially easier than his ride to Sacramento. Although he drew a pair of GOP primary opponents, there was no factional warfare, and McCarthy won 86% of the vote. He brings with him to Congress experience learned in the do-or-die atmosphere of California's term-limit-driven legislature. The most difficult job in a term-limited legislature is that of a rookie. Mastering Sacramento's learning curve is akin to scaling Mt. Everest, where the summit is shrouded in a fog of policy and politics, the climb begins even before one is sworn into office, it must be made with a minimum of missteps, and there are few if any veterans to help show the way.

McCarthy mastered the basics—and beyond. Chosen in 2004 as California Journal's Rookie of the Year, his swift rise to power exceeded all expectations. Capitol insiders regarded the entire freshman class as exemplary. Several among the Assembly's 31 rookies soared quickly to the top of the house itself. One was elected speaker, McCarthy was elected Republican Party leader, a third chaired the Rules Committee, and a fourth took on the Budget Committee. So singling out McCarthy was a particular honor.

Not that McCarthy didn't endure a few stumbles and fumbles. Although he protected all vulnerable GOP incumbents in the 2004 election, McCarthy and his political team were unable to oust several highly vulnerable Democrats despite ample resources and help from Governor Arnold Schwarzenegger. More significant, McCarthy's biggest failure took place in his backyard—Bakersfield—where GOP missteps allowed Democrat Nicole Parra to win re-election in District 30. McCarthy failed to recruit a strong candidate to oppose Parra, and then stubbornly continued to fund his deeply flawed nominee. It was a problem repeated in San Bernardino County, also considered McCarthy's bailiwick.

Before being elected to the Assembly in 2002, McCarthy was Thomas's district director, and that pedigree gave him the money and resources to win a hard-fought and close 2002 primary against Bakersfield City Councilman Dave Maggard. The primary win was tantamount to winning the seat, and McCarthy coasted through his 2002 general election campaign. Ironically, he replaced Republican Roy Ashburn, a Thomas foe who won a seat in the state Senate.

In replacing his mentor, McCarthy can't replicate Thomas's clout. A junior member of the minority party, McCarthy will not be able to wield a fraction of the influence accorded the chairman of Ways and Means.

BIOGRAPHY: Born: Bakersfield, January 26, 1965. Home: Bakersfield. Education: BS, CSU Bakersfield; MBA, CSU Bakersfield. Military: None. Family: wife Judy, two children. Religion: Decline to state.

OFFICES: Capitol: Rayburn Building 2208, Washington, DC 20515, Phone: (202) 225-2915, Fax: (202) 225-8798, email: kevin.mccarthy@mail.house.gov. District: 4100 Empire Drive, Suite 150, Bakersfield, CA 93309, Phone: (661) 327-3611, Fax: (661) 637-0867; 5805 Capistrano Avenue, Suite C, Atascadero, CA 93422, Phones: (805) 461-1034, (805) 549-0390, Fax: (805) 461-1323.

COMMITTEES: Agriculture; House Administration

ELECTED: 2006

ELECTION HISTORY: State Assembly, 2002–2006.

2006 ELECTION: McCarthy (R) 71%
                 Beery (D) 29%

RATINGS: Newly Elected.

HOWARD "BUCK" McKEON (R)
25th Congressional District

Counties: Los Angeles, San Bernardino, Inyo, Mono
Cities: Palmdale, Santa Clarita, Lancaster, Barstow, Bishop, Victorville, Adelanto
Ethnicity: 57% White, 27% Latino, 8% Black, 4% Asian
Voter Registration: 35% D – 44% R – 17% DS
President 04: 59% Bush, 40% Kerry

In the previous decade, the 25th District was concentrated in Santa Clarita, extending east to Palmdale and no further north than the Los Angeles–Kern county line. The district was relatively compact and safely Republican. Then, mapmakers took over for the 2001 reapportionment, and the original condensed district was blown east and north like a gawky triangular balloon. The new district follows U.S. Route 395 north more than 240 miles past Death Valley and Mammoth Lakes to take in, among other chunks of population-free territory, all of Mono County. District voters are concentrated in and around the old district lines, although sprawl is inching east-

Howard McKeon

ward into the high desert. With high-growth areas of the Inland Empire rapidly filling with refugees from Orange and Los Angeles counties, the region around Victorville now absorbs some of the flight. The 25th is a fairly typical congressional district by U.S. standards with a median family income of $53,500—only slightly above the national average of $50,046.

Incumbent Republican Howard "Buck" McKeon first won the seat in 1992 when he bested a small platoon of GOP contenders, including former Congressman John Rousselot, Los Angeles Assessor John Lynch, and Assemblyman Phil Wyman. McKeon, whose family owns a chain of western-wear shops, was the first mayor of Santa Clarita when he sought a seat in Congress and had little trouble outpacing the Republican field. Soon after he arrived in Washington, his district was hammered by defense downsizing, especially the decision to terminate the B-1 bomber—built in Palmdale by the Northrop Corporation. He has used his position on the House Armed Services Committee to help offset that loss by helping secure a portion of the contract to construct the Joint Strike Fighter at Northrop's Palmdale facility.

Generally a conservative vote, McKeon occasionally breaks with his caucus and with Republican orthodoxy, as he did in 2005 by joining 50 House Republicans to vote for increased funding for federal stem cell research—a position opposed by the Bush administration. He helped pull together a bipartisan coalition to expand the Pell Grant Program, which helps low-income students attend college—part of his focus on jobs and the workforce. A defense hawk, he has supported the war in Iraq, including giving the Bush administration full funding for its efforts in Iraq and Afghanistan.

His most notable legislation in the 109th Congress was a bill that granted 240 acres of excess BLM land to a local Indian tribe, the Utu Utu Gwaitu Paiute Tribe. The land will be added to the Benton Paiute Reservation near Bishop for a health center and small business park. As part of the settlement, the tribe agreed not to conduct gaming activity on the newly acquired land.

Politically, McKeon has few troubles, regularly topping 60% of the vote in his district. Soon, he may be able to win re-election merely on the strength of his family. McKeon and his wife have six children and 26 grandchildren.

BIOGRAPHY: Born: Los Angeles, September 9, 1939. Home: Santa Clarita. Education: BS, Brigham Young University. Military: None. Family: wife Patricia, six children, 26 grandchildren. Religion: Mormon.

OFFICES: Capitol: Rayburn Building 2351,Washington, DC 20515, Phone: (202) 225-1956, Fax: (202) 226-0683, email: tellbuck@mail.house.gov. District: 26650 The Old Road, Suite 203, Santa Clarita, CA 91381, Phone: (661) 254-2111, Fax: (661) 254-2380; 1008 West Avenue M-14, Suite E-1, Palmdale, CA 93551, Phone: (661) 274-9688, Fax: (661) 274-8874.

COMMITTEES: Armed Services; Education and the Workforce.

ELECTED: 1992
ELECTION HISTORY: William S. Hart School Board, 1978–1987; Santa Clarita City Council, 1987–1992; Mayor, 1987–1988.
2002 ELECTION: McKeon (R*) 65%
 Conaway (D) 31%
 Consolo (L) 4%
2004 ELECTION: McKeon (R*) 65%
 Willoughby (D) 35%
2006 ELECTION: McKeon (R*) 60%
 Rodriguez (D) 36%
 Erickson (L) 4%

RATINGS:

ACU	ADA	AFL-CIO	CoC	GO	LCV	NTU	PIRG
84	0	13	93	A-	8	54	8

JERRY McNERNEY (D)
11th Congressional District

Counties: Alameda, Contra Costa, San Joaquin, Santa Clara
Cities: Stockton, Dublin, Danville, Tracy, San Ramon, Pleasanton, Morgan Hill
Ethnicity: 64% White, 20% Latino, 3% Black, 9% Asian
Voter Registration: 37% D – 43% R – 16% DS
President 04: 54% Bush, 45% Kerry

Jerry McNerney

The national earthquake that ended Republican control of the Congress sent one fault line into California, and it ended here, among the growing suburbs and shrinking farms of California's Central Valley. It claimed one casualty—seven-term incumbent Republican Richard Pombo. The benefactor of this seismic activity is Democrat Jerry McNerney, a mathematician and wind-power expert from Pleasanton who lost to Pombo just two years ago and by a significant margin. A seat in Congress is McNerney's first elective office.

Pombo's demise was swift but not entirely unexpected, given the scandals and trends that plagued Republicans all over the country. Pombo represented the district since 1992 when, as a 31-year-old Tracy councilman, he defeated Democrat Patti Garamendi—wife of then-Insurance Commissioner John Garamendi. The election was excruciatingly close, with Pombo's margin of victory only 900 votes out of 165,000 cast in the election. Because of his narrow victory, congressional Democrats targeted Pombo in 1994, but he rode what was then a Republican tide to re-election and never looked back—until 2006.

In Congress, Pombo sewed the seeds of his eventual defeat by exercising both his ultra-conservative values and his hubris. He took on the Endangered Species Act and in 1995 headed a task force that rewrote the law. The result was more reasonable for his large agricultural constituency but a point of outrage for environmentalists.

Over the years, Pombo had made his mark as a member of the Republican majority, and he used his growing influence to help his district. He chaired the House Resources Committee and sat on the Agricultural Committee. But he took a leave from the Transportation and Infrastructure Committee—of vital interest to a district that includes auto-loaded sections of a commuter route between Bay Area jobs and San Joaquin Valley bedroom communities. Those communities represented the way Pombo's district changed during his congressional tenure—from one focused on agriculture to another at the epicenter of suburban sprawl where priorities, not to mention constituents, change. Among his other troubles, Pombo did not adjust to that change.

But Pombo had other troubles related to scandals plaguing all manner of congressional Republicans. He was linked to Jack Abramoff, a once-powerful lobbyist who pled guilty in 2006 to charges of bribery and political corruption and who began to cooperate with federal prosecutors. No one has suggested that Pombo broke the law, but his documented association with Abramoff provided plenty of fodder for Pombo's opponents during both ends of the 2006 election cycle—primary and general.

The incumbent's troubles began in the Republican primary where an old warhorse—former U.S. Rep. Pete McCloskey—emerged from political retirement to challenge Pombo. McCloskey, who once ran for president against Richard Nixon, previously represented the Palo Alto area. He did not have much cash but ran a spirited campaign fueled in large measure by free media, and he hammered Pombo ceaselessly for his Abramoff connections, and for his efforts to gut the Endangered Species Act and turn public land over to private investors. Pombo fired back, arguing that McCloskey was no longer a Republican. Pombo won the primary, but McCloskey polled a third of the vote—a troubling sign for the incumbent.

Sensing an upset in a year when every seat inched the party closer to control of the House, Democrats opened their wallets and resources on behalf of McNerney—who had not been their first choice to win their own primary. But after he defeated airline pilot Steve Filson, Democrats solidified behind him and continued to pound Pombo, using the same themes inflicted on the incumbent by McCloskey. The negatives, coupled with voter frustration over the war in Iraq, crystallized in the few weeks before the election—Pombo's consultant feared the worst when district voters began telling him it was time for change in Washington. Republicans scrambled to shore up their candidate. President Bush made an appearance in Stockton in early October, a visit that McNerney claimed helped him more than Pombo by stirring up the president's foes. Laura Bush arrived the week before the election for Pombo, and former Pres. Bill Clinton stumped for McNerney. Congressional Democrats provided a field general and daily advice. Pombo out-raised McNerney nearly four-to-one, but independent expenditures helped level the field, especially the $1 million spent by environmental groups to oust Pombo.

The district's big voting bloc, and its most reliably Republican base, is San Joaquin County, which provides 56% of registered voters. Pombo won San Joaquin, but only by 2,000 votes out of 110,500 cast in the county. It wasn't nearly enough to offset the beating he took elsewhere in the district. McNerney won the sliver of Alameda County by 8,500 votes, even though the Democratic edge there is less than 1,000 votes. He won Contra Costa County by 4,000 votes in the face of an 8,000-vote registration edge by Republicans. He won the seat with 53% overall.

McNerney's challenge now is to hold the seat in 2008, and Democrats already have moved to place him in positions where he can exercise some clout. Speaker Nancy Pelosi, for instance, gave him a spot on the Democratic Policy Committee. Still, compared with a hardened conservative like Pombo, the rangy McNerney comes off like Jefferson Smith, the Jimmy Stewart character in Frank Capra's "Mr. Smith Goes to Washington."

The district itself remains marginally Republican, thanks to the 2001 redistricting. When the deal was sealed between Republicans and Democrats, the 11th District was treated to a facelift. The old version centered on Stockton, with its southern boundary anchored on Manteca and the northern portion wrapping around metropolitan Sacramento from the south and east. By the end of the previous decade, it was relatively secure for Republicans even though Democrats held a slight, 2% registration edge.

Enter the mapmaker.

The district's top half still centers on Stockton but includes very little of the city itself, instead surrounding it on three sides. The northern portion stops at Galt, some 20 miles short of metropolitan Sacramento. In place of all that lost territory and population, the district slides south and west. Morgan Hill, Pleasanton, Dublin, San Ramon, and Danville—affluent Santa Clara County and East Bay communities—make the district a poster child for "mixed use," combined as they are with agricultural areas in San Joaquin and Santa Clara counties. Registration between the parties is no longer close; the district is decidedly Republican, and that poses a stiff challenge for McNerney

BIOGRAPHY: Born: Hays, Kansas, June 18, 1951. Home: Pleasanton. Education: BA, MA, PhD, University of New Mexico. Military: None. Family: wife, Mary, three children. Religion: Catholic.

OFFICES: Capitol: Rayburn Building 2411, Washington, DC 20515, Phone: (202) 225-1947, Fax: (202) 226-0861, email: jerry.mcnerney@mail.house.gov. District: 2495 West March Lane, Suite 104, Stockton, CA 95207, Phone (209) 951-3091, Fax: (209) 951-1910; 3000 Executive Parkway, Suite 216, San Ramon, CA 94583, Phone: (925) 866-7040, Fax: (925) 866-7064.

COMMITTEES: Transportation and Infrastructure Committee.

ELECTED: 2006

ELECTION HISTORY: None.

2004 ELECTION: Pombo (R*) 61%
                     McNerney (D) 39%

2006 ELECTION: McNerney (D) 53%
                     Pombo (R*) 47%

RATINGS: Newly Elected.

JUANITA MILLENDER-McDONALD (D)
37th Congressional District

Counties: Los Angeles
Cities: Long Beach, Carson, Compton, Los Angeles
Ethnicity: 17% White, 43% Latino, 25% Black, 12% Asian
Voter Registration: 57% D – 21% R – 18% DS
President 04: 74% Kerry, 25% Bush

Juanita Millender-McDonald

Before the 2001 reapportionment, the 37th District cut a compact swath through urban Los Angeles, from Lynwood to Long Beach, bordered on the east and west by Highways 110 and 710. It was overwhelmingly Democratic and ethnically diverse, with a black power structure and growing Latino population. Voters, however, were indifferent. In 2000, incumbent Juanita Millender-McDonald took 82% of the vote in winning a third term. But her raw vote total was only slightly more than that of the Democratic loser in the neighboring 38th District, who captured only 47% of the vote.

Reapportionment left most of the district intact, tinkering instead on the fringes where mapmakers collapsed the old Republican-leaning 38th District. Lynwood was removed in the north as the boundary extended west to take in more of Signal Hill and south to capture the lion's share of Long Beach. The changes didn't make the district any more affluent. A quarter of the population lives below the federal poverty line, while only 63% of those 25 and older have a high school diploma (the national average is 80 percent).

For many years, Democrat Mervyn Dymally, a former state legislator and lieutenant governor, represented the area in Congress. In 1992 Dymally, who has since launched yet another career in the state legislature, retired from Congress and tried to hand the district to his daughter. But she lost a crowded and contentious primary to Walter Tucker III—at the time the dynamic young mayor of Compton who then settled in for what promised to be a long tenure in the House. Unfortunately, Tucker's career ran off a cliff; in 1995 he was convicted of soliciting bribes, among other infractions, while mayor. The 1996 special election to replace Tucker featured a pair of Assembly members—Willard Murray and Juanita McDonald (who has since added her maiden name), as well as the wife of the disgraced incumbent. McDonald won a narrow victory in the primary, blew through the runoff and has not been seriously challenged since in either the old or new district.

A former teacher and once the vice mayor of Carson, Millender-McDonald first took a seat in the state Assembly by winning the 1992 primary against not one but two incumbent Democrats—Dave Elder and Dick Floyd. The veteran lawmakers, both white, had been thrown together by the insensitivities of nonpartisan, court-appointed mapmakers during the 1992 redistricting process. Millender-McDonald visited even greater insensitivities on them by taking 45% of the primary vote, leaving Elder and Floyd to split the rest.

During her rookie year in Congress, Millender-McDonald's most notable event did not involve legislation but occurred when she arranged for the director of the CIA to attend a public meeting in her district. The session followed close on the heels of revelations in the *San Jose Mercury News* that the CIA had been involved in drug trafficking in urban Los Angeles, with the proceeds used to fund anti-Contra activities in Nicaragua. The event was a fiasco, with Millender-McDonald's constituents heckling her guest.

Millender-McDonald has worked to expand health care coverage to underinsured and poor ethnic populations and to enhance federal funding for stem cell research—a bill that puts her in direct conflict with the Bush administration. It isn't the only issue over which the liberal lawmaker has clashed with the conservative president. She has been a vocal and persistent opponent of the war in Iraq, voting against the 2002 resolution authorizing the use of force in Iraq and most subsequent appropriations to finance the war. She has invested much time of late in helping the troubled King-Drew Medical Center, a critical provider of health care for her district.

BIOGRAPHY: Born: Birmingham, AL, September 7, 1938. Home: Carson. Education: BS, University of Redlands; MA, CSU Los Angeles. Military: None. Family: husband James, five children, five grandchildren. Religion: Baptist.

OFFICES: Capitol: Rayburn Building 2233, Washington, DC 20515, Phone: (202) 225-7924, Fax: (202) 225-7926, email: juanita.millender-mcdonald@mail.house.gov. District: 970 West 190th Street, Suite 900, Torrance, CA 90502, Phone: (310) 538-1190, Fax: (310) 538-9672.

COMMITTEES: House Administration; Small Business; Transportation and Infrastructure.

ELECTED: 1996

ELECTION HISTORY: Carson City Council, 1990–1992; State Assembly, 1992–1996.

2002 ELECTION: Millender-McDonald (D*) 73%
　　　　　　　　 Velasco (R) 23%
　　　　　　　　 Peters (L) 4%

2004 ELECTION: Millender-McDonald (D*) 75%
　　　　　　　　 Van (R) 20%
　　　　　　　　 Peters (L) 5%

2006 ELECTION: Millender-McDonald (D*) 82%
　　　　　　　　 Peters (L) 18%

RATINGS:

ACU	ADA	AFL-CIO	CoC	GO	LCV	NTU	PIRG
0	90	93	33	F-	92	13	88

GARY MILLER (R)
42nd Congressional District

Counties: Orange, Los Angeles, San Bernardino
Cities: Mission Viejo, La Habra, Anaheim, Yorba Linda, Diamond Bar
Ethnicity: 54% White, 24% Latino, 3% Black, 17% Asian
Voter Registration: 29% D – 50% R – 18% DS
President 04: 62% Bush, 37% Kerry

Gary Miller

When incumbent Republican Gary Miller ran his final race in the old 41st District, the GOP registration edge had slipped to 2%. Miller wasn't bothered by that slim margin, winning in 2000 by more than 20 points. But a politician, and his party, can't be too careful. So when it came time for the 2001 reapportionment, Miller's old district, built around a compact Chino-Pomona-Yorba Linda triangle, was messed with—like a jackhammer messes with a soufflé. The new (now 42nd) district bears an uncanny resemblance to Italy, with the northern region stretching from Whittier in the west to Chino in the east. The "boot" angles southeast through wilderness to its heel at Rancho Santa Margarita and toe at Mission Viejo. Gone to other worlds are Pomona and Montclair.

The northern part of the district still is one of the smog capitals of California, complete with some of the nation's most clogged commuter routes—including infamous Highways 91 and 60, which transverse the district south of Yorba Linda and along its northern boundary. Much of the area once was orange groves and dairy farms that gave way long ago to blobbed-together suburbs and commercial strips. Although once settled by refugees from high home prices in Orange and Los Angeles counties, the district itself now is relatively affluent, with a median family income more than 50% above the national average. Only 4.2% of families live below the federal poverty line.

Miller came to Congress in 1998 after one term in the state Assembly, the beneficiary of scandal. His predecessor was Republican Jay Kim who, in 1992, became the first Korean American ever elected to the House. Kim was immediately engulfed in controversy stemming from a *Los Angeles Times* series that detailed conflicts of interest in his campaign fundraising. That prompted multiple criminal investigations, and Kim spent the next two elections under a darkening cloud. The lack of an indictment against Kim greased his re-elections in 1994 and 1996, but the situation soon soured. By 1998 he had been indicted and convicted, yet refused to bow out, choosing instead to seek a fourth term. He was challenged in the primary by, among others, Miller, a one-term assemblyman who had profited from another political scandal to win a seat in the legislature.

Ultimately, the Kim-Miller race proved once and for all that "house arrest" is not good for one's political resumé. In March 1998 Kim was sentenced to two months confinement—in Virginia, making it all but impossible to campaign in his district. The place of confinement didn't matter; Kim had become an embarrassment to the GOP, and it was willing to back anyone with a chance to rid it of a convicted felon. Miller, a Diamond Bar councilman before going to Sacramento, easily beat Kim and two other challengers, amassing nearly 50% of the primary vote and scoring a solid if unspectacular victory in November.

It was not the first time that Miller had stepped over the carcass of a fellow Republican. In 1995 he won a special election to the Assembly, prompted by the recall of Republican Paul Horcher—another former Diamond Bar official who gained lasting notoriety when, in the wake of the 1994 elections, he voted for Democrat Willie Brown as speaker of the Assembly and thus denied his own party control of the house. Horcher's treachery threw the Assembly into a year of chaos, and his constituents rewarded him less than a year later by replacing him with Miller. When Republicans finally took control of the Assembly, Miller was named chairman of the Budget Committee—an unprecedented achievement for a rookie. Over the years, Miller financed his campaigns (including two failed attempts to win a state Senate seat) with infusions of his own cash, wealth earned as a real-estate developer.

As a congressman, Miller has been a reliable conservative vote for the Bush administration, most recently siding with the president's stand against increased federal funding for stem cell research. He has supported all phases of the war on terrorism, including the use of military force in both Afghanistan and Iraq. His legislative priorities are increased efforts to bring more water to southern California, easing traffic congestion on Highway 91, and improving the supply of affordable housing. His current legislative load is relatively light but does include an effort to repeal the excise tax on telephone and other communications services.

During the 2006 election season, Miller was subjected to unflattering publicity in the pages of the *Los Angeles Times*. Several former staff members accused Miller of using his position to unduly influence decisions that affected his pocketbook. In one instance, it was alleged that Miller engineered the sale of 165 acres to the Monrovia City Council to be used for a wilderness preserve. Miller, who owned the land, made a profit of $10 million on the sale. At the time, he claimed that the city had forced him to sell under the threat of eminent domain, which allowed him to shelter the profits. The city disputed the claim. In securing the deal, Miller's aides alleged that he pressured them to secure an appointment for one of the Monrovia councilmen to an advisory board for the National Park System—an action his staff warned could be interpreted as a bribe. The *Times* documented several instances where Miller used his official clout to enhance his business dealings, including collecting $25,000 in rent when his campaign operation was housed in property he owned. Miller collected the rent in 2006 even though he ran unopposed. He also was accused of insisting that aides perform personal tasks for him, such as helping his kids with their schoolwork. A federal watchdog group has asked the IRS to open an investigation.

BIOGRAPHY: Born: Huntsville, AR, October 16, 1948. Home: Diamond Bar. Education: Attended Mount San Antonio College. Military: U.S. Army (Vietnam era). Family: wife Cathy, four children. Religion: Calvary Chapel.

OFFICES: Capitol: Rayburn Building 2438, Washington, DC 20515, Phone: (202) 225-3201, Fax: (202) 226-6962, email: gary.miller@mail.house.gov. District: 1800 East Lambert Road, Suite 150, Brea, CA 92821, Phone: (714) 257-1142, Fax: (714) 257-9242; 200 Civic Center, Mission Viejo, CA 92691; Phone: (949) 470-8484.

COMMITTEES: Financial Services; Transportation and Infrastructure.

ELECTED: 1998

ELECTION HISTORY: State Assembly, 1996–1998.

2002 ELECTION: G.Miller (R*) 68%
                     Waldron (D) 29%
                     Yee (L) 3%

2004 ELECTION: G.Miller (R*) 68%
                     Myers (D) 32%

2006 ELECTION: G.Miller (R*) 100%

RATINGS:

ACU	ADA	AFL-CIO	CoC	GO	LCV	NTU	PIRG
96	0	14	92	A-	0	65	0

GEORGE MILLER (D)
7th Congressional District

Counties: Contra Costa, Solano
Cities: Richmond, Vallejo, Concord, Martinez
Ethnicity: 43% White, 21% Latino, 17% Black, 14% Asian
Voter Registration: 5% D – 22% R – 18% DS
President 04: 67% Kerry, 32% Bush

George Miller

One of the distinct features of the 7th District is the Carquinez Strait, a mile-wide waterway between Benicia, which in 1853–54 served as the state's capital, and Martinez, a center of petroleum refineries and railroad traffic. The straight is a key part of the state's fragile water supply and a major route for migrating salmon.

Wealthy landowner General Mariano Vallejo provided the first ferry between the two cities. Today, commuters cross the strait on Interstate 680 via the Benicia-Martinez Bridge, also known as the George Miller Jr. Bridge, named for a member of the state legislature until 1968. That also happens to be the name of the incumbent congressman—a happy coincidence for any politician to have his name on a sign seen from 18 million cars a year.

The bridge, which links Contra Costa and Solano counties, is a good place to observe the central features of the district. Deepwater ports are busy with tankers for oil refineries and ships carrying cars from Japan, which are unloaded in Benicia. Railroad lines lace the area. A few miles to the east, two bridges carry traffic on Interstate 80 between the Bay Area and points east and north.

Between Vacaville and Richmond, the northern and southern extremities of the district on I-80, the district displays its varied past and future: strip malls, farms, fields, and residential housing that climbs the edges of the Coastal Range. Solano County produces more than 70 agricultural commodities such as fruit, nuts, and livestock. Closer to Richmond, development becomes more concentrated, and Casino San Pablo, operated by the Lytton Band of Pomo Indians, looms close to the highway.

That casino—and the controversy that surrounds it—owes much of its existence to George Miller, who played a key role in securing land for the Lytton Band of Pomo Indians. In 2000, Miller wrote an amendment to an appropriations bill that restored land for the casino to the tribe, which had lost its federally recognized land in Sonoma County. A political firestorm erupted in 2005 when the tribe and Governor Arnold Schwarzenegger announced an agreement for a casino with 5,000 slot machines—bigger than many Las Vegas casinos. The tribe backed down—some—but Senator Dianne Feinstein introduced a bill supported by the Bush administration that would undo Miller's action.

Miller has been in Congress since the Earth cooled, while his father served in the state legislature for 22 years between 1946 and 1968. In this part of the Bay Area, "Miller" is as recognizable a public name as "Bonds." In past elections, a majority of residents voted Democratic, and Miller rarely faces trouble in election years. In 1998 and 2002, he trounced his opponents, scoring over 70% of the vote. The district rejected the 2003 Davis recall by 60%, and voters opted for Democratic candidate Cruz Bustamante by 10 points. All this points to a lasting Democratic pedigree.

Elected to the seat in 1975, the liberal Miller has steadily gained power and notoriety. He has served on influential congressional and Democratic Party committees. Miller claims the "No Child Left Behind Act" as one of his most substantial legislative accomplishments, although he is careful to point out that the Bush administration's implementation of the bill is far from ideal.

Miller was an author of the 1992 Central Valley Project Improvement Act, signed by the first President Bush. The law seeks to limit irrigation water for farmers in the Central Valley and increase flows of fresh water to protect fisheries in the delta and the Carquinez Strait. A strong environmentalist, Miller has spent the years of Republican congressional control fighting a rearguard action, trying to prevent the undoing of environmental laws passed when Democrats controlled the House.

When Democrats regained the House in 2006, Miller was poised to resume a position of influence, especially since the new Speaker was one of his closest political allies. Miller assumed the chairmanship of the Education and the Workforce Committee, but not all of his efforts went smoothly. For instance, Miller was one of those who urged Speaker Nancy Pelosi to nominate liberal Pennsylvanian John Murtha as Democratic floor leader—a notion that ran afoul of the Democratic caucus, which voted to give the number-two post to Maryland moderate Steny Hoyer. Miller downplays his influence with Pelosi, but he is regarded now as the main voice and point man for the Democrats' domestic agenda. Among his priorities for the 110th Congress are universal preschool, expanded Head Start programs, and increased grants for needy college students. He also plans to seek adequate funding for the "No Child Left Behind Program."

BIOGRAPHY: Born: Richmond, May 17, 1945. Home: Martinez. Education: BA, San Francisco State; JD, UC Davis. Military: None. Family: wife Cynthia, two sons, four grandchildren. Religion: Catholic.

OFFICES: Capitol: Rayburn Building 2205, Washington, DC 20515, Phone: (202) 225-2095, Fax: (202) 225-5609, email: george.miller@mail.house.gov. District: 1333 Willow Pass Road, Suite 203, Concord, CA 94520, Phone: (925) 602-1880, Fax: (925) 674-0983; 3220 Blume Drive, Suite 281, Richmond, CA 94806, Phone: (510) 262-6500, Fax: (510) 222-1306; 375 G Street, Suite 1, Vallejo, CA 94592, Phone: (707) 645-1888, Fax: (707) 645-1870.

COMMITTEES: Education and the Workforce (chair); Resources.

ELECTED: 1974

ELECTION HISTORY: None.

2002 ELECTION: Geo.Miller (D*) 71%
Hargrave (R) 27%
Wilson (L) 3%

2004 ELECTION: Geo.Miller (D*) 76%
Hargrave (R) 24%

2006 ELECTION: Geo.Miller (D*) 84%
McConnell (L) 16%

RATINGS:

ACU	ADA	AFL-CIO	CoC	GO	LCV	NTU	PIRG
0	100	93	35	F-	100	17	95

GRACE NAPOLITANO (D)
38th Congressional District

Counties: Los Angeles
Cities: Pomona, Norwalk, Pico Rivera, Montebello, La Puente, Hacienda Heights, East Los Angeles, Whittier, South San Gabriel, Santa Fe Springs
Ethnicity: 14% White, 71% Latino, 4% Black, 11% Asian
Voter Registration: 56% D – 23% R – 17% DS
President 04: 65% Kerry, 34% Bush

Looking at the demographics of the newly crafted 38th District, it is hard to imagine that this is part of the California that launched Richard Nixon's political career 60 years ago. Although Nixon's hometown of Whittier was removed from the district in 2001, it still contains communities such as Santa Fe Springs, Montebello, and Pico Rivera that were white suburbs in the years following World War II. That California has fled to Orange County and the Inland Empire, leaving these same communities to host the influx of Hispanics, Pacific Islanders, and Asians, that has made the region a cultural stew.

Grace Napolitano

The 1992 reapportionment was the result of a non-partisan process, and the district it fashioned for this area—bearing the number 34—was relatively compact and centered on Pico Rivera and Whittier. The new version—now the 38th—was created by a partisan deal designed to produce safe districts. The upshot: a geographic mess. It begins with a rather solid chunk from Montebello in the north to Norwalk in the south, and then oozes west to bulge around La Puente and Industry. A small corridor between Walnut and Diamond Bar connects the district to its western frontier—a daub of paint flung on top of Pomona. Taken as a whole, it looks like the aftermath of a Jackson Pollock temper tantrum or what might be left on your shoe after squashing an earwig.

Economically, it aspires to be a middle-class enclave, with the median household income slightly above the national average and the poverty level hovering around 16%.

Incumbent Grace Napolitano inherited the physical hodgepodge that is now the 38th District. Once the mayor of Norwalk, Napolitano first came to Congress in 1998 after serving three terms in the Assembly. At the time, her election surprised many political observers because the grandmotherly politician was competing for an open seat vacated when veteran Democrat Esteban Torres retired after eight terms in Congress. Torres timed his announcement only days before the filing deadline to narrow the field of potential contenders and help his chosen successor, who happened to be his chief of staff and son-in-law, James Casso. But Napolitano, who had been gearing up for a tough state Senate primary against Martha Escutia, rushed to file at the last moment. The two then engaged in a bare-knuckle primary, with prominent Latinos lined up on both sides. Napolitano emerged by a scant 618 votes and has never looked back.

In the House, the liberal Napolitano is regarded as a reliable vote on Democratic causes, especially the environment and immigration. She does not wield substantial influence, although she serves as chair of the Hispanic Congressional Caucus and is a member of the House Resources Committee where she has made removal of uranium tailings stored in Utah a major legislative crusade. Like most Democrats, she is no friend to the Bush administration, voting in 2002 against authorizing the use of force in Iraq and against oil drilling in the Arctic National Wildlife Refuge.

Politically, local Democrats have not entirely conceded the seat to Napolitano, and she has endured primary challenges in 2002 and 2004. The incumbent swept both pretenders aside, but each captured at least 20% of the vote—a signal to Napolitano that she must continue to tend the home front so as not to give some local upstart an opening to launch a more aggressive ambush. She did not draw a primary opponent in 2006.

BIOGRAPHY: Born: Brownsville, TX, December 4, 1936. Home: Norwalk. Education: LA Trade Tech; Southmost College; Cerritos Community College. Military:

None. Family: husband Frank, five children, 14 grandchildren. Religion: Catholic.

OFFICES: Capitol, Longworth Building 1610, Washington, DC 20515, Phone: (202) 225-5256, Fax: (202) 225-0027, email: grace.napolitano@mail.house.gov. District: 11627 East Telegraph Road, Suite 100, Santa Fe Springs, CA 90670, Phone: (562) 801-2134, Fax: (562) 949-9144.

COMMITTEES: Resources; Transportation and Infrastructure; International Relations.

ELECTED: 1998

ELECTION HISTORY: Norwalk City Council, 1986–1996 (Mayor, 1989); State Assembly, 1992–1998.

2002 ELECTION: Napolitano (D*) 71%
Burrola (R) 26%
Cuperus (L) 3%

2004 ELECTION: Napolitano (D*) 100%

2006 ELECTION: Napolitano (D*) 75%
Street (R) 25%

RATINGS:

	ACU	ADA	AFL-CIO	CoC	GO	LCV	NTU	PIRG
	0	100	100	35	F-	100	12	92

DEVIN NUNES (R)
21st Congressional District

Counties: Fresno, Tulare
Cities: Fresno, Clovis, Visalia, Tulare, Dinuba, Porterville
Ethnicity: 46% White, 43% Latino, 2% Black, 5% Asian
Voter Registration: 34% D – 50% R – 13% DS
President 04: 65% Bush, 34% Kerry

Devin Nunes

The 21st District once occupied territory to the south of its current version and there was held by one of the most powerful members of Congress—then-House Ways and Means Committee chairman Bill Thomas of Bakersfield. But thanks to population growth over the last decade of the 20th century, California was able to add an additional congressional district, and in the machinations used by mapmakers to create that new district, the 21st was shoved north into Fresno and Clovis. Along the way, it picked up some pristine landscape in Kings Canyon and Sequoia national parks. Kern and San Luis Obispo counties were dropped, with Thomas's home displaced to the neighboring 22nd District.

Not that the 21st left the Thomas orbit. Designed as an open seat with the potential to elect a Latino Republican, the 21st fulfilled its promise in 2002 with the election of Thomas protégé Devin Nunes.

Despite backing from Thomas, Nunes's road to Congress was not a sure thing when he declared for the 2002 GOP primary. Because the 21st was a newly created open seat, with serious GOP overtones, seven Republicans filed to run, among them former Fresno Mayor Jim Patterson and incumbent Assemblyman Mike Briggs. Ironically, it was Briggs's presence that made the entire contest competitive; it stirred conservatives to pump money and resources into Patterson's campaign. The reason: In 2002 Briggs was one of only four Republican legislators to join Democrats and vote for the state budget. That brought the wrath of Republican chieftans down on him—and that wrath materialized in the form of support by the Washington, D.C.–based Club for Growth. Why Patterson? Conservatives didn't much care for Thomas either, hence their support for the cash-strapped Patterson. Without that help, Patterson never would have been able to broaden his base of support beyond Fresno.

Unfortunately, Patterson's financial foundation was confined to conservatives because of Nunes and Thomas. With Thomas's help, the 28-year-old dairy farmer built up a $500,000 campaign treasury, allowing him to take up residence in district mailboxes and develop a strong media campaign in vote-rich Fresno County. Nunes, thanks to Thomas' arm-twisting, was endorsed by nine members of the California congressional delegation, as well as *The Fresno Bee*—hometown paper for both Briggs and Patterson. More significant, Nunes's alliance with Thomas shut down Beltway money to anyone else.

Ultimately, geography played a role in the outcome. Fresno and Tulare counties provide equal numbers of GOP voters, but Patterson and Briggs split the Fresno vote. Patterson won Fresno County, but his margin of victory over Nunes was too small to offset Nunes's bulge in his home base of Tulare County. Had either Patterson or Briggs been alone in the race, the outcome might have been different. Nunes dispatched his token Democratic opponent to assume his place in Washington.

The Thomas connection helped Nunes once he arrived in the Capitol. He secured a seat on Thomas's Ways and Means Committee and served as assistant majority whip. A Republican Latino of Portuguese descent, he serves as vice chair of the Congressional Hispanic Conference and can be expected to move up in leadership as the party tries to showcase its diversity.

For the most part, Nunes has tacked right, as evidenced by ratings from various interest groups. He broke with Thomas in 2005 over stem cell research, voting against extended federal funding. Before the 109th Congress adjourned in December 2006, Nunes tried to resolve a dispute over restoration of the San Joaquin River, but his efforts were stonewalled in the U.S. Senate. He has promised to take up the issue again in 2007, but he will be dealing with a Democrat-controlled Congress which places more emphasis on environmental concerns than did the GOP House.

With Thomas now gone from Congress, and the House controlled by Democrats, Nunes's immediate fortunes are uncertain. He faces no electoral threat at home, but the extent of his influence is sharply curtailed as a minority member without a powerful mentor.

BIOGRAPHY: Born: Tulare, October 1, 1973. Home: Visalia. Education: BS, MS, Cal Poly, San Luis Obispo. Military: None. Family: wife Elizabeth. Religion: Catholic.

OFFICES: Capitol: Longworth Building 1013, Washington, DC 20515, Phone: (202) 225-2523, Fax: (202) 225-3404, email: devin.nunes@mail.house.gov. District: 113 North Church Street, Suite 208, Visalia, CA 93291, Phone: (559) 733-3861, Fax: (559) 733-3865; 264 Clovis Avenue, Suite 206; Clovis, CA 93612, Phone: (559) 323-5235, Fax: (559) 323-5528.

COMMITTEES: Agriculture; Resources; Ways and Means (on leave).

ELECTED: 2002

ELECTION HISTORY: None.

2002 ELECTION: Nunes (R) 71%
LaPere (D) 26%
Richter (L) 3%

2004 ELECTION: Nunes (R*) 73%
Davis (D) 27%

2006 ELECTION: Nunes (R*) 67%
Haze (D) 30%
Miller (G) 3%

RATINGS:

ACU	ADA	AFL-CIO	CoC	GO	LCV	NTU	PIRG
84	5	29	96	A-	0	59	0

NANCY PELOSI (D)
8th Congressional District

Counties: San Francisco
Cities: San Francisco
Ethnicity: 43% White, 16% Latino, 9% Black, 30% Asian
Voter Registration: 55% D – 10% R – 29% DS
President 04: 84% Kerry, 14% Bush

Nancy Pelosi

It is called the marble ceiling, and for more than 200 years it remained an impenetrable barrier for ambitious women. It layered most aspects of the American power structure, but it provided an especially tough obstacle in the Congress, where the influence of women was muted by tradition, seniority, and institutional procedure. The first woman member did not even serve until 1916 when Jeannette Rankin won a seat from Montana. The first senator, Hattie Caraway of Arkansas, arrived in 1932 to replace her late husband. Since that time, 230 women have served in one house or the other, but not one rose to lead her party. Not even the White House was as unaffected as Congress to the steady advancement of feminine power. First Ladies dating back to Abigail Adams and including Edith Wilson, Eleanor Roosevelt, Nancy Reagan, and Hilary Clinton have strongly influenced their president husbands.

But Congress largely remained immune.

Until November 16, 2006. On that historic date, congressional Democrats, who regained the House majority in the 2006 elections, selected San Franciscan Nancy Pelosi to be Speaker of the House of Representatives—arguably the most powerful position in Congress and second in line for the presidency behind only the vice president.

For 40 years, just three people have represented eastern San Francisco in the House, and two of them rose to within striking distance of the speakership. The first was Democrat Phil Burton. Elected to the state Assembly in 1956 and Congress in 1964, he built a powerful political dynasty as he climbed the political ladder in Sacramento and Washington, coming within one vote of becoming House Majority Leader in 1976. In San Francisco, Burton's political machine launched the careers of Assembly Speaker Willie Brown, Mayor George Moscone, and state Senate President pro Tem John Burton, Phil's younger brother.

The second occupant was Burton's wife Sala, who filled it when he died of a heart attack in 1983. Four years later, she died of cancer but not before hand-picking her successor—Nancy Pelosi, at the time a party activist close to the Burton machine.

Politics was part of Pelosi's blood. Born into a prominent Baltimore political family, she was the daughter of five-term Democratic Congressman and three-term Mayor Thomas J. D'Alesandro, Jr. Her older brother also served as mayor. At home, Pelosi learned back scratching by maintaining a file of constituents who came to her father for help and could be asked to return the favor during campaign season. But it was Pelosi's connection to Burton that propelled her to Congress and started her climb to become the nation's first Speaker.

Although technically a political novice, Pelosi had been preparing to run her entire life. After college, she married Paul Pelosi. The couple moved to San Francisco, where Paul made millions as an investor. As she raised her five children, Pelosi volunteered in Democratic causes. Over the years, she went from hosting small get-togethers at the family's Pacific Heights home in the early 1970s to serving as chair of the California Democratic Party and finance chair of the Democratic Senatorial Campaign Committee in the early and mid-1980s. Pelosi accepted Sala Burton's request to run and narrowly prevailed over gay San Francisco Supervisor Harry Britt and a dozen other candidates—spending $1 million, more than all of her rivals put together.

She remains one of the top fundraisers in Congress, and the millions she showered on colleagues helped her when she needed to call in favors of her own, starting with her first leadership run in the early 1990s. She became whip in 2001, and when Minority Leader Dick Gephardt left to take another stab at the presidency in 2004, Pelosi locked up the votes she needed to succeed him.

As she rose, fellow Democrats labeled Pelosi an "airhead" and "dilettante," while Republicans called her—worse—a "San Francisco liberal." Although she has a history of being pragmatic, putting aside her own issues when necessary, she has consistently tacked to the left of her party. When gay marriage issues engulfed the political world in 2004, Pelosi supported marriage even as California's Democratic senators, Barbara Boxer and Dianne Feinstein, moderated their stances.

As Speaker, Pelosi's pragmatic side must emerge if she is to keep her party in power. Many Democrats elected for the first time in 2006 represent districts where moderation is a virtue, and if they are to keep those seats in 2008—when wounded Republicans make a dogged effort to return to power—they must hew to the center. The Speaker must hew with them, and that journey already has upset some of her more outspoken and leftist San Francisco constituents. Pelosi represents more than 80% of the city's residents and every part of the city except the Sunset and Twin Peaks districts in the southwest quadrant. It is one of the safest seats in Congress, and one of the most liberal, and it will give Pelosi plenty of running room as Speaker—even as it gives her an occasional earful about her pragmatic approach.

Pelosi's challenges as Speaker are enormous, not the least of which is keeping her often fractious party caucus unified and productive. The Republican-controlled 109th Congress was savaged during the 2006 election campaign for its scandals, but also for accomplishing little to address such problems as the federal deficit, health care reform, terrorism and homeland security, and education—not to mention the war in Iraq. Democrats must now deal with these issues, and Pelosi is responsible for lashing them to the grindstone and developing an agenda for governing. She also must keep Democrats from exacting revenge for the way Republicans ran the House over the past dozen years.

Her first step down the leadership road was anything but steady or unifying. On the day she was elected Speaker, Pelosi tried to have a key ally, Pennsylvanian John Murtha, elected majority leader. It was not a popular choice, even though Murtha had become a cult hero for his outspoken opposition to the war in Iraq. Most of Pelosi's colleagues—including many from the California delegation—backed an old Pelosi rival, Steny Hoyer of Maryland. Pelosi sought a confrontation over the post, and she lost—badly. The internal struggle over Murtha highlighted rifts within the Democratic caucus, and Pelosi worked hard in succeeding months to soothe them over.

One focal point was her insistence that the Democratic Congress set an agenda to serve as a counterpoint to the Bush administration, and she promised an aggressive drive to enact a flurry of bills within the first few months of Democratic control. High on her list were an increase in the minimum wage, a new ethics package to govern congressional behavior and regulate lobbyists, a cut in interest rates on student loans, reform of the congressional practice of earmarking, reviewing subsidies to oil companies, funding for stem cell research, and revisiting the No Child Left Behind program. She plans an ambitious effort to create an "innovation agenda" in cooperation with the high-tech industry in California and elsewhere. It is an effort she launched in 2006 and calls for huge funding increases for the National Science Foundation, educating more than 100,000 scientists, engineers and mathematicians, and making permanent a research tax credit.

More significant, Pelosi and her Senate counterpart, Democrat Harry Reid of Nevada, must forge a relationship with the Bush administration, which had its way with the Republican Congress. Early on, Pelosi signaled a willingness to work with the president, saying that voters want an end to bipartisan bickering. She resisted calls for impeaching the president over Iraq and declared that Democrats would not withhold funds to prosecute the war, saying Congress would support American troops as long as they remained on dangerous ground. That said, she warned that Congress would work with the administration but not do its bidding.

Pelosi's greatest achievement as Speaker may already have occurred—the not-so-simple act of taking a jackhammer to that marble ceiling. "There is a role-model effect," one observer told the San Francisco Chronicle. "When you see someone who looks like you in a position of power, you think, 'I can do it, too.'"

BIOGRAPHY: Born: Baltimore, MD, March 26, 1940. Home: San Francisco. Education: AB, Trinity College. Military: None. Family: husband Paul, five children, five grandchildren. Religion: Catholic.

OFFICES: Capitol: Cannon Office Building 235, Washington, DC 20515, Phone: (202) 225-4965, Fax: (202) 225-8259, email: sf.nancy@mail.house.gov. District: 450 Golden Gate Avenue, Suite 145378, 14th Floor, San Francisco, CA 94102, Phone: (415) 556-4862, Fax: (415) 861-1670.

COMMITTEES: Speaker of the House.

ELECTED: 1988

ELECTION HISTORY: None.

2002 ELECTION: Pelosi (D*) 80%
German (R) 13%
Pond (G) 6%
Spivack (L) 2%

2004 ELECTION: Pelosi (D*) 85%
DePalma (R) 12%
Dowell (PF) 4%

2006 ELECTION: Pelosi (D*) 80%
DeNunzio (R) 11%
Keefer (G) 7%
Berg (L) 1%

RATINGS:

ACU	ADA	AFL-CIO	CoC	GO	LCV	NTU	PIRG
0	95	93	36	F-	100	11	89

GEORGE RADANOVICH (R)
19th Congressional District

Counties: Fresno, Madera, Stanislaus, Mariposa
Cities: Fresno, Turlock, Madera, Modesto, Chowchilla
Ethnicity: 60% White, 28% Latino, 4% Black, 5% Asian
Voter Registration: 36% D – 47% R – 13% DS
President 04: 61% Bush, 38% Kerry

When mapmakers finished with the 19th District, it looked like a rhinoceros facing west, with its horn extending north into Sierra foothills between Sonora and Stockton. The district added a largely uninhabited chunk of Tuolumne County in the north,

George Radanovich

as well as a southern footpad extending from Fresno to Mendota and Firebaugh. Its scenic beauty is unparalleled for inland California, containing as it does Yosemite National Park. The Republican registration edge, which tightened at the time the new map was drawn, has ballooned to 11% thanks to trends in the Central Valley. It includes the wealthier parts of Fresno, as well as some of the former "Condit Country" stripped from the 18th District to persuade Democrat Gary Condit to abandon his re-election after a scandal rocked his career.

Little more than a decade ago, the district was represented by a Democrat—Rick Lehman, who now is a lobbyist in Sacramento. Lehman nearly lost the seat in 1992, and campaigned vigorously for re-election in 1994. But that year was marked by a national Republican tide that helped take down Lehman. The Republican who replaced him was George Radanovich, a former Mariposa County supervisor, who beat Lehman by running an aggressive anti-incumbent campaign that lashed Lehman to then-President Bill Clinton. That Lehman spent a good portion of the election distancing himself from Clinton made no difference, and Radanovich had himself a seat in the House.

A vintner, local banker, and substitute teacher, Radanovich made an immediate mark in Washington as the elected president of the 74-member freshman class—a historic group of Republicans who helped restore GOP control of the Congress after four decades of minority status. As such, he helped write the "New America" vision statement that outlined the classic Republican themes that have guided the Congress for more than a decade: smaller federal government and a focus on family, religion, and business enterprise. He has continued to follow the conservative standard on most issues. In 2005, for instance, he supported the Bush administration position and voted against federal funding for extended stem cell research. In a show of support for beleaguered House Majority Leader Tom DeLay, Radanovich voted to weaken House ethics rules that threatened DeLay with censure or investigation. The ploy didn't work, and DeLay resigned in 2006. Radanovich sponsored a bill in 2005 to prevent firearm manufacturers from being held liable for damages resulting from the misuse of their products. A consistent enemy of new taxes, he was honored by the National Tax Limitation Committee with its annual "tax fighter" award for 2006.

Radanovich has ambitions within the House, as evidenced by his brief foray for a leadership position in 1998 when he sought the post of Republican conference chairman. He eventually backed a rival—Oklahoman J. C. Watts. In 1998 he became chairman of the Western Caucus, a post he relinquished in 2001. In the 109th Congress, he served as chair of the Water and Power Subcommittee of the Resources Committee—a position he relinquished when Democrats took control in 2007.

BIOGRAPHY: Born: Mariposa, June 20, 1955. Home: Mariposa. Education: BS, Cal Poly, San Luis Obispo. Military: None. Family: wife Ethie, one son. Religion: Catholic.

OFFICES: Capitol: Rayburn Building 2367, Washington, DC 20515, Phone: (202) 225-4540, Fax: (202) 225-3402, email: george.radanovich@mail.house.gov. District: 1040 East Herndon, Suite 201, Fresno 93720, Phone: (559) 449-2490, Fax: (559) 449-2499; 121 Main Street, Suite D, Turlock, CA 95380, Phone: (209) 656-8660, Fax: (209) 656-8649.
COMMITTEES: Energy and Commerce; Resources.
ELECTED: 1994
ELECTION HISTORY: Mariposa County Board of Supervisors, 1988–1992.
2002 ELECTION: Radanovich (R*) 67%
Veen (D) 30%
McHargue (L) 3%
2004 ELECTION: Radanovich (R*) 66%
Bufford (D) 27%
Mullen (G) 7%
2006 ELECTION: Radanovich (R*) 61%
Cox (D) 39%
RATINGS:

ACU	ADA	AFL-CIO	CoC	GO	LCV	NTU	PIRG
92	0	21	96	B-	0	64	6

DANA ROHRABACHER (R)
46th Congressional District

Counties: Los Angeles, Orange
Cities: Huntington Beach, Costa Mesa, Palos Verdes
Ethnicity: 63% White, 17% Latino, 2% Black, 18% Asian
Voter Registration: 31% D – 47% R – 17% DS
President 04: 57% Bush, 42% Kerry

Dana Rohrabacher

The 46th District is nestled along the southern California coast—and even off the coast, because the district traverses 26 miles of blue water to encompass Avalon—and includes Huntington Beach and Seal Beach, as well as the affluent enclaves of Rolling Hills Estates, Rancho Palos Verdes, and Palos Verdes Estates. The 2000 census showed a median household income approaching $100,000 and the median cost of a home in the area at more than $500,000—a figure that is woefully out of date, given the recent skyrocketing of home values. The solidly white, Republican district, its boundaries rewritten in the last reapportionment, straddles the line between Los Angeles and Orange counties and includes some of the most spectacular ocean-front real estate in California. George Bush did well here in 2004, harvesting both votes and campaign donations. The 46th is often viewed as an Orange

County district, despite its spillover into Los Angeles County, and part of the reason for that is Dana Rohrabacher, the conservative but pragmatic Republican, a surfer and former Orange County newspaper editorial writer, who has represented the area in Congress for nearly two decades.

Rohrabacher, a former special assistant and speech writer to Ronald Reagan, is probably known as much for his penchant for surfing as for his work in Congress, where he is the ranking California member of the House Science and International Relations committees and has served as chairman of the Oversight and Investigations Subcommittee of the House International Relations Committee. A lesser-known fact: Rohrabacher is an Eagle Scout and co-chairs the House Scouting Caucus.

Perhaps Rohrabacher's defining issue is illegal immigration. He was an early supporter—some say author—of Proposition 187, the anti–illegal immigration initiative that voters approved in 1994 after a bitter campaign, and he campaigned heavily on behalf of the measure, most of which was later tossed out by the courts as unconstitutional. But a decade later, illegal immigration remains a transcendent political issue in California, especially in Orange County, and Rohrabacher remains heavily involved in the debate.

Rohrabacher's re-election campaigns have been uneventful, with two exceptions. In 1998 he fended off a significant challenge from Democrat Patricia W. Neal, which developed from the skullduggery of Rohrabacher's staff—including an aide, Rhonda Carmony, who would later become his wife—in the successful recall effort against former Assembly Speaker Doris Allen of Cypress. Allen briefly held the Assembly's top post after she broke ranks with the GOP and parlayed with Democrats to curry support—much to the fury of local Republicans.

The local district attorney, Republican Michael Capizzi, investigated election-linked complaints in the recall, including the allegation that the Rohrabacher staff members recruited a fake Democratic candidate to help Rohrabacher's hand-picked Republican choice, Scott Baugh, succeed Allen. There were other allegations of electoral wrongdoing, too. In the end, after assorted indictments, two trials, a guilty plea by Carmony to two felonies, dismissals by a judge, and assorted other actions, the scandal finally subsided—but only after giving a brutal picture of the political hardball played in Orange County.

Carmony married Rohrabacher in 1997—she was more than just an aide, it turned out—and the couple now are the happy parents of triplets. In the 1998 General Election, Rohrabacher defeated Neal three-to-two.

A comical footnote to Rohrabacher's political career occurred in 2004, when he faced Robert "B-1 Bob" Dornan in the March primary. The voluble Dornan, a veteran Orange County congressman who was defeated by Loretta Sanchez in 1998, was thirsting to get back into Congress and thought that Rohrabacher was vulnerable. Rohrabacher won in a landslide.

In 2006 Rohrabacher spearheaded efforts to present an alternative federal budget, one that would end deficit spending by the year 2011. He also called on the federal government to withdraw aid to Nicaragua should Daniel Ortega be elected president. Ortega won, but the Bush administration has thus far ignored Rohrabacher's advice.

BIOGRAPHY: Born: Corona, June 21, 1947. Home: Coronado. Education: BA, Long Beach State; MA, USC. Military: None. Family: wife Rhonda, three children. Religion: Baptist.

OFFICES: Capitol: Rayburn Building 2338, Washington, DC 20515, Phone: (202) 225-2415, Fax: (202) 225-0145, email: dana.rohrabacher@mail.house.gov. District: 101 Main Street, Suite 380, Huntington Beach, CA 92648, Phone: (714) 960-6483, Fax: (714) 960-7806.

COMMITTEES: International Relations; Science

ELECTED: 1988

ELECTION HISTORY: None

2002 ELECTION: Rohrabacher (R*) 62%
　　　　　　　　　Schipske (D) 35%
　　　　　　　　　Gann (L) 3%

2004 ELECTION: Rohrabacher (R*) 62%
　　　　　　　　　Brandt (D) 33%
　　　　　　　　　Lash (G) 4%
　　　　　　　　　Gann (L) 2%

2006 ELECTION: Rohrabacher (R*) 60%
　　　　　　　　　Brandt (D) 37%
　　　　　　　　　Chang (L) 4%

RATINGS:

ACU	ADA	AFL-CIO	CoC	GO	LCV	NTU	PIRG
96	5	7	81	A	17	76	17

LUCILLE ROYBAL-ALLARD (D)
34th Congressional District

Counties: Los Angeles

Cities: Los Angeles, Culver City, Bell Gardens, Bell, Huntington Park, Maywood, Downey, Bellflower, Vernon.

Ethnicity: 12% White, 77% Latino, 5% Black, 6% Asian

Voter Registration: 57% D – 21% R – 18% DS

President 04: 69% Kerry, 30% Bush

Pity the poor Republicans who live in Downey and Bellflower. They were embroidered on this district (formerly the 33rd) to increase GOP registration, which had been a paltry 14% just prior to the 2001 reapportionment. Unfortunately, that creative needlework raised the Republicans' share to just 21%—still a galaxy shy of competitive. With the exception of those two communities, the district remained much the same—downtown Los Angeles, East L.A., and the largest Latino share of any California congressional district.

The 34th District is illustrative of the state's have-not society—it is poor, ill educated, and politically disengaged. The median family income of $32,000 is well below the U.S. average, while 22% of district families live on the wrong side of the federal

Lucille Roybal-Allard

poverty line. Less than half the adult population has a high school diploma, and more than three-fourths of those over age five speak a language other than English at home. The 34th District also holds the unenviable record for fewest registered voters in a congressional district—165,923. By comparison, the district with the most registered voters—the 4th around Sacramento and the Sierra foothills—has over 400,000.

Incumbent Lucille Roybal-Allard has represented the area since 1992 when the previous reapportionment created a new district. At the time, Roybal-Allard was a three-term assemblywoman with a sterling political pedigree for this part of southern California: She is the daughter of Ed Roybal, the legendary figure who served in Congress for more than 30 years before his retirement in 1992.

Roybal-Allard herself entered elective office in 1987 after winning a special Assembly election to replace Democrat Gloria Molina, who had been elected to the Los Angeles City Council. She filled out Molina's term and was elected twice more before jumping to Congress. Her decision to seek the new congressional seat virtually cleared the field, allowing her to win both the primary and general elections in a walk—an unusual bow to her reputation given how few opportunities for lifetime employment surface in California. Her election provided a historical footnote as well; she was the first Hispanic woman ever elected to Congress.

Roybal-Allard arrived in Washington determined to work in areas critical to her blighted district, which at the time had just endured spillover damage from the 1992 riots that plagued South Central Los Angeles. Her focus was housing, education, and health care. But two years later, Republicans took control of the House, forcing Roybal-Allard to play defense just to preserve vital programs already in place.

In seven congressional elections, Roybal-Allard has never been pressed, allowing her the freedom to play internal politics, although she has continued to be attentive to conditions back home. More than most, she has benefited from the overall expansion of Latino power. In 1998, for instance, she became the first woman to chair the Congressional Hispanic Caucus and was rewarded with a seat on the Appropriations Committee. That assignment allows her to pursue her legislative passions by serving on the subcommittee for health care and education. Her influence in the area will be enhanced now that Democrats form a majority of the House.

A consistent foe of U.S. intervention in Iraq, Roybal-Allard in 2002 voted against the resolution authorizing the use of force against Sadam Hussein's government. That same year, she opposed creation of the Department of Homeland Security. In 2006, she sponsored a bill to curb teenage drinking—HR 864. President George Bush signed it into law just before the end of the year. It is billed as the nation's first comprehensive effort to attack underage drinking.

BIOGRAPHY: Born: Los Angeles, June 12, 1941. Home: Bell Gardens. Education: BA, CSU Los Angeles. Military: None. Family: husband Edward, four children, four grandchildren. Religion: Catholic.

OFFICES: Capitol: Rayburn Building 2330, Washington, DC 20515, Phone: (202) 225-1766, Fax: (202) 226-0350, email: lucille.roybal-allard@mail.house.gov. District: 255 East Temple Street, Suite 1860, Los Angeles, CA 90012-3334, Phone: (213) 628-9230, Fax: (213) 628-8578.
COMMITTEES: Appropriations.
ELECTED: 1992
ELECTION HISTORY: State Assembly, 1987–1993.
2002 ELECTION: Roybal-Allard (D*) 74%
　　　　　　　　Miller (R) 26%
2004 ELECTION: Roybal-Allard (D*) 75%
　　　　　　　　Miller (R) 25%
2006 ELECTION: Roybal-Allard (D*) 77%
　　　　　　　　Miller (R) 23%
RATINGS:

ACU	ADA	AFL-CIO	CoC	GO	LCV	NTU	PIRG
0	90	93	43	F-	100	10	93

ED ROYCE (R)
40th Congressional District

Counties: Orange
Cities: Orange, Fullerton, Anaheim, Villa Park, Placentia, Buena Park, Los Alamitos
Ethnicity: 49% White, 30% Latino, 2% Black, 16% Asian
Voter Registration: 32% D – 47% R – 17% DS
President 04: 60% Bush, 38% Kerry

Ed Royce

Reapportionment overhauled this safe Republican district in 2001, creating instead one that is—well—slightly safer for Republicans. Perhaps the previous version was too compact. Perhaps mapmakers were on a roll after carving Daliesque works of art in districts 38 and 39. Whatever the reason, the old district (39 at the time) was cut in half, with Artesia, Cerritos, and La Mirada sliced away in the west. In their place is an eastern leg from Placentia in the north to Orange and Villa Park in the south, producing a district that fits like a wig around Democratic precincts in Anaheim. Economically, the 40th is an upper-middle-class region with only 7% of families living below the poverty line and the median household income some 20% above the national average. The median cost of a home is twice the national average.

Incumbent Republican Ed Royce has never suffered much of a challenge and likely won't now that the GOP registration edge has been enhanced. Royce first went to Congress in 1992 when the district's previous occupant—Republican William Dannemeyer—made a disastrous attempt to win a seat in the U.S. Senate. At the time, Royce was one of the most conservative members of the state Senate, where he had spent 10 years as an undistinguished backbencher. His most notable legislative achievement in Sacramento was a 1987 bill that automatically revoked the driver's license of anyone who refused to take a roadside sobriety test. Otherwise, Royce left few footprints, often carrying a light legislative load and restricting his floor and committee activity to "no" votes.

In Congress, Royce has been livelier and benefited from the Republican takeover of 1994. Regarded as a loyal soldier, Royce nonetheless has not gained the influence shared by several delegation colleagues who chair the most powerful committees in Congress. Royce's committee assignments—notably as a member of the House International Relations Committee—did not gain center stage until after the terrorist attacks of 9/11. As chair of the subcommittee on international terrorism and nuclear proliferation, Royce stood near the epicenter of two highly charged international debates. He serves on the Financial Services Committee and has been a House-Senate conferee on several key issues, including legislation on corporate accountability. He is a solid vote for the Bush administration on most issues, including stem cell research and support for the wars in Iraq and Afghanistan. A proponent of a fence on the Mexican border, Royce used his waning days as chair of a subcommittee on international terrorism to castigate incoming Speaker Nancy Pelosi for supporting an amnesty program for illegal immigrants.

An accountant for a cement company, Royce's introduction to California's political wars came through involvement with Young Americans for Freedom.

BIOGRAPHY: Born: Los Angeles, October 12, 1951. Home: Fullerton. Education: BA, CSU Fullerton. Military: None. Family: wife Marie. Religion: Catholic.

OFFICES: Capitol: Rayburn Building 2185, Washington, DC 20515, Phone: (202) 225-4111, Fax: (202) 226-0335, email: ed.royce@mail.house.gov. District: 305 North Harbor Boulevard, Suite 300, Fullerton, CA 92832, Phone: (714) 992-8081, Fax: (714) 992-1668.

COMMITTEES: Financial Services; International Relations.

ELECTED: 1992

ELECTION HISTORY: State Senate, 1983–1993

2002 ELECTION: Royce (R*) 68%
　　　　　　　　 Avalos (D) 30%
　　　　　　　　 McGlawn (L) 3%

2004 ELECTION: Royce (R*) 68%
　　　　　　　　 Williams (D) 32%

2006 ELECTION: Royce (R*) 67%
　　　　　　　　 Hoffman (D) 31%
　　　　　　　　 Inman (L) 3%

RATINGS:

ACU	ADA	AFL-CIO	CoC	GO	LCV	NTU	PIRG
96	0	0	77	F-	17	79	18

LINDA SANCHEZ (D)
39th Congressional District

Counties: Los Angeles
Cities: South Gate, Lynwood, Lakewood, Cerritos, Paramount, Artesia, La Mirada, Whittier
Ethnicity: 21% White, 61% Latino, 6% Black, 10% Asian
Voter Registration: 50% D – 29% R – 17% DS
President 04: 59% Kerry, 40% Bush

Linda Sanchez

In the 2001 reapportionment, Steve Horn drew the short straw. A progressive, five-term Republican incumbent from Long Beach, Horn had been squatting on Democratic territory since 1992 when he captured a district that had been vacated by the retirement of Democrat Glenn Anderson. A former university president, he more often than not voted with Democrats on key issues and likely was the only Republican who could have held a district that, by 2000, sported a 22% Democratic registration edge. Still, his election campaigns were always tense; in 2000 he won his fifth term by a mere 2%.

So when it came time to reapportion the state in 2001, Democratic and Republican negotiators agreed that Horn's old 38th District would be dismantled to accommodate the additional House seat accorded to California because of population growth. Created out of whole cloth, that new district became the 39th. Horn took one look at the new map—with its large Latino population and 35% Democratic edge—and promptly called it quits.

On paper, the 39th is not quite the chaotic mess as the neighboring 38th District. Nor, however, is it compact. Shaped like a horseshoe, its western arm includes South Gate, Lynwood, and Paramount. From there, it swoops through Lakewood, Artesia, and Cerritos before shooting north through La Mirada to the Sycamore Canyon area above Whittier. It has a middle-class feel, with the median household income about 10% above the national average. But 37% of its adults have failed to graduate from high school, and about 16% of the population lives below the poverty line.

In 2002 the new district created a scramble among Democrats, with six candidates filing for the primary—two of whom had an electoral base while a third brought a political pedigree. Those with a base were Assemblywoman Sally Havice and South Gate Councilman Hector De la Torre. The pedigree belonged to Linda Sanchez, an attorney and labor official who happened to be the sister of U.S. Representative Loretta Sanchez.

Havice polled well at the outset, but her early stature proved to be an illusion puffed up by her name identification and the fact that she had spent three terms in the legislature. Never a strong fundraiser or campaigner, Havice was soon eclipsed by both of her two main competitors. De la Torre, too, was flawed, but his problem was one of proximity. As an elected official from South Gate, he was tarred with the scandals and recalls that beset that community throughout the late 1990s and early 2000s. Although not the subject of investigations or indictments—he was, in fact, a reformer who helped clean up the troubled city—De la Torre's campaign suffered from guilt by association, a notion reinforced by the fist-in-the-chops campaign waged by Sanchez. At one point, Sanchez accused De la Torre of taking campaign contributions from a trash hauler who did business with the city—an allegation denied by De la Torre and repudiated by other South Gate officials. Sanchez refused to back down.

It was that kind of campaign, especially at the end when De la Torre accused Sanchez of seat shopping—moving into the district from Orange County just to run for Congress.

With Latinos the principal voting bloc, both sides piled up long lists of prominent Hispanic endorsements, but Linda Sanchez held the trump card: her sister. Loretta Sanchez became something of a cult heroine in 1996 when she knocked off one of the nation's most bombastic Republicans—Bob Dornan—to take an Orange County congressional seat. A charismatic, trend-setting Latina, Loretta Sanchez lent both resources and persona to her sister's effort. It was enough, as Sanchez beat De la Torre by 1,300 votes, with Havice a distant third. Linda Sanchez sealed her victory in the 2002 general election, making the Sanchez sisters the first siblings to serve in Congress at the same time. De la Torre, meanwhile, was elected to the state Assembly in 2004.

During her brief tenure in Congress, Sanchez has established herself as a reliable liberal vote on most issues. She is pro-choice, pro-labor, pro–gun control, pro-environment, and against armed intervention in Iraq.

BIOGRAPHY: Born: Orange, January 28, 1969. Home: Lakewood. Education: BA, UC Berkeley; JD, UCLA. Military: None. Family: Single. Religion: Catholic.

OFFICES: Capitol: Longworth Building 1222, Washington, DC 20515, Phone: (202) 225-6676, Fax: (202) 226-1012, email: linda.sanchez@mail.house.gov. District: 4007 Paramount Boulevard, Suite 106, Lakewood, CA 90712, Phone: (562) 429-8499, Fax: (562) 938-1948.

COMMITTEES: Judiciary; Government Reform.

ELECTED: 2002

ELECTION HISTORY: None.

2002 ELECTION: Sanchez (D) 55%
Escobar (R) 41%
Newhouse (L) 4%

2004 ELECTION: Sanchez (D*) 61%
Escobar (R) 39%

2006 ELECTION: Sanchez (D*) 66%
Andion (R) 34%

RATINGS:

	ACU	ADA	AFL-CIO	CoC	GO	LCV	NTU	PIRG
	0	100	93	30	F-	100	13	97

LORETTA SANCHEZ (D)
47th Congressional District

Counties: Orange
Cities: Santa Ana, Anaheim, Garden Grove, Fullerton
Ethnicity: 17% White, 65% Latino, 2% Black, 14% Asian
Voter Registration: 43% D – 37% R – 17% DS
President 04: 50% Bush, 49% Kerry

Loretta Sanchez

A classic example of the power of redistricting, Orange County's 47th Congressional District is solidly Latino and solidly Democratic, and that's exactly how the Democrat-controlled legislature, which conceived the latest reapportionment, wanted it. This dense, urban district includes a small piece of Fullerton, about half of Anaheim, three-fourths of Garden Grove, and almost all of Santa Ana. The mapmakers who drew it had two goals, and they did their work well. First, they wanted to carve out an area with a solid Democratic registration edge, and they managed to get registered Democrats over Republicans by 14%. Second, they sought to enfold a large Latino population to protect incumbent Loretta Sanchez, the first woman and first Latino elected to Congress from Orange County. Here, too, they succeeded. The district is two-thirds Latino; in Santa Ana, nearly nine out of 10 voters are Latino. The district is vibrant and less affluent than the rest of the county. In Santa Ana, the median family income is two-thirds of the county average, and better than 16% of the families live below the poverty line, more than double the county proportion as a whole.

For two decades, much of the area had been represented by Robert Dornan, a former television commentator and Air Force pilot who became known as "B-1 Bob" in Congress for his support of military spending, and who had an unenviable reputation for invective, bombast, and the low blow. For years, he seemed unbeatable—and was. But in 1996 he launched a run for president, labeled Bill Clinton a womanizing draft-dodger, and scurried around the country to campaign. The result was that he didn't pay attention to his district, and Sanchez exploited the vacuum.

A financial analyst by training, Sanchez, largely unknown, mounted an early advertising campaign to build name recognition and worked the precincts 24/7. She used her maiden name in the race, instead of her married name, Brixey, in what critics said was a transparent ploy to appeal to Latino voters. State and national Democrats, stunned to see a woman Latino candidate with a chance against Dornan, gave her support. President Clinton, happy to whack Dornan, paid a visit. Considered a long shot, Sanchez beat Dornan by 984 votes in an election that transfixed the country.

Never one to go anywhere quietly—including into the political sunset—Dornan cried fraud, refused at first to give up his seat, and launched a court battle to toss out the election—a battle that captured national attention and embarrassed nearly everyone connected with it. Toward the end, even Republicans in Congress wanted Dornan to go away. Sanchez kept the seat and, a decade later, still has it.

After the 1996 campaign, everything was downhill. Dornan made a run at her again in 1998, and Sanchez won handily. During that campaign, Dornan's poll numbers were so bad going into the race that Sanchez hoped to face Dornan again in the general election, rather than a better-funded, more formidable Republican candidate. Some Sanchez supporters, holding their noses, reportedly urged followers to vote for Dornan in the open primary to head off a stronger GOP threat.

Sanchez generated some negative publicity of her own in 2000 when she scheduled a fundraiser at Hugh Hefner's mansion in Los Angeles. Ordinarily, the event would pass unnoticed—except for the fact that it took place in the middle of the Democratic National Convention in Los Angeles. At the time, Democrats were trying to put a galaxy between themselves and the sex scandals that had engulfed President Clinton, and Hefner was regarded as a symbolic whoopee cushion because of his Playboy reputation. Sanchez was roundly criticized for choosing the venue, and when she refused to cancel her event, Democrats removed her as a convention speaker even though she was vice chair of the Democratic National Committee.

Sanchez's normally uneventful re-election campaign was marked by an unseemly incident involving her Republican opponent, Tan Nguyen, whose campaign was responsible for a letter sent to 14,000 newly registered district residents with Hispanic surnames. The letter, written in Spanish, warned that it was illegal for immigrants to vote and threatened jail time for those who tried. The letter was universally condemned, including by Scott Baugh, the former Assembly floor leader who serves as chairman of the Orange County Republican Party. Baugh called on Nguyen to drop out of the race, but he refused, agreeing to cooperate with law enforcement agencies investigating the letter.

After her re-election, Sanchez stood first in line for a subcommittee chairmanship dealing with homeland security issues. The subcommittee has jurisdiction over, among other things, airports and ports. She plans to use her chairmanship to more closely scrutinize the work of the Homeland Security Department.

BIOGRAPHY: Born: East Los Angeles, January 7, 1960. Home: Anaheim. Education: BS, Chapman University; MBA, American University. Military: None. Family: husband Stephen Brixey. Religion: Catholic.

OFFICES: Capitol: Longworth Building 1230, Washington, DC 20515, Phone: (202) 225-2965, Fax: (202) 225-5859, email: loretta.sanchez@mail.house.gov. District: 12397 Lewis Street, Suite 101, Garden Grove, CA 92840, Phone: (714) 621-0102, Fax: (714) 621-0401.

COMMITTEES: Armed Services; Homeland Security; Education and the Workforce (on leave).

ELECTED: 1996

ELECTION HISTORY: None

2002 ELECTION: Sanchez (D*) 61%
                Chavez (R) 35%
                Marsden (L) 4%

2004 ELECTION: Sanchez (D*) 60%
Coronado (R) 40%
2006 ELECTION: Sanchez (D*) 62%
Nguyen (R) 38%
RATINGS: ACU ADA AFL-CIO CoC GO LCV NTU PIRG
16   90   87   52   F- 100   22   84

ADAM SCHIFF (D)
29th Congressional District

Counties: Los Angeles
Cities: Glendale, Alhambra, Burbank, Pasadena, Altadena, San Gabriel, Monterey Park
Ethnicity: 39% White, 26% Latino, 6% Black, 25% Asian
Voter Registration: 43% D – 31% R – 22% DS
President 04: 61% Kerry, 37% Bush

Adam Schiff

The 29th District—which before reapportionment bore the number 27—was the scene of a ferocious election battle in 2000 where Democratic state Senator Adam Schiff took out one of the Democratic Party's most reviled Republican incumbents—James Rogan. It wasn't so much that Rogan was a poster boy for conservative values. His support for Proposition 187 and school vouchers and his opposition to gun control and abortion were issues that Democrats exploited during the campaign, but not enough to make the affable Rogan the nation's number-one congressional target. He earned that honor the old-fashioned foolish way: his high-profile role as House manager for the effort to impeach then-President Bill Clinton following the Monica Lewinsky sex scandal. That put Rogan squarely in Democratic crosshairs.

Republicans, naturally, hurried to Rogan's defense, both emotionally and financially, and the resulting nuclear cash war produced the most expensive congressional race in U.S. history. Before it was over, the two sides had spent $11 million in an effort to influence 206,000 voters. Although Rogan never backed away from his impeachment responsibility, Schiff barely mentioned it, concentrating instead on Rogan's voting record and calling it far too conservative for the district. It proved a feasible tactic and helped the Democrat fashion a 9% victory. The district had changed in the four years since Rogan first won the seat in 1996, and faced with a viable alternative, his constituents chose someone whose philosophy closely mirrored their own. It helped that Schiff was no raving liberal; a former prosecutor, he had charted a moderate course in the Senate. He earned a unique distinction when, as a freshman, he was appointed to chair a committee: the first time that anyone who had never held public office was tapped to head a standing committee of the Senate.

When it came time for reapportionment, Democrats sought to strengthen their hold on the district by running it through a Quisinart. Although Democratic registration remained the same, that of the Republicans dropped 5%. La Canada Flintridge was sliced away in the north, while the new district dipped south of Pasadena to pick up South Pasadena, Alhambra, San Gabriel, and Temple City. Thoughtful mapmakers were careful to shape the district around Republican voters in San Marino, however.

As a state legislator, Schiff had a knack for the spotlight, using his chairmanship of the Judiciary Committee as a springboard for oversight hearings on such matters as the national tobacco settlement. In Congress, Schiff sought and won several small leadership posts, including president of the 2001 Democratic Freshman Class, subsequently winning the same post in 2002. In 2001 *Roll Call* named him one of 10 rookies to watch. He worked issues ranging from theft of intellectual property to improving mass transit in the San Gabriel Valley. A member of the House International Relations Committee, Schiff has been all over the map in his support for the war in Iraq. He originally voted for the Bush administration's resolution of war but a year later opposed an $87 million supplemental appropriation to fund the effort. In 2004 he backed a similar $78 million outlay.

A decent fundraiser, Schiff ended 2004 with more than $1 million in the bank—more than enough to deter any serious threat to his House career. Meanwhile, he reaped an immediate reward in 2006 after Democrats took control of the House—a seat on the Appropriations Committee, where he joins fellow California Democrats Sam Farr and Lucille Roybal-Allard. His first crusade of the new Congress dealt with military affairs, however. He is pushing for a new attack submarine to be christened the U.S.S. California.

BIOGRAPHY: Born: Framington, MA, June 22, 1960. Home: Burbank. Education: BS, Stanford; JD, Harvard. Military: None. Family: wife Eve, two children. Religion: Jewish.

OFFICES: Capitol: Cannon Office Building 326, Washington, DC 20515, Phone: (202) 225-4176, Fax: (202) 225-5828, email: adam.schiff@mail.house.gov. District: 87 North Raymond Avenue, Suite 800, Pasadena 91103, Phone: (626) 304-2727, Fax: (626) 304-0572.

COMMITTEES: Judiciary, International Relations; Appropriations.

ELECTED: 2000

ELECTION HISTORY: State Senate, 1996–2000.

2002 ELECTION: Schiff (D*) 63%
　　　　　　　　　　Scileppi (R) 33%
　　　　　　　　　　Brown (L) 4%

2004 ELECTION: Schiff (D*) 65%
　　　　　　　　　　Scolinos (R) 31%
　　　　　　　　　　Koebel (G) 3%
　　　　　　　　　　Brown (L) 2%

2006 ELECTION: Schiff (D*) 64%

Bodell (R) 28%
Paparian (G) 6%
Keller (L) 2%
Llamas (PF) 2%

RATINGS:

ACU	ADA	AFL-CIO	CoC	GO	LCV	NTU	PIRG
0	85	93	42	F-	100	12	96

BRAD SHERMAN (D)
27th Congressional District

Counties: Los Angeles
Cities: Los Angeles, Burbank
Ethnicity: 45% White, 37% Latino, 5% Black, 11% Asian
Voter Registration: 47% D – 29% R – 19% DS
President 04: 59% Kerry, 39% Bush

Brad Sherman

To explain the miles that mapmakers traveled to manufacture a new district for Democrat Brad Sherman, one needs to find the intersection of Highway 101 and I-405. Those two arteries met in the extreme eastern part of Sherman's old 24th District, between Encino and Van Nuys. Today, the 405 slices Sherman's new 27th district almost in half, while Route 101 forms the southern boundary. They meet almost dead center at the bottom of Sherman's new territory. As a result, the district grew away from the coast to concentrate more heavily in the San Fernando Valley. It is more Democratic and more Latino than Sherman's previous district.

As a politician, Sherman is a survivor blessed with good timing. The veteran Democratic lawmaker began his political career in 1990 when he won a seat on the State Board of Equalization. At the time, the BOE served as an obscure political outpost rather than its current function as a holding tank for termed-out legislators waiting for better opportunities. He won re-election to the BOE in 1994, putting him in the right place at the right time for a seat in Congress.

That seat—the old 24th—came available in 1996 when longtime incumbent Democrat Tony Beilenson decided to retire rather than endure another tough re-election. When such Democratic luminaries as Assemblyman Richard Katz took a pass on the race, the mantle fell to Sherman. The 1996 election was not easy; eager Republicans nominated Richard Sybert, who had nearly knocked off Beilenson two years before. But Sybert turned out to be a train wreck as a candidate, even sending out a mailer that implied a nonexistent endorsement from Colin Powell. Sherman won by 7% and crushed another highly touted GOP candidate in 1998.

As a congressman, Sherman likes to portray himself as more moderate than his predecessor, Beilenson. In 2002, he voted to authorize the use of force in Iraq and has since backed administration requests for additional funds to prosecute the war. But as his ratings demonstrate, he is far more liberal than "Blue Dog Democrats" such as Ellen Tauscher and Dennis Cardoza. A CPA and attorney by trade, he is a former board member for California Common Cause and a Democratic activist who helped on scores of campaigns before dipping into elective office himself. Self-deprecating to a fault, the balding Sherman often makes light of his nerdy appearance; his favorite campaign tchotchke, for instance, is a comb emblazoned with his name. He is not without ambition, however. In 1994, he filed letters of intent for four offices before seeking another term on the Board of Equalization.

In Congress Sherman has focused on presidential succession, hybrid vehicles, and bankruptcy laws. His 2006 legislation allows owners of hybrid vehicles to use car-pool lanes. He has been an ardent supporter of Israel and called for sanctions against Iran in the wake of that country's effort to build a nuclear weapon.

BIOGRAPHY: Born: Los Angeles, October 24, 1954. Home: Sherman Oaks. Education: BA, UCLA; JD, Harvard. Military: None. Family: Single. Religion: Jewish.

OFFICES: Capitol: Longworth Building 1030, Washington, DC 20515, Phone: (202) 225-5911, Fax: (202) 225-5879, email: brad.sherman@mail.house.gov. District: 5000 Van Nuys Boulevard, Suite 420, Sherman Oaks, CA 91403, Phone: (818) 501-9200, Fax: (818) 501-1554.

COMMITTEES: Financial Services; International Relations; Science.

ELECTED: 1996

ELECTION HISTORY: State Board of Equalization, 1990–1995.

2002 ELECTION: Sherman (D*) 62%
                            Levy (R) 38%

2004 ELECTION: Sherman (D*) 62%
                            Levy (R) 34%
                            Carter (G) 4%

2006 ELECTION: Sherman (D*) 69%
                            Hankwitz (R) 31%

RATINGS:

	ACU	ADA	AFL-CIO	CoC	GO	LCV	NTU	PIRG
	0	100	93	41	F-	100	12	93

HILDA SOLIS (D)
32nd Congressional District

Counties: Los Angeles

Cities: West Covina, El Monte, Baldwin Park, South El Monte, Los Angeles, Duarte, Azusa, Irwindale

Ethnicity: 15% White, 62% Latino, 3% Black, 19% Asian

Voter Registration: 51% D – 26% R – 20% DS
President 04: 62% Kerry, 37% Bush

Hilda Solis

The politics of the district formerly known as "31" did not change much when the 2001 reapportionment changed its number to 32. It remained solidly Democratic and overwhelmingly Latino. Located east of downtown Los Angeles, it lost San Gabriel and Alhambra but picked up Covina and West Covina. It still includes legendary Irwindale where city fathers once tried to build a stadium to lure the Oakland Raiders back to southern California. Economically, the district is slightly better off than its immediate neighbors. The median household income is only a few hundred dollars less than the national average of $41,994, although 14% of district families live below the poverty line. Nearly 42% of the district population is foreign-born, however, and over 68% of residents speak a language other than English at home.

Since 2000, the district has been represented by Democrat Hilda Solis, a former state legislator who first captured the seat by ousting an unpopular incumbent—Matthew "Marty" Martinez—in the Democratic primary. Taking on a nine-term incumbent, even one with a record as pockmarked as Martinez's, was a bold ploy by Solis, but her confidence was bolstered early on when Helen Lujan, Martinez's sister, endorsed her.

The election was no contest. Backed by U.S. Senator Barbara Boxer, EMILY'S List, and the state Democratic Party, Solis dealt one of the most thorough primary thrashings ever administered to an incumbent congressman, beating Martinez better than two-to-one. Even Martinez's staunchest allies—the vaunted Berman-Waxman machine that created his career some two decades earlier—took a pass. Solis campaigned on her championing of labor as a state legislator, which earned her financial and ground support from the Los Angeles Federation of Labor. She raised three times as much money as Martinez and beat him over the head with the cash, using it to remind voters that Martinez had compiled one of the worst attendance records in Congress and that he had been virtually invisible in the district for years.

When the March primary was over, Martinez was a lame duck with nine months left in Congress, and he responded to his loss with a temper tantrum. He abruptly resigned from the Democratic Party and spent what was left of his career as a Republican.

When she took on Martinez, Solis was in the middle of her second and final term in the Senate after serving one term in the Assembly, and with one notable exception she had made few ripples in either house. In 1994, when she replaced Democrat Art Torres in the Senate, she was, at 37, the youngest member of that body, and she spent her time on labor issues and tried to hike the minimum wage.

In 1997, Solis took on Governor Pete Wilson and business leaders in an effort to secure better environmental protections for ethnic communities, where enforcement of environmental law was regarded as haphazard. Although Wilson vetoed her first effort, Solis persisted and by 1999, her environmental justice bill was law thanks to a signature from newly elected Governor Gray Davis. A year later, her efforts earned Solis one of the most prestigious public service honors in the nation—the John F. Kennedy "Profile in Courage Award," given annually by the Kennedy Library in Boston.

To date, Solis's congressional agenda focused on issues of importance to the Latino community and women. She has sponsored bills to reduce barriers to job training for legal immigrants who are not proficient in English and provide funding for special courts dealing with domestic violence.

After the Democrats won control of the House in 2006, Solis was tapped by Speaker Nancy Pelosi to be vice chair of the Democratic Steering Committee, a significant post on a panel that develops the party agenda and recommends committee assignments and chairmanships. The position puts Solis squarely in the middle of Pelosi's leadership team for 2007–2008.

BIOGRAPHY: Born: Los Angeles, October 20, 1957. Home: El Monte. Education: BA, Cal Poly, Pomona; MPA, USC. Military: None. Family: husband Sam. Religion: Catholic.

OFFICES: Capitol: Longworth Building 1414, Washington, DC 20515, Phone: (202) 225-5464, Fax: (202) 225-5467, email: hilda.solis@mail.house.gov. District: 4401 Santa Anita Avenue, Suite 211, El Monte, CA 91731, Phone: (626) 448-1271, Fax: (626) 448-8062; 4716 Cesar Chavez Avenue, Building A, East Los Angeles, CA 90022, Phone: (323) 307-9904, Fax: (323) 307-9906.

COMMITTEES: Energy and Commerce.

ELECTED: 2000

ELECTION HISTORY: State Assembly, 1992–1994; State Senate, 1994–2000.

2002 ELECTION: Solis (D*) 69%
Fishbeck (R) 27%
McGuire (L) 4%

2004 ELECTION: Solis (D*) 85%
Faegre (L) 15%

2006 ELECTION: Solis (D*) 83%
Faegre (L) 17%

RATINGS:

ACU	ADA	AFL-CIO	CoC	GO	LCV	NTU	PIRG
0	100	93	35	F-	100	15	96

FORTNEY "PETE" STARK
13th Congressional District

Counties: Alameda
Cities: Fremont, Hayward, Alameda, San Lorenzo, Union City
Ethnicity: 38% White, 21% Latino, 7% Black, 30% Asian
Voter Registration: 53% D – 20% R – 23% DS
President 04: 71% Kerry, 28% Bush

Pete Stark

The 13th District moved slightly north in the 2001 reapportionment, shedding its sliver of San Jose and Milpitas while sticking a finger into Alameda. Politically, it remains solidly Democratic and heavily Asian, with a large number of decline-to-state voters.

The current incumbent is neither decline-to-state nor Asian. He has been in Congress since Vietnam was a war. Fortney Stark, known to the world as "Pete," first won election to the House in 1972—the year Richard Nixon won re-election as president and some of his operatives committed a third-rate burglary at the Watergate. During some of those 34 years, Stark wielded power and influence as chair of a Ways and Means subcommittee on health, from which he repeatedly pushed efforts at health care reform. He once called for a constitutional amendment that would guarantee every citizen the right to health care. And he once so enraged the American Medical Association that it bankrolled his 1986 opponent to the tune of $200,000—a maharajah's ransom in those days. Stark breezed to re-election anyway.

He made his mark in the East Bay during the Vietnam War when in 1963 he started a bank in Walnut Creek and used peace symbols on the checks. That drew depositors from all across the Bay Area and gave him the foundation to create a second bank. By age 31, he was well on his way to financial independence. His skills as a banker, however, did not save him from the check cashing scandal that plagued the House bank during the 1990s—Stark was one of many members accused of bouncing checks.

Stark's influence faded after Republicans took control of the House in 1994, but his loss of clout did not turn down the volume on his often-acerbic rhetoric. He took on for-profit HMOs, railing at what he saw as their indifference toward beneficiaries. He reserved a special place in his vitriol for Blue Cross of Northern California, which he called a "greed-driven vampire" after it went from nonprofit to for-profit during the 1990s. During the Clinton administration's last years, Stark cosponsored the Patients' Bill of Rights and fought to extend Medicare benefits to teachers, police, and firefighters.

The Democratic resurgence of 2006 found him still on Ways and Means and still throwing himself into health issues. His favored target of late is PhRMA—the association of drug manufacturers. One of his bills attempted to make the industry accountable for drug safety, and the introduction to his legislation claims that many people die because the industry sells them drugs it knows to be unsafe. He is actively engaged in efforts to prevent Bush administration moves to privatize Social Security.

Although now approaching his mid-70s, Stark shows no signs of slowing down politically—much to the annoyance of younger East Bay politicians scouting for a landing place in this era of term-limited legislators. Democratic control means he could resume his subcommittee chairmanship. That ought to make the drug industry giddy with delight.

BIOGRAPHY: Born: Milwaukee, WI, November 11, 1931. Home: San Lorenzo. Education: BS, MIT; MBA, UC Berkeley. Military: U.S. Air Force. Family: wife Deborah, seven children, eight grandchildren. Religion: Unitarian.

OFFICES: Capitol: Cannon Office Building 239, Washington, DC 20515, Phone: (202) 225-5065, Fax: (202) 226-3805, email: pete.stark@mail.house.gov. District: 39300 Civic Center Drive, Suite 220, Fremont, CA 94538, Phone: (510) 494-1388, Fax: (510) 494-5852.

COMMITTEES: Ways and Means; Joint Economic Committee

ELECTED: 1972

ELECTION HISTORY: None

2002 ELECTION: Stark (D*) 71%
 Mahmood (R) 22%
 Grundmann (AI) 2%
 Stroberg (L) 3%
 Bambey (RF) 2%

2004 ELECTION: Stark (D*) 71%
 Bruno (R) 25%
 Stoberg (L) 4%

2006 ELECTION: Stark (D*) 75%
 Bruno (R) 25%

RATINGS:

ACU	ADA	AFL-CIO	CoC	GO	LCV	NTU	PIRG
0	90	93	32	F-	100	24	87

ELLEN TAUSCHER (D)
10th Congressional District

Counties: Contra Costa, Alameda, Sacramento, Solano
Cities: Fairfield, Antioch, Concord, Livermore, Walnut Creek
Ethnicity: 65% White, 15% Latino, 6% Black, 10% Asian
Voter Registration: 45% D – 33% R – 18% DS
President 04: 59% Kerry, 40% Bush

Interests of voters in the 10th District are surprisingly homogenous given its diverse population. The district includes recently added Solano County, with its mixture of rural and suburban life in communities like Dixon and Fairfield, to the north. At the district's southern tip is the booming town of Livermore with its high-tech bedroom communities and the Lawrence Livermore and Sandia national laboratories. To the west lie the upscale Contra Costa County communities of Orinda, Walnut Creek, and Alamo and the newly added towns of El Cerrito, Kensington, and Concord. To the east are the quickly developing towns of Antioch and Oakley. The northern end tilts blue collar, while the rest leans white collar. The district includes the headquarters of Longs Drugs, the Jelly Belly factory, and a Budweiser brewery.

All this Democratic goodness and light was added to the district during the 2001 reapportionment, but, at the time, it simply made incumbent Ellen Tauscher grumpy.

Ellen Tauscher

Tauscher first won the previous version of the 10th District in 1996 by taking out an incumbent Republican—Bill Baker—who was considered too conservative and who refused to moderate his views, especially on gun control.

When cartographers finished retooling her district, Tauscher publicly protested, saying the new district lacked cohesiveness because it was divided between agricultural and suburban interests, and was too geographically divided to be properly represented. She alleged the legislature gave her such a varied district because she backed Maryland's Steny Hoyer over San Franciscan Nancy Pelosi for minority whip. It didn't help Tauscher that State Senate pro Tem John Burton, a close ally of Pelosi, oversaw the drawing of new congressional districts. The redrawing was something of a poke in the eye to Tauscher, but it did not discomfort her come election time, given that Democratic registration had actually increased.

In the redistricting process, Tauscher was in danger of losing the liberal, upscale "Lamorinda" area, comprising Lafayette, Moraga, and Orinda. But she held on, thanks to a mobilization of voters in that area horrified at the prospect of being represented by Republican Richard Pombo of Stockton. She quickly endeared herself to voters in the new communities by becoming an advocate for the military personnel at Travis Air Force Base near Fairfield. As an Armed Services Committee member, she has continually lobbied for low-cost housing for troops and city planning around the base.

As a member of the House's moderate "Blue Dog" coalition, Tauscher seeks to build bridges to Republican colleagues. The first woman to gain a seat on the New York Stock Exchange, she is pro-business and debt-conscious. Socially, she is more progressive: anti-war and against a constitutional amendment banning gay marriage. She is in tune with three key district concerns: transportation, education, and national security.

Traffic congestion is a frequent topic of newspaper articles and political measures. The county is home to a number of traffic morasses, including the 580-680 interchange in Walnut Creek. Transportation is a recurring subject of clashes between environmentalists who favor growth control and advocates for wider freeways. In 2004, a Solano County measure that would have taxed voters for freeway improvements and expanded public transportation failed. Contra Costa County voters did decide to renew the transportation sales tax to add a fourth bore to the Caldecott Tunnel and extend BART service into the county. Tauscher's seat on the Highways and Transit Subcommittee, which authorizes federal contributions for transportation projects, has been helpful in securing funds for East Bay improvements.

In a district that includes Travis and two national defense laboratories, national security and armed services and veterans' benefits are top concerns. Tauscher sits on the House Armed Services Committee and is actively involved in such issues. She was a leading voice in getting former lab workers who suffer long-term illnesses proper compensation.

In the 110th Congress, controlled by Democrats and led by Pelosi, Tauscher will become chair of the New Democrat Coalition, a 62-member panel that leans to the middle on fiscal issues (as opposed to the moderate "Blue Dog Democrats" who tack right on social issues). That puts Pelosi in Tauscher's orbit, rather than the other way around, because the new Speaker must trundle the entire Democratic caucus toward the center if she hopes to extend the party's control beyond one term. The coalition's most controversial stand in 2006 was support for reform of bankruptcy laws, which liberals saw as favoring businesses at the expense of the middle class.

BIOGRAPHY: Born: Newark, NJ, November 15, 1951. Home: Alamo. Education: BA, Seton Hall University. Military: None. Family: Divorced, one daughter. Religion: Catholic.

OFFICES: Capitol: Rayburn Building 2459, Washington, DC 20515, Phone: (202) 225-1880, Fax: (202) 225-5914, email: ellen.tauscher@mail.house.gov. District: 2121 North California Boulevard, Suite 555, Walnut Creek, CA 94596, Phone: (925) 932-8899, Fax: (925) 932-8159; 420 West 3rd Street, Antioch, CA 94509, Phone: (925) 757-7187, Fax: (925) 757-7056; 2000 Cadenasso Drive, Suite A, Fairfield, CA 94533, Phone: (707) 428-7792.

COMMITTEES: Armed Services; Transportation and Infrastructure

ELECTED: 1996

ELECTION HISTORY: None

2002 ELECTION: Tauscher (D*) 75%
Harden (L) 25%

2004 ELECTION: Tauscher (D*) 66%
Ketelson (R) 34%

2006 ELECTION: Tauscher (D*) 67%
Linn (R) 34%

RATINGS:

ACU	ADA	AFL-CIO	CoC	GO	LCV	NTU	PIRG
8	90	93	52	F-	100	17	87

MIKE THOMPSON (D)
1st Congressional District

Counties: Del Norte, Humboldt, Lake, Mendocino, Napa, Sonoma, Yolo

Cities: Davis, Eureka, Napa, West Sacramento, Mendocino, Fort Bragg, Arcata, Crescent City, Willits, Woodland

Ethnicity: 71% White, 18% Latino, 2% Black, 4% Asian

Voter Registration: 45% D – 29% R – 19% DS

President 04: 60% Kerry, 38% Bush

California's 1st Congressional District was little changed by the 2001 reapportionment. Resembling an elongated fairway with a narrow green, it sweeps down the coast from the Oregon border and then doglegs into the heart of the Napa-Sonoma wine country northeast of San Francisco Bay. It extends a finger into Yolo County to pick up Davis, Woodland, and West Sacramento—the only significant difference between the old and new maps. A swath along I-80 between Vallejo and Davis was removed from

Mike Thompson

the district, including Travis Air Force Base in Fairfield and the prison and commuter town of Vacaville.

To the north, it is an area dependent on tourism, small farms, and the increasingly depressed lumber and fishing industries. Del Norte County on the Oregon border sports a cottage industry that caters to the state's most notorious prison at Pelican Bay near Crescent City. The north gradually gives way to lush vineyards and inflated real estate values of Mendocino, Napa, and Somona counties. To the east, where it snuggles up to the state capital, the district is home to a University of California campus at Davis.

Most small towns along the north coast have struggled for years, both financially and socially, as the area's thriving counterculture clashes often with more conservative refugees who have moved north from the Bay Area. One of the flash points, for citizens and law enforcement alike, is the region's economic reliance on marijuana—the district's largest cash crop—that is grown in isolated areas throughout the district. The lucrative trade in herbal jade often turns violent, with growers and poachers sometimes engaged in remote shootouts.

The district remains ground zero for confrontations between the increasingly hard-pressed lumber industry and radical environmentalists struggling to stop logging in the old-growth forests that sprawl across parts of the northern and central landscape. The 1st District was the scene of skirmishes over logging in the Headwaters Forest and for some notable environmental activism, such as tree-sitting by the likes of Julia Butterfly Hill, who lived in a redwood tree for 738 days in 1998 and 1999. Finally, the district is home to one of the state's more entertaining alternative newspapers—the weekly *Arcata Eye*, with its eclectic "police log."

Throughout the 1990s, the district bounced between Republicans and Democrats, finally settling into political stability with the election of Democrat Mike Thompson in 1998. Thompson first won elective office in 1990 when he captured the 4th state Senate District. The next year reapportionment put his home in the neighboring 2nd District, and he took a calculated risk by running in a special election in that district despite having two years remaining on his original term. He won, and remained in the Senate until 1998. In 1995 he took over as chairman of the Senate Budget Committee, a high-profile job made all the more significant because Republicans at the time controlled the Assembly.

By the time he ran for office, Thompson, the first Vietnam veteran elected to the state Senate, was also a Capitol veteran, having worked for seven years as chief of staff to then-Assemblywoman Jackie Speier. Prior to Speier, he served in the same role for Democrat Lou Papan, who was chairman of the Assembly Rules Committee and one of the most powerful members of the "old Assembly." Thompson also taught political science at several area universities.

Once in Congress, Thompson aligned himself with the Blue Dog Caucus of conservative and moderate Democrats, which gained much influence in Washington during the Clinton presidency. Although a member of the House minority, he sits on the powerful Ways and Means Committee and co-chairs (what else?) the 250-member

Congressional Wine Caucus. He has backed increased support for renewable energy, sponsored legislation to help restore spawning grounds for salmon and steelhead, and has been active in efforts to restore the Klamath River. As expected from someone who represents wine country, Thompson supported a 2005 decision by the U.S. Supreme Court to allow small and midsize wineries to ship directly to consumers rather than through wholesalers, filing an amicus brief on behalf of wineries.

Thompson was under consideration to head the Democratic Congressional Campaign Committee in the next session of Congress, but Speaker Nancy Pelosi chose Maryland's Chris Van Hollen instead. Still, Thompson remains one of Pelosi's closest advisors, and his influence over Democratic policy likely will increase during the 110th Congress.

BIOGRAPHY: Born: St. Helena, January 24, 1951. Home: St. Helena. Education: BA, MA, CSU Chico. Military: U.S. Army. Family: wife Janet, two sons. Religion: Catholic.

OFFICES: Capitol: Cannon Office Building 231, Washington, DC 20515, Phone: (202) 225-3311, Fax: (202) 225-4335, email: mike.thompson@mail.house.gov. District: 1040 Main Street, Suite 101, Napa, CA 94559, Phone: (707) 226-9898, Fax: (707) 251-9800; 317 3rd Street, Suite 1, Eureka, CA 95501, Phone: (707) 269-9595, Fax: (707) 269-9598; 430 North Franklin Street, Fort Bragg, CA 95437, Phone: (707) 962-0933, Fax: (707) 962-0934; 712 Main Street, Suite 1, Woodland, CA 95695, Phone: (530) 662-5272, Fax: (530) 662-5163.

COMMITTEES: Ways and Means

ELECTED: 1998

ELECTION HISTORY: State Senate, 1996–1998

2002 ELECTION: Thompson (D*) 64%
Wiesner (R) 32%
Bastian (L) 4%

2004 ELECTION: Thompson (D*) 68%
Wiesner (R) 28%
Elizondo (L) 4%

2006 ELECTION: Thompson (D*) 66%
Jones (R) 29%
Elizondo (L) 3%
Stock (PF) 2%

RATINGS:

ACU	ADA	AFL-CIO	CoC	GO	LCV	NTU	PIRG
16	90	87	48	C-	92	18	83

MAXINE WATERS (D)
35th Congressional District

Counties: Los Angeles
Cities: Los Angeles, Inglewood, Gardena, Hawthorne, Lawndale
Ethnicity: 10% White, 47% Latino, 34% Black, 6% Asian

Voter Registration: 65% D – 16% R – 16% DS
President 04: 79% Kerry, 20% Bush

Maxine Waters

A decade ago, a previous edition of the "California Political Almanac" referred to the urban territory known as the 35th District as "the center of . . . infamous riots" with a "constancy to the issues here—poverty, crime, drugs, lack of community facilities, poor schools, substandard housing, and a police force still viewed as insensitive to those problems."

Not much has changed. Reapportionment added some wealthier Los Angeles neighborhoods west of Inglewood where the district now approaches Marina del Rey and where the Pacific Coast Highway slices through it before jogging south toward Manhattan Beach. But the bulk of the 35th District encompasses its previous troubled self, with its rugged economic profile. Away from the ocean, a quarter of the district population lives below the federal poverty line, 42% of those over age 16 are "not in the labor force," and 69% of households have incomes below the national average. This was the epicenter of the 1992 riots that followed acquittal of the police who beat Rodney King.

A quarter century ago, when Watts was burning, the area was mostly black. But an influx of Latino immigrants has scrambled the area's cultural tapestry, and half the population now is Hispanic. Blacks make up a third of the district's population but still dominate its power structure, and that has caused friction in the halls of power and brutal combat on the streets. One notable brawl took place between Latino and black students at a district high school in the spring of 2005.

Political power in this part of Los Angeles rests firmly in the hands of the official who has represented the area in one place or another for the past 28 years: Democrat Maxine Waters. She most recently displayed that power during the 2005 mayoral contest where she was credited with helping the eventual winner, Antonio Villaraigosa, add essential African-American support to the ethnic coalition that swept him to victory over incumbent James Hahn. Her support for Villaraigosa came at a critical time in the campaign and blunted Hahn's attempts to shore up support among black voters. In 2001, Waters had also backed the winner, helping Hahn defeat Villaraigosa. In another critical matter, she has effectively used her clout and presence to crusade against closure of the troubled King/Drew medical center, which serves her constituency.

Although 68 years old, Waters has lost none of the brass and fire that has characterized her public persona for the past three decades. In Sacramento, where she spent 14 years in the Assembly, Waters was known as "Mama Doc" for an absolutist approach to politics, often conducted at decibel levels worthy of the most sophisticated boom box. "She has a tongue that could open a wall safe," a colleague once said of her.

Waters grew up in the urban war zone known as East St. Louis, Illinois, and began her involvement with the district as a Head Start teacher and civic organizer in Watts. She worked for a Los Angeles councilman when she won an Assembly seat in 1976.

When Willie Brown became speaker four years later, Waters began her ascent into the realm of power, holding key committee assignments that allowed her to wage war on behalf of women, the poor, and the nonwhite. She was elected to Congress in 1990, and although the Washington stage was substantially larger than in Sacramento, Waters did not shrink but continued to expand her range, serving as a confidant and advisor to the likes of the Reverend Jesse Jackson. She was the focus of media attention during the Rodney King conflagration, constantly referring to it as an insurrection rather than a riot. She served as honorary co-chair of the 1992 Clinton-Gore presidential campaign, although her characterization of the senior George Bush as a racist caused some disquiet among Democrats. Still, her work for the ticket reaped at least one reward; her husband, Sidney Williams, was named ambassador to the Bahamas.

Waters's influence expanded during the Clinton administration, although she clashed with the moderate president on several issues—notably the massive welfare-reform bill signed into law during Clinton's first term. In Clinton's second term, Waters, as a member of the Judiciary Committee, was one of the president's staunchest and most vocal defenders during impeachment hearings.

Waters's institutional power receded after Republicans captured control of Congress in 1994, although she continued to be a force in Democratic politics. In 2002, she was named vice chair of the Democratic Steering Committee—which makes committee assignments. On policy matters, she has kept an especially watchful eye on political events in the Caribbean, notably in Haiti where she has been a continuing champion of President Jean-Bertrand Aristide, warning in 2004 about events designed to topple his government. She has been an irrepressible opponent of the war in Iraq, the Patriot Act, and creation of a Department of Homeland Security. She opposed the appointment of fellow Californian, state Supreme Court Justice Janice Rogers Brown, to the federal bench, calling Brown—also an African American—"hostile to the cause of civil rights." She lost that fight.

As active as she has been in Washington through the years, Waters continues to exert significant influence at home through a controversial political machine with tentacles all through south Los Angeles. In December 2004, she generated some unwanted publicity when the *Los Angeles Times* chronicled the ways Waters and her family often profit from her political stature. She continues to run a lucrative slate-mailer operation—L.A. Vote—and has been criticized because members of her family sometimes benefit from campaigns endorsed by Waters. Some observers complain that Waters's stubborn defense of all things black creates disharmony in her now multicultural district—especially as blacks jockey with Latinos for power. Her support for Antonio Villaraigosa notwithstanding, Waters was criticized in 2005 for a tirade against what she called the "Mexican Mafia" during a subcommittee hearing of the House Judiciary Committee.

Closer to home, Waters was engaged in a personal dust up with community activist Najee Ali. A parking-lot confrontation during the 2006 campaign led to each side requesting a restraining order against the other, with Waters declaring that Ali repeatedly confronted her over the years. Ali, according to the *Los Angeles Times*, was the first to seek the order. The altercation occurred as Waters and Ali arrived at what was supposed to be a campaign appearance by Gov. Arnold Schwarzenegger at Mount Moriah Baptist Church in South Los Angeles. Waters had protesters in tow and accused Ali and others of pandering to the governor. The argument then escalated into a shouting match. Both sides subsequently dropped requests for a restraining order, but not their mutual animosity.

BIOGRAPHY: Born: St. Louis, MO, August 15, 1938. Home: Los Angeles. Education: BA, CSU Los Angeles. Military: None. Family: husband Sidney Williams, two children, two grandchildren. Religion: Christian.

OFFICES: Capitol: Rayburn Building 2344, Washington, DC 20515, Phone: (202) 225-2201, Fax: (202) 225-7854, email: maxine.waters@mail.house.gov. District: 10124 South Broadway, Suite 1, Los Angeles, CA 90003, Phone: (323) 757-8900, Fax: (323) 757-9506.

COMMITTEES: Banking and Financial Services; Judiciary
ELECTED: 1990
ELECTION HISTORY: State Assembly, 1977–1990
2002 ELECTION: Waters (D*) 78%
               Moen (R) 19%
               Mego (AI) 3%
2004 ELECTION: Waters (D*) 80%
               Moen (R) 16%
               Mego (AI) 2%
               Tate (L) 2%
2006 ELECTION: Waters (D*) 84%
               Ireland (L) 8%
               Mego (AI) 9%

RATINGS:

	ACU	ADA	AFL-CIO	CoC	GO	LCV	NTU	PIRG
	8	95	93	32	F-	100	19	91

DIANE WATSON (D)
33rd Congressional District

Counties: Los Angeles
Cities: Los Angeles, Culver City
Ethnicity: 20% White, 35% Latino, 30% Black, 13% Asian
Voter Registration: 64% D – 12% R – 19% DS
President 04: 83% Kerry, 16% Bush

The 33rd District is a cultural soup, symbolized by its wealth of diverse neighborhoods and ethnicities. The African-American communities of Ladera Heights, Baldwin Hills, and Crenshaw anchor it and control its politics. Ladera Heights and Baldwin Hills represent Los Angeles's affluent black communities, while Crenshaw is more modest although prime with re-development.

The northern portion of the district was added in the 2001 reapportionment and includes upper-income white areas such as Hancock Park and the hills of Hollywood, Silver Lake, and Los Feliz. Hancock Park has old tree-lined streets, reminiscent of

Diane Watson

homes in the Midwest and East Coast. Adjacent to Hancock Park is Korea Town, with its bustling economy and Korean culture. Historically Jewish Culver City is now ethnically diverse, while South Los Angeles has traditionally been black but is increasingly home to Latino immigrants.

Democrat Diane Watson first won the congressional seat in a 2001 special election to replace longtime and popular incumbent Julian Dixon, who had died unexpectedly. At the time, Watson was the Clinton administration's ambassador to Micronesia—a post she took in 1999 after being termed out of the state Senate, where she had been the first black woman elected to the upper house. Prior to her election to the legislature, she was the first black woman elected to the Los Angeles Board of Education, serving from 1975 to 1978, when she went to Sacramento. She once ran for the Los Angeles County Board of Supervisors, losing an invective-laced election to Yvonne Burke.

Watson won her congressional seat by defeating a pair of well-known Democrats—state Senator Kevin Murray and Los Angeles City Councilman Nate Holden. Murray, especially, proved a thorn. Son of Willard Murray, a former legislator influential in area politics, Kevin was backed by Dixon's widow and by U.S. Representative Maxine Waters—an old Watson nemesis. But Watson used her stronger name and more potent electoral and public service pedigree to brush aside both of her opponents, then easily defeated millionaire travel agency maven Noel Irwin Hentschel in the runoff. Hentschel had run for statewide office in 1998, making a credible showing in the GOP primary for lieutenant governor, and few could understand why she chose to undertake the impossible task of winning such a heavily endowed Democratic district. Hentschel spent some $700,000 of her own money, with predictable results. She pulled in just 20% of the vote.

Not that Watson didn't have her vulnerabilities. While a legislator, she was known as one of the Capitol's most contentious and demanding members, one who always appeared to be mad at someone or something. In 1989 her office was investigated by the Sacramento County District Attorney's office over allegations that she used staff and state resources to help prepare her doctoral dissertation. The probe led nowhere when investigators concluded that legislative record-keeping had been too shoddy to provide any proof. In 1989 she caused a stir by voting against legislative ethics reform, and again during a 1991 ethics workshop when she harrumphed, "We're not ordinary people."

Ordinary or not, in 2002 Watson was one of the few Democrats who opposed a resolution authorizing the use of force in Iraq, speaking against the Bush administration's plan on the House floor. She continued to question the wisdom of the administration's Iraq policy, and expressed disappointment once the invasion was launched in March 2003. In another House speech, she called for the resignation of Secretary of Defense Donald Rumsfeld after events proved her right and took delight when, in 2006, he finally quit the post following the November election. Watson has not had a Republican opponent since 2002.

BIOGRAPHY: Born: Los Angeles, November 12, 1933. Home: Los Angeles. Education: AA, Los Angeles City College; BA, UCLA; MS, CSU Los Angeles; PhD, Claremont Graduate Schoool. Military: None. Family: Single. Religion: Catholic.

OFFICES: Capitol: Cannon Office Building 125, Washington, DC 20515, Phone: (202) 225-7084, Fax: (202) 225-2422, email: diane.watson@mail.house.gov. District: 4322 Wilshire Boulevard, Suite 302, Los Angeles, CA 90010, Phone: (323) 965-1422, Fax: (323) 965-1113.

COMMITTEES: International Relations; Government Reform

ELECTED: 2001

ELECTION HISTORY: Los Angeles Unified School Board, 1975–1978; State Senate, 1978–1998.

2002 ELECTION: Watson (D*) 83%
Kim (R) 14%
Tate (L) 3%

2004 ELECTION: Watson (D*) 89%
Weber (L) 11%

2006 ELECTION: Watson (D*) 100%

RATINGS:	ACU	ADA	AFL-CIO	CoC	GO	LCV	NTU	PIRG
	4	95	93	37	F-	100	13	95

HENRY WAXMAN (D)
30th Congressional District

Counties: Los Angeles
Cities: Los Angeles, Beverly Hills, Santa Monica, West Hollywood
Ethnicity: 77% White, 8% Latino, 3% Black, 10% Asian
Voter Registration: 50% D – 25% R – 21% DS
President 04: 66% Kerry, 33% Bush

Prior to the 2001 reapportionment this district had a different number—the 29th—and was located entirely on what is known as the Westside, home to Hollywood stars. Beginning just east of downtown at the Silver Lake Reservoir, it meandered west, taking in affluent and well-known communities such as Los Feliz, Hollywood, West Hollywood, Beverly Hills, Bel Air, Brentwood, Westwood, Pacific Palisades, and Santa Monica. This is Governor Arnold Schwarzenegger's home district, for instance.

Reapportionment changed it. Where once it just grazed the sea at Santa Monica Bay, the district now sprawls along the coast and Highway 1 from Santa Monica to well past Malibu. La Brea Boulevard is its eastern boundary, although a finger sticks to the east to encompass Hollywood Bowl. Added to the district to make up for population lost in the east are Malibu, the Santa Monica Mountain cities of Hidden Hills, Calabasas, Agoura Hills, and Westlake Village, and the San Fernando Valley communities of Woodland Hills, Canoga Park, West Hills, and Chatsworth.

Henry Waxman

Most of the district is white, with a substantial Jewish population, gays centered around West Hollywood, and a significant Iranian community. Democrats outnumber Republicans two-to-one, with Republican voters concentrated around Chatsworth at the far northern edge.

Incumbent Henry Waxman has represented the area in one place or another for more than 35 years. Long known as one of the sharpest intellects in Congress, he joined with fellow Democrat Howard Berman to form one of the most significant power bases in southern California during the 1970s and 1980s—the Berman-Waxman organization.

In Congress, he has focused his considerable talents and energies on health care, clean air, and the problems of the elderly. When Democrats controlled the House, he was one of its most influential voices on health care policy—losing a substantial amount of clout when Republicans took over in 1994. He gained national prominence during the late 1990s when he subpoenaed tobacco company executives who claimed, under his questioning, that their products were not habit-forming.

Since 1997 he has used his position as ranking member of the House Government Reform Committee to initiate probes of, among other issues, Bush administration connections to Enron, the high cost of prescription drugs, conditions in nursing homes, Medicare, and overcrowded schools. Waxman initially voted to support U.S. military action in Iraq, although he has become a vocal critic of the Bush administration's handling of the war and its aftermath, eventually voting against the president's request for additional funds for operations in Iraq. As befitting both his heritage and constituency, he is an ardent supporter of all things Israel, including the Israeli government's plans to build a fence in the West Bank. He has opposed congressional efforts to ban same-sex marriages.

Back in the 1990s, Waxman gained some notoriety during the House banking scandal when it was revealed that he bounced some 434 checks written on the House bank. Although he amassed one of the highest totals in the House, Waxman refused to discuss the matter, saying it was private. His constituents apparently agreed with him because the incumbent has never had to sweat an election.

Democratic control of the House returned in 2007, and Waxman was one of the chief beneficiaries of the return to power. He chaired the Government Reform Committee, which has the authority to probe nearly every government operation—complete with subpoena power for documents from the Bush administration. That makes him the Sherlock Holmes of Congress, and the reconstruction of Iraq and aftermath of Hurricane Katrina are but two super-size subjects likely to come under Waxman's magnifying glass. When Republicans controlled the House, Waxman often would conduct his part of an investigation by issuing detailed letters to various officials, complete with footnotes and questions. The letters were inserted into the public record. Now, he has the power to use a much more forceful instrument for his investigations.

BIOGRAPHY: Born: Los Angeles, September 12, 1939. Home: Los Angeles. Education: BA, JD, UCLA. Military: None. Family: wife Janet, two children, three grandchildren. Religion: Jewish.

OFFICES: Capitol: Rayburn Building 2204, Washington, DC 20515, Phone: (202) 225-3976, Fax: (202) 225-4099, email: henry.waxman@mail.house.gov. District: 8436 West Third Street, Suite 600, Los Angeles, CA 90048, Phones: (323) 651-1040, (818) 878-7400, (310) 652-3095, Fax: (323) 655-0502.

COMMITTEES: Government Reform; Energy and Commerce.

ELECTED: 1974

ELECTION HISTORY: State Assembly, 1969–1975.

2002 ELECTION: Waxman (D*) 70%
                 Gross (R) 30%

2004 ELECTION: Waxman (D*) 71%
                 Elizalde (R) 29%

2006 ELECTION: Waxman (D*) 72%
                 Jones (R) 26%
                 Cannon (PF) 2%

RATINGS:

ACU	ADA	AFL-CIO	CoC	GO	LCV	NTU	PIRG
0	100	93	38	F-	100	15	98

LYNN WOOLSEY (D)
6th Congressional District

Counties: Marin, Sonoma
Cities: Santa Rosa, Petaluma, San Rafael
Ethnicity: 76% White, 15% Latino, 2% Black, 5% Asian
Voter Registration: **51% D – 24% R – 19% DS**
President 04: 70% Kerry, 28% Bush

Lynn Woolsey

Encompassing all of Marin County, most of Sonoma County, and Muir Woods in between is one of the most affluent, white liberal congressional districts in the country. And the southern edge of Marin County tends to be the most affluent, liberal, and culturally extreme portion of the district. Perched on mountains sloping up from San Fancisco Bay, the constituency can be as exotic as their panoramic views of San Francisco and the Bay. Moving further north into Novato and Sonoma County, the cultural landscape tends to be less eclectic but still heavily Democratic and liberal.

Reapportionment removed the city of Sonoma, solidifying the wine country in the neighboring 1st District, but left most everything else intact. Over the years, the area has become suburbanized; San Francisco is the nation's fifth largest metropolitan area. Locals try to control this with slow-growth initiatives, but closing the valve in one town merely causes increased pressures elsewhere. Very unsuburban are the coastal communities in the western edge of the district including bohemian Stinson Beach and Bolinas, recreational Point Reyes, Dillon Beach, Bodega Bay, and the resort town of Guerneville on the Russian River.

Democrat Lynn Woolsey, who has represented the district since 1992, hails from Petaluma, located in the geographic center of the district. She was elected after surviving a contentious, nine-candidate Democratic primary in 1992 made necessary when Barbara Boxer vacated the seat to run for the U.S. Senate. She faced Republican Bill Filante in a bittersweet general election. Filante, a doctor, was a popular member of the state Assembly who had been diagnosed with a brain tumor not long after declaring for Congress. Filante refused to bow out, even though he was forced to suspend his campaign following surgery. His wife filled in on the hustings, but the combination of Woolsey's Democratic pedigree and Filante's illness led to a sweeping Democratic victory. Filante died not long after the election.

Woolsey served on the Petaluma City Council from 1984 to 1992. A former welfare mom and the mother of a gay son, she brought a compelling personal story to her political career and has taken an independent route at times. She opposed President Clinton's 1996 Welfare Reform Act, opposed banning gays in the military, and carried a bill in Congress that was soundly defeated by a vote of 362–12 to revoke the federal charter for the Boy Scouts because of the group's ban on gays.

Although a seven-term incumbent, Woolsey attracts her share of Democratic opponents. In 2004 she faced Renn Alexander Vara, who shared her liberal politics but believed she wasn't effective enough. Vara did not run a competitive race, receiving just 16% of the vote. In 2002, Woolsey beat back a challenge from a more formidable opponent, Mayor Mike Martini of Santa Rosa, the district's largest city. Martini targeted Woosley as too liberal and ineffective in a Republican-controlled Congress. He did better than Vara two years later but still only received 20% of the vote.

In 2006, Woolsey faced her toughest competitor—Assemblyman Joe Nation, who announced his candidacy more than a year before the June 2006 primary. Nation was termed out of the Assembly and had no viable route to the state Senate. In making his announcement, Nation took pains to praise Woosley rather than denigrate her, saying only that he wanted to give voters a chance to evaluate another option. That rhetoric hardened as the campaign progressed, and he accused Woolsey of being ineffective and of promoting a ferry terminal at Port Sonoma while accepting contributions from those who benefited from the terminal. Nation stumped on his Assembly record, especially on his environmental record and his advocacy of alternative fuels. For her part, Woolsey accused Nation, a moderate by district standards, of promoting business interests. The two clashed over Iraq, with Woolsey demanding an immediate pullout of American troops and Nation arguing for a gradual withdrawal.

Woolsey's stiffest electoral challenge ended with the incumbent capturing two-thirds of the vote and breezing to re-election in November.

BIOGRAPHY: Born: Seattle, WA, November 3, 1937. Home: Petaluma. Education: Attended University of Washington; BS, University of San Francisco. Military:

None. Family: Divorced, four children, four grandchildren. Religion: Presbyterian.

OFFICES: Capitol: Rayburn Building 2263, Washington, DC 20515, Phone: (202) 225-5161, Fax: (202) 225-5163, email: lynn.woolsey@mail.house.gov. District: 1101 College Avenue, Suite 354, Santa Rosa, CA 95404, Phone: (707) 542-7182, Fax: (707) 542-2745; 1050 Northgate Drive, Suite 140, San Rafael, CA 94903, Phone: (415) 507-9554, Fax: (707) 542-2745.

COMMITTEES: Education; Science.

ELECTED: 1992

ELECTION HISTORY: Petaluma City Council, 1984–1992.

2002 ELECTION: Woolsey (D*) 67%
                      Erickson (R) 30%
                      Barton (L) 2%
                      Rainforth (RF) 1%

2004 ELECTION: Woolsey (D*) 72%
                      Erickson (R) 28%

2006 ELECTION: Woolsey (D*) 70%
                      Hooper (R) 26%
                      Friesen (L) 4%

RATINGS:

ACU	ADA	AFL-CIO	CoC	GO	LCV	NTU	PIRG
8	100	93	33	F-	100	19	93

8

The Counties

California has over 5,000 local governments—from its 58 counties to a myriad of cities, special districts, and agencies—and how to fund them adequately has vexed policymakers for more than a generation. Basically, local governments—including counties—get revenue from three sources: property and sales taxes and the vehicle license fee (VLF). The money pays for a variety of programs and services—health care, law enforcement, libraries, social services, some educational needs, transportation, to name a few.

Much of the dilemma over local government finance can be traced to the passage of Proposition 13, the 1978 initiative that dramatically altered the revenue available from property taxes. Before 1978 property taxes financed schools and community colleges. But in 1979, the state took on the responsibility for funding education and used property taxes to pay for local government. Unfortunately, the initiative reduced the amount of money available from this tax. In addition, the state has raided the pool of local government money during tough fiscal times to gin up the General Fund, using the resources to pay for other programs. This practice pits local programs against state funded health care, education, and social services.

The system—"chaos" might be the more appropriate word—for parceling out money to local governments also created competition between cities and counties and between counties and various special districts. Until 2004, locals grumped about the situation but did little politically to secure a more reliable and equitable source of funding from the state. But the grumping turned to action in 2004 when newly elected Governor Arnold Schwarzenegger reduced the VLF—an action that blew a $4 billion

| Ten Largest Counties in California ||
County	Population
1. Los Angeles	10,292,723
2. San Diego	3,084,634
3. Orange	3,083,894
4. San Bernardino	2,016,277
5. Riverside	2,004,608
6. Santa Clara	1,791,869
7. Alameda	1,514,909
8. Sacramento	1,396,353
9. Contra Costa	1,034,874
10. Fresno	909,399

hole in an already steroid-driven state budget deficit and, more significantly, took the funds directly out of the hide of local government.

The action evolved into an alliance between the counties and cities during negotiations over the 2004–2005 state budget, when the two main local government entities became politically active for the first time in years. Fronted by the League of California Cities and the California State Association of Counties, the alliance used as a club the threat of an initiative that locked up funds for local government under terms dictated, not by the governor or legislature, but by locals themselves. Not long after the initiative qualified for the November 2004 ballot as Proposition 65, the governor and lawmakers negotiated a deal with cities and counties that helped the administration address the budget deficit in exchange for future funding guarantees. That deal also appeared on the November 2004 ballot as Proposition 1A.

The dueling ballot measures created some comic relief in an otherwise maudlin election. Once the deal was struck, cities and counties abandoned their stepchild—Proposition 65—and urged voters to support Proposition 1A. That essentially made local governments the chief *opponent* of their own initiative.

Meanwhile, California's magnesium-hot real estate market produced a serious up-tick in property tax revenues flowing into county coffers in 2004–2006, so much so that counties that once faced revenue shortages of their own reported surpluses. Los Angeles County, for instance, reported a $300 million-plus surplus for 2004–2005. The real-estate market, however, slowed considerably in late 2006, threatening another plunge in local revenues.

Key issues for counties during the 2007–2008 legislative session are growing concerns over unfunded pension liabilities at the local level and the expansion of Indian gaming into urban areas. Local governments, including the association of counties, exercised their political muscles during the November 2006 election with mixed results. They led the charge to defeat Proposition 90 that would have severely restricted

| Fastest-Growing Counties Based on Percent Change ||
County	Percentage Growth (2000–2006)
1. Riverside	28.6
2. Placer	27.9
3. Kern	19.7
4. Yuba	19.0
5. San Joaquin	18.5
6. Imperial	18.3
7. Madera	18.2
8. Merced	17.9
9. Sutter	17.1
10. San Bernardino	17.1
California	9.8
Source: Department of Finance	

the use of eminent domain condemnations to aid local development. It lost by some 400,000 votes. Counties (and cities) were not so fortunate with another initiative on that same ballot: Proposition 83, which regulates where convicted sex offenders may live after release from prison. It won with more than 70 percent of the vote, but a federal judge issued a restraining order on the day after the election calling the measure unconstitutional. That legal fight is far from over, and many of the state's rural counties are concerned that, if ultimately implemented, the new law would adversely impact them. The law mandates that sex offenders cannot live within 2,000 feet of a park or school—a prohibition that rural counties fear will preclude offenders from living in urban areas.

Alameda County

Area: 738 sq. mi.; Population: (2005 est.) 1,497,251, (2000) 1,443,741; (1990) 1,279,182, (1980) 1,105,379; Registration (Oct. 2006): D-55.2%, R-17.5%, DS-21.8%; 2006 voter turnout (rank): 61.2% (19); County supervisors: Scott Haggerty, Gail Steele, Alice Lai-Bitker, Nate Miley, Keith Carson; 1221 Oak St., Rm. 536, Oakland 94612, Phone: (510) 272-6347, Fax: (510) 272-3784; Assembly Districts 14, 15, 16, 18, 20; Senate Districts 9,10; Congressional Districts 9, 10, 11, 13; Budget (2006-2007): $2.19 billion; Median income: $61,017; Median home value (Sept 2006): $595,000; Ethnicity: White-40.9%, Latino-19.0%, Asian-20.4%, Black-14.9%; Largest cities (2006): Oakland (411,765), Fremont (210,158), Hayward (146,398), Berkeley (105,385).

The largest burg in Alameda County is Oakland, once dismissed by writer Gertrude Stein with the remark, "There's no there there." Stein wasn't referring to politics but to the fact that the Oakland of her childhood had disappeared. Politically, the remark could apply to the Republican Party in Alameda County for much the same reason. As of October 2006, nearly 30,000 more Alameda County voters registered "decline-to-state" than Republican, a fact reflected in election results over the past 16 years.

Alameda County stretches along the eastern shore of San Francisco Bay, and although Republicans have made strides in some of the fast-growing, affluent suburbs—Livermore and Pleasanton, for instance—Democratic strongholds in Oakland, Hayward, and Berkeley dominate the county. Berkeley, especially, is a GOP desert; as many voters register for the Green Party as Republican while four times as many voters register "decline-to-state" as Republican. In 18 elections for president, governor, and U.S. Senate since 1990, the GOP has cracked 30 percent of the vote only three times—Pete Wilson for governor in 1990 and 1994, and Arnold Schwarzenegger in 2006. Neither Wilson nor Schwarzenegger actually carried the county, however. President George W. Bush captured less than a quarter of the Alameda County vote in 2000 and 2004, and 70 percent of Alameda voters opposed the 2003 recall of former Governor Gray Davis—making Alameda one of only nine counties statewide to vote against recall. In the election to replace Davis, Democratic Lieutenant Governor Cruz Bustamante outpolled Republican Arnold Schwarzenegger 53.5 percent to 25.6 percent.

True to its Democratic roots, in the 2006 governor's race, Alameda was one of only five counties to favor Democratic gubernatorial candidate Phil Angelides over Schwarzenegger. In that same election, Democratic incumbent U.S. Senator Dianne Feinstein breezed through Alameda, winning 75 percent of the vote, while her GOP opponent, Richard Mountjoy, received a paltry 17 percent.

Although a Republican represents a sliver of the county in the state Assembly (District 15), the rest of Alameda's state and federal legislators are Democrats. In the high-profile race for Congress from District 11, Alameda played a pivotal role in the defeat of seven-term incumbent Republican Richard Pombo. Pombo managed only 38 percent of the Alameda vote, losing by 6,000 votes. Despite the fact that Alameda contributed only 15 percent of the district's electorate, it gave Pombo's opponent, Democrat Jerry McNerney, more than half of his 11,000 margin of victory.

The county's most recognizable politicians are Democrats Jerry Brown, Bill Lockyer, and Don Perata. Brown, the former governor, served as mayor of Oakland from 1998 to 2006, then continued his unique, four-decade political odyssey by getting elected state attorney general in 2006. He replaces Lockyer, the Hayward native who played the game of musical offices by being elected state treasurer in 2006. Perata, a former Alameda supervisor from Oakland, is the president pro tem of the state Senate, a position that makes him one of the most powerful legislators in Sacramento. Termed out in 2008, Perata likely will see his power wane over the next two years as his Democratic colleagues pressure him to step aside before his Senate career comes to a close.

Shifts inherent in Alameda demographics and development were highlighted at the close of 2006 when one of the region's premier sports franchises, baseball's Oakland Athletics, announced that the team was leaving Oakland. Team owners had partnered with software giant Cisco Systems to relocate in Fremont, another Alameda

County burg that is only half Oakland's size but with a 145-acre chunk of undeveloped land—perfect for a new stadium.

Alpine County

Area: 743 sq. mi.; Population: (2005 est.) 1,242, (2000) 1,208, (1990) 1,113, (1980) 1,097; Registration (Oct. 2006): D-35.7%, R-35.0%, DS-23.0%; 2006 voter turnout (rank): 71.7% (4); County supervisors: Henry "Skip" Veatch, Donald Jardine, Terry Woodrow, Gunter Kaiser, Phillip Bennet; P.O. Box 158, Markleeville 96120, Phone: (530) 694-2287, Fax: (530) 694-2491; Assembly District 4; Senate District 1; Congressional District 3; Budget (2005-2006): $22 million; Median income: $41,875; Median home value: $184,200; Ethnicity: White-66.9%, Latino-7.8%, Asian-0.1%, Black-0.6%; Largest cities (2000): Markleeville (197), Mesa Vista (182).

The population boom that has blessed—some might say cursed—California over the past 20 years has bypassed Alpine County, which remains the state's smallest county in terms of population. Nestled against the Nevada border along the spine of the Sierras south of Lake Tahoe, Alpine grew by just 95 people between 1980 and 2000—an increase of slightly over 8 percent. Whites are the predominant ethnic group, while Native Americans outnumber Latinos nearly three to one. Winter sports, centered on the ski resorts at Kirkwood and Bear Valley, are a major source of income for county residents, although unemployment has remained near 10 percent since 1990.

Politically, this former conservative bastion has been trending left. Republicans who once dominated county politics found themselves on the short end of registration —by six registrants—on the eve of the 2006 general election. In 2003, Alpine backed the recall of former Democratic Governor Gray Davis and gave his successor, Republican Arnold Schwarzenegger, 52.5 percent of the vote. A year later, Democratic presidential hopeful John Kerry and Democratic U.S. Senator Barbara Boxer both captured the county.

The county split its party allegiance in 2006. In his re-election bid, Schwarzenegger bagged 54 percent of the Alpine vote against Democrat Phil Angelides, while Democratic U.S. Sen. Dianne Feinstein won Alpine with 57 percent of the vote. In the most competitive of the statewide races, the Democratic candidate for lieutenant governor—John Garamendi—won the county with 48 percent of the vote against conservative Republican state Sen. Tom McClintock.

More significant, Alpine blessed Democrat Cruz Bustamante's effort to move from lieutenant governor to insurance commissioner—making the small rural county one of the few in the state to favor Bustamante over the eventual winner, Republican Steve Poizner. In other signals that Alpine has moved to the political center, the county opposed, by a two-to-one margin, a measure that would have required parental notification before a minor could obtain an abortion. It also approved taxes on tobacco and oil to fund health care and development of alternative energy technology.

Amador County

Area: 593 sq. mi.; Population: (2005 est.) 38,221, (2000) 35,100, (1990) 30,309, (1980) 19,314; Registration (Oct. 2006): D-34.9%, R-46.5%, DS-13.2%; 2006 voter turnout (rank): 69.3% (6); County supervisors: Richard Escamilla, Richard Forster,

Theodore Novelli, Louis Boitano, Mary Ellen Welsh; 500 Argonaut Lane, Jackson 95642, Phone: (209) 223-6470; Assembly District 10; Senate District 1; Congressional District 3; Budget (2006-2007): $74 million; Median income: $42,280; Median home value: $153,600; Ethnicity: White-76.4%, Latino-8.9%, Asian-1.0%, Black-3.9%; Largest cities (2004): Ione (7,129), Jackson (3,989), Sutter Creek (2,303).

Deep in Mother Lode territory, Amador County has seen its population grow nearly 82 percent over the past 20 years as urban Sacramento spreads east into the Sierra foothills. Inmates at Mule Creek State Prison in Ione represent some of the growth, but most of it has come in the form of flatland refugees. The growth has caused some frictions between old-time mountaineers and newcomers.

Politically conservative, Amador has voted Republican in all but two top-of-the-ticket statewide races since 1990 (Dianne Feinstein for U.S. Senate in 1992 and Gray Davis for governor in 1998), although its voting patterns have been galloping to the right in recent years. Republican Tom Campbell carried the county against Feinstein in 2000, while Republican Bill Simon finished 20 points ahead of Davis in the 2002 gubernatorial race. Two-thirds of Amador voters backed Davis's recall in 2003, and conservative GOP state Senator Tom McClintock polled even with Democratic Lieutenant Governor Cruz Bustamante (18%) in the contest to replace Davis. Both finished well behind Republican Arnold Schwarzenegger's 58 percent. In 2004, President George Bush took 62 percent of the vote, while Republican U.S. Senate candidate Bill Jones carried Amador over incumbent Democrat Barbara Boxer. Two years later, Amador provided Feinstein with one of her few county losses, giving her opponent, Republican Richard Mountjoy, 50 percent of its vote. Some 72 percent of county voters backed Schwarzenegger's re-election bid.

In true conservative fashion, Amador voted down three of four infrastructure bonds (for transportation, schools, and affordable housing) on the November 2006 ballot despite Schwarzenegger's heavy support for the bonds. Alpiners did approve bonds for flood control.

Butte County

Area: 1,639 sq. mi.; Population: (2005 est.) 216,401, (2000) 203,171, (1990) 182,120, (1980) 143,851; Registration (Oct. 2006): D-34.6%, R-41.1%, DS-17.8%; 2006 voter turnout (rank): 60.8% (20); County supervisors: Bill Connelly, Jane Dolan, Maureen Kirk, Curt Josiassen, Kim Yamaguchi; 25 County Center Drive, Oroville 95965, Phone: (530) 538-7631; Assembly Districts 2, 3; Senate District 4; Congressional Districts 2, 4; Budget (2006-2007): $375 million; Median income: $31,924; Median home value: $129,800; Ethnicity: White-74.0%, Latino-10.5%, Asian-3.3%, Black-1.4%; Largest cities (2004): Chico (71,300), Paradise (26,408), Oroville (13,004).

When he first ran for president in 1992, Democrat Bill Clinton defeated incumbent Republican George H. W. Bush by 1 percent in Butte County. Until 2006, that marked the last time a Democrat carried Butte at the top of the ticket. Even Clinton himself was walloped there in 1996.

In 2006, Democrats scored something of a breakthrough when U.S. Sen. Dianne Feinstein eked out a 700-vote victory over Republican Richard Mountjoy in her bid for a fourth term. But Feinstein was the only Democrat statewide to carry Butte.

A rural enclave in the geographic center of northern California, Butte was for a time the most watched county in California. In 1989, 1990, and 1991, it came within days of becoming the first county in the United States to file for bankruptcy—a calamity narrowly averted by last-second state bailouts. A combination of events and decisions contributed to the problem, including the loss of taxing territory to city annexations and the refusal of Butte voters to approve either tax hikes or bond measures. When Interstate 5 was extended north from Sacramento to the Oregon border it bypassed Butte, causing some developers to take investment dollars elsewhere.

Like many rural counties, Butte is politically conservative despite the presence of California State University, Chico. In top-of-the-ticket races, Butte voters nearly always give Republicans the nod. Republican Bill Simon defeated Democratic incumbent Gray Davis here by some 22 points in the 2002 race for governor, and nearly 65 percent of Butte voters backed Davis's recall a year later. Republican Arnold Schwarzenegger was the county's clear choice to replace Davis. In 2004, Republicans George W. Bush and Bill Jones won Butte in contests for president and U.S. Senate. Two years later, Butte gave two-thirds of its vote to Schwarzenegger's re-election effort.

Calaveras County

Area: 1,020 sq. mi.; Population: (2005 est.) 45,711, (2000) 40,554, (1990) 31,998, (1980) 20,710; Registration (Oct. 2006): D-33.9%, R-44.8%, DS-15.4%; 2006 voter turnout (rank): 57.5% (26); County supervisors: Alan "Bill" Claudino, Steve Wilensky, Merita Callaway, Thomas Tryon, Russell Thomas; 891 Mountain Ranch Road, San Andreas 95249, Phone: (209) 754-6370, Fax: (209) 754-6733; Assembly District 25; Senate District 1; Congressional District 3; Budget (2006-2007): $106 million; Median income: $41,022; Median home value: $156,900; Ethnicity: White-84.4%, Latino-6.8%, Asian-0.9%, Black-0.7%; Largest cities (2004): Angels Camp (3,440), San Andreas (2,615).

Calaveras County could well be the most famous of California's nonurban counties, thanks to a 125-year-old short story by Mark Twain. Jumping frogs aside, this Sierra foothill county's population has doubled since 1980 and could, if mid-decade trends hold, jump another 25 percent by 2010. The county is intersected by scenic Highway 49, which carries sightseers and tourists up from the Sacramento Valley into Gold Country and provides some economic stability. Unemployment, in double digits as late as 1995, shrank to 6 percent in 2001 only to spike back to 8 percent in 2003 as northern California's recession deepened.

Conservative Calaveras has voted for only one top-of-the-ticket Democrat since 1990—Dianne Feinstein's initial race for the U.S. Senate in 1992. Incumbent Feinstein lost the county in 1994, 2000, and 2006. Two-thirds of Calaveras voters supported the 2003 recall of Governor Gray Davis, while conservative Republican Tom McClintock hauled in 20 percent of the vote in the replacement election. Republican Arnold Schwarzenegger won the county with 53.8%, upping his take to 70 percent in his 2006 re-election. In 2004, President George Bush captured 61 percent of the county vote, and Republican Bill Jones beat Democratic incumbent Barbara Boxer. In 2006, Republican Richard Mountjoy beat Feinstein for U.S. Senate in Calaveras.

The county tilts right on ballot measures as well. In November 2006, it defeated every initiative on the ballot save one—a measure meant to restrict government use of eminent domain to condemn private property for private development as well as public use. Calaveras also defeated three of four infrastructure bond proposals, giving the nod only to one earmarked for flood control.

Colusa County

Area: 1,151 sq. mi.; Population: (2005 est.) 21,315, (2000) 18,804, (1990) 16,274, (1980) 12,791; Registration (Oct. 2006): D-35.6%, R-46.5%, DS-14.3%; 2006 voter turnout (rank): 57.3% (27); County supervisors: Dan Yerxa, Tom Indrieri, Mark Marshall, Gary Evans, Kim Vann; 546 J Street, Colusa 95932, Phone: (530) 458-0508; Assembly District 2; Senate District 4; Congressional District 2; Budget (2006-2007): $43.6 million; Median income: $35,062; Median home value: $107,500; Ethnicity: White-48.0%, Latino-46.5%, Asian-1.2%, Black-0.5%; Largest cities (2004): Coulsa (5,625), Williams (3,670).

Many travelers pass through the 1,100 square miles of Colusa County farmland each day, but few stop to shop because they are locked in autos, trucks, and buses on Interstate 5, heading north from Sacramento to Oregon. As a result, the most noticeable fact about Colusa County is its chronic, double-digit unemployment rate, which hit a high of 21.5 percent in 1992 and 1993 and has since leveled off around 19 percent. Agriculture supports the county's economy, with rice the primary crop. But without a natural resource to exploit for tourism, and too far from Sacramento to provide bedroom communities, Colusa has little hope of diversifying.

The county is doggedly Republican—no Democratic presidential, gubernatorial, or U.S. Senate candidate carried Colusa County in the 1990s or 2000s. The effort to recall Governor Gray Davis garnered 75 percent of Colusa's vote in 2003, while Republican Arnold Schwarzenegger captured 64 percent of the vote in the Davis replacement election. He added another 10 percent to that percentage in his 2006 re-election effort. President George Bush received more than two-thirds of the Colusa vote, while the county was one of the few statewide where losing Republican U.S. Senate candidate Bill Jones reached 60 percent of the vote. Republican Richard Mountjoy didn't breach that threshold against Democratic incumbent Dianne Feinstein in 2006, but still captured 54 percent in winning the county.

Contra Costa County

Area: 720 sq. mi.; Population: (2006 est.) 1,029,377, (2000) 948,816, (1990) 803,732, (1980) 656,331; Registration (Oct. 2006): D-48.1%, R-29.6%, DS-18.1%; 2006 voter turnout (rank): 61.5% (16); County supervisors: John Gioia, Gale Uilkema, Mary Nejedly Piepho, Susan Bonilla, Federal Glover; 651 Pine St., Martinez 94533, Phone: (925) 335-1900, Fax: (925) 335-1098; Assembly Districts 11, 14, 15; Senate Districts 7, 9; Congressional Districts 1, 10, 13; Budget (2006-2007): $1.22 billion; Median income: $63,675; Median home value: $559,000; Ethnicity: White-57.9%,

Latino-17.7%, Asian-11.0%, Black-9.4%; Largest cities (2006): Concord (124,436), Richmond (103,468), Antioch (100,945).

Contra Costa County, its western nose nuzzled against San Francisco Bay, is one of California's more schizophrenic counties. The north and west portions are home to blue-collar, sometimes poor areas such as Richmond, Martinez, Pittsburg, and Antioch, with their sprawling oil refineries and industrial complexes. But the inland eastern areas include tony, booming Walnut Creek, Moraga, Orinda, and Lafayette.

These affluent suburbs have benefited from the lion's share of a 20-year growth spurt that has seen the county's population increase by 50 percent since 1980. That growth has transformed Contra Costa from a bucolic bedroom community for San Francisco and Oakland into a thriving upscale metropolis as well as a freeway conduit for workers forced to move even farther east into the San Joaquin Valley in search of affordable housing. The pressure on traffic throughout Contra Costa County has increased exponentially over the past 15 years, especially on arteries such as Highway 4, Interstates 580 and 680, and the notorious Vasco Road, where 11 people died in accidents during an 18-month stretch in 2003-2004. As a result, traffic issues tend to dominate local races.

The poorer areas of the county may well see some economic improvement, although with a price. Native American tribes with visions of casino grandeur have come calling on Contra Costa, especially around Richmond and the I-80 corridor that leads to San Francisco. The Lytton Band of Pomo Indians, based in Santa Rosa, signed a 2004 compact with Governor Arnold Schwarzenegger that would allow it to expand its small San Pablo casino near Richmond into a mega-gambling facility adjacent to Interstate 80. The expansion received the blessing of the area's powerful congressman, Democrat George Miller, but ran afoul of other local officials who succeeded in halting it temporarily through legislative action. Despite initial concerns about increased traffic and congestion, the casino has become an important source of jobs and revenue that has allowed San Pablo to increase services for youth programs and public safety.

Close on the heels of the Lytton Band come two more tribes, each with casino plans for the Richmond vicinity and each trailing controversy in its wake. The Scotts Valley Band of Pomo Indians and the Guidivulle Band of Pomo Indians want casino complexes, but neither currently owns land. Richmond wants the development; the county does not, putting the two at odds. Both tribes require federal approval—and an exemption from current federal law—to purchase land and build a casino.

Other parts of the county also are experiencing development controversies. In Concord, for instance, city officials were blindsided late in 2006 when the U.S. Navy announced plans to sell the mothballed, 5,000-plus acre Concord Naval Weapons Station to a private developer. The Navy and city officials had been dickering over plans for the base—one of the biggest parcels of undeveloped land in the San Francisco Bay Area. Local officials and the area's congressional delegation vowed to fight the sale, arguing that the city and county would have little say over future development on base property.

Politically, the county mostly votes Democratic, although Republican Pete Wilson captured the county in his 1994 re-election race against Democrat Kathleen Brown. Contra Costa voters rejected the recall of former Governor Gray Davis in 2003, although they gave Republican Arnold Schwarzenegger a narrow nod over Lieutenant Governor Cruz Bustamante to replace Davis. In 2004, the county aligned itself solidly behind Democratic presidential hopeful John Kerry and U.S. Senator Barbara Boxer.

In 2006, Republican Schwarzenegger won 53 percent of the Contra Costa vote in his re-election bid against Democrat Phil Angelides, while Democratic U.S. Sen. Dianne Feinstein took 68 percent of its vote. County voters contributed to the defeat of Republican incumbent U.S. Representative Richard Pombo in District 11, giving his Democratic challenger, Jerry McNerney, 54 percent of their vote.

On a local level, Contra Costa provided a significant milestone for the Green Party when Gayle McLaughlin was elected mayor of Richmond in November 2006, making Richmond the biggest city in the nation with a Green at the helm. McLaughlin is the first Green elected mayor of a city where whites are in the minority, perhaps broadening the appeal of a party primarily known for its environmental activism.

Del Norte County

Area: 1,008 sq. mi.; Population: (2005 est.) 29,355, (2000) 27,482, (1990) 23,460, (1980) 18,217; Registration (Oct. 2006): D-36.5%, R-39.2%, DS-18.2%; 2006 voter turnout (rank): 56.7% (29); County supervisors: Leslie McNamer, Martha McClure, Mike Sullivan, Gerry Hemmingsen, David Finigan; 981 H St., Crescent City 95531, Phone: (707) 464-7204; Assembly District 1; Senate District 4; Congressional District 1; Budget (2006-2007): $42 million. Median income: $29,642; Median home value: $121,100; Ethnicity: White-65.0%, Latino-13.9%, Asian-2.3%, Black-4.3%; Largest cities (2004): Crescent City (7,550).

Prisons as the basis for an economy are two-edged. They bring jobs and pump income into a community, but they bring social problems that often accompany families of inmates who attempt to settle near the prison. Those problems include increased welfare rolls and a culture clash between new urban arrivals and locals accustomed to a more exurban lifestyle. The problems are exacerbated if the prison houses some of the state's most hardened criminals. So it is with Del Norte County after Crescent City landed one of California's most notorious prisons—Pelican Bay, which houses California's most dangerous inmates.

Pelican Bay was supposed to help alleviate economic problems caused when the county's historic industries—lumbering and commercial fishing—fell on hard times during the 1970s and '80s. It hasn't always worked out that way. The population has increased 50 percent since 1980, and unemployment dropped to 8.5 percent in 2003 down from a peak of 15.4 percent in 1992. But the median household income hovers around $30,000, and that includes well-paid prison guards.

The two political parties are close in registration, but the county usually votes Republican. George W. Bush handily defeated Al Gore here in the 2000 presidential election and repeated that performance over John Kerry in 2004. Republican Bill Simon won the county in the 2002 gubernatorial race, as did the GOP's Bill Jones in the 2004 contest for U.S. Senate against incumbent Barbara Boxer. The 2003 recall of Governor Gray Davis captured 62 percent of the Del Norte vote.

In 2006, Del Norte shifted gears, but only slightly, supporting the re-election of Democratic incumbent U.S. Sen. Dianne Feinstein, although Feinstein captured less than 50 percent of the local vote and was the only statewide Democratic candidate to win Del Norte. On the same November ballot, Gov. Arnold Schwarzenegger enjoyed a 16-point margin over his Democratic opponent. Even uber-conservative Republican Tom McClintock won the county in his bid to become lieutenant governor. Del Norte voted against all four infrastructure bonds in November 2006, approving only two of 13 ballot measures—restrictions on where sex offenders may live and limits on the use of eminent domain condemnations by local governments.

El Dorado County

Area: 1,711 sq. mi.; Population: (2005 est.) 175,550, (2000) 156,299, (1990) 125,995, (1980) 85,812; Registration (Oct. 2006): D-30.7%, R-46.5%, DS-17.5%; 2006 voter turnout (rank): 51.4% (41); County supervisors: Rusty Dupray, Helen Baumann, Jack Sweeney, Charles Paine, Norma Santiago; 330 Fair Lane, Placerville 95667, Phone: (530) 621-5390, Fax: (530) 622-3645; Assembly Districts 4, 10; Senate District 1; Congressional District 4; Budget (2006-2007): $474 million; Median income: $51,484; Median home value: $480,000; Ethnicity: White-80.4%, Latino-9.3%, Asian-2.1%, Black-0.5%; Largest cities (2004): South Lake Tahoe (23,600), Placerville (10,150).

El Dorado County, the scene of a classic gold rush in the 1850s, is currently the setting for a rush for riches that is only slightly less frantic at both ends of the county. At its western edge, migrants from Sacramento are pushing urban sprawl far into the Sierra foothills, while its eastern reaches, which extend to the Nevada border and include the southern shore of Lake Tahoe, have seen extensive resort and vacation development. As a result, El Dorado County's population grew 82 percent between 1980 and 2000, then added another 20,000 folks in the next half decade. With growth have come prosperity and jobs—unemployment hit a low of 3.9 percent in 1999 at the height of the state's economic boom. It has since risen to over 5 percent as California battled a recession.

The bulk of El Dorado's growth has been suburban, in communities such as Cameron Park, El Dorado Hills, and Placerville along busy trans-Sierra Highway 50—the main corridor bearing weekend traffic from the San Francisco Bay Area and Central Valley to the resort and winter sports mecca around South Lake Tahoe.

Suburban growth has driven county politics to the right, and Republicans now dominate every election. No Democrat has carried El Dorado County at the top of the ticket in 16 years— and that includes five statewide efforts by no less an institution than Senator Dianne Feinstein. Republican Bill Simon captured nearly 60 percent of El Dorado's vote in the 2002 gubernatorial contest against incumbent Democrat Gray Davis, while El Dorado voters backed the Davis recall a year later by 71.5 percent. El Dorado gave George Bush 61 percent in his 2004 re-election and supported Republican Bill Jones' unsuccessful attempt to deny Democrat Barbara Boxer a third term in the U.S. Senate.

In 2006 Feinstein lost the county once again, even as she was overwhelmingly re-elected to a fourth term. Republican Gov. Arnold Schwarzenegger captured 73 percent of the El Dorado vote in his 2006 re-election. And true to its Republican hue, the county helped its embattled congressman, Republican incumbent John Doolittle, survive a dogged challenge from Democrat Charlie Brown, giving Doolittle nearly half his 8,000-vote margin of victory.

Fresno County

Area: 5,963 sq. mi.; Population: (2005 est.) 892,325, (2000) 799,407, (1990) 667,490, (1980) 587,329; Registration (Oct. 2006): D-39.5%, R-45.3%, DS-11.6%; 2006 voter turnout (rank): 54% (33); County supervisors: Phil Larson, Susan Anderson, Henry Perea, Judy Case, Bob Waterston, Vacancy; 2281 Tulare St., Room 301, Fresno 93721, Phone: (559) 488-3529; Assembly Districts 29, 30, 31; Senate Districts 13, 16; Congressional Districts 18, 19, 20, 21; Budget (2006-2007): $1.65 billion; Median income: $34,725; Median home value: $299,000; Ethnicity: White-39.7%, Latino-44.0%, Asian-8.1%, Black-5.3%; Largest cities (2004): Fresno (456,100), Clovis (80,900).

Fresno County, in the middle of California, represents the state's agricultural heritage as well as its new urban focus. It was here that the term "agribusiness" was coined, and large-scale agriculture remains an economic staple, with Fresno rated the number-one farm county in the nation. But its leading city—Fresno—is a rapidly expanding urban center whose population has increased more than 50 percent in the past decade. But growth hasn't necessarily brought prosperity as the county's unemployment rate has hovered around 14 percent during the past dozen years.

As Fresno County has grown, it has become increasingly Republican and conservative. Part of the change is reflected in the demographics of age. Between 1990 and 2000, the number of Fresnans between ages 20 and 39 increased 9%, while the population between 40 and 70 increased 34 percent. Older voters tend to be more conservative, as do many of the white middle-class migrants who came to the Central Valley to escape rising housing costs in Los Angeles and the San Francisco Bay Area. The change is reflected in voter registration. In October 1996, Democrats held a 47-41 percent edge. Eight years later, that dynamic had flipped, with the GOP claiming 47 percent of registered voters and Democrats only 40 percent.

Fresno's voting patterns reflect its Republican nature. Top-of-the-ticket Democratic candidates have captured Fresno County only three times since the 1990 gubernatorial race: Bill Clinton's 1992 presidential contest and Dianne Feinstein's 2000 and 2006 re-election bids to the U.S. Senate. Two-thirds of Fresno voters approved the 2003 recall against Governor Gray Davis, and more than half of them gave the nod to Republican Arnold Schwarzenegger to replace Davis. The leading Democratic candidate, Lieutenant Governor Cruz Bustamante, got only 28 percent of the vote, an extremely poor performance given that Bustamante hails from Fresno.

Bustamante did little better in 2006 when he ran for state insurance commissioner against little-known Republican Steve Poizner, who was making his first run for statewide office. Native son Bustamante managed less than a third of the vote in Fresno County, losing to Poizner here by more than 40,000 votes. Poizner, in fact, gained more raw votes in Fresno County than did Arnold Schwarzenegger. On the same ballot, Feinstein polled 52 percent to win a fourth term in the Senate.

Bustamante's various debacles notwithstanding, the fact that he was lieutenant governor at all shows that Fresno's growth has made it a better launching pad for politicians with statewide ambition. That wasn't always the case. Until the mid-1990s, Fresno politicians—even those as locally popular as the late state Senator Ken Maddy—fell flat in attempts to parlay regional appeal onto a broader stage. Jones, a former legislator, broke through in 1994 when he was elected to the first of two terms as secretary of state, but he failed when trying to move up to governor in 2002 or get elected to the U.S. Senate in 2004. Bustamante was elected in 1998.

Fresno County GOP politics can be problematic, and Fresno has strutted some seamy stuff on the political stage in recent years. Mike Briggs won an Assembly seat in 1998 despite having once pled no contest to statutory rape. He failed to win a 2002 congressional seat, largely because he voted with Democrats to pass the 2002 budget. He was replaced by Republican Steve Samuelian, who won the district after a brutal primary fight. Samuelian's tenure ended after one term when the police accused him of frequenting an area of Fresno known for prostitution. He declined to run for re-election and was replaced in 2004 by Mike Villines, who had to survive a gutter-level GOP primary.

Villines, on the other hand, scored a coup not long after the 2006 election when he was chosen Assembly GOP leader, ousting George Plescia. In part, Villines victory was an effort to return the Republican caucus to its conservative roots and give it a harder edge in negotiations with majority Democrats and Governor Schwarzenegger, a moderate Republican.

Glenn County

Area: 1,327 sq. mi.; Population: (2005 est.) 28,523, (2000) 26,453, (1990) 24,798, (1980) 21,350; Registration (Oct. 2006): D-32.5%, R-47.3%, DS-16.0%; 2006 voter turnout (rank): 64.6% (12); County supervisors: Tom McGowan, Tracey Quarne, John Amaro, Mike Murray, Keith Hansen; 526 West Sycamore Street, Willows 95988, Phone: (530) 934-6400, Fax: (530) 934-6419; Assembly District 2; Senate District 4; Congressional District 2; Budget (2006-2007): $74.3 million; Median income: $32,107; Median home value: $94,900; Ethnicity: White-62.6%, Latino-29.6%, Asian-3.4%, Black-0.6%; Largest cities (2004): Orland (6,525), Willows (6,375).

Glenn County is a quiet, rural enclave midway between Sacramento and the Oregon border. Its primary industry is agriculture, featuring rice, almonds, prunes, and dairy products. One of its largest employers is a Wal-Mart in Willows. Interstate 5 bisects the county, but the traffic streaming north and south between Oregon and Sacramento has had little impact on Glenn's economy or culture. Unemployment has stayed at 12 percent since 1990.

As with most rural northern California counties, Glenn is conservative and Republican. No top-of-the-ticket Democrat has carried the county in the last 15 statewide elections, and three-quarters of Glenn's voters approved the recall of Governor Gray Davis. In the race to replace Davis, conservative Republican state Senator Tom McClintock outpolled Democratic Lieutenant Governor Cruz Bustamante—although both finished well behind Republican Arnold Schwarzenegger. President George Bush received two-thirds of the county's vote in 2004, while Republican Bill Jones topped 60 percent in his failed effort to defeat Democratic incumbent U.S. Senator Barbara Boxer.

The county's conservative bent emerged in 2006 as well as it voted against infrastructure bonds for transportation, schools, and affordable housing, approving only those for flood control. And, once again, Republicans swept the county in statewide contests, including the U.S. Senate race where Republican Richard Mountjoy won 57 percent of the local vote against incumbent Dianne Feinstein. Democratic gubernatorial candidate Phil Angelides barely registered on the Glenn vote-o-meter, capturing 19 percent compared with 77 percent for Schwarzenegger.

Humboldt County

Area: 4,052 sq. mi.; Population: (2005 est.) 132,434, (2000) 126,518, (1990) 119,118, (1980) 108,525; Registration (Oct. 2006): D-41.4%, R-28.9%, DS-20.4%; 2006 voter turnout (rank): 53.5% (34); County supervisors: Jimmy Smith, Roger Rodoni, John Woolley, Bonnie Neely, Jill Geist; 825 Fifth Street, Eureka 95501, Phone: (707) 476-2384, Fax: (707) 445-7299; Assembly District 1; Senate District 2; Congressional District 1; Budget (2006-2007): $242.4 million; Median income: $31,226; Median home value: $133,500; Ethnicity: White-81.6%, Latino-6.5%, Asian-1.7%, Black-0.9%; Largest cities (2004): Eureka (26,250), Arcata (16,651), Fortuna (10,497).

On California's ruggedly beautiful North Coast, Humboldt County has undergone an economic and cultural transition during the past two decades. Historically, its economy was based on timber and commercial fishing, both of which fell on hard times during the 1980s and 1990s. As the influence of those industries faded, tourism became more important to the economy and urban refugees more influential on the culture. Marijuana became an important cash crop as remnants of the 1960s Hippie culture fled urban San Francisco and southern California for more remote climes. And environmentalism—always at loggerheads with the timber industry—exerted more and more influence over local politics.

Timber companies still employ many county residents; Pacific Lumber and Simpson Lumber are among the two biggest employers. But the political influence of immigrants has been evident since the early 1980s, and Democrats now win most elections, although not by overwhelming margins. Humboldt did vote against the recall of Governor Gray Davis in 2003, even as Republican Arnold Schwarzenegger narrowly carried the county in the replacement election. The Green Party has significant influence, evidenced by Green gubernatorial candidate Peter Camejo's strong showing in the replacement election. Democrat John Kerry won 58 percent of the Humboldt vote in 2004, while Democratic U.S. Senator Barbara Boxer outpolled Republican Bill Jones 59 percent to 35 percent in her successful 2004 re-election.

In November 2006, Schwarzenegger again captured the county with 49 percent of the vote, but Camejo's 7 percent was a respectable performance. Except for governor, Democrats captured the local vote in every other statewide race, and the county approved all four infrastructure bonds (for transportation, affordable housing, flood control, and schools). Befitting the area's strong environmental tendencies, Humboldt voters approved a tax on oil companies to fund development of alternative energy sources that lost statewide.

Imperial County

Area: 4,175 sq. mi.; Population: (2005 est.) 164,221, (2000) 142,361, (1990) 109,303, (1980) 92,110; Registration (Oct. 2006): D-55.3%, R-26.3%, DS-15%; 2006 voter turnout (rank): 33.3% (58); County supervisors: Victor Carrillo, Larry Grogan, Joe Maruca, Gary Wyatt, Wally Leimgruber; 940 Main St., El Centro 92243, Phone: (760) 482-4220, Fax: (760) 482-4215; Assembly District 80; Senate District 40; Congressional District 51; Budget (2006-2007): $285.3 million; Median income: $31,870; Median home value: $100,000; Ethnicity: White-20.2%, Latino-72.2%, Asian-2.0%, Black-4.0%; Largest cities (2004): El Centro (40,500), Calexico (32,600), Brawley (23,800).

Carved away from the eastern section of San Diego County in 1908, Imperial was the 58th and final county created in California. In November 2006, it was dead last in a less-savory category: Imperial's 33.3 percent voter turnout ranked it 58 out of California's 58 counties in civic engagement.

Imperial is largely agricultural, but one of its major crops is human. It also is home to a pair of maximum-security state prisons at Brawley and Calpatria. And, situated on the U.S.-Mexico border, Imperial sees a steady stream of illegal immigrants pour across its open, sandy, uninhabited desert.

Its hot climate allows Imperial farmers to grow two or three crops a year and keeps the fragile economy afloat. Unemployment is among the highest for any county in the state, up to 31 percent in 1992 and hovering above 21 percent as late as 2001 before dipping to 15 percent in 2003.

Political registration heavily favors Democrats, who have won 10 of 14 top-of-the-ticket statewide races here since 1990. But the recall of Democratic Governor Gray Davis captured 63 percent of the vote in Imperial County, and Republican Arnold Schwarzenegger was favored to replace Davis. Schwarzenegger won the county, narrowly, in his 2006 re-election effort against Democrat Phil Angelides.

As 2006 demonstrated once again, Democrats, despite their registration edge, have trouble getting voters to the polls and often lose legislative races as a result. In November 2006, incumbent Republican Bonnie Garcia won a third and final term, defeating former Assemblymember Steve Clute by only 2,200 votes out of nearly 75,000 cast. Imperial is home to nearly 30,000 registered Democrats, yet Clute managed fewer than 8,000 votes from the county. Garcia won the Democratic county by 1,500 votes, the third time she out-hustled Democrats on what should be their home turf. At the same time, Imperial County gave incumbent Democratic U.S. Sen. Dianne Feinstein 61 percent of its vote. In 2004, Democratic presidential hopeful John Kerry won the county with 54 percent of the vote over President George Bush.

Inyo County

Area: 10,227 sq. mi.; Population: (2005 est.) 18,599, (2000) 17,945, (1990) 18,281, (1980) 17,895; Registration (Oct. 2006): D-32.1%, R-45.1%, DS-17.2%; 2006 voter turnout (rank): 51% (44); County supervisors: Linda Arcularius, Jim Billyeu, Beverly Brown, Susan Cash, Richard Cervantes; P.O. Box N, Independence 93526, Phone: (760) 878-0373; Assembly District 34; Senate District 18; Congressional District 25; Budget (2006-2007): $79.9 million; Median family income: $42,100;

Median home value: $161,300; Ethnicity: White-74.4%, Latino-12.6%, Asian-0.9%,
Black-0.2%; Largest cities (2004): Bishop (3,630).

Inyo County had a rare distinction among California counties during the 1990s—
its population actually *declined* by 336 people. That wiped out most of the gain of
the 1980s, although a recent surge brought the county population back over 18,000.
Sprawling along the Nevada border, the huge, scenic county is home to Mt. Whitney
and second only to San Bernardino County in size. Some 85 percent of Inyo is owned
by the federal government, and the economy is based on tourism, small Indian gaming
operations, mining, and ranching. Unemployment was a modest 6.4 percent in 2003.

Solidly Republican, Inyo gave Michael Huffington a 39-point victory over Democrat Dianne Feinstein in the 1994 U.S. Senate race and saw Republican Bill Simon
trample Governor Gray Davis in 2002. Two-thirds of Inyo voters subsequently approved Davis's recall a year later. Inyo backed President George Bush and Republican
U.S. Senate candidate Bill Jones in 2004 and gave Gov. Arnold Schwarzenegger 65
percent of its vote in 2006.

Kern County

Area: 8,161 sq. mi.; Population: (2005 est.) 770,424, (2000) 661,645, (1990)
543,477, (1980) 403,089; Registration (Oct. 2006): D-35.7%, R-47.4%, DS-13.2%;
2006 voter turnout (rank): 51.9% (38); County supervisors: Jon McQuiston, Don Ma-
ben, Mike Maggard, Ray Watson, Michael Rubio; 1115 Truxtun Avenue, Bakersfield
93301, Phone: (661) 868-3601, email Board@kern.co.ca.us; Assembly Districts 30,
32, 34; Senate Districts 16, 18; Congressional Districts 20, 22; Budget (2006-2007):
$1.3 billion; Median income: $35,446; Median home value: $285,000; Ethnicity:
White-49.5%, Latino-38.4%, Asian-3.4%, Black-6.0%; Largest cities (2004): Bakers-
field (279,200), Delano (38,824), Ridgecrest (24,947).

In many ways, Kern County in 2007 is much the same as Kern County in 1980—
conservative, Republican, and fueled by agriculture and oil. But there are tectonic
shifts at work as well, mostly in the growth experienced in the southern end of the
county around Bakersfield, its chief city. The population of Kern County increased
more than 72 percent between 1980 and 2002 and now exceeds 700,000. Bakersfield
itself is fast approaching 300,000.

Much of the growth is the result of spread of the Los Angeles metropolitan area
north across the Tehachapis. Although Kern County is counted as part of the Central
Valley, UCLA is closer to Bakersfield than is the Central Valley's new campus in
Merced.

Kern is staunchly Republican; the GOP has won every top-of-the-ticket race in
the county since 1990. In the 2003 recall election 76 percent of Kern voters chose to
bounce Gov. Gray Davis. Pres. George Bush defeated Democrat John Kerry two to
one in the 2004 presidential race, and Republican U.S. Senate candidate Bill Jones
ran 20 points ahead of Democratic incumbent Barbara Boxer. Even venerable Dianne
Feinstein failed to breach 40 percent of the vote in her 2006 re-election bid against
conservative Republican Richard Mountjoy, a little-known former state senator from
Monrovia. Gov. Arnold Schwarzenegger took 72 percent of the vote in 2006.

But in 2006 this decidedly Republican county also provided the margin of victory for a Democratic legislator as Republicans failed for the third time in this decade to transfer top-of-the-ticket success to an Assembly candidate. Incumbent Democrat Nicole Parra won a third and final term in 2006, even though three of the four counties in her district voted for her Republican opponent, Dan Gilmore. Kern went for Parra, giving her 65 percent of its vote and a nearly 6,000-vote margin. Districtwide, she won by less than 1,600 votes.

Although Republicans dominate the political landscape, both parties have experienced internal strife in recent years. The leading Republican is former U.S. Rep. Bill Thomas of Bakersfield, who served as powerful chair of the Ways and Means Committee when Republicans controlled the House. Thomas retired from Congress in 2006 but still heads a local machine that includes his congressional replacement, former Assemblyman Kevin McCarthy. But Thomas, a moderate by modern Republican standards, is not without his more conservative detractors who often chafe under what they consider his autocratic rule.

Democrats, too, have experienced factional skirmishes between those beholden to former Kern County Supervisor Pete Parra (father of Nicole) of Bakersfield and state Senator Dean Florez of Shafter. That dust-up came to a head in March 2004 when Pete Parra was ousted from the board in favor of Michael Rubio, a Florez ally. Florez's mother is said to be preparing to run for Nicole Parra's Assembly seat in 2008, when the incumbent is termed out.

Kings County

Area: 1,391 sq. mi.; Population: (2005 est.) 146.487, (2000) 129,461, (1990) 101,469, (1980) 73,738; Registration (Oct. 2006): D-37.9%, R-46.8%, DS-11.8%; 2006 voter turnout (rank): 51.4% (41); County supervisors: Joe Neves, Jon Rachford, Tony Oliveria, Tony Barba, Alene Taylor; 1400 West Lacey Blvd., Hanford 93230, Phone: (559) 582-3211, Fax: (559) 585-8047; Assembly District 30; Senate District 16; Congressional District 20; Budget (2006-2007): $183 million; Median income: $35,749; Median home value: $97,600; Ethnicity: White-41.6%, Latino-43.6%, Asian-3.1%, Black-8.3%; Largest cities (2004): Hanford (46,300), Corcoran (22,150), Lemoore (19,712).

Although it sits in the middle of San Joaquin Valley farmland and suffers a habitual unemployment rate around 15%, Kings County has experienced unusual growth over the past two decades as its population increased more than 75 percent. Part of the reason is the county's diverse economic base. Along with agriculture, manufacturing, the military, prisons, and tourism generate jobs. The county's two prisons are in Avenal and Corcoran, the latter one of the state's more troubled institutions thanks to allegations of guard brutality.

Kings County is decidedly Republican when it comes to statewide office; top-of-the-ticket Democrats have won only two of 16 elections since 1990, and the county voted overwhelmingly to recall Governor Gray Davis in 2003 and replace him with Republican Arnold Schwarzenegger. That said, through 2004, the county was represented by Democrats in the state legislature and in Congress—thanks in part to its being attached to Democratic precincts in Fresno and Kern counties.

In 2006, the county continued to back Republicans, including U.S. Senate candidate Richard Mountjoy, who won the county by 400 votes over incumbent Democrat Dianne Feinstein. Schwarzenegger and his putative running mate for lieutenant governor, conservative state Sen. Tom McClintock, each took over 60 percent of the local vote. Voting patterns were eclectic when it came to initiatives in 2006. The county approved bonds for transportation, affordable housing, and flood control but narrowly defeated a bond proposal for schools.

Lake County

Area: 1,258 sq. mi.; Population: (2005 est.) 64,180, (2000) 58,309, (1990) 50,631, (1980) 36,366; Registration (Oct. 2006): D-43.3%, R-32.0%, DS-19.1%; 2006 voter turnout (rank): 50.5% (47); County supervisors: Ed Robey, Jr., Jeff Smith, Denise Rushing, Anthony Farrington, Rob Brown; 255 North Forbes St., Lakeport 95453, Phone: (707) 263-2368; Assembly District 1; Senate District 2; Congressional District 1; Budget (2006-2007): $148.6 million; Median income: $29,627; Median home value: $122,600; Ethnicity: White-74.8%, Latino-11.4%, Asian-0.1%, Black-2.1%; Largest cities (2004): Clearlake (13,950), Lakeport (4,820).

An hour from San Francisco, Lake County is a tourism and retirement mecca dominated, as its name implies, by Clear Lake. Mostly middle-class retirees fuel the local economy, where pension and Social Security checks are major sources of income. The 2000 Census revealed that 40 percent of the county's population was older than 50. Ranching and geothermal development also stimulate the local economy.

The county trends Democratic, but can't be taken for granted. It narrowly voted to recall Governor Gray Davis in 2003 and backed the candidacy of his eventual successor, Republican Arnold Schwarzenegger. The county split its loyalties in 2006, giving U.S. Sen. Dianne Feinstein a convincing win over Republican Richard Mountjoy, but giving Schwarzenegger an equally convincing win over Democrat Phil Angelides for governor. Republican Steve Poizner carried the county in his successful campaign for insurance commissioner against Lt. Gov. Cruz Bustamante.

Other contests reflect flexible county attitudes. Although Democrats won races for lieutenant governor and secretary of state, margins of victory for John Garamendi and Debra Bowen, respectively, were three percent or less. Lake County voters turned their backs on statewide bonds for schools and transportation, approving other bond proposals for affordable housing and flood control.

Lassen County

Area: 4,720 sq. mi.; Population: (2005 est.) 35,696, (2000) 33,828, (1990) 27,598, (1980) 21,661; Registration (Oct. 2006): D-28.9%, R-46.6%, DS-18.3%; 2006 voter turnout (rank): 61.3% (17); County supervisors: Bob Pyle, Jim Chapman, Lloyd Keefer, Brian Dahle, Jack Hanson; 221 South Roop Street, Suite 4, Susanville 96130, Phone: (530) 251-8333, Fax (530) 257-4898, email coadmin@co.lassen.ca.us; Assembly District 3; Senate District 1; Congressional District 4; Budget (2006-2007): $87.3 million; Median income: $36,310; Median home value: $106,700; Ethnicity: White-70.6%, Latino-13.8%, Asian-0.7%, Black-8.8%; Largest cities (2004): Susanville (18,100).

Government, in all its varied forms, is the largest employer in Lassen County, which lies along the Nevada border in extreme northern California. Among those government employers, the most profound and influential is the Department of Corrections with two state prisons in Susanville.

After government, the largest employers include Sierra Pacific Industries (logging) and Wal-Mart (merchant to everyone). Ranching and tourism—a portion of Lassen Volcanic National Park is here, although not the volcano itself—supply some jobs. Although not considered prosperous, Lassen has a modest unemployment rate, pegged at 6.3 percent in 2003 and down from near 10 percent in 1990—before the Susanville prison expanded. The expansion itself was opposed by locals, evidence of the county's conservative nature.

This is Republican territory; President George W. Bush took two-thirds of the vote here in 2000 and 71 percent in 2004. Three-fourths of county voters backed the 2003 recall of Democratic Governor Gray Davis. Sixty percent favored Republican Arnold Schwarzenegger to replace Davis. In 2004, Republican Bill Jones took 63 percent of the county vote in his unsuccessful bid for the U.S. Senate against Democratic incumbent Barbara Boxer.

Results from November 2006 showed not the slightest change in Lassen politics. Schwarzenegger swept two-thirds of the vote in his re-election, while Republican Richard Mountjoy scored a 20-point win over incumbent Democrat Dianne Feinstein in the race for U.S. Senate. Conservative state Sen. Tom McClintock doubled Democrat John Garamendi's vote count in the campaign for lieutenant governor, and Lassen voted down all four infrastructure bonds despite heavy backing from Schwarzenegger.

Los Angeles County

Area: 4,061 sq. mi.; Population: (2005 est.) 10,223,055, (2000) 9,519,338, (1990) 8,863,164, (1980) 7,477,517; Registration (Oct. 2006): D-49.7%, R-27%, DS-19.0%; 2006 voter turnout (rank): 51.4% (41); County supervisors: Gloria Molina, Yvonne Burke, Zev Yaroslavsky, Don Knabe, Michael Antonovich; 500 West Temple Street, Los Angeles 90012, Phone: (213) 974-1411, Fax: (213) 620-0636; Assembly Districts 35-61; Senate Districts 17, 19-30, 32; Congressional Districts 22, 25-39, 42, 46; Budget (2006-2007): $20.04 billion; Median income: $42,189; Median home value: $520,000; Ethnicity: White-31.1%, Latino-44.6%, Asian-11.9%, Black-9.8%; Largest cities (2004): Los Angeles (3,912,200), Long Beach (487,100), Glendale (205,300), Santa Clarita (164,900), Pomona (158,400).

The story of Los Angeles County begins with numbers. More than one in four Californians live in the county—2,344 people per square mile, more than 10 times the state average. Of these, 18 percent live below the poverty line (compared with 14 percent statewide). Thirty-six percent of county residents were born in another country (compared with 26 percent statewide). In 2002, a fourth of the $206.4 billion spent by the federal government in California was spent in Los Angeles County. The county budget passed $20 billion for 2006-2007. More than 80 languages are spoken in its schools, and 89 incorporated cities lie within its boundaries.

The sheer size of Los Angeles County prompts questions about its governability, and those questions have led to efforts to it break up. In 2002, the city of Los Angeles was the subject of a secessionist movement by the San Fernando Valley, whose residents complained they were given short shrift by City Hall when it came to police and fire protection, social services, traffic control, parks, and libraries. At the same time, the Valley remains a major economic engine for Los Angeles County, adding 7,600 jobs in 2003—compared with 36,700 jobs lost countywide. (That trend abated somewhat in 2004, with job growth up a modest 1.7 percent over 2003).

The secession revolt culminated in Measure F on the November 2002 ballot. Then-Mayor James Hahn took the lead in fighting the proposal while promising Valleyites his administration would be more attentive to their needs. To a lesser degree, the Hollywood area also sought to break away from the city. Narrowly approved in the Valley, Measure F failed the other threshold for passage—a majority vote in Los Angeles citywide. As a result, the secessionist movement has retreated, but the issue is far from dead.

In fact, the city of Los Angeles has taken the cue and is mulling over seceding from the county and forming its own city-county, a la San Francisco. The *Los Angeles Times* reported that the secessionist effort is spearheaded for the moment by City Councilwoman Jan Perry, with preliminary studies due by mid 2007.

To date, no breakup has been successful, although some—like the San Fernando Valley effort—have proven expensive and cantankerous. A year before Measure F, education groups had petitioned the State Board of Education for permission to allow L.A. voters to decide whether to decentralize the massive school district, home to 700,000 students and 37,000 teachers and administrators. The state board based its denial on the notion that LAUSD would lose a third of its potential bonding power while remaining accountable for nearly 90 percent of the students. Essentially, the board punted, not wishing to immerse itself in local squabbles.

The board's lack of chutzpah is understandable. Los Angeles County wields cultural, economic, and political influence on a global scope. There are huge enclaves of Latinos, Blacks, Koreans, Armenians, Chinese, Vietnamese, Japanese, Iranians, Russians, Cambodians, and other ethnic groups, and each plays a role in shaping the society that has become Los Angeles. They participate in an economy that is as diverse as the state and includes manufacturing, Pacific Rim trade, finance, high-tech, entertainment, tourism, and sweatshops.

The cities and towns of Los Angeles County hum with 24-hour-a-day freeway traffic that remains the county's most pervasive feature and the core of the region's intractable smog problem. For more than two decades, traffic has worsened as the megalopolis known as Los Angeles has spilled into neighboring counties such as Orange, Riverside, San Bernardino, and Ventura—all connected by concrete sinews of freeways. The motivator is the search for affordable housing. Attempts to reintroduce rail traffic via Metrolink have barely put a dent in Angelenos' love affair with the automobile.

Economically, Los Angeles has recovered from the dark days of the early 1990s when the region—including parts of the Inland Empire—lost nearly half a million jobs. In fact, while other parts of the state, notably the San Francisco Bay Area and its Silicon Valley neighbor, suffered through recession in the early 2000s, Los Angeles prospered. The region is expected to add nearly 170,000 jobs a year over the next decade, according to the Center for the Continuing Study of the California Economy. Its population is expected to increase by 13 percent by 2012.

County politics became more Democratic in flavor in the late 1990s, with top-of-the-ticket Democrats regularly pulling in 60 percent of the vote—a trend broken when Governor Gray Davis was held to 56 percent in his 2002 re-election. The 2003 recall against Davis failed in Los Angeles County, but only by 2%, while Republican Arnold Schwarzenegger—a hometown celebrity—carried the county in the election to succeed Davis. Republican voters have fled Los Angeles County for outlying areas, making neighboring counties—especially in the Inland Empire—safe GOP territory.

Because of its sheer size and the number of votes it commands, Los Angeles is the state's Democratic behemoth. Democrats must win here, sometimes by significant numbers, to win statewide. As a result, voter registration figures released prior to the November 2006 election could be troubling. Despite overwhelming negative publicity for Republicans nationwide, and a momentous surge on the part of Democrats, the percent of voters registered Democratic actually *fell*—dropping below 50 percent for the first time in recent memory.

Despite that drop, Democrats fared well in the 2006 general election. U.S. Sen. Dianne Feinstein won over two-thirds of the vote in her re-election, while the election's lowest-scoring Democrat, Lt. Gov. Cruz Bustamante, captured the county in his unsuccessful effort to become insurance commissioner. The county even turned its back on homeboy Arnold Schwarzenegger, giving its nod to Democrat Phil Angelides, though Angelides won less than 50 percent of the county vote.

Despite its Democratic leanings, county politics runs to extremes. Some of the state's most conservative and most liberal officeholders hail from its legislative and congressional districts. The central and western portions—downtown Los Angeles, South-Central, East Los Angeles, Beverly Hills, Santa Monica, and Westwood—remain strongly Democratic. But Long Beach and Anglo suburbs on the fringes of the county lean Republican. The San Fernando Valley is a toss-up.

Over the past decade, the influx of Latino immigrants has made Hispanics the largest ethnic group in the county, with 44 percent of the population; whites now comprise only 31 percent. Despite traditional low voter turnout, Latinos (and to some degree Asians) have elected key officeholders, especially to the legislature and Congress. Sheriff Lee Baca and District Attorney Rocky Delgadillo are Latino, as is Supervisor Gloria Molina.

But the county's most visible Latino politician is not a county official at all but the mayor of its largest city. Antonio Villaraigosa, a former Assembly speaker, defeated Kenneth Hahn for mayor in 2005 and instantly vaulted into the nation's pantheon of top-tier political figures. His smiling photo has graced the covers of national news magazines, and he easily tops the handful of potential Democratic candidates for governor in 2010. Villaraigosa put his stamp on county politics in 2006 when he steered a bill through the state legislature that grants the mayor more authority over Los Angeles schools. Rebuffed in his effort to hand-pick a new superintendent for LAUSD in 2006, Villaraigosa served notice that education will be a centerpiece of his political agenda.

Villaraigosa's stature notwithstanding, the most powerful political entity in the county—perhaps the most powerful local board in the nation—is the five-member

Los Angeles Board of Supervisors. Each supervisor represents nearly 2.5 million constituents, employs a huge personal staff, and helps oversee a budget in excess of $20 billion. Given that there is no elected head of county government, the five supervisors—three men and two women—wield vast authority over land use, transportation, and health care.

The county's political split is reflected in the board—three are Democrats and two Republican. The Democrats are Zev Yaroslavsky from the largely Jewish west side; Yvonne Brathwaite Burke, an African American and former congresswoman who represents South-Central Los Angeles; and Gloria Molina, a former legislator and city councilwoman. The Republicans are Don Knabe, whose coastal district includes the ports of Los Angeles and Long Beach and Los Angeles International Airport; and Mike Antonovich, a former state legislator who represents the San Fernando Valley and north-county suburbs.

As befits its size, Los Angeles exerts great political influence statewide. The four most-recent speakers of the Assembly each hailed from Los Angeles: Democrats Villaraigosa, Robert Hertzberg, Herb Wesson and Fabian Nunez. Although state Senate leadership has rested with northern California politicians of late, former City Council President Alex Padilla was elected to the state Senate in November 2006 and has made no secret of his desire to become Senate president pro tem—sooner rather than later. Five of the last six governors came from the region: Ronald Reagan, Jerry Brown, George Deukmejian (Long Beach), Gray Davis, and Arnold Schwarzenegger. The new secretary of state, Debra Bowen, hails from Marina del Rey, while the new state controller is John Chiang of Los Angeles.

The November 2006 approval of $43 billion in infrastructure bonds is expected to provide a financial boon to the county, especially money raised for highways and schools—both critical needs for the sprawling county. One estimate indicates that the county's transportation needs alone exceed $95 billion, far in excess of the $30 billion available to address those needs.

But the county also received some negative publicity in 2006 on another money matter—the funds owed to parents who depend on child support. The county supposedly reformed its tracking and collection system in 2001 to ensure that kids receive timely support from a parent who owes the money. But an investigation by the *Los Angeles Times* revealed that the county has one of the worst collection rates in the country, with only 45 percent of the money owed actually reaching the custodial parent.

Madera County

Area: 2,153 sq. mi.; Population: (2005 est.) 142,837, (2000) 123,109, (1990) 88,090, (1980) 63,116; Registration (Oct. 2006): D-33.7%, R-49.2%, DS-13.6%; 2006 voter turnout (rank): 52.1% (37); County supervisors: Frank Bigelow, Vern Moss, Ronn Dominici, Max Rodriguez, Tom Wheeler; 209 West Yosemite Avenue, Madera 93637, Phone: (559) 675-7700, Fax: (559) 673-3302, email supervisors@madera-county.com; Assembly Districts 25, 29; Senate Districts 12, 14; Congressional Districts 18, 19; Budget (2006-2007): $170.3 million; Median income: $36,286; Median home value: $290,000; Ethnicity: White-46.6%, Latino-44.3%, Asian-1.3%, Black-4.1%; Largest cities (2004): Madera (48,350), Chowchilla (11,127).

Madera County is Central Valley farm and foothill country, home to ranches, a growing number of retirees, and a portion of Yosemite National Park. Grapes and cattle are the agricultural staples, while the county attracts some tourism from the Yosemite gateway and Millerton and Bass lakes. Although not considered a candidate for urban sprawl, the county's population more than doubled between 1980 and 2005.

Whites and Latinos are nearly equal parts of that population, although whites still dominate the political landscape. Republicans are consistent winners here. GOP senatorial candidate Richard Mountjoy took 53 percent of the Madera vote in 2006 against incumbent Democrat Dianne Feinstein, while Gov. Arnold Schwarzenegger buried Democrat Phil Angelides under a 72 percent landslide in the 2006 gubernatorial campaign. Schwarzenegger came to power in the 2003 recall of Governor Gray Davis, which won here with 72 percent in favor.

Marin County

Area: 828 sq. mi.; Population: (2005 est.) 252.195, (2000) 247,289, (1990) 230,096, (1980) 222,592; Registration (Oct. 2006): D-51.7%, R-22.4%, DS-20.6%; 2006 voter turnout (rank): 51.8% (39); County supervisors: Susan Adams, Harold Brown, Jr., Charles McGlashan, Steve Kinsey, Cynthia Murray; 3501 Civic Center Drive, Room 329, San Rafael 94903, Phone: (445) 499-7331, Fax: (445) 499-3645; Assembly District 6; Senate District 3; Congressional District 6; Budget (2006-2007): $387 million; Median income: $71,306; Median home value: $795,000; Ethnicity: White-78.6%, Latino-11.1%, Asian-4.5%, Black-2.9%; Largest cities (2004): San Rafael (56,900), Novato (49,400).

Marin County is California's in-house joke—the subject of songs, comedy routines, movies, and satirical novels. In some ways, California's reputation as a left coast kooksville, deserved or not, is predicated on Marin's worldwide reputation for hot tubs, oddballs, and individualism.

But Marin is a study in contrasts. The northern edge of the Golden Gate Bridge touches down in Marin at Sausalito, where a small slice of the posh population lives on houseboats. It has a spectacular coastline, dotted with communities that thrive on tourists. It also has the state's most famous prison, San Quentin, home to California's death row.

In Marin County, one of the wealthiest counties in the nation, unemployment is miniscule. Nonetheless, Marin is home to the Buck Trust, a multi-million dollar fund established in the 1950s and dedicated exclusively to aiding the county's poor. Efforts to expand the trust's scope to other, perhaps more deserving parts of the Bay Area have failed, mostly due to dogged opposition by the Marin County Board of Supervisors.

This is northern California wealth, liberal in outlook and potent in its ability to influence policy, locally and statewide. The county, for instance, has largely succeeded in curtailing growth. The population increased only 13 percent in the quarter century between 1980 and 2005—far below the average statewide and nowhere near what could be expected in so attractive a slice of the Bay Area. The environmental movement is especially strong here.

But the clamp on growth inside Marin has had an impact. Housing prices have gone through the roof as the median price of a home soared close to $800,000, driving out lower- and middle-class residents (and making it more challenging for the Buck Trust to meet its mission of serving the poor inside Marin). Stopping growth in Marin could not stop it elsewhere, however, as regions to the north and east expanded and as urban migrants commuted through Marin to reach more affordable housing in neighboring communities.

Marin is decidedly Democratic in its politics. U.S. Senator Barbara Boxer began her elective career as a Marin County supervisor, and the county gave her 71 percent of its vote in her 2004 re-election. A current supervisor is Harold Brown, Jr., cousin of state Attorney General (and former governor) Jerry Brown and former state Treasurer Kathleen Brown. Two-thirds of Marin voters opposed the 2003 recall of Governor Gray Davis while giving Democratic Lieutenant Governor Cruz Bustamante one of his few county victories as Davis's replacement. Less than a third of Marin voters backed the eventual winner—Republican Arnold Schwarzenegger. In the 2004 presidential election, Democrat John Kerry won 73 percent of the Marin vote.

In 2006, Marin softened its attitude toward Republicans. Schwarzenegger lost Marin in his re-election bid, but did so by only 1,000 votes out of more than 70,000 cast. Republican Steve Poizner actually captured Marin in his campaign for insurance commissioner, outpolling Democrat Cruz Bustamante 47 percent to 40 percent. Democrats won all other statewide contests in the county, including Democratic U.S. Sen. Dianne Feinstein, who got three-quarters of the county vote in her re-election effort. Marin was one of a handful of counties that approved taxes on cigarettes and oil (Props. 86 and 87) in November 2006.

Mariposa County

Area: 1,463 sq. mi.; Population: (2005 est.) 18,281, (2000) 17,130, (1990) 14,302, (1980) 11,108; Registration (Oct. 2006): D-32.2%, R-46.8%, DS-14.6%; 2006 voter turnout (rank): 69% (7); County supervisors: Brad Aborn, Lyle Turpin, Janet Bibby, Diane Fritz, Bob Pickard; P.O. Box 784, Mariposa 95338, Phone: (209) 966-3222, Fax: (209) 966-5147; Assembly District 25; Senate District 14; Congressional District 19; Budget (2006-2007): $91.8 million; Median income: $34,626; Median home value: $141,900; Ethnicity: White-84.9%, Latino-7.8%, Asian-0.7%, Black-0.7%; Largest cities (2000): Bootjack (1,588), Mariposa (1,373).

Mariposa County's population grew by 65 percent between 1980 and 2005. At that, it ended the 22-year period with fewer residents than would attend an NBA game in Sacramento. That's not to say that a lot of people don't set foot in Mariposa County during the course of a year—hundreds of thousands do as visitors to Yosemite National Park and the gold-rush towns that dot its rolling foothills.

Politically, Mariposa mirrors other rural Central Valley and northern California counties—it is conservative and solidly Republican. Even Republican U.S. Senate candidate Richard Mountjoy won in Mariposa County against Democratic incumbent Dianne Feinstein in 2006, capturing 51 percent of the county vote, compared with only 35 percent statewide. In the same election, Gov. Arnold Schwarzenegger won easily here over Democrat Phil Angelides. In 2004, both top-of-the-ticket Republicans— President George Bush and U.S. Senate hopeful Bill Jones—won the county handily.

Mendocino County

Area: 3,878 sq. mi.; Population: (2005 est.) 90.487, (2000) 86,265, (1990) 80,345, (1980) 66,738; Registration (Oct. 2006): D-46.3%, R-24.9%, DS-19.5%; 2006 voter turnout (rank): 65.9% (11); County supervisors: Michael Delbar, Jim Wattenburger, John Pindus, Kendall Smith, J. David Colfax; 501 Low Gap Road, Room 1090, Ukiah 95482, Phone: (707) 463-4221, Fax: (707) 463-4245, email bos@co.mendocino.ca.us; Assembly District 1; Senate District 2; Congressional District 1; Budget (2006-2007): $206.5 million; Median income: $35.996; Median home value: $170,200; Ethnicity: White-74.9%, Latino-16.5%, Asian-1.2%, Black-0.6%; Largest cities (2004): Ukiah (15,900), Fort Bragg (7,026), Willits (5,073).

Mendocino County ignited something of a political firestorm in 2004 when it became the first county in California—and one of the first jurisdictions anywhere—to ban the planting of genetically altered seeds. The grass-roots campaign succeeded in the face of intense lobbying and heavy financial investment by the industries that produce and support genetically altered crops. That battle now has moved to the Legislature where opponents of the ban hope to circumvent local ordinances.

It is not surprising that Mendocino County residents, especially the urban refugees who migrated here during the 1960s and 1970s, would go to war over the environment, given that the county's greatest asset is its physical beauty, highlighted by its miles of coastline. Those migrants helped transform the economy and the culture from its historic anchor in logging and commercial fishing to tourism.

But such are the progressive politics of this ruggedly beautiful North Coast tourist mecca where the environmental movement has been shaped by decades of battle with the area's fading but still potent timber industry. In further testimony to environmentalist strength, Green Party gubernatorial candidate Peter Camejo polled 7 percent of the vote—one of his best showings statewide—in the 2003 recall election against Gray Davis. Mendocino voters rejected the recall and the eventual winner—Republican Arnold Schwarzenegger—giving Democratic Lieutenant Governor Cruz Bustamante one of his few county victories.

Schwarzenegger fared better in 2006, winning the county with 46 percent of the vote over Democrat Phil Angelides. Bustamante, on the other hand, did a little worse. He took the county in his failed effort to become state insurance commissioner, but by less than 1,000 votes. True to its environmental roots, the county voted to tax oil companies (Prop. 87) to support alternative energy.

Merced County

Area: 1,972 sq. mi.; Population: (2005 est.) 244,320, (2000) 210,554, (1990) 178,403, (1980) 134,558; Registration (Oct. 2006): D-45.0%, R-41.0%, DS-11.2%; 2006 voter turnout (rank): 45.8% (53); County supervisors: John Pedrozo, Kathleen Crookham, Mike Nelson, Deidre Kelsey, Jerry O'Bannion; 2222 M Street, Merced 95340, Phone: (209) 385-7366, Fax: (209) 726-7977; Assembly District 17; Senate District 12; Congressional District 18; Budget (2006-2007): $373 million; Median income: $35,532; Median home value: $350,000; Ethnicity: White-40.6%, Latino-45.3%, Asian-6.8%, Black-3.8%; Largest cities (2004): Merced (69,800), Los Banos (25,869), Atwater (23,113).

In the heart of the Central Valley, Merced County has been buffeted by the severe growth pressures in this region as the San Francisco Bay Area spreads south and east into what had been farmland. The county population increased 82 percent between 1980 and 2005, while the city of Merced alone grew 10 percent between 2000 and 2004. The widening of Highway 152 facilitated commutes between the Santa Clara Valley and once-rural Los Banos, which now considers itself part of the Bay Area.

The economy is in transition as well. Although a list of the county's largest employers still includes processed meat giant Foster Farms, dairies, and canning companies, the influx of Silicon Valley refugees is promoting growth for other kinds of service industries, including health-related employers such as hospitals and clinics. A new University of California campus at Merced is expected to add a new dimension to the local economy and fuel additional growth.

The politics of Merced County reflect its transition, not that many voters are paying attention. In 2006, for instance, less than 46 percent of registered voters bothered to turn out for the November gubernatorial election—the sixth worst turnout among California's 58 counties.

Those who do vote tend to be all over the map. The 2001 redistricting lumped Merced into what became two of the hottest legislative contests of 2002—Senate District 12 and Assembly District 17. Republicans and Democrats split the results, with Democrats capturing the Assembly district and Republican Jeff Denham scoring an upset victory over Democrat Rusty Areias in the Senate contest. Democrat Dennis Cardoza represents the county in Congress.

In 16 top-of-the-ticket elections between 1990 and 2006, the county voted eight times for the Democrat and eight times for the Republican. Lately, voters have been trending to the GOP. George W. Bush carried the county in 2000 and 2004, as did GOP gubernatorial candidate Bill Simon in 2002. The county voted for the recall of Governor Gray Davis in 2003, and for Republican Arnold Schwarzenegger as Davis's replacement. Democratic U.S. Senator Barbara Boxer won the county in her 2004 re-election bid against Republican Bill Jones, although her margin of victory was a scant 3 percent compared with President Bush's 14-point margin over Democrat John Kerry.

In 2006, Schwarzenegger hauled in 63 percent of the county's vote against Democrat Phil Angelides, while Democratic U.S. Sen. Dianne Feinstein captured 54 percent in her re-election effort against conservative Republican Richard Mountjoy. Republicans did well in down-ticket statewide races, however, and voters made Merced one of the few counties to approve Prop. 85, the failed initiative that would have required parental consent before a minor could obtain an abortion.

Modoc County

Area: 4,203 sq. mi.; Population: (2005 est.) 9,813, (2000) 9,449, (1990) 9,678, (1980) 8,610; Registration (Oct. 2006): D-30.2%, R-49.3%, DS-15.9%; 2006 voter turnout (rank): 68.2% (8); County supervisors: Dan Macsay, Mike Dunn, Patricia Cantrall, Ray Anklin, David Bradshaw; P.O. Box 130, Alturas 96101, Phone: (530) 233-6201, Fax: (530) 233-2434; Assembly District 2; Senate District 1; Congressional District 4; Budget (2006-2007): $33 million; Median income: $27,522; Median *home value: $69,100; Ethnicity: White-81.1%, Latino-11.5%, Asian-0.6%, Black-0.7%; Largest city (2004): Alturas (2,840).*

Modoc County sits at the very northeast tip of California, bordered by Nevada and Oregon. It is rugged, remote, and extreme in its weather. The economy, such as it is, centers on ranching and timber, although the single largest employer is government—including CalTrans and the U.S. Bureau of Land Management.

The population is overwhelmingly white and Republican. Nearly 75 percent of county voters backed the recall of Governor Gray Davis in 2003, while Democratic Lieutenant Governor Cruz Bustamante polled less than 15 percent in his quest to succeed Davis. Republican Arnold Schwarzenegger won the county with 60.5 percent of the vote, with conservative GOP state Senator Tom McClintock a distant second with 20%—still well ahead of Bustamante. In 2004, it gave President George Bush 73 percent of its vote and Republican U.S. Senate candidate Bill Jones two-thirds—one of his largest county margins of victory. Two years later, Schwarzenegger took 75 percent of the vote in his re-election, while Republican Richard Mountjoy rolled up 57 percent in his futile effort to deny incumbent Democrat Dianne Feinstein a fourth term in the U.S. Senate.

Ironically, the county's love of all things Republican cost it the title of California's bellwether county. Between 1912 and 1992, Modoc had voted for every presidential winner. That streak ended when it cast its lot with Republican losers George H. W. Bush in 1992 and Bob Dole in 1996.

Mono County

Area: 3.044 sq. mi.; Population: (2005 est.) 13,512, (2000) 12,853, (1990) 9,956, (1980) 8,577; Registration (Oct. 2006): D-31.1%, R-38.6%, DS-24.3%; 2006 voter turnout (rank): 59.8% (22); County supervisors: Tom Farnetti, Duane Hazard, Vicki Magee-Bauer, John Cecil, Byng Hunt; P.O. Box 237, Bridgeport 93517, Phone: (760) 932-5533, Fax: (760) 932-5531; Assembly District 25; Senate District 1; Congressional District 25; Budget (2006-2007): $45.5 million; Median income: $44,992; Median home value: $236,300; Ethnicity: White-72.5%, Latino-11.7%, Asian-1.1%, Black-0.5%; Largest city (2004): Mammoth Lakes (7,475).

Mono County is a long way from Los Angeles, but its fate has been tied to that southern California megapolis for more than 70 years. That's when L.A. began pulling water out of rivers and streams on the eastern slope of the Sierras, the same watersheds that feed Mono County's most dominant features—Mono Lake and the geologic formations that make it a unique environmental landmark.

The county battled Los Angeles in court for years, seeking to slow the water diversions and preserve the shrinking lake. The court battles ended in 1994 when the county and various environmental groups struck a deal with Los Angeles to keep the lake level deep enough to preserve it.

Tourism from the lake, and from the Mammoth Lakes ski resort, fuel Mono County's economy, although the area took something of a hit in the 1980s when it was discovered that the resort was sitting atop an active volcano. That hasn't stopped people from coming, either as tourists or residents. The county's population grew 36 percent between 1990 and 2005.

Despite a strong environmental movement, which has fought for Mono Lake and tends to support Democrats, the county is Republican territory. Local voters supported the 2003 recall of Governor Gray Davis nearly two to one and heavily backed Republican Arnold Schwarzenegger to succeed Davis. Prior to 2004, the last top-of-the-ticket Democrat to carry the county was Davis in the 1998 gubernatorial contest, but Davis's margin of victory was a mere one-tenth of 1 percent. He then lost the county by 16 percent when he sought re-election in 2002 against Republican Bill Simon.

In 2004 and 2006, Mono reversed course, giving Democratic U.S. Sen. Barbara Boxer a 6 percent margin in her 2004 re-election effort against Republican Bill Jones. In that year's presidential contest, Democrat John Kerry beat incumbent Republican George Bush by a mere seven votes out of more than 5,200. In that context, U.S. Sen. Dianne Feinstein rolled up a virtual landslide in her 2006 re-election effort against Republican Richard Mountjoy, winning Mono by 159 votes. On the same ballot, Republican Schwarzengger provided bipartisan balance by doubling the vote total of his Democratic rival, Phil Angelides.

The county's conservative nature surfaced in 2006 on votes for a package of infrastructure bonds for transportation, education, flood control, and affordable housing. Although all four measures passed statewide, each was voted down in Mono County.

Monterey County

Area: 3,322 sq. mi.; Population: (2005 est.) 425.055, (2000) 401,762, (1990) 355,660, (1980) 290,444; Registration (Oct. 2006): D-48.2%, R-30.8%, DS-17.1%; 2006 voter turnout (rank): 42.7% (56); County supervisors: Fernando Armenta, Louis Calcagno, Simon Salinas, Jerry Smith, Dave Potter; 240 Church St., Salinas 93901, Phone: (831) 755-5066; Assembly Districts 27, 28; Senate Districts 12, 15; Congressional District 17; Budget (2006-2007): $879.8 million; Median income: $48,305; Median home value: $595,000; Ethnicity: White-40.3%, Latino-46.8%, Asian-6.0%, Black-3.7%; Largest cities (2004): Salinas (152,200), Seaside (33,300), Monterey (30,250).

Even in a state blessed with an abundance of natural beauty, Monterey County is special. It has a rugged coastline, stately forests, quaint towns, and perfect weather. But local politics can be stormy when it comes to protecting those assets. Not surprisingly, those who have already captured a piece of Monterey for themselves jealously guard it against outsiders. Most development projects spark heated controversy.

But it has not been entirely possible to close off growth and development. The 1993 closure of Fort Ord took a toll on the county's economy, but the area surrounding the mothballed installation has recovered with commercial development—thanks in part to the creation and expansion of a California State University campus in the old military compound. The city of Monterey's world-class aquarium and refurbished Cannery Row form a solid base of tourism for the entire Monterey Peninsula.

Economic and cultural differences divide the county, with wealthy seaside enclaves such as Carmel contrasting starkly with rural inland towns that depend on the price of locally grown produce. Development conflicts occur at the perimeters of the

Peninsula as agriculture gives way to the pressures of suburban development from San Jose and Silicon Valley to the north along Highways 101 and 17.

Culturally, the county's two main population centers—Monterey and Salinas—could be on different planets. Further south along 101, a large state prison bolsters the economy of Soledad. Despite suburban growth, Salinas and other inland communities remain blue collar and rely on agriculture. And while the politics of Monterey and Carmel lingers in the hands of Anglos, the politics of Salinas and much of the rest of Monterey County is being shaped by the emerging political power of Latinos, now the largest ethnic group in the county.

The county has become more Democratic, although voters are not averse to sending a moderate Republican to the legislature. Bruce McPherson, a former newspaper publisher from Santa Cruz who represented the area in the state Senate since 1996, was termed out in 2004. He subsequently was appointed secretary of state in 2005, following the resignation of incumbent Democrat Kevin Shelley. McPherson's old Senate district was shattered, with the number—15—moving south toward Santa Barbara County.

In 2006, homeboy McPherson ran for secretary of state on his own and carried his home county, although he lost statewide to Democrat Debra Bowen. Two other Republicans captured the Monterey vote while winning statewide—Gov. Arnold Schwarzenegger and Steve Poizner, the GOP candidate for insurance commissioner.

Schwarzenegger is the first top-of-the-ticket Republican to carry the county since Pete Wilson in 1994. Even the 2003 recall election against Democratic Gov. Gray Davis failed in Monterey County. Democrats John Kerry and Barbara Boxer both carried the county with 60 percent of the vote for president and U.S. Senate, respectively, in 2004. In 2006, incumbent Democrat Dianne Feinstein took 65 percent of the county's vote while winning a fourth term in the U.S. Senate.

Schwarzenegger notwithstanding, Monterey County mostly stayed home in November 2006, with less than 43 percent of its registered voters bothering to cast a ballot—nearly 10 percent below statewide turnout. That ranked Monterey third from the bottom among the state's 58 counties.

The 2001 redistricting was not kind to Monterey County, especially when it came to Senate districts. Essentially, Monterey was split between districts 12 and 15, both of which are represented by Republicans. District 15 was created as a GOP seat and combines portions of Monterey with larger population centers in Santa Clara and San Luis Obispo counties. In 2004, Monterey went along with the rest of SD 15 in supporting Republican Assemblyman Abel Maldonado, who defeated a Democratic San Luis Obispo supervisor. Senate District 12 is nominally Democratic, even though a conservative Republican (Jeff Denham) won it in 2002 and was re-elected in 2006. It stretches into the Central Valley, where the biggest chunk of votes is cast in Stanislaus and Merced counties.

Napa County

Area: 754 sq. mi.; Population: (2005 est.) 133,526, (2000) 124,279, (1990) 110,765, (1980) 99,199; Registration (Oct. 2006): D-46.1%, R-31.4%, DS-17.2%; 2006 voter turnout (rank): 46.1% (52); County supervisors: Brad Wagenknecht, Mark Luce, Diane Dillon, Bill Dodd, Harold Moskowitz; 1195 Third St., Napa 94559, Phone:

(707) 253-4386; Assembly District 7; Senate District 2; Congressional District 1; Budget (2006-2007): $276.4 million; Median income: $51,738; Median home value: $615,000; Ethnicity: White-69.1%, Latino-23.7%, Asian-3.0%, Black-1.3%; Largest cities (2004): Napa (75,900), American Canyon (9,774).

The political struggle for Napa County was distilled in the 1990s battle over a train—a private wine train that ran up through the Napa Valley to St. Helena, carrying diners and tourists on a genteel lunch or dinner excursion through the county's world-famous wine country. Tourists loved it. Locals hated it. The train stayed.

The blessings and curses associated with Napa County's economic success are wrapped up in the train and in the traffic that clogs county highways most weekends and every day throughout the summer tourist season. The county's economy is tied to wine, from vineyard to cask, and that has transformed this once-rural valley into a tourist draw of international proportions. Napa Valley symbolizes California's—indeed the nation's—wine industry, and its close proximity to San Francisco only exacerbates its problems. Unemployment is low (4.6%); growth is moderate (21 percent from 1990 to 2005); the economy is robust; property values are skyrocketing; and local tempers are frayed, even as locals trek to the bank.

Politically, Napa County usually votes Democratic, although Republican Gov. Arnold Schwarzenegger and new GOP Insurance Commissioner Steve Poizner won it in 2006. It was the second time Schwarzenegger had been given the local nod, having finished first in the 2003 election following the recall of Gov. Gray Davis. The county opposed the recall itself, however, sends Democrats to the legislature and to Congress, and in 2004 strongly backed both presidential hopeful John Kerry and U.S. Sen. Barbara Boxer. Two years later, another Democrat, U.S. Sen. Dianne Feinstein, won nearly two-thirds of the county vote in her re-election.

Nevada County

Area: 958 sq. mi.; Population: (2005 est.) 100,227, (2000) 92,033, (1990) 78,510, (1980) 51,645; Registration (Oct. 2006): D-32.2%, R-43.0%, DS-18.4%; 2006 voter turnout (rank): 51.5% (40); County supervisors: Nate Beason, Sue Horne, John Spencer, Hank Weston, Ted Owens; 950 Maidu Ave., Nevada City 95959, Phone: (530) 265-1480, Fax: (530) 265-9836; Assembly District 3; Senate Districts 1, 4 ; Congressional District 4; Budget (2006-2007): $168.7 million; Median income: $45,864; Median home value: $457,000; Ethnicity: White-87.7%, Latino-5.7%, Asian-0.8%, Black-0.3%; Largest cities (2004): Truckee (13,984), Grass Valley (12,050), Nevada City (3,001).

The population of this slice of the Sierra foothills nearly doubled between 1980 and 2005, topping the 100,000 mark and making growth and its attendant problems a key issue in local politics. Growth brought some prosperity, but it also clogged roads and dotted once-pristine vistas with homes.

The county's cultural life centers on the Nevada City–Grass Valley area, with art galleries and theater companies that attract tourists the year around. It is a magnet for retirees seeking a mild climate within hailing distance of mountain sports. In 2000, a quarter of the population was over 60. The local economy, bolstered by retail trade and electronics, has been relatively stable since the late 1990s, with unemployment falling to a low of 3.6 percent in 2000. By 2003, the recession had driven it back to 4.7 percent .

As with many smaller, mountain counties, Nevada is Republican. Until 2006, a top-of-the-ticket Democrat hadn't carried the county for more than a decade, but U.S. Sen. Dianne Feinstein broke that string by defeating Republican Richard Mountjoy by 1,500 votes. More characteristic of county voting patterns, 63 percent of local voters approved the 2003 recall of Gov. Gray Davis. A year later, President George Bush beat Democrat John Kerry by 5,000 votes—a large margin in a small county. Republican U.S. Senate hopeful Bill Jones carried Nevada County by 2,000 votes over incumbent Democrat Barbara Boxer. In 2006, Gov. Arnold Schwarzenegger beat his Democratic challenger by more than 12,000 votes. The county voted against bond measures to fund schools, transportation, and affordable housing, but approved bonds for flood control.

Orange County

Area: 948 sq. mi.; Population: (2005 est.) 3,061,094, (2000) 2,846,289, (1990) 2,410,556, (1980) 1,932,921; Registration (Oct. 2006): D-30.1%, R-47.9%, DS-18.0%; 2006 voter turnout (rank): 50.5% (47); County supervisors: John Moorlach, Bill Campbell, Chris Norby, Thomas Wilson, Vacancy; 10 Civic Center Plaza, Santa Ana 92701, Phone: (714) 834-3550; Assembly Districts 56, 60, 67-73; Senate Districts 29, 33, 34, 35; Congressional Districts 40, 42, 46, 47, 48; Budget (2006-2007): $5.56 billion; Median family income: $75,700; Median home value: $630,000; Ethnicity: White-49.1%, Latino-32.3%, Asian-15.3%, Black-1.5%; Largest cities (2006): Santa Ana (351,697), Anaheim (345,317).

This is not your daddy's Orange County. Not in demographics, not in image, and certainly not in politics. For decades, political strategists knew—had to know—only four true facts about Orange County: It was rock-solid conservative, suburban, white, and Republican. The conventional wisdom—built to unassailable levels in election after election—held that Republican success statewide required that the GOP capture two-thirds of the vote in Orange County to overcome Democratic strength elsewhere.

But Orange County wasn't merely Republican. It was conservative Republican. The kind of conservatism that sent John Birch Society uber-member John Schmitz to Sacramento and "B-1" Bob Dornan to Washington. It was a political culture influenced by a large, patriotic military presence and the libertarian *Orange County Register*. In fact, the three defining icons of the county still make it the only place in America where a visitor can fly into an airport named for an ersatz war hero (John Wayne), spend a few days at the Happiest Place on Earth (Disneyland), and take a side trip to Richard Nixon's grave (Yorba Linda). As Orange County native Scott Harris wrote, "The county styled itself as a wholesome, family-oriented, flag-waving sort of place, built on some innocent fakery and a certain amount of grandstanding."

But all that began to change in the 1980s and 1990s as immigrants from Mexico and Southeast Asia altered the demographic and political landscape. Once overwhelmingly Anglo, the county is now less than half white. Latinos account for nearly a third of the population, with Asians at 15 percent plus.

The growing ethnic diversity has prompted ethnic tensions that often surface during elections. In 2006, for instance, those tensions flared during a congressional campaign in District 47. Republican Tan Nguyen, who is Vietnamese, sent a racially charged mailer warning Latinos about penalties for illegal voting. The mailer earned Nguyen a stiff rebuke from his own party, but his actions highlighted an increasingly fierce struggle for political power.

Currently, Latinos hold more of that clout. The mayor of the county's largest city, Santa Ana, is Latino, and in 2001, Santa Ana became the site of the first U.S.-Mexico International Trade Center—a symbolic gesture that underscored the county's new status. In 2006, Santa Ana became the largest city in the country with an all-Latino city council.

Vietnamese influence is growing, however. In 2004, the county elected the first Vietnamese American ever to serve in a state legislature—Republican Van Tran of Garden Grove. The Vietnamese have been flexing financial muscle in recent elections. Tran pulled in more than $800,000 in his quest for the Assembly, mostly from local Vietnamese although a substantial portion came from Vietnamese around the country. Westminster Councilman Andy Quach raised nearly $200,000 in his unsuccessful bid for mayor. Besides Tran and Quach, Janet Nguyen was elected to the Garden Grove City Council. These fund-raising efforts and candidacies affirmed that Vietnamese are becoming a political force in Orange County.

In 2006, a state Senate candidate, Republican Lynn Daucher, invested much of her time going door-to-door in the county's Little Saigon, raising her profile dramatically among Southeast Asian voters and allowing her to compete with Democrat Lou Correa, a county supervisor who is Latino. Correa won by a narrow margin—but not in Little Saigon.

The growing diversity helped erode the conservative Republican grip on county politics. Republican voter registration has continued to erode from its high point of 55 percent in the 1990s to less than 48 percent today. In 1996, Democrats ousted two of the county's most recognizable GOP lawmakers, U.S. Representative Bob Dornan and state Senator Rob Hurtt. More significant, the county no longer gives Republican statewide candidates two-thirds of its vote, reducing its ability to influence statewide elections. Republican Arnold Schwarzenegger captured just shy of 70 percent of the county vote in the 2006 gubernatorial election, but he was the first top-of-the-ticket Republican to clear the two-thirds hurdle since Pete Wilson's 1994 re-election as governor.

Although Orange County no longer routinely gives two-thirds of its vote to the GOP, Republican candidates still win the county. The county did its part to get rid of Democratic Gov. Gray Davis in 2003 by voting 73 percent for his recall, while Schwarzenegger captured 64 percent of the vote in the election to replace Davis. Pres. George Bush received just under 60 percent in 2004.

In 2006, the county voted for every Republican statewide candidate, including Richard Mountjoy, who won only a third of the vote elsewhere in his unsuccessful effort to unseat incumbent U.S. Senator Dianne Feinstein. Conservative Republican Tom McClintock took 60 percent of the Orange County vote in his losing campaign for lieutenant governor against Democrat John Garamendi.

Scandals and loss of registration have helped embolden more moderate Republicans to vie for party leadership. Two groups—Republicans for New Directions and the New Majority Committee—elected members to the county central committee, while moderates such as County Supervisor Charles Smith and Assembly members Tom Harman and Lynn Daucher have loosened the conservative grip on elective office.

Daucher almost provided Republicans with their one bright legislative light in 2006, coming within a whisker of retaking a state Senate seat (District 34) that had been held by Democrat Joe Dunn, who was termed out. Daucher eventually lost to Orange County Supervisor Lou Correa, a Democrat, whose campaign was aided by the kind of mini-scam that has come to characterize local politics. Democrats funded a write-in campaign by another Republican candidate, Otto Bade, that siphoned votes away from Daucher.

The write-in effort was reminiscent of a Republican trick in the 1995 recall of former Assemblywoman Doris Allen, a Republican who had allied herself with legislative Democrats in 1995 and been rewarded, briefly, with the speakership. In truth, Allen had no GOP support and was branded a traitor by party regulars who sought to oust her in a recall. The effort succeeded but fostered charges that Republicans had tampered with the electoral process. Among Republicans targeted in the subsequent investigation were U.S. Rep. Dana Rohrabacher, then-Assembly Speaker Curt Pringle (now the mayor of Anaheim), and candidate Scott Baugh, who later became Assembly GOP leader. They were accused of a variety of violations, including trying to get a bogus Democrat onto the ballot to replace Allen, hoping to siphon votes away from a popular Democratic candidate. Although no elected official was convicted, the investigation produced convictions for staff aides to Rohrabacher and Pringle.

Orange County has recovered from two debilitating problems of the 1990s—political scandal and the 1995 bankruptcy. In some cases, the two were intertwined. The bankruptcy evolved from risky investments made by then-County Treasurer–Tax Collector Robert Citron, who was sentenced to jail for his part in engineering the investments—known as "derivatives." Several of his assistants and two county supervisors were hauled into court by then-District Attorney Michael Capizzi. Although the supervisors were acquitted, their political careers were over.

Finally, the county continues to battle a perennial image problem with its mammoth neighbor to the north—Los Angeles. In 2004, Anaheim Mayor Pringle expressed deep displeasure that the county's major league baseball franchise—the Anaheim Angels—would return to its historic roots and rename itself the "Los Angeles Angels." Pringle subsequently sued the team, whose friendly contract at the municipally owned "Big A" Stadium is predicated on continued use of the term "Anaheim Angels." The city lost that suit in 2006 and felt little solace when the Angels called themselves "The Los Angeles Angels of Anaheim."

Placer County

Area: 1,503 sq. mi.; Population: (2005 est.) 313,931, (2000) 248,399, (1990) 172,296, (1980) 117,247; Registration (Oct. 2006): D-28.7%, R-51.47%, DS-16.2%; 2006 voter turnout (rank): 52.9% (35); County supervisors: F.C. Rockholm, Robert Weygandt, Jim Holmes, Ted Gaines, Bruce Kranz; 175 Fulweiler Avenue, Auburn 95603, Phone: (530) 889-4010, Fax: (530) 889-4009, email bos@placer.ca.gov; As-

sembly Districts 3, 4; Senate Districts 1, 4; Congressional District 4; Budget (2006-2007): $688.7 million; Median income: $57,535; Median home value: $430,000; Ethnicity: White-83.4%, Latino-9.7%, Asian-2.9%, Black-0.8%; Largest cities (2004): Roseville (96,900), Rocklin (36,300), Auburn (12,462).

To say that Placer County's population increased over the past quarter century would be like saying Barry Bonds bulked up. Thanks to the explosive expansion of metropolitan Sacramento, Placer County in 2005 was home to 168 percent more people than lived there in 1980. In the half decade since the 2000 Census, it is estimated that Placer grew by 65,000—an increase of 26 percent in five years. Much of that growth has taken place in the county's western section, which butts against Sacramento and contains a pulsating area around Roseville and Rocklin. Roseville itself is home to a prosperous computer and software industry that spilled out of the Silicon Valley a decade ago and settled in the suburbs around Sacramento. Hewlett-Packard, NEC Electronics, and Oracle Software are among the county's biggest employers—as is the Union Pacific Railroad, which maintains one of the largest railroad yards in the world in Roseville.

But Placer County is much more than high-growth suburbs. In reality, the county is three distinct regions. Beyond the Roseville and Sacramento suburbs lies the Mother Lode gold country, home to the picturesque county seat at Auburn. Further east, Placer spills over the Sierras to touch the Nevada border and is home to some of California's premier resorts, including Squaw Valley and Alpine Meadows.

Growth, in all its manifestations, has been a key political issue for a decade and was responsible for the defeat of several pro-growth county supervisors in 1994. Although a slow-growth majority then dominated the Board of Supervisors, it did little to slow the county's rapidly expanding population.

Politically, Placer County votes Republican. Since 1990, the only top-of-the-ticket Democrat to carry the county was Dianne Feinstein in her first election to the U.S. Senate in 1992—and Feinstein's margin over Republican John Seymour was .02 percent. More recently, Feinstein lost the county to Republican Richard Mountjoy by six points in her 2006 re-election bid. The county supported the 2003 recall of Gray Davis with 72 percent of the vote, giving Republican Arnold Schwarzenegger a wide margin as Davis's successor. President George Bush captured 63 percent of the vote in his 2004 re-election, while Republican Bill Jones defeated incumbent Democrat Barbara Boxer by 17 percentage points. In his 2006 re-election, Schwarzenegger took nearly three of every four votes cast in Placer for governor. Placer is now the most Republican county in the state—surpassing even Orange County.

Not surprisingly, county voters in 2006 approved statewide bond measures to provide more money for highways and flood protection, but they rejected bonds targeting affordable housing and schools.

Plumas County

Area: 2,554 sq. mi.; Population: (2005 est.) 21,557, (2000) 20,824, (1990) 19,739, (1980) 17,340; Registration (Oct. 2006): D-33.4%, R-43.8%, DS-17.4%; 2006 voter turnout (rank): 69.6% (5); County supervisors: Bill Powers, Robert Meacher, Sharon Thrall, Rose Comstock-Correi, Ole Olsen; 520 Main Street, Room 309, Quincy 95971,

Phone: (530) 283-6170, Fax: (530) 283-6288, pcbs@countyofplumas.com; Assembly District 3; Senate District 1; Congressional District 4; Budget (2005-2006): $83 million; Median income: $36,351; Median home value: $137,900; Ethnicity: White-86.3%, Latino-5.7%, Asian-0.5%, Black-0.6%; Largest cities (2004): Portola (2,190), Quincy (1,879).

Plumas is another of those northern California counties with miles of vistas, few people, and a decidedly rural, iconoclastic outlook. The nearest population center is Reno, Nevada, 80 miles to the southeast. Most of the county is owned by the U.S. Forest Service, most of the residents are white, and a majority of the voters are Republican. Its growth rate is minimal—24 percent in the quarter century between 1980 and 2005—and locals like it that way.

For decades, the economy relied on the timber industry, which has fallen on hard times of late, keeping the unemployment rate around 10 percent since 1997. Still, that marks an improvement over the 15 percent rate of 1993.

County voters gave George W. Bush better than 60 percent of their votes in the 2000 and 2004 presidential elections and Republicans Bill Simon and Bill Jones 55 percent in the 2002 gubernatorial race and 2004 U.S. Senate contest, respectively. Voters were overwhelmingly for the 2003 recall of Governor Gray Davis and for Republican Arnold Schwarzenegger as Davis's replacement.

Not much changed in 2006. Schwarzenegger's re-election was backed by 70 percent of county voters, who again rejected a Democratic incumbent U.S. senator—in this case, Dianne Feinstein. The county rejected all four infrastructure bonds on the November 2006 ballot (for transportation, schools, affordable housing, and flood control).

Riverside County

Area: 7,303 sq. mi.; Population: (2005 est.) 1,931,437, (2000) 1,545,387, (1990) 1,170,413, (1980) 663,199; Registration (Oct. 2006): D-34.4%, R-45.7%, DS-15.8%; 2006 voter turnout (rank): 49.4% (50); County supervisors: Bob Buster, John Tavaglione, Jeff Stone, Roy Wilson, Marion Ashley; 4080 Lemon Street, 5th Floor, Riverside 92501, Phone: (951) 955-1111; Assembly Districts 64-66, 71, 80; Senate Districts 31, 36, 37, 40; Congressional Districts 41, 44, 45, 49; Budget (2006-2007): $3.94 billion; Median income: $41,646; Median home value: $421,000; Ethnicity: White-51.0%, Latino-36.2%, Asian-3.7%, Black-6.2%; Largest cities (2004): Riverside (277,000), Moreno Valley (142,381), Corona (124,966), Hemet (58,812), Temecula (57,716).

Together with neighboring San Bernardino County, Riverside County forms the Inland Empire, a basin with roughly four million people. Laced with interstate highways, it is the heart of California's fastest-growing region. Riverside County alone added 1.3 million newcomers (a phenomenal growth rate of 191%) between 1980 and 2005, and the Inland Empire as a whole now boasts as many people as Oregon. In the half decade since the 2000 Census, it is estimated that Riverside County grew by 386,000 people—or 25 percent in only five years. Some estimates predict that Riverside alone will be home to over 3 million people by 2025. Two of the eight fastest growing counties in the continental United States, Riverside and San Bernardino also have the worst ozone pollution and the most endangered species.

The city of Corona epitomizes the county's growth problems. Between 1990 and 2000, its population nearly doubled. Unincorporated county land adjacent to the city erupted with housing tracts, causing a strain on city roads, parks, and libraries and prompting the city to threaten to secede from the county. Further south on I-15, Temecula and Murrieta—cities that didn't exist until 1989—blanket the valleys and hillsides. Avocado and orange groves have given way to red-tiled subdivisions and generic malls. Residents are buffeted by furious residential growth, mind-numbing commutes, and lousy air. The I-10 corridor east to the desert resorts of Palm Springs and Palm Desert is becoming a tourist hub thanks to the explosion of Indian casino gambling.

The downsides are part of a pact with the devil, for Riverside County's growth has been spurred by affordable housing, good schools, great weather, and an ideal location, just an hour's drive from the desert, the mountains, or the beach. Unfortunately, since their jobs did not move with them the migrants have to commute whence they came—Orange, Los Angeles, and San Diego counties. Thus, the county's foremost problem is traffic congestion.

Riverside tried to address the problems with an ambitious local planning effort known as the Riverside County Integrated Project—an attempt to draft a new general plan, transportation plan, and habitat conservation plan all at the same time. Meanwhile, the county has approved new subdivisions in rural areas and fast-tracked some industrial projects. The object, local officials note, is not to limit growth but to manage it.

Politically, the county remains staunchly Republican, although Democrats have been known to carry the top of the ticket. Dianne Feinstein defeated Republican Richard Mountjoy in her 2006 re-election bid to the U.S. Senate, and Democrat Gray Davis won the county in his first election for governor in 1998. He lost it four years later, and his 2003 recall gained 70 percent approval in Riverside. In 2004, Riverside gave the nod to Pres. Bush (58%) and Republican U.S. Senate candidate Bill Jones (a more modest 49%). Although Democrat Feinstein won the county in 2006, Republican Gov. Arnold Schwarzenegger took two-thirds of Riverside's vote in the same election.

Republican domination of local and legislative races has led to some factionalism. In 2002, GOP rivals went after each other in the 64th Assembly District primary when a disaffected faction claimed the leading conservative candidate was ineligible because he did not live in the district. A court agreed and tossed the candidate off the ballot, which was supposed to clear the way for a more moderate nominee. But conservatives rallied around a third candidate—John Benoit—who won the primary and the seat. Benoit has been elected twice more, opening the way for another round of factional infighting in 2008 when he is termed out.

Sacramento County

Area: 966 sq. mi.; Population: (2005 est.) 1,379,103, (2000) 1,223,499, (1990) 1,041,219, (1980) 783,381; Registration (Oct. 2006): D-42.6%, R-34.5%, DS-18.2%; 2006 voter turnout (rank): 57.9% (25); County supervisors: Roger Dickinson, Jimmy Yee, Susan Peters, Roberta Macglashan, Don Nottoli; 700 H Street, Suite 2450, Sacra-

mento 95814, Phone: (916) 440-5411, Fax: (916) 440-7593; Assembly Districts 4, 5, 9, 10, 15; Senate Districts 1, 4, 6; Congressional Districts 3, 5; Budget (2006-2007): $2.66 billion; Median income: $43,816; Median home value: $359,500; Ethnicity: White-57.8%, Latino-16.0%, Asian-11.0%, Black-10.0%; Largest cities (2004): Sacramento (441,000), Elk Grove (109,100), Citrus Heights (87,000), Folsom (65,600).

Not long ago, 40 percent of Sacramento County's workforce drew some kind of government paycheck. State government, with the Capitol anchoring Sacramento's economy, supplied a good portion of that income. But with three major military installations (McClellan and Mather Air Force bases and the Sacramento Army Depot) and numerous agencies located here, the federal government was a significant employer.

State government has downsized in recent years, and all three military bases closed during the 1980s—a one-two economic punch that could have soured many communities. But Sacramento was in the early stages of a transformation that began in the late 1970s when soaring housing costs and clogged streets and roads in the Bay Area began pushing development outward. With its cheaper land and easy lifestyle, Sacramento became an attractive location for employers looking to relocate. Although government remains the backbone of the area's economy, private sector development has diversified the region. A glance at a current list of the county's largest employers highlights the diversity: Apple Computers, Campbell Soup, Intel Corporation, Teichert Construction, Kaiser Hospitals, EDS Corporation, and USAA Insurance, to name a few. Sacramento's downtown has been revived with a plethora of high-rise office buildings, tony restaurants, and first-class hotels. The 2002-2003 recession caused barely a ripple in the area as the county's unemployment rate went from 4.2 percent in 2000 to 5.6 percent in 2003.

But there have been downsides to the growth that has seen population increase 76 percent since 1980. The election of a pro-development Board of Supervisors in the 1990s led to new housing tracts that have welded once-isolated suburbs into a far-flung metropolitan area centered on the city of Sacramento. North and South Natomas extend the city's reach to the north along Interstate 5 toward Sacramento International Airport, while in the south, Sacramento and Elk Grove have been sprouting houses and shopping malls on land that once grew alfalfa. The two cities are linked by Interstate 5 and Highway 99, and both corridors have seen startling development that has obliterated all traces of the region's once vibrant agricultural community. Housing prices have soared throughout the county, with some neighborhoods experiencing doubling or tripling home values in less than a decade.

Not surprisingly, traffic congestion and worsening air quality have followed in the wake of development and growth. The area is beset by a mish-mash of government that rivals the Tower of Babel. Sacramento is only part of a metropolitan area that includes huge unincorporated but urbanized areas and several newly formed cities. Attempts at city-county consolidation failed in 1974 and 1990, while a controversial proposal to create regional government was hooted down in 2003 by the county and smaller cities afraid of the reach and power of more liberal Sacramento.

Complicating matters is the fact that a sizeable amount of growth is taking place on the edge of—but beyond the boundaries of—Sacramento County, in Yolo, Placer and El Dorado counties to the east and west. Those new regional centers heavily impact traffic congestion in, out of, and through Sacramento, yet local authorities have little control over this growth.

Although much of the area's political energy centers on the state Capitol, city politics has produced its share of entertainment in recent years. During the mid-1990s, then-Mayor Joe Serna of Sacramento ran a reform slate that took over the Sacramento Unified School District board, which was rendered virtually useless by factionalism and dissent. The new board made some progress toward improving local schools, but by 2003, it, too, had splintered into factions—with the centerpiece issue a new retirement program that had seen top administrators receive handsome retirement packages. The result was the defeat, in 2004, of one of the most notable reformers.

Meanwhile, the city council has been split over whether to help finance a new basketball arena for the city's NBA franchise, the Kings, on city land near downtown Sacramento. Despite opposition to spending public dollars for the project, Mayor Heather Fargo and others pushed for a public vote on the matter, with some support from the council. Fargo and arena backers got their wish in November 2006, but the result was a vague proposal to raise the county sales tax by a quarter cent, coupled with an advisory that authorized spending some of the revenue for an arena. The vagueness and advisory avoided a two-thirds vote for passage. But both failed in part because of boorish behavior by the Kings' owners, who complained that a generous arena offer from the city wasn't good enough.

Sacramento County's reputation as a dependable Democratic stronghold has eroded significantly over the past decade as Republicans have made inroads in the sprawling new suburbs, especially in the southern and eastern portions of the county. Dramatic evidence of this erosion occurred in November 2006 when Sacramento native Phil Angelides, the Democratic candidate for governor, barely managed a third of the county's vote in his effort to defeat incumbent Republican Gov. Arnold Schwarzenegger. Four years earlier, incumbent Democratic Gov. Gray Davis also lost Sacramento County to a neophyte Republican politician, Bill Simon. In 2003, the county voted overwhelmingly to recall Davis and install Schwarzenegger as his successor.

Democratic U.S. Sen. Dianne Feinstein fared better in 2006, winning the county by 56 percent against Republican Richard Mountjoy. But she had few coattails. Conservative Republican state Sen. Tom McClintock won the county against another regional homeboy, Democrat John Garamendi of Walnut Grove, in McClintock's unsuccessful effort to become lieutenant governor. Republican Secy. Of State Bruce McPherson also captured Sacramento County, as did the GOP candidate for insurance commissioner, Steve Poizner. In 2004, Democrat Barbara Boxer took 55 percent of the county vote en route to re-election to a third term in the U.S. Senate, but Democratic presidential hopeful John Kerry beat Pres. George Bush by only 1,000 votes out of half a million cast.

Nor does there seem to be much middle ground when it comes to electing lawmakers. Sacramento County elects either liberals (state legislators Darrell Steinberg, Dave Jones, and U.S. Rep. Doris Matsui) or conservatives (U.S. Reps. Dan Lungren and John Doolittle and state legislators Dave Cox and Alan Nakanishi).

San Benito County

Area: 1,389 sq. mi.; Population: (2005 est.) 57,700, (2000) 53,234, (1990) 36,697, (1980) 25,005; Registration (Oct. 2006): D-45.1%, R-33.9%, DS-17.0%; 2006 voter turnout (rank): 58.6% (24); County supervisors: Donald Marcus, Anthony Botelho, Pat Loe, Reb Monaco, Jaime De La Cruz; 481 4th St., Hollister 95023, Phone: (831) 636-4000, Fax: (831) 631-4010, sbcbos@hollinet.com; Assembly District 28; Senate District 12; Congressional District 17; Budget (2006-2007): $107.8 million; Median income: $57,469; Median home value: $284,000; Ethnicity: White-46.0%, Latino-47.9%, Asian-2.4%, Black-1.1%; Largest cities (2004): Hollister (37,000).

San Benito County used to be a quiet, out-of-the-way agricultural area nestled in rolling hills between the San Francisco Bay Area and the Monterey Peninsula. That was before the Bay Area pushed south in the mid 1980s and 1990s, before San Benito County's population increased 130 percent between 1980 and 2005, and before farm towns such as Hollister became bedroom communities for San Jose.

The growth has brought service jobs to the local economy, diversifying beyond agriculture, and this has helped lower the unemployment rate—which hit a high of 17.3 percent in 1992. It has been nearly halved in the years since but still hovers just below 10 percent.

The growth has brought enormous pressure on the county's political, fiscal, and physical infrastructure. In November 2006, the *San Jose Mercury News* ran a two-part special report on troubles in San Benito County, focusing on Hollister where a secret society known as "Los Valientes" has taken on slow-growth factions. Accusations of corruption, bribery, and blackmail now dot the political landscape and have embroiled the local district attorney.

The county's largest ethnic group is Latino, which helps make San Benito County relatively solid Democratic territory for now, although voters narrowly approved the 2003 recall of Governor Gray Davis and gave Republican Arnold Schwarzenegger nearly 50 percent of their vote to succeed Davis. Schwarzenegger took the county in his 2006 re-election, but so did Democratic U.S. Sen. Dianne Feinstein. Other Republicans such as Secy. of State Bruce McPherson and insurance commissioner hopeful Steve Poizner, both of whom hail from neighboring regions, did well in 2006. San Benito is part of relatively safe Democratic legislative and congressional districts largely because it is lumped with heavily Democratic precincts in Santa Clara and Monterey counties.

San Bernardino County

Area: 20,052 sq. mi.; Population: (2005 est.) 1,977,822, (2000) 1,709,434, (1990) 1,418,380, (1980) 895,016; Registration (Oct. 2006): D-37.6%, R-42.4%, DS-16.0%; 2006 voter turnout (rank): 45% (55); County supervisors: Bill Postmus, Paul Biane, Dennis Hansberger, Gary Ovitt, Josie Gonzales; 385 N. Arrowhead Ave., 5th Floor, San Bernardino 92415, Phone: (909) 387-5417, Fax: (909) 387-5430; Assembly Districts 32, 34, 36; Senate Districts 17, 18, 29, 31, 32, 59-63, 65; Congressional Districts 25, 26, 41, 42, 43; Budget (2006-2007): $3.27 billion; Median income: $42,066; Median home value: $363,250; Ethnicity: White-44.0%, Latino-39,2%, Asian-4.7%,

California Political Almanac

Black-9.1%; Largest cities (2004): San Bernardino (196,300), Ontario (167,900), Fontana (128,929), Rancho Cucamonga (127,483).

Physically, San Bernardino County is the largest county in California. In fact, it's the largest county in the United States. Most of that territory is federally owned and sparsely populated. Most residents of San Berdoo, as it is known, live in a small western sliver that abuts Los Angeles County to the west, Orange County to the southwest, and Riverside County to the south. And there are a lot of residents, for this is the heart of the Inland Empire—the fastest-growing region of California, where the population has been mushrooming for more than two decades.

It is unusual when a county with a population close to 900,000 more than doubles in size over 25 years, but that has been the fate of San Bernardino. Some growth has been fueled by retirees seeking cheaper housing and warmer climes for their golden years. But a huge amount of the increase resulted from circumstances in Orange, San Diego, and Los Angeles counties, where the cost of homes has skyrocketed, forcing middle-class workers east into San Bernardino County in search of affordable housing. Their jobs did not migrate with them, and the result has been near catastrophic for San Bernardino's infrastructure, especially its ability to cope with traffic. The character of the area has changed drastically as small towns such as Yucaipa have grown into cities and the their once-resplendent orange groves have given way to malls, golf courses, and housing developments.

San Bernardino County struggles with problems other than growth: fires that ravage southern California nearly every year take an especially heavy toll as population pressures cause houses to be built in areas once considered wilderness, and where forest fires now consume more than trees. The county's air quality is, at times, among the worst in the state thanks to pollution blown east from Los Angeles and corralled by the San Bernardino Mountains.

The county has prospered in other ways that are not without controversy. Late in 2004, county officials discovered that San Berdoo had amassed a $113 million budget surplus due to higher revenues and smaller cuts from the state. Supervisors began squabbling over how to spend the extra cash, and, at one point, they voted to block Board Chairman Dennis Hansberger from spending any money in his district while approving firehouses and other projects in their own backyards.

Growth has caused other fights. For instance, an Upland corporation sued the county because it had failed to provide flood-control protection even though it had approved new commercial and residential development, forcing developers themselves to provide the protection. A divided county board of supervisors settled the case for more than $100 million late in 2006, prompting fears that other lawsuits—and settlements—may be in the offing.

The influx of migrants from western counties has altered county politics, and the pressures associated with growth have thrust local politicos into a high-powered world laced with corruption. Voter registration was dead even between Republicans and Democrats in 1996 but since has trended toward the GOP. San Bernardino, Fontana, and Ontario remain Democratic strongholds, but many surrounding cities—where much of the growth has taken place—are Republican.

Newer communities, those that have grown whole from the desert and absorbed the urban migrants, are among the most conservative in California. Some 70 percent of San Bernardino County voters approved the recall of Governor Gray Davis in 2003, although the county has gone for both Republicans and Democrats in top-of-the-ticket races over the past decade. Democrat Bill Clinton carried the county in the 1996 presidential race, while Republican George Bush narrowly won it in 2000. That same year, Democrat Dianne Feinstein easily defeated Republican Tom Campbell for U.S. Senate. Two years later, Republican Bill Simon captured the county's gubernatorial nod over Davis, who had won the county four years earlier. In 2004, San Berdoo voters split on the top of the ticket, supporting Bush over John Kerry for president but giving the nod to Democratic incumbent U.S. Senator Barbara Boxer.

In 2006, Gov. Arnold Schwarzenegger easily outpaced his Democratic rival, while Democratic U.S. Sen. Dianne Feinstein also won, albeit by a narrower margin over Republican Richard Mountjoy. Republicans swept most of the down-ticket statewide offices, and voters approved four statewide infrastructure bonds on the November 2006 ballot—a no-brainer for a county desperate for revenues to improve transportation, schools, housing, and flood control.

Local politics have been plagued with corruption, with county officials charged with accepting bribes in exchange for lucrative contracts to private vendors. In 2000, two successive county chief administrators pleaded guilty to charges that they delivered bribes. Two years later, two former Colton mayors, among others, admitted to accepting bribes in exchange for helping businessmen develop a city-owned trailer park. In 2002, Supervisor Jerry Eaves, a former Democratic assemblyman, was indicted on bribery charges and resigned as part of a plea bargain.

San Diego County

Area: 4,526 sq. mi.; Population: (2005 est.) 3,057,000, (2000) 2,813,833, (1990) 2,498,016, (1980) 1,861,846; Registration (Oct. 2006): D-34.2%, R-39.5%, DS-21.7%; 2006 voter turnout (rank): 57% (28); County supervisors: Greg Cox, Dianne Jacob, Pam Slater-Price, Ron Roberts, Bill Horn; County Administration Center, 1600 Pacific Highway, San Diego 92101, Phone: (619) 531-5600, Fax: (619) 531-6098; Assembly Districts 66, 73-79; Senate Districts 36, 38-40; Congressional Districts 49-53; Budget (2006-2007): $4.19 billion; Median income: $47,067; Median home value: $498,500; Ethnicity: White-55.0%, Latino-26.7%, Asian-8.9%, Black-5.7%; Largest cities (2004): San Diego (1,294,000), Chula Vista (173,556), Oceanside (161,029), Escondido (133,559).

San Diego's climate is as spectacular as ever, Balboa Park remains unsurpassed, the beaches gleam, and memories of the wonderful fare at the Old Town Tamale Factory transcend time.

But the little Navy town that mushroomed after World War II is long gone, replaced by a pastiche of freeways, shopping centers, suburban housing tracts, coastal development, and congestion, overlaid by increasingly polluted air drifting north from the Mexican border. Freeway traffic is miserable; three out of five families can't afford the soaring home prices; and the inexorable crush of population has transformed once-charming neighborhoods into clogged, depressing hives. Mission Valley resembles a strip mall crisscrossed by freeways, a huge bumper-to-bumper north-south bottleneck on most weekdays. An upscale population flows to the coast—gentrified, once-seedy neighborhoods in Ocean Beach and South Mission look good—or to the North County, one of the nation's premier retirement havens.

San Diego's downtown core has been invigorated by Horton Plaza shopping mall in an area that once included a scruffy park and a spate of second-run movie theaters. Nearby, south of Broadway, the Gaslight District has become an enticing restaurant and entertainment nexus. Indeed, urban San Diego is delightful and livable—an increasing rarity in any major city.

Livable as it may be, the county sits on the Mexican border and is ground zero in the struggle over illegal immigration. A vigilante group known as the "Minutemen" took up occasional residence along the border, ostensibly aiding federal border agents in the hunt for those trying to enter the U.S. illegally. Their presence—alternatively praised and condemned by Gov. Arnold Schwarzenegger—has been controversial. At least one county municipality, Escondido, attempted to deal with illegals by passing an ordinance to punish landlords for renting to illegal aliens. A federal judge issued a temporary restraining order in November 2006, preventing Escondido from enforcing the law and pending a hearing on issuance of a preliminary injunction early in 2007.

Beneath San Diego's surface beauty, the region is awash in political shenanigans and inevitable fallout from same. The latest involved one of the area's congressmen—Republican Randy "Duke" Cunningham—whose bribery by defense contractors reached breathtaking proportions. Cunningham, since removed from Capitol Hill to a federal prison in North Carolina, confessed to using his position on the House Armed Services Committee to steer as much as $70 million worth of business to the defense contractors who bribed him. Cunningham resigned in March 2006 and was replaced in a heated special election by Republican Brian Bilbray.

Cunningham's downfall resulted from the ethical lapses of one individual. But the city of San Diego—the county's largest burg—faces fiscal dilemmas that have resulted from chronic mismanagement of its pension fund, a situation that threatens to push the nation's seventh-largest city into bankruptcy. In November 2006, the federal Securities and Exchange Commission declared that the city had defrauded investors—those who buy its bonds—because it never told those investors that its pension fund had a massive deficit. The SEC said the city could not be trusted to manage its money and ordered San Diego to hire an independent monitor who would report directly to the SEC.

At one point, the fund had a shortfall of about $1.6 billion, which includes about $545 million in retiree medical benefits. To help fix the problem, the city may borrow money and push up the retirement age from 55 to 62. The issue reverberated in the elections, as Mayor Dick Murphy won a squeaker over challenger Donna Frye, a city council member who ran as a last-second write-in candidate. Scandal subsequently drove Murphy and his temporary successor from office, forcing another special election in July 2005. Frye ran again as a conventional candidate but lost to Jerry Sanders.

Prior to the Murphy scandal, three San Diego City Council members were accused of taking money from Las Vegas–based strip club operators in return for backing repeal of a San Diego law barring patrons and dancers from touching each other. The case, which originated in 2003, is still pending in federal court, and two of the principals on the Las Vegas end have pleaded out.

The ghosts of earlier miscues hover over the latest scandals: Mayor Roger Hedgecock—now a popular talk-radio host—resigned in 1985 after being convicted of conspiracy and perjury for campaign finance violations. A decade later, three Superior Court judges and a local lawyer were convicted of corruption when the judges took cash payments from the attorney.

In the 1960s and 1970s, the scandals included the indictment of a slew of officials on bribery and conspiracy charges for taking money in return for backing a rate increase for the Yellow Cab Company. Soon after, another scrape captured nationwide headlines when the national Republican convention was yanked from San Diego and moved to Miami amid disclosures of a controversial $400,000 offer from IT&T to underwrite the convention. At the time, there were fears that the city would become a mecca for political protesters. To polish its tarnished image, then-Mayor Pete Wilson and others pushed through San Diego's official sobriquet of "America's Finest City"—which remains to this day. Wilson's reform-minded efforts raised his political profile and propelled him to the U.S. Senate and governorship.

In this potent political stew, Republicans outnumber Democrats, but voters are fickle and independent minded, and party lines aren't sacrosanct. So San Diego tends to be moderate, even progressive. Independent presidential contender H. Ross Perot took 26 percent of the county vote in 1992, decline-to-state strength remains high, and Democrats are abundant in San Diego's Republican-dominated state Senate, Assembly, and congressional delegations.

The November 2006 elections continued the trend of San Diego's split loyalties. Republican Gov. Arnold Schwarzenegger won two-thirds of the county vote in his reelection, while Democratic U.S. Sen. Dianne Feinstein also captured the county. This top-of-the-ticket split mirrored results from 2004 when Republican Pres. George Bush and Democratic U.S. Sen. Barbara Boxer both won the county.

San Francisco County

Area: 232 sq. mi.; Population: (2005 est.) 794,850, (2000) 776,733, (1990) 731,700, (1980) 678,974; Registration (Oct. 2006): D-54.4%, R-10.9%, DS-28.9%; 2006 voter turnout (rank): 60.5% (21); County supervisors: Jake McGlodrick, Michela Alioto-Pier, Aaron Peskin, Ross Mirkarimi, Chris Daly, Sean Elsbernd, Bevan Duffy, Tom Ammiano, Sophie Maxwell, Gerardo Sandoval, Vacancy; 1 Dr. Carlton B. Goodlett Place, Room 244, San Francisco 94102, Phone: (415) 554-5184, Fax: (415) 554-5163, email board.of.supervisors@sfgov.org; Assembly Districts 12, 13; Senate Districts 3, 8; Congressional Districts 8, 12; Budget (2006-2007): $2.7 billion; Median income: $55,221; Median home value: $759,000; Ethnicity: White-43.6%, Latino-14.1%, Asian-30.8%, Black-7.8%; Largest cities (2004): San Francisco (792,700).

Politics in San Francisco is not about Democrats and Republicans. There virtually are no Republicans. The GOP is barely an afterthought and nearly 2.5 times as many voters register "decline to state" as Republican. The last GOP candidate to win a legislative office from San Francisco was state Senator Milton Marks back in the early 1980s—shortly before he switched to the Democratic Party. In 2004, San Franciscans gave Democrats John Kerry and Barbara Boxer 83 percent of their votes for president and U.S. Senate, respectively. Two years later, they gave their former mayor, U.S. Sen. Dianne Feinstein, 81 percent of the vote in re-electing her to a fourth term. More significant, they awarded Democrat Phil Angelides 63 percent of their vote in his effort to unseat Republican Gov. Arnold Schwarzenegger. Statewide, Angelides managed less than 40 percent.

Politics in San Francisco is about Democrats, and about the various shades of being a Democrat. It is perhaps the only county in California where being liberal is not enough.

That said, San Francisco's political pantheon underwent a transition between 2004 and 2006. Out went the man who had dominated the political landscape for decades by bridging all facets of party ideology—Willie Lewis Brown, Jr., who served as mayor from 1996 to 2004 after representing San Francisco in the state legislature for three decades including a stint as the longest serving Speaker of the Assembly in state history.

In came the first woman ever to serve as Speaker of the U.S. House of Representatives, Nancy Pelosi, whose rise to one of the most powerful positions in American politics occurred when Democrats took control of the House following the November 2006 elections. Now third in line for the presidency, Pelosi is not a local bridge in the mold of Brown. In fact, San Francisco Democrats immediately registered displeasure with Pelosi, who to secure the speakership was forced to accommodate conservatives in her own party.

Despite her national prominence and safe congressional district, Pelosi will never be a local icon like Brown. San Francisco, like Brown, is unique. It is California's only consolidated city-county government and, as such, the County Board of Supervisors functions as the city council, and the mayor traditionally wields strong powers over appointments and policy.

Brown was first elected mayor in December 1995 by defeating the incumbent—a decent but drab former police chief named Frank Jordan. As he had during his legislative career as the self-described "ayatollah of the Assembly," Brown governed San Francisco by force of will. When his tenure was complete in January 2004, it marked the end of a career in elective politics that began in 1964—when Pat Brown was governor of California. And when Willie Brown turned over the reins of government to his handpicked successor, Supervisor Gavin Newsom, San Francisco passed to a new generation of politicians: Newsom was born during Brown's second term in the Assembly.

Brown characterized his time as mayor as "the most enjoyable eight years of my political existence." His accomplishments, as he saw them, were a string of day-care centers, a spruced-up waterfront, and construction of Pac-Bell Park, the trend-setting downtown ballpark that replaced Candlestick Park as home of baseball's San Francisco Giants.

But Brown's legacy—and the San Francisco he left behind—is not easily described. As the *San Francisco Chronicle* noted, Brown's policies helped reshape the city, for good and ill. He was the driving power behind a $300 million restoration of City Hall, complete with a $400,000 gilded dome. The Ferry Building was restored to the tune of $100 million. The city built a new main library, new airport terminals, new homes for the Asian Art Museum and the deYoung art museum, and expanded the Moscone Convention Center.

San Francisco was a major beneficiary of personal and corporate wealth accumulated during the dot-com era of the mid and late 1990s. Huge financial resources flowed into the city, financing new construction and raising the demand for pricey inner-city housing by newly minted paper millionaires who sought San Francisco's cosmopolitan lifestyle.

The Brown administration was more than willing to cooperate. The mayor had consolidated political power during his first term by appointing eight supervisors (of 11 total) to vacancies created when incumbents moved on to higher office or state and federal appointments. In exchange for Brown's patronage, the board majority became a rubber stamp for the mayor's pro-development policies, and gussied up major portions of the central business district. High-tech office buildings and live-work lofts sprouted in many areas of the city, often replacing blight with glitz.

But the development changed the character of working-class neighborhoods, causing unrest and discontent among blue-collar workers forced to relocate. Blue-collar means labor, and labor means union power that eventually turned against Brown and his allies. Dissatisfaction among voters with the pace and character of development led to a showdown at the ballot box in 2000. A year after Brown was overwhelmingly re-elected to a second term, voters tossed out several of his allies on the Board of Supervisors, installing others who had campaigned against the kind of development Brown had fostered. Among those elected was Matt Gonzalez, a member of the Green Party who became president of the board and Newsom's most formidable challenger for mayor.

In some ways, the 2003 election to replace Brown was a clash of cultures. Newsom, a wealthy businessman and Brown's hand-picked successor, represented a continuation of his policies, especially toward corporate San Francisco. Gonzalez, a public defender who mounted a grass-roots effort that expanded his base far beyond the Green Party, was far more willing to take on corporate forces that had fueled San Francisco's transformation during the Brown years. Among those who endorsed Gonzalez were Dolores Huerta, cofounder of the United Farm Workers, and the Harvey Milk LGBT Democratic Club—a major political organization in the city's powerful gay and lesbian community.

The Gonzalez-Newsom contest exemplified what is unique about San Francisco and its politics. It is not enough to be a liberal Democrat; Newsom is a liberal Democrat. A candidate has to be a *progressive*. Newsom himself best summed it up for the *New York Times* when he explained that "Only in San Francisco can you be pro-choice, pro-gay marriage, anti-death penalty, pro-gun control, pro-rent control and be considered the conservative or moderate."

Newsom won a run-off and immediately moved to shore up his progressive credentials, especially among gays and lesbians. Not long after taking the oath of office in January 2004, he began performing marriage ceremonies for gay and lesbian couples even though the practice is illegal in California. His actions put San Francisco in the spotlight of a national debate over the issue of gay marriage, and although Newsom's efforts eventually were undone by the courts, which invalidated the marriages, Newsom made no apologies for being a social scofflaw.

But the issue of gay marriage is merely a diversion for both Newsom and San Francisco. The problem of homelessness continues to sit at the top of voter concerns, and it is significant that fixing that problem was at the top of Willie Brown's agenda when he became mayor in January 1996. The *Chronicle* called homelessness Brown's "most profound failure," one he conceded during his first year in office when he said the problem "may not be solvable." Events proved him correct. Despite spending millions of dollars on services and the construction of shelters, San Francisco still harbors thousands of homeless who sleep in park encampments, under freeways, in transit kiosks, or on the street.

They are now Newsom's concern, but homelessness is not his only challenge. Traffic congestion remains formidable at all hours, even though the dot-com collapse put a damper on the city economy, and Oakland long ago supplanted San Francisco as the Bay Area's premier shipper of air-, land-, and sea-borne freight.

San Francisco continues to lose corporate headquarters and white-collar jobs to suburban centers across the bay in Contra Costa and Alameda counties and to the South Bay. Skyrocketing real estate prices drove many middle-class whites to the suburbs, and gentrification has obliterated many African American enclaves. The only place that has not benefited is Hunter's Point, a sore spot that continues to suffer high rates of poverty, bad air, crime, and blight.

The city now stands to lose something more tangible. In October 2006, the city's venerable pro football franchise, the San Francisco '49ers, announced it was moving south to Santa Clara because it could not come to an agreement with the city over renovations to Monster Park (formerly Candlestick Park). The collapse of those negotiations affected more than football. The city was in the thick of bidding for the 2016 Olympic Games, and an improved stadium was vital to its bid. When the '49ers opted out, the stadium deal collapsed, forcing San Francisco to withdraw its bid for the Olympics.

City politics remain intense and are marked by ethnic and social divides as Asians, gays, and others vie for slices of power. Every San Franciscan, it seems, belongs to one of the dozens of political pressure groups that range in scope from ethnic to lifestyle to issue-oriented. Most are reactive rather than pro-active, mobilizing primarily to oppose any perceived threat to their value systems.

In a previous era, much of the factionalism was contained by a power structure centered on the late Philip Burton—a forceful Democratic congressman of enormous political talent. His brother John recently stepped down as president pro tempore of the state Senate, arguably the most powerful position in Sacramento short of governor. Brown was part of the Burton machine, but its influence is fading as its core ages and retires, and no single faction seems capable of filling the vacuum. Brown tried, but his minions on the Board of Supervisors were mostly rejected at the polls. His choice for district attorney, Kamala Harris, won election alongside Newsom, but the new mayor seems more interested in charting an independent course and less capable of welding the various factions into a cohesive political whole. Nor does he have the patronage at his disposal that bolsters machine politics. Those powers were weakened during Brown's second term by a more hostile board, which stripped the mayor of some of his appointments.

Nor were suspicions and tensions among groups helped in recent years by internal troubles in San Francisco's election system. In 2001, for instance, the state had to monitor a run-off after post-primary ballot boxes were found floating in San Francisco Bay and many blank ballots turned up weeks later.

Meanwhile, the relationships that underlie San Francisco's old-time politics emerged at the center of yet another scandal, this time involving one of the city's favorite sons—Secretary of State Kevin Shelley, whose father once served as mayor. Shelley, a former supervisor and state assemblyman, was able to steer a state grant to one of his backers—Julie Lee, a prominent businesswoman in the city's influential Chinese community who sought the money to build a senior-citizens center. The center was never built, and money from the grant found its way into Shelley's campaign coffers. The resulting scandal eventually led to Shelley's resignation as secretary of state. Another investigation centered on Mabel Teng, the county's assessor-recorder. Late in 2004, Teng was forced to call in auditors from the state Board of Equalization to peek into her office and its property records. Critics charged that her staff gave tax breaks to political donors. The county would have to pay for the audit, and the tab could run as high as $500,000.

Still, San Francisco remains a font of progressive innovation. In 2004, a unique "instant run off" procedure for city and county elections allowed voters to cast three ballots in each election—for their first, second, and third choices. If no candidate gets 50 percent of the vote in a given election, second and third place votes are tabulated to determine a winner. Unfortunately, the system hit a glitch during its 2004 run when the large turnout caused computers to malfunction and results were withheld until weeks after the election.

San Joaquin County

Area: 1,426 sq. mi.; Population: (2005 est.) 664,369, (2000) 563,598, (1990) 480,628, (1980) 347,342; Registration (Oct. 2006): D-42.4%, R-40.6%, DS-13.3%; 2006 voter turnout (rank): 50.1% (49); County supervisors: Steve Gutierrez, Frank Ruhstaller, Victor Mow, Ken Vogel, Leroy Ornellas; 222 East Weber Avenue, Room 701, Stockton 95202, Phone: (209) 468-2350, Fax: (209) 468-3694; Assembly Districts 10, 15, 17, 26; Senate Districts 5, 14; Congressional Districts 11, 18; Budget (2006-2007): $1.36 billion; Median income: $41,282; Median home value: $429,000; Ethnicity: White-47.4%, Latino-30.5%, Asian-11.4%, Black-6.7%; Largest cities (2004): Stockton (269,100), Lodi (56,999), Tracy (56,929), Manteca (49,228).

When Silicon Valley exploded with jobs and high-tech development in the 1980s, it caused a flood to the east, over Altamont Pass and down into the farmlands of the Central Valley. The channel for that flood was Interstate 580, which connects the southern and eastern San Francisco Bay Area with San Joaquin County.

When converted garages in Palo Alto began to sell for $1 million and up, middle-class refugees sought affordable housing elsewhere, and the end of the rainbow was Tracy, Manteca, and other once sleepy farm towns in San Joaquin County, where county population grew 77 percent between 1980 and 2002.

With that kind of influx, growth—and how to control and manage it—became a major issue throughout the region, sometimes pitting San Joaquin County against its neighbors to the west. Some communities, such as Tracy, have encouraged the area's emergence as a Bay Area bedroom, but those local decisions have spawned widespread repercussions. Several communities in Alameda and Contra Costa counties have threatened to sue San Joaquin cities over issues such as traffic congestion caused as commuters pour through Livermore and Pleasanton en route to homes on the eastern slope of the coast range.

Politically, Republicans hold a narrow registration edge in San Joaquin, but this part of the Central Valley has become a key political battleground. Two of the state's most competitive legislative districts are in San Joaquin (Senate District 5, Assembly District 17), and top-of-the-ticket races have bounced back and forth between Republicans and Democrats in recent years. George Bush carried the county over Al Gore in the 2000 presidential contest by a mere 1%, increasing his margin to 8 percent in 2004. In the two most recent contests for U.S. Senate, voters opted for Democrats Barbara Boxer (2004) and Dianne Feinstein (2006). In 2002, Republican Bill Simon won San Joaquin in his bid to unseat incumbent Gov. Gray Davis, and a year later, county voters overwhelmingly approved Davis's recall and the election of Republican Arnold Schwarzenegger to succeed him. Schwarzenegger captured over 60 percent of the San Joaquin vote in his 2006 re-election. Republicans did well in other statewide races in 2006, including conservative state Sen. Tom McClintock, who edged San Joaquin homeboy Democrat John Garamendi who won the statewide race for lieutenant governor.

As in years past, the county provided the state's hottest district race in 2006—the contest for Congressional District 11. Incumbent Richard Pombo, a Stockton native, had represented the area in Congress since 1992. But Pombo was caught in a series of unfortunate events, some of his own making and some whistling in from elsewhere. Beset by a whiff of scandal and regarded as out of touch with constituents, many of them transplants from the Bay Area, Pombo was defeated after a bruising campaign by Democrat Jerry McNerney, a mathematician and political neophyte. Even repeated help from Bush, who came to the district for a Pombo fund raiser, could not salvage the incumbent's career. Half the district electorate resides in San Joaquin County, and Pombo had to win big on his home turf to offset McNerney's strength in Santa Clara and Alameda counties. Pombo won San Joaquin by 2,000 votes—less than McNerney's margin in the tiny sliver of Santa Clara County included in the district.

San Luis Obispo County

Area: 3,616 sq. mi.; Population: (2005 est.) 262,593, (2000) 246,681, (1990) 217,162, (1980) 155,435; Registration (Oct. 2006): D-35.1%, R-41.8%, DS-17.3%; 2006 voter turnout (rank): 63.4% (14); County supervisors: Harry Ovitt, Bruce Gibson, Jerry Lenthall, Katcho Achadjian, Jim Patterson; County Government Center, Room 370, San Luis Obispo 93408, Phone: (805) 781-4540, Fax: (805) 781-1350, taritt@co.slo.ca.us; Assembly District 33; Senate District 15; Congressional Districts 22, 23; Budget (2006-2007): $434.5 million; Median income: $42,428; Median home value: $540,000; Ethnicity: White-76.1%, Latino-16.3%, Asian-2.7%, Black-2.0%; Largest cities (2004): San Luis Obispo (44,200), Atascadero (26,411), El Paso de Robles (24,297).

In the heart of the Central Coast, midway between San Francisco and Los Angeles, sits San Luis Obispo County—a heaven of low mountains, rugged coastline, sandy beaches, temperate weather, and laid-back lifestyle. Hearst Castle towers above the coast near the picturesque town of Cambria. Pismo Beach, with its ancient pier and beach life, is here.

But San Luis Obispo County is no backwater. It has become a haven for urbanites—both north and south—who have cashed in on inflated home prices and moved to a less-hurried pace along the coast. As a result, property values are increasing—as is the population, which has grown 69 percent since 1980. Agriculture, tourism, and education form the backbone of the local economy, where the unemployment rate was only 3.4 percent in 2003.

County politics are decidedly Republican, although Republicans here tend to be more moderate than their inland brethren—especially on the environment. One of the key local issues centers on the potential development of Hearst Ranch, which surrounds Hearst Castle. The house itself was given to the state years ago and remains a state park. But the surrounding property still is under control of the Hearst Corporation, and development plans met with fierce local opposition before an agreement was reached.

Despite the presence of a university (Cal Poly-San Luis Obispo) and many government workers, Democrats do not fare well. The only top-of-the-ticket Democrats to carry the county in the last decade were Gray Davis in his first bid for governor in 1998 and U.S. Sen. Dianne Feinstein in her re-election effort in 2006. Davis lost the county in his 2002 re-election and saw 63 percent of San Luis voters favor his recall in 2003.

In 2004 the county played a pivotal role in a hotly contested legislative race between Republican Abel Maldonado and Democrat Peg Pinard. Maldonado won, in part because San Luis provided 75 percent of his margin of victory. Pres. George Bush and Republican U.S. Senate hopeful Bill Jones carried the county in 2004, and two years later, Gov. Arnold Schwarzenegger doubled the San Luis vote total of his Democratic rival in winning re-election.

San Mateo County

Area: 741 sq. mi.; Population: (2005 est.) 721,350, (2000) 707,161, (1990) 649,623, (1980) 587,329; Registration (Oct. 2006): D-49.4%, R-24.5%, DS-22.2%; 2006 voter turnout (rank): 56.2% (31); County supervisors: Mark Church, Jerry Hill, Richard Gordon, Rose Gibson, Adrienne Tisser; 400 County Center, Redwood City 94063, Phone: (650) 363-4653, Fax: (650) 599-1027; Assembly Districts 19, 21; Senate Districts 8, 11; Congressional Districts 12, 14; Budget (2006-2007): $1.59 billion; Median income: $70,819; Median home value: $760,000; Ethnicity: White-49.8%, Latino-21.9%, Asian-20.0%, Black-3.5%; Largest cities (2004): Daly City (103,300), San Mateo (92,482), Redwood City (75,402), South San Francisco (60,442).

Lying directly south of San Francisco, San Mateo County isn't very big. But it contains enormous social and economic extremes. The hill country is as wealthy as it gets in California, with tree-shaded byways and multi-million-dollar estates in communities such as Atherton, Hillsborough, Portola Valley, and Woodside. Closer to San

Francisco, the area around San Francisco International Airport is blue-collar and middle class, with incomes less than a third of those found in the county's more exclusive areas. At the southern edge of the county along the Bay sits East Palo Alto, a mostly African American community where the median per capita income was little more than $13,000 at the height of the state's economic boom less than a decade ago.

Population growth has been snail-like during the past two decades, increasing only 23 percent between 1980 and 2005. That hasn't prevented the housing market from blowing through the roof with the median home value now $760,000. High-tech has been a boon and a problem for San Mateo County, providing jobs and economic boom times for cities such as Menlo Park and Redwood City. As a result, San Mateo contributes to traffic congestion in both directions—heading out of the county toward San Francisco and into the county for work in South San Francisco, Foster City, and Burlingame. Unemployment doubled between 1990 and 2003, soaring to 5.1 percent from 2.6 percent.

Politically, the county is increasingly Democratic, with those opting for "decline to state" approaching a quarter of the registered voters and nearly equaling Republican registration. As a result, no Republican has carried the county at the top of the ticket in 14 years, and that includes Gov. Arnold Schwarzenegger, who in 2006 lost San Mateo by 160 votes out of nearly 200,000 cast for governor. Democrat Dianne Feinstein polled three-fourths of the county vote in her successful re-election to the U.S. Senate, while Republican Steve Poizner, a native of nearby Santa Clara County, won San Mateo County in his successful effort to become state insurance commissioner, besting Democrat Cruz Bustamante by nearly 9,000 votes. County voters approved all four infrastructure bonds on the November 2006 ballot, backing oil and tobacco taxes (Pros. 87 and 86) that were defeated statewide.

Santa Barbara County

Area: 2,737 sq. mi.; Population: (2005 est.) 419,678, (2000) 399,347, (1990) 369,608, (1980) 298,694; Registration (Oct. 2006): D-40.4%, R-35.5%, DS-18.9%; 2006 voter turnout (rank): 52.4% (36); County supervisors: Saluda Carbajal, Janet Wolf, Brooks Firestone, Joni Gray, Joseph Centeno; 105 East Anapamu St., Santa Barbara 93101, Phone: (805) 568-2190, cao@co.santa-barbara.ca.us; Assembly Districts 33, 35; Senate Districts 15, 19; Congressional Districts 23, 24; Budget (2006-2007): $757 million; Median income: $46,677; Median home value: $461,000; Ethnicity: White-56.9%, Latino-34.2%, Asian-4.1%, Black-2.3%; Largest cities (2004): Santa Barbara (90,500), Santa Maria (85,300), Goleta (55,204), Lompoc (41,103).

Santa Barbara County went through a growth spurt between 1980 and 1990, its population increasing by an alarming 25%, alarming because quality of life is a seminal issue in this tony coastal enclave. Alarming, too, because much of that growth pressure came from Los Angeles—the megalopolis separated from Santa Barbara only by Ventura County. Since then, local activists have blocked most major developments, and growth slowed during the 1990s so the county population increased by only 30,000, or 8%, during the decade. According to estimates, another 20,000 have taken up residence in the half decade since the last census.

Still, the character of Santa Barbara County is schizophrenic: upscale wine-and-brie folks in the south and blue-collar, working-class communities in the north. As a result, a move is afoot to split the county along a north-south axis at the Santa Ynez Mountains and create a new "Mission County." Santa Ynez, Solvang, Lompoc, and Santa Maria would be the population centers of Mission County; Santa Barbara, Carpinteria, and Goleta would remain in a truncated Santa Barbara County. This is the sixth attempt to split the county in the past 150 years, with the most recent occurring in 1978 when a proposed "Los Padres County" was trounced at the polls. The "Mission County" proposal didn't fare much better, managing less than 20 percent of the vote in June 2006.

The county is moderate in its politics, especially on the Republican side. The 2001 redistricting and reapportionment was not particularly kind to Santa Barbara County, splitting it between two congressional districts and a pair of state Senate districts. In the U.S. House, the southern portion of the county is tacked onto Ventura County to make a safe seat (24) for Republicans, while its Democratic precincts are joined with San Luis Obispo and a slice of Ventura to make a safer Democratic seat (23).

The state Senate slice-and-dice was much worse for the county. The northern half is part of a large Central Coast district (15) that extends all the way to Monterey County and is marginally Republican, with moderate sensibilities that mirror Santa Barbara's own. The southern half (19) was given a Ventura County tail that snakes into Los Angeles County to include Simi Valley and Santa Clarita. The state senator who holds the seat, Republican Tom McClintock, is one of the legislature's most conservative members. As a candidate for governor in the 2003 recall election, McClintock gained only 16.5 percent of the vote from Santa Barbara County. He fared much better in his 2006 campaign for lieutenant governor, capturing the county with 50 percent of the vote against Democrat John Garamendi, the winner statewide.

On its own, the county has voted mostly Democratic in top-of-the-ticket races since 1990, although it backed Republican Bill Simon over Democratic incumbent Gray Davis for governor in 2002. It supported Davis's recall a year later and the election of Republican Arnold Schwarzenegger to replace Davis. Top-of-the-ticket Democrats dominated in 2004 as presidential nominee John Kerry and U.S. Sen. Barbara Boxer both won. In 2006 Democrat Dianne Feinstein carried the county in her re-election to the U.S. Senate, but so did Schwarzenegger.

Santa Clara County

Area: 1,304 sq. mi.; Population: (2005 est.) 1,760,741, (2000) 1,682,585, (1990) 1,497,577, (1980) 1,295,071; Registration (Oct. 2006): D-44.9%, R-26.8%, DS-24.5%; 2006 voter turnout (rank): 58.8% (22); County supervisors: Donald Gage, Blanca Alvarado, Peter McHugh, Ken Yeager, Liz Kniss; County Government Center, 70 West Hedding Street, San Jose 95110, Phone: (408) 299-5001; Assembly Districts 20-24, 27, 28; Senate Districts 10, 11, 13, 15; Congressional Districts 11, 14-16; Budget (2006-2007): $3.7 billion; Median income: $74,335; Median home value: $677,000; Ethnicity: White-44.2%, Latino-24.0%, Asian-25.6%, Black-2.8%; Largest cities (2004): San Jose (926,200), Sunnyvale (131,760), Santa Clara (102,361), Mountain View (70,708), Palo Alto (58,598).

Santa Clara County is one of the engines that drive the San Francisco Bay Area economy—indeed, the California economy—and a list of the county's major employers reflects its power: Agilent Technologies, Apple Computers, Applied Materials, Cisco Systems, Flextronics International, Hewlett-Packard, IBM, Intel, KLA-Tencor, Lockheed Martin Space Systems, Solectron, and Sun Microsystems. Each is connected with the computer-electronics industry and Silicon Valley, centered in Santa Clara County. So, too, is Stanford University, which supplies much of the brain power and business acumen that has made Silicon Valley an economic—and more recently, political—powerhouse.

But Santa Clara County has been on a roller-coaster ride during the past half-dozen years, its economy soaring and plummeting then inching upward again. The soaring came during the late 1990s when a "dot-com boom," spurred by expansion of the Internet, virtually eradicated unemployment. What Federal Reserve Board Chairman Alan Greenspan called an "irrational exuberance" drove stock prices of Internet-driven companies—some of which had never made a dime—through the roof.

Greenspan was right, of course. The dot-com revolution that had put more than 1.1 million people to work in Santa Clara and San Mateo counties came to a crashing halt in 2000. The region lost 200,000 jobs between January 2000 and May 2004—one in six Silicon Valley workers. "Outsourcing"—the export of jobs to other countries where labor costs are substantially cheaper—became a bugaboo to the labor force, a savior to corporations.

The local economy took an enormous hit. Rental rates for commercial property dropped 62 percent in four years. Average annual pay declined from a peak of $81,700 in 2000 to $62,400 in 2003. Still, Silicon Valley's cost of living remained 47 percent higher than that of the nation as a whole.

Despite the bust, the boom times altered the character and culture of what had been a Bay Area backwater. The most prominent physical evidence of the county's emergence as an economic powerhouse is the transformation of its largest city—San Jose, the third-largest city in the state. The effort, led by then-Mayors Tom McEnery and Susan Hammer and civic leaders such as the late David Packard, started in the 1990s and included construction of a downtown trolley system, convention center, high-tech museum and sports complex, and an improved airport.

Late in 2006 the county pulled off another coup by luring one of the Bay Area's premier sports franchises—the National Football League '49ers—out of San Francisco and to a new home in the city of Santa Clara, where a developer announced plans to build an 80,000-seat palace surrounded by commercial and residential property. The county had out-hustled its more famous neighbor to the north, where the move deprived San Francisco of a virtually new facility at Candlestick Point and proved a crushing blow to that city's dream of hosting the 2016 Olympic Games.

Population and job growth have led to increased problems with traffic congestion and the cost of living for anyone without a portfolio of stock options. The median price of a home soared more than $300,000 between 1990 and 2000—up 131 percent. It more than doubled in the next half decade. A two-bedroom apartment rented for $1,800 a month. Other property values exploded accordingly as the county added seven jobs for every new housing unit—far in excess of what housing experts considered a healthy ratio of 1.5 jobs per home. That ratio forced many who work in the Silicon

Valley to seek housing elsewhere—south toward Gilroy and east into Central Valley communities such as Tracy, Stockton, and Lodi. And that migration created enormous traffic problems for the Silicon Valley, the Central Valley, and all points in between.

Not everyone in the county shared in the region's prosperity. According to the Bay Area United Way, 121,000 county households live below a "self-sufficiency standard" developed by the National Economic Development and Law Center and generally seen as a more accurate measure than federal poverty standards when determining how families cope. According to the study, an adult with a preschool child would require a wage of $27 per hour—nearly five times the minimum wage in California—to "make it" in Santa Clara County. As a result, Santa Clara and neighboring San Mateo counties helped redefine the notion of who is and who is not poor. In Santa Clara County, a family earning less than $60,000 is considered "low income." Teachers, firefighters, nurses, and others considered middle class in most locales often show up at food banks and homeless shelters in Silicon Valley.

Santa Clara County is fascinated with the road to riches, and a few of its billionaire entrepreneurs have plunged into political waters either as candidates or those who bankroll candidates and causes. The most notable example is Steve Poizner, who made a fortune in software development, some of which he applied to a 2004 campaign for the state Assembly. Although the roughly $7 million Poizner spent in that election could be considered pocket change for the candidate, it smashed all spending records for a legislative race. Records aside, it wasn't enough to overcome the "R" attached to Poizner's name in a district that was solidly—and, it turns out, loyally—Democratic. Poizner reversed his fortunes in 2006 by spending another huge chunk of change to win election as state insurance commissioner.

The county itself votes Democratic in most contests, as evidenced by the fact that nearly 60 percent of the county electorate opposed the 2003 recall of then-Governor Gray Davis and gave Democratic Lieutenant Governor Cruz Bustamante a narrow nod over Republican Arnold Schwarzenegger to replace Davis.

Schwarzenegger changed that dynamic in his 2006 re-election, winning 52 percent of the Santa Clara vote and becoming the first top-of-the-ticket Republican to carry the county in recent memory. Poizner, too, won the county in 2006. But that was the extent of Republican success here. U.S. Sen. Dianne Feinstein took 70 percent of the vote in her 2006 re-election. In 2004, the county gave both top-of-the-ticket Democrats—John Kerry and Barbara Boxer—nearly two-thirds of its vote for president and U.S. Senate.

Santa Cruz County

Area: 607 sq. mi.; Population: (2005 est.) 260,634, (2000) 255,602, (1990) 229,734, (1980) 188,141; Registration (Oct. 2006): D-53.0%, R-20.3%, DS-19.5%; 2006 voter turnout (rank): 50.6% (46); County supervisors: Jan Beautz, Ellen Pirie, Neal Coonerty, Tony Campos, Mark Stone; 701 Ocean Street, Room 500, Santa Cruz 95060, Phone: (831) 454-2200, Fax: (831) 454-3262; Assembly Districts 27, 28; Senate Districts 11, 15; Congressional Districts 14, 17; Budget (2006-2007): $549.2 million; Median income: $53,998; Median home value: $712,000; Ethnicity: White-65.5%, Latino-26.8%, Asian-3.4%, Black-1.0%; Largest cities (2004): Santa Cruz (56,300), Watsonville (48,300).

Santa Cruz County was never quite the same after the University of California opened what became an unconventional campus in the city of Santa Cruz in 1965. Prior to that, this tiny county was a conservative seaside enclave that fed on tourism and agriculture. The university changed that dynamic, attracting a liberal faculty and student body to half the county (the city of Santa Cruz), while leaving the rest of the county bucolic. Politics changed as well, as the city of Santa Cruz rivaled Berkeley and Santa Monica as bastions of liberal thought and activism.

Tourism is one cornerstone for the local economy given that the county has six state parks and six state beaches. But agriculture, centered near Watsonville, plays a part—giving the county a schizophrenic outlook on jobs and employment. The region is known for its artichoke and strawberry production.

The role of agriculture in the county makes immigration a key issue. Migrant farm hands still work the fields around Watsonville, making the late Cesar Chavez an icon even today. In September 2006, federal immigration agents arrested and deported 87 people in the Watsonville area.

Environmentalism anchors local politics, and the county has been represented in Sacramento and Washington over the years by some of the legislature's and Congress's most ardent conservationists. The Santa Cruz Board of Supervisors has been a launching pad for legislative office over the years, with Democrats Fred Keeley and John Laird jumping from the board to the Assembly.

Politically, the county is solid Democratic territory; no top-of-the-ticket Republican has won here since before 1990. The 2003 recall of Governor Gray Davis failed badly here, and Santa Cruz County provided Lieutenant Governor Cruz Bustamante one of his rare county victories in the election to replace Davis. Republican Arnold Schwarzenegger received only one-third of the vote, while Green Party nominee Peter Camejo pulled in a respectable 7 percent. In 2004, the fact that U.S. Senator John Kerry of Massachusetts failed to oust Republican President George Bush was no fault of Santa Cruz County, which gave Kerry 73 percent of its vote. Kerry outpolled Democratic U.S. Senator Barbara Boxer, who received only 71 percent in her successful re-election.

The county followed local tradition in 2006, becoming one of only five counties statewide to favor Democrat Phil Angelides over incumbent Governor Arnold Schwarzenegger. Democrats carried the county in every statewide race, including for secretary of state where Debra Bowen narrowly defeated incumbent homeboy Republican Bruce McPherson (92 votes out of 70,000 cast). McPherson, a moderate and former publisher of the *Santa Cruz Sentinel*, represented the county in the state Senate from 1996 to 2004. He was appointed secretary of state in 2005 by Schwarzenegger when the Democratic incumbent, Kevin Shelley, resigned in the wake of a scandal.

If the November 2006 election produced any surprise, it came in the vote over Measure G, which would have raised the minimum wage to $9.25 an hour. Similar measures passed in several states, and a hike in the minimum wage is a centerpiece for the new majority Democrats in Congress. But the effort failed in Democrat-dominant Santa Cruz County after the local business community spent $60,000 to defeat Measure G. More than 60 percent of the Santa Cruz electorate voted "no."

The county also exhibited an anti-growth attitude in 2006 by passing a pair of measures designed to inhibit growth at the University of California. One denied municipal services to the campus unless the university covers related costs, while the other authorized the city of Santa Cruz to withhold water and sewer service to the campus.

Redistricting splintered Santa Cruz County when Democratic legislators sliced off friendly precincts to bolster a state Senate district centered on San Mateo and Santa Clara counties. The rest was attached to a nominally Republican district that extends down the coast to San Luis Obispo County. The result: no member of the state Senate will hail from—or be beholden to—Santa Cruz County.

Shasta County

Area: 3,847 sq. mi.; Population: (2005 est.) 180.984, (2000) 163,256, (1990) 147,036, (1980) 115,715; Registration (Oct. 2006): D-30.1%, R-49.2%, DS-16.2%; 2006 voter turnout (rank): 66.8% (9); County supervisors: David Kehoe, Mark Cibula, Glenn Hawes, Linda Hartman, Les Baugh; 1815 Yuba Street, Suite 1, Redding 96001, Phones: (530) 225-5557, (800) 479-8009; Fax: (530) 225-5189; Assembly District 2; Senate District 4; Congressional District 2; Budget (2005-2006): $273 million; Median income: $34,335; Median home value: $120,800; Ethnicity: White-86.4%, Latino-5.5%, Asian-1.9%, Black-0.8%; Largest cities (2004): Redding (87,300).

Shasta is one of California's least ethnically diverse counties, with 86 percent of the population white and less than 6 percent Latino. Politically, it brandishes the kind of conservatism that saw Republican state Senator Tom McClintock gain 20 percent of the vote in the 2003 election to replace recalled Governor Gray Davis while the leading Democrat, Lieutenant Governor Cruz Bustamante, polled 17 percent. In 2006, McClintock, a candidate for lieutenant governor, polled 65 percent of the vote, while in the contest for U.S. Senate conservative Republican Richard Mountjoy received 10,000 more votes in Shasta than Democratic incumbent Dianne Feinstein.

Shasta County has had its share of fiscal problems, especially in the late 1980s when the county library system shut down and voters refused to approve a tax hike to reopen it. The county hospital went bankrupt in 1987. Although the county has rebounded from those dark days, more than 11 percent of its families live below the poverty line, and unemployment was nearly 8 percent in 2003. Sierra Pacific Industries continues to be one of the county's biggest employers, but its presence here is lumber manufacturing rather than timber harvesting. Government is another large employer.

As noted, when it comes to elections in Shasta County, Democrats need not apply. The only Democrat since 1990 to break 40 percent of the vote (43.3) at the top of the ticket was Gray Davis in the 1998 gubernatorial race against Republican Dan Lungren, and Davis lost the county by 10 points. Even Feinstein failed to muster 40 percent in her 2006 re-election. More than 70 percent of Shastans voted to recall Davis in 2003, and nearly 60 percent chose to replace him with Republican Arnold Schwarzenegger. Schwarzenegger got 74 percent in his 2006 re-election. When it comes to ballot measures, Shasta mostly votes "no," although local voters did approve one of the statewide infrastructure bonds in November 2006—for flood control. They dinged schools, highways, and affordable housing bonds.

Sierra County

Area: 962 sq. mi.; Population: (2005 est.) 3,514, (2000) 3,555, (1990) 3,318, (1980) 3,073; Registration (Oct. 2006): D-31.1%, R-42.8%, DS-18.8%; 2006 voter turnout (rank): 73.7% (3); County supervisors: Arnie Gutman, Peter Huebner, Bill Nunes, Brooks Mitchell, Patricia Whitley; P.O. Drawer D, 100 Courthouse Square, Suite 11, Downieville 95936, Phone: (530)289-3295, Fax: (530) 289-2830; Assembly District 3; Senate District 1; Congressional District 4; Budget (2006-2007): $18.1 million; Median income: $35,827; Median home value: $128,600; Ethnicity: White-90.3%, Latino-6.0%, Asian-0.2%, Black-0.2%; Largest cities (2004): Loyalton (880).

Sierra is one of California's least populated counties. In fact, population estimates from the Department of Finance indicate that the county actually *lost* residents during the first five years of the 21st century. Almost no Asians or Blacks live here, and few Latinos. Unemployment is high, nearly 12%—not surprising for a county whose economy relies on logging and sawmills. Sierra Pacific maintains saw and planing mills, while Hood Logging of Loyalton is one of the county's biggest employers. There is some mining, the Sierra Buttes attract a few tourists, and the state and federal governments keep large payrolls.

Sierra has the distinction of being the only county in California without a public library, a situation county officials tried to remedy in 2006 by raising money for a multi-purpose facility in Loyalton. It was designed for books, classrooms, and a children's center, but rising construction costs threatened final approval—even though the county had raised more than $2.3 million in grants.

The county is Republican and conservative, so the fights are internal and revolve around local issues. Sierra has a natural east-west split that often lies at the center of those fights and keeps meetings of the Board of Supervisors lively. Meanwhile, a Democrat such as Dianne Feinstein can consider it a victory when she polls as much as 40 percent of the Sierra vote, as she did in her 2006 re-election bid. No other statewide Democratic candidate reached that mark.

At least Sierra voters—few as they may be—turn out on Election Day. The county's turnout rate of 73.7 percent ranked third in the state.

Siskiyou County

Area: 6,287 sq. mi.; Population: (2005 est.) 46,410, (2000) 44,301, (1990) 43,531, (1980) 39,732; Registration (Oct. 2006): D-35.5%, R-42.3%, DS-16.7%; 2006 voter turnout (rank): 54.9% (32); County supervisors: Jim Cook, LaVada Erickson, Michael Kobseff, Bill Overman, Marcia Armstrong; 311 4th St., Yreka 96097, Phone: (530) 842-8081; Assembly District 2; Senate District 4; Congressional District 2; Budget (2005-2006): $114.5 million; Median income: $29,530; Median home value: $100,300; Ethnicity: White-79.5%, Latino-7.6%, Asian-1.2%, Black-1.3%; Largest cities (2004): Yreka (7,325), Mt. Shasta (3,621).

Physically, Siskiyou is the largest of the northern California counties. Situated along the border with Oregon, it is more part of the Beaver State than the Golden State. In fact, there have been periodic efforts over the past half century to unite Siskiyou with its neighboring counties in southern Oregon to form a new state called "Jefferson."

The county, whose dominant landmark is Mount Shasta, experienced mild population growth during the 1980s (about 10%), but tough economic times in the timber industry saw unemployment rise as high as 15.6 percent in the early and mid 1990s, and that helped slam the brakes on even this modest growth. The county gained fewer than 1,000 people between 1990 and 2000, another 2,000 in the half decade since. Among the county's biggest employers are RCO Reforesting and Roseburg Forest Products. The Union Pacific Railroad has a large work force centered in Dunsmuir. Some tourism, clustered around the county's dominant physical landmark—Mount Shasta—has diversified the economy during the past decade.

Siskiyou is Republican, and GOP candidates have won every top-of-the-ticket race here since 1990, including big victories for Pres. George Bush in 2004 and Arnold Schwarzenegger in 2006. Republican Richard Mountjoy enjoyed a 10 percent margin over Democrat Dianne Feinstein in the U.S. Senate race in 2006.

Local voters rejected all but three ballot measures in November 2006, only approving proposals that require transportation funds be spent for transportation (Prop. 1A), curtail the use of eminent domain (Prop. 90), and restrict where convicted sex offenders may live (Prop. 83). If ultimately implemented, this last may impact the county because the restrictions could force many of the affected felons into rural counties—such as Siskiyou.

Solano County

Area: 907 sq. mi.; Population: (2005 est.) 422,094, (2000) 394,542, (1990) 340,421, (1980) 235,203; Registration (Oct. 2006): D-48.6%, R-29.1%, DS-18.5%; 2006 voter turnout (rank): 64.1% (13); County supervisors: Barbara Kondylis, John Silva, Jim Spering, John Vasquez, Mike Reagan; 1410 Georgia Street, Vallejo 94590, 580 Texas St., Fairfield 94533, Phone: (707) 421-6100, Fax: (707) 421-7975; Assembly Districts 7, 8; Senate Districts 2, 5; Congressional Districts 3, 7, 10; Budget (2006-2007): 870 million; Median income: $54,099; Median home value: $458,000; Ethnicity: White-49.2%, Latino-17.6%, Asian-12.7%, Black-14.9%; Largest cities (2004): Vallejo (121,100), Fairfield (103,600), Vacaville (95,100).

It wasn't so long ago that Solano County was a quiet blend of small cities separated by wide tracts of farmland and bordered by the upper reaches of San Francisco Bay. But that was before the San Francisco Bay Area and Sacramento began to grow toward each other, turning Solano County into a bedroom community for both metropolitan areas. Solano's population has increased 80 percent since 1980 and transformed small towns along Interstate 80 into strings of housing tracts separated by shopping malls and outlet stores.

In the past, the military played a large role in Solano's economy, and the county managed a draw when the Pentagon downsized during the 1980s and 1990s. Vallejo lost its naval base, but Fairfield retained Travis Air Force Base, complete with its large hospital. Six Flags Marine World helped Vallejo offset the loss of the Navy, while Genentech and a 24/7 construction industry helped keep the economy vibrant.

Solano has one of the state's most ethnically diverse populations, with no group a majority and all four major ethnic groups each contributing at least 12 percent of the population. The politics lean Democratic. Democrats win most top-of-the-ticket races in Solano, which voted against the recall of Governor Gray Davis in 2003. Republican Arnold Schwarzenegger captured the county in his successful effort to replace Davis, although he gained only 43 percent of the vote. He did better in his 2006 re-election against Democrat Phil Angelides, winning 54 percent of the county vote. U.S. Sen. Dianne Feinstein doubled the vote total of her GOP opponent, Richard Mountjoy, while Republican Steve Poizner beat Lt. Gov. Cruz Bustamante in the race for insurance commissioner.

Sonoma County

Area: 1,576 sq. mi.; Population: (2005 est.) 478,724, (2000) 458,614, (1990) 388,222, (1980) 299,681; Registration (Oct. 2006): D-50.2%, R-25.7%, DS-17.9%; 2006 voter turnout (rank): 75.5% (2); County supervisors: Valerie Brown, Mike Kerns, Tim Smith, Paul Kelley, Mike Reilly; 575 Administration Dr., Santa Rosa 95403, Phone: (707) 565-2241, Fax: (707) 565-3778; Assembly Districts 1, 6, 7; Senate Districts 2, 3; Congressional Districts 1, 6; Budget (2006-2007): $1.18 billion; Median income: $53,076; Median home value: $535,000; Ethnicity: White-64.3%, Latino-17.3%, Asian-3.1%, Black-1.4%; Largest cities (2004): Santa Rosa (154,400), Petaluma (55,900), Rohnert Park (42,236).

When the powers that be put the clamps on growth in Marin County during the 1970s, they burst a pipe in its neighbor to the north—Sonoma County. The county entices residents and tourists alike with internationally recognized wineries and cuisine, not to mention scenic beauty of rolling hills and a rugged coastline. Between 1980 and 1990, Sonoma's population increased by 88,000, or 30%, as commuters moved up Highway 101 in search of affordable housing. The county gained another 70,000 (18%) over the next decade. By 2004, it had increased another 3 percent and could grow to a projected 540,000 over the next decade. The economy has been resilient, as housing, employment growth, and taxable sales continue to rise. Home values skyrocketed as towns such as Petaluma and Santa Rosa blossomed. The city of Windsor is the county's fastest-growth community. Sonoma is not a retirement haven; the biggest population gains were in ages 40 to 59—prime working years, although the over-60 crowd has a higher percentage of the population here than statewide.

Not surprisingly, the economy is oriented toward services, and the largest employers tend to be government, hospitals, grocery chains, and school districts. Unemployment fell to a ridiculously low 2.6 percent by 2000—climbing with the recession to a still-modest 4.9 percent by 2003.

Sonoma County is heavily Democratic. It voted overwhelmingly against the recall of Gov. Gray Davis in 2003 and gave Democratic Lt. Gov. Cruz Bustamante one of his few countywide victories in the replacement election. U.S. Sen. Barbara Boxer took two-thirds of the county vote in her 2004 re-election, as did Democratic presidential candidate John Kerry.

But the county experienced something of a change of heart in November 2006, especially when it came to Bustamante, this time running for state insurance commissioner. His Republican opponent, Steve Poizner, won the county with 45 percent of the vote; Bustamante gaining only 40 percent. Republican Gov. Arnold Schwarzenegger captured the county, defeating Democrat Phil Angelides 48 percent to 44 percent.

In both races, the county followed the state trend. Democrats, however, took everything else, including legislative and congressional races.

In local matters, county voters showed a preference for what had been termed the "smart train," a mass transit system that would link the county with its neighbor—Marin. Marin voters rejected the proposal, however, leaving it in limbo.

An anti-casino mood also seems to be gaining strength in Sonoma County. Voters in Petaluma passed a measure in November 2006 that gives the city license to oppose development of a casino just south of the city. The gambling mecca is proposed by the Dry Creek Band of Pomo Indians, which has a Las Vegas–style casino in Geyserville. The tribe has proposed three casinos for the county, all strung along a 50-mile stretch of Highway 101, which links the county with San Francisco. Several cities elected new council members who ran on anti-casino platforms, and the new Assembly member from District 6, Jared Huffman, gained wide support in his campaign from the "Stop the Casino 101 Coalition."

Stanislaus County

Area: 1,494 sq. mi.; Population: (2005 est.) 510,858, (2000) 446,997, (1990) 370,522, (1980) 265,900; Registration (Oct. 2006): D-40.2%, R-42.2%, DS-13.3%; County supervisors: Bill O'Brien, Thomas Mayfield, Jeff Grover, Dick Monteith, Jim Demartini; 1010 10th St., Modesto 95354, Phone: (209) 525-4494, Fax: (209) 525-4410; Assembly Districts 17, 25, 26; Senate Districts 12, 14; Congressional Districts 18, 19; Budget (2006-2007): $899.9 million; Median income: $40,101; Median home value: $368,000; Ethnicity: White-37.6%, Latino-31.7%, Asian-4.2%, Black-2.6%; Largest cities (2004): Modesto (206,200), Turlock (64,200), Ceres (34,609).

Like other counties in the heart of the Central Valley, Stanislaus has experienced explosive increases in population during the past 25 years; in this case, 92 percent. The influx has changed the character of a once agricultural region to one of suburbs and seam-popping small cities. Agriculture still wields significant influence, but the problems that county government grapples with more often deal with traffic, sprawl, and overcrowded schools than water use and agricultural runoff. The county's top agricultural commodity is livestock—dairy cows, chickens, and cattle—which generates problems as housing developments spread toward farms and feedlots.

Unemployment is relatively high, peaking at 16.7 percent in 1993 and gradually improving over the succeeding decade, but not much; 11.5 percent of the county workforce still was jobless in 2003.

Voter registration slightly favors Republicans, but since 1990 the two parties have shared victories at the top of the ticket. Republican candidates for governor, U.S. Senate, and president have won eight of 14; Democrats the other six. Recent voting patterns favor the GOP, although U.S. Sen. Dianne Feinstein captured the county in her 2006 re-election.

The county was split during the 2001 redistricting, with Democratic precincts added to Senate (12) and Assembly (17) districts to enhance Democratic majorities there. But in 2002, the strategy backfired because, historically, Central Valley Democrats are not always the most loyal voters. They tend to be more conservative than their urban brethren, and that was reflected in the contest for state Senate where conservative Republican Jeff Denham defeated Democrat Rusty Areias in District 12. Denham was easily re-elected in 2006.

County voters supported the 2003 recall of Gov. Gray Davis and favored Republican Arnold Schwarzenegger as Davis's replacement. Conservative Republican Tom McClintock came away from Stanislaus with 24 percent of the vote—one of his best showings in any county. He won the county in 2006 when he ran for lieutenant governor against John Garamendi. In 2004 George Bush received nearly 60 percent of the vote.

Sutter County

Area: 609 sq. mi.; Population: (2005 est.) 90,627, (2000) 78,930, (1990) 64,415, (1980) 52,246; Registration (Oct. 2006): D-32.3%, R-49.5%, DS-12.5%; 2006 voter turnout (rank): 46.3% (51); County supervisors: Larry Montna, Stan Cleveland, Larry Munger, Jim Whiteaker, Dan Silva; 1160 Civic Center Boulevard, Suite A, Yuba City 95993, Phone: (530) 822-7106, Fax: (530) 822-7103; Assembly District 2; Senate District 4; Congressional District 2; Budget (2005-2006): $159.3 million; Median income: $38,375; Median home value: $120,700; Ethnicity: White-60.2%, Latino-22.2%, Asian-11.3%, Black-1.9%; Largest city (2004): Yuba City (50,800).

Sutter County's main population center lies half in Sutter County (Yuba City) and half in Yuba County (Marysville). County boundaries are but technicalities because the fate of both cities (if not their respective counties) is linked to Sacramento 40 miles to the south. The state capital has been spreading out in every direction during the past two decades, and Sutter and Yuba counties have not escaped the impact of that sprawl. The population of Sutter County alone has grown 74 percent since 1980 (Yuba County a more modest 38%).

Development has been fueled by land that is cheaper than in adjacent Sacramento County, and Sutter officials have been friendlier to developers. Still, the impacts are felt on a daily basis, especially for those who drive the main connector between Sacramento and Yuba City—Highway 99, known locally as "blood alley." Jobs haven't caught up with population growth, and the county's unemployment rate was 13.6 percent in 2003—only .4 percent lower than in 1990.

Sutter is home to the state's largest concentration of Sikhs, who live in and around Yuba City and Marysville. The county also harbors the world's smallest mountain range—the Sutter Buttes.

Politically, Sutter County is about as Republican as it gets. U.S. Sen. Dianne Feinstein failed to crack 40 percent of the vote here in 2006, while Democratic gubernatorial candidate Phil Angelides couldn't muster a quarter of the vote. His opponent, Gov. Arnold Schwarzenegger, received 73 percent. Local voters can pony up in their own interests, however. Of the four infrastructure bonds on the November 2006 ballot, Sutterites approved those for flood control and transportation while defeating bonds for schools, affordable housing, and parks.

Tehama County

Area: 2,962 sq. mi.; Population: (2005 est.) 61,378, (2000) 56,039, (1990) 49,620, (1980) 38,888; Registration (Oct. 2006): D-33.3%, R-45.3%, DS-15.5%; 2006 voter turnout (rank): 62.1% (15); County supervisors: Greg Avilla, George Russell, Charles Willard, Bob Williams, Ron Warner; 332 Pine Street, Red Bluff 96080, Phone: (530) 527-4655; Assembly District 2; Senate District 4; Congressional District 2; Budget (2006-2007): $20 million; Median income: $31,206; Median home value: $103,100; Ethnicity: White-78.5%, Latino-15.8%, Asian-0.8%, Black-0.6%; Largest cities (2004): Red Bluff (13,550), Corning (6,741).

Back in the late 1980s, Tehama County supervisors went eyeball-to-eyeball with state government, threatening to shut down county services because they did not have enough money to fund state mandates. The result was a compromise: supervisors backed down and the state stepped in to partially fund trial courts.

Tehama County can foot the bills these days, but the county still struggles economically. Tehama lives off timber and agriculture, plus whatever traffic spills off Interstate 5 en route between the rest of California and Oregon. The county does not attract much tourism, as befitting a place whose principal city—Red Bluff—often is identified as the hottest place north of Death Valley.

Tehama County votes Republican. The last top-of-the-ticket Democrat to carry the county was Bill Clinton, who eked out a .4 percent victory over George H. W. Bush in the 1992 presidential election. Four years later, Clinton lost the county to Republican Bob Dole by 15 points. Democratic U.S. Sens. Barbara Boxer and Dianne Feinstein each received less than 40 percent of the vote in their 2004 and 2006 re-elections. The 2003 recall of Gov. Gray Davis was supported by 73 percent in Tehama, while Republican Arnold Schwarzenegger finished first in the replacement election with 58 percent. In his 2006 re-election, Schwarzenegger took three-fourths of the county's vote.

Tuolumne County

Area: 2,235 sq. mi.; Population: (2005 est.) 58,215, (2000) 54,501, (1990) 48,456, (1980) 33,928; Registration (Oct. 2006): D-36.3%, R-43.7%, DS-14.8%; 2006 voter turnout (rank): 66.7% (10); County supervisors: Liz Bass, Paolo Maffei, Jim Peterson, Mark Thornton, Richard Pland; 2 South Green St., Sonora 95370, Phone: (209) 533-5521, Fax: (209) 533-5510; Assembly District 25; Senate District 14; Congressional District 19; Budget (2006-2007): $122.7 million; Median income: $38,725; Median home value: $149,800; Ethnicity: White-81.2%, Latino-8.2%, Asian-0.7%, Black-2.1%; Largest city (2004): Sonora (4,650).

Tuolumne is another of the mid-Sierra counties that has experienced rapid growth during the past 25 years; in this case, 72 percent. Mining still plays a part in the economy of an area that was born during the Gold Rush era, but so do recreation and retirement. More than 35 percent of the county's population is older than 50.

Politics in Tuolumne are conservative and Republican. The only top-of-the-ticket Democrat to carry the county since 1990 was Dianne Feinstein in her initial bid for the U.S. Senate in 1992. She has lost the county ever since, including her 2006 re-election effort. The county voted overwhelmingly for the recall of Gov. Gray Davis in 2003 and gave Republican Arnold Schwarzenegger the nod as Davis's replacement. Republicans George Bush and Bill Jones carried the county in 2004 in contests for president and U.S. senator respectively, while Schwarzenegger swept up 70 percent in his 2006 re-election.

Trinity County

Area: 3,179 sq. mi.; Population: (2005 est.) 14,025, (2000) 13,022, (1990) 13,063, (1980) 11,858; Registration (Oct. 2006): D-35.9%, R-39.1%, DS-17.1%; 2006 voter turnout (rank): 76.9% (1); County supervisors: Judy Pflueger, Jeff Morris, Roger Jaegel, Howard Freeman; Wendy Reiss; 101 Court St., Weaverville 96093, Phone: (530) 623-1217, Fax: (530) 623-8365; Assembly District 1; Senate District 4; Congressional District 2; Budget (2006-2007): Not available; Median income: $27,771; Median home value: $112,000; Ethnicity: White-84.9%, Latino-4.0%, Asian-0.5%, Black-0.4%; Largest city: Weaverville (3,554—unincorporated).

Trinity County boasts a distinction that only one other California county (Inyo) can claim. During the 1990s, it actually *lost* population. Trinity, which gets its name from the Trinity Alps, is the only California county with no incorporated cities; its largest town is Weaverville. Unemployment runs a tad over 11%, while a third of the workforce toils for government—mostly school districts and the county itself.

Republicans win most elections in Trinity, although Reform Party presidential candidate Ross Perot carried the county in 1992. The 2003 recall of Gov. Gray Davis won here two to one, although Davis did carry the county in his first bid for governor in 1998. He was trounced by Republican Bill Simon four years later. Until she finally broke through with a 500-vote margin in 2006, even Dianne Feinstein had lost Trinity County in her four previous elections (governor in 1990 and U.S. Senate in 1992, 1994 and 2000). Republican Arnold Schwarzenegger easily took the county in his 2006 re-election as governor.

If residents of every GOP-leaning county in California performed their civic duty with the panache of Trinity voters, Republicans might dominate the state. Nearly 77 percent of local registered voters cast ballots in 2006, placing Trinity atop all 58 counties when it comes to voter turnout.

Tulare County

Area: 4,824 sq. mi.; Population: (2005 est.) 417,287; (2000) 368,021, (1990) 311,921, (1980) 245,738; Registration (Oct. 2006): D-34.5%, R-48.0%, DS-14.2%; 2006 voter turnout (rank): 45.3% (54); County supervisors: Allen Ishida, Connie Conway, Phil Cox, Steve Worthley, Mike Ennis; 2800 West Burrell Ave., Visalia 93291, Phone: (559) 733-6531, Fax: (559) 733-6318; Assembly Districts 30, 31, 34; Senate Districts 16, 18; Congressional District 21; Budget (2006-2007): $764.6 million; Median income: $33,983; Median home value: $260,000; Ethnicity: White-41.8%, Latino-50.8%, Asian-3.3%, Black-1.6%; Largest cities (2004): Visalia (102,700), Tulare (47,700) Porterville (39,615).

Tulare County, which sits in the middle of the Central Valley, tried hard during the 1990s to diversify its economy and succeeded in attracting some industrial facilities, especially around Visalia. The county's population grew 50 percent between 1980 and 2000, then exploded—adding another 50,000 residents in the first half of the new century. That's an overall growth rate of 70 percent.

But prosperity did not follow either the effort to diversify or the growth. By the end of the 1990s, more than 16 percent of the population was unemployed, and nearly 19 percent of families lived below the poverty line. Agriculture still provided more jobs than any other industry, with the exception of health and education.

Latinos are the major ethnic group, but whites still dominate the political structure—as evidenced by the county's strong Republican credentials. In 16 elections since 1990 (including the 2003 recall against Governor Gray Davis), no Democrat has carried the county for president, governor, or U.S. Senate. More than 72 percent of Tulare voters supported Davis's 2003 recall, while Republican Arnold Schwarzenegger reaped 55.5 percent of the vote as Davis's replacement. In 2004, Pres. George Bush wiped the floor with Democrat John Kerry, polling two-thirds of the county's vote, while Democratic incumbent U.S. Sen. Barbara Boxer lost big to Republican Bill Jones.

In 2006, Schwarzenegger breezed to victory with 71 percent of the vote against Democrat Phil Angelides, while U.S. Sen. Dianne Feinstein, a popular Democrat elsewhere, lost the county to conservative Republican Richard Mountjoy, 53 percent to 42 percent.

Ventura County

Area: 2,208 sq. mi.; Population: (2005 est.) 815,528, (2000) 753,197, (1990) 669,016, (1980) 529,174; Registration (Oct. 2006): D-38.1%, R-39.8%, DS-17.6%; 2006 voter turnout (rank): 56.4% (30); County supervisors: Steve Bennett, Linda Parks, Kathy Long, Peter Foy, John Flynn; 800 South Victoria Avenue, Ventura 93009, Phone: (805) 654-3656; Assembly Districts 35, 37, 38, 41; Senate Districts 17, 19, 23; Congressional Districts 23, 24; Budget (2006-2007): $1.5 billion; Median income: $59,666; Median home value: $598,500; Ethnicity: White-56.8%, Latino-33.4%, Asian-5.3%, Black-1.9%; Largest cities (2004): Oxnard (186,100), Thousand Oaks (117,005), Simi Valley (111,361), San Buenaventura (Ventura city) (100,916).

It may be hard to believe, but Ventura County once was rural southern California, home of oil wells, cattle ranches, and citrus operations. That was before freeways connected it to the San Fernando Valley and developers began buying farmland to grow houses instead of crops.

As a result, Ventura County has been swallowed by Los Angeles, with all the attendant problems associated with rapid growth and urbanization. The county's population grew 54 percent between 1980 and 2005. Manufacturing and recreation replaced agriculture as the local economic mainstays, although government—in all its forms—remains the county's biggest employer. The U.S. Navy maintains a large presence in Ventura County, thanks to the Naval Air Weapons Center at Point Mugu and a construction operation at Port Hueneme. Large private employers include Amgen

(Newbury Park), Kavlico (Moorpark) and Technicolor Video Services (Camarillo). The unemployment rate is a modest 5.3 percent.

Development continues to be a catalyst. For instance, as unlikely a place as Port Hueneme is ticketed for a $300 million resort hotel and condo complex, converting what is now a parking lot into the largest building on the coast between San Francisco and Los Angeles. Approval is expected in 2007. Meanwhile, another kind of development—controversial on the face of it—affects the county: an $800 million liquefied natural gas processing plant and terminal in the Pacific some 14 miles offshore. The county's air quality board ruled in November 2006 that the plant should comply with strict clean-air standards, a decision that could delay development.

Ventura County politics trend Republican, as evidenced by the GOP's registration edge, although Democrats can do well here. Former Democratic state Sen. Jack O'Connell, now state superintendent of public instruction, twice carried Ventura County as a legislator. The 2003 recall of Gray Davis succeeded here with 63.5 percent in favor, but home-grown state Senator Tom McClintock, a Simi Valley Republican, finished well behind Arnold Schwarzenegger in the race to succeed Davis. In 2006, McClintock easily carried the county in his quest to become lieutenant governor, besting Democrat John Garamendi. The county split its top-of-the-ticket vote in 2004, giving the nod to Republican Pres. George Bush and Democratic U.S. Sen. Barbara Boxer. It did the same thing in 2006, voting for Schwarzenegger for governor and incumbent Democrat Dianne Feinstein for U.S. Senate.

Ventura County did not fare well in the 2001 redistricting of state legislative districts, as county precincts were used to bolster Republican and Democratic margins. As a result, the county was shattered. In the Assembly, Ventura and Oxnard were tacked onto coastal Santa Barbara County to create a marginally safe Democratic district (35), while Thousand Oaks, Simi Valley, Camarillo, and Moorpark were added to two other districts (37, 38) considered safe for Republicans. The county was divided into three parts for Senate districts. Republican districts (17, 19) picked up the coastal hills and Thousand Oaks–Simi Valley, while Oxnard was added to a Democratic district (23) where political power resides in Los Angeles communities such as Santa Monica, West Hollywood, Malibu, and Beverly Hills.

Yolo County

Area: 1,013 sq. mi.; Population: (2005 est.) 188,858, (2000) 168,660, (1990) 141,092, (1980) 113,374; Registration (Oct. 2006): D-46.2%, R-27.5%, DS-20.6%; 2006 voter turnout (rank): 61.3% (17); County supervisors: Mike McGowan, Helen Thomson, Max Rexroad, Mariko Yamada, Duane Chamberlain; 625 Court St., Woodland 95695, Phone: (530) 666-8195; Assembly Districts 2, 8; Senate District 5; Congressional Districts 1, 2; Budget (2006-2007): $299.2 million; Median income: $40,769; Median home value: $405,000; Ethnicity: White-41.8%, Latino-25.9%, Asian-9.9%, Black-2.0%; Largest cities (2004): Davis (64,500), Woodland (49,151), West Sacramento (38,000).

Not long ago, Yolo County was an agricultural enclave, anchored by the University of California's "aggie school" at Davis. But just as UC Davis has outgrown its aggie label, so, too, has Yolo County diversified its economy. A list of the top 15 employers countywide includes only one related to agriculture—Pacific Coast Producers, which deals in preserved fruits and vegetables. The other large employers are in government, research, and service industries.

Yolo County's future is dominated by geography. It sits astride Interstate 80 between Sacramento and the San Francisco Bay Area, and like its brother counties along the same route, Yolo has experienced population growth as the two metropolitan areas continue to inch toward each other. Yolo's population grew 67 percent between 1980 and 2005. Davis, once a university town, has become a bedroom community for both Sacramento 12 miles away, and the Bay Area some 60 miles in the other direction. The I-80 causeway is lined with commuter traffic and the landscape with housing developments.

Sacramento's boom has benefited West Sacramento, once Yolo County's poorest city. Although 17 percent of its families still live below the federal poverty line, the beginnings of a new prosperity are visible in "West Sac," especially along the riverfront facing the capital city. Raley's Markets moved its corporate headquarters there during the late 1990s, and the Sacramento River Cats—a Pacific Coast League baseball franchise affiliated with the Oakland Athletics—built a stadium in West Sacramento at the foot of the Capital Avenue bridge. The port of Sacramento is in West Sacramento and has fostered service and transportation businesses that transcend the port itself.

Since expanding out of its agricultural roots, Yolo has been trying to balance growth with conservation. Davis has classified itself as a slow-growth community, yet rising housing costs have created pressure for new development, which in turn has met resistance from longtime Davis residents. Notably, Davis voters rejected Measure X in 2005, which would have created a large new housing development. In 2006, however, voters approved Measure K, which allows for construction of a Target store.

The county also pays attention to growth elsewhere. In 2006, for instance, the city of Davis challenged the development of a $250 million racetrack in the nearby community of Dixon, in Solano County. Davis officials claimed that the track would impact traffic and other facilities in Yolo County and threatened to sue Dixon to stop construction.

Yolo County politics are dominated by Democrats, although voter registration is nearly even between the two parties in the county seat of Woodland. Yolo was one of only a handful of counties to defeat the 2003 recall against Gov. Gray Davis, although Republican Arnold Schwarzenegger did carry the county in the replacement election. He also won Yolo in his 2006 re-election against Democrat Phil Angelides, who hails from Sacramento just across the river.

In 2004, Yolo voted heavily for both top-of-the-ticket Democrats—presidential hopeful John Kerry and U.S. Sen. Barbara Boxer. But the county's most significant contribution to Democratic fortunes may have come in state Senate District 5, where Yolo support saved the career of incumbent Mike Machado in the most fiercely contested legislative race of the year. Machado defeated Stockton Mayor Gary Podesto in a district retooled in 2001 to bolster Democrats. The boost came from Yolo County, which was added to the previous version of District 5 and performed exactly as redistricting architects imagined it would.

In 2006, Republicans made inroads in Democrat-dominated Yolo. Not only did Schwarzenegger prevail, but county voters elected Woodland Mayor Max Rexroad, a

Republican, to the board of supervisors. Republican Steve Poizner carried Yolo against Democrat Cruz Bustamante in the race for state insurance commissioner.

Those three contests marked the boundary of GOP gains as Democrats took all other races in Yolo County. For instance, U.S. Sen. Dianne Feinstein received 65 percent of the local vote in her re-election effort, while the county voted to send Democrat Mike Thompson back to the U.S. House.

Not surprisingly, Green Party candidates did well in environmentally sensitive Yolo County, consistently running well ahead of the party's statewide performance. Yolo was one of a handful of counties to vote for Proposition 86—an initiative to dramatically increase the sales tax on cigarettes. The measure lost statewide.

Yuba County

Area: 631 sq. mi.; Population: (2005 est.) 68,618, (2000) 60,219, (1990) 58,228, (1980) 49,733; Registration (Oct. 2006): D-34.0%, R-42.5%, DS-18.1%; 2006 voter turnout (rank): 40% (57); County supervisors: Dan Logue, John Nicoletti, Mary Jane Griego, Dan Schrader, Hal Stocker; 915 8th St., Marysville 95901, Phone: (530) 749-7575, Fax: (530) 749-7312; Assembly District 3; Senate District 4; Congressional District 2; Budget (2006-2007): $296 million; Median income: $30,460; Median home value: $89,700; Ethnicity: White-53.2%, Latino-17.4%, Asian-7.5%, Black-3.2%; Largest city (2004): Marysville (12,800).

Given that its county seat and largest city—Marysville—sits in the path of urban sprawl from Sacramento, Yuba County has grown at a modest 38 percent rate over the past 25 years. Much of that growth has taken place in and around Marysville, which lies across the Feather River from Yuba City, county seat of Sutter County. Confused?

Yuba County lies north and east of Sutter County, which has absorbed most of the growth. Agriculture still plays a big part in the county's economy, as does Beale Air Force Base near Marysville—home to the U-2 spy plane. The county did not suffer when the military presence in California was downsized during the 1980s and 1990s because Beale's mission actually expanded. The Air Force notwithstanding, county unemployment is high—14.2 percent in 2003, more than twice the statewide average.

Politically, the county is Republican and conservative. Democrats have lost every top-of-the-ticket race in Yuba County since 1990, and three out of four Yuba voters backed the 2003 recall of Gov. Gray Davis. Republican Arnold Schwarzenegger received 62 percent of the vote to replace Davis. In his 2006 re-election, Schwarzenegger captured 73 percent. That same year, Democrat Dianne Feinstein lost her re-election vote in Yuba to conservative Republican Richard Mountjoy. Pres. George Bush took more than two-thirds of the Yuba vote in his 2004 re-election. Yuba voters did back two locally important statewide bond proposals in November 2006: Prop. 1B to fund highways, and Prop. 1D to fund flood control measures.